The Blackwell Companion to the Qur'ān

Blackwell Companions to Religion

The Blackwell Companions to Religion series presents a collection of the most recent scholarship and knowledge about world religions. Each volume draws together newly-commissioned essays by distinguished authors in the field, and is presented in a style which is accessible to undergraduate students, as well as scholars and the interested general reader. These volumes approach the subject in a creative and forward-thinking style, providing a forum in which leading scholars in the field can make their views and research available to a wider audience.

Published

The Blackwell Companion to Judaism
Edited by Jacob Neusner and Alan J. Avery-Peck

The Blackwell Companion to Sociology of Religion
Edited by Richard K. Fenn

The Blackwell Companion to the Hebrew Bible
Edited by Leo G. Perdue

The Blackwell Companion to Postmodern Theology
Edited by Graham Ward

The Blackwell Companion to Hinduism
Edited by Gavin Flood

The Blackwell Companion to Political Theology
Edited by Peter Scott and William T. Cavanaugh

The Blackwell Companion to Protestantism
Edited by Alister E. McGrath and Darren C. Marks

The Blackwell Companion to Modern Theology
Edited by Gareth Jones

The Blackwell Companion to Christian Ethics
Edited by Stanley Hauerwas and Samuel Wells

The Blackwell Companion to Religious Ethics
Edited by William Schweiker

The Blackwell Companion to Christian Spirituality
Edited by Arthur Holder

The Blackwell Companion to the Study of Religion
Edited by Robert A. Segal

The Blackwell Companion to the Qur'ān
Edited by Andrew Rippin

The Blackwell Companion to Contemporary Islamic Thought
Edited by Ibrahim M. Abu-Rabiʾ

The Blackwell Companion to the Bible and Culture
Edited by John F. A. Sawyer

The Blackwell Companion to Catholicism
Edited by James J. Buckley, Frederick Christian Bauerschmidt, and Trent Pomplun

The Blackwell Companion to Eastern Christianity
Edited by Ken Parry

Forthcoming

The Blackwell Companion to the New Testament
Edited by David E. Aune

The Blackwell Companion to the Qur'ān

Edited by

Andrew Rippin

WILEY-BLACKWELL
A John Wiley & Sons, Ltd., Publication

This paperback edition first published 2009

Edition history: Blackwell Publishing Ltd (hardback, 2006)
Blackwell Publishing was acquired by John Wiley & Sons in February 2007. Blackwell's publishing program has been merged with Wiley's global Scientific, Technical, and Medical business to form Wiley-Blackwell.

Registered Office
John Wiley & Sons Ltd, The Atrium, Southern Gate, Chichester, West Sussex, PO19 8SQ, United Kingdom

Editorial Offices
350 Main Street, Malden, MA 02148-5020, USA
9600 Garsington Road, Oxford, OX4 2DQ, UK
The Atrium, Southern Gate, Chichester, West Sussex, PO19 8SQ, UK

For details of our global editorial offices, for customer services, and for information about how to apply for permission to reuse the copyright material in this book please see our website at www.wiley.com/wiley-blackwell.

Library of Congress Cataloging-in-Publication Data

The Blackwell companion to the Qur'ān / edited by Andrew Rippin.
p. cm. – (Blackwell companions to religion)
Includes bibliographical references and index.
ISBN: 978-1-4051-8820-3 (paperback : alk. paper)
1. Koran—Criticism, interpretation, etc. 2. Koran—Appreciation.
I. Rippin, Andrew, 1950– . II. Title: Companion to the Qur'ān. III. Series.
BP130.4.B57 2006
297.12226—dc22
200524135

A catalogue record for this book is available from the British Library.

Set in 10 on 12.5 pt Photina by SNP Best-set Typesetter Ltd., Hong Kong
Printed in Singapore by C.O.S. Printers Pte Ltd

1 2009

Contents

Contributors

Binyamin Abrahamov, Dean, Faculty of Humanities, Professor of Islamic Theology and Qurʾānic Studies, Bar-Ilan University, Israel.

Herbert Berg, Associate Professor, Department of Philosophy and Religion, University of North Carolina, Wilmington, USA.

Christopher Buck, Independent scholar and attorney in Pennsylvania, having taught at Michigan State University, Quincy University, Millikin University, and Carleton University.

Michael Carter, Professor of Arabic, University of Oslo (until 2005), Honorary Professor at the Centre for Medieval Studies of Sydney University, Australia.

François Déroche, Professor, École pratique des hautes études, Paris, France.

Salwa M. S. El-Awa, Lecturer in Qurʾān and *ḥadīth*, Department of Theology and Religion, University of Birmingham, UK.

Reuven Firestone, Professor of Medieval Judaism and Islam at Hebrew Union College, Los Angeles, senior fellow at the University of Southern California's Center for Religion and Civic Culture and co-director of the Center for Muslim-Jewish Engagement.

Anna M. Gade, Senior Lecturer, Religious Studies Programme, Victoria University of Wellington, New Zealand.

Alan Godlas, Associate Professor, Department of Religion, University of Georgia, USA.

Rosalind Ward Gwynne, Associate Professor of Islamic Studies, Department of Religious Studies, University of Tennessee, USA.

Avraham Hakim, Arabic teacher and lecturer on Islam, The Lowy School for Overseas Students, Tel Aviv University, Israel.

Navid Kermani, writer, Cologne, Germany.

Leah Kinberg, Senior Lecturer, Department of Middle Eastern and African History, Tel Aviv University, Israel.

Marianna Klar, Research Associate, Centre of Islamic Studies, School of Oriental and African Studies, London, UK.

Jane Dammen McAuliffe, President and Professor of History, Bryn Mawr College, Pennsylvania, USA.

Mustansir Mir, University Professor of Islamic Studies, Department of Philosophy and Religious Studies, Youngstown State University, Ohio, USA.

Khaleel Mohammed, Associate Professor of Religion, San Diego State University, California, USA.

Jawid Mojaddedi, Assistant Professor, Department of Religion, Rutgers University, New Jersey, USA.

Angelika Neuwirth, Professor, Seminar für Semitistik und Arabistik, Freie Universität, Berlin, Germany, and director of the Project Corpus Coranicum at the Berlin-Brandenburgische Akademie der Wissenschaften.

A. Kevin Reinhart, Associate Professor, Department of Religion, Dartmouth College, New Hampshire, USA.

Andrew Rippin, Dean, Faculty of Humanities, Professor of History, University of Victoria, Canada.

Uri Rubin, Professor, Department of Arabic and Islamic Studies, Tel Aviv University, Israel.

Abdullah Saeed, Sultan of Oman Professor of Arab and Islamic Studies, Director of the Centre for the Study of Contemporary Islam, University of Melbourne, Australia.

Walid Saleh, Associate Professor, Department of Religion and Department of Near and Middle Eastern Civilizations, University of Toronto, Canada.

Aliza Shnizer, Department of Arabic and Islamic Studies, Tel Aviv University, Israel.

Tamara Sonn, Kenan Professor of Religion, Professor of Humanities, College of William and Mary, Williamsburg, Virginia, USA.

Diana Steigerwald, Assistant Professor, Department of Religion, California State University, Long Beach, USA.

Roberto Tottoli, Associate Professor, Università degli Studi di Napoli "L'Orientale", Italy.

Brannon Wheeler, Professor of History. Director of the Center for Middle East and Islamic Studies, United States Naval Academy, Annapolis, Maryland, USA.

A. H. Mathias Zahniser, Professor Emeritus of Religious Studies, Asbury Theological Seminary, Wilmore, Kentucky, USA, and Scholar in Residence at Greenville College, Illinois, USA.

Kate Zebiri, Senior Lecturer in Arabic and Islamic Studies, School of Oriental and African Studies, London, UK.

Preface

Andrew Rippin

The publication of a volume devoted to the Qur'ān in the "companion" genre marks the emergence of the text of Muslim scripture within the canon of world literature in a manner particularly appropriate to the twenty-first century. This companion is explicitly designed to guide the reader who may have little exposure to the Qur'ān beyond a curiosity evoked by the popular media. It aims to provide such a person with the starting point of a general orientation and take him or her to a well-advanced state of understanding regarding the complexities of the text and its associated traditions. However, a "companion" volume such as this is also an opportunity for scholars to extend the boundaries of what might be deemed to be the "accepted" approaches to the text of the Qur'ān because such a volume provides, it is to be hoped, the material which will inspire future generations of scholars who first encounter the Qur'ān in the classroom and for whom new avenues of exploration provide the excitement of research and discovery.

Organization

This companion has been organized in order to facilitate its usefulness for the groups of readers who may wish to embark on a deeper understanding of the Qur'ān in its historical context and as an object of scholarly study. Part I functions as an introduction to the text but its three chapters are oriented in different, yet complementary ways. All readers, but especially those who are coming to the Qur'ān with little foreknowledge of the text and/or the scholarly study of it, will find these chapters the place to start. "Introducing" the Qur'ān (chapter 1) means orienting the reader to the basic facts, themselves coming from a variety of perspectives both internal and external to the text. "Discovering" the Qur'ān (chapter 2) speaks to the experience of a student and considers how one might integrate the Qur'ān within a framework of religious studies. "Contextualizing" the Qur'ān (chapter 3) orients the reader to a Muslim scholarly perspective, putting the emphasis on the historical context in which the facts about the

Qur'ān are to be understood. Each chapter thus adds a level of complexity to the task of approaching the Qur'ān, although each chapter recognizes certain common elements which pose a challenge to the reader, especially the question of the choice of "lens" through which one should read the text.

Part II addresses the text of the Qur'ān on both the structural and the historical level, two dimensions which have always been seen in scholarly study as fully intertwined. Issues of origin and composition lie deeply embedded in all of these concerns because, it is argued, the structure of the text – which is what makes the book a challenge to read – must be accounted for through the process of history. However, the final aim of these attempts at explaining the Qur'ān is directed towards a single end, that of coming to an understanding of the text. The internal structure of the Qur'ān is the focus of chapter 4. These observations are complemented by an intricate series of observations about the nature of the text and its language, including the patterns of address used in the text (chapter 5), language – especially its use of literary figures – in chapter 6, the relationship between poetry and language as it affects the Qur'ān (chapter 7), and the range of the vocabulary of the text that is thought to come from non-Arabic sources in chapter 8. All of these factors – structure, language, and vocabulary – combine and become manifested in the emergence of a text of the scripture within the context of a community of Muslims (chapter 9), creating the text which emerges as sacred through the complex passage of history (chapter 10), which is then transmitted through the generations of Muslims, the focus of chapter 11. All of this happens in a historical context of the early community which is shown to be foundational to the understanding of the text in both the person of Muḥammad and his life (chapter 12) as well as that of the early leader ʿUmar b. al-Khaṭṭāb (chapter 13).

Such details provide an understanding of the text on a linguistic and historical level but the overall nature of its message is fundamentally ignored in such considerations. Part III thus turns to consider some of the major topics which characterize that message. Muslims have, in fact, seen the Qur'ān as all-encompassing in its treatment of human existence and an inventory of themes can really only provide examples of ways of analyzing and categorizing the contents of the scripture: there is little substitute for a rigorous study of the text itself if one wishes to gain a clear sense of what it is really about as a whole. However, certain aspects do provide key ideas and provide the opportunity to illustrate methods of approach. Dominating all of the message of the Qur'ān is, of course, the figure of Allāh, the all-powerful, one God revealed in the Qur'ān just as He is in the biblical tradition (chapter 14), through a process of revelation brought by prophets (chapter 15), an important one of whom within the Muslim context is Moses (chapter 16), although, of course, figures such as Abraham and Jesus play a central role in the Qur'ān as well. The message those prophets (including Muḥammad in the Qur'ān) bring argues for belief in God (chapter 17) among reflective, thinking human beings (chapter 18). However, the prophets also bring a message of how life should be lived in both love (chapter 19) and war (chapter 20).

This text of the Qur'ān, as all of the preceding material has made clear, is a complex one that Muslims have always known needed interpretation. This might be said to be the nature of divine revelation which poses the problem of how the infinity and absoluteness of God can be expressed in the limited and ambiguous format of human language. Such a situation calls for a hermeneutics that is elaborated within the framework of Islam (chapter 21) which can also draw its inspiration from a multitude of sources always filtered through Islamic eyes and needs (chapter 22). Differing approaches to Islam developed in the Muslim world, variations which the Qurʾān facilitated through its conduciveness to interpretation: thus Ṣūfīs (chapter 23), Rūmī, (chapter 24), Twelver Shīʿites (chapter 25) and Ismāʿīlīs (chapter 26) all sought strength and support for their ideas in the text of the Qurʾān and developed their own principles by which to understand the scripture.

However, the Qurʾān has far more significance within Muslim life than as an object functioning as a ground for exegesis. The world of the Qurʾān extends much further, becoming the basis of scholastic consideration and development of learning within the context of exegetical elaboration (chapter 27), theology (chapter 28), and jurisprudence (chapter 29). It is a touchstone for every discussion of ethical issues in the modern world (chapter 30) just as it was the basis for literary development in the classical world (chapter 31). Underlying all of that, however, is the status of the Qurʾān not so much as a rational launching pad for further thought but as a text of devotion as displayed in the attention to its orality and manifestation in recitation (chapter 32). The application of the Qurʾān thus extends through the many aspects of Muslim day-to-day life.

Technical Considerations

A work such as this depends upon a significant number of scholars interested in making their academic work accessible to a broad reading public and a new generation of students. As editor of the volume, I would like to express my appreciation to all of the contributors – a truly international gathering of scholars – for their efforts. There is a delicate balance in a work such as this between documenting and annotating every thought and being mindful of the variety of readers who are the potential audience; thus, the number of references and endnotes has been drastically reduced but not totally eliminated, for it is in such supporting apparatus that there lies one of the sources of research directions for future generations of scholars. As well, it is notable that there clearly continues to be a need to justify many points of discussion with reference to original and secondary sources; it is perhaps indicative of the still-developing nature of Qurʾānic studies that it is not possible to assume an agreed-upon core of basic data and interpretation that would simplify much of the documentation in a volume such as this.

In an attempt to eliminate some of the "clutter" that is often associated with academic work, the bibliographical references for each chapter have been consolidated into one overall bibliography at the end of the volume. The exercise of compiling this bibliography has been, for the editor, and for the publisher's copy-editor as well, a task made all the more complex because of the lack of standard editions of many works of constant reference in the field – an aspect aggravated by the loose control over the reprinting of works by different publishers in many parts of the Arab world who make no reference to the source of the original print and who often times use slightly variant page numbering even in direct reprints of a text; thus, for some items in the bibliography, several prints will be listed because those are the ones available to individual writers and only seldom has it been possible to consolidate different editions. The situation does not exist solely with reprints of Arabic texts in the Arab world, although it certainly afflicts that area far more extensively; the record of the European publishing project of the *Encyclopaedia of Islam* is equally complex, although the correlations between the multiple versions of that work are at least somewhat more straightforward. For ease of citation, all references to the *Encyclopaedia of Islam* New Edition (= second edition) in this book have been reduced to *EI2* (2004) meaning the CD-ROM version which is a direct reproduction of the printed work in English which appeared in twelve volumes (plus supplements) between 1954 and 2004 (and which is now also available in a Web version). The now emerging third edition appears to be planned under English head words, so no correlation with that edition will likely be possible.

References to the Qurʾān are cited generally in the format "Q *sūra* number: *āya* number," numbered according to what is commonly called the Cairo text. Dates are generally cited in the format "Hijrī/Gregorian" unless otherwise indicated.

PART I

Orientation

CHAPTER 1

Introducing

Tamara Sonn

The Qurʾān ("Koran" in archaic spelling) is the sacred scripture of Islam. The term *qurʾān* means "recitation" or "reading," reflecting the Muslim belief that it is the word of God, not of the prophet who delivered it. Although the Qurʾān was revealed (or "sent down," *munzal*, as the Arabic term has it) in the first/seventh century, Muslims believe that it is nonetheless timeless, the word of God, revealed word for word in the Arabic language through God's final messenger, Muḥammad (d. 11/632). Sunnī Muslims (approximately 85 percent of the world's Muslim population) believe the Qurʾān is therefore uncreated; like God, whose speech it is, it has always existed. The Qurʾān says that its words reflect a divine archetype of revelation, which it calls "the preserved tablet" (*al-lawḥ al-maḥfūẓ*, Q 85:22). This allows for interpretation of the term *qurʾān* as "reading," even though Muḥammad is described by the Qurʾān as unlettered or illiterate (Q 7:157; 62:2). Rather than "reading" a message, Muḥammad is described as delivering a message that God had imprinted upon his heart (e.g., Q 26:195). At one point the Qurʾān refers to Gabriel (Jibrīl) as the one "who has brought it [revelation] down upon your heart" (Q 2:97). As a result, traditional interpreters claim that Gabriel was the medium through whom Muḥammad received God's revelation.

The Qurʾān uses the term *qurʾān* seventy times, sometimes generically referring to "recitation" but usually referring to revelation. The Qurʾān also refers to itself, as it does to the Torah and the Gospels, as simply "the book" (*al-kitāb*), a term used hundreds of times to refer to recorded revelation. Muslims therefore frequently refer to the Qurʾān as "The Book." Muslims also commonly use terms such as "noble" (*al-Qurʾān al-karīm*), "glorious" (*al-Qurʾān al-majīd*), and other terms of respect for the Qurʾān. They commemorate annually the beginning of its revelation on the "night of power" (or "destiny," *laylat al-qadr*), during the last ten days of Ramaḍān, the month of fasting. So important is the revelation of the Qurʾān that the Qurʾān describes *laylat al-qadr* as "better than a thousand months" (Q 97:4).

Muslims' respect for the Qurʾān is demonstrated by the fact that only those who are in a state of spiritual purity are allowed to touch it. It is the miracle of Islam; Muḥammad brought no other. The Qurʾān tells us that when people asked Muḥammad to demonstrate the authenticity of his prophecy by performing miracles, as other prophets had done, he offered them the Qur'ān. The beauty of its language is believed to be beyond compare, and impossible to imitate. (This belief is conveyed in the doctrine of the inimitability of the Qur'ān, *i'jāz*.) Whereas Jesus' life was miraculous and forms the basis of Christianity, the Qur'ān itself is the basis of Islamic life. It forms the core of Islamic ritual and practice, learning, and law.

Structure of the Text

The Qur'ān consists of 114 chapters, called *sūras* (plural: *suwar*). The verses of the chapters are called *āyāt* (singular: *āya*). The chapters range in length from 7 to 287 verses. The first *sūra* is very short, but the remaining *sūras* are arranged roughly in descending order of length, that is, from longest to shortest, rather than in chronological order.

The chronological order in which the chapters were delivered is determined based on both internal evidence and traditional literature concerning the circumstances of revelation (*asbāb al-nuzūl*). Although not all scholars agree on the precise dating of all the verses of the Qur'ān, there is general agreement that approximately ninety of the chapters were delivered during the earlier period of revelation, while Muḥammad and his community lived in Mecca. The remaining chapters were delivered after the emigration (*hijra*) to Medina (1/622). Accordingly, scholars often refer to chapters as being Meccan or Medinan. The former tend to be shorter (and therefore placed at the end of the Qur'ān), poetic in form, passionate in tone, and characterized by general references to monotheism; the glory, power, mercy and justice of God (Allāh, from the Arabic *al-ilāh*: the [one] god); and the need for submission (*islām*) to the will of God in order to achieve the great rewards promised in the afterlife and avoid divine retribution. The Medinan *sūras* tend to be longer (and therefore found at the beginning of the Qur'ān), more prosaic in form, and deal with more practical issues such as marriage and inheritance.

Each chapter of the Qur'ān has a name, such as "Opening" (Q 1), "Women" (Q 4), and "Repentance" (Q 9). These names were ascribed after the Qur'ān was canonized (established in its authoritative form) and typically derive from major references in the chapters. All but one chapter (Q 9) begins with the phrase "In the name of God, the Merciful, the Compassionate." Twenty-nine chapters of the Qur'ān are also preceded by a letter or brief series of Arabic letters, whose meaning is unclear. Some scholars believe they refer to elements within the chapter itself, some believe they refer to early organizational components of the chapters, while others believe they have mystical or spiritual meanings. Whatever their significance, these letters are considered to be part of revelation itself.

Voice and Audience

The Qur'ān often speaks in the first person ("I" or "We," used interchangeably), indicating that it is the voice of God. For example, as in the verse about the first night of revelation (*laylat al-qadr*) cited above, the Qur'ān says, "Surely We sent it [revelation] down on the night of power" (Q 97:2). In this voice, the Qur'ān frequently addresses itself to Muḥammad, instructing him to "say" or "tell" people certain things, sometimes in response to specific issues. For example, when people were doubting Muḥammad's role as prophet, the Qur'ān instructs him: "Say, 'O people, indeed I am a clear warner to you. Those who believe and do good works, for them is forgiveness and generous blessing" (Q 55:49–50). The Qur'ān also offers advice to Muḥammad. When people accused him of being a mere poet or even a fortune-teller, the Qur'ān says, "Do they say that you have forged [the Qur'ān]? Say, 'If I have forged it, my crimes are my own; but I am innocent of what you do' " (Q 11:36). The Qur'ān also offers encouragement to Muḥammad when his efforts seem futile: "Have we not opened your heart and relieved you of the burden that was breaking your back?" (Q 94:1–2). At other times, the Qur'ān speaks directly to the people about Muḥammad. Concerning the issue of the authenticity of his message, the Qur'ān addresses the community, saying, "The heart [of the prophet] was not deceived. Will you then dispute with him about what he saw?" (Q 53:12–13). The Qur'ān is the word of God throughout, but many of the longer verses appear in the voice of Muḥammad, addressing the community with the word of God and referring to God in the third person. For instance, we are told, "There is no compulsion in religion. Right has been distinguished from wrong. Whoever rejects idols and believes in God has surely grasped the strongest, unbreakable bond. And God hears and knows" (Q 2:257).

The audience addressed by the Qur'ān is assumed to be the community of seventh-century Arabia, where Muḥammad lived, although its message is meant for all times and places. Interestingly, and uniquely among monotheistic scriptures, the Qur'ān assumes both males and females among its audience, and frequently addresses the concerns of both. For example, it tells us that God is prepared to forgive and richly reward all good people, both male and female:

> Men who submit [to God] and women who submit [to God],
> Men who believe and women who believe,
> Men who obey and women who obey,
> Men who are honest and women who are honest,
> Men who are steadfast and women who are steadfast,
> Men who are humble and women who are humble,
> Men who give charity and women who give charity,
> Men who fast and women who fast,
> Men who are modest and women who are modest,
> Men and women who remember God often. (Q 33:36)

History of the Text

Unlike earlier scriptures, the history of the Qur'ān is well known. The Qur'ān was delivered by Muḥammad to his community in Arabia in various contexts over a period of twenty-two years, 610 to 632 CE. According to tradition, Muḥammad's followers sometimes recorded his pronouncements, while others of his followers memorized and transmitted them orally during his lifetime. After the death of Muḥammad (11/632), and with the deaths of some of those who memorized the Qur'ān (*ḥuffāẓ*), the prophet's companions decided to establish a written version of the Qur'ān so that it could be preserved accurately for posterity. This process was begun by a close companion of Muḥammad, Zayd b. Thābit (d. 35/655), who collected written records of Qur'ānic verses soon after the death of Muḥammad. The third successor (caliph) to the prophet, ʿUthmān b. ʿAffān (d. 36/656), is credited with commissioning Zayd and other respected scholars to establish the authoritative written version of the Qur'ān based upon the written and oral records. Thus, within twenty years of Muḥammad's death, the Qur'ān was committed to written form. That text became the model from which copies were made and promulgated throughout the urban centers of the Muslim world, and other versions are believed to have been destroyed. Because of the existence of various dialects and the lack of vowel markers in early Arabic, slight variations in the reading of the authoritative versions were possible. In order to avoid confusion, markers indicating specific vowel sounds were introduced into the language by the end of the third/ninth century, but seven slightly variant readings remain acceptable.

The Qur'ān was copied and transmitted by hand until the modern era. The first printed version was produced in Rome in 1530 CE; a second printed version was produced in Hamburg in 1694. The first critical edition produced in Europe was done by Gustav Flügel in 1834.

The numbering of the verses varies slightly between the standard 1925 CE Egyptian edition and the 1834 edition established by Flügel, which is used by many Western scholars. (Editions from Pakistan and India often follow the Egyptian standard edition with the exception that they count the opening phrase, "In the name of God, the Merciful, the Compassionate," of each chapter as the first verse. This is the numbering followed in the citations given in this text.) The variations in verse numbering comprise only a few verses and reflect differing interpretations of where certain verses end.

The Qur'ān is considered to be authentic only in Arabic. Even non-Arabic speaking Muslims pray in Arabic, the language serving as a great symbol of unity throughout the Muslim world. Nevertheless, numerous translations of the Qur'ān have been produced. The first Latin translation was done in the twelfth century CE, commissioned by Peter the Venerable, abbot of the monastery of Cluny in France. It was published in Switzerland in the sixteenth century. The Qur'ān is now readily available in virtually all written languages.

Relationship of the Qur'ān to Other Scriptures

The Qur'ān contains numerous references to the earlier monotheistic scriptures, which it identifies as the Torah and the Gospels, and assumes people are familiar with those texts. As a result, it does not recount their historic narratives. Instead, the Qur'ān uses characters and events familiar to Jews and Christians to make specific moral or theological points. References to Adam, Noah, Abraham, Isaac and Jacob, Moses, and Jesus, for example, therefore appear frequently but not in chronological order.

The Qur'ān refers to the monotheistic tradition as simply "the religion" (*al-dīn*), meaning the monotheistic religion that began with the initiation of the covenant between God and humanity at the time of Abraham (Ibrāhīm). It informs its audience that Muḥammad's revelation is part of the same tradition: "He has laid down for you as religion what He charged Noah with, and what We have revealed to you, and what We charged Abraham with, Moses and Jesus: 'Practice the religion, and do not separate over it' " (Q 42:14).

The Qur'ān calls upon believers to recognize the religion of Abraham, clearly positioning itself as revelation in the same tradition:

> And they say, "Be Jews or Christians and you shall be guided." Say: "No, rather the creed of Abraham, a true believer; he was no idolater." Say: "We believe in God, and in what has been revealed to us and revealed to Abraham, Ishmael, Isaac and Jacob, and the tribes, and what was given to Moses and Jesus and the prophets from their Lord; we make no division between any of them, and to Him we surrender." (Q 2:136–7; cf: 26:193–8)

Although this monotheistic religion was accurately revealed before the time of Muḥammad, the Qur'ān says that the communities that received those scriptures had become confused about it (Q 42:13). Whether through ignorance or by deliberately distorting the message, many Jews and Christians had fallen into disagreement, each claiming to have the truth. The Qur'ān advises that if they understood their scriptures properly, there would be no dispute and, what is more, they would recognize that the Qur'ān truly confirms what had been revealed before. "This is a blessed scripture We have revealed, confirming that which was before it" (Q 6:93).

The Qur'ān thus presents itself as confirmation and clarification of the true religion of monotheism, the religion of Abraham, which Jews call Judaism and Christians call Christianity but which is really a single tradition. "This Qur'ān narrates to the children of Israel most of what they disagree about. It is a guide and a merciful gift for believers" (Q 27:77–8). Muḥammad is presented as an integral part of the succession of prophets sent by God to reveal the divine will, just as Jesus and Moses were sent before him:

> And when Moses said to his people, "O my people, why do you hurt me, though you know I am the messenger of God to you?" . . . And when Jesus, son of Mary, said, "Children of Israel, I am indeed the messenger of God to you, confirming the Torah that is before me, and giving good tidings of a messenger who shall come after me, whose name shall be Aḥmad;" then when he brought them clear signs, they said, "This is sheer sorcery." (Q 61:6–7)

"Aḥmad" in this passage refers to Muḥammad. Muslims believe that the specific prediction of the coming of Muḥammad was deleted from Christian scriptures or, at least, that the general prediction of someone coming after Jesus (for example, John 16:6–33) has been misinterpreted. The Qur'ān makes a number of similar clarifications of the previous messages. For example, when Abraham demonstrated his submission (*islām*) to the will of God by agreeing to sacrifice his son, the son in question is identified as Ishmael (Ismāʿīl), not Isaac (Isḥāq), as Jews and Christians believe. As well, Abraham's act is described as personal; its reward was not bequeathed to successive generations. The patriarch serves as a model for others to follow, but each individual must earn her own reward from God by likewise submitting to the divine will:

> Those to whom We gave the book and who follow it accurately, they believe in it; and whoever disbelieves in it, they are the losers. Children of Israel, remember My blessing with which I blessed you, and that I have preferred you above all others; and fear a day when no soul shall substitute for another, and no ransom will be accepted from it, nor any intercession will help it, and they will not be assisted. And when his Lord tested Abraham with certain words, and he fulfilled them. He said, "I make you a leader for the people." He said, "And what of my progeny?" He said, "My covenant does not extend to oppressors." (Q 2:122–5)

Similarly, the Qur'ān corrects those who believe that Jesus is the son of God. The Qur'ān says that Jesus was a great prophet; in fact, he is called "Messiah" (Q 3:46) and the Qur'ān recounts miracles he performed that do not appear in Christian scriptures. But the Qur'ān calls Jesus the "son of Mary," not the son of God (Q 2:88; 2:254; 3:46, etc.). He was a messenger (Q 4:172). God is the creator of all that exists, the Qur'ān says, not the progenitor of children. Nor is Jesus above being a servant of God (Q 4:172–3). Furthermore, the Qur'ān says that Jesus was not crucified. The Qur'ān says that it only appeared as if he had been killed, but really God "took him up to himself" (Q 4:158).

The Qur'ān also refers to prophets unknown to Jews and Christians. For example, there is a chapter named for an Arab messenger, Hūd (Q 11), who warned his community to follow God, but they rejected him. The same community then rejected another messenger, Ṣāliḥ, and they were punished with tragedy. Similarly, the Qur'ān relates the story of the Midianites, who were done away with when they rejected their messenger Shuʿayb. The point of these stories, like that of the people of Lot, is that people reject the message of God at their own risk.

The Qur'ān then confirms that it is the final clarification of the message. Those who accept the message brought by Muḥammad are called "the best community brought forth to people, enjoining good and forbidding evil, and believing in God" (Q 3:111). The "People of the Book" – those who have received the earlier scriptures – will suffer if they reject true prophets. "Some of them are believers," the Qur'ān claims, "but most of them are sinful" (Q 3:112–13). The Qur'ān is the perfect expression of the divine will; no other is necessary. As the Qur'ān puts it in a verse delivered toward the end of Muḥammad's life, "Today I have perfected your religion for you, and I have completed my blessing upon you and approved submission (*al-islām*) as your religion. Whoever is forced by hunger to sin . . . God is forgiving, merciful" (Q 5:4). Therefore, the succession of prophets ends with Muḥammad. The Qur'ān calls him the "seal of the prophets" (Q 33:41). The fact that the communities of earlier prophets have separated over their interpretations is accepted as the will of God: "If your Lord had so willed, He would have made mankind one community, but they continue to remain divided" (Q 11:119; cf. Q 2:213; 10:19). Now, rather than disputing over doctrine, all who claim to believe should simply "compete with one another in good works." Muslims believe this message is intended for all people and is sufficient for all time.

Themes of the Qur'ān

As noted above, the Qur'ān is the basis of all Islamic life. It provides guidance concerning worship and ritual, as well as personal piety, and family and community relations. In fact, the Qur'ān frequently refers to itself, as well as the Torah and the Gospels, as "guidance for humanity" (Q 2:186, for example). That guidance turns on a set of interrelated themes. Chief among them are the oneness of God (*tawḥīd*) and divine mercy (*raḥma*).

The Arabic term for monotheism is *tawḥīd*. Derived from the Arabic term for "one," *tawḥīd* does not appear as such in the Qur'ān (although other forms of the term do). But it conveys the rich complexity of the Qur'ān's insistence on the oneness of God. *Tawḥīd* means not only that there is only one God, the god (*al-ilāh*), Allāh, but that God is without partners and without parts. None of the deities worshiped by the Meccans is actually divine, the Qur'ān asserts (see Q 53:20), nor is God part of a trinity, as the Christians believe (see Q 4:172; 5:74). But the oneness of God carries further implications in the Qur'ān, particularly in view of modern Islamic thinkers. There is only one God, and there is only one creator of all human beings. The one God is also the sole provider, protector, guide, and judge of all human beings. All human beings are equal in their utter dependence upon God, and their well-being depends upon their acknowledging that fact and living accordingly. This is both the will and the law of God. Modern Islamic commentators such as the Egyptian Muḥammad ʿAbduh (d. 1905), Muslim Brotherhood ideologue Sayyid Qutb (d. 1966), and Iranian leader Ayatollah Khomeini (d. 1989) stress, therefore, that *tawḥīd* implies that society must be ordered in accordance with the will of God. A *tawḥīd*-based society is one in which people devote themselves to serving God by safeguarding the dignity and equality in which all were created. Submission (*islām*) to that will is the route to our happiness both in this life and the hereafter.

Thus, *tawḥīd* not only describes God but also commands that humans create a society reflecting the divine will. Demonstrating God's mercy, the Qur'ān provides the guidance necessary to do that. Although the Qur'ān frequently warns of perdition for those who violate the will of God and vividly describes the scourges of hell, its overriding emphasis is on divine mercy. "The Merciful" (*al-raḥmān*) is one of the most frequently used names of God, equivalent to Allāh (*al-ilāh*). As noted above, all but one chapter of the Qur'ān begin by invoking the name of God, "the Merciful, the Compassionate." Divine mercy is often paired with forgiveness. "God is forgiving and merciful" is a common refrain. At times, especially in the early Meccan chapters, the Qur'ān sternly warns people that they ignore its message at their own risk: "Woe to the slanderer and backbiter, who collects wealth and counts it continually. He thinks his wealth will bring him eternal life, but no, he will certainly be thrown into hell" (Q 104:2–5). "Have you seen the one who makes a mockery of faith? He is the one who neglects the orphan, and does not encourage feeding the poor. Woe to those who pray but do so only to impress others. They like to be seen [praying] but [then] do not give charity" (Q 107:2–8). The Qur'ān balances these warnings with expressions of understanding of the weaknesses of human nature: "Indeed, the human being is born impatient. When evil touches him he is anxiety-ridden, and when good things happen to him, grudging" (Q 70:20–22). In this context it offers advice and encouragement:

> As for the human being, when God tests him and honors him and blesses, he says, "My Lord has favored me." But when God tests him and restricts his livelihood, he says, "My Lord has forsaken me." No; you do not honor orphans or work for the well-being of the poor, you take over [others'] inheritance and are overly attached to wealth. (Q 89:16–21)

> [W]hen you are aboard ships and they sail with a fair breeze and they are happy about it, then a violent wind overtakes them and the waves come from every side and they think they are drowning, then call upon God, practicing religion properly [and saying] if you spare us from this we will be indeed grateful. But when He has rescued them, indeed they begin oppression on earth. O people, your oppression will only hurt yourselves! (Q 10:23–4)

At the same time, the Qur'ān promises mercy and forgiveness. "My mercy encompasses everything" (Q 7:157).

> On the day when every soul is confronted with what it has done, good and evil, they will desire a great distance from [evil]. God asks you to beware; God is full of pity for servants. Say: "If you love God, follow me." God will love you and forgive you your sins. God is forgiving, merciful. (Q 3:29–31)

Thus the Qur'ān describes God's judgment and mercy as two aspects of the same phenomenon, both within the context of the divine command to submit to the divine will by establishing a just society. It also sets an example for people to emulate and provides specific guidelines for that society. Fair-dealing, honesty, and justice are central: "O Believers, be steadfast [for] God, giving testimony in justice, and do not let a people's hatred cause you to act without justice. Be just, that is nearer to righteousness" (Q 5:9). "Believers, establish justice, being witnesses for God, even if it [works] against yourselves or against your parents or relatives; regardless of whether [those involved are] rich or poor, God has priority for you" (Q 4:136).

The Qur'ān places particular emphasis on justice and compassion for the most vulnerable members of society. It mentions orphans often, calling for their care and protection. Their well-being is routinely mentioned as the measure of the piety of both individuals and society. For example, the Qur'ān instructs Muḥammad to tell people when they ask about orphans: "Promotion of their welfare is great goodness" (Q 2:21).

> True piety is this: to believe in God and the last day, the angels, the book, and the prophets, to give of one's substance, however cherished, to relatives and orphans, the needy, the traveler, beggars, and to ransom the slave, to perform the prayer, to pay alms. And those who fulfill their promises, and endure with fortitude misfortune, hardship and peril, these are the ones who are true in their faith; these are the truly God-fearing. (Q 2:178)

The Qur'ān also acknowledges the institution of slavery but says that moral superiority lies in freeing slaves, as well as feeding the hungry and orphans (Q 90:5–17). Freeing slaves and feeding the hungry is enjoined as a way of making up for sins (Q 5:90).

Among the Qur'ān's most detailed legislation is that designed to improve the status of women. The Qur'ān is the only major religious text to acknowledge misogyny and enjoin correctives. For example, the Qur'ān criticizes those who are disappointed by the birth of girls (Q 16:59–60; 43:18). It forbids female infanticide, a common practice at the time of Muḥammad. Wives are not to be bought from their families, as they were in many cultures in the Middle East at the time; instead, the Qur'ān stipulates that the bridal gift (dower) be given to the bride herself in an amount to be agreed upon between the bride and groom (Q 4:25). The dower is referred to in the Qur'ān as the woman's wages, indicating that women's work is valuable and should be compensated. Nevertheless, the marriage relationship is not simply a contract for services. The Qur'ān describes it as mutually beneficial. Spouses are described in the Qur'ān as protective "garments" for one another (Q 2:188; 9:71). Their relationship is to be one of "love and mercy" (Q 30:22). Men are encouraged to be patient with their wives (Q 4:20). Divorce is allowed, but only after two trial separations, during which arbiters are chosen from both families to try to arrange reconciliation (Q 4:36; cf. 4:129). Then the couple may part, but without rancor, and the husband is required to provide support for the divorced wife, "according to justice, an obligation on those who are righteous" (Q 2:242). A woman may also obtain a divorce if she and her husband agree on a financial consideration (Q 2:230). Overall, the Qur'ān treats women and men as moral equals. It specifies that believing men and women "are protectors of one another. They enjoin good and forbid evil, and observe prayer, give charity, and obey God and his messenger" (Q 9:71). The social structure envisioned by the Qur'ān is unquestionably patriarchal. Women are granted rights "similar to those appropriately over them, but men are one degree higher" (Q 2:229). Similarly, men are considered to be "responsible for women because God has favored some over others and because they spend of their wealth" (Q 4:35). As a result, women must obey their husbands, and men have the right to discipline their wives or even divorce them for disobedience (Q 4:35). Nevertheless, the Qur'ān clearly insists that women, particularly in view of their financial dependency on males, be treated justly.

The Qur'ān stresses that people can be judged only by God and that God will judge based upon their efforts to comply with the divine command to "establish justice." Those who "believe and do good works," the Qur'ān states repeatedly, will have nothing to fear in the afterlife; they will be richly rewarded. "Believers, bow down and prostrate yourselves in prayer and worship your Lord and do good deeds, and you will prosper. And struggle for God as you should struggle" (Q 22:78–9). This struggle "on the path of God" (*fī sabīl Allāh*), as the Qur'ān often puts it, is the root meaning of the term *jihād*. Thus, the Qur'ān presents a challenge to humanity. Using Muḥammad as the model and remembering the forgiveness and mercy of God, people must strive to create a just society. As in the case of past examples, communities as a whole will be judged in history; God does not allow oppressive societies to flourish indefinitely. But individuals will be judged in the afterlife, based upon whether or not they attempted to contribute to this effort:

> To God belongs whatever is in the heavens and earth. He forgives whom He will and punishes whom He will. God is forgiving, merciful. Believers, do not consume usury, doubling

> and redoubling [the amount]. Do your duty to God and you will be successful. Protect yourselves from the fire prepared for disbelievers. And obey God and the messenger, and you will find mercy. And compete with one another for forgiveness from your Lord, and for paradise as great as the heavens and earth, prepared for the righteous. Those who spend in [times of] prosperity and adversity, and those who control their anger and who pardon others; God loves those who do good; and those who, when they commit an offense or wrong themselves, remember God and beg forgiveness for their sins – and who can forgive sins except God – and who do not repeat knowingly what they have done; these are the ones whose reward from their Lord is forgiveness and gardens with rivers flowing beneath, where they will abide, a great reward for those who work. Indeed there have been ages before you, so travel the earth and see what was the end of those who deny [messengers]. This is a clear sign for people and guidance and a warning to the righteous. Do not give up or grieve, and you will certainly prosper if you are believers. . . . And God will make clear those who believe and blot out the disbelievers. Do you think that you will enter heaven without God recognizing those of you who struggle and those who are steadfast? (Q 3:130–43)

Role of the Qur'ān in Islamic Life: Ritual and Art

The Qur'ān is the foundation of all Islamic ritual. It is the source of all prayer and the basis of communal worship. Muslims are required to pray five times daily, at sunrise, midday, mid-afternoon, sunset and evening. At each of these times, verses of the Qur'ān are recited in a specified order and number of repetitions (ranging from twice at morning prayer to four times at evening prayer). Extra prayers may be added individually but, again, they are based on the Qur'ān. The weekly congregational prayer (at midday on Fridays) follows the same pattern, although it includes a sermon (*khuṭba*), often based upon a Qur'ānic theme. As well, devout Muslims read the entire Qur'ān during the holy month of fasting, Ramaḍān. The book is divided into thirty sections for this purpose.

Qur'ān recitation (*tajwīd*) and Qur'ānic calligraphy are the most respected art forms in Islam. Both follow traditional standards developed over the centuries and transmitted from master to student. *Tajwīd* follows set patterns of pronunciation and intonation, characterizing it as chanting rather than singing. Its basic use is to call worshipers to prayer at the appointed times, but "spiritual concerts" (*samā*ʿ) by respected chanters (*qāri'*; plural: *qāri'ūn*) are also common. Such concerts are particularly popular among Muslim mystics (Ṣūfīs) and those drawn toward spirituality. In addition to its spiritual purposes, the tradition of oral recitation of the Qur'ān has also allowed scholars to be certain of the correct pronunciation of Qur'ānic Arabic.

Muslims display enormous reverence for the Qur'ān. It is still common for young boys to memorize the entire Qur'ān. Such an accomplishment is often marked by great celebration, as a kind of rite of passage from childhood to adulthood. Popular Qur'ān chanters can attract great followings and are often invited to open important events in Muslim communities. Many people maintain belief in the miraculous protective power of the words of the Qur'ān itself. It is very common for Muslims to wear verses of the Qur'ān around their necks, and hang beautifully reproduced verses on walls, or have them stitched into fabric, or carved into wood or stone as decorative or architectural elements of their homes or public buildings. Each year during the pilgrimage season, for example, a special cloth embroidered in gold with Qur'ānic verses is created to drape the Ka'ba (the sanctuary in Mecca which is the object of the annual Islamic pilgrimage, the *ḥajj*). Some people believe there are statistical miracles in the Qur'ān, for example, that there are exact equivalences in the mention of opposite terms such as "heaven" and "hell" or "angels" and "devils," or that the proportion of the number of times the terms "land" and "sea" are used equals the proportion of the earth that is covered by each element respectively.

The Qur'ān in Law

Perhaps the most fundamental use of the Qur'ān in Islamic society is as the basis of Islamic law. As indicated above, the Qur'ān does provide some specific legislation, but it is not essentially a book of legislation. It uses the term "law" or "legislate" only four times. The Qur'ān describes the basic elements of Islamic life, including the essential duties of all believers (the "five pillars" of Islam: bearing witness that there is no God but God, prayer, charity, fasting, and pilgrimage). It also prohibits various actions that undermine both personal and social well-being, such as murder, theft, dishonesty, slander, adultery, drunkenness, and gambling. All such specific rulings carry the force of law in Islam. But much of the Qur'ān consists of moral guidance and ideals – such as justice, honesty, charity, mercy, and compassion – rather than specific rulings. Furthermore, the prophet and the community he established are presented as perfect examples of Islamic life (Q 33:22; 60:4–6). However, during the lengthy historical period of Qur'ānic revelation, from about 610 CE until Muḥammad's death in 11/632, the prophet's community progressed from being a small, marginalized group in Mecca to being the dominant power in the region. As specific historical circumstances changed, so did the Qur'ān's judgment on specific topics.

Islamic legislators are therefore presented with a number of challenges. First, they must distinguish between those elements of the Qur'ān that describe specific, changeable historic circumstances, and those that contain eternal principles, applicable in all times and places. As scholars often put it, they must distinguish between description and prescription in the Qur'ān. For example, as noted above, the Qur'ān treats women and men as moral equals; they share the same religious duties and are equally responsible before God for their efforts in creating a just society. Yet the Qur'ān also claims that men "are a degree higher" in social responsibility, that men are responsible for women, that they may marry up to four women if the women are in need and the men can treat them equally, and that wives must be obedient toward husbands. Those who seek to replicate the Qur'ān's example in different times and places must then determine whether or not the Qur'ān's patriarchy is an ideal (prescription) or simply a reflection of the reality at the time of revelation (description), whose injustices the Qur'ān sought to offset by prohibiting misogynistic practices. Would the insistence on women's subservience to men conflict with the Qur'ān's overall egalitarianism if economic conditions no longer dictated that women were financially dependent upon men?

Islamic legislators must also determine which of the Qur'ān's often diverse judgments on specific topics carry the force of law. A common example of such diversity is found in the Qur'ān's statements about war. In *sūra* 16, Muslims are told that "those who emigrated in God's cause after they were wronged, We shall surely lodge them in this world in a goodly lodging, and the wage of the world to come is better" (Q 16:42). No advice is given for seeking a redress of grievances. A little later, those who have suffered oppression are told to "call [the oppressors] to the way of your Lord with wisdom and good advice, and dispute with them in the better way. . . . And if you punish, do so as you have been punished; and yet surely if you are patient, it is better for those who are patient" (Q 16:126–7). However, Q 22:40 declares, "Permission is given to those [who fight] because they were wronged; surely God is able to help them." Similarly, "Fight in the way of God those who fight you, but do not commit aggression; God does not love aggressors" (Q 2:191). In this instance, retaliation is allowed in cases of self-defense or defense of property. The chapter continues:

> And kill [those who fight against you] wherever you find them and drive them out from where they drove you out; persecution is worse than killing. But do not fight them at the holy mosque unless they fight you there. Then, if they fight you, fight them. That is the recompense of unbelievers. But if they stop, surely God is forgiving and merciful. Fight them until there is no persecution and religion is God's. Then if they stop, there [shall be] no aggression except against the oppressors. (Q 2:191–4)

Islamic legal scholars are therefore presented with a rich and complex array of precedent and advice from which to extract legislation suitable to diverse and ever-changing circumstances.

Principles and Practice of Qur'ānic Interpretation

Fortunately, the Qur'ān itself provides guidance for interpretation. It acknowledges that some verses are more difficult to interpret than others. The Qur'ān describes itself as containing different kinds of verses. The book is entirely from God and it contains the truth and confirms previous revelations carried in the Torah and the Gospel; it is guidance for people (*hudan li'l-nās*) and a means of distinguishing right from wrong (*al-furqān*). However, in a verse that is among the most difficult of the entire Qur'ān to translate, the Qur'ān says that it contains some verses that are *muḥkamāt* and others that are *mutashābihāt* (Q 3:4–8). *Muḥkam* (the singular of *muḥkamāt*) can be interpreted as "clear," "decisive in meaning," "accurate," "solid," "reinforced," "perfect," or "well-planned," among other things. *Mutashābih* (the singular of *mutashabihāt*) can mean "ambiguous," "indistinct," or "obscure." The verse in which these terms are used to describe some verses of the Qur'ān amplifies its meaning, saying that the verses that are *muḥkamāt* are "the mother" or "basis of the book," while "no one except God knows the interpretation" of the *mutashābihāt*. The Qur'ān does not indicate which verses are which, or how many of each type it contains. This fascinating verse seems to be a caution against excessive confidence among interpreters. It seems to encourage instead the ongoing struggle to elicit inspiration from the Qur'ān.

The Qur'ān's most specific advice concerning the legislative impact of its content is contained in passages describing its abrogation (*naskh*) of some verses. "Whatever verse we abrogate or cause to be forgotten, we bring one better than that or else one like it" (Q 2:107; cf. Q 16:102; 13:40). Some scholars believe this applies only to the Qur'ān's abrogation of earlier scriptures, but many believe it applies to verses within the Qur'ān itself. This principle of abrogation has been used, for example, to establish the Islamic prohibition of alcohol, even though the Qur'ān at one point says simply that people should not pray under the influence (Q 4:44) and, at another, only that wine should be avoided (Q 5:91). Nevertheless, the verses which state that drinking wine is a grievous sin whose evil outweighs its usefulness (e.g., Q 2:220) are taken as definitive, superseding the earlier verses because they were delivered later. In other cases, however, such as the verses on oppression, all the verses are applicable, depending upon the circumstances for which people are seeking guidance. In some circumstances, suffering patiently is recommended, such as when those suffering are so weak that rebellion would undoubtedly result in utter defeat, whereas in other cases retaliation or retribution might be an effective means of ending oppression.

In order to determine the applicability of diverse judgments such as these, scholars refer to the circumstances of revelation (*asbāb al-nuzūl*) of each verse. The circumstances of revelation are conveyed in reports known generically as *ḥadīth* (plural: *aḥādith*; sometimes translated as "traditions"). A rich source of the early history of Islam, *ḥadīths* are reports of things Muḥammad said or did, and include things that were said or done in the presence of the prophet and his reaction to them. As noted above, these circumstances assist in dating the various verses, a critical element in determining the applicability of the principle of abrogation. But they also provide the context for various Qur'ānic statements, allowing scholars to define the circumstances in which the various verses carry the force of law.

Since the death of Muḥammad, Islam's most revered scholars have devoted themselves to elaboration of the Qur'ān in commentaries known as *tafsīr*. Based on detailed study of language, logic, and history transmitted through *ḥadīth*, *tafsīr* attempt (among other things) to provide guidance to Muslim legists in their efforts to derive legislation from the Qur'ān.

The study of the Qur'ān for the sake of determining Islamic law is considered the highest science in Islam (*fiqh*). Relying on *ḥadīth* reports and *tafsīr*, scholars set about the process of deriving legislation from the Qur'ān. But in view of the dynamic nature of society and the fallibility of human judgment, Islamic legislation has never been monolithic. Even though the Qur'ān is considered perfect and applicable for all time, Islam has always tolerated a range of interpretations of its legal implications. By the tenth century, the Muslim community recognized five major schools of Islamic legal thought (*madhāhib*; singular: *madhhab*). Each was named for a major scholar who was believed capable of deriving fresh legal rulings from the Qur'ān and the *sunna*. These were Ja'far al-Ṣādiq (d. 148/765), Abū Ḥanīfa (d. 150/767), Mālik ibn Anas (d. 179/795), al-Shāfi'ī (d. 205/820), and Ibn Ḥanbal (d. 241/855), producing, respectively, the Ja'farī *madhhab* which is dominant among Shī'ī Muslims as well as the Sunnī Ḥanafī, Mālikī, Shāfi'ī, and Ḥanbalī schools.

Overall, Qur'ānic legislation is characterized as being of two kinds: those regulations concerning humans' responsibility to God (*'ibādāt*), and those concerning human beings' interaction (*mu'āmalāt*). The former concern requirements for prayer, charitable giving, fasting, and pilgrimage. The latter deal with all social matters, including marriage, divorce, inheritance, the treatment of orphans and slaves, murder, theft, retaliation, and war. In the Qur'ān, however, these issues are not always separate, as is clear from the popular verse quoted above:

> True piety is this: to believe in God and the last day, the angels, the book, and the prophets, to give of one's substance, however cherished, to relatives and orphans, the needy, the traveler, beggars, and to ransom the slave, to perform the prayer, to pay alms. And those who fulfill their promises and endure with fortitude misfortune, hardship and peril, these are the ones who are true in their faith; these are the truly God-fearing. (Q 2:178)

Instead of a neat division of duties into those concerned with the divine and those concerned with the mundane, then, the entire world for the Qur'ān is of divine concern, and thus potentially sacred. Indeed, the Qur'ān may be described as charging humanity with the task of sanctifying all aspects of human life by bringing them into accord with the will of God.

Further reading

Translations of the Qur'ān

Ali, Abdullah Yusuf (1934) *The Holy Qur'ān: Text, Translation and Commentary.* Shaikh Muḥammad Ashraf, Lahore. (Accessible translation; includes voluminous footnotes describing interpretations of various verses. Generally follows Egyptian standard edition verse numbering. Many reprints exist.)

Arberry, A. J. (1955) *The Koran Interpreted.* Allen & Unwin, London. (Poetic translation in somewhat anachronistic style. Follows Flügel edition verse numbering.)

Bell, Richard (1937–9) *The Qur'ān Translated, with a critical re-arrangement of the Sūrahs.* 2 vols. T. & T. Clark, Edinburgh. (Classic translation, based on Flügel edition. Some critical comments and *sūra* arrangement considered problematic by Muslim scholars.)

Khan, Muḥammad Zafrulla (1971) *The Quran.* Curzon Press, London. (Arabic text with English translation, often reflecting modern interpretations. Uses common Indian/Pakistani verse numbering, similar to Egyptian standard system except that it counts the opening "In the name of God, the Merciful, the Compassionate" as the first verse.)

Pickthall, Mohammed Marmaduke (1930) *The Meaning of the Glorious Koran: An Explanatory Translation.* A. A. Knopf, London. (Classic English translation, following Egyptian standard verse numbering and based on traditional interpretations.)

Secondary sources

Bijlefeld, William A. (1974) Some recent contributions to Qur'anic studies. Selected publications in English, French, and German, 1964–1973. *The Muslim World* 64, 79–102, 172–9, 259–74.

Cragg, Kenneth (1971) *The Event of the Qur'ān: Islam in its Scripture.* Allen & Unwin, London.

Cragg, Kenneth (1973) *The Mind of the Qur'ān: Chapters in Reflection.* Allen & Unwin, London.

Izutsu, Toshihiko (1964) *God and Man in the Koran: Semantics of the Koranic Weltanschauung.* Keio Institute of Cultural and Linguistic Studies, Tokyo.

Jeffery, Arthur (1937) *Materials for the History of the Text of the Koran.* E. J. Brill, Leiden. (Classic study of the history of Qur'ān text, although showing little sensitivity for Muslims' concerns about its uniqueness and authenticity.)

Kassis, Hanna E. (1983) *A Concordance of the Qur'ān.* University of California Press, Berkeley. (Essential tool for Qur'ānic study; concordance of Arberry's translation keyed to the Arabic text.)

Mawdudi, Sayyid Abu al-A'la (1988) *Towards Understanding the Qur'ān.* Trans. Zafar Ishaq Ansari. Islamic Foundation, Leicester. (Commentary by early Islamist, combining traditional and modern themes.)

Rahman, Fazlur (1980) *Major Themes of the Qur'ān.* Bibliotheca Islamica, Minneapolis. (Modern classic on the basic teachings of the Qur'ān.)

Wansbrough, John (1977) *Quranic Studies: Sources and Methods of Scriptural Interpretation.* Oxford University Press, Oxford; reprint with annotations Prometheus Press, Amherst NY, 2004. (Controversial study suggesting Jewish and Christian influence in the Qur'ān.)

Watt, W. Montgomery (1977) *Bell's Introduction to the Qur'ān.* Edinburgh University Press, Edinburgh. (Contains a discussion of the seven acceptable variant readings of the Qur'ān.)

CHAPTER 2

Discovering

Christopher Buck

Why the Qur'ān?

The Qur'ān, the holy book of Islam, may well be the most powerful book in human history, with the arguable exception of the Bible. Both in world history and contemporary affairs, it is doubtful that any other book now commands, or has in the past exerted, so profound an influence. Objectively, one of every five people on earth today is Muslim, each of whom subjectively believes that the Qur'ān actually supersedes the Bible, and that it is the Qur'ān – not the Bible – that is unsurpassed. Since Muslims see Islam as the last of the world's religions, they view the Qur'ān as the latest and greatest book. Even if one does not share this view, the sheer magnitude of its influence commands respect, and one cannot be cross-culturally and globally literate without some understanding of this monumental text. The purpose of this chapter is to inspire and assist readers in discovering the Qur'ān for themselves, with the helpful synergy of insider and outsider – religious and secular – perspectives.

Academic Study of the Qur'ān

The study of the Qur'ān in an academic setting has raised a number of legal and pedagogical issues in recent decades, some of which have thrust the scripture into the public eye in a way that has not been previously experienced. Of course, religion in general is a controversial topic within education, and demands inevitably arise to know why the Qur'ān should (or even can) be taught in a publicly funded university. The situation in the United States, for example, is one that has provoked legal discussions and challenges. Doesn't the study of the Qur'ān in the university violate the Establishment Clause of the First Amendment? What about the separation of church and state?

These very concerns were recently raised in US federal courts. A national academic and legal controversy erupted in summer 2002 when the University of North Carolina

(UNC) at Chapel Hill required incoming freshmen, as part of its Summer Reading Program, to read and discuss Michael Sells' *Approaching the Qurʾān: The Early Revelation* (Sells 1999). This text – a fresh translation and elucidation of the early Meccan *sūras* of the Qurʾān – was recommended by UNC Islamicist Carl Ernst in order to promote an understanding of Islam, especially in light of the events surrounding the September 11, 2001 terrorist attacks (Burdei 2002).

Alleging that UNC violated the Establishment Clause and abridged students' rights to religious free exercise by forcing incoming freshmen and transfer students to study Islam against their will, a conservative-Christian activist group, the Family Policy Network (FPN) filed suit in US District Court, Middle District of North Carolina (MDNC), on July 22, seeking a preliminary injunction to keep UNC from conducting its summer program. The case was captioned (named) *Yacovelli v. Moeser* (after James Yacovelli, an FPN spokesman, and James Moeser, UNC Chancellor). When the FPN lost, it immediately appealed to the 4th Circuit Court of Appeals, but lost again. This case was widely reported (see Euben 2002), both nationally and internationally, but was not judicially "reported" (that is, the district and appellate decisions were not published).

A later challenge was filed in 2004 but was lost on appeal. Without going into the technicalities of the *Lemon* test, which the Court applied along with the endorsement and coercion tests, the challenge failed. In his decision, Chief Judge N. Carlton Tilley, Jr. ruled:

> *Approaching the Qurʾān* simply cannot be compared to religious practices which have been deemed violative of the *Establishment Clause*, such as posting the Ten Commandments, reading the Lord's Prayer or reciting prayers in school. The book does include Suras, which are similar to Christian Psalms. However, by his own words, the author endeavors only to explain Islam and not to endorse it. Furthermore, listening to Islamic prayers in an effort to understand the artistic nature of the readings and its connection to a historical religious text does not have the primary effect of advancing religion. (*Yacovelli v. Moeser*, 2004 US Dist. LEXIS 9152 [MDNC May 20, 2004], *aff'd Yacovelli v. Moeser* [University of North Carolina, Chapel Hill], 324 F.Supp.2d 760 [2004].)

This ruling is consistent with the US Supreme Court's endorsement of the academic study of religion in public schools and universities, when Justice Tom C. Clark in 1963 declared that "one's education is not complete without a study of comparative religion or the history of religion and its relationship to the advancement of civilization" (*Abington v. Schempp*, 374 US 203, 224, n. 9 [1963]). It is the secular approach that makes the academic study of religion constitutionally permissible: "Nothing we have said here indicates that such study of the Bible or of religion, when presented objectively as part of a secular program of education, may not be effected consistently with the First Amendment" (*Abington v. Schempp*, 374 US 203, 224, n. 9 [1963]). As Justice Powell has said more recently: "Courses in comparative religion of course are customary and constitutionally appropriate" (*Edwards v. Aguillard*, 482 US 578, 607 1987] [Powell and O'Connor, JJ., concurring]). Based on Justice Clark's statement as it applies to the Qurʾān specifically, university officials now argue that – in addition to being constitutionally permissible – one's education is not complete without a study of the

Qur'ān (as well as the history of Islam) and its relationship to the advancement of civilization.

How to Read the Qur'ān?

A nineteenth-century mystic once said that the Qur'ān eclipses all of the miracles of all of the previous prophets, for the miracle of the Qur'ān, alone, remains (Shirazi 1950; Lawson 1988). That is to say, the staff of Moses may have turned into a serpent and swallowed up the magicians' snakes in Pharaoh's court, but that prophetic scepter has vanished. Moses may well have parted the Red Sea, as Muslims themselves believe, but that prodigy is long gone. No empirical evidence of either miracle remains today. What alone abides is the "miracle" of the Qur'ān – its prodigious ability to transform the lives of those who believe and accept the Qur'ān as the best guide for their lives. This transformation is spiritual alchemy, taking the base appetites that most of us are born with and transmuting these into the pure gold of a refined moral and spiritual character. The Qur'ān can transform a pair of horns into a set of wings, changing the pious believer from a devil into an angel. Such is the nature of Muslim belief about the Qur'ān.

The Qur'ān can and should be taught in the university – not to convert students into pious Muslims, but to convert pious Muslim beliefs into something students can understand, so that they can appreciate the power of the book to influence those who believe in it. However, beyond the question of why the Qur'ān should be taught, there is the problem of how it should be taught. In whatever course and context it may be taught, the challenge is to engage readers in the study of this text, to assist them in discovering the Qur'ān for themselves.

Reading the Qur'ān is far easier said than done. The Qur'ān is a challenging text. To the uninitiated, the book is both simplistic and enigmatic. To the untrained eye, the Qur'ān, on first impression, may strike one as arcane, florid, repetitive, or otherwise impenetrable to Westerners wholly unprepared to study the text dispassionately. However, there is a deeper hermeneutical issue involved, one of attitude and assumptions as to the authority and nature of the text.

The Qur'ān makes its own particular truth-claims, which are quite audacious. It tells the reader that its source is an archetypal "mother of the book" (*umm al-kitāb*) in heaven. The Qur'ān is therefore of divine origin. It is not only authorized, it is actually authored by God Himself. This is an extraordinary claim, indeed. As such, from a Muslim perspective the element of divine revelation is of paramount importance. God wrote the Qur'ān, Muslims believe, and thus the book commands their respect. But should it command the respect of those who have not been raised in its culture, who might consider it in the university? Absolutely. So where does one begin? There are methodological considerations that must first be addressed. The Qur'ān may be a difficult text for non-Muslims, but it is not unfathomable.

The still-predominantly Christian West may have serious misgivings as to the truth of such claims. Isn't the Qur'ān an ersatz version of the Bible – a derivative imitation?

Table 2.1 Polarities in the study of the Qurʾān

Western	Muslim
Secular academic	Traditional academic
Analytic	Synthetic
Tendency to over-differentiate	Tendency to harmonize
Use of reason and bias	Use of reason and faith
Sometimes offensive	Sometimes defensive

This very assumption largely biased the Western reception of the Qurʾān from the very start, and affected (infected) its study until now. As a result, polarities in the study of the Qurʾān have emerged, although these are beginning to disappear. The great divide in Qurʾānic studies has historically been the tension between traditional Muslim approaches and Western academic approaches. Although problematic for gaining a coherent understanding and appreciation of the Qurʾān, these two competing paradigms are somewhat synergistic. If you combine the two, you get what Wilfred Cantwell Smith (Smith 1959: 53; but cf. McCutcheon 1999) regarded as the insider–outsider dynamic. In principle, he suggested that the best approach to the study of the Qurʾān and Islam is to be able to enter into a believer's (emic) perspective while maintaining some degree of relative objectivity (etic perspective). Indeed, Smith's canon of believer intelligibility requires that "no statement about a religion is valid unless it can be acknowledged by that religion's believers." This "creative principle" offers the best of both worlds, for it "provides experimental control that can lead" scholars "dynamically towards the truth." However, unless one adheres to Smith's principle, polarities will inevitably arise. Table 2.1 highlights the nature of these polarities.

The table shows a complement of productive and reductive approaches. The method of reading largely determines what is read and how it is understood. The Muslim approaches the Qurʾān reverentially and with full faith in the truth it enshrines. The Western secular approach can be just the opposite: it is skeptical and analytic. But it does not have to be. Where there are apparent difficulties and even apparent contradictions in the text, the Muslim will try to resolve those anomalies by harmonizing them on a higher plane of understanding, while a person approaching the text from a secular perspective (the Westerner) may be dismissive of the Qurʾān as simply a human enterprise where inconsistencies and errors are to be expected. Such a conclusion is not only misguided according to any knowledgeable Muslim, it is also an attack upon the integrity of a sacred text that is divinely revealed.

This concept of the Qurʾān as a revealed scripture is basic to an appreciation as to why Muslims both revere the Qurʾān and orient their entire lives according to its dictates, for the Qurʾān and the *ḥadīth* (oral traditions that report the sayings and actions of the Muḥammad) are the two principal sources of authority for Muslim doctrine and praxis. So, to the questions of where to begin in discovering the Qurʾān, it only makes sense to start with the concept of revelation.

Revelation and the Abrahamic Faiths

Scholars have long recognized that claims of revelation are central to the three Abrahamic faiths of Judaism, Christianity, and Islam. What these faiths have in common is that each is monotheistic. That is, they each preach a belief in a supreme Being, a one-and-only, all-powerful God. Historically, monotheism is a conscious revolution against the archaic, pre-monotheistic mind-set. This revolution was not prevalently theoretic but dynamic. It effected a radical shift in the concentration of what some scholars call the *numinosum*, or the locus of the supernatural. Archaic ("primitive" or "primal") culture is founded on the idea of an anthropocentric correspondence of microcosm and macrocosm, of part-to-whole, as in astrology. In the archaic worldview, the *numinosum* is situated in and around nature, whereas in a monotheistic framework, the *numinosum* is a supreme being, located outside nature. Monotheism disenchants the universe by exorcizing the very existence of gods, demons, and sprites. The nature spirits disappear, ghosts vanish, and the astrological basis of fate and predestination collapses. Experimental science of a pre-modern type could not have been born without the demythologization of nature that monotheism put into motion. By moving God outside of nature, monotheism contributes to the revaluation of the ideas of infinity and the void.

This revolution in worldview – disenchanting nature and seeing divinity as its prime mover – gave rise to two major defining features of Western civilization: historicism and technique. The first affects the human sciences; the other impacts the physical sciences. The argument that Islam is one of the unacknowledged roots of Western civilization flows from this historical perspective: Islamic philosophy and science impacted the high medieval and renaissance cultures to produce Western civilization, especially after the Enlightenment.

Within the monotheist worldview that is central to Islam, the Qur'ān is the literary amber of revelation – the primary mode of disclosure of God's will for humanity. The Qur'ān speaks of itself as a revealed text. Phenomenologists of religion have identified five characteristics or phenomena typically associated with revelation (Dininger 1987: 356). There are two prime characteristics. (1) *Origin or source*: All revelation has a source – God, or something supernatural or numinous communicates some kind of message to human beings. *Waḥy* is the technical term for revelation in the Qur'ān. The fundamental sense of *waḥy* seems to be what those steeped in the European romantic ethos would call a "flash of inspiration," in the sense that it is sudden and unpremeditated; (2) *Instrument or means*: Revelation is communicated supernaturally, through the agency of dreams, visions, ecstasies, words, or sacred books. *Nuzūl* is a synonym for revelation, but with the explicit notion that the Qur'ān was "sent down" from its archetypal original in the spiritual realm known as the heavens.

Other key phenomena of revelation, all of which the Qur'ān exemplifies, are: (3) *Content or object*: Revelation is the communication of the didactic, helping, or punishing presence, will, being, activity, or commission of the divinity. In this case, the Qur'ān is a revelation from God, pure and simple, communicated through a series of revelations imparted to Muḥammad over the course of twenty-three lunar years. Thus, it would be error and sacrilege to speak of Muḥammad as the "author" of the Qur'ān.

(4) *Recipients or addressees*: The Qur'ān itself is a revelation of the universal type. It is a message from God to the world; (5) *Effect and consequence for the recipient*: Revelation transforms its recipient. As the agent of revelation, Muḥammad was commissioned with a divine mission to present the Qur'ān as the voice of God, calling the entire world to righteousness and justice, to morality and decency, and to a life of prayer and fasting, and surrender to the will of God. The fact that Muḥammad was commissioned with a divine mission does not make Muḥammad himself divine, as the Qur'ān itself states: "He would never order you to take the angels and the prophets as Lords" (Q 3:74). This idea may be seen in an early Christian text: "Neither is there salvation in believing in teachers and calling them lords" (*Homilies* 8:5 in Roberts and Donaldson 1989–90).

How the Qur'ān Was Revealed

With an understanding of revelation generally, the specifics of the revelation of the Qur'ān may now be addressed. Such considerations focus on the person identified as the prophet of Islam, Muḥammad.

It was Muḥammad's practice to meditate prayerfully in a cave on Mt. Ḥirā'. He was practicing *taḥannuth*, some sort of pious exercise, when he first encountered the archangel Gabriel, who revealed the Qur'ān to him over the next twenty-three lunar years. Tradition is unanimous that Gabriel was the agent of revelation, even though he is mentioned only twice in the Qur'ān. The Qur'ān itself explains how God reveals: "It belongs not to any mortal that God should speak to him, except by revelation, or from behind a veil, or that He should send a messenger and he reveal whatsoever He will, by His leave; surely He is All-high, All-wise" (Q 42:50). In other words, while the prophet revealed the Qur'ān, it was God who authored it, according to Muslim belief.

The Qur'ān is modeled on an archetypal *al-lawḥ al-maḥfūẓ*, the "preserved tablet" (Q 85:22), having been sent down to the nearest heaven on the "night of power" (Q 97) in the holy month of Ramaḍān, in order for Gabriel to transmit it to Muḥammad. The text of Qur'ān is from God, Muslims believe, while the recording and editing of Qur'ān is by men. It is important to understand the implications of the Qur'ān being originally revealed over a period of time, and thereafter collected and edited. Just as the Qur'ān cannot be read from cover to cover in quite the same way that one reads a novel or treatise, the Qur'ān was not written from cover to cover as well. Just as writers have flashes of inspiration, Muḥammad experienced flashes of revelation. These cumulatively became the Qur'ān.

The *ḥadīth* literature provides many anecdotes as to how revelations would come upon Muḥammad. The descriptions vary. The agent of revelation Gabriel taught Muḥammad to recite the first passages of the Qur'ān. Most frequently the accounts speak of revelations "descending" upon Muḥammad such that he would hear the sound of buzzing, or of bells, or would feel a great weight come upon him, or would enter a trance, after which the words of the Qur'ān would become indelibly inscribed in his heart, and subsequently dictated to scribes. The revelations of the Qur'ān were first recorded by scribes who wrote down the verses on whatever writing materials were available: leaves and branches of palm trees, white stones, leather, shoulder blades of sheep, ribs. One early account states that a revelation was actually eaten by a domestic animal, because it had been recorded on something organic and edible.

After Muḥammad's death in 11/632, there was no authoritative record of the revelations. They had to be collected. The process of assembling, collating, and codifying the Qur'ān was not informed by a great deal of available information as to dating and other historical information on which to base the traditional form that the Qur'ān eventually took. According to tradition, the decision to preserve the Qur'ān was taken after hundreds of reciters were killed in the Battle of Yamāma (12/633). ʿUmar (who was to become the second Caliph) suggested to Abū Bakr that the Qur'ān be collected and written down. Finally, the text was fixed under ʿUthmān, in the dialect of the Quraysh tribe (that of Muḥammad), said to be the clearest of dialects, according to tradition. Where difficulties in establishing the text arose, the dialect of the Quraysh, the tribe to which the prophet belonged, was given preference. Written texts required attestation from reciters, who had heard and memorized the Qur'ān by heart. Thus, the canon of the Qur'ān was fixed as well as the order of the *sūras* and the integrity of the consonantal text.

The urgency with which the text became fixed under the decree of the caliph ʿUthmān afforded precious little opportunity for a systematic, much less scientific ordering of the text. Its preservation was more important than its sequencing, and it was left to later Muslims scholars to provide a critical apparatus for more fully appreciating the pieces that made up the larger whole. How much editing and how intrusive or interpretive such editing may have been is largely a modern question that has occupied much of Western scholarship on the Qur'ān.

Soon after the Qur'ān was revealed, it spread like wildfire, racing with the Arab conquerors during the first two centuries of Arab expansion. The rapidity and breadth of that expansion was dramatic. At this stage, the Qur'ān had not yet achieved its status as a world text, for the simple reason that it was considered an "Arab" book (or, rather, "the" Arab book, since the Qur'ān is the first book in Arabic). Non-Arab converts were at first obliged to attach themselves to various Arab tribes, in a kind of process of spiritual and social adoption. It did not take long before non-Arabs, especially the Persians, took umbrage with this. How could a scripture with a universal message, they argued, be restricted to just a single ethnicity? And, if not, on what grounds were Arabs justified in relegating to non-Arabs a secondary status, when the category of "Muslims" constitutes a spiritual and social "nation" that embraces all races and nations, yet transcends them? Was not the prophet Abraham a Muslim ("one who surrenders" to the will of God)? And is not anyone who professes belief in the oneness of God and in the authenticity of the prophet Muḥammad to be accounted as a believer, on equal footing with every other? And so it came to be: the appeal to the Qur'ān's universalisms, expressive of its egalitarian ethic, prevailed. Thus Islam, although based on a message revealed in Arabic, was transposed to other cultures and climes, although it took centuries before the Qur'ān itself was actually translated into other languages. This singular revelation became a universal scripture.

In its final form, the Qur'ān's 114 *sūras* are arbitrarily arranged by the longest *sūra* first (except for the short "opening" chapter). The traditional dating of these *sūras* has the "early Meccan *sūras*" spanning the first thirteen lunar years (with early, middle, and final periods), shifting to the period of "Medinan *sūras*" in 1/622, coinciding with the first year of the *hijra* or migration of the early Muslim community from Mecca to Medina, followed by the "later Meccan *sūras*" on the prophet's triumphal return to his oasis-city of Mecca shortly before the end of his life in 11/632.

Taking what has become a classic, two-part division of Muḥammad's life (Watt 1953, 1956), the early Meccan *sūras* exemplify Muḥammad's role as "prophet" while the Medinan and later Meccan *sūras* present Muḥammad's vocation as "statesman." Thus the earlier revelations are intended to kindle hope and to strike the fear of God into the heart of the hearer by the promise of heaven and the threat of hell. Accordingly, the prophet's role is that of a "warner" who has come to make people alive to the threat of impending doom and death unless they repent and surrender to the will of God.

First warned, later governed – this is basically the purpose of the revelations and the logic of their sequence. The later Qur'ānic revelations enshrine laws and principles for Muslims to follow. Once a Muslim community had formed (the migration of Muslims to Mecca in 1/622 effectively created the first Muslim state), laws were needed. Accordingly, Muḥammad became a statesman in addition to his role as prophet, and began revealing the laws and ethical principles that later became the foundation for the four Sunnī schools of law and a distinctive way of life.

Sources of Revelation?

Whether the Qur'ān is informed by previous sources is a vexed question. To suggest that the Qur'ān somehow derives from predominantly Jewish or Christian sources is tantamount to discrediting the Qur'ān as a document of revelation. For Muslims, the question should be the other way around. The Qur'ān is the gold standard of divine truth. Since it is pure and unadulterated, it is previous scriptures that should be measured against the Qur'ān, not the other way around. Indeed, the Qur'ān comprehends all previous scriptures:

> Within itself, the Qur'ān provides Muslims with a view of the Bible. Mention is made of the "scrolls" of Abraham and Moses, the *Tawrāt* (Torah) of Moses, the *Zabūr* (usually understood as the Psalms) of David and the *Injīl* (Gospel) of Jesus, all conceived as direct revelation from God to the prophet concerned: "Surely we sent down the Torah wherein is guidance and light" (Qur'ān 5.48); "And we sent, following in their footsteps, Jesus son of Mary, confirming the Torah before him; and we gave to him the Gospel, wherein is guidance and light" (Qur'ān 5.50). In this way, all previous scriptures are pictured within the revelatory and compositional image of the Qur'ān itself. (Rippin 1993: 250)

To say that Muḥammad was "influenced" by his religious world and that the Qur'ān is a hodge-podge of intermixed influences is not only highly reductionist, but suggests that the prophet was himself the author of the Qur'ān and not God. Surely God had no need to borrow from previous scripture or religious lore, from the Muslim perspective. So the tension between traditional Muslim and Western academic approaches is perhaps nowhere more intense than in discussing this question.

One approach that is both methodologically sound as well as religiously acceptable is to look at the foreign vocabulary of the Qur'ān and also the religious technical terms and concepts that the Qur'ān mentions. This area of study has proven fruitful for elucidating the text. But then, again, what exactly is being proved? If used as evidence that the Qur'ān is derivative, then this crosses over from a purely descriptive phenomenology into an explanatory phenomenology that is inherently reductive. This latter approach tries to "explain away" the Qur'ān, presenting it as the product of past influences rather than as an original work that absorbs and reconfigures its cultural content to produce an Islamic civilization of world-historical proportions.

For Muslims, the only pre-Islamic source for the Qur'ān is the archetypal "mother of the book" of which the earthly Qur'ān is a faithful copy. But Muslim scholars will readily admit that the Qur'ān speaks to its historical-contemporary world, which includes the immediate past. Thus we find specific references to practices from the pre-Islamic period that the Qur'ān explicitly forbids. This is "influence" in the other direction. For instance, the pre-Islamic practice of female infanticide was quite common, where parents would bury their infant daughter in the hot, desert sand, if they thought it too much of a financial burden to raise a girl. So, in this respect, Islam functioned as a women's protectionist movement. Suffice it to say that knowledge of pre-Islamic Arabia is the natural starting place for developing a fuller understanding and appreciation for how the Qur'ān represents a significant moral and social advancement after the pre-Islamic "age of ignorance."

Major Themes of Revelation

Knowing something of the history of the revelation of the Qur'ān and its codification provides a necessary orientation. But the real heart of the Qur'ān is its message. One useful way of approaching the Qur'ān is to see it as the vehicle for expressing profound truths regarding God and the universe, and humankind and its civilizations. God is the creator, and humankind the creative. The themes of the Qur'ān, therefore, are the organizing principles of Islamic religion and civilization. What follow are several of the major themes of the Qur'ān. Most of the Qur'ān's religious principles are common to the Abrahamic faiths, and many of its morals may be appreciated as universal ethical truths.

Exaltation

One feels the presence of God in the Qur'ān, which makes it such a powerful text. Since Muḥammad is the revealer, not author, the pious read the text as the voice of God Himself. This is not a mere poetic device, as the voice of God in the Puritan poet Michael Wigglesworth's "God's Controversy with New England" (1662). The Qur'ān is the real thing, like a whole book of the Ten Commandments and more. This direct communication of God to man is charged with a power and authority that Muslims feel makes the Qur'ān inimitable, and without peer. No other text can compare with it, except previous scriptures. And rarely are they so direct and compelling. The Qur'ān is a conduit to the presence of God, and to follow the Qur'ān's dictates is to manifest the will of God.

Creation

The Qur'ān accounts for the creation of the world – not as a scientific treatise, but rather as a prophetic narrative. Scholars call this cosmogony. The important thing to remember is that cosmogony often functions as "sociogony" – the genesis of society. Just as God is the creator of the physical universe, the Qur'ān is the great moral and social civilizer of human (Muslim) society, when ideally applied.

Revelation

We have stated earlier that the Qur'ān is a revelation (actually a series of revelations) direct from God. In practice that means that everything the Qur'ān says is taken as truth. This fact is clearly of profound importance in appreciating the status and authority of the Qur'ān. While all of the Qur'ān is God's revealed truth, the Qur'ān does not contain all of God's revelations. The Qur'ān "confirms" the truth of previous revelations, as embodied in the Jewish and Christian scriptures. Much of the Qur'ān, in fact, is retrospective. It harks back to the days of previous prophets and relates what became of them and tells of the fate of peoples who rejected and persecuted the warners and messengers that God sent to them. These historical narratives have a didactic (edifying) function. They are homilies on religious history, and thus serve a religious purpose.

With its dire warnings of the day of judgment, the Qur'ān is prospective as well as retrospective. It endows history with teleology – a purpose and a final result. While this teleology is predestined, the individual can largely choose the outcome for his or her salvation. Here, salvation is not absolution from sin, but a resolution to abide by the will of God. This is true for entire societies as well, since they are aggregates of individuals and families. That is to say, an entire social order can be transformed by following the way of life illuminated by the Qur'ān. Thus, revelation contains within it the seeds of a higher civilization.

And so it happened: Islam reigned as the world's "superpower" during the so-called dark ages of Europe, when great Muslim civilizations exerted a moralizing, philosophical and scientific influence on the West. Historically, Islam is one of the catalysts that sparked the Renaissance. Ideally, revelation is the genesis of ideal civilization.

Consummation

The Qur'ān is not just one of a series of progressive revelations sent by God to help steer the course of civilization. The Qur'ān literally is the latest and greatest revelation to date. We know this because we are told that Muḥammad is the "seal of the prophets"

– that is, the final messenger. He has, in a real sense, completed the series of revelations. The Qur᾿ān is therefore the capstone of God's messages to the world.

Muḥammad's station as the "seal of the prophets" is of fundamental importance in Islam. This appellation comes from the famous "seal verse" (Q 33:40). Although interpretations of this key verse did vary in early Islam (Friedmann 1986), there is now a consensus among Muslims that the term "seal" means "last," in the sense of both "latest" and "final." While Muḥammad is considered fully human and not divine (Islam rejects the doctrine of incarnation), this truth-claim easily rivals – in both its audacity and centrality of dogma – that of Jesus being the son of God. Rather than a person being the "word" of God, for Muslims the Qur᾿ān is the word of God literally. However, that Muḥammad is the seal of the prophets is a major truth-claim and is effectively non-negotiable. It has achieved the status of a dogma, and one learns not to debate this point with Muslims if friendship is a priority. Accepting Muḥammad as the seal of the prophets is absolutely fundamental to Muslims everywhere. And this belief is firmly anchored in the Qur᾿ān itself.

Salvation

For Muslims, salvation consists in much more than simply being forgiven for one's past sins and transgressions. The act of repentance itself effects much of this. Indeed, the true test of one's sincerity is a matter of public record, purely in terms of one's actions. This record is not simply what gets recorded in the proverbial "Book of Deeds," to be read back to each individual on the day of judgment. Rather, pious deeds both manifest and further nurture purity of heart and soul. Here, salvation is active, not passive. One's salvation is a matter of degree, not of status. But Islam sees a spiritual life beyond forgiveness. Salvation is not a change of status that magically and suddenly averts God's wrath. Salvation is a process, a refinement of one's character over time.

A deeper walk with God on the "straight path" of Islam can come about through spiritual growth and transformation. But how does one do this? What can serve as an infallible spiritual guide? For Muslims, the way to bring one's life into greater conformity with God's will is through following the laws of the Qur᾿ān and the example of Muḥammad. The truest sign of one's transformative faith is conformity and dedication to the principles and teachings of Islam which are preserved, first and foremost, in the Qur᾿ān itself. The single most important act of piety is to surrender one's own will to that of the will of God. The word "Muslim" means "one who has submitted" or surrendered to the will of God. "Surrender" is not the best translation, because following God's will is an act of free will, a vigilant choice, a matter of strength through commitment and practice.

Then what is the will of God? There is a Zoroastrian scripture that states: "The will of the Lord is the law of holiness" (the Ahunwar, the most sacred formula in Zoroastrianism, a common refrain found throughout the Zend Avesta – see Vendidad, Fargard 19, and *passim*). This means that, rather than trying to divine what the will of God is in terms of making important life-decisions, the will of God is not so much what one believes, or what one is, but what one does. What a Muslim believes and what a Muslim does combine to produce what a Muslim is.

Surrendering to the will of God begins with professing one's self to be Muslim, by proclaiming that "There is no god but God" and that "Muḥammad is the messenger of God." As a general rule, Muslims pray more frequently than in any other religion. They also fast longer, for thirty days during the holy month of Ramaḍān (the dates of which annually vary because Islam is based on a lunar calendar). Once one is properly oriented towards God, and is conscious of God throughout the day, it becomes much easier to fulfill one's moral obligations as a pious Muslim. For salvation to be complete, it must be perfected. But salvation is not an all-or-nothing proposition. It is a process of drawing ever nearer to God, which process involves becoming more God-like in one's deeds. Here is where faith and works combine to effect salvation.

Therefore, the requirements of the Qur'ān for the true believer may be described, in Christian terms, as a "faith of works." In other words, Islam is ideally a "faith at work" (in Christian terms, a "way of life") and thus a "faith that works" – for the benefit of individual and society alike. If, as Christians often say, "faith without works is dead," the "faith with works" is very much alive. This is the spiritual life that Islam breathes into the physical lives of pious Muslims. Readers may be familiar with the way in which Martin Luther dichotomized faith and works. Individuals would not be "saved" by unaided efforts, but by faith alone. Islam has no such doctrine of salvation by grace. The most efficacious grace is not to give up on the sinner and allow another to die in his place as in Christianity. The better way is to promote the spiritual and moral growth of the individual. This takes discipline as well as a certain amount of faith. Daily obligatory prayer and following the laws and precepts of the Qur'ān is the truest salvation by grace, because works and faith combine to become, in the words of the beloved spiritual, "Amazing Grace."

Civilization

Salvation is not just for the individual. There is collective salvation as well. The purpose of the Qur'ān is to communicate God's will for humankind – all of humanity. Through its laws and moral principles, the Qur'ān is meant to benefit the world through restructuring human society, to infuse it with the consciousness of God and to make it alive to the will of God for human society. It is a call to righteousness and brotherhood, to human solidarity in a community of principle and commonality of values. The Qur'ān is nothing less than an attempt to reorder human society, to rescue it, Muslims would say, from the moral appetites and turpitude that threaten to make the West morally uncivilized while remaining technologically advanced. Islam offers to fill a spiritual vacuum to which Western society has largely turned a blind eye. Islamic spirituality can be harmonized with the best of Western – Christian as well as contemporary secular – traditions of civic virtues, of moral decency and of family values, informed by the West's traditional Judeo-Christian ethic. Just as the biblical "ten commandments" are still relevant, the Qur'ān still has much to say, although even some Muslims would say that it needs to be understood anew within the changed circumstances of modernity and postmodernity.

Final destination

Few other sacred texts depict the afterlife so vividly as the Qur'ān. Whether literal or metaphorical, paradise is described as the abode of the righteous, dwelling in peace in Edenic gardens inhabited by dark-eyed damsels that seem to represent higher passions rather than lower ones. Conversely, the Qur'ān portrays hell in equally graphic terms, as a pit of fire and brimstone, with a descriptive immediacy that the sermons of Jonathan Edwards can scarcely rival. Indeed, it is said that around a full one-third of the Qur'ān is eschatological, dealing with the afterlife in the next world and with the day of judgment here on earth at the end of time. As in Christianity, the day of resurrection plays a prominent role in the Qur'ān with a focus on inevitable moral accountability, both individual and collective in nature. Through promise and threat, the Qur'ān instills a healthy fear of God in the believer, who is constantly taught to respect divine authority and to expect the consequences of one's own actions.

Reading Revelation

The Qur'ān presents a number of challenges for interpreter and reader alike. Many Western readers have complained that the Qur'ān is dull and repetitive. If the Qur'ān were read as a novel from cover to cover, there might be some truth to this. But just as the Qur'ān was revealed in piecemeal fashion, so also should it be read. The final redaction of the Qur'ān obscures this fact. There are few obvious markers that will signal, to the untrained eye, the beginning and end of various discrete, revelatory sections known as pericopes. The best examples of a piece of revelation preserved in its entirety and discretely identifiable would be most of what are known as the early Meccan *sūras*.

The Qur'ān was not intended to be read as a book in one or two sittings. The more that one reads, the more the reader will have the sense that the Qur'ān repeats itself. Some expressions recur like a refrain. They have a rhetorical purpose, in that they are repeated for stress. The reiterative nature of the Qur'ān notwithstanding, certain passages have achieved such renown that they have come to be known as what al-Ghazālī (d. 505/1111) referred to as the "jewels of the Qur'ān." These include such celebrated passages as the "throne verse" (Q 2:255) and the "light verse" (Q 24:35).

Shifting from the mystical to the perplexing, some Qur'ānic passages defy easy explanation. The most obvious examples are the so-called "mysterious letters of the Qur'ān," which occur at the very beginning of twenty-nine chapters. Muslims themselves often have a mystical relationship with the Qur'ān that does not require that they understand the text, divine its enigmas or derive mystical meaning by probing its depths. In popular or "folk" Islam, instead of trying to divine its truths, Muslims may turn to the

Qur'ān as a source of divination. One common practice is to consult the Qur'ān as a kind of oracle. If a person wishes to know the solution to a personal problem, he or she can look to the Qur'ān for personal guidance by carefully meditating on the passage that first falls into view.

It is instructive enough simply to be able to see the different modes of discourse that give texture and vitality to the Qur'ān. Although the Qur'ān does not have a definite structure in any kind of systematic method, it has a complex of structures within it. These have been identified in various ways by Muslim and Western scholars alike. One way to discern the various shifts in revelatory content is to perform a genre analysis of a *sūra* or part of a *sūra* in question. The major genres, or the various styles of Qur'ānic revelations, are as follows.

Prophetic revelations

A narrative is simply a story. If the story is true, it qualifies as history. Some narratives have a purely edifying (instructive) function. Whether historically verifiable or not, all of the Qur'ānic narratives are morally true. Such a distinction will probably be lost on those pious Muslims who take the sacred text at its word (literally). Take for instance the story of Jesus as a young boy. The Qur'ān states that, as a child, Jesus would fashion birds out of mud, then breathe life into them, and the birds would fly away:

> And He [Jesus] will teach him the book, the wisdom, the Torah, the Gospel, to be a messenger to the Children of Israel saying, "I have come to you with a sign from your Lord. I will create for you out of clay as the likeness of a bird; then I will breathe into it, and it will be a bird, by the leave of God. I will also heal the blind and the leper, and bring to life the dead, by the leave of God." (Q 3:43)

Despite the abundance of miracle narratives in the four gospels, this particular prodigious ability of Jesus is unreported in the gospels found today in the New Testament. Thus, as the Qur'ān itself states, some stories it relates may be traced back to previous scriptures, and some not. This is a case of one that is not.

Prophetic narratives are what they purport to be – stories of the prophets. The Qur'ān has many such narratives. Indeed, the Qur'ān speaks much more about past prophets than about the prophet Muḥammad himself. These narratives, for the most part, are partial, even fragmentary. The only complete prophetic narrative in the Qur'ān is the *sūra* of Joseph (Q 12). The nature of these narratives is referential and homiletic. They serve an edifying purpose.

Many of the Qur'ān's prophetic narratives will no doubt be familiar to readers who are conversant with the Hebrew scriptures and the New Testament. However, in addition to the "new" material on Jesus just mentioned, the Qur'ān contains many other stories that are not to be found anywhere in the Bible. For many readers, this adds to the Qur'ān's mystique. Whether such stories are those of Moses and Khiḍr (Q 18), the story of the Seven Sleepers (Q 18), or other nonbiblical narratives that add to the overall impression, the reader must not assume that these stories are untrue or merely apocryphal. Whether they are or not is not the point. For Muslims, the Qur'ān confirms much material found in previous scriptures, and adds new material as well. Even if such stories may be found in Jewish lore or elsewhere, it is safe to say that the Qur'ān presents these as morally true and as paradigmatically important. The stories are authoritative and, by virtue of their status as revelation, are true for Muslims howsoever they may be nuanced or explained.

Edifying revelations

While the majority of narratives are stories of the prophets, other narratives have a purely edifying purpose. One example is the Qur'ān's use of parables. These function in quite the same way as the parables of Jesus. Maxims, aphorisms, and other wisdom sayings enrich the didactic dimension of the Qur'ān. This material regulates the lives of Muslims in ways that laws cannot. Laws may govern outward actions, and conform them to moral and religious standards. But the Qur'ānic wisdom literature is the heart of piety, which can take on mystical dimensions not contemplated by observant praxis alone.

Legal revelations

As stated earlier, the Qur'ān is one of the two major sources of Islamic law. The other is the *ḥadīth* literature, which is a body of traditions that report the extra-canonical sayings and actions of Muḥammad. Together, the Qur'ān and *ḥadīth* make up the *sunna*, the way of the prophet, which, in turn, becomes the *sharīʿa*, the code that Muslims should follow. If the Qur'ān is the revealed word of God, then the life and sayings of Muḥammad represent the will of God. Muḥammad is the perfect Muslim. Therefore, the pious Muslim will try to emulate the prophet in just about every way, beyond his singularly prophetic mission.

Given the harsh realities of the day, the Qur'ān can at times be uncompromising. Some of its corporeal punishments are objectionable and unacceptable in the modern world today. Some Muslim reformers advocate dispensing with the letter of certain Islamic laws yet preserving principles and social goals that stand behind them.

Liturgical revelations

The Qur'ān has liturgical value because it is used in private and public worship. Among the many and varied devotional uses of the Qur'ān, the first *sūra* is used in daily obligatory prayer (*ṣalāt*). Qur'ānic recitation – that is, chanting the verses of the Qur'ān according to stylized canons of intonation and cadence – became an art-form in itself, just like Qur'ānic calligraphy. In a sense, Qur'ānic recitation re-enacts those original, revelatory moments of the spoken Qur'ān as they were first dictated by Muḥammad to his scribes.

The Qur'ān loses much of its force on the barren printed page. Emotions thrill to the spirited invocation of Qur'ānic passages, as a whole religious culture comes alive. One does not have to know Arabic to be struck by the emotional depth that is conveyed by Qur'ānic recitation. The hearts of the pious are swept with awe and fascination by the measured accents of the text, as it is experienced in the depth of the soul.

Polemical revelations

To promote Islam is also to defend it. Secular as well as religious charges were leveled at the prophet of Islam. Muḥammad was variously accused of being a crazed poet, soothsayer, or sorcerer, as well as a liar. In all of these cases, Qur'ānic polemics are to be seen as both actual and theoretical. They may be historical and localized, or doctrinal and generalized. Sometimes the Qur'ān directly cites the charges it refutes. The important thing to remember is that the Qur'ān, despite its exalted claims to revelation, is personalized through the formative experience of Islam as a historical movement. Muḥammad and the early Muslims faced challenges, debates, and outright persecution. Under these circumstances, polemics served an immediate purpose, yet had a paradigmatic value as Islam spread to countries outside Arabia, where Islam was just as new then as before.

Another aspect of Qur'ānic polemics is apologetic in nature. Among the detractors of Islam were Jewish communities. This fact becomes problematic in the modern context and has fueled charges of a latent Muslim anti-Semitism. The many references to Judaism, however, are for instructive purposes, and a much greater focus is placed on the prophethood of Moses, who is really a prototype of Muḥammad himself.

The Qur'ān has a certain degree of affection for Christians. During times of persecution in the early days of Islam, Christians tended to be the most sympathetic of onlookers. Muslims share a great deal in common with Christians. However, the Qur'ān brooks no tolerance for the Christian doctrine of the trinity. Although the Qur'ān affirms the virgin birth, it does not accord Jesus the status of the son of God (nor that of God, for that matter). The Qur'ān also views original sin as absolute injustice and complete predestination. Pure Christianity is pure Islam, since there is only one true religion. What would Jesus do if he met Muḥammad? Muslims would say that Jesus would embrace the truth of Muḥammad's revelation, considering the fact that the Qur'ān states that Jesus prophesied the advent of Muḥammad.

Assessing the Qur'ān

Is the Qur'ān a revelation sent down by God, as Muslims claim? This is clearly a theological question. If the answer were yes, Christians and others might feel compelled to become Muslims. The simplest solution is to recognize Islam for what it is – a system of salvation at the center of which is the Qur'ān, which is functionally and effectively the word of God, entirely independent of what non-Muslims have to say about its truth claims. The Qur'ān invites all humanity to respond to the call of God. It sees itself as the latest and fullest testimony of God and the most direct expression of the divine purpose for humanity. This is a monumental truth-claim, and must be taken very seriously when studying the text. Readers will wish to keep this salient fact in mind because it goes far to explain the power of the Qur'ān to command allegiance and serve as the effective constitution of entire Islamic societies.

An understanding of the Qur'ān is analogous to music appreciation, although saying so is by no means meant to trivialize the purpose or process of gaining that understanding. Muslims have a coherent worldview, one that originates from the Qur'ān itself. To appreciate the Qur'ān is to develop a sensitivity to the operation of the divine in a culture removed for centuries from the Euro-American world but now increasingly an integral part of it. One can only gain from such an understanding. Indeed, one can only be enriched by it, but only if one's prejudices are first abandoned. The Qur'ān is a world unto itself, a palatial architecture of meaning that is multidimensional and comprehends the totality of the human experience. On the moral and spiritual foundation of the Qur'ān, an entire history and civilization has been built. The West can continue to clash with Islam – which is the religion of the Qur'ān – or embrace it.

To acknowledge the beauty and depth of the Qur'ān is not to convert to Islam, but to converse with it and with Muslims who are enlivened by it. Yes, the Qur'ān is a text of monumental historical importance. But it may have an even greater contemporary relevance, for in an increasing number of Western nations the population of Muslims is beginning to surpass the number of Jews. Thus the religion of Islam is rapidly entrenching itself as a French religion, as part of UK society, as a feature of the Canadian mosaic, and as an essential element of the spiritual landscape of the United States.

To know the Qur'ān is to better prepare oneself for inevitable encounters with Muslims both in America and abroad – not as the exotic "other" somewhere in the distant Orient, but as the religion and way of life of our fellow compatriots at home – friends, neighbors and, through increasing religious intermarriage, that of our immediate and extended families. The events of September 11, 2001 have riveted world attention on Islam (albeit radical Islam). Sales of the Qur'ān and texts on Islam have skyrocketed.

For the non-Muslim, reading the Qur'ān is an act of moderation, a significant form of communication, an act of intellectual and perhaps spiritual empathy, and, for some, a religious moment without a religious commitment, and a gesture of understanding. It is an act of humanity. Moreover, the Qur'ān is a text of world-historical proportions that institutions of higher learning can scarcely afford to ignore, because our domestic life, as well as international affairs, will be increasingly informed by it. Discovering the Qur'ān on a personal basis can be rewarding for its own sake. Studying the Qur'ān will equip university students with a competence they are sure to find useful in an increasingly multicultural world, one-fifth of which is already under Islam's spiritual, political, and cultural authority – with an even greater part of the world affected by it. The US courts have already weighed in on the University of North Carolina Qur'ān controversy. While reading the Qur'ān cannot be required, it is required reading for religious, political, cultural, and global literacy. In its own way, it is a democratic as well as academic enterprise.

Further reading

Bausani, Allesandro (1974) Islam as an essential part of western culture. In: *Studies on Islam: A Symposium on Islamic Studies Organized in Cooperation with the Accademia dei Lincei in Rome, Amsterdam, 18–19 October 1973.* North-Holland Publishing Company, Amsterdam, pp. 19–36.

Buck, Christopher (2006) University of North Carolina's Qur'an controversy. In: Ahmad, M. (ed.) *The State of Islamic Studies in American Universities.* Alta Mira Press, Lanham MD.

Friedmann, Yohanan (1986) Finality of prophethood in Islam. *Jerusalem Studies in Arabic and Islam* 7, 177–215.

Rippin, Andrew (1993) Interpreting the Bible through the Qur'ān. In: Hawting, G. R. and Shareef, A.-K. (eds.) *Approaches to the Qur'ān.* Routledge, London and New York, pp. 249–59.

Sells, Michael (1999) *Approaching the Qur'ān: The Early Revelations.* White Cloud Press, Ashland, OR.

Watt, William Montgomery (1953) *Muhammad at Mecca.* Clarendon Press, Oxford.

Watt, William Montgomery (1956) *Muhammad at Medina.* Clarendon Press, Oxford.

CHAPTER 3

Contextualizing

Abdullah Saeed

For many non-Muslims, and even Muslims who are not familiar with the Qurʾān, reading it in translation or in the original Arabic and understanding it is a very difficult task for a variety of reasons: lack of familiarity with the context of the Qurʾān; the time, place, people, and circumstances of the text, and the structure of the text provide barriers to immediate comprehension of its meaning. In the following discussion, I will rely largely on traditional Muslim accounts of the nature of the Qurʾān, its structure, context, and understanding as well as the life of the prophet Muḥammad. The broad features of these accounts are still generally accepted in Muslim communities across the world who share a common view (even if frequently unenunciated) on the context within which the Qurʾān must be understood.

The Broad Historical Context of the Qurʾān

The Qurʾān is situated in the broader political, social, intellectual, and religious context of Arabia in general, and Mecca and Medina in particular, in the early seventh century CE. An understanding of the key aspects of this context will help the reader to make connections between the Qurʾānic text and the environment that led to the emergence of the text.

Great empires

In the sixth century CE, much of the region we today call the Middle East was dominated by two great powers: the Byzantine Empire and the Sassanid Empire. Much of Arabia, however, except for the north and south, remained outside the direct influence of these two empires. Mecca, where Islam emerged, happened to be in the region where the empires did not hold sway. The two empires had fought endless wars (directly or by proxy) and were still doing so in the early seventh century.

The Byzantine Empire was on the whole Christian, the Sassanid Empire predominantly Zoroastrian. However, Sassanids had in their midst a number of other religious traditions such as Judaism, Christianity, and Buddhism. Christians, Jews, and pagan communities were scattered throughout Arabia. Mecca itself was largely pagan; its people worshiped a large number of idols housed in the sanctuary Kaʿba (called "House of God"). However, a few people in Mecca shunned the worship of idols and believed in a supreme God. The interaction, through trade, of Meccans with adherents of religions such as Judaism and Christianity appears to have been common, particularly with communities in neighboring regions such as Yathrib (later known to be as Medina), which had three large Jewish tribes, and Abyssinia, which was largely Christian.

Mecca: The birthplace of Islam

In the early seventh century, Mecca was rather marginal. Apart from the importance some Arab pagans gave to the Kaʿba in Mecca and the caravan trade in which the Meccans were engaged, the town appears to have been insignificant. The people of Mecca were predominantly of one large tribe, the Quraysh, which was made up of several clans. Some clans were rich and powerful and dominated the political scene, while others took on the responsibility of looking after the sanctuary and its visitors. The affairs of Mecca were managed by a collective of influential elders and the rich through an informal consultative process. There was no ruler or a formal state. In general, the clan (a subset of the tribe) provided safety and security for its members. This custom dictated that when a person from a tribe or a clan was threatened, it was the duty of the entire tribe or clan to defend that person, if necessary by going to war.

Life in Mecca and surrounding regions was harsh. The land was generally arid. No agriculture of note existed. While Mecca itself was a settled community, there were plenty of nomadic tribes around Mecca which were constantly on the move in search of water and vegetation for their animals, primarily camels and goats. Raids by one tribe on another were common. Settled communities had to enter into understandings and agreements with nomadic tribes to protect their communities and caravan trade from raids. Such unexpected raids and the insecurity associated therewith, coupled with the general hardships and uncertainties associated with life, gave the inhabitants a rather fatalistic view of the world.

Education largely comprised basic skills in survival, in the use of armaments such as swords and arrows, and in camels and horse riding. Only a few people were literate. In Muslim tradition, Muḥammad himself is considered to have been illiterate. For Muslims, the notion of an illiterate prophet provides strong support for the doctrine of the divine revelation of the Qurʾān. If the prophet was unable to read or write, the argument goes, he could not have composed a text such as the Qurʾān.

However, the Meccans had a particular love of language. Poetry and poets were revered. Beautifully expressed language was considered the pinnacle of intellectual activity. At certain times of the year, competitions were held in Mecca and surrounding regions for poets and orators. Only a few texts were written; these included the eloquently and beautifully expressed Arabic poetry. Several famous poems were reportedly written and displayed in important places like the Kaʿba.

It was in this environment that Muḥammad began to preach his message in Mecca in 610 CE. The Qur'ān is connected to that context, and many Qur'ānic texts reflect the realities of that context. Muslims in general prefer to ignore the matter of context and argue instead that a close connection between the Qur'ānic text and its socio-historical context is not relevant to belief and interest in the Qur'ān. However, understanding the context helps us to understand why the Qur'ān dealt with particular issues and why it emphasized certain issues over others at particular times. It dealt with problems and issues that concerned the community.

Related to this broad context is also the life of the prophet. Thus, a historical overview of the prophet's life and of the early Muslim life would be helpful to the student of the Qur'ān in making sense of the text. Without this basic framework, it is difficult to contextualize the Qur'ān.

Outline of Muḥammad's Life as a Framework for Understanding the Qur'ān

Muḥammad's father died before he was born and his mother died before he was six. He was then looked after by his relatives: his grandfather until he was eight and thereafter his uncle, Abū Ṭālib. At the age of twenty-five, he married Khadīja, a wealthy widow of Mecca, and they lived together until her death. All of his children (except one) were borne by Khadīja. He continued working in his wife's business and lived an unremarkable life until the age of forty. Unlike his compatriots, Muḥammad liked to spend time apart for reflection and meditation, often in a cave outside Mecca. Muslim tradition holds that it was during one of those retreats in a cave near Mecca that he experienced his first revelation in 610 CE. According to tradition, while in the cave, Muḥammad heard a voice which commanded him to "read." Three times the voice asked him to "read." Each time, Muḥammad replied by saying, "I cannot read." The third time, the voice commanded him to utter the following:

> Recite: In the name of thy Lord who created, created man from a blood-clot. Recite: for thy Lord is Most Generous, who taught by the pen, taught man what he knew not. (Q 96:1–5)

This was the first of the "revelations" which Muḥammad received. In the Qur'ān as we have it today, it is part of *sūra* (chapter) 96 (verses 1–5). Initially, Muḥammad was not sure what to make of this. In fear, he hurried to Mecca to his family. Khadīja comforted him and later took him to one of her cousins, Waraqa, a Christian with knowledge of Christian scripture, who assured Muḥammad that what he had received was similar to that which prophets before him had received: revelation from God. Over the first three years, Muḥammad received more messages and began to teach them to his close friends and family. He then began to teach the message to the wider Meccan community. The initial message was that Meccans should accept that there was only one God, that this

God was the creator and sustainer of everything, and that Muḥammad was sent by this God as a messenger to the Meccan people. These early messages also emphasized that Meccan people should be mindful of the needy and disadvantaged in their midst and that they should not forget the favors God had bestowed on them.

Naturally, many were skeptical and refused to accept the teachings of Muḥammad. However, a number of Muḥammad's relatives and close friends and some marginalized people in Mecca followed him. Slowly, his teaching began to be accepted, but his opponents also began to work to marginalize him and put obstacles in his way by punishing those who followed him, particularly the slaves. Such persecution led Muḥammad to instruct his small group of followers to flee Mecca and seek protection with the Christian ruler of Abyssinia, Negus. It was under the protection of Negus that the first Muslim migrant community was able to practice its religion.

After thirteen years of preaching in Mecca, Muḥammad had been unable to convince the vast majority of Meccans to profess his new teachings. The tribes surrounding Mecca also rejected him. But he managed to convince a few people from Yathrib (Medina), to the north of Mecca, to accept his teachings (Islam). These new converts promised Muḥammad that, if he decided to leave Mecca and settle in Medina, they would protect him and support his work. Fortunately for Muḥammad, a large number of Medinan people professed Islam readily and within a very short time. When his Meccan opponents began planning to kill Muḥammad, he and his remaining followers fled to Medina and settled there. Of the five tribes in Medina (two non-Jewish, three Jewish), only the non-Jewish tribes professed Islam. In Medina, Muḥammad established the first Muslim "state," which comprised Muslims from both Mecca and Medina. He concluded agreements with the Jewish tribes for the common defense of Medina against external threats, particularly from the Meccans. Muslims and Jews lived together peacefully at first, but tensions began to emerge which led to the expulsion of the Jewish tribes from Medina within a few years of the prophet's arrival. Much of the Qur'ānic critique of Jews belongs to this period and particularly in relation to Jews in Medina.

In Mecca, the opponents of the Muslims watched the new developments in Medina with increasing dismay. As Medina was not far from the caravan trade route to the north, Muslims could easily interfere with the trade activities of the Meccans. The first major conflict with the Meccans occurred in the second year after the migration (*hijra*) of the prophet and was closely associated with the attempt by Muslims to block the passage of a Meccan caravan returning from the north to Mecca. In this battle (named the "Battle of Badr"), the Muslims, although numerically smaller, defeated the Meccans. It was the first major victory for Muslims against their Meccan opponents. Thereafter, several military confrontations between the two groups occurred until the final occupation of Mecca by Muslim forces in the eighth year after *hijra* (630 CE). By the time Muḥammad died in 11/632, Muslims had an established "state" and controlled much of Arabia, with their followers numbering, according to tradition, over 100,000.

While the Qur'ān does not provide a systematic narrative of Muḥammad's life or the life of his community, there are occasional references to both. In *sūra* 105, reference is made to a group of people, called "Companions of the Elephant," who reportedly came to attack Mecca, probably in the same year as Muḥammad was born (570 or 571 CE).

Another short *sūra* refers to the caravan trade of the Quraysh and their journeys in winter and summer to the north and south as part of that trade, and to how God provided them with food and security. No details are given about the events; the emphasis is on the basic message that God was the one who protected Mecca from the attackers and that God bestowed favors on the Quraysh by facilitating their trade. The *sūra* reads as follows:

> For the covenants [of security and safeguard enjoyed] by the Quraysh. Their covenants [covering] journeys by winter and summer. Let them adore the Lord of this house, who provides them with food against hunger, and with security against fear [of danger].

This approach to historical events is quite consistent across the Qur'ān. It is not particularly interested in providing details of the time, place, characters, and circumstances of events; it emphasizes only the point of the message. Even the prophet's name Muḥammad is mentioned only four times in the Qur'ān. Often, he is referred to as the prophet (*nabī*) or messenger (*rasūl*). Rarely does the Qur'ān mention the names of Muḥammad's contemporaries. In one case, one of the opponents of Muḥammad, his uncle Abū Lahab, is mentioned, in another, his adopted son Zayd.

The Qur'ān as "Revelation" in Arabic

The Qur'ān is the most sacred religious text for Muslims. It is the foundation of Islam and remains the primary source of guidance in all aspects of life: spiritual, legal, moral, political, economic, and social. It is considered to be the speech of God communicated to Muḥammad (i.e. "revelation") between 610 and 632 CE in Arabia. Many Muslim theologians believed that the most common form of the revelation of the Qur'ān to the prophet was from God via the angel Gabriel. From their point of view, the angel brought the word of God to the prophet *verbatim*, in Arabic, the language that the prophet spoke (Q 26:195). The Qur'ān stresses that the prophet was required only to receive the sacred text and that he had no authority to change it (Q 10:15). The Qur'ān strongly denies that it is the speech or the ideas of the prophet or, indeed, of any other human being. It challenges those who consider it the speech of Muḥammad to produce a book similar to it or even one *sūra* like it (Q 2:23). The Qur'ān affirms that the revelation came directly from God and in Arabic so that it would be without human-induced errors or inaccuracies: "Do they not consider the Qur'ān [with care]? Had it been from any source other than God, they would surely have found therein much discrepancy" (Q 4:82).

For Muslims, the angel was entrusted with a direct message *in Arabic*, not simply with meanings and ideas. The revelation was intended to be comprehensible to ordinary people. The Qur'ān says: "Verily this is a revelation from the Lord of the worlds: with it came down the spirit of faith and truth to your heart and mind, that you may admonish in the perspicuous Arabic tongue" (Q 26:192–5). Given that Muḥammad's own language was Arabic and the community to whom he began preaching his message was Arab, the religious text that he used to support his preaching was also in

Arabic. The Qurʾān says that all prophets received their "revelations" or "scriptures" in their own language to facilitate communication with their communities. Although most Muslims today do not speak Arabic, they recite the Qurʾān in Arabic. One of the first things that Muslims are taught from early childhood is how to recite the Qurʾān in Arabic.

For non-Muslims, perhaps, who do not relate to it in terms of faith, the Qurʾān is just like any other text. To Muslims, however, the Qurʾān is not just a text to be understood and read; it is also something to be listened to. The reciter of the Qurʾān is an important figure in the Muslim community and his or her presence is sought eagerly for important celebrations or events. Qurʾānic recitation is an art that is cultivated in Muslim seminaries and mosques. The voice of the reciter and the beauty of the recitations are equally appreciated by Muslims around the world (Sells 1999: 1–3). For devout Muslims, whether they understand the meaning of the recitation or not, there is something very moving about it. A person is attracted to it by simply listening to the beautiful voice of the reciter. Perhaps this can be compared to the culture of singing in Christianity.

For Muslims, the voice captivates individuals and groups alike. In fact, recitation of the Qurʾān on a daily basis is a common practice among devout Muslims. If they do not recite it themselves, they may make an effort to listen to it. When Muslims listen to Qurʾānic recitation they believe that they are hearing the word of God, through the voice of the reciter. The fact that many Muslims do not understand the meaning is of little importance or relevance to them. The main issue for them is that they are able to recite and listen to the word of God.

Muslims believe that this extraordinary power of the word of God through the voice of the reciter was equally important in the early Islamic times during Muḥammad's time. In fact, one of the ways the prophet reportedly attracted a large number of Meccans to his mission was through the beautiful and powerful words of God that he recited to Meccan audiences. Given that the Meccans had, according to the tradition, an extraordinary sensitivity to beautiful words and language, they were captivated by the beauty of the Qurʾān. Even the most ardent opponents of the prophet were said to have been captivated by its majestic power. One such enemy was ʿUmar b. al-Khaṭṭāb, who converted to Islam and came to be one of the most influential Muslims after Muḥammad.

The Qurʾān as Scripture

There are several verses which appear to indicate that, during the time of Muḥammad, the Qurʾān came to be conceived of as scripture, not just spoken word. It thus became a book, a scripture (*kitāb*) much like the earlier scriptures given to the prophets before Muḥammad (Q 98:1–3): "God has sent down to you the book and wisdom and taught you what you knew not before" (Q 4:113; also see 2:231; 4:105). Certainly, the Qurʾān considered itself as scripture or book: "And recite what has been revealed to thee of the book of thy Lord: none can change His words" (Q 18:27). This is reiterated in the verse: "We have revealed for you a book in which is a message for you" (Q 21:10). In fact, the

Qur'ān uses *kitāb* ("scripture") to refer to itself more than seventy times in various contexts, indicating that the concept of the Qur'ān as a book or scripture was well established before Muḥammad's death in 11/632 (Q 2:176; 3:7; 4:105; 6:154–7; 16:64; 29:47). However, it was not put together or compiled into one volume at that stage.

At first, the Qur'ān remained largely in the memories of Muḥammad and his immediate followers (known as the "Companions"); but, immediately after the death of Muḥammad in 632, a number of the followers began to think about "collecting" all the parts of the Qur'ān into one volume to safeguard it against corruption and distortion. For Muslims, since the collection was completed very early on and in the presence of those who had witnessed the revelation and retained what had been revealed in their memory and in documents, there was the opportunity to prepare a historically reliable and accurate version. Those who were entrusted with the task of putting together the Qur'ān, according to Muslim tradition, were a committee of senior companions who were among those most closely associated with the Qur'ān during the time of Muḥammad.

One may wonder whether the collected material which now exists in the Qur'ānic text represents the totality of what was revealed to the prophet. Whatever the actual case, for a Muslim, the Qur'ān, as collected during the reign of ʿUthmān, represents the historical, authentic codification of the revelation. Any texts which may have been excluded from the final codified text of the Qur'ān were not considered by those who compiled it to be essential parts of the text. The standard Sunnī Muslim view is that such exclusions, if any, were based on Muḥammad's instructions. Early Shīʿī scholars expressed the view that certain texts that made references to the family of the prophet were excluded by the committee that compiled the Qur'ān. Today, however, such views among the Shīʿites are not common and both the Sunnīs and Shīʿites accept the Qur'ānic text as it is. There are no different versions of the Qur'ān today among Muslims. From a Muslim point of view, the authenticity and reliability of the codified text that became the basis of Islam is not to be seriously questioned, notwithstanding the arguments advanced by scholars such as Wansbrough (1977).

Central Themes of the Qur'ān

The Qur'ān deals with many themes but one theme that stands out is that of God and the relationship of God to human beings. All other issues revolve around this central theme. From the beginning, the Qur'ān talked about God and God's relationship to the creation of human beings and the universe in general. The Qur'ān relied on the understanding that pre-Islamic Arabs, including Meccans, had of God. References to God were not entirely foreign to those people. They knew of "God"; they had a sanctuary that was referred to as the "House of God" and they interacted with Christians and Jews, who talked about "God."

One God

The Qur'ān affirmed the existence of one God. It rejected the belief that there were many gods in addition to a higher god, as the Meccans believed. For the Meccan people, the lesser gods functioned as intermediaries between the higher god and themselves. In the Qur'ān, the one God is often referred to as Allāh or is given other attributes such as the Merciful, the Compassionate, the Creator, the Sustainer, the Everlasting, the Omnipotent, the Just, the Revengeful, and the Wise. Muslim tradition records ninety-nine names or attributes of God, and these are widely used in the Qur'ān. Despite these attributes, the Qur'ān emphatically denies that there is any similarity or any likeness of God to anything which we can imagine or think of, while still using attributes that are understandable in the human context. Muslim theologians argued endlessly about this; one helpful view is that these attributes function like ideals or goals for human beings to aim at. For example, if God is forgiving, human beings should strive to adopt this value of forgiving.

There is nothing that escapes God, who created everything and who sustains that creation. It is in God's power to destroy everything and bring it back to life. Another associated theme is that God will bring all human beings back to life after they die and will judge them on the day of judgment. These ideas were particularly difficult for the Meccans, who often asked Muḥammad rather despairingly how human beings could be brought back to life. With reference to this, the Qur'ān says: "They [Meccans] say: 'When we are bones and mortal remains, will we be raised up in some flesh creation?' " (Q 17:49, 98).

Spiritual beings

The Qur'ān acknowledges that there are other beings beside God that might be considered spiritual, beings that we do not have any understanding or experience of, such as angels. Angels are referred to frequently in the Qur'ān, and some of them are said to have specific functions, such as bringing revelation to prophets or forewarning of death. In fact, one of the six "pillars" of faith in Islam is a belief in angels. In one of the verses, the Qur'ān makes this connection between belief in God and belief in angels: "The messenger [Muḥammad] believes in what has been sent down to him from his Lord, and so do believers [Muslims]; everyone believes in God and His angels, His scriptures and His messengers [prophets]" (Q 2:285).

Below the angels, there are other beings referred to as *jinn*. Unlike angels, these are beings that may or may not be obedient to God. There are many references to *jinn*, and sometimes *jinn* and human beings are referred to in the same verse. For example, Q 51:56 says, "I have only created *jinn* and human beings so they may worship me." From a Qur'ānic point of view, *jinn* are like human beings in terms of obedience or disobedience to God but their nature is different.

Satan as the symbol of evil

The symbol of disobedience to God is Satan (Iblīs), a figure seen by the Qur'ān as a *jinn* in origin but which somehow came to be associated with angels (Q 18:50). In the Qur'ānic story of creation, at a certain point, God wanted to create a human being, called Adam. God informed the angels of this. Some angels protested and said that this being would create havoc on earth. God rejected their arguments and created the being, known as Adam. God then asked all the angels to bow down to Adam. All the angels obeyed God, with the exception of Iblīs (Satan), who objected to God's command and argued that he, Iblīs, was superior to Adam (Q 2:30–8). Iblīs thus rebelled against God. God, however, gave him the opportunity to do whatever he wanted until the end of the time. As a result, according to Muslim belief, Iblīs is engaged in leading human beings astray and away from God, a task he promised God that he would do. From the Qurʾānic point of view, the force of good is God and the force of evil is Satan, and these two forces exist side by side. The Qurʾān presents Satan as a perpetual force of evil until the end of the world as we know it.

Creation of human beings and God's guidance through prophets

According to the Qurʾān, once God had created the first human being, Adam, He provided that human with a partner (known in the Islamic tradition as Hawwaʾ (Eve). The Qurʾān accepts that Adam and his partner committed the sin of disobeying God by eating from a certain tree that was prohibited for them. For this, they were moved out of their abode, which the Qurʾān calls a *janna* ("garden"), into the mundane world. The Qurʾān says that all people are descendants of Adam and Eve and thus form a single family. It also states that all people on earth receive God's instructions or guidelines on how to live correctly in the world. These messages come through prophets and messengers; some messengers receive revelation in the form of scriptures, others do not receive a formal revelation but are somehow "inspired." According to tradition, there are thousands of prophets and messengers. However, only twenty-five are mentioned by name in the Qurʾān. They include Adam, Noah, Abraham, Isaac, Jacob, Joseph, Moses, Zachariah, David, Solomon, Jesus, and Muḥammad. The Qurʾānic view is that every community, without exception, had received "warners" (prophets and teachers) from God. The basic message they taught was that God is the creator and sustainer of the universe and that human beings should recognize this and lead an ethical and moral life. The Qurʾān goes into some detail regarding Adam and the first human family, Noah and the great flood, Moses, Pharaoh and the children of Israel, Joseph and his time in Egypt, Jesus and his teachings and miracles, Mary and the birth of Jesus. The purpose of these accounts is not to provide a historical account of what happened with dates, place names, and people's names. Instead, these stories are "addressed to the human soul. [They depict] in vivid terms the ups and downs, the trials and vicissitudes of the human soul in terms of accounts of bygone people which were not only true about such and such a people and time but concern the soul here and now" (Nasr 1971: 51).

Life after death

The Qurʾān talks about the hereafter and about issues related to life after death in great detail. From the Qurʾānic point of view, while this world is important, what comes after is more important because it is everlasting; it is then that the final fate of human beings will be decided. The world as we know it will come to an end. All human beings will be raised one day and be accountable for all their actions. On that day, God will judge between all people; those who followed God's path will enter the "garden" or "paradise" (*janna*) and those who followed Satan's path will enter "hell" (*jahannam*). Description of both paradise and hell are covered in many *sūras*, particularly the Meccan.

Moral and legal matters

Another important theme of the Qur'ān is law and related matters such as how the affairs of the Muslim community should be conducted. This includes how to worship God through prayer, fasting, and pilgrimage; marriage and divorce; the restriction of polygyny; the regulation of slavery; spending money to help the poor and needy; relations between the sexes; children and custody; punishment for crimes such as theft, murder, adultery, and slander; prohibition of gambling; war and peace; commercial transactions; inheritance. It also covers moral injunctions such as moderation in behavior, justice, fairness, forgiveness, honesty, kindness to one's parents and relatives, generosity, and the keeping of promises. It warns against superstition, telling lies, malicious gossip, and spying. While references are made to legal and ethical-moral issues frequently, the Qur'ān, according to Fazlur Rahman (1966: 37), "is primarily a book of religious and moral principles and exhortations, and is not a legal document. But it does embody some important legal enunciations issued during the community-state building process at Medina." The number of legal verses in the Qur'ān ranges from 100 to 500, depending on the definition of the term "legal," which is a relatively small portion of the entire text of the Qur'ān with its approximately 6,300 verses.

Understanding the Sūra

Books as we know them today often deal with one main topic only but are divided into sub-topics, which makes it relatively easy to follow the structure and argument of the book. However, the Qur'ān is different. For the beginning student of the Qur'ān, the topics it deals with can appear haphazardly ordered. Long *sūras* usually jump from one topic to another, and it can be difficult to see the links between the topics. For example, the second *sūra* of the Qur'ān begins by referring to the Qur'ān as a book about which there is no doubt and then listing the characteristics of the believers (Muslims). It then moves to an exposition of what it calls *munāfiqūn* ("religious hypocrites") in Medina and their attitudes towards Muslims. A. Yusuf Ali, whose translation of the meanings of the Qur'ān is used widely today, provides a summary of key themes covered in *sūra* 2:

Verses	
1–29	Description of the three kinds of people (believers, religious hypocrites and unbelievers)

30–39	Story of creation of the first human being and his partner, the destiny intended for him, his fall and the hope held out to him
40–86	Story of the Israelites and the privileges they received and how they responded to God's call
87–121	Moses, Jesus and their struggles with their people; the People of the Book (Jews and Christians) and their rejection of Muḥammad
122–141	Abraham, the father of Ishmael and Isaac, and the building of the Kaʿba (the sanctuary in Mecca) and the Abrahamic tradition
142–167	The Kaʿba as the center of universal worship and the symbol of Islamic unity
168–242	The Muslim *umma* ("community") and ordinances for the social life of the community related to food and drink, bequests, fasting, war and peace, gambling, treatment of the disadvantaged; treatment of women
243–253	Story of Goliath and David and of Jesus
254–283	That true virtue lies in practical deeds of kindness and good faith
255	God and throne
284–286	Exhortation to faith, obedience, personal responsibility and prayer.

While *sūra* 2 is the longest and has many themes within it, the short *sūras* usually deal with one matter only. An example of a short *sūra* is Q 107:

> Have you seen someone who rejects religion? That is the person who pushes the orphan aside and does not promote feeding the needy. It will be too bad for the prayerful who are absent-minded as they pray, who aim to be noticed, while they hold back contributions. (Q 107:1–7)

Chronology of the verses in the sūra

The content of the *sūra* (particularly the long ones) is not usually chronologically ordered. The verses of a *sūra* may come from very different times of the prophetic mission, between 610 and 632 CE. While short *sūras* are more likely to have been revealed as a unit at the same time, the verses of the long and medium-length *sūras* may have come at different times. More problematic for the reader is that it is often difficult to identify which parts of the *sūra* were revealed when. When Muslims read a *sūra* and attempt to understand what it says, they often do not think about when a particular text was revealed and the reason for its revelation. Questions like these are of enormous importance for Muslim jurists but seem less so for ordinary Muslims. When they recite a particular *sūra*, they would be more concerned about its broader message than any emphasis on when that message came, about whom or what. For the average Muslim, the Qurʾān is, first and foremost, a sacred religious text, and the circumstances of its revelation are irrelevant. However, earlier Muslim scholars studied the Qurʾān and commented upon it, interpreted it, and made significant attempts at understanding when a particular *sūra* or significant parts thereof were revealed. Thus the reader will find at the beginning of each *sūra* a reference as to where the *sūra*, or at least the larger part of the *sūra*, was revealed: Mecca or Medina. Understanding this helps situate the *sūra* and its content in the timeframe of Muḥammad's mission.

Early and later texts

It is important to note that the *sūras* at the beginning of the Qur'ān as it exists now are not necessarily from early in the prophet's mission. The very early Qur'ānic revelations are actually at the end of the Qur'ānic text as we have it today. Most of the *sūras* from the Meccan period deal with matters such as God as creator and sustainer, how human beings should be grateful to God and how they should relate to God. The early *sūras* also address social justice issues, including the treatment of the poor and needy. They state that God has given many favors to the people of Mecca and the surrounding regions. The following is an example of one of the earliest *sūras* (in Mecca), which reminds Muḥammad of God's favor towards him and the exhortation to help those in need:

> By the morning bright, and at night all is still. Your Lord has not forsaken you [Muḥammad], nor is He annoyed. The hereafter will be even better for you than the first [life] was. Your Lord will soon give you something which will leave you satisfied. Did He not find you an orphan and sheltered [you]? He found you lost and guided [you]. He found you destitute and made you rich. Thus the orphan must not be exploited; and the beggar should not be brushed aside. Still tell about your Lord's favor. (Q 93:1–11)

There are many references to past prophets and how their communities responded to the missions of those prophets, often as a form of consolation to Muḥammad that what he was facing in Mecca was not unique. From a Qur'ānic point of view, this is, in fact, the history of the confrontation between good and evil, between God's guidance and Satan's temptation.

In the Medinan texts of the Qur'ān, while these themes continue to an extent, much more emphasis is given to providing guidance to the prophet on managing a community in its legal, economic, and political spheres. Matters such as war and peace, and punishment for offences such as murder, theft, and adultery, come from the Medinan period. This is simply because, in Mecca, Muḥammad and his small number of followers had little influence politically and there was no possibility of establishing a Muslim "state" there; in Medina, however, the prophet and his followers from both Mecca and Medina formed the first Muslim "state," in which Muḥammad functioned as both judge and political and military leader. There was also a small band of opponents called hypocrites, from among Muslims and opposition from the Jewish community of Medina. Tensions between these groups and critiques of their beliefs and attitudes are prominently covered in the Medinan parts of the Qur'ān.

Shifts in voice

In reading the *sūras*, the beginner reader might find quite often the sudden shift in voice quite bewildering (Sells 1999: 20–1). Although throughout the Qur'ān the speaker is considered to be God, it is not clear when or for what purpose the speaker changes from the first person to the third person, and even to the second person. God is often referred to in the third person; for example: "Anyone who obeys God and His messenger will be admitted to gardens through which rivers flow, to live there for ever" (Q 4:13). At times, He is referred to in the first person singular: "I have only created *jinn* and human beings so they may worship Me" (Q 51:56), while at other times it is first person plural: "We shall test you with a bit of fear and hunger" (Q 2:155). At other times, God is referred to in the second person: "We worship Thee." Confusion arises as a result of the use of the first person plural (We) to refer to God. "We" does not refer to a multiplicity of gods; rather, it is similar to the royal "We" used in English.

The Qur'ān takes it for granted that it is God who is speaking throughout and it rarely uses "God says." Sometimes the text addresses the prophet directly: "O prophet, heed God and do not obey disbelievers and hypocrites" (Q 33:1). At other times it addresses people in general: "O people"; the "believers" (Muslims) or the "unbelievers"; or the "People of the Book." Whatever the voice, it is always assumed that the message is from God through the medium of Muḥammad.

Understanding Parts of the Qur'ān with the Help of Other Parts

For Muslims, the Qur'ān is a coherent whole with a unified purpose. This means that often difficult sections or verses of the Qur'ān can be clarified in another part of the text. An ambiguous verse may have its explanation in another verse or verses. An issue raised by one verse may be elaborated on by another verse (Ibn Taymiyya 1392: 93). An example of an explanation of one verse by another is as follows. Q 2:37 states: "Thereupon Adam received words [of guidance] from his Sustainer, and He accepted his repentance: for verily, He alone is the Acceptor of repentance, the Dispenser of grace." This verse indicates that Adam received certain "words" (*kalimāt*) from God. However, it does not elaborate on what these words were. This elaboration is provided by Q 7:23, which states: "The two [Adam and Eve] said: 'Our Lord! We have wronged our own souls. If You do not forgive us, and do not bestow upon us Your mercy, we shall certainly be lost.' "

Another form of explanation of one set of verses by others is related to cases where the Qur'ān makes reference to a particular issue, event, or person in more than one place or *sūra*. While for the novice this may seem to be repetition, the emphasis in each place is usually on a different aspect of the issue. To get a clearer picture of the issue at hand, it is important to bring together all the verses that deal with that issue. For instance, the Qur'ān, on several occasions, refers to the "people of Thamūd," a northwestern Arabian people. Their story is scattered throughout the Qur'ān: Q 7:73–9; 11:61–8; 26:141–59; 27:45–53; 51:43–5; 53:50–1; 54:23–31; 69:4–5; and 91:11–15. Without bringing together all these verses from different *sūras* it will be difficult to get a clear picture of the scope of the Qur'ān's treatment of this issue. Even then, there may be significant gaps. Exegetes of the Qur'ān usually go to external sources to fill in these gaps. They consult the Bible, for instance, on matters related to Moses or Jesus.

Muslim exegetical tradition mentions instances in which Muḥammad explained certain parts of the Qur'ān to his followers. According to the Qur'ān, one of the functions of the prophet was to explain the text to the people: "And upon you have We bestowed from on high this reminder [Qur'ān] so that you explain to the people what has been revealed to them" (Q 16:44). An example of Muḥammad's reported explanation is as follows. It is reported that Muḥammad's companions could not grasp what the Qur'ān meant by "wrongdoing" (*ẓulm*) in the following verse: "Those who have attained to faith and who have not obscured their faith by wrongdoing (*ẓulm*) – it is they who shall be secure since it is they who have found the right path" (Q 6:82). The companions said to Muḥammad, "O messenger of God, who from among us has not committed [any] wrong?" The companions here appear to have understood *ẓulm* in its literal sense of wrongdoing. The prophet reportedly explained this by saying that "wrongdoing" here refers to "ascribing divine powers to beings other than God" as in Q 31:30 (Ibn Ḥajar 1990–3: I, 123).

Although questions related to the meaning of verses would have been directed to Muḥammad, there is no indication that he held special sessions to expound the meaning of the Qur'ān. The practice was *ad hoc* and depended entirely on circumstances. The most common practice seems to have been that Muḥammad simply recited to those present at the time what he received as revelation and assumed that they understood the text. Of course, not all verses would have been equally understood by everyone, especially with regard to some metaphorical expressions. Most of the prophet's interpretation to his followers was practical (indirect), rather than expository (direct). An indirect interpretation would be of the performance of *ṣalāt*, which the Qur'ān commands Muslims to perform but does not give any details as to how this is to be accomplished. Muḥammad taught Muslims how to perform *ṣalāt* in practice. In direct interpretation, what is noticeable is that his interpretation is generally in the form of "it means [such and such]," and the general meaning of the verse or phrase is then given. There is no philological, linguistic, or semantic analysis, which indicates that the prophet was more interested in conveying the practical implications of the Qur'ān as it applied to a particular circumstance.

Based on the two sources, the Qur'ān and Muḥammad's guidance, Muslim scholars have developed a great number of Qur'ānic exegetical works over the past 1,400 years. Some of these rely very heavily on the Qur'ān and the reported explanations of Muḥammad; others draw on a range of additional sources to expound the meanings of the Qur'ān. Some have produced mystical, linguistic, literary, philosophical, theological, or legal exegetical works. In the modern period, a rich array of exegetical works has been produced.

Concluding Remarks

This chapter aimed to provide an overview of some of the key ideas that may help in approaching the Qur'ān and making some sense of it. Given that many students who are attempting to read the Qur'ān today may or may not be Muslim, I have tried to be as neutral as possible in dealing with this topic while attempting to be as close as possible to mainstream Muslim positions. Readers may find elsewhere more detailed expositions and critiques of Muslim positions on a range of issues covered in this chapter. For students who do not have advanced Arabic skills, there are many translations of the Qurʾān or, as Muslims would like to refer to them, "translations of the meanings of the Qurʾān." Even for a reader with advanced Arabic skills, the language of the Qurʾān can be quite daunting, and an accessible translation with some commentary in English can be helpful. Some translations are accompanied by commentary in the form of extensive footnotes (as is the case with Muḥammad Asad's (1980) *The Message of the Qurʾān* or A. Yusuf Ali's (1934) *The Holy Qurʾān* or Abu al-Aʿla Mawdudi's (1988) *Towards Understanding the Qurʾān*, a popular modern commentary originally written in Urdu but translated into English). The quality and standard of the available English translations vary enormously. The search for the ideal translation goes on because most existing translations have their share of problems, ranging from accuracy in rendering the meanings of the Arabic text to distortions that may occur as a result of the authors' theological, sectarian, or religious disposition. For this reason, it is important for the beginning reader to have access to a good annotated bibliography of the translations of the Qurʾān into English before deciding on which translation and commentary to use.

Further reading

Ayoub, Mahmoud (1984) *The Qurʾān and its Interpreters. Volume One.* State University of New York Press, Albany.

Draz, M. A. (2000) *Introduction to the Qurʾān.* I. B. Tauris, London.

Esack, Farid (2002) *The Qurʾān: A Short Introduction.* Oneworld, Oxford.

Nasr, Seyyed Hossein (1971) *Ideals and Realities of Islam.* Allen and Unwin, London.

Rahman, Fazlur (1980) *Major Themes of the Qurʾān.* Bibliotheca Islamica, Minneapolis.

Robinson, Neal (1996) *Discovering the Qurʾan: A Contemporary Approach to a Veiled Text.* SCM Press, London.

Saeed, Abdullah (2006) *Interpreting the Qurʾān: Towards a Contemporary Approach.* London: Routledge.

Sells, Michael (1999) *Approaching the Qurʾān: The Early Revelations.* White Cloud Press, Ashland.

Sherif, Faruq (1995) *A Guide to the Contents of the Qurʾān.* Garnet Publishing, Reading.

Wansbrough, John (1977) *Quranic Studies: Sources and Methods of Scriptural Interpretation.* Oxford University Press, Oxford; reprint with annotations Prometheus Press, Amherst NY, 2004.

Wild, Stefan (ed.) (1996) *The Qurʾān as Text.* E. J. Brill, Leiden.

PART II

Text

CHAPTER 4

Linguistic Structure

Salwa M. S. El-Awa

Many non-Arabic-speaking readers of the Qurʾān complain that they cannot understand the interrelations between the different parts of its long *sūras*, and sometimes of its shorter *sūras* as well. This does not come as a surprise to the Arabic-speaking reader of the same text. Though the latter is more familiar with the style of the Qurʾān, she does not seem able to explain its textual relations more readily. The difference between the two readers, however, is that the non-Arabic-speaking reader struggles to understand the overall meaning of the *sūra* and appreciate its textuality, whereas the Arabic-speaking reader seems happier and less likely to complain; to her, the meaning of the text is clear enough, and, therefore, the question of interrelations is not an urgent one. In this chapter, I will explain why these relations are problematic to readers of the Qurʾān and propose an alternative approach to understanding them. In this introduction, I will shed light on some of the general problems in understanding the structure of the Qurʾānic text and the main viewpoints from which they can be addressed. In the second section I will follow the development of these approaches throughout the history of Qurʾānic studies. I will then discuss from a text-analytical point of view why textual relations are a problem in the Qurʾānic text. Finally, I will propose a new framework for understanding these relations rooted in an appreciation of the role of context in explaining the structure and the meaning of the text.

The Problem

The following example demonstrates the problem; it is composed of the three middle sections of a relatively short Qurʾānic *sūra* (Q 75). The numbers preceding each line are the verse numbers. A reading of this text shows that, contrary to what would normally be expected from three consecutive parts of one text, these sections do not form a unit, nor do they display any obvious connectivity/coherence.

14 But man is a witness against himself.
15 Even though he might tender his excuses.

***

16 Move not your tongue to hasten with it.
17 Verily, upon Us is its gathering and its recitation.
18 Thus, when We recite it follow its recitation.
19 And then, verily, it is upon Us to clarify it.

***

20 No indeed. But you love the world that hastens away,
21 and you forsake the hereafter.
22 Faces will on that day be radiant,
23 gazing to their Lord.
24 And faces will on that day be scowling,
25 knowing that a backbreaking is about to befall them.

The following are only some of the questions that would occur to the non-Arabic-speaking reader of this text:

1 What is the relation between the first and the second sections? The second section seems to be completely unconnected; it has no semantic or grammatical connection with the surrounding sections.
2 Is it possible, given the history of the text, that this section has been misplaced?
3 Who is the addressee of the second section? Is it the same as the addressee of the third section? The third section begins with what seems to be an answer to a question. What is that question and where is it?

These questions are divided into three groups. This division corresponds to three very common ways in which people tend to think of text structure. The questions in the first group tackle the problem from a thematic viewpoint. They try to find a common theme that links the three sections together and then come up with one topic that could include the three sections together as parts of one large unit of meaning, or, perhaps, three closely related topics, through whose relation one can justify the arrangement of the three sections one after the other. In the case of this particular text, many readers who have attempted to explain it from thematic viewpoints have failed. Although one may find a possible relation between the first and third sections, there seems to be no obvious reason why the second section should be where it is. Why should a section about man trying to find excuses for his deeds be followed immediately by a section on the revelation of the Qur'ān and the manner of its recitation, followed by a third on how people will look on judgment day?

Around the middle of the last century, this approach to the study of the structure of the Qur'ān became very popular in the Muslim world thanks to the works of two prominent exegetes who published two full commentaries trying to discover a thematic unity in each and every *sūra* of the Qur'ān. The outcome of their works will be discussed in a later section of this chapter. Meanwhile, we continue to consider other angles from which this problem might be tackled.

The second group of questions suggests that it is not right to place the second section where it is. Fundamentally, this suggestion has to do with our existing information about the text's history. If people did not know, for example, about the difficulties the Arabs had in finding writing materials, or if they knew more facts about text memorization in early oral cultures, perhaps this kind of question would not be asked in exactly the way it is. Our knowledge or lack of knowledge of the text's history determines to a large extent what questions we feel we can ask about its composition and structure. The fact that the text has been revealed (according to Muslims)/composed (according to non-Muslims) over a period of some twenty-three years, and that the final written codex was not completed and made official for more than a decade after the death of Muḥammad, have influenced the way researchers have approached the problems they encounter when trying to understand the structure of the text. This association has led a number of scholars to attempt a rearrangement of the Qur'ān according to the historical order of the revelations (i.e. trying to produce a sequence by which verses revealed earlier were placed first and the later ones placed after them and so on). In spite of the interesting and useful insights into the stylistic differences between the earlier and the later *sūras* which Nöldeke's work (1909–38) contains, and the more thematically coherent text and the lengthy notes on style and grammatical problems in Bell's critical rearrangement of the Qur'ān (1937–9), such attempts have been largely unsuccessful. The fact of the matter is, they do not solve the central problem in response to which they were written: they do not make reading the Qur'ān and understanding its structure any easier.

Another problem with this approach, which would perhaps be more important to a structuralist text critic, is that this type of question undermines the text's authority as an independent piece of writing that should be understood and studied on its own merits and sets a limit on the interpreter's ability to explain the text in ways beyond the obvious. It implies a suggestion that the text as it stands now should be dismissed and replaced by another with a different arrangement. Modern text critics cannot welcome such a suggestion. In this day and age, when a postmodern poem does not make much sense in terms of the relations between its lines, or when a few pages of a novel contain a description of a fictional character that is to appear only in the last chapter, critics do not wonder whether a huge mistake has taken place during the editing process. Instead, they engage in an active process of interpretation, aiming to come as close as possible to the intended meaning and purpose of the unusual style.

For all the reasons discussed above, and with the growing interest in structuralism as a literary approach that could benefit the study of the Qur'ān as a text, this approach did not develop much after the second third of the last century. Instead, scholars redirected their efforts towards the study of the Qur'ān as a literary text using tools derived from both linguistics and literary criticism.

I now turn to the third group of questions, which focuses mainly on the linguistic structure of the text. It tries to find in the linguistic components of the three sections some indicators as to what might be the relations between the different parts of the text. Various grammatical and non-grammatical elements influence our understanding of text structure. In the case of this text, pronouns were questioned. Pronouns are words that writers use to refer to other entities known to the recipient of the text (either by having been mentioned in previous parts of the text or from the extra-linguistic context). When recipients find it difficult to work out what the references of the pronouns are, they feel that the text is ambiguous or incoherent. Take, for example, the question about the addressees of sections two and three above. There are no explicit referents to the addressee pronouns in either section. However, because one expects that a pronoun must have a referent, the reader tries to search for any clues as to who might be the addressees of the two sections, and whether they could be the same person. The addressee of section two is instructed to read the Qur'ān slowly, specifically, not to "hasten" in its recitation. The addressee of section three, on the other hand, is rebuked for loving the world which "hastens" away. Could this be an indicator that the two pronouns refer to the same person? Might it be a person whose haste in recitation is just a symptom of his love of this world and impatience which leads him to forsake the hereafter?

In this particular case, this question can be partly answered by reference to the Arabic origin of the text where we find that the addressee of section two is in the singular and of section three in the plural (which some translations have indicated by use of the old English versions of the pronoun which retain the distinction between singular and plural). However, establishing that the addressees of the two sections are different does not solve the problem; it only sends us back to square one where we did not know who is addressed by each section because the pronoun reference is not clear, and where there was no indication of what links the two sections together.[1]

One element, however, can help us to explore more possible answers to all the above questions. In reading the discussions above, it will have been noticed that there were several items of information whose absence from my discussions has possibly added to the complexity of the matter, and if they were to be borne in mind perhaps the case would not have been as problematic as it now appears to be. In general, could it be possible that reading these textual relations would have been easier if the whole of the *sūra* were available to us and used to support the various elements in the discussion? For example, verse 14 begins with a "but" indicating contradiction with a previous statement to which we have no access in this reading. Similarly, it is possible that there is a story behind those instructions on the manner of recitation which, if we knew it, might shed some light on the reason why verses 16–19 are placed where they are.

Now that I have given an overview of the type of problems that the study of textual relations involves, and before I begin analyzing some examples from the text to show how these problems occur, I shall briefly review the ways in which scholars have approached Qur'ānic textual relations from the early days of Qur'ānic studies up to the present day.

Previous Works

Scholarly interest in understanding the structure of the Qur'ān goes back to the early stages of Qur'ānic studies and the so-called "golden age of Islamic scholarship." The earliest work known to us which emphasizes the textual relations element of the meaning of the Qur'ān is the substantial commentary *Mafātiḥ al-Ghayb* by Fakhr al-Dīn al-Rāzī (d. 606/1209). His work is representative of the way in which scholars thought of textual relations at the time, which is best described as "linear." At every point where a change of subject matter takes place, al-Rāzī tries to explain the relations between the subject matter of the preceding and the following section, at times on a broad thematic basis and, at others, by trying to find a hidden clue, thematic or linguistic, to a link between the sections. He applies this method throughout the entire Qur'ān. At the end of each *sūra*, he searches for an explanation of the relation between the last verse of the *sūra* and the first of the following one and so on, through to the last verse of the last *sūra*. This forms a long line of relations linking Qur'ānic verses like a chain in which some links are bigger than others, according to the different lengths of the sections. Since the section division itself was arbitrary, as the borderlines between them are often not clear-cut, different scholars would apply different divisions to the *sūras* and hence the same verse does not belong to the same section in every commentary.

Although the explanations in these commentaries are diverse and interesting, they remain intuitive and individual. Each commentator had his own different interpretations of the relations between sections, based on his personal understanding of *sūras* and influenced by his political or religious affinity, which only proved that these relations were indeed ambiguous and in need of a more rigorous approach to unravel them. The efforts of the early commentators have therefore remained unhelpful for the modern day reader, especially in terms of their methodology, and have left modern scholars with more or less the same problem as that with which their predecessors had to deal.

In the 1950s two scholars, one in the Indian Subcontinent and one in the Middle East, wrote two very similar commentaries on the Qur'ān with a focus on interrelations and structures of *sūras*. Preoccupied with the then popular idea in literary theory that the text has to possess "organic unity" in order for it to possess textuality and be of a literary quality, the two scholars have come up with the idea of a core theme that links the seemingly unrelated passages of a given *sūra*. According to Amīn Aḥsan Iṣlāḥī of Pakistan (b. 1906, d. 1997) and Sayyid Quṭb of Egypt (d. 1966), each Qur'ānic *sūra* has a central idea as its unique message and around this idea every theme or topic within the *sūra* evolves: to elaborate, detail, exemplify, or explain.

Iṣlāḥī refers to this idea as an *ʿamūd* (pillar) and Quṭb uses *miḥwar* (axis), and it would usually be one of the ideas central to the message of Islam. It is irrelevant where in the *sūra* the verses expressing the central idea occur. It is the work of the interpreter to read, reread and reflect on the meanings of the different sections until she has found out what the *ʿamūd*/*miḥwar* is. It is also the interpreter's work to decide what the sections are, where they begin and where they end. What did not seem to be one of the aims was the establishment of a new structure for the *sūra*, one that corresponds to the location of the *ʿamūd* section and organization of the remaining sections around it. That remained random, or at least, linear.

These two scholars endeavor to explain every single passage of each *sūra* in relation to what they presume is the central idea. In addition to deep reflection on the meanings of verses and *sūras*, the two scholars suggest some methodological principles to guide the work of the interpreter. Iṣlāḥī, following on the work of his teacher

Imām Farāḥī (d. 1930), stipulates six principles as grounding for any legitimate interpretation; they are listed in Mir (1986). Quṭb, on the other hand, emphasizes the significant role of context, which is also one of Iṣlāḥī's principles, in understanding the Qur'ānic text.

The works of these two scholars have paved the way for today's scholars to begin their postmodern search for Qur'ānic textual relations with two very important ground rules in mind: (a) context plays a vital role in understanding the text of the Qur'ān and therefore should be carefully considered when trying to study any aspect of its meaning; and (b) *sūras* consist of passages, not only verses. The borders between passages are arbitrary but are possible to determine.

Two tasks have thus been set for today's scholars searching for and trying to unravel Qur'ānic textual relations: to establish a methodologically profound argument for section divisions of *sūras* and to try to explain the relations between these sections within context on rigorous theoretical grounds.

In the last two decades scholars have begun their search for identifiable thematic borders and points of intersection within the long *sūras*. Neuwirth (1981) pioneered the explicit theoretical discussion of the division of Meccan *sūras* into distinctive subjects. Robinson (1996; 2000; 2001) applied a modified version of Iṣlāḥī's theory to *sūra* 2, and later analyzed the section division of *sūras* 6 and 23, producing a more linguistically and contextually aware explanation of section divisions and textual relations in the three *sūras*. Zahniser (2000) with special interest in *sūras* 2 and 4, and with reference to Robinson's and Iṣlāḥī's works, scrutinizes their section divisions, proposing new structures to the *sūras* and making some enlightening remarks on patterns and markers of section divisions.

El-Awa (2005) works on the same issue with an analysis of *sūras* 33 and 75 in an attempt to propose a theoretical framework for an interpretation based on understanding the mutual role of the passages as context to each other, focusing once again on trying to find more definitive markers of beginnings and ends of sections and, in doing so, adding a number of indicators to Zahniser's list and introducing a new linguistic framework for explaining Qur'ānic textual relations. The structure of *sūras* suggested by this work is more an interwoven fabric than a chain of topics or a core around which various objects revolve.

A New View of Qur'ānic Structure

The matter of connectivity between parts of the multiple-theme Qur'ānic *sūras* has been a problem for scholars and commentators throughout the centuries. In their endeavor to find a suitable explanation for this problem, their main preoccupation has been the apparent disconnectivity of passages covering variant topics. They have tried to explain the structure of the Qur'ān in such a way that this appearance of disconnectivity would be removed, on the assumption that disconnectivity is a form of deficiency in literary texts.

In the rest of this chapter I want to move from this point of view to another. I want to establish by linguistic analysis that (a) the Qur'ānic *sūras* are composed of structurally independent (or disconnected) units and (b) that this characteristic does not really pose any threat to the perception of the Qur'ān as a highly literary text, nor does it affect communication of its message. Before I do so, however, it is important to define the units of the Qur'ānic discourse that I shall be discussing here. The peculiar format of the Qur'ān in *sūras* rather than chapters, and those *sūras* being composed of strings of verses with hardly any punctuation marks, rather than clearly defined paragraphs or sections, makes the question of connectivity between the elements a highly complicated one; it involves more than simply the question of the overall coherence of the text. One needs to know what the relations between those strings of sentences are, how they are represented, and what the role is of each one of them in forming the overall message of the *sūra*.[2]

In what follows, I shall focus on textual relations between verses in the Qur'ānic *sūra* as they appear in their text; I shall not try to group them in sections or paragraphs. The aim is to show, by close examination, a special characteristic of sentence structure in the Qur'ān, and then to suggest that the same applies to units larger than a sentence.[3] Equally, verses that are composed of units smaller than the sentence are not discussed here.

Textual relations

Text is composed of linguistic units of various lengths, the smallest unit being a word and the largest being a text. A number of words linked together make a sentence; a number of sentences normally make a paragraph; a number of paragraphs make the text.

Sentences within paragraphs, and paragraphs within texts, are usually expected to have some kind of connection with each other. This connection may be semantic, structural/grammatical, or both. When the relation between two units (sentences or paragraphs) is expressed physically, in actual words or marks (such as punctuation marks that act as connectives), I will refer to it as "structural." Connectives indicate to the reader what the author of the text thinks the relation between the two units is. On the other hand, when no such indicator is apparent in the text and the relation can be understood only from the meaning, I will refer to it as "semantic." Sometimes the two types of relations are combined, and sometimes they are not. Our understanding of textual relations in a given text is based on observation and understanding of these two types of relations.

There are four logical possibilities for these two types of relations working together within text. A relation between two units may be evident in the explicit words and meanings of the two units; or it may be evident in either of them; or it may be unclear in either of them. Thus, I divide these four possibilities into four categories, each representing one possibility. In the following four sections I will show how such relations are formed and discuss their effect on the recipients' understanding of textual relations. I will use a variety of examples from everyday conversation, literary texts and the Qur'ān. It is important to bear in mind that the majority of textual-relation problems arise when the relation is not clear between two sentences that come at the point of thematic transition. Since the aim of this chapter is to examine the causes of the problem and how it occurs from a linguistic point of view, and in order to avoid the added complexity of the question of where sections actually begin and end, simple examples from any location in the text suffice to illustrate the situation. The analysis and the problems, however, apply to points of transition between sections and themes as much as they apply to any two sentences in the text.

Semantic and structural connectedness

The first category of relations I introduce here is that of semantic and structural connectedness, which is where both the meaning and the connectives work together to indicate the relation between two sentences. When sentences are linked together using cohesive ties, such as "and" or "therefore," they are grammatically connected; there is a clear relation between them and one or more words are used to indicate this relation. Such words are known in general linguistics as cohesive ties and they create structural connectivity. Without cohesive ties sentence relations might not be equally clear to all readers.

Consider the following examples:

Sentence 1 Ahmad is the taller.
Sentence 2 He is six feet tall.

The two sentences are full grammatical sentences and can be used completely independently of one another. We may understand sentence 1 with reference to two persons indicated by the speaker in a context where both the hearer and the speaker know who the second person is, and where "he" in sentence 2 is a reference to a third person, outside the comparison in sentence 1, who is six feet tall. In this case, the two sentences are not at all connected and so are unconnected grammatically and semantically.

However, we may think of another scenario in which the two sentences are used in connection with one another, if "he" in sentence 2 is understood to be a reference to Ahmad, the subject of sentence 1, in which case we assume that the height of the second person is known to both the speaker and the hearer and is less than six feet.

A writer using the two sentences may wish to make sure the relation between the two sentences is clear to all readers beyond doubt, by using the word "as" in the function of a cohesive tie:

Sentence 3 Ahmad is the taller as he is six feet tall.

Or, he could do so by using the semi-colon:

Sentence 4 Ahmad is the taller; he is six feet tall.

In both sentences 3 and 4 the cohesive tie used indicates that the pronoun "he" must be a reference to the noun at the beginning of the first sentence, and so the two sentences are seen as dependent both in terms of their meanings and their grammatical structure.

This type of structure is often used in the Qurʾān, but is not the most common category of cross-sentence relations in the Qurʾān. It is more common within long verses than across verses.[4] Consider the following example (Q 2:5):

> They are following guidance from their Lord
> And they are the ones who will prosper.

The use of the conjunction "and" (*wāw*) before the second sentence indicates that the two occurrences of the pronoun "they" (*ulāʾika*) refer to the same people. However, an additional aspect of the relations between the two sentences may be inferred. The second sentence may be a consequence of the first. Those who follow the guidance from God are those who will succeed. Their success follows from their choice to follow the guidance, rather than just being an accidental conjunct/coordinate as would be indicated without the inference of this additional connotation of the relation. Accordingly, the *wāw* ("and") in this context means "so" or "therefore."

However, this example, in spite of the ambiguity of the relation resulting from the choice of *wāw* here, does not seriously hinder the understanding of the broad textual relations in the *sūra* because this verse occurs in the middle of a passage that is coherent overall. When such connectivity is apparent, whether in the middle or on the borders of passages, textual relations are not normally problematic for the reader. It is when the connection is between two consecutive sentences, each falling on the border of a passage, which have no apparent relation, either structurally or semantically or both, that the recipient fails to work out why one of those passages should follow the other. The discussions of the following two categories show how this happens.

Semantic and structural disconnectivity

The second category is opposite to the first, focusing on disconnectivity. When two different sentences are grammatically unconnected and when their meanings are not clearly related, they are considered to be semantically and structurally disconnected.

If a sentence is part of a text with which the reader cannot see its connection, either grammatical or semantic, it is thought to be incoherent with the text. This is similar to the case of the second section of the *sūra* discussed at the beginning of this chapter. However, there might be some more obscure semantic relation(s) holding between such a sentence and the text to which it belongs. In that case, it is said that the meaning of this relation is open to interpretation. This feature is more common in literary language. However, if the relation is too hard to work out, it is often thought that the text is incoherent. Applying this to my initial example, it is clear that verse 16 has no apparent connection with verse 15, and verse 19 has no apparent connection with verse 20. The two sections as a whole have neither a structural nor a semantic relation between them.

15 Even though he might tender his excuses.

***

16 Move not your tongue to hasten with it.
17 Verily, upon Us is its gathering and its recitation.
18 Thus, when We recite it follow its recitation.
19 And then, verily, it is upon Us to clarify it.

***

20 No indeed. But you love the world that hastens away,

It is useful in such cases to consider the overall meaning of a number of verses belonging to one section as one proposition expressed by this section, then to look for a possible semantic relation. But when a relation cannot be found, textual relations between those sentences are deemed problematic.

Semantic connectivity and structural disconnectivity

The third category is when the semantic relation between two sentences, paragraphs, or sections of a text is apparent but without any physical indication of this relation, that is, they are semantically related but structurally unrelated. In such cases, context is used to infer the relation between the two.

Consider the following example from a poem by Ott (1998):

Sentence 5 Look into my eyes.
Sentence 6 The same gradual fire.

Sentences 5 and 6 are two lines of a postmodern poem. Sentence 5 ends with a full stop indicating structural discontinuity. However, the reader is inclined to draw a relation between the two sentences on the basis of several items of information drawn from outside the actual words of the text:

a Seeing fire in someone's eyes is a common metaphor to indicate anger or other feelings;
b The invitation to look into the speaker's eyes in sentence 5 must be to see something unusual in those eyes. People do not normally ask one another to look into their eyes for no reason. Sentence 6 provides a reason: the speaker wants the addressee to see the fire in her eyes;
c Usually when two sentences are placed one after the other, recipients assume this particular arrangement must be due to their being related, particularly if there is no clear indication that the intention is otherwise.

For all these reasons, and perhaps there may be others too, one is entitled to think that sentence 6 comes by way of explanation of what is to be seen in the eyes of the speaker if the addressee agrees to the request made in sentence 5. On the other hand, it is possible that a different interpretation of the poem may explain the relation differently and even reach the conclusion that there is no such direct relation between the two sentences.[5]

It is not unusual to see this type of structure interpreted into a variety of meanings, since the author has, probably deliberately, not included within the text a clear indication of what the particular relation between the consecutive units of text is. Because different readers process the text using different sets of assumptions, in the absence of any guidance from the text it is to be expected that they would arrive at different interpretations. Thus, the meaning of this kind of structure is inherently ambiguous.

This type of semantic relatedness and structural disconnectivity is the most common type of relations in the Qur'ānic text: many of the problems in the study of Qur'ānic textual relations are due to the inherently ambiguous nature of this kind of structure. Consider the following Qur'ānic example which occurs at a point of thematic transition in *sūra* 2 (Q 2:5–6):

5 They are following guidance from their Lord and they are the ones who will prosper.
6 Those who disbelieve, verily, it makes no difference whether you warn them or not: they will not believe.

Verse 5 is the end of the introductory section (verses 2–5), and verse 6 is the introductory verse of the second section of the *sūra* with an apparently new topic of the disbelievers.[6] There are no words to indicate a direct connection between the two sections or direct the reader to the type of relation intended. On the contrary, verse 6 begins with a "separator," *inna*, rather than a connective. *Inna* is a sentence initial introducing a new subject and emphasizing the information content that is to follow.

However, the relation between the two sections is not seen as a problematic relation because there is a semantic connection holding the meanings of the two sections together. The first section speaks of the believers who accept the guidance of the Qur'ān and the next speaks of the unbelievers who do not do so. By way of comparison between two kinds of people, the logical relation between the two different sections has been made clear and placement of the two as consecutive sections has been justified.[7] As the following sections of the *sūra* unfold, this understanding of the relation is consolidated.

Semantic disconnectivity and structural connectivity

The fourth logical type of textual relations is where structural connectedness exists but with no obvious semantic relation. According to the function of cohesive ties as indicators of semantic connectedness, it would be against the principles of communication to add a physical link between things that have no relation whatsoever. However, in some cases a connective is used, presumably indicating the existence of a semantic relation, where the semantic relation it indicates is not obvious. In this case, it is to be assumed that the linguistic connective is added to indicate to recipients that there is some fine relation between the two sentences but it is for the recipient to work it out.

Consider this example from Q 110:2–3.

2 When you see people embracing God's faith in crowds
3 then, celebrate the praise of your Lord and ask His forgiveness: He is always ready to accept repentance.

The relation in question is that between seeing people embrace God's faith (verse 2) on the one hand, and asking the Lord's forgiveness (verse 3) on the other. Grammatically, the two sentences are connected by the use of "when" (*idhā*) and "then" (*fa*), a grammatical structure that indicates the second sentence is a consequence of the first. But this connection is not very clear from the meaning of the two sentences; in the recipient's mind, seeing people embrace faith is not normally something that people would respond to by asking God's forgiveness. Religious people would ask for God's forgiveness when they commit a sin, not when they see other religious people.

I assume that it is because of this lack of clarity in the relation between the two sentences that commentators have often associated this *sūra* with a report that when Abū Bakr (Muḥammad's companion and friend) heard this *sūra* for the first time as a new revelation, he considered it an indication that the prophet would soon die. If the tradition is true, Abū Bakr's assumption would be based on establishing the missing semantic relation between the two sentences as follows:

a The fact that crowds of people had started to embrace Islam indicates completion of the prophet's mission;
b It is near their death that religious people tend to ask intensely for God's forgiveness;
Conclusion:
c If the prophet's career has come to an end, and he is being asked to ask God for forgiveness, it must mean he is going to die soon.

It is by working out which assumptions to use to fill the gaps between the meanings of the different sentences that one can make some sense of relatedness between them and hence justify their arrangement. However, if one fails to work out such helpful assumptions, relations between the sentences in similar structures remain highly problematic.

The reason for the ambiguity of Qur'ānic textual relations is therefore assumed to be that most of them belong to the second and third categories: they encompass complete and independent units of meaning lined up one after the other with few grammatical connectives, and with relations between those complete units of meaning that are not always straightforward and easy to work out.

Table 4.1 shows the four types of possible relations between sentences and their effects on recipients' understanding of textual relations.

Relevance

In the above discussions and examples I have shown that a Qur'ānic *sūra* is composed of separate linguistic units whose relations are not always obvious, and have discussed

Table 4.1 General categories of textual relations

	Structural relation	Semantic relation	Textual relations
1 Semantically related and structurally connected	Yes	Yes	Clear except when the connective is ambiguous
2 Semantically unrelated and structurally disconnected	No	No	Problematic
3 Semantically related and structurally disconnected	Yes	No	Possibly ambiguous
4 Semantically unrelated and structurally connected	No	Yes	Problematic

a number of possible reasons for this lack of clarity. This now raises the question: how do such separate units make sense together in order to communicate the intended message of the text?

In order to answer this question I shall draw on a number of tenets from Pragmatics, the discipline dealing with the non-linguistic aspects of a text's meaning.[8]

Sentence meaning and the intended meaning

A central problem for the study of meaning is that sentence meaning vastly undermines a speaker's meaning. What this means is that the intended meanings of text are not understood simply by working out what the meanings of its units are. In fact, in most cases, the meanings of the words are only a very small aspect of the message communicated. Take for example the following sentence:

Sentence 7 It is raining.

There are many cases in which sentence 7 would not be taken as merely informative of the fact that it is raining. For example, if the speaker and the addressee were planning a picnic, the intended meaning would not be just to inform the hearer of the state of affairs that it is raining. Instead, it could be:

Sentence 7a The picnic will have to be cancelled.

In another scenario, if the speaker is responding by sentence 7 to sentence 8 below:

Sentence 8 I do not need to take my umbrella with me.

The intended meaning of sentence 7 would in this case be:

Sentence 7b Yes, you do need to take your umbrella with you.

Which is not what the words of the sentence say. Sentence 7, with its two scenarios, represents many other sentences that we use, hear, and read where understanding the meanings of their words is not alone sufficient to communicate the intended meanings. In both scenarios, if the hearer of sentence 7 took the sentence as merely informative of a state of affairs not related to her present situation, and continued preparing for the picnic or went out without her umbrella, communication of the intended meaning would have failed. In cases of successful communication of the intended meaning, the message communicated by the sentence is more than what its words simply said.

What is it, then, that one needs in order to work out the intended meaning of sentences? If we continue using the example above, we shall be able to see that it is the context of the conversation that is used, in both scenarios, to reach the correct understanding of the intended meaning. Sometimes this context comes from outside the text (first scenario), and at other times from the rest of the text (second scenario). In the first scenario, it is the information, known to both the speaker and the hearer, that they were planning to go on a picnic, and the general knowledge that people do not normally go on picnics while it is raining. In the second scenario, it is the speaker's knowledge of the hearer's intention to go out without an umbrella, as understood from sentence 8 being the preceding part of the conversation, and the commonsense knowledge that if people go out while it is raining they take umbrellas with them in order to avoid getting wet.

This brief analysis highlights three aspects of knowledge used in the comprehension of a text's intended meaning: (a) general knowledge/commonsense knowledge; (b) knowledge common to the speaker and addressee or writer and reader; and (c) knowledge from other parts of the text. Aspects (a) and (b) are non-linguistic context since information drawn from them does not form part of the text, whereas (c) is linguistic context because it draws on information gained by recovering the meanings of other parts of the text. These are three broad divisions of information from outside the text in question that recipients use to understand the intended meaning.

The role of contextual information

As we have seen above, recipients need contextual information to understand the intended meaning. If such information is not accessible to them, they are likely to fail to understand the speaker's intended meaning. Similarly, if recipients of the Qur'ānic text lack access to the knowledge they need to process the meanings of its language, they are unlikely to succeed in uncovering the intended meanings, including those meanings indicated by the relations between the themes/sections of *sūras*.

A verse such as "May the hands of Abū Lahab be ruined, and may he be ruined too" (Q 111:1) is not understandable in the absence of the knowledge of who Abū Lahab is, whereas the following verse (Q 111:2), "Neither his wealth nor his gains will help him," can be understood as a general reference to man, especially in the light of the fact that this reinforces a meaning central to the message of the Qur'ān; that is, if man does not believe in God and the day of judgment, wealth and worldly deeds will not be of any use to him on that day. Similarly, the third verse of the same *sūra*, "and so will his wife, the fire-wood carrier," would be understood metaphorically rather than literally, as is the case in its standard Sunnī interpretation, if one is not aware of the history of the situation commented on by the *sūra*. In fact, if information about the historical situation is not available to interpreters, the meaning of the whole *sūra* may be turned into an image of man and his female partner being punished in hellfire for their disbelief.

The only difference between the Qur'ān and any other text, literary or non-literary,[9] in this respect is that the contextual information required for interpreting each text varies according to the nature of the text and its content. Advertising language, for example, is understood in the light of knowledge about modern daily life and commodities, whereas understanding contemporary media language requires knowledge of current affairs and modern lifestyles and a certain linguistic knowledge. A pre-Islamic poem would be understood by using contextual information from history and Arab culture of the time in addition to commonsense and general linguistic knowledge of Arabic. As for the Qur'ān, in addition to general linguistic knowledge of Arabic and Arabic language at the time of the revelations, knowledge of pre- and early Islamic Arab culture and history and basic Islamic knowledge (e.g., *ḥadīth* and *sīra*) are essential.

However, it is only reasonable to assume that not all recipients, given their varied backgrounds, will have access to all the information they need from outside the text. Thus, generally speaking, contextual information may be divided into two broad types: linguistic or immediate context, and non-linguistic context. *Sūra* 111 above is an example of the latter. It remains to clarify what the linguistic context of the Qur'ān is.

As with any text, the linguistic context of any given part of the Qur'ān is the preceding and the following verses. Due to their physical proximity to the text in question they can be referred to as the immediate context. The information provided by the immediate context is naturally the most immediately accessible information that can be relied on for working out the meaning of the text in question, which gives it a prime role in the comprehension process. However, accessibility of contextual information does not guarantee successful communication. Indeed, most of those who have considered the text of the Qur'ān to be confused and incoherent were specialists in this particular field of knowledge, Arabic and Islamic studies.

Context and relevance

A major hurdle in the way of successful communication of the intended meaning is that there is often too much contextual information to choose from. To solve this problem, relevance theoreticians hold that human cognition has evolved in the direction of increasing efficiency and, therefore, out of the huge amount of information available to recipients of a text (via memory, perception, and inference), the most relevant will be selected and used in processing the language of the text in order to maximize relevance.[10] Relevance theoreticians define relevance as a property of text[11] that makes it worth processing. For a text to be relevant it has to make a difference to the recipient's cognitive environment, that is, it must enhance their knowledge of the world.

The outcome of the interaction between the propositions expressed by the text and information derived from context is known as "cognitive effect," of which there are three possible types:

1 Addition of new information to already existing knowledge.
2 Contradiction of already existing knowledge.
3 Confirmation of already existing knowledge.

Relevance is measured against two factors: the number of cognitive effects and the effort put into achieving them. The more the effects, the more relevant the text is, while the less effort one puts into processing an item of information, the more its relevance.

Consequently, the answer to the question of which items of contextual information to use in processing a unit of discourse lies in maximizing relevance. In other words, as an automatic cognitive process, recipients tend to choose the aspect of context that is most easily accessible and that will interact with the text to yield the maximum possible effects; it will enhance recipients' cognitive environment in the most possible ways.

Thus, in the case of sentence 7 above, to understand "it is raining" as merely informative of a state of affairs outside the recipient's situational context is to minimize the relevance of the utterance because it only adds one item of information to the recipient's general knowledge, an item that is not likely to enhance the recipient's knowledge of her present situation. To understand it in the ways suggested above adds more to the recipient's existing knowledge both of the world and of her present situation, making it the optimal explanation of the sentence.

Similarly, the Qurʾān as a whole should be seen as a highly accessible source of information needed to work out the intended meaning of a given verse. Just as the preceding and following utterances in a conversation contribute towards understanding any part of it, previous verses provide background information for understanding a verse in question, and following verses soon act as context for those after them, the end result being that each part of the text is equally important for comprehension of all the other parts, because they reduce the effort required in the process of comprehension, thus maximizing relevance.[12] The picture of the discourse, then, is as Diane Blakemore (1987: 112) describes it: "one in which the interpretation of utterance (that is the prepositional content and its contextual effect) contribute towards the contexts for interpreting subsequent utterances. That is, as discourse proceeds, the hearer is provided with a gradually changing background against which new information is processed."

It is from this idea that the importance of the immediate context arises: information made accessible by the verses nearest to those being processed is easily accessible to the reader and so they help to minimize the costs of processing text for comprehension.

So meanings achieved by using the immediate context are more likely to be the intended meanings. In a later section I shall shed more light on the role of the immediate context as a tool that speakers/authors use to direct hearers/readers towards their intended meanings, knowing that they are likely to use them before any other source of context.

Maximizing the relevance of Qur'ānic verses

The idea of maximization of relevance by increasing the cognitive effect of utterances is evident in the Qur'ān, and in particular in the relatively loose connections between verses. In accordance with the framework explained above, the greater the number of linguistic ties used to direct recipients towards a particular understanding of the intended meaning of a verse, the more restricted that verse will be to its immediate context. Such ties function as constraints on the relevance of the verse because the relation they create between the verse and the information surrounding it is effectively a limitation of interpretational possibilities (as they direct the recipient to select one particular item of contextual information and ignore all the others). On the other hand, the fewer restraints there are, the greater the potential for multiple interpretations and the more universal the intended meaning of the message becomes.

Universal meanings and loose ends

The majority of Qur'ānic verses feature what is known in the study of Arabic literary styles as *ījāz*, that is, a property of literary language whereby the maximum possible meaning is encompassed in the minimum possible number of words to produce high intensity of meaning and a kind of universality that would allow the same sentence to be used in multiple contexts.[13] The detailed discussions of *ījāz* in Arabic rhetoric come to the conclusion that *khayr al-kalām mā qalla wa dall* ("the best composition is the least in size but the greatest in semantic outcomes"). As such, this criterion takes into consideration the size of the utterance/text to be processed for comprehension relative to the outcome of the comprehension process and is thus vaguely similar to the notion of relevance, with the contextual information factor omitted. By default, the stylistic feature of *ījāz* requires authors who aim at the best literary language to maximize the effect of their sentences. It requires sentences to lead to the inference of more meanings so that, to use relevance theory language, the reader perceives them to be worth her while and is therefore prepared to put time and effort into processing them.

The majority of Qur'ānic verses express universal meanings and refer to situations whose occurrence is likely for everyone at some point in time. The text's use of very few linguistic connectives allows it to live up to its promise to be a message for humanity applicable in all places at all times. Consider, for example, the verses on Islamic dress code (Q 33:53, 55, 59; 24:30–1, 60). The generalized and broad manner in which the verses are phrased only enhances the flexibility of their application. The addition of any details to the texts would impose more constraints and hence limit applicability. When information from the relevant contexts such as *ḥadīth* and *sīra* is employed to explain the intended form and shape of women's dress, it only re-emphasizes the broadness of these limits. Several items of information (from various narratives) are available concerning the wide variety of dress that women wore during the lifetime of Muḥammad. This must mean to the Islamic legislator that an equivalent level of variety and flexibility should be permissible in modern days. Any limitation of this flexibility would be against the texts' intended meaning as indicated by the way they are phrased and by their context.

The same method of understanding works for the way textual relations are structured: the lack of obvious ties between verses leaves them as free agents, to be used in any possible context. The more a verse is tied to its immediate context, the less its applicability outside that particular context. The loose structure of Qur'ānic texts has the effect of maximizing the cognitive effects of verses by making them true and valid for contexts other than their immediate ones.

This quality has resulted in the fact that Qur'ānic expressions have become highly quotable in a huge variety of contexts, sometimes even in situations that are not in the slightest related to the original contexts in which they occur. For example, it is very common to see on the façades of juice shops in the Arab world the Qur'ānic phrase (Q 37:46): "White, delicious to those who taste it." If this verse were phrased more tightly so as to link it with its immediate context by including a specific reference to which drink and where it is, it would not have become possible for juice sellers to use it so wittily! One could very easily compose a long list of such examples, which would prove the same point; the deliberate lack of constraints on the structure of the Qur'ānic text is one major factor contributing to the effectiveness of the communication of its universal message.

Conclusions

A close analysis of the structure of verses in Qur'ānic *sūras* reveals that they do indeed have a distinctly loose structure, but one which is explicable in terms of maximization of the effect of those verses on recipients' understanding of the whole text of the Qur'ān and hence their own cognitive environments.

This is not to suggest that the answer to the ultimate question of whether Qur'ānic *sūras* possess textual relations is that they do not. On the contrary, Qur'ānic textual relations within any given *sūra* are explicable through a different understanding of the role of the linguistic/Qur'ānic unit known as a "verse" as a source of contextual information that can be used to aid comprehension of the Qur'ānic meaning both in the same *sūra* and in other *sūras*. The role of verses as contexts to one another is the justification of their own relevance. In any sequence of verses, the proposition expressed by a preceding verse is an "immediate context" that is automatically used by recipients in processing any following verse. When a verse is read, its words, or general meanings, work as a stimulus directing the brain to access other verses, which would have been read previously, to be used as sources of contextual information needed to assist in recovering the meaning of that verse.

The traditional view of the comprehension process requires Qur'ānic verses to be superficially connected regardless of the effect this may have on the delivery of the overall intended message. The framework of understanding I have proposed here gives rise to an appreciation of the mutual role of verses as the most accessible sources of contextual information. This mutuality leads to the minimalization of the effort put into the comprehension process, and thus justifies their relevance.

Notes

1 Robinson (1996: 138ff.) tries to draw a connection between the two sections from the repetition of words derived from the stem "hasten" but he fails to reach a definitive conclusion because of the lack of other affirmative indicators. For a detailed discussion of the structure of this *sūra* see also: Robinson (1986) and El-Awa (2005).
2 A similar question regarding cross-*sūra* relations arises here, but is not within the scope of this chapter.
3 In El-Awa (2006), I have treated the section and the paragraph as possible units of the Qur'ānic *sūra* and shown how sections may be equal in value to sentences in that they also express one proposition that makes a contribution to the overall meaning of the *sūra*.
4 Though it is rare, we may observe some tendencies, and detect certain literary effects for whose achievement this particular structure of relations is used across verses. For example, the connection is often "and," which, in Arabic, indicates the mere existence of a relation, without stipulating what this relation is. This function is similar to the function of a semicolon joining two sentences. In many cases, therefore, textual relations remain ambiguous to some extent.
5 This analysis does not take into consideration the rest of the poem, which might lead to the inference of a completely different meaning.
6 In order to maintain the flow of the discussion, and because section divisions are not in question here, I do not question them. Instead, I use the topic as a broad indicator of switches in subject matter. In another analysis, one that is dedicated to determining where sections end and begin, one would be obliged to rely on many more indicators than I do here.
7 Indeed, in Robinson (1996: 200ff.) the two sections are considered parts of one major section of the *sūra*.
8 The views and analysis of examples in this section are based on relevance theory as explained by Sperber and Wilson (1995; 2004).
9 Fabb (1997) shows how the process involved in understanding everyday language is not different from that involved in understanding literary language. The same principles of human communication are in operation. In El-Awa (2006), examples from Arabic literature have been used to establish the same point.
10 This is based on the cognitive "principle of relevance" that human cognition tends to be geared towards maximization of relevance.
11 The theory extends to other aspects of human communication, but for the purpose of this chapter, and to avoid confusion, I refer only to text.
12 According to this understanding, Qur'ānic repetitions are highly effective tools of maximizing relevance. Each repetition provides access to other occurrences of the same theme, phrase, or word in other places of the Qur'ān and in so doing it adds the effects of the contexts of the repetitions to the present context resulting in more cognitive effects. For more details on this role of repetition see El-Awa (2004).
13 The most typical Qur'ānic example favored by almost all classical critics and linguists who have written on this stylistic feature is the infamous Qur'ānic statement commending

capital punishment as a gift of life for those who possess wisdom (Q 2:179): "Life is in fair retribution." Books have been written to elaborate how and why this verse is considered the peak of Arabic eloquence, but what concerns us here is that it represents the ultimate example of how a few words can, through their interaction with the right set of contextual information, express an infinity of meanings related to a huge legal and human argument about why the existence of capital punishment is beneficial for society.

Further reading

El-Awa, S. M. S. (2004) Qur'ānic repetition: A relevance based explanation of the phenomenon. *Islamic Studies* 42:4, 577–93.

El-Awa, S. M. S. (2005) *Textual Relation in the Qur'ān: Relevance, Coherence and Structure.* Routledge, London.

Mir, M. (1986) *Coherence in the Qur'ān.* American Trust Publications, Indianapolis.

Robinson, N. (1986) The Qur'ān as the word of God. In: Linzey, A. and Wexler, P. (eds.) *Heaven and Earth: Essex Essays in Theology and Ethics.* Churchman, Worthington, pp. 38–54.

Robinson, N. (1996) *Discovering the Qur'an: A Contemporary Approach to a Veiled Text.* SCM Press, London.

Robinson, N. (2000) The structure and interpretation of *Sūrat al-Mu'minūn. Journal of Qur'ānic Studies* 2:1, 89–106.

Robinson, N. (2001) Hands outstretched: Towards a re-reading of *Sūrat al-Mā'idah. Journal of Qur'ānic Studies* 3:1, 1–19.

Zahniser, Mathias (2000) Major transitions and thematic borders in two long *sūras*: al-Baqara and al-Nisā'. In: Boullata, Issa J. (ed.) *Literary Structures of Religious Meaning in the Qur'ān.* Curzon Press, Richmond, pp. 22–55.

CHAPTER 5

Patterns of Address

Rosalind Ward Gwynne

To the extent that Muslims regard the Qurʾān as a blessing for all humanity, they consider that its every word addresses the audience in some fashion. Over the centuries scholars have exhaustively analyzed these ways, classified them, and distinguished them from or assimilated them to one another. Classical works on Qurʾānic sciences deal with patterns of address (*khiṭāb, mukhāṭabāt*) but do not always separate those parts that address the Qurʾān's audience from those in which one character in the Qurʾān addresses another, as in the exchanges between Abraham and his father.

In this chapter we shall examine the most prominent forms of address: vocatives and those whom they designate, imperatives and the actions they prescribe, and the effects that the passages have on their intended audiences. Muslim scholars did not confine a passage to a single category, however; they were acutely aware that a historical precedent or a parable, for example, though in the form of a third-person narrative, is a form of address, and its surrounding apparatus places it in one or more of the first three categories.

My two principal sources for this chapter, besides the Qurʾān itself, are the encyclopedic *al-Burhān fī ʿulūm al-Qurʾān* ("The Proof in the Qurʾānic Sciences") by the Egyptian Shāfiʿī scholar Badr al-Dīn al-Zarkashī (d. 794/1392), and *al-Itqān fī ʿulūm al-Qurʾān* ("The Perfection in the Qurʾānic Sciences") by his successor Jalāl al-Dīn al-Suyūṭī (d. 911/1505), who credits al-Zarkashī generously in the introduction to *Itqān* but rarely mentions him in context, even when he lifts whole passages from *Burhān*. While making my own additions, deletions, and rearrangements, I shall nevertheless rely upon these works for two reasons. First, in dealing with the Qurʾān as a whole they do not classify a given passage under a single rubric but where possible offer multiple analyses. Second, adopting their approach acquaints the reader with not one but two levels of Islamic discourse, the Qurʾān itself and the methods of classical Qurʾānic scholars.

Particles, Pronouns, and Other Methods of Designating the Audience

Who is the audience for the Qur'ān? The first, of course, was the prophet Muḥammad, and the first revelation was, by most accounts, a command to him: *iqra'*, "Read!" or "Recite!" As we shall see, the most common command in the Qur'ān is understood to be directed at the prophet as well: *qul*, "Say!" In countless passages, the Qur'ān famously shifts from general to particular, from singular to dual to plural, and from first to second to third person, offering scholars opportunity to disagree over both textual and extra-textual referents. The beginning of al-Zarkashī's and al-Suyūṭī's chapters on patterns of address (chapters 42 and 51, respectively) make the basic distinction among all these possibilities: is the addressee general (*ʿāmm*) or particular (*khāṣṣ*)? These are not synonymous with "plural" and "singular," however, for al-Zarkashī includes both categories. "It is God who created you (*khalaqakum*), then gave you sustenance" (Q 30:40). "O humanity (*yā ayyuhā 'l-insān*)! What has beguiled you (*mā gharraka*) from your gracious Lord?" (Q 82:6). The addressee in both is generic, but only the first uses the plural, second-person pronoun to refer to the addressee (al-Zarkashī 1988: II, 349).

The particular, likewise, may be either grammatically plural or singular. All humanity will see the day of judgment, but only those bound for hell, with faces black and gloomy, are addressed at the end of Q 3:106: "Did you [plural] disbelieve after believing?" There is only one possible addressee in Q 5:67: "O apostle (*yā ayyuhā al-rasūl*)! Deliver the message that has been sent down from your Lord" (al-Zarkashī 1988: II, 349).

The non-identity of general and particular with plural and singular generate al-Zarkashī's next two considerations. The first concerns passages that appear to address a particular person but are in fact directed at a general audience, while the second notes general forms that actually address particular persons or groups. One of the best-known examples of the former comes in Q 65:1: "O prophet (*yā ayyuhā 'l-nabī*)! When you [plural] divorce women . . . ," followed by several long verses concerning the laws of divorce. As al-Zarkashī says, "The discourse opens with the prophet, while the intended audience is whoever is in a position to divorce" (al-Zarkashī 1988: II, 349). A much more difficult verse is Q 33:50 on the subject of legal marriage: first the prophet is addressed, then women whom "you" (masculine singular) may marry, then women who are legal only for the prophet. Al-Zarkashī quotes Abū Bakr al-Ṣayrafī (like al-Zarkashī, a Shāfiʿī, d. 330/941–2): "The beginning of the address is to [Muḥammad], and when it said that the one who gives herself is 'only for you', he knew that what came before that was for himself and others" (al-Zarkashī 1988: II, 350).

Certain "general" references may, in fact, be particular, leading to various controversies. For example, a long verse in *sūrat al-nisā'* enumerates the women whom a Muslim man may not marry. It begins, "Forbidden to you are your mothers and daughters," but, in effect, it exempts new converts from divorcing wives within these degrees, as it ends with the phrase "except what has gone before; God is Forgiving and Merciful" (Q 4:23). Al-Zarkashī occasionally engages in the popular practice of identifying particular individuals associated with seemingly general verses. He says that Q 2:13 –

"When it is said to them, 'Believe as the people believe' [they say, 'Shall we believe as the fools believe?']" – actually refers to ʿAbd Allāh b. Salām, a rabbi who eventually accepted Islam (al-Zarkashī 1988: II, 352; cf. Guillaume 1955: 240, 262).

Many examples of general and particular concern matters of law, and, though al-Zarkashī does not say so specifically, interpretation depends largely upon legal reasoning that was not systematized until centuries after the revelation. He gives a short example from *sūrat al-nisāʾ*: "O people, fear your Lord" (Q 4:1) but says, "Children and the insane are not included" (al-Zarkashī 1988: II, 352). Particularization of a general rule might come at the end of a verse (e.g. Q 4:4: "And give women their dowers . . . but if they freely give some back, then take it") or at the beginning (Q 2:229: "Divorce is only permissible twice; after that . . ."). It might come from another verse in the same *sūra* (e.g. Q 8:16 and 65, concerning the obligation to fight in battle); or it might come from another *sūra* altogether. A passage in *sūrat al-baqara* stipulating that widows in general must wait four months and ten days before marrying again (Q 2:234) is qualified by one from *sūrat al-ṭalāq* that requires pregnant widows to give birth first (Q 65:4) (al-Zarkashī 1988: II, 352–3).

The scope of address decreases as al-Zarkashī progresses in his analysis. He isolates passages that address the genus (*al-jins*) but not every individual, the "species" (*al-nawʿ*), and the individual (*al-ʿayn*). The phrase "O people! (*yā ayyuhā ʾl-nās*)" in Q 2:21 ("O people! Worship your Lord who created you"), according to al-Zarkashī, applies to the genus but not to individuals who are not legally responsible; it predominates in addresses to the people of Mecca. A more delicate question is whether the same phrase in the command, "O people! Fear your Lord!" includes the prophet. Al-Zarkashī says that legal scholars have affirmed that it does. The command begins a *sūra* in the first half of the Qurʾān (*sūra* 4, *al-nisāʾ*) and a *sūra* in the second half (*sūra* 22, *al-ḥajj*); the first passage deals with creation, the second with the hereafter, "so consider this arrangement – how steeped it is in eloquence!" In still other contexts, the word may actually refer to "people of virtue, not those who are given the name 'people' out of tolerance" (al-Zarkashī 1988: II, 356–7).

In this chapter, the only example al-Zarkashī gives of addressing the "species" is from Q 2:40, where God's command to remember His benefits and keep His covenant is addressed to the Children of Israel but, he says, really means "the sons of Jacob." Individuals whom God addresses include Adam, (Q 2:35), Noah (Q 11:48), Abraham (Q 37:104–5), Moses (Q 7:144), and Jesus (Q 3:55). Muḥammad, however, is never addressed by his personal name but as *yā ayyuhā ʾl-nabī* (Q 8:64) or *yā ayyuhā ʾl-rasūl* (Q 5:41) (al-Zarkashī 1988: II, 357).

After a digression upon the topics of praise and blame, favor, humiliation, and sarcasm (discussed below along with other effects upon the audience), al-Zarkashī focuses upon increasingly intricate questions of audience identification. His analysis uses grammatical terminology – singular, dual, plural – to make even more minute distinctions than the genus/species/individual division. A plural may be addressed in the singular, a singular in the plural, both singular and plural in the dual, a dual in the singular; or a combination may be addressed sequentially. Al-Suyūṭī's contribution is to subdivide al-Zarkashī's five sections dealing with this topic into ten. Simply enumerating these possibilities hints at the potential exegetical challenges.

A comparatively simple example of addressing the plural in the singular is "O humanity (*yā ayyuhā ʾl-insān*)! What has beguiled you [singular] from your bountiful Lord?" (Q 82:6). That this is addressed to everyone al-Zarkashī proves by referring to Q 103:2–3: "Truly humanity (*al-insān*) is in a state of loss, except those who believe" (al-Zarkashī 1988: II, 360).

Addressing a singular in the plural presents far more alternatives, hence more opportunities for disagreement. Thus, asserts al-Zarkashī, when God speaks to the prophets as a group – "O messengers (*yā ayyuhā ʾl-rusul*)! Eat of the good things and do good works" (Q 24:51–4) – he is really addressing Muḥammad, "because there was no prophet with him . . . or after him." "Those of favor and ample means among you" who must not refrain from helping family and the needy (Q 24:21) actually signifies Abū Bakr, who withheld a Badr veteran's share from him for his involvement in the slander of ʿĀʾisha (al-Zarkashī 1988: II, 361; cf. Guillaume 1955: 495–7). The prophet is sometimes addressed in the plural (Q 11:14, 13), and God may be addressed and speak of himself in the "plural of majesty" (Q 23:99; 43:32; al-Zarkashī 1988: II, 361–2). Yet we note that the most commonly repeated *sūra* addresses God in the singular: "It is You [singular] Whom we worship and You whom we ask for help" (Q 1:5). Other possible plural audiences include humans and *jinn* (Q 6:130; al-Zarkashī 1988: II, 363).

Examples of singular and plural addressed in the dual and dual in the singular come from passages concerning Moses and Aaron (e.g., Q 10:89; 20:49), but at least one refers to a dispute between two of Muḥammad's wives (Q 66:4).

Perhaps the most convoluted example of sequential address (al-Zarkashī 1988: II, 365–7) comes in Q 10:87: "We revealed to Moses and his brother, 'Provide houses for your [dual] people in Egypt; and make your [plural] houses places of worship and perform prayer [plural]; and give [singular] good news to the believers.' "

Sometimes one person – Muḥammad or another – is addressed when the intended audience may be someone else. Al-Zarkashī disposes of anything that seems to contradict Muḥammad's immunity from sin (*ʿiṣma*): " 'O prophet! Fear God and do not obey the unbelievers and hypocrites!' (Q 33:1): the address is to him but the believers are meant; because he was pure; far be it from him to obey the unbelievers and hypocrites!" This point, al-Zarkashī says, is proven by the next verse. Other verses treated similarly include Q 10:94 and 104, and 9:43 (al-Zarkashī 1988: II, 367).

To illustrate how the Qurʾān goads its audience to awareness, al-Zarkashī cites passages that invite "contemplation" of sacred history or other phenomena. Thus Ṣāliḥ addresses his people after their destruction by earthquake (Q 7:79); the prophet is told to say, "Travel in the earth and see [how God originated creation] . . ." (Q 29:20); and all are told to observe the fruits of the earth as signs for believers (Q 6:99) (al-Zarkashī 1988: II, 368–9; cf. Gwynne 2004: 25–58).

Al-Zarkashī next covers instances in which the Qurʾān addresses one person, then turns to another. Most useful for our purposes is one of al-Suyūṭī's examples: "We have sent you [singular] as a witness, a bringer of good tidings, and a warner, so that you [plural] may believe in God and His apostle" (Q 48:8–9). First God speaks to the prophet, then turns to human beings in general (al-Suyūṭī 1951: II, 34; cf. al-Zarkashī 1988: II, 369).

The next related topic is *talwīn* ("variegation"). Without first defining the word, al-Zarkashī (1988: II, 369) cites only two short examples that he has already used in other contexts: "O prophet! When you [plural] divorce women . . ." (Q 65:1) and "Who is your [dual] Lord, O Moses?" (Q 20:49). But then he notes that rhetoricians call this *iltifāt* and that he will deal with it under that heading. Indeed he does, in a section that is eighty-six pages long! He begins by describing the purpose of *iltifāt*:

> It is the transition of speech from one style to another, rendering it fresh and abundantly rich for the hearer, renewing his vital energy, and safeguarding his mind from the boredom and irritation that the persistence of a single style [would have] on his hearing. (al-Zarkashī 1988: III, 380)

More specifically, it signifies the abrupt transition from speaking in the first person (*takallum*) to the second (*khiṭāb*) or third (*ghayba*), or any combination thereof; the great length of the section gives some idea of the differences of opinion possible when interpreting such passages. A single example must suffice, from a description of the joys of paradise. "Enter [plural] the garden, you [plural] and your spouses, to be made glad . . . Dishes of gold and cups will be passed among them . . . And you [plural] will be there eternally" (Q 43:70–1); first comes an address in the second person, then a third-person narrative, then another second-person address.

Is the audience only human beings? Al-Zarkashī (1988: II, 369–70) illustrates "addressing inanimate objects as a rational being would be addressed" by citing Q. 41:11, "He said to [the sky] and the earth, 'Come willingly or unwillingly!' The two of them said, 'We come willingly.'" There are disagreements, he says, as to whether this is meant literally or metaphorically, but the wording cannot be denied: sky, earth, and mountains (Q 34:10) are addressed as members of God's audience.

The attention that Muslim exegetes and rhetoricians have devoted to every letter of the Qur'ān is epitomized in these systematic examinations of all possible Qur'ānic formulae of designating the audience, with all their possible interpretations from the most concrete to the most speculative, excluding only the possibility of human authorship. The impatience and preconceptions of some non-Muslim scholars of Islam have often prevented them from seeing such change and variety in the text as anything other than an exasperating inconsistency.

Effects on the Audience

After the Qur'ān designates the audience for a given passage, how does the discourse proceed? Al-Zarkashī treats the broad topic of Qur'ānic rhetoric in his chapter 46, which occupies nearly half of the book's four volumes; that is where we find his treatment of *iltifāt*, for example. In chapter 42, however, he arranges the remaining categories of address according to the effects they are intended to produce rather than their rhetorical patterns.

He begins with "praise" (*al-madḥ*). Interestingly, this is where he classifies all passages beginning with the phrase "O you who believe" (*yā ayyuhā 'lladhīna āmanū*), which occurs some ninety times in the Qur'ān. According to al-Zarkashī, this formula addresses

> the people of Medina who believed and performed the *hijra*, to distinguish them from the people of Mecca. As mentioned previously, every verse in which *yā ayyuhā 'l-nās* occurs is for the people of Mecca; and the reason for that is that after *yā ayyuhā 'l-nās* comes the command for basic belief, while after *yā ayyuhā 'lladhīna āmanū* comes the command for the particulars of the religious law. (al-Zarkashī 1988: II, 357)

Al-Zarkashī also includes here the passages in which God addresses Muḥammad, whether as prophet (*yā ayyuhā 'l-nabī*, Q 8:64) or as messenger (*yā ayyuhā 'l-rasūl*, Q 5:41), as appropriate for his role in the passage. Thus Q 5:67 deals with divine law appropriate for all: "O messenger! Convey what has been sent down to you from your Lord." The other sort addresses the prophet as an individual: "O prophet! Why have you forbidden [yourself] what God has made lawful for you?" (Q 66:1, concerning a disputed incident in Muḥammad's family life; cf. al-Qurṭubī 1997: XVIII, 117–22).

Next, logically, comes "blame" (*al-dhamm*). "O you who disbelieved (*yā ayyuhā 'lladhīna kafarū*)! Make no excuses on this day! [You are only being paid back for what you have done]" (Q 66:7). "Say: O disbelievers (*yā ayyuhā 'l-kāfirūn*)!" (Q 109:1) "And because of the humiliation that it contains, it [i.e. direct address to unbelievers] does not occur in the Qur'ān except in these two places." Al-Zarkashī contrasts this with how often believers are addressed in the second person, pointing out that in all other places those who reject faith are addressed in the third person:

> turning away from them, as in His statement, "Say to those who reject faith that if they cease, they will be forgiven for what is past, and if they return [to their old ways] – well, the example of the ancients has already been set." (Q 8:38; al-Zarkashī 1988: II, 358; cf. Gwynne 1993: 457, 459–60)

"Favor" or "honor" is dealt with briefly in only two examples, each of which is an invitation, one to Adam and his spouse (Q 7:19) and the other to the righteous (*al-muttaqīn*, Q 15:45–6), to enter the garden. "Humiliation" (*al-ihāna*) resumes the note of "blame" struck earlier. But these verses are addressed either to Iblīs (Q 15:36–7; 17:64–5) or to sinners in hell (Q 23:108), not directly to the Qur'ān's audience who are hearing or reading the words in this life. Al-Zarkashī's use of the term *ihāna*, "humiliation," applies to one of only two instances in which disbelievers are addressed directly (Q 109:1; al-Zarkashī 1988: II, 359). For those in hell, however, such humiliation is part of the punishment (Gwynne 2002).

"Sarcasm" (*al-tahakkum*) is again mostly directed to residents of hell, where they are offered the "hospitality" of bitter fruit and boiling water (Q 56:52–6, 93), the "shade" of black smoke (Q 56:42–3), and the "warmth" of hellfire (Q 56:94). An inhabitant of hell whom al-Zarkashī identifies as Abū Jahl is told, "Taste this! Truly you are the mighty (*al-ʿazīz*), the noble (*al-karīm*)" (Q 44:49), using two of the divine names for one of the prophet's chief enemies. As for those in the audience who hide their wealth rather than spend it in the way of God, the prophet is told, "Give them the good news of a painful punishment!" (Q 9:34; al-Zarkashī 1988: II, 359–60).

After completing his second sequence on identification of audiences, al-Zarkashī again discusses how the Qur'ān affects them. This sequence demonstrates how the text elicits positive results by the proper management of emotions usually classed as negative. One of these is called "provocation." Characteristic of all his examples are phrases such as "if you are believers" and "if you are Muslims." For example, Q 2:278 states, "O you who believe, fear God and give up what remains of the usury due you, if you are believers!" The author says, "He – may He be glorified – has already characterized them by belief when He addresses them, then said 'if you are believers' intending to prod them into abandoning usury, as it is proper for them to do that" (cf. Q 8:1, 41; 10:84; al-Zarkashī 1988: II, 370).

Al-Zarkashī's next section deals with "affront" – literally, "causing rage" (*ighḍāb*) – against "those who fought you for your religion and expelled you from your homes and supported your expulsion" (Q 60:9); against Iblīs: "Do you take [Satan] and his progeny as protectors rather than Me?" (Q 18:50); and against the hypocrites: "They want you to reject faith as they have so that you will be like them" (Q 4:89) (al-Zarkashī 1988: II, 370).

Al-Zarkashī first defines the next topic, "encouragement and agitation," as "encouraging one to distinguish oneself by fine qualities." Q 61:4 states, "God loves those who fight in His path," which applies to those who remain firm and pious in battle (Q 3:125), who do not turn their backs (Q 8:16) because they trust God's promise of victory (Q 3:126; 4:104). On the other hand, those preparing to fight must also exercise prudence and deliberation (Q 2:195; 8:60). Finally, he glosses the title with a pair more familiar in theological texts, *al-targhīb wa 'l-tarhīb* ("awakening desire and arousing fear"), as found in the tales of reward of the blessed and punishment of the wretched (al-Zarkashī 1988: II, 371).

What is more negative than fear? For al-Zarkashī it is a verse the purpose of which is "to render offensive." When banning suspicion and slander among Muslims, the verse asks, "Would anyone among you like to eat the flesh of his dead brother? You would hate it!" (Q 49:12). Al-Zarkashī (1988: II, 371) notes the juxtaposition of positive and negative: the virtues of asking questions whose purpose is actually censure and reprimand, and the joining of extreme repugnance with brotherly love. It is not just human flesh, but one's brother; and it is not just one's brother, but one's dead brother. Also, "the slanderer is addressed in the third person; thus he cannot rebut what has been said about him, so he is like the dead man."

Now positive effects reappear, first "tenderness and affection," and then "endearment." The distinction appears to be that the former indicates God's feeling for His servants, while the latter describes family relations. "Tenderness and affection" is illustrated by Q 39:53: "Say, 'O my servants who have transgressed against their souls, do not despair of God's mercy; [truly God forgives all sins].' " For "endearment", the illustration is Abraham addressing his father concerning the latter's gods (Q 19:42), Luqmān, his son on God's knowledge and power (Q 31:16), and Aaron, his brother Moses on his attempt to do Moses' bidding without causing a split among the Children of Israel (Q 20:94). Al-Zarkashī (1988: II, 372) compares these to the prophet's customary address to his uncle: "O ʿAbbās, O uncle of the messenger of God!" In this section, the Qur'ān does not address its audience in the second person but demonstrates proper piety and respect with third-person examples that believers are to emulate.

Al-Zarkashī next covers three confrontational patterns: "challenge" or "exposing weakness," "causing grief and regret," and "exposing lies." "Challenge" (*taʿjīz*) has always had a special place in treatments of the "miraculous inimitability" (*iʿjāz*) of the Qurʾān, because it dares the audience to produce a single *sūra* like it (Q 2:23), or ten *sūras* (Q 11:13), or indeed any speech (Q 52:34). It is understood in the text (Q 2:24; 11:14) and among Muslims that that condition has never been met. Al-Zarkashī (1988: II, 372) adds a challenge of more immediate concern to the audience, that of evading death. Those who did not fight at Uḥud say that their brethren who did and were killed could have avoided their fate; the Qurʾān answers, "Say, 'Then avert death from yourselves, if you are speaking the truth!' " (Q 3:168).

"Causing grief and regret" is not further defined and is illustrated by a single partial verse. "Say [to the hypocrites who bite their fingers in concealed rage], Die in your rage! God knows what is in your hearts!" (Q 3:119). But many other passages serve the same purpose, especially descriptions of hell that emphasize the mental states of its residents: God will not speak to them nor look at them on the day of resurrection (Q 3:77); or he will speak to them, but only to tell them, "God hates you more than you hate yourselves" (Q 40:10; Gwynne 2002).

"Giving the lie," contains only two verses and no definition, yet the second example is tied linguistically to an important covenantal element, that of witness. The first example challenges the Children of Israel to bring proof from the Torah that it was God and not they themselves who imposed their dietary laws (Q 3:93). The second example addresses polytheists: "Say, 'Bring your witnesses (*shuhadāʾakum*) who will testify (*yashhadūn*) [that God has forbidden this'] . . ." (Q 6:150; al-Zarkashī 1988: II, 372). As I have demonstrated elsewhere (Gwynne 2004: 12–13, 99–103; cf. Mendenhall and Herion 1992: 1181, 1184), the notion of witness is a basic component of the covenant between God and humanity and an important element in Qurʾānic legal reasoning (cf. Q 2:282–3 on contract law). The root *sh-h-d* occurs some 160 times in the Qurʾān, only rarely implying martyrdom (e.g., Q 57:19). Significantly, al-Zarkashī's first example of "challenge" also contains the first Qurʾānic occurrence of "witness": "If you are in doubt about what We have revealed to Our servant, then bring a *sūra* like it, and call your witnesses besides God if you are telling the truth" (Q 2:23).

The opposite of "humiliation" forms yet another category. "Conferring honor is everything in the glorious Qurʾān addressed by *qul* [Say!], such as in *al-qalāqil* [i.e. the *sūras* beginning with the word *qul*: 109, 112, 113, and 114]." The only example al-Zarkashī quotes is two words from *sūrat Āl ʿImrān*:

> "Say, 'We believe!' " (Q 3:84), and it is an honor from Him (may He be praised) to the whole Muslim community, in that He is addressing them without an intermediary so that all may gain the honor of being addressed. (al-Zarkashī 1988: II, 372–3)

Construing the singular *qul* as an honorific address to a group is an original approach to a word that creates one of the most vexed questions of Qurʾānic rhetoric. Al-Zarkashī (1988: II, 373) explains his reasoning:

> It would not be eloquent for the messenger to say to the one to whom he is sent, "The One who sent me said to me, 'Say such-and-such' "; and because it could not be omitted, that indicates that it is intended to remain [in the text]. Thus there must be some reason for leaving it in, to be a command from the speaker to the one spoken to about that whereof he is to speak, a command which He gave orally with no intermediary, as when you say to one whom you are addressing, "Do this!"

Most occurrences of *qul* are presumably addressed to the prophet; al-Zarkashī's only example, however, does not address the messenger alone but the entire community. Discussing this command, given in the singular to the community as a whole, partly avoids the logical problem of how the word "Say!" is both an instruction and part of what is to be said. The grammarian Ibn Khālawayh (d. 370/980–1), on the other hand, deals with the word as addressing only the prophet, whose name he understands to be interpolated: "Say, O Muḥammad, 'Say, He, God, is One' " (Q 112:1). Perhaps it is no coincidence that two of the early codices, those of Ibn Masʿūd and Ubayy, are said to have lacked *qul* (Gwynne 2004: 81–2; Ibn Khālawayh 1960: 228; see also Radscheit 1997).

As a bit of an anticlimax but logically placed, al-Zarkashī's last section concerns "addressing that which does not [yet] exist" (*al-maʿdūm*). "O sons of Adam" (Q 7:26), says al-Zarkashī (1988: II, 373), "is an address to people of that time and to all after them, somewhat like the procedure of giving counsel in a person's address to his son, and his son's son – whoever descended from him – to fear God and obey Him."

But what of the instances in which addressing the nonexistent is the very process that brings it into existence? "Our utterance to a thing, when We have willed it, is to say to it 'Be! and it is (*kun fa-yakūn*)" (Q 16:40, cf. Q 36:82, 2:117). The Shāfiʿī al-Zarkashī gives two solutions to the theological problem, one from the Ashʿarīs and the other from the Ḥanafīs. The former hold that the existence of the world came about through the imperative *kun*, while the latter argue that "creation is eternal existing by the nature of the Creator . . . not that it comes into existence at [the letters] *kāf* and *nūn*." The Ashʿarīs answer that if they were not separate, the word *kun* would have no meaning. The Ḥanafīs reply that they are speaking of the reason that it exists and that it does not possess meaning by itself: saying that *kun* existed at creation is not the same as either comparing [God] to anything or denying all his attributes (al-Zarkashī 1988: II, 373–4).

Patterns of Utterance

In chapter 45 on the patterns of Qurʾānic meaning, al-Zarkashī discusses the many ideas concerning its divisions: they are unlimited, there are only two, there are ten or nine or eight or seven, and so forth; he himself opts for six, which I have retained. We have already encountered all or most of them in examples of the patterns of address and production of psychological effects; now I shall briefly examine their grammar.

I must point out, however, that while other chapters in al-Zarkashī (1988) deal with such common literary topoi as "the literal and the metaphorical" (chapter 43), "metonymy and allusion" (chapter 44), "rhetorical styles" (chapter 46), and "grammatical particles" (chapter 47), the aim of chapter 45 is to distinguish form from meaning. Thus a sentence that has the form of an ordinary verb-subject or subject-predicate statement may in fact be a command, a blessing, a curse, a promise, or a threat. Space does not permit examination of all possible permutations and combinations of form and meaning – al-Zarkashī's analysis runs to fifty-four pages – but I shall at least alert the reader to some significant distinctions.

Information

Al-Zarkashī (1988: II, 425) says that the aim of this first pattern "is to inform the addressee, but it is also pervaded by other meanings." Comparisons between the Qurʾān, the Hebrew Bible, and the New Testament often turn on stories of the prophets, and it is usually noted that *sūra Yūsuf* (12), "the most beautiful of stories" (Q 12: 4–101), is the only one that consists (for the most part) of a single, continuous, third-person narrative. Nevertheless, it directly addresses the audience before (Q 12:1–3), during (Q 12:7, 22, 56–7, etc.), and after the narrative (Q 12:102–11). Many other *sūras* contain sequences of prophetic episodes (e.g., Q 6:74–90; 7:59–155; 19:41–58; 21 *passim*), and one might expect to find this sort of passage included under the rubric of information (*khabar*). But nowhere have I found that al-Zarkashī includes "stories," except in a quotation. His priorities suit my purposes well, however, as they concentrate much more specifically on "address."

Oddly, the first locution classed as information (*khabar*) is "wonder" or "astonishment:" Q 18:5, in denying that God has a son, states, "How excessive is the word that comes out of their mouths! They only speak lies!" This is a surprisingly long section because of theological questions implicit in the relevant grammatical structures. Briefly, one may be astonished by God's works but not use such constructions as *mā aʿẓama ʾllāh* because of the grammatical implication that God was made great by something greater than He; and God may cause humans to wonder but not himself express wonder at his own works, since wonder arises from ignorance (al-Zarkashī 1988: II, 425–8).

"Command" and "prohibition" may appear as simple subject-predicate sentences. "Divorced women shall wait for three monthly periods" (Q 2:228). "None shall touch [the Qurʾān] except those who are [ritually] pure" (Q 56:79). "Promise" and "threat" form another pair with important theological ramifications. "We shall show them Our signs on the horizons" (Q 41:53). This is al-Zarkashī's sole example of the first, but it may, given its context, be interpreted equally well as an example of the second. "Those who do wrong – what a reverse they shall suffer!" (Q 26:227).

The single example of "rejection and rebuke" is, "Taste this! Truly you are the mighty, the noble" (Q 44:49). Already cited as "sarcasm," it is an example of information delivered in the form of a command (al-Zarkashī 1988: II, 429).

A number of *khabar*-locutions qualify as address only in an indirect sense, as examples of certain human speech-acts: prayer (*duʿāʾ*; e.g., Q 1:5), wish (*tamannī*; e.g., Q 7:53), hope (*tarajjī*) (al-Zarkashī 1988: II, 429–30, 432; cf. Gwynne 2004: 105–9).

The long section that al-Zarkashī calls "proclamation," using the grammatical term for "vocative" (*nidāʾ*), combines many elements also found in chapter 42. He defines it as "the demand – by means of a special word – that the one addressed respond to the addressor, most often accompanied by a command or prohibition." Most are indeed characterized by a particle: "O people (*yā ayyuhā ʾl-nās*)! Worship your Lord!" (Q 2:21); but a subclass does omit it. Besides commands and prohibitions, there may be questions: "O you who believe, why do you say that which you do not do?" (Q 61:2). There may be information (*khabar*): "O My servants! There shall be no fear upon you" (Q 43:68); and there are other subclasses. He quotes al-Zamakhsharī (d. 538/1144) to the effect that all instances of *nidāʾ* are accompanied by some aid to understanding the religion; it is al-Zamakhsharī who, finally, includes the genre "stories" (*qiṣaṣ*) (al-Zarkashī 1988: II, 430–2).

Inquiry

The question with which al-Zarkashī begins and shapes this very long, much subdivided section is, "What is the difference between *istikhbār* [seeking information] and *istifhām* [seeking understanding]?" Philologists' answers turn upon points such as whether the question precedes the address or follows it; whether the question is worded positively or negatively; whether the point is explicit or implicit; and whether the purpose is affirmation, reproof, or rebuke, declaring two things equal, or one of the themes already mentioned.

God's questions to the Qurʾān's audience, of course, can hardly be requests for either information or understanding: the Lord only poses such questions to listeners in order to affirm them in their faith and remind them that they have learned the truth on that point. "Whose word is truer than God's?" (Q 4:87) (al-Zarkashī 1988: II, 433). A prominent example of a negatively worded question comes in Q 7:172, the passage that establishes the covenant. "[God said] 'Am I not your Lord?' They said, 'Yes (*balā*), we so witness'!" The presence of the word *balā* in this question is theologically crucial, as it is the proper particle for introducing an affirmative answer to a negative question. Had the reply been *naʿm*, it would have meant "Yes, you are not our Lord" and would have constituted rejection of faith (*kufr*) (al-Zarkashī 1988: II, 439).

A number of earlier categories reappear in this section. God's question to Jesus, "Did you say to the people, 'Worship me and my mother as deities'?" (Q 5:116) is a rebuke to the Christians for claiming that Jesus was divine (al-Zarkashī 1988: II, 441). A negative imperative is implied in Q 9:13: "Are you afraid of them? But God is more worthy that you should fear Him!" (II, 443). Motivation ("awakening desire") is exemplified by Q 61:10: "O you who believe! Shall I guide you to a transaction that will save you [from a painful punishment]?" (al-Zarkashī 1988: II, 444).

Condition

Conditional constructions are prominent in the Qurʾān; al-Zarkashī sets out eleven rules for them, again with multiple variants. As before, space allows for only basic examples of some of them.

His first rule is that a "full conditional statement" consists of two clauses of which the first is verbal and the second may be nominal or verbal. When they are combined, they form a single sentence: "And whoever, male or female, does good deeds and is a believer, they [plural] will enter the garden" (Q 4:124). "If you will help God, He will help you" (Q 47:7) (al-Zarkashī 1988: II, 453–5). The second rule is that it is the nature of condition and fulfillment that the latter depends on the former. "If you believe and ward off [evil], He will give you your rewards" (Q 47:36); this also illustrates the third and fourth rules covering the relationship of the two in time (al-Zarkashī 1988: II, 456–60).

The fifth rule is that grammatical particles set up the conditional: "if" (*in*) or nouns that contain the same meaning, such as "whoever" (*man*), "whatever" (*mā*), or such adverbs as "wherever" (*ayna, aynamā*), "whenever" (*matā*), and so on. "So if (*fa-immā*) you fear treachery from any people, then cast [their covenant] back at them [so as to be on equal terms]" (Q 8:58). "If (*in*) [My enemies] find you, they will be your enemies, and stretch their hands and their tongues out against you with an evil purpose, and desire that you reject religion" (Q 60:2). The sixth rule is that an impossible or absurd condition must be joined with an impossible or absurd result. "If there were in [the heavens and the earth] a deity besides God, they would both have come to ruin" (Q 21:22) (al-Zarkashī 1988: II, 460–5; see also Gwynne 2004: 170–84).

Oath and consequent

Al-Zarkashī describes his next category, "the oath and its consequent," as "two clauses with the same relation as the conditional antecedent and consequent." He does not include full treatment in this section, however, but in chapter 46 on Qurʾānic rhetoric, a chapter that occupies nearly one-half of this four-volume work. Oaths form the eighteenth part of the first "style" analyzed, which is "emphasis." Al-Zarkashī notes that in seven locations God swears by himself, in the rest by his creations. "Then, by the Lord of heaven and earth, it is the truth" (Q 51:23; cf. 10:53; 70:40). "But no! I swear by the setting of the stars – and that is a powerful oath, if you only knew" (Q 56:75–6). People have asked what role the oath plays, since the believer will believe simply by being informed, and the unbeliever will not profit from it. Al-Qushayrī (d. 465/1072) answered that judgment proceeds either by witness or by oath, and that both are in the Qurʾān. If it is asked how God can swear by created things when humans are forbidden to do so, there are three possible answers: that the expression "Lord of" has been omitted; that it was the custom among Arabs of the time; that one must swear by something greater than oneself, but God's oaths all point to the Creator (al-Zarkashī 1988: III, 121–3).

What has usually been overlooked in discussions of Qurʾānic oaths is that oaths are an integral part of the covenant between God and human beings. "When your Lord brought forth from the children of Adam, from their loins, their descendants, and made them testify concerning themselves. 'Am I not your Lord?' They said, 'Yes, we so witness'" (Q 7:172). Elsewhere I have discussed the topic of oaths at some length (Gwynne 2004: 16, 20–2, 103–5), but al-Qushayrī's pairing of witness and oath is one characteristic of the prototypical covenant in the Abrahamic/Mosaic religions (Mendenhall and Herion 1992: 1181–2, 1184–5). These two elements – God's oaths and evidence of the fates of earlier peoples – are what assure humans that God will keep his promises and carry out his threats, since there is no superior power to force him. Humans who abide by the covenant will be rewarded, because God has bound himself to do so.

Command

The covenant is the condition for every aspect of the relationship between God and humanity (Gwynne 2004: 1–24), particularly divine command. By most accounts, the first revelation to Muḥammad came in the form of a command: "*Iqra'* [Recite]!" (Q 96:1). We have already seen that God's very act of creation was a command, "Be (*kun*)!" given to an entity that did not yet exist (Q 16:40; cf. Q 36:82; 2:117). As Toshihiko Izutsu (1956: 52–3; see also Gwynne 2004: 67) has shown, command may actually be the primary mode of all speech. Commands have their own logic: the one who issues the command must have the authority to do so, and the command must be justified (Rescher 1966). In human terms, authority (or power) and justification are not the same thing, otherwise they amount to an argument from force, a classic fallacy (*argumentum ad baculum*). But that distinction disappears when both command and justification come from God. "He is not to be asked about what He does; it is they who are to be asked" (Q 21:23). The covenant is the assurance that God's acts are not arbitrary or capricious; in addition, much if not most of the Qur'ān is explanation for God's actions and – especially – his commands (Gwynne 2004: 67–82). "O people, worship your Lord Who created you and those who came before you, thus may you protect yourselves [against evil]" (Q 2:21). "Do not set up any other deity with God, lest you be thrown into hell, blamed and banished" (Q 17:39) (Gwynne 2004: 77).

Al-Zarkashī's treatment of commands here (1988: II, 474) is curiously short, no doubt because he has discussed them in so many other places. In the section on *khabar* in the same chapter, he specifically notes that the locution called "proclamation" often concludes with a command, as does the conditional clause. But a quick review of the verses previously cited will yield multiple examples of command in virtually every section.

Qur'ānic imperatives and other rules are so varied and inclusive that they are the basis for the structure of Islamic law, whether in the field of devotions (*'ibādāt*) or that of transactions (*mu'āmalāt*). Legal scholars have determined that the Qur'ān commands, encourages, permits, discourages, and forbids particular actions; and while particulars of the "five types of action" (*al-aḥkām al-khamsa*) are beyond the scope of this essay, we may offer examples of each. "Your Lord has decreed that you [plural] worship none but Him, and that you be kind to parents" (Q 17:23). The command to worship God is obligatory (*wājib*) and needs no elaboration, but it is worth noting that disobedience to parents is a cardinal sin, and that Q 17:23 is the first proof-text in that section of *Kitāb al-kabā'ir* ("Book of Major Sins") by al-Dhahabī (d. 748/1348 or 753/1352–3; 1976: 41–9). Extra acts of charity are the classic example of "recommended" acts. "If you give [extra] charity openly, it is good; and if you hide it and give it to the poor, it is better for you" (Q 2:271).

An example of a "permitted" action may be found in Q 24:60: "Such women as are past childbearing and do not hope for marriage, there is no blame upon them if they put aside their wraps . . . but it is better to refrain." Al-Qurṭubī says of this passage, "They are permitted what is not permitted to others, and the trouble of observing a tiresome precaution is lifted from them" (al-Qurṭubī 1997: XII, 203). The usual example of a "repugnant" act is divorce, but let us examine a verse that represents the term more literally. "God has only forbidden you carrion and blood and the meat of pigs, and what has had the name of another deity invoked over it; but whoever is forced to, not wanting to and not repeating the act, there is no sin upon him" (Q 2:173). Al-Qurṭubī (1997: II, 151) says, quoting Mujāhid, "Forced to do it like the man seized by the enemy, when they force him to eat pork, or some other sin against God Almighty: the use of force permits that, to the utmost force." A simple example of a "forbidden" action may be found in Q 5:72: "Whoever joins other deities with God, God has forbidden him paradise, and the fire will be his abode."

Negation

Negation, says al-Zarkashī, is half of speech; the other half is affirmation. He does not include the negative imperative here, perhaps because he has included its one-line section as part of *khabar*, right after the positive imperative. Here he discusses points relevant only implicitly to Qur'ānic address: whether the negation is valid or invalid; whether it is general or particular; and whether the negative particle refers to the past or the future, "always more common than the past." The believer will profit from contemplating both what God does and what he does not do, and what people have and have not done. "God does not destroy towns wrongfully, when their people are unaware [of the truth]" (Q 6:131). "We did not destroy towns except when their people were evildoers" (Q 28:59). "God does not change a benefit He has bestowed upon a people until they change what is in their hearts" (Q 8:53) (al-Zarkashī 1988: II, 474–9).

As more and more people claim the right to interpret the Qur'ān, analysis of Qur'ānic address is the first step to understanding audience response to the Qur'ān, as it is the first step to understanding the context of any passage. Such scholars as al-Zarkashī demonstrate where one may find freedom for interpretation and where one encounters the necessity for restraint.

Further reading

Gwynne, Rosalind W. (1993) The neglected sunna: sunnat Allāh (the sunna of God). *American Journal of Islamic Social Sciences*, 10, 455–63.

Gwynne, Rosalind W. (2002) Hell and hellfire. In: McAuliffe, Jane Dammen (ed.) *Encyclopaedia of the Qur'an*. Brill, Leiden, vol. II, pp. 414–20.

Gwynne, Rosalind W. (2004) *Logic, Rhetoric, and Legal Reasoning in the Qurʾān: God's Arguments.* RoutledgeCurzon, London and New York.

Izutsu, Toshihiko (1956) *Language and Magic.* The Keio Institute of Cultural and Linguistic Studies, Tokyo.

Mendenhall, G., and Herion, G. (1992) Covenant. In: Freedman, D. N. (ed.) *The Anchor Bible Dictionary.* Doubleday, New York, vol. I, pp. 1179–1202.

Radscheit, Matthias (1997) Word of God or prophetic speech? Reflections on the Quranic *qul*-statements. In: Edzard, L. and Szyska, C. (eds.) *Encounters of Words and Texts: Intercultural Studies in Honor of Stefan Wild.* Georg Olms Verlag, Hildesheim.

Rescher, Nicholas (1966) *The Logic of Commands.* Routledge and Kegan Paul, London.

CHAPTER 6

Language

Mustansir Mir

The Qurʾān's statement that it has been revealed in Arabic is the basis of the dogma that only the Arabic Qurʾān can be called the Qurʾān, that only the Arabic Qurʾān can be recited in prayers, and that only the Arabic Qurʾān can be the proper subject of study and interpretation. The dogma thus foregrounds the language of the Qurʾān, and this language is then taken as providing the principal access to the meaning of the scripture. Consequently, a thorough knowledge of Qurʾānic Arabic has always been regarded as a prerequisite for all areas of Qurʾānic scholarship – theology, law, history, and others.

The Qurʾān as a "Clear" Book

The Qurʾān calls itself a "clear" book. The Arabic word it frequently uses for "clear" is *mubīn*: The Qurʾān is *kitāb mubīn* or *al-kitāb al-mubīn* ("a clear book" or "the clear book," Q 5:15; 12:1; 26:2; 27:1; 28:2; 44:2), its language is *ʿarabī mubīn* "clear Arabic," Q 16:103; 26:195), and the prophet presents *al-balāgh al-mubīn* ("the clear communication," Q 5:92; 16:35, 82; 24:54; 29:18; 64:12); in two verses, *mubīn* is used as an adjective qualifying *Qurʾān* itself (Q 15:1; 36:69). The word *mubīn* means both "clear in itself" and "that which clarifies (something else)." Thus, the Qurʾān claims both that it yields its meaning unambiguously and that it elucidates matters, dispelling doubt and eliminating error. One must keep both meanings of *mubīn* in mind for a correct understanding of the Qurʾānic claim to be "clear."

Doubtless, many matters in the Qurʾān require explanation, the large number of commentaries written to explicate Qurʾānic thought and language being proof. The need for explanation remains even after allowing for the temporal gap between the present-day readership and Muḥammad's first audience; the Qurʾān attests to companions of Muḥammad coming to him for elucidation of Qurʾānic verses, and there are anecdotes about companions spending long periods of time to study portions of the

Qur'ān (for example, the reports about ʿUmar and his son ʿAbd Allāh, al-Qurṭubī 1967: I, 152). Furthermore, the Qur'ān itself says that some of its verses have a "firm" or "stable" meaning whereas others are "ambiguous" (Q 3:7).

If the Qur'ān indeed is a clear book, then how does one explain, on the one hand, the difficulty encountered by Muḥammad's companions in comprehending parts of the Qur'ān and, on the other hand, the Qur'ān's acknowledgment of the presence of ambiguity in it? The answer is twofold. First, the claim of any book to be clear does not necessarily mean that all its readers, regardless of their backgrounds – that is, their age, experience, mental acumen, level of knowledge, and linguistic ability – will understand it equally well or fully. Second, clarity is not to be confused with simplicity: a document will be called "clear" if it treats its subject in language that is clear relative to that subject. This brings out the relevance of the two meanings of the word *mubīn*. The Qur'ān is clear not only in a passive sense – "clear in itself" – but also in an active sense – it clarifies the particular subject it treats, it is suitable for presenting a certain subject, and judgment on its clarity should be passed in reference to that subject. In fact, in the case of the Qur'ān, the first meaning of the descriptive adjective *mubīn* – "clear in itself" – arises as a corollary of the second – "that which clarifies (something else)."

The language of the Qur'ān is "clear" in the sense that it presents its message clearly. This view is supported by each of the sixteen above-cited verses if they are read in context. For example, Q 5:15 tells the People of the Book that the Qur'ān is a "light" from God, the next verse adding that God "guides by means of it those who seek His pleasure." The verse immediately following Q 12:1 reads: "We have revealed it ['the Clear Book' of verse 1] as an Arabic Qur'ān, so that you may use reason." The words "so that you may use reason" (*laʿallakum taʿqilūn*) provide the rationale for revealing the Qur'ān in Arabic. Had the Qur'ān been revealed in a language other than Arabic, the addressees – the Meccan Arabs – would have taken an easy alibi, arguing that, not knowing that language, they were incapable of judging or evaluating the Qur'ān and, as a result, could not be blamed for not accepting its message.

The general rule governing the revelation of a scripture in a particular language is laid down in Q 14:4: "We have not sent a messenger except in the language of his nation, so that he might explicate matters to them" (Q 26:198–9 makes the same point). Q 26:2 is followed by "Perhaps you will strangle yourself to death [out of frustration] that they will not become believers," again indicating that the Qur'ān is dealing with the issue of belief and disbelief. What has been said about Q 5:15, 12:1, and 26:2 is true of the remaining thirteen verses cited. As remarked above, since "clarity" is not to be reduced to "simplicity," the above-quoted verses cannot be taken to mean that Qur'ānic language will not raise issues of interpretation, that different readers will not understand the Qur'ānic text differently, or that the extensive historical discussion and debate about the various aspects of the Qur'ānic language go against the Qur'ānic claim to clarity.

If the Qur'ānic claim to clarity pertains basically to message rather than to language, then the issue of foreign vocabulary in the Qur'ān (see Jeffery 1938; Watt and Bell 1970: 84–5) will appear in a different light. The view that the Qur'ān is free of non-Arabic words is based on such verses as Q 16:103, which says that the person whom Muḥammad's opponents have identified as his informant speaks a language other than

Arabic whereas the Qur'ānic language is *lisān ʿarabī mubīn* ("clear Arabic language"). But even here, as in the verses cited above, the issue at stake is that of belief and lack of belief. First, Q 16:103 speaks of language in general and not of individual vocabulary items. That the language of a certain book is Arabic does not necessarily imply that that language does not contain a single word from another language; such a notion of linguistic purity has no Qur'ānic basis, and there are no rational grounds for denying the existence of well-attested linguistic relationships between the Arabic of the Qur'ān and other languages. Second, a Qur'ānic passage very similar to Q 16:103 is Q 26:192–9, which begins by saying that Gabriel has "brought it [Qur'ān] down on your [Muḥammad's] heart . . . in clear Arabic language [*bi-lisān ʿarabī mubīn*]" but ends by explaining the purpose of the revelation of the Qur'ān in Arabic thus: "And had We sent it down on one of the non-Arabs and he had read it to them [Arabs], they would not have reposed belief in it." Once again, the Qur'ān is saying that a nation receives scripture in its language; it is not addressing the issue of whether a given language includes or does not include words from another language.

Valorization

The language of the Qur'ān is both similar to and different from the language of pre-Islamic Arabia (cf. Watt and Bell 1970: 83–4). The vocabulary of the Qur'ān, though familiar to the Arabs, had a much smaller base – the number of the Arabic roots in the Qur'ān is well under two thousand – which made the Qur'ān accessible to a wider and more diverse audience. At the same time, that audience could not help but feel that the Qur'ān's language was markedly different from the language of their poets and orators. The Qur'ān invested ordinary words with special meanings, coined special terms, and then embedded these terms in a well-articulated worldview and placed them in a complex web of relationships. The net effect of this exercise was to create a coherent scheme of religious thought, the refashioned Arabic language serving as the gateway to that scheme. Thus, the language of the Qur'ān is best viewed as a vehicle for the expression of a set of philosophical, religious, and cultural perspectives that the Qur'ān introduced into the Arabian setting of the seventh century. In a word, the Qur'ān valorizes the Arabic language. This valorization, evident throughout the Qur'ān, occurs at several levels.

To begin with, serving as keys to the Qur'ānic discourse are terms of various types – terms that occur in the Qur'ān too often to need chapter-and-verse citation: (1) terms pertaining to faith and lack of faith: *hudā* ("guidance"), *ḍalāla* ("misguidance"), *īmān* ("belief"), *islām* ("submission"), *kufr* ("rejection of truth"), *nifāq* ("hypocrisy"), *mīthāq* ("covenant"), *al-ṣirāṭ al-mustaqīm* ("the straight path"), *ḥaqq* ("truth"), *bāṭil* ("falsehood"), *fawz* ("success, salvation"), *khusrān* ("loss"); (2) terms designating people: *ahl al-kitāb* ("people of the book"); *aṣḥāb al-janna* ("people of paradise"), *aṣḥāb al-nār* ("people of hellfire"); (3) terms describing ritual practices and legal prescriptions: *zakāt* ("mandatory giving"), *ṣiyām* ("fasting"); *ḥudūd Allāh* ("the limits prescribed by God"); (4) attributes of the Divinity, as in Q 59:22–4; (5) terms representing the prophetic vocation: *rasūl* ("messenger"), *nabī* ("prophet"), *bashīr* ("giver of good tidings"), *nadhīr* ("warner"); (6) terms pertaining to the Qur'ān or to scripture in general: *sūra* ("chapter"), *āya* ("verse"), *furqān* ("criterion"), *āyāt bayyināt* ("manifest verses *or* signs"); (7) terms representing virtues and vices or virtuous and evil conduct: *taqwā* ("God-consciousness"); *iṣlāḥ* ("setting things right"); *fasād* ("corruption"); *ẓulm* ("wrongdoing"); *jihād* or *jihād fī sabīl Allāh* ("striving" or "striving in the way of God"); *infāq* or *infāq fī sabīl Allāh* ("spending" or "spending in the way of God"). Some of the Qur'ānic terms are multivalent, for example, *dīn*, which, depending on the context, may mean "allegiance," "retribution," "judgment," or "religion"; *tawba*, which, depending on its subject, may mean "repentance" (of sin by a human being) or "forgiveness" (granted by God); and *shāhid*, which may mean "one who is present," "witness," or "martyr."

At the next level, a large number of phrases and expressions not only sums up important aspects of the Qur'ānic worldview, but also frames the Qur'ānic discussions of matters. To take a few examples: (1) *li-llāh mā fī 'l-samāwāt wa-mā fī 'l-arḍ* ("To God belongs all that is in the heavens and the earth"); (2) *inna 'llāh ʿalā kull shayʾ qadīr* ("Indeed, God has the power to do anything"); (3) *inna 'llāh maʿa 'l-ṣābirīn* ("Indeed, God is with those who remain steadfast"); (4) *wa-ilā 'llāh turjaʿu 'l-umūr* ("And to God are referred all matters"); (5) *aṭīʿu llāh wa'l-rasūl* ("Obey God and the messenger"); (6) *inna 'lladhīna āmanū wa-ʿamilū 'l-ṣāliḥāt* ("Indeed, those who have believed and done good deeds"); (7) *yaʾmurūna bi'l-maʿrūf wa-yanhawna ʿan al-munkar* ("They enjoin good and forbid evil"); (8) *ittaqū 'llāh* ("fear God"); (9) *lā tattabiʿū khuṭuwāt al-Shayṭān* ("Do not follow in the footsteps of Satan"); (10) those who enter paradise – *lā khawfun ʿalayhim wa-lā hum yaḥzanūn* ("They shall have no fear, and they shall have no regrets either"); (11) *jannatun tajrī min taḥtihā 'l-anhār* ("gardens [of paradise] with streams flowing underneath").

Also representative of Qur'ānic language are the relatively long and often quite vivid passages describing, among other things, the following: (1) the phenomena of nature as evidence of such verities as the oneness of God (Q 2:21–2, 164) and the coming of the last day (Q 78:6–17; 81:1–14); (2) the conduct, in this world, of the believers (Q 78:31–5) and the disbelievers (Q 70:22–34; 78:21–5); (3) the rewards of heaven (Q 76:5–21; 88:8–16) and the suffering of hell (Q 88:2–7); (4) the punishment stories of disbelieving nations of former times (for example, in *sūras* 11 and 26).

Another form of the Qur'ānic valorization of the Arabic language may be called sublimation. Often, the Qur'ān takes a well-known expression and, by subtly modifying it or using it in a new context, raises it to a higher plane of meaning. Let us look at a few examples.

The Arabs compared a backbiter to a carrion eater. The phrase *akala laḥmahū* (with variations) occurs in their poetry in the sense of "to backbite" or "to slander" (Mir 1989a: 42–3 [*ʾ-k-l*]) and draws the image of a dead animal that is lying defenseless against a predator – *al-sabʿ al-ḍarīmī*, as one poet calls the predator – that feasts on the corpse at leisure. One who is backbitten is, likewise, at the mercy of the backbiter, who "nibbles" at the victim's reputation without fear of being challenged. The Arabs called backbiting a dastardly act; in the Qur'ān, a religious value is added to the act. Q 49:12, providing an example of backbiting, says: *a-yuḥibbu aḥadukum an yaʾkula laḥma akhīhi maytan fa-karihtumūh*, "Would any of you like to eat the flesh of his dead brother? You would abhor it!" The word *akh*, "brother," in the verse means "brother in religion," as borne out generally by the context and specifically by the declaration in verse 10 of the same *sūra*, "The believers are but brothers to one another" (*innama ʾl-muʾminūn ikhwa*). The addition of a single word transforms the familiar Arab image of backbiting in that the act now conjures up not merely the picture of an animal devouring a dead animal, but the picture of a human being devouring the flesh of a dead human being – or, rather, of a brother devouring the flesh of a dead brother. The verse is saying: carrion-eating is repugnant, cannibalism is worse, and acting like a cannibal brother is the ultimate in heinousness.

Another instance of the strategic use of the word *akh* is found in Q 2:178, which, laying down the law of *qiṣāṣ*, or retaliation, says that the punishment for taking a human life is death. According to the verse, the killer's life may be spared if the heirs of the person killed accept blood money. This dispensation is introduced with the words, *fa-man ʿufiya lahū min akhīhi shayʾ* ("But if one is pardoned something by his brother"). The use of the word *akh* here makes a subtle but strong appeal, namely, that the option of blood money be considered by the heirs, for, in the end, Muslims are brothers to one another, and – the verse is suggesting – acceptance of blood money might mitigate the rancor and hostility between the aggressor party and the aggrieved party, eventually leading to reconciliation between the two (Iṣlāḥī 2000: I, 432). In pre-Islamic times, acceptance of blood money by a tribe was considered a sign of weakness – "accepting milk [that is, milk camels as blood money] in exchange for blood" was the contemptuous expression used on such occasions (see, for example, al-Marzūqī 1951–3: I, 216, verse 2). The Qurʾān, rejecting the vendetta motif and allowing for the possibility of reconciliation between two estranged parties, not only allows the taking of blood money, but, by using the word *akh*, casts its vote in favor of blood money, thus wiping out the feeling of disgrace attached to acceptance of blood money.

We will take one more example of the Qurʾān's infusion of religious and moral meaning into the Arabic language. *Taraktuhū kadhā*, "I left him in such-and-such a state," was a common Arabic expression, often used by poets in a context of war, the poet-warrior boasting that he felled his opponent and left his corpse unattended in the battlefield. A representative use of the construction is found in the *muʿallaqa* of ʿAntara (al-Tibrīzī 1964: 239):

> *Fa-taraktuhū jazara ʾl-sibāʿi yanushnahū*
> *Ma bayna qullati raʾsihī waʾl-miʿṣamī*
> (I left him there, butchered meat for predators, which devoured him
> From the top of his head to his wrists.)

In Q 54:15, the verbal form of the phrase *tarakahū kadhā* is retained, but the context undergoes a change. The verse, referring to the event of the rescue of Noah and the drowning of his opponents, says: *wa-laqad taraknāhā āyatan fa-hal min muddakir* ("And We left it [the land, or story, of Noah] to serve as a sign, so, are there any who would take remembrance?"). The first audience of the Qurʾān, on hearing this apparently simple statement, must have made a mental comparison between the Qurʾānic and pre-Islamic Arabic uses of *tarakahū kadhā*. ʿAntara's use of the phrase, it is not difficult to see, is devoid of the moral dimension of history encapsulated in the Qur'ānic verse.

Above and beyond the individual terms, phrases, and passages that may be cited to illustrate the Qur'ānic valorization of the Arabic language is the "climate" of the Qur'ānic language. Even a cursory reading of the Qur'ān, whether in the original or in translation, will bring out the religious character of the Qur'ānic language. In all but six of the 114 *sūras*, God is referred to either as *Allāh*, *Rabb*, or *Raḥmān* or by means of a pronoun for God. But even in those six *sūras* – all of them short (Q 101, 102, 103, 107, 109, and 111) – God is clearly in the background. And it is not simply a question of referring to God. In the Qur'ān, God is mentioned as the central point of reference for all existence and the central point of validation for all activity. The mention of God or reference to him, thus, serves to give a distinctive sacral character to Qur'ānic language.

Orality

The language of the Qur'ān is oral, but the nature of Qur'ānic orality should be understood clearly. The Qur'ān was presented by Muḥammad in an oral situation, but this does not mean that the Qur'ānic speech is colloquial. The Qur'ān does not say or imply that its language is one of the dialects spoken in a certain town or region of Arabia – Mecca, Ṭā'if, Medina, or some other – but simply that it has been revealed *bi-lisān ʿarabī mubīn*, as was noted above. The adjective *mubīn* in this phrase connotes "standard." Of the sixteen verses that were cited earlier in discussing the word *mubīn*, some belong to Meccan and others to Medinan *sūras*. This means that the Qur'ānic claim to be *mubīn* was made both in Mecca and in Medina, and there is no indication in the Qur'ān or in other sources that the claim was challenged at any time during the period of revelation, in Mecca or in Medina. This fact in itself supports the view that a standard version of Arabic was well-established, at least in the Ḥijāz and possibly in all of Arabia, at the time of Muḥammad and that Qur'ānic language represented that version. We will note two characteristics of Qur'ānic orality.

Sajʿ

The usual translation of this word, "rhymed prose," while not entirely incorrect, places Qur'ānic language in the category of prose, denoting, additionally, that that language happens to be rhymed. This description runs the risk of compromising the rhythmic quality of Qur'ānic language. The language of the Qur'ān partakes of both poetry and prose and is certainly more poetic in some parts and more prose-like in others, but it is difficult to generalize and say that it is primarily prose or poetry. Perhaps the best way to describe it is to say that it is *sui generis*. Because of its rhythmic quality, Qur'ānic language is eminently chantable. Rhyme, while found throughout the Qur'ān, is conspicuous in many of the early or middle Meccan *sūras*, in which the relatively short verses throw the rhyming words into prominence. The following passage (Q 81:1–14), which draws, in almost epic dimensions, a picture of the world coming to an end, comes very close to being poetry (the rhyming syllables are given in bold):

*idhā 'l-shamsu kuwwi**rat***
*wa-idhā 'l-nujūmu n-kada**rat***
*wa-idha 'l-jibālu suyyi**rat***
*wa-idha 'l-ʿishāru ʿuṭṭi**lat***
*wa-idha 'l-wuḥūshu ḥushi**rat***
*wa-idha 'l-biḥāru sujji**rat***
*wa-idha 'l-nufūsu zuwwi**jat***
*wa-idha 'l-mawʿudatu suʾi**lat***
*bi-ayyi dhanbin quti**lat***
*wa-idha 'l-ṣuḥufu nushi**rat***
*wa-idha 'l-samaʾu kushi**ṭat***
*wa-idha 'l-jaḥīmu suʿʿi**rat***
*wa-idha 'l-jannatu uzli**fat***
*ʿalimat nafsun mā aḥḍa**rat***

A change of rhyme in a *sūra* usually signals a change in the subject. For example, in *sūra* 81, from which the above lines have been quoted, a few oaths are sworn next, in verses 15–19, which have a different rhyme. (For another example of the change of rhyme indicating a change of subject, see Q 79:1–5 (*gharqā, nashṭā, sabḥā, sabqā, amrā*), 6–14 (*rājifa, wājifa, khāshiʿa, ḥāfira, nakhira* [partial rhyme], *khāsira, wahīdā, sāhira*), 15–26 (*Mūsā, Ṭuwā, ṭaghā, tazakkā, fa-takhshā, al-kubrā, ʿasā, yasʿā, fa-nādā, al-aʿlā, al-ūlā, yakhshā*). Similarly, in *sūra* 96, the change of rhyme from one set of verses to another (1–2, 3–5, 6–14, 15–18) marks a change of subject, the only exception being the "stand-alone" last verse. Often, rhyme in the Qurʾān is mixed in with assonance.

The Qurʾānic use of rhyme and assonance sets the Islamic scripture apart from soothsayer utterances (cf. Watt and Bell 1970: 77–9). In the Qurʾān, rhyme and assonance are ancillary to the content of the scripture, whereas in the Arab soothsayers' speech, they bear no necessary connection with the content of the soothsaying – not to mention that Arab soothsaying lacked the ethical orientation of the Qurʾān.

Iltifāt

This term refers to shifts of person, number, and tense in a discourse (Abdel Haleem 2000: 184–210; Robinson 1996: 245–52). Such shifts, quite frequent in the Qurʾānic text, are a significant marker of orality. Like a speaker addressing a live audience, the Qurʾān may begin by speaking to one segment of the audience – say, the believers – and then, with little advance notice, may turn its attention to another segment – the disbelievers, for example. We also have to imagine that the speaker – the Qurʾān in this case – cognizant of the dynamic oral situation, responds to questions asked by some members of the audience, answers objections made by others, and comments on issues that, even though not verbally raised by any member of the audience, may be present in the audience's minds and, thus, be part of the overall situation. An example of *iltifāt* of person is Q 2:74–5, in which the People of the Book and, immediately afterwards, Muslims are addressed. An example of *iltifāt* of number is the opening words of *sūra* 65: "O prophet, when you divorce [*ṭallaqtum*] your wives." Instead of the expected singular *ṭallaqta*, the Qur'ān uses the plural form *ṭallaqtum* and continues to use the plural verb form until verse 6, implying that the prophet is being addressed as a representative of the Muslim community and that the injunction applies not only to him but to all of his followers as well. A simple shift of number thus widens the scope of application of the injunction. Finally, Q 2:214 is an example of *iltifāt* of tense:

> Do you think that you will enter heaven even though you have not yet experienced the like of what those who lived before you experienced? They suffered from hunger and distress, and they were shaken up, until the prophet and those with him say, "When will God's help come?" Lo, God's help is on hand!

The reference to previous nations is made by means of the perfect tense, except in the phrase "until the prophet and those with him say," the verb "say" being imperfect in the original (*yaqūlu*) when one would expect it to be in the perfect (*qāla*). The strategic use of the imperfect links up the past ages with the present: it establishes an identity between the ordeals of the previous prophets and their followers on the one hand and that of Muḥammad and his followers on the other. The net effect of the identification is to console Muḥammad and his companions, who are being assured that God will help them just as he helped earlier prophets in similar situations.

A proper appreciation of *iltifāt* in the Qur'ān will yield a more satisfactory explanation of some of its verses. Consider Q 6:52:

> And do not spurn those who call upon their Lord day and night, seeking His face [that is, pleasure]; you do not share any of their responsibility, and they do not share any of your responsibility – lest you should spurn them and thereby become a wrongdoer.

Many commentators think that all the third person plural pronouns in the verse refer to the believers, the verse commanding the prophet to be kind to them (see, for example, al-Qurṭubī 1967: VI, 432). On this understanding, the verse would be saying: Muḥammad, do not spurn the believers, who call upon God day and night. But there is one problem: the middle part of the verse, "you do not share any of their responsibility, and they do not share any of your responsibility," is a strong statement – it is particularly strong in Arabic (*mā ʿalayka min ḥisābihim min shayʾin wa-mā min ḥisābika ʿalayhim min shayʾ*) – and its curt tone, no less than its words, is unlikely to be used of the believers, the disbelievers being the only possible referent. If so, then it would make sense to regard the disbelievers as the antecedent of the pronouns in *min ḥisābihim* and *ʿalayhim*, but the believers as the antecedent of the pronoun in *fa-taṭrudahum*. The meaning of the verse now will be: Muḥammad, do not, in the interest of converting the unbelievers, ignore or spurn those who have already believed, for the unbelievers, if they persist in their unbelief, will have their own answering to do, just as you will have your own answering to do, neither of you being responsible for the beliefs or actions of the other; you must not, therefore, spurn the believers, for, doing so will make you a wrongdoer. This interpretation itself is subject to an objection. If the plural pronouns in the verse have more than one antecedent – the disbelievers in the case of two pronouns and the believers in the case of one – then why does the Qur'ān itself not make that distinction so as to avoid all confusion? Here, the point made above about Qur'ānic orality should be recalled: a speaker addressing a live audience can point to two different sections of the audience and use the pronoun "you" to speak to each, without causing any confusion. The situation in Q 6:52 is similar. The Qur'ān, addressing the prophet, who has to be imagined as facing an audience composed of both believers and unbelievers, points first to the believers and says, "these people over here," then to the unbelievers and says, "these people over here," and, finally, again to the believers and says, "these people over here." In a scenario like this, the use of the same pronoun for two – or even more – groups of people would create no confusion as long as the nonverbal components of the situation are taken to identify the addressee in each case.

Genres

Several genres of Qur'ānic discourse may be distinguished – narrative, poetic, hortatory, hymnal, and legal. The narrative genre is conspicuous in *sūras* that relate historical events – for example, *sūras* 11, 21, and 23, which contain accounts of previous nations' response to the divine message and describe their fate; the fairly long *sūra* 12 (111 verses) is devoted to the story of Joseph. However, on very few occasions does one find in the Qur'ān sustained narration. As a rule, in a given place, only a certain portion of a story – the portion bearing on the subject under discussion – is given, other portions being related in other contexts. Furthermore, Qur'ānic narration is selective in that it presents only those elements of a story that are significant from the viewpoint of illustrating a certain moral. For the same reasons, Qur'ānic characters are not drawn in detail. These characters appear to be types, though a close study will show that most of the characters also have peculiar or distinctive traits. Often, the onset of a story is marked by a word or expression like *idh* or *wa-idh* ("when" or "and when") or *udhkur* ("remember!"), as in Q 2:49–66, in which *wa-idh* is used no fewer than ten times, and in *sūra* 19, in which the stories of Mary, Abraham, Moses, Ishmael, and Idrīs are each introduced with *wa-dhkur* (verses 16, 41, 51, 54, 56). Narrative in the Qur'ān often includes dialogue, of which there is considerable variety (Mir 1992).

It is often remarked that the Qur'ān is poetic without being poetry. We have already mentioned an important element in the poetical repertoire of the Qur'ān, namely, *saj'*, especially when it occurs in the crisply short verses of early and middle Meccan *sūras* (e.g., Q 55; 78; 91; 92; 93; 99; 100). Another is the balanced phrasal construction, as in Q 96:13–16, each of its four verses consisting of a noun and a qualifying adjective that occupy the same syntactical position in the sentences in which they occur:

Fīhā sururun marfū'a
wa-akwābun mawḍū'a
wa-namāriqu maṣfūfa

> *wa-zarābiyyu mabthūtha*
> (In it [paradise], there are couches raised high,
> and cups set out,
> and carpets aligned,
> and cushions lying all around.)

Verses 17–20 of the same *sūra* provide another example of such construction.

Only a small number of texts in the Qur'ān can be called hymns if a hymn is defined as a song in praise of a deity. But the Qur'ān is not entirely without hymnal elements. Consider Q 22:18:

> Have you not seen that God is one to whom bow down all who are in the heavens and the earth and the sun, the moon, and the stars, and the mountains, the trees, and animals, and many people. And there are many to whom punishment is rightly due. And the one whom God humiliates will find no one to confer honor. Indeed, God does what He wishes.

Two other examples are Q 24:41–4 and 30:20–7.

Qur'ānic legalese – if the expression be allowed – is notable for its matter-of-factness, and also for a degree of complexity that arises from a statement of law that covers exceptions, dispensations, and contingent circumstances. Thus, Q 2:282–3 (1) commands the believers to record in writing a loan transaction made for a stated period of time; (2) instructs the scribe to record the transaction faithfully and the debtor – or, in some cases, his representative – to dictate the terms of the transaction; (3) specifies the number and qualifications of witnesses; (4) admonishes the witnesses to discharge their obligation willingly and diligently; (5) stresses the importance of recording the transaction in writing, but validates verbal agreement when "ready merchandise" is involved; (6) emphasizes the need to take witnesses and ensure the safety of both scribe and witness; and (7) allows the taking of pledges by creditors in case loan transactions have to be made during travel. Q 4:12, which lays down rules for the distribution of a person's property among the heirs, is the basis of the Islamic law of inheritance. Qur'ānic legal language reflects the ethical vision that informs the Qur'ānic legislative material. Thus, statements of laws are frequently accompanied by exhortations to cultivate piety and to remember that the law is being given by an all-knowing, all-wise deity. The legal passages in the Qur'ān contain maxim-like statements. For example, after laying down the law of *qiṣāṣ*, Q 2:179 says, "And in [the law of] *qiṣāṣ*, there is life for you, O people of wisdom, that you may acquire piety!"

It remains to add that the various modes of discourse in the Qur'ān do not occur discretely, but rather interpenetrate – especially in longer Medinan *sūras* – thus giving rise to a distinctive Qur'ānic discourse.

Verbal Economy

The saying "The best speech is that which is brief and yet effectively conveys the meaning" (*khayru 'l-kalām mā qalla wa dalla*) is often cited as the motto of Classical

Arabic rhetoric. As a rule, the principle of economy of expression, enshrined in this saying, is adhered to in the Qurʾān. The two main forms taken by the principle, terseness and ellipsis, are abundantly attested in the Qurʾān.

Terseness

Compactness frequently marks not only individual sentences but also passages and extended descriptions in the Qurʾān. Sometimes the essential details of a story are presented briefly; sometimes, different types of statements – for example, commands and prohibitions or promises and threats – are combined; and sometimes aspects of the Qurʾānic doctrine, philosophy, or worldview are summed up with proverbial force. Q 29:14–15 summarizes the story of Noah and his people:

> We sent Noah to his people, and he stayed among them for a thousand years save fifty. Then a typhoon overtook them – wrongdoers as they were. And We rescued him and the people of the boat, and We made the event a sign for the people of the world.

Q 11:44 describes how the floodwaters that drowned Noah's people were made to recede by God:

> It was said, "Earth, swallow up your water! Skies, stop!" The water shrank; the matter was decided; and it [the Ark] sat perched atop [Mt.] Jūdī. And it was said, "Away with the wrongdoers!"

Q 2:51, referring to the Israelites' defeat of the Philistines, speaks of David as the hero of the battle and as the recipient of special wisdom from God. The verse also lays down a law of history:

> They defeated them by God's will. David killed Goliath, and God gave him kingdom and wisdom, teaching him whatever He pleases. And if God were not to repulse one people by means of another, the earth would be filled with corruption. God, however, is bountiful toward the world.

Q 29:40, summing up the accounts of destruction of earlier nations, describes the inexorable application of the divine law to nations, the forms of punishment meted out in the past (described in detail in other places of the Qurʾān), and the principle underlying the punishment:

> Each one of them [nations] We seized on account of its sins: there were some whom We caused to slide into the land; there were some who were overtaken by a crashing thunder; and there were some whom We caused to drown. God was not the One to wrong them. Rather, they had wronged themselves.

Ellipsis

In its simple form, ellipsis involves suppression of a word or phrase in a statement. Joseph's half-brothers, trying to convince their father that Jacob's son (who was Joseph's real brother) was held back in Egypt through no fault of theirs, say: "And ask the town we were in" (Q 12:82). They mean "the people of the town," the word *ahl* in the Arabic phrase *ahl al-qarya* having been omitted (al-Qurṭubī 1967: IX, 246). The omission is justified because it does not detract from clarity.

At a slightly higher, and more technical, level, a correlative term or an antithetical unit is suppressed, the context pointing to the suppression. Q 6:13 says: "To Him belong what remains still during the night and [moves during] the day." Here, the words in brackets are omitted and are to be taken as understood (Iṣlāḥī 2000: III, 6). Q 27:86 is similar: "Have they not observed that We have made the night that they might take rest in it, and the day an illuminator [that they might seek God's bounty during it]?" Again, the words in brackets are taken as understood, as suggested by other Qur'ānic verses – for example, Q 28:73, which says: "It is a manifestation of His mercy that He has made for you night and day, that you might take rest in it and seek His bounty." Taking rest goes with the night, seeking God's bounty (i.e., engaging in economic activity) with the day (Iṣlāḥī 2000: V, 703).

Sometimes, one or more links in a chain of thought or one or more steps in an argument are omitted, the readers or listeners often being expected to supply the missing steps or links from their knowledge of other relevant parts of the scriptural text. To take an example, Q 43:54 says that Pharaoh "made light of his people and so they obeyed him." The complete argument is as follows:

A Pharaoh made light of his people
B *his people let themselves be taken lightly*
C *he gave them orders*
D they obeyed him

B and C, that is to say, are implied.

Parataxis

Being in the style of Classical Arabic, the Qur'ānic text makes sparing use of transitional expressions, which spell out the causal relationships between clauses, sentences, and paragraphs. The technical term for the resulting coordinate construction, which the Qur'ān prefers over the subordinate construction, is parataxis (*irdāf*). Sometimes parataxis is easy to notice, as in Q 7:31, *kulū wa-shrabū wa-lā tuṣrifū*, in which the first *wāw* means "and," but the second, an adversative, means "but," the translation being: "Eat and drink, but do not be extravagant." Other cases may be a little more complex. Consider Q 18:50, which says, in reference to Satan, *abā wa-stakbara wa-kāna min al-kāfirīn* ("He refused [to bow to Adam] and he became proud and he was [*or* became] one of the unbelievers"). Let us look at the first two of the three sentences. It is possible that Satan heedlessly refused to obey the injunction to bow to Adam, so that it was only *after* he had done so that he became proud of his act, his pride validating his act in his own eyes. But it is also possible that his refusal constituted a studied, rather than hasty, act on his part, stemming from an already strong sense of pride, so that he refused to bow to Adam *because* he was proud (the Arabic *wa-stakbara* in this case could be taken as a parenthetic conditional clause (*wa-qadi stakbara*). Now let us look at the last two verbs in the original. It is possible that Satan acted arrogantly and, *as a result*, became a disbeliever. But the Arabic verb *kāna* can mean "to be" as well as "to become." As such, it is possible that Satan always was a disbeliever and his disbelief was the cause rather than the result of his arrogance. A close study of Qur'ānic parataxis can reveal complexities hidden behind seemingly simple constructions.

On another level, parataxis raises the issue of coherence in the Qur'ānic discourse. The first twenty-nine verses of *sūra* 2 distinguish between those who believe and those who disbelieve in the message that has been sent down to Muḥammad. The next ten verses (30–9) narrate incidents from the story of Adam and Eve. The beginning of the passage – *wa-idh qāla rabbuka li'l-malā'ika innī jāʿilun fī 'l-arḍ khalīfa* ("And when your Lord said to the angels, 'I am going to install a caliph on the earth") – seems to introduce a new subject altogether, making one wonder about the nature of the connection of this passage with the preceding verses. In cases like these, it helps to remember that, as a rule, the Qur'ān tells a story to illustrate a theme already under discussion. Accordingly, when one comes upon a story in the Qur'ān and wonders about its relevance in a particular place, it is advisable to reread the story in light of the subject that has led up to that point. Q 2:30–9, upon close reading, will be found to have a bearing on the different reactions to the prophetic message that the preceding verses have outlined. In this passage, an arrogant Satan disobeys the Divine command to bow to Adam, whereas the angels, after they have received from God a satisfactory answer to their query about the need to create the human species, obey God and bow before Adam. The story of Adam, thus, corresponds with the first twenty-nine verses of the *sūra* (Iṣlāḥī 2000: I, 152–4). Similarly, Q 6:74–90 relates a certain incident from Abraham's life and then makes brief references to a number of other prophets – Isaac, Jacob, David, Solomon, Job, Joseph, Moses, and Aaron among them. No transitional expressions exist to link up this passage with the preceding part of the *sūra*. But the passage offers a refutation of idol worship, which is a prominent theme of much of the *sūra* from the beginning up to this point (for example, verses 14–24 and 56–67). *Sūra* 6 tells the people of Mecca that their idolatry belies their claim to be the heirs of Abraham the monotheist, and it is in this context that verses 74–90 occur (Iṣlāḥī 2000: III, 84).

Repetition

The Qur'ān does not share the view that repetition is necessarily a demerit. There is considerable repetition in the Qur'ān – both of theme and expression – as one would expect from a book that calls itself *dhikr* ("remembrance, reminder") and is preoccupied with the task of explicating its message to doubters and objectors no less than to believers and submitters. From a Qur'ānic standpoint, the only relevant question is whether repetition serves a purpose, and there is sufficient reason to believe that repetition in the Qur'ān is purposeful. Apart from putting more than ordinary emphasis on a statement, repetition may bring into sharp relief a certain doctrine of the religion.

For example, Q 5:110 enumerates some of the miracles of Jesus, the addition of *bi-idhnī* ("by My [i.e., God's] will") in each case ensuring that God is understood as the source of all miracles and Jesus only as an instrument for performing them: "and when you [Jesus] created from clay a shape like that of a bird by My will and breathed into it, and it became a bird by My will; and you healed the blind and the leper by My will; and when you raised people from the dead by My will" (cf. Q 3:49, in which Jesus repeats the phrase "by God's will" with the same signification). In some cases, repetition is scarcely noticeable in that the repeated words, being short and simple, are quickly processed in the mind as they occur, deflecting attention away from themselves and to the main argument. This happens in Q 7:195, in which four questions, the first introduced by *a-lahum* ("Do they have . . . ?") and the last three by the correlative *am-lahum* ("Or do they have . . . ?"), are asked in quick succession, followed by a challenge that represents a climactic moment:

> Do they have feet they walk with?
> Or do they have hands they hold with?
> Or do they have eyes they see with?
> Or do they have ears they hear with?
> Say: "Call those you associate [with God], then play your tricks
> against me, and give me no respite!"

Q 7:195 is an instance of repetition turning attention away from itself and thus becoming practically unnoticeable (two other examples are Q 27:60–4, in which *am man* ["Or who is the one who . . . ?"] occurs five times, and Q 36:33–41, in which *wa-āyatun lahum* ["And a sign for them is . . ."] occurs thrice [Q 30:20–5 is similar to the latter example]). In other cases, the exact opposite result may be produced by repetition, which may consist not of a short or simple expression but of a substantial phrase whose syntactic position requires the reader to linger with it, paying it close attention. In *sūra* 54, for example, repetition takes the form of an ominous-sounding refrain, namely, the pointed question *fa-hal min muddakir* ("So, are there any who would take remembrance?"), which occurs six times (verses 15, 17, 22, 32, 40, 51), four times immediately preceded by *wa-laqad yassarnā 'l-Qur'ān li'l-dhikr* ("And we have certainly made the Qur'ān easy for purposes of remembrance"). Each of the six instances of *fa-hal min muddakir* concludes a verse, carrying the burden of part of the argument and, at the same time, contributing to the argument being made in the larger passage.

Sometimes repetition draws attention to an important theme of the whole *sūra*, as in *sūra* 26, which consists of 227 verses and in which the refrain-like statement, *inna fī dhālika la-āyatan wa-mā kāna aktharuhum mu'minīn* ("In this, certainly, there is a sign, but most of them are not believers"), occurs eight times (verses 8, 67, 103, 121, 139, 158, 174, 190), indicating, and bearing a direct relationship to, a principal theme of the *sūra*. Q 26:105–90 tells the stories of five prophets – Noah, Hūd, Ṣāliḥ, Lot, and

Shuʿayb – and their nations. The five parts into which the long passage may be divided (105–22, 123–40, 141–59, 160–75, 176–91) have almost identical beginnings (for example, "The people of Noah gave the lie to the messengers" and "The ʿĀd [Hūd's nation] gave the lie to the messengers") and the same ending ("And, indeed, your Lord alone is the One Mighty, Merciful"), and have several other features in common.

The verbal and conceptual repetition in these passages brings home several points, namely, that all prophets before Muḥammad taught the same essential message; that all prophets invited their nations to ground their conduct in sound belief; that Muḥammad should not lose heart over the stubborn opposition he is facing, for prophets before Muḥammad, too, were rejected by their nations; and that Muḥammad's opponents, if they do not mend their ways, will be dealt with by God in the same way as previous rebel nations were. In *sūra* 16, the construction *inna fī dhālika la-āyatan li-qawmin yatafakkarūn* ("In this, indeed, there is a sign for people who would reflect") occurs in verse 11. The construction is repeated four times, except for the verb, on which a variation is made: *yadhdhakkarūn* ("who take remembrance" [verse 13]), *yasmaʿūn* ("who listen" [verse 65]), and *yaʿqilūn* ("who use reason" [verse 67]). Then, in verse 69, the first verb, *yatafakkarūn*, is repeated. The use of different verbs underscores the need to give full consideration to the claims of the prophetic message, the use of *yatafakkarūn* at both ends of the passage creating a sort of envelope structure.

Imagery

Like pre-Islamic Arabic poetry, the Qurʾān is rich in imagery. A reader of the ancient Arabic odes will be struck by their well-drawn images of the elements of nature, of heroic action on the battlefield, of the camel speeding along with its rider through the trackless desert, of the precious wine brought in from distant lands, and of the wistful lover passing, years later, through the ruins of the dwellings where he once dallied with his beloved. But this imagery, though delightfully vivid, is self-referential in the sense that it does not provide any significant leads to philosophical or moral reflection. Qurʾānic imagery, on the other hand, adds to its graphic quality a clear focus of thought and is, in the end, instrumental in the sense that it reinforces the structures of Qurʾānic thought. (In this respect, the imagery of the Qurʾān invites comparison with that of the Bible.) We can discuss Qurʾānic imagery under three heads.

Simile (Watt and Bell 1970: 81–2)

Many Qurʾānic similes pertain to the "last day," a key notion in the Qurʾān. To the Arabs, mountains symbolized permanence, *khawālid* ("eternal ones") being one of the words they used to describe them. When the Qurʾān related the cataclysmic happenings of the last day, many sarcastically asked: "What about the mountains – will they, too, perish?" The Qurʾān replied that the mountains, on that day, would lose their integrity, floating around "like clouds" (Q 27:88). Q 55:37 says that, on the last day, the sky will split up, "turning red like [freshly peeled] skin," its blue changed to red.

Called out to gather at a certain place on the last day, human beings will, obeying the command, come running "as if they were rushing to appointed marks" (Q 70:43; in modern terms, as if they were eager to reach the finishing line or – not to make it sound too modern – to score a goal).

A few miscellaneous similes, each firmly tied to some aspect of the Qur'ānic religious teaching, may be noted. Q 74:50–1 says that the disbelievers shy away from the divine message "as if they were frightened asses running away from a lion." The crescent moon, obeying the law God has laid down for it, passes through many phases and, after becoming a full moon, begins to diminish until it comes to look "like an old twig" (Q 36:39). Q 7:171, referring to a pact that Israel had made with God, speaks of God's act of causing the mountain to hang over the Israelites' heads "as if it were a canopy." And in a simile that would seem exotic today but must have seemed entirely appropriate to seventh-century Arabs, the houris of paradise are compared to "hidden eggs" (Q 37:49), a reference to ostrich eggs, which the male of the species jealously guards – hiding them from predators – until they are hatched. The maiden egg was considered especially lovely because of its creamy yellow color, and poets frequently compared a pretty woman's complexion to it. The simile, thus, describes the houris as chaste, delicate, well-taken-care-of, and beautiful. A notable feature of the Qur'ānic similes is the likening of the abstract to the concrete (Quṭb 1982: 39). A good example is Q 14:18, which says that, on the last day, the unbelievers' supposedly good actions will be of no avail to the disbelievers, those actions becoming "like ashes that a strong wind sweeps about on a stormy day."

Metaphor (Watt and Bell 1970: 82)

The metaphors of the Qur'ān, like its similes, occur in a well-defined religious context. Q 3:7, dividing the Qur'ānic verses into "firm" or "unmistakable" and "ambiguous," calls the former "the mother of the book" (*umm al-kitāb*). The word *umm* (literally, "mother") suggests that the "firm" verses are of foundational importance and furnish criteria for settling differences and judging matters, the metaphor assigning to such verses hermeneutic value (Iṣlāḥī 2000: II, 25).

The Arabs engaged in trade and commerce (Mecca reaped the benefits of transit trade, while agriculture dominated Medinan economic life), and several metaphors relate to this background. Q 2:141 speaks of the actions performed by humans in this world as earnings, for one "earns" paradise or hell in the next world on the basis of one's conduct in this world. In Q 9:111, we read that God has "bought" from the believers their lives and wealth in exchange for the promise that they shall have paradise in the next world. To spend one's wealth in the way of God, especially in a war, is called advancing a "good loan" to God, who will repay it manifold (Q 2:245; 57:11). The hypocrites of Medina are criticized in these words (Q 2:16): "They are the ones who bought misguidance in exchange for guidance [i.e., preferred misguidance to guidance], and so their transaction yielded no profit." Q 35:29 says that those who read the book of God, regularly offer the prayer, and generously spend of the gift of wealth they have received from God can rightfully expect to have made a profitable transaction. Q 61:10–12 makes the prophet say:

> O those who have believed, shall I tell you of a transaction that will deliver you from a painful punishment: That you believe in God and His messenger, and fight in the way of God with your wealth and your souls. This is better for you if you knew; and He will forgive you your sins and make you enter gardens with streams flowing underneath and good dwellings in gardens of eternity. This is the great success!

Parable (Watt and Bell 1970: 81)

The Qur'ānic parables (or similitudes – I will use the two words interchangeably), too, add point and color to the Qur'ānic argument or statements. Unlike a simile or a metaphor, a parable cannot be analyzed in such a way as to establish a one-to-one correspondence between the persons, situations, or objects compared, the focus of attention being the main point the parable is trying to make. On the other hand, by virtue of its relative length, the parable has greater potential than a simile or metaphor has to develop a thought. The central theme of the Qur'ān is monotheism. In Q 14:24–5, the monotheistic creed is called the "good word" (*kalima ṭayyiba*), and is contrasted with idolatry, which is called the "evil word" (*kalima khabītha*):

> Have you not seen how God has struck a similitude – that of a good word? It is like a good tree whose root is entrenched and whose branches are up in the heavens; it yields its fruit every time, by the command of its Lord. And God strikes similitudes for people that they might take remembrance. And the similitude of an evil word is that of an evil tree that has been uprooted from the top of the ground, lacking as it does all stability.

The parable can be interpreted to mean that belief in monotheism has a solid basis in nature and reason and is productive of good conduct, whereas idolatry has no firm basis, neither in reason nor in nature, and is therefore false (Iṣlāḥī 2000: IV, 14–17). Q 24:39, using two parables, brings into relief the Qur'ānic theme that faith and works are integrally related:

> As for those who have disbelieved, their actions are like a mirage in a plain which a thirsty man takes to be water, until, when he gets to it, he finds it to be nothing, and finds by it God, Who will settle his account fully; and God is quick of recompense. Or they [actions] are like layers of darkness in a deep ocean, a wave covering it, on top of which is another wave, on top of which are clouds – one layer of darkness atop another: when he puts out his hand he can scarcely see it; and he whom God gives no light has no light.

One of the best-known verses of the Qur'ān is Q 24:35. It makes the point that God is the source of all knowledge and understanding, and it does so by presenting a similitude of surpassing literary beauty:

> God is the light of the heavens and the earth! His light, in terms of a similitude, is like a niche in which there is a lamp – the lamp is in a glass, the glass as if it were a brilliant star – that is being kindled by [the oil of] a blessed olive tree that is neither [of the] eastern nor [of the] western [side]: its oil would all but light up, even though no fire were to touch it. Light upon light! God guides to His light whomever He likes.

The Qur'ān also uses parable as a vehicle of social comment. In several parables, the Quraysh, the oligarchs of Mecca, who were opposed to Muḥammad, are criticized for their reluctance to share their wealth with the poor members of their society. In Q 68:17–33, for example, the Quraysh are compared to the owners of an orchard who had forgotten that they owed their affluence to God and, in their arrogance, neglected the poor of their community.

> We have put them [Quraysh] to the test, just as We put the people of the garden to the test, when they swore an oath that they would definitely pick the [fruit of the] garden early in the morning – and they were making no exceptions! But there came upon it [garden] a calamity from your Lord as they slept, and it became like a field mowed down. In the morning, they called out to one another: "Get to your fields early if you do intend to pick." And so they set out, whispering to one another: "Let no poor man under any circumstances accost you today." And they set out early, in earnestness, and in full control [of the situation]! But when they saw it [garden], they said, "We have lost our way! No, we have been deprived!" The most reasonable man among them said, "Did I not tell you? Why do you not glorify God?" They said, "Glory to our Lord! We were the wrongdoers." Then they started to blame one another. They said, "Woe to us, it is we who are the transgressors. Perhaps our Lord will give us something better in place of it; we turn to our Lord." This is how the punishment is! And the punishment of the hereafter is severer. Only if they knew!

The meaning of the parable is clear: the wealth given by God to people in this world is meant to test them, and failure in the test will result in the loss of that wealth in this life and in a harsher punishment in the next. The particular point of the parable is that the Quraysh, like the men of the orchard, have monopolized Mecca's sources of income, denying the needy any share of their prosperity, thus failing in their moral obligation to look after the welfare of the community as a whole. For this failure, they are warned of dire consequences in this world and the next. They are also told that, after a certain time, repentance will be of no avail.

Concluding Remarks

A more exhaustive study than the present one will examine many other features of the Qur'ānic language. To mention a few such features: (1) Certain *sūras* – for instance, Q 1–2, 7, and 10–15 – open with the so-called "broken letters," for which no completely satisfactory explanation exists. That the letters posed no special problems to the Qur'ān's first audience suggests that the use of such letters at the beginning of orations – perhaps with the purpose of drawing and focusing the audience's attention – was familiar to the Arabs. There may be some connection of theme and content between two or more *sūras* sharing one or more of the broken letters (Iṣlāḥī 2000: I, 82–4). (2) The Qur'ānic oaths, often regarded as rhetorical flourishes, have been cogently explained by the Indian scholar Ḥamīd al-Dīn al-Farāhī (d. 1938) as well-constructed arguments (Mir 1989b). (3) The relationship between sound and sense in the Qur'ān (Sells 1993) constitutes a subject that deserves more attention than it has received. (4) Q 3:54, "And they used a secret stratagem and God used a secret stratagem" (*wa-makarū wa-makara 'llāh*), represents a category of verses that have caused theological worries – for, how can wiliness be attributed to God? But such verses can be explained as instances of *mushākala* (formal equivalence), a stylistic feature in which identity of form does not necessarily imply identity of content. For example, the repetition of the verb *makara* in Q 3:54, this time with God as its subject, only signifies that God "paid them in the same coin," thus thwarting their evil attempts. In the same way, Q 2:190, *fa-man iʿtadā ʿalaykum fa ʿtadū ʿalayhi bi-mithli mā ʿtadā ʿalaykum* (literally, "So, anyone who transgresses against you, you may transgress against them the way they have transgressed against you") only means that one has the right to respond to aggression and not that one has the license to become an aggressor oneself, for the Qurʾān declares in unambiguous terms that "God does not love those who commit transgression" (for example, Q 2:190).

A linguistic feature like *mushākala* highlights the need to emphasize the distinction between language and logic. The language of the Qurʾān must not be parsed, analyzed, and discussed as if it were a treatise of logic. A proper understanding of that language requires that it be seen as belonging to the living context which gave rise to it; we saw, for example, how, viewed as part of a dynamic oral situation, *iltifāt* becomes not a type of the so-called "elegant variation" but a normal element in the interaction between a speaker and a live audience. Part of the challenge of studying the language of the Qurʾān consists in reconstructing, through study of Classical Arabic poetry and through an imaginative or empathetic exercise, that living context.

Further reading

Abdel Haleem, M. (2000) *Understanding the Qur'an: Themes and Style.* I. B. Tauris, London.

Boullata, Issa J. (ed.) (2000) *Literary Structures of Religious Meaning in the Qurʾān.* Curzon, Richmond.

Boullata, Issa J. (2003) Literary structures of the Qurʾān. In: McAuliffe, Jane Dammen (ed.) *Encyclopaedia of the Qurʾān.* Brill, Leiden, vol. III, pp. 192–205.

Gilliot, Claude, and Larcher, Pierre (2003) Language and style of the Qurʾān. In: McAuliffe, Jane Dammen (ed.) *Encyclopaedia of the Qurʾān.* Brill, Leiden, vol. III, pp. 109–35.

Kadi (al-Qadi), Wadad, and Mir, Mustansir (2003) Literature and the Qurʾān. In: McAuliffe, Jane Dammen (ed.) *Encyclopaedia of the Qurʾān.* Brill, Leiden, vol. III, pp. 205–27.

Mir, Mustansir (1989a) *Verbal Idioms of the Qurʾān.* Center for Near Eastern and North African Studies, University of Michigan, Ann Arbor, MI.

Mir, Mustansir (1989b) The Qurʾānic oaths: Farahi's interpretation. *Islamic Studies* 29:1, 5–27.

Mir, Mustansir (1992) Dialogue in the Qurʾān. *Religion and Literature* 24:1, 1–22.

Robinson, Neal (1996) *Discovering the Qur'an: A Contemporary Approach to a Veiled Text.* SCM Press, London.

Sells, Michael (1993) Sound and meaning in Sūrat al-Qāriʿa. *Arabica* 40, 403–30.

CHAPTER 7

Poetry and Language

Navid Kermani

The prophet Muḥammad lived from 570 to 632 CE. He had his first visions at the age of 40 and, more importantly, his first auditions which continued to recur up to his death twenty-two years later. He recited these revelations to his countrymen, primarily to the people of Mecca, but also to the Arab people as a whole. He conveyed an "Arabic recitation," *Qurʾān ʿarabī*. The word Qurʾān literally means "recitation" or "that to be recited," often mentioned in the early *sūra*s without an article, hence not yet used as a proper noun (as-Said 1975; Graham 1987; Neuwirth 1996). The Qurʾān always distinguishes between an "Arabic" and some "foreign language" (*aʿjamī)* revelation, which is not specifically addressed to Arabs (Izutsu 1964). Indeed, I cannot think of any other historical religious text that refers so often and so explicitly to the foregone conclusion that the revelation is expressed in a specific language.

> If We had made it a non-Arabic Qurʾān (*Qurʾān aʿjamī*), they would assuredly have said: "Why are its verses not clear? What! A non-Arabic Qurʾān and an Arabic messenger?" (Q 41:44)

Muḥammad claimed to be the "Arabic" proclaimer of a message sent by God to all people. "We have sent no messenger save with the tongue of his people, that he might make all clear to them" (Q 14:4). This notion presupposes that Arabs felt part of one society, distinct from other non-Arabic societies and peoples. What is now taken to be a matter of fact is not at all so if we consider the political situation, geographical boundaries, and the tribal structure of society on the Arabic peninsula in the seventh century. The Arabs of the *jāhiliyya* or pre-Islamic era did not form an alliance nor did they share a common political platform. On the contrary, tribes fought with one another and blood feuds racked the country. The single major organization was the tribe, influencing the worldview and personal ties of each individual. Yet the numerous, warring tribes did feel united as a people. It was the language that constituted the unifying element transcending all conflicts on the seventh-century Arabic peninsula. While many tribal dialects were mutually unintelligible, the formalized language of poetry, the *ʿarabiyya*, towered above all dialects (Zwettler 1978; Versteegh 1997). Poetry forged a common identity, overcoming this fragmentation to provide the basis for a homogeneous memory.

The situation might be compared to Germany at the turn of the nineteenth century when literature helped small, miniature states to develop a cohesive, specifically "German" identity. And yet it was different. The Arabs of the early seventh century were Bedouins or desert nomads, linked only by caravans of traders and frequent wars between the tribes, who constituted an independent economic sector. Otherwise, there was little or no contact between the tribes and virtually no means of communication. The written word was not widely disseminated, and most people were, in fact, illiterate and the differences between dialects made communication difficult. Yet still, throughout the Arabic region, which was a third of the size of all Europe, and spread from Yemen in the south to Syria in the north, from the borders of modern Iraq to the borders of Egypt, old Arabic poetry with its formal language, sophisticated techniques and extremely strict norms and standards was identical. "How this was achieved, we do not know and most probably shall never learn," remarked the Israeli Orientalist, Shlomo D. Goitein, on this astonishing phenomenon (Goitein 1966: 6).

Old Arabic poetry is a highly complex phenomenon. The vocabulary, grammatical idiosyncrasies and strict norms were passed down from generation to generation, and only the most gifted students fully mastered the language. A person had to study for years, sometimes even decades under a master poet before laying claim to the title of poet. Muḥammad grew up in a world which almost religiously revered poetic expression. He had not studied the difficult craft of poetry, when he started reciting verses publicly. Initially, the Qurʾān was not a written work; it consisted of a variety of separate recitations which were later compiled in one body of work. The first *sūras* were dominated by gripping, apocalyptic scenarios, appeals for a return to spiritual and moral values, the equality of man and his responsibility to himself and others. The language was extremely powerful, captivating contemporary audiences with its pulsating rhythms, striking use of sound patterns, and a fantastical matrix of images (Sells 1999; Boullata 2000). Yet Muḥammad's recitations differed from poetry and from the rhyming prose of the soothsayers, the other conventional form of inspired, metrical speech at that time. The norms of old Arabic poetry were strangely transformed, the subjects developed differently, and the meter was abandoned. While poetry was, in political terms, generally conservative, reinforcing the moral and social order of the day, the whole impetus of the early Qurʾān, its topics, metaphors, and ideological thrust, was towards revolutionary change. All this was new to Muḥammad's contemporaries. On the other hand, however, the way the verses were used conformed to the rules of old Arabic poetry. And, more important still, the Qurʾān was written in the *ʿarabiyya*, the code, as it were, of contemporary poetry. Therefore, despite the discrepancies in form and content, many listeners initially perceived Muḥammad as a poet.

The Qurʾān traces its own reception to an extent which seems unprecedented for a revelatory text: it documents the reactions of both believing and unbelieving audiences in series of citations and comments. The Qurʾān itself reveals that the criticism most likely to incense the prophet was the claim that he was a mere poet. Although in later *sūras* the response to this claim is rather stereotypical, the minuteness of detail, especially in early accounts, indicates that this allegation must have been seen as a real threat. It is safe to assume that certain actions, conduct, or speeches led to Muḥammad being labeled a poet, especially in the first phase of the revelation. If, after all, nothing in his performance evoked this comparison, his opponents would have sought other ways of undermining his claim to be a prophet. They could have accused him of being a liar, a thief, or a charlatan: "But what they said was: he just composes poetry, he is a poet" (Q 21:5). The claim by Muḥammad's opponents that the Qur'ān was poetry cannot have been purely polemic, but must have reflected what many people felt: not because the collective consciousness identified the Qur'ān with poetry, but because poetry (and the other genres of inspired speech) were the only ones people could relate it to at all, it being "the least different." Early Muslim sources regularly note that the people of Mecca consulted poets and other literary masters for advice on how to technically categorize Muḥammad's recitations. These "experts" – both astonished and fascinated – most often replied that the Qur'ān was neither poetry nor rhyming prose, thus defining the boundaries for evaluating the Qur'ān. "I know many Qasides and *rajaz* verses, and am even familiar with the poems of the Jinnee. But, by God, his recitation is like none of them" remarked one famous poet, Walīd b. Mughīra (Ibn Kathīr 1987: I, 499) echoing the perception of many of Muḥammad's contemporaries, how it was memorized by later generations. Yet while sources consistently insist that the poets and orators were aware of the stylistic difference of the Qur'ān, they acknowledged that simple people found it hard to clearly distinguish between poetry and revelation. The tradition tells how the poet and prophet's companion, ʿAbd Allāh b. Rawāḥa, was surprised and challenged by his wife as he was leaving a concubine's chambers. She had long harbored the suspicion that he was having a clandestine affair. Knowing that ʿAbd Allāh had sworn never to recite the Qur'ān unless he was ritually pure (which he would not have been after an act of adultery), she asks him to read from the Qur'ān in order to show him up. The poet immediately reads three verses of a poem that sound so like the Qur'ān that his wife exonerates him, thinking "it was a Qur'ān" (Ibn Manẓūr 1956: VII, 183).

The danger of being wrongly identified as poetry forced the Qur'ān to distance itself from it. The poets were, after all, direct rivals, since they both used the same formal language, the *ʿarabiyya*, both invoked heavenly powers and, like the prophet, both claimed to be the supreme authorities of their communities (Zwettler 1991). "And the poets – the perverse follow them" (Q 26:24). The polemic against poets can only be understood in this context, and a good example can be found in *sūra* 26. The argument had nothing to do with literary rivalry. It was a contest for leadership, but not just the leadership of a single tribe, as enjoyed by the poets. The entire tribal structure of Arabic society with its polytheism was challenged by the Qur'ān, since it proclaimed the principle of unity, i.e. the unity of God and the unity of the community. Poets, on the other hand, represented more than any other social group the social and spiritual order of the *jāhiliyya*, which was characterized politically by tribalism, and spiritually, by polytheism. Contrary to popular claims, the Qur'ān is not generally anti-poetry. Poets are criticized in a very concrete context, some of them being labeled as those who insist on their leadership role and are inspired by demons. In the same passage specifically excluded from this criticism are poets who "believe, and do righteous deeds, and remember God oft" (Q 26:227).

Obviously, the prophet succeeded in this conflict with the poets, otherwise Islam would not have spread like wildfire. The Qurʾān itself just obliquely refers to the reasons for its success. It may reflect upon the situation at the time of the revelation, mentioning real events and developments, but it does so for audiences already familiar with these events. So, unlike the history books, it does not relate what happened on a particular day, but just relies on keywords to jolt the memory of the listener. Modern readers, who in general accept Muslim historiography as a relevant source, often have to consult secondary sources to reconstruct the historical context, including biographies, history books or writings on the "occasions of revelation" (*asbāb al-nuzūl*).

In the Western view of the early development of Islam, it was social, ideological, propagandistic, or military reasons for the success of Muḥammad's prophetic mission. Western historians have acknowledged the prophet's charisma and his egalitarian message. Yet Muslim sources paint a different picture. Over the ages they have emphasized the literary quality of the Qurʾān as a decisive factor for the spread of Islam among seventh-century Arabs. They refer to the numerous stories in Muslim literature that recount the overwhelming effect of Qurʾān recitation on Muḥammad's contemporaries, tales about people spontaneously converting, crying, screaming, falling into ecstasy, fainting or even dying while hearing verses from the Qurʾān. Over the centuries, Muḥammad's conflict with the poets was more and more portrayed in terms of a literary struggle, enacted partly in the imagery of a classical poet's duel. The following – clearly invented (Nöldeke 1967; Kister 1980) – anecdote by the greatest Arabic poet, Labīd b. Rabīʿa (d. ca. 40/660–1), is proof of this. As a sign of his supremacy, Labīd nailed his poems to the entrance to the Kaʿba. None of Labīd's rivals dared challenge his authority by pinning their own verses next to Labīd's. One day, though, a group of followers of Muḥammad approached the gate. At that time, Muḥammad was denounced by contemporary pagan Arab society as an obscure sorcerer and deranged poet. They pinned up a passage from the second *sūra* of the Qurʾān and called upon Labīd to read it aloud. The King-Poet laughed at their impudence. Still, either to pass the time or to mock them, he agreed to recite the verses. Overwhelmed by their beauty, he converted to Islam on the spot (Lane 1843: 88).

This type of conversion is a recurring image in early Muslim historical sources, and the later these sources are, the more embellished the aesthetic power of the Qurʾānic looks (Juynboll 1974; Kermani 2000). One story tells of the story of the poet and nobleman al-Ṭufayl b. ʿAmr al-Dawsī. When he arrived at Mecca some men of the Quraysh called on him, warning him about Muḥammad's magic speeches. They urgently advised him not to listen to his recitations. "By God, they were so persistent that I indeed decided neither to listen to anything he said nor to speak to him," al-Ṭufayl is quoted as saying in Ibn Isḥāq's early biography of the prophet. The poet even stuffed wool in his ears, "fearing that some of his words still might get through, whereas I did not want to hear any of it." In the Kaʿba, al-Ṭufayl eventually met the prophet performing his prayer. "Here I am, an intelligent man and poet, I can distinguish between the beautiful and the repulsive," he said to himself. "So what is to prevent me from listening to what this man is saying?" He took the wool out of his ears, followed Muḥammad to his house and asked him to recite something. On the spot al-Ṭufayl converted to Islam, stating "By God, never before have I heard a word more beautiful than this." He returned to his clan and won the majority of his companions over to Islam (Ibn Hishām n.d.: 175f.). The Sirens in the twelfth book of Homer's *Odyssey* could not have been more seductive.

The idiosyncratic nature of these identical accounts of conversion – which, incidentally, always feature one or more protagonists who do not like or do not know of the prophet, listen to a few verses from the Qurʾān and convert to Islam on the spot – is obvious if we search for comparisons in other religions. The phenomenon of a conversion inspired – in the narrow sense – by an aesthetic experience often recurs even in later Islam but is relatively seldom found in Christianity. Neither in the Gospels nor elsewhere are similar accounts reported in any comparable frequency. As far as we know from autobiographical testimonies, the legendary conversions and initiation events in Christian history – Paul, Augustine, Pascal, or Luther, for instance – were triggered by other, equally remarkable but not primarily aesthetic experiences. It is not the beauty of divine revelation but the moral and ethical message which is the most striking feature of these accounts. This does not imply that the evolution and practice of Christianity – or any other religion – can be imagined without the aesthetic fascination of specific sites, texts, hymns, images, scents, actions, gestures, and garments. Protestantism would never have spread so quickly in the German-speaking regions if it had not been for the rhetorical force of Luther's Bible. Yet in the portrayal of their past by the Christian, or more specifically, Protestant community, the aesthetic momentum is less significant, however relevant its role in religious practice. Few Christians would claim that the disciples followed Jesus because he was so handsome or spoke so eloquently. In turn, Christian religious instruction would hardly teach that the triumph of Christianity was due to the stylistic perfection of the Gospels. Surely there were conversions to Christianity inspired by the beauty of the scriptures, but these are not treated as a literary topos in the body of testimonies on the propagation of Christianity. They are also not treated as a topos in the literature on the history of the salvation of humankind by God. But, for Muslims, the aesthetic fascination with the Qurʾān is an integral part of their religious tradition. It is this collective awakening, interpretation of theological reflection on the aesthetics of the text which specifically defines the religious world of Islam – and not the aesthetic experience as such, which seems to occur during the reception of any sacred texts. Only in Islam did the rationalization of aesthetic experience culminate in a distinct theological doctrine of poetics, the *iʿjāz*, based on the superiority and inimitability of the Qur'ān (Neuwirth 1983). For a Christian, the reasoning of the *iʿjāz* is highly peculiar: I believe in the Qurʾān because the language is too perfect to have been composed by man. One can see this as an aesthetic proof of God or truth. In Western civilization, virtually no equivalent exists in the sphere of religion. The nearest we get is perhaps our subjective response to certain works of, say, Bach or Mozart. Typically enough, audiences often refer to them as "divine."

For centuries, the relationship between revelation and poetry in Arabic cultural history was as close as at the start of the revelation. In fact, literary study owes its existence to the Qurʾān. If the miracle of Islam is the language of revelation, then the language of the Qur'ān must be analyzed in literary terms and, to prove its superiority, be compared to other texts, that is, poetry. The initial thrust was apologetic, but literary interest soon departed from the theological context. Particularly beginning in the fourth/tenth to sixth/twelfth centuries, great works on Arabic poetics were produced, anticipating many of the findings of modern linguistics and literary studies. Arabic rhetoricians discussed the Qur'ān and poetry together, refusing to play one off against the other. The most fascinating example of this kind of scholarship seems to me the Iranian ʿAbd al-Qāhir al-Jurjānī (d. 471/1078 or 474/1081), a leading theologian and literary scholar of the fifth/eleventh century, who consistently focused on the specific merits of the poetical language as such, be it in the Qur'ān or in poetry. Anticipating many findings of twentieth-century structuralism and semiotics, al-Jurjānī analyzed the specifics of the poetical use of language by comparing the Qur'ān and poetry – an interweaving of theology and literary studies hardly conceivable in today's Arabic world, both in terms of academic precision and theological legitimacy (al-Jurjānī 1984; Abu Deeb 1979).

I have spoken of literary studies which, inspired by the Qur'ān, was soon to become autonomous. The Qur'ān had a paradoxical effect on poetry itself, secularizing it in a way. Following the triumph of Islam, poets initially relinquished their metaphysical claim and focused on secular motives instead, such as love, court and urban life, and the virtues. Later, in the second/eighth and third/ninth century, they repositioned themselves in the ʿAbbāsid courts and cities by distancing themselves from Islam. In deliberate rivalry to prophetic revelation, they sought other sources of inspiration than the concept of one God, such as the *jinn* and Satan. The best known satanic verses were written by Abū Nuwās (d. ca. 198/813), probably the best known poet in Arabic literature. Yet, similar to Europe in the modern era, the recourse to transcendental powers was more a literary motif than one based on real experience. The aim was to break Islam's monopoly on inspiration. Poets competed with the Qur'ān, striving to surpass it stylistically. In the second/eighth century, poets and writers like Bashshār b. Burd (d. ca. 167/784), Ṣāliḥ b. ʿAbd al-Quddūs (d. ca. 167/783), ʿAbd al-Ḥamīd b. Yaḥyā al-Kātib (d. 132/750) met in literary circles, above all in Basra. They spurred each other on with comments like "Your poem is better than this or that verse in the Qur'ān," or "That line is more beautiful than such and such a verse in the Qur'ān," and so forth (Goldziher 1889/90: II, 402). Up to the middle of the fifth/eleventh century, in fact, intellectuals like al-Mutanabbī (d. 354/965) or al-Maʿarrī (d. 449/1058) continued to challenge the superiority of Qur'ānic language. Nevertheless, the Qur'ān remained a model or yardstick even for those who denied the miraculous character of Qur'ānic language. Indeed, one of the mentioned poets of Basra, Bashshār b. Burd, reportedly boasted that one of his own poems, recited by a singer in Baghdad, was superior even to the 59th *sūra*. Surely, he was convinced by his own poetry – but even he seems not to have thought badly at all of the stylistic quality of the Qur'ān.

As much as poets contested the Qur'ān, theologians criticized poetry. Arabic poetry was the revelation's main rival, posing an even greater threat than other religions gaining ground in Muslim regions. The relationship between the two was, and in some ways, still is highly ambivalent. In Arabic tradition, poetry was the only medium, apart from the revelation – and later mystical discourses – that was acknowledged to have access, albeit limited in transcendental reality, to supernatural inspiration. This occurs even where poetry is rejected, because this claim is accepted (otherwise, being insignificant, it could have been dismissed), despite being seen as dangerous and blasphemous.

This view of poetry as potentially blasphemous became one of the fundamental themes of Arabic literature. As long as it remained secular, it was rarely subjected to moral or political restrictions within Muslim culture. Yet, once it competed directly with religion, be it via reference to divine sources of inspiration or attempts to imitate and surpass the Qur'ān stylistically, poets became targets of religiously motivated criticism and were sometimes persecuted. From a modern perspective, these attacks on orthodox or simply traditional religion link them to "the Promethean enterprise of modern poetry," as Octavio Paz describes it, that is, the wish to create "a new sacred order to challenge the modern Church" (Paz 1990: 148). The Syrian poet Adonis (b. 1930) is one of the major figures in the Arabic world committed to this ancient yet new undertaking. His work can be read as a passionate, at times violent, at times tender exploration of his own intellectual and aesthetic tradition. There is a religious thrust to his work but one which makes it impious. Adonis does not write religious poetry, that is, poetry that serves the cause of religion; his poetry actually contests the status of religion. In this, he identifies with the role of the poet in the *jāhiliyya*, whose prophetic claims are rejected by Islam, and, furthermore, with mystical poets like al-Ḥallāj (d. 309/922) and al-Niffarī who wrote in the fourth/tenth century. The mystical poets, however, helped reinstate the metaphysical seriousness of poetry, which had been more or less secularized by Islam, and the invocation of demons, angels, or Satan was more a formal device than an expression of a real transcendental experience. They elevated poetry to the level of prophetic vision. At the same time, they dismissed the canon of rules governing Arabic poetic tradition in an effort to forge a new linguistic and intellectual reality, just as, says Adonis, the Qur'ān had done in bygone times, and as he also does in his own poetry. Unlike mystical poets, who saw themselves as Muslims and justified their breach of conventional aesthetic and religious norms in religious terms, Adonis rejects any Islamic connotation whatsoever. He sheds religion, but instead of ignoring it like many of his contemporaries, he analyzes the shedding process.

Today I burnt the phantom of Saturday
I burnt the phantom of Friday
Today I threw away the mask of the house
And replaced the blind God of stone
And the God of seven days
With a dead God (Adonis 1998: 52)

Adonis epitomizes the aforementioned ambivalence between the Qur'ān and poetry. He substitutes the God of seven days with a dead God. Yet this is the very poet who praises the Qur'ān as the source of modernity in Arabic poetry (Adonis 1985: 50f.). In his theoretical work, Adonis analyzes the language of the Qur'ān in detail, its literary and aesthetic provocative power, and its breach with traditional norms.

Indeed, the Qur'ān enriched Arabic poetry more than any other text. It liberated it from the narrow framework of existing genres and inspired new approaches to language, imagery, and the use of motifs. Conventional standards, and the theoretical analysis of language and literature can both be traced to the hermeneutics of the Qur'ān. Just as theologians referred to poetry to analyze the language of the Qur'ān, the reverse also happened and still does: poets and literary scholars refer to the Qur'ān in order to analyze poetry. One example is the movement of so-called "modernists" (*muḥdathūn*) in Arabic poetry, who dominated literary debate in the second/eighth and third/ninth centuries. The imagery of the Qur'ān and its stylistic departures from the strict formal rules of poetry inspired the "modernists" to introduce new rhetorical devices and replace traditional norms. In the purely literary-aesthetic discussion of poetry conducted by the modernists, the Qur'ān was the obvious key reference point because of its poetic structure.

Adonis, too, is in fact an example of the literary power of the Qur'ān. The language of his poetry absorbs the language of the Qur'ān, reconstructing it and dismantling it from within. And the language he chooses is none other than the *ʿarabiyya*, the 1,500-year old literary language of the Arabs. It is both a curse and a blessing: a language which even in pre-Islamic times had already matured into a structure of breath-taking complexity, regularity, and semantic density, largely removed from the common vernacular, which consisted of dozens of dialects. A language which still retains virtually the same form and structure has hardly changed, and whose strict metrical norms are still taught. The durability of the language is mainly due to the Qur'ān, whose use of the idiom of old Arabic poetry has given it unique normative power (Fück 1950). Apart from Sanskrit, Arabic grammar may be the only grammar in which the rules are not based on linguistic reality. In both theory and practice, these are based on one single book, whose grammatical reality – unchanged since the era of pre-Islamic poetry – ignored everyday communication to become a truly absolute standard.

Roman Jakobson once raised the following question: how would Russian literary language have flourished "if the Ukrainian poet Gogol had not appeared on the scene speaking poor Russian" (Jakobson 1993: 68f.). The Arabic world may have had also its Gogols, but the existence of a divine model did prevent the transformation of its linguistic norms as it has happened within the Russian language. Uniquely, Arabic grammatical rules and the aesthetic norm are scarcely affected by the inexorable passage of time. Instead, for centuries, a historical expression of language has been enshrined as the ideal; only the finer points are examined and described in increasing depth by grammarians, and while it is judged inaccessible, it is the duty of every literary scholar and rhetorician to try to understand it.

Arabic is thus an extreme example of how sacral languages are consciously kept static and, while unable to prevent it totally, very effectively block the evolution of a language. Yet, at the same time, colloquial language continues to evolve just like in every other culture; external influences, for instance, seep into the language keeping sources of lively perception and description alive in a dynamic environment. Clifford Geertz (1976: 1490) spoke of a "linguistic schizophrenia" – the formal language is upheld as the only, true language, although it has become increasingly removed from real, everyday language and has to be learnt almost as a foreign language. None of the Arabic dialects developed into a formally distinct language as happened in Italian. Even if the dialects virtually constitute a separate language as in Maghreb, they are not seen as such. Although the differences between the local vernacular and educated language are greater than between Latin and Italian, they are still defined as dialects. The reason is that Arabs still define themselves – Muslim Arabs, Christians, and even Jewish Arabs well into the twentieth century – as a community solely defined by the language, that is, the 1,400-year-old language of poetry and the Qur'ān (Chejne 1969: 18ff.).

But, unlike Latin, classical Arabic is still a living language, existing parallel to the dialects. It is the official language, and the language of science and poetry. This unique resilience is due to the Qur'ān, which, written in the idiom of old Arabic poetry, acquired unique normative power. However, one is rarely conscious that modern educated Arabic is not identical to the language of the Qur'ān, but is grammatically, morphologically, and acoustically far more simple. Nevertheless, the listener unconsciously perceives modern high Arabic as an old, venerable language and instinctively equates it with ancient Arabic literature. As a result, Arabic poets who have mastered the subtleties of classical Arabic find it easy to generate a mythical aura. It is far harder to imbue this language with a sense of contemporaneity. Modern Arabic poetry regularly attempts this, often with considerable success.

At the same time, vernacular poetry continues to flourish today. Great poets and singers spontaneously compose poetry during performances and enjoy enormous prestige among all classes of society. But this poetry was and still is assigned to popular culture, which is strictly divorced from high culture. Now, however, some young poets are consciously opting for simple, modern language, and, instead of wrestling with classical standards, choose to simply ignore them. At an intellectual and culturo-political level, this is innovative and honest, but at an aesthetic level, as far as I can see, it has not been too successful. Many young poets simply do not bother with the rules and tonal diversity of Arabic literary language, which must be mastered in order to destroy it. Their poetry is closer to colloquial language, their delivery as monotonous and commonplace as poetry readings in Europe nowadays. In a milieu steeped in bathos, this new brashness could have a quality of directness, but judging from the poems of the young poets I have read or listened to while I was living in Cairo, it tends to fall flat. Their poetry possesses none of the immediacy of spontaneous popular poetry inspired by the people, nor the aura, tonality, or rhythmic quality of classical literary language.

As evidence that the Arabic language may generate some form of verbal magic, and the pure sound of the precisely accentuated words evoke a strangely solemn, almost sacred yet vigorous mood which is totally separate from the semantic meaning, one need only attend a Qur'ānic recitation or a public reading by one of the greatest contemporary poets. Both have preserved the extreme differentiation of the consonants, the wealth of phonetic nuances and the sometimes exorbitantly lengthy vowels. Both are a concert of tone and rhythm. The fascination they hold even for listeners who do not speak fluent Arabic is partly due to the succession of highly differentiated, compressed consonants which culminate in a momentous semantic-acoustic explosion, with the vocals extremely drawn out to achieve an air of solemnity. Both the differentiation of the consonants and the melodic vowels are rare, and do not occur in colloquial Arabic. Colloquial Arabic languages have, naturally, reduced the variety of nuances and cropped the vowels to a manageable length. The entire acoustic range of classical Arabic has only been preserved in poetry and, more extensively, in Qurʾānic recitations (Nelson 1985).

Yet this fascination contains its dangers: since, in Muslim interpretation, God chose the wonderful Arabic language to address mankind, it has acquired a status which many of its speakers still find binding, elevating, and sometimes oppressive. This makes Arabic particularly open to stagnation, mythologization, formalization, kitsch, and ideological exploitation, or demagoguery. It is the fascination and danger of all verbal magic, that great, controversial theme of the twentieth century, which preoccupied thinkers like Scholem, Wittgenstein, Benjamin and Karl Krauss. Anyone who has witnessed a well-phrased, rousing public speech in an Arabic country has felt the powerful, "magical" effect of the language upon the audience.

It is difficult to imagine how such a speech might sound in a different language, removed from the constant presence of a 1,500-year-old language with strong sacral overtones in society, in its theology, literature, and politics. The "mythical" power of language in an Arabic milieu is apparent. A politician, theologian, or poet who starts speaking in classical Arabic uses a tool which, provided he is a good orator, is sure to captivate a wide audience. Language operates here as a kind of time machine, effectively transporting all present back to a mythical epoch. Even television broadcasts of a speech by, say, Arafat, Qaddafi, or Saddam Hussein have the same effect. But how much more impressive were Nasser's great speeches, whose uprising was due to his extraordinary rhetorical skill.

In the Egyptian film *Nasser 57*, broadcast throughout the Arabic world some years ago, it became clear just how consummately Nasser, portrayed by the actor Aḥmad Zakkī, could manipulate the various levels of the Arabic language, shifting from popular to high Arabic, captivating and persuading audiences by the sheer power of his rhetorical skill. He is proof that the dramatic delivery of punctuated formal Arabic phrases at a crucial moment, even a simple "old-fashioned" turn of phrase like *yā ayyuhā ʾl-ikhwa* ("O brethren") can electrify audiences and link the orator to a 1,500-year-old line of ancestors. Even the crowded cinema in Beirut, where I saw the film in 1996, vibrated with an incredible tension. When, at last, in the final scene, Nasser addressed his audience in the classical vocative, emitting familiar classical phrases from a mask-like face, the tension in the audience was palatable. And, at the end of the speech, when, from the pulpit of Azhar University, Nasser, the socialist, cries out *Allāhu akbar* four times, punctuated by short, pregnant pauses, the wheel comes full circle and he is back where his own history began: he becomes a prophet.

Modern Arabic leaders, like the Mubaraks, the Assads, and the young monarchs, do not possess Nasser's rhetorical skill, which accounts for their lack of effect. Thus, rival leaders are driven even more to resort to the *ʿarabiyya*, the ancient language of the poets, the language of the Qurʾān, which is both a treasure and a weapon. The fascination of fundamentalism is also bound up with language. Their leaders try to speak pure Arabic, untainted by dialects or foreign words. Except superficially, this generally has little to do with the Qurʾān or its dynamics, since the Qurʾān vibrates with energy and a richness of sound, and its fascination lies in its breach of norms. The Arabic spoken by modern fundamentalists is often appallingly trite, puritanical, conformist and, in fact, artificial. It is, however, perceived as pure and religious, mythical and, in a dull, banal sense, sublime. The mere code of the language becomes a tool used to legitimate their claim to the status of a sacred authority.

Watching Osama bin Laden's first video broadcast after the start of the American air offensive on Afghanistan, I was struck by the exquisite Arabic he spoke. Not once did he slip into dialect, as usually happens with the modern generation of Arabic leaders, nor did he confuse the complicated flectional endings, a mistake made even by intellectuals. He chose antiquated vocabulary, familiar to educated Arabs from religious literature and classical poetry, and avoided neologisms. It was, in a way, the stiff, puritanical, conformist, even artificial Arabic already mentioned, with one significant difference. For the first time, I witnessed a person use the puritanical form so naturally that even I fell under its spell.

The crucial rhetorical point of the speech was not its beauty as such: Osama bin Laden evoked the unadulterated purity of the language. It sounded like a traditional speech. In reality, though, his rhetoric represents a complete break with tradition. The real heirs of this tradition, the Arab theologians of today, speak very differently – if they are rhetorically well educated – with their exquisitely varying enunciation of high Arabic consonants, precise modulation and length of vowels, the result of many years of learning during which they are taught Qur'ānic recitation and eloquence. Osama bin Laden lacks this training, and although he speaks antiquated Arabic, it sounds simple, clear, and modest. In fact, his rhetoric works precisely because of the lack of rhetorical ornament, and the conscious modesty of expression. This linguistic asceticism marks a rejection of the burden of tradition, a return to pure roots – also symbolized by his attire and location, namely the cave – all the props needed to create a prophetic aura. Even the lack of accentuation in his rhetoric echoes the puritanical Wahhābī spirit, which is allegedly identical with the divine spirit of the prophet. This break with prevailing tradition was most obvious when Osama bin Laden cited phrases from the Qur'ān: while other speakers grotesquely raise and lower their voices when they recite the revelation, Osama bin Laden proceeded in the same solicitous tone, as if he wished to persuade his audience through the clarity of his message alone.

Osama bin Laden rejects the factual history of Islam in order to return to an alleged primordial origin, but he also turns his back on the predominant rhetorical tradition. He rejects ornamentation of any kind, rhetorical devices, in fact, the entire history of interpretation of the Qur'ān, to return to the unadulterated, original wording, the pure, naked scripture. It is no coincidence that, in Christianity, this explicit eschewal of aesthetic splendor is found in Protestantism, particularly Pietism. The rejection by the new Muslim puritans of excessively musical Qur'ānic recitations, especially in Saudi Arabia, is an essential one. A fundamentalist reading of a source text in literary terms could be defined as the assertion of a single, eternally valid, literal interpretation. Thus, a fundamentalist exegesis negates the diversity of the possible interpretations which, in the theological tradition of Islam, like Judaism, was always seen as a merit.

Classical Muslim interpreters agreed that no verse of the Qur'ān could be reduced to one single, absolute meaning, insisting that the Qur'ān was *dhū wujūh*, implying that it has many faces, similar to the many *pānīm* or faces that Jewish scholars find in the Torah. Today, virtually all secular readings by modern Muslim scholars subscribe to this fundamentalist principle of Muslim exegesis: they insist upon the heterogeneous meaning of the text, including – implicitly or explicitly – the poetry of the Qur'ān, its poetically structured language, since any poetic text can be read and interpreted from many perspectives without affecting its irreproducible singularity. The very heterogeneity of meaning defines the text as poetic, indeed, it stops being poetic once it is unambiguous. It is then reduced to a mere treatise, an ideological manifesto or – in the case of the Revelation text – a mere book of laws. For scholars like the Egyptians Amīn al-Khūlī, Muḥammad Aḥmad Khalaf Allāh and Naṣr Ḥāmid Abū Zayd or the Iranians ʿAbdolkarim Sorush and Moḥammad Mojtahed Shabestarī, this insistence on the heterogeneous meaning of the text and the innovative, variable act of interpretation is related to an emphasis on its aesthetic features (Kermani 1996; Speicher 1997; Taji-Farouki 2004). They know that if the Qur'ān is accepted as a revelation and as a literary monument and body of sound, this will open up a whole cosmos of signs, meanings, and interpretations, and allow it to be read in a multitude of different ways. This relationship to the revelation is diametrically opposed to the claim to a monopoly of interpretation, as more or less advocated by Islamist movements. Therefore, they warn against arbitrariness, stressing the clarity of the divine word and thus neglecting its beauty. The intellectual and often physical conflict surrounding the Qur'ān which is being played out today in the Islamic world is also a conflict about its aesthetic dimension, which some feel is in danger of being lost.

I spoke earlier of the Sirenic effect of Qur'ānic recitation. I would like to finish with a citation from Franz Kafka: "Now the Sirens have an even more terrible weapon than singing: their silence" (Kafka 1983: 58).

Author note

This chapter contains some thoughts and reflections, addressed to a general reader, which were, to a large part, discussed more comprehensively and with detailed bibliographical notes in Kermani 1999. A first version of this chapter was published in German in *Kursbuch* 149 (September 2002), pp. S145–60. A shortened English version of it was also published in the *Times Literary Supplement* (London) for October 1, 2004. As I do not deal with the Qur'ān as such, but solely with its reception within Arab Muslim communities, I leave out questions of Muḥammad's historicity and the genesis of the text. The foundational history of Islam is taken here as it is memorized by the community, not as a historical fact. For a methodological outline of that approach cf. Assmann 1992.

Further reading

as-Said, L. (1975) *The Recited Koran: A History of the First Recorded Version* (ed., trans. Weiss, B., Rauf, M. A. and Berger, M.). Darwin Press, Princeton.

Chejne, A. (1969) *The Arabic Language: Its Role in History*. University of Minnesota Press, Minneapolis.

Graham, William (1987) *Beyond the Written Word: Oral Aspects of Scripture in the History of Religion*. Cambridge University Press, Cambridge.

Kermani, Navid (1999) *Gott ist schön. Das ästhetische Erleben des Koran*. C. H. Beck, Munich.
Kermani, N. (2000) The aesthetic reception of the Qur'an as reflected in early Muslim history. In: Boullata, Issa J. (ed.) *Literary Structures of Religious Meaning in the Qur'ān*. Curzon, Richmond, pp. 255–76.
Nelson, K. (1985) *The Art of Reciting the Qur'an*. University of Texas Press, Austin.
Taji-Farouki, S. (ed.) (2004) *Modern Muslim Intellectuals and the Qur'an*. Oxford University Press, London.
Versteegh, K. (1997) *The Arabic Language*. Edinburgh University Press, Edinburgh.
Zwettler, M. (1978) *The Oral Tradition of the Classical Arabic Poetry: Its Characters and Implications*. Ohio State University Press, Columbus.
Zwettler, M. (1991) A mantic manifesto. In: Kugel, J. (ed.) *Poetry and Prophecy: The Beginning of a Literary Tradition*. Cornell University Press, Cornell, pp. 75–120.

CHAPTER 8

Foreign Vocabulary

Michael Carter

The Qurʾān proclaims itself to be an "Arabic Qurʾān" (*Qurʾān ʿarabī*, Q 12:2; 20:113; 39:28; 41:3; 42:7; 43:3) revealed in "a clear Arabic tongue" (*lisān ʿarabī mubīn*, Q 16:103; 26:195). In Q 16:103 and 41:44 there is an explicit contrast between "Arabic" *ʿarabī*, and "non-Arabic, foreign," *ʿajamī*. Interpretations differ on the circumstances and meaning of these last two verses, but the implications are unmistakable: this revelation was delivered in a language familiar to its audience, though it is not certain whether "Arabic" denotes the natural speech of the people around Muḥammad or the elevated diction of public address, as in the utterances of soothsayers and poets. For the purposes of this chapter the distinction is not important: medieval Muslims regarded the language of the Qurʾān as formally identical with that of poetry, differing only in its divine source of inspiration. In this framework, *mubīn* has to be understood literally as "making or being clear," and there is no need for the speculation (see Zammit 2002: 37 for references to Corriente) that it meant "falling between, intermediate," that is, between everyday Arabic and the archaic, fully inflected language of poetry.

Clear though it was intended to be, the Qurʾān contains at least five kinds of acknowledged obscurity. There are the famous "mysterious letters" at the beginning of twenty-nine *sūras*, there are the *mutashābihāt*, the "ambiguous verses," there are the numerous "strange, rare" (*gharīb*) expressions, mostly native words, which puzzled the lexicographers, there are the textual variants (*qirāʾāt*), and there are the words which look and sound "foreign" (*ʿajamī*, *aʿjamī*). The presence of foreign words in the Qurʾān was recognized from the start – by none less than the prophet's cousin and father of exegesis, ʿAbd Allāh b. ʿAbbās (d. ca. 68/686) – and the early commentators of the second/eighth century were apparently unconcerned by these non-Arabic elements (Versteegh 1993: 89ff. lists the languages mentioned by the first generation of exegetes).

This chapter takes no position on the alleged debt of Islam to earlier religions which has been inferred from these foreign words, and the striking overlap in biblical and

Qur'ānic content is left for others to interpret. Kronholm's laconically objective review of 150 years of scholarship on this theme (1982–3) is recommended as the best coverage of this battleground of conflicting opinions. All it lacks (apart from a little updating, e.g. Luxenberg 2000; Rippin 1991) is a reference to one S. Mahdihassan (for example, 1953, on *kursī*, "throne," is just one example of his work), who appears to believe that several Qur'ānic words are derived from Chinese.

Attitudes of the Medieval Arabs

The Arabs were sensitive to the foreignness of many Qur'ānic words (al-Suyūṭī lists more than a hundred; see Rippin 2003), and it behooves us to respect their *Sprachgefühl*, as they identified a number of items recognized as foreign by Western scholars also. Jeffery's account of their efforts is somewhat patronizing, and his secondary sources even more so; he cites (1938: 30, n. 4) Dvořák's notion that some etymologies were motivated by a simple desire to conceal ignorance, a criticism which is directed against Jeffery himself by Tritton (1939–42) regarding the supposed Ethiopian origin of *khayma*, "tent."

The medieval Arabs' knowledge of foreign languages is more empathetically described by Baalbaki, who shows that there were systematic criteria for distinguishing foreign words (1983; also set out in Kopf 1961, *EI2* 2004: *muʿarrab*). A word betrays its foreign origins if it has no known Arabic root, contains an abnormal sequence of phonemes or is of a shape not commonly found in native Arabic. Thus the patterns *fāʿal* and *fuʿlān* are characteristic of loan words, such as *khātam*, *ʿālam*, *burhān*, *buhtān*, *sulṭān* and most famously *qur'ān* itself. A delicate case is the name *alyasaʿ*, "Elisha," whose first element could be mistaken for the definite article *al-* (cf. Jeffery 1938: 68) but al-Farrā' (d. 207/822) (1955–72: I, 342), points out that the article is not normally prefixed to proper names beginning with the letter *yā'*.

Sībawayhi (d. ca. 180/796), the founder of grammatical science, states that "God's servants were addressed in their own way of speaking and the Qur'ān came to them in their own language" (1881–5: I, 139; 1898–1900: I, 167), echoing Q 14:4 "We have only sent apostles in the tongue of their people," but the theological implications of foreign words did not arouse his curiosity. His interest is limited to their morphology and its consequences for their inflection (1881–5: II, 18f.; 1898–1990: II, 19 = chapter 300): assimilated foreign words are fully inflected (he cites the Qur'ānic *zanjabīl*, "ginger," and *Nūḥ*, "Noah," among others), while words which do not fit into the Arabic pattern system are only partially inflected, for example, *Ibrāhīm*, "Abraham," *Firʿawn*, "Pharaoh." But he was chided for including the "Arab" prophet Hūd among the foreign names! Elsewhere in Sībawayhi's *Kitāb* (1881–5: II, 375–6; 1898–1900: II, 342–3 = chapters 524–5) he discusses the assimilation (or not) of foreign words to native patterns and the phonetic changes the borrowings may undergo, but again he mingles Qur'ānic and secular vocabulary indiscriminately.

The Qur'ānic passage which caused the most difficulty is Q 41:44, where Muḥammad, probably in answer to an objection from his audience, asks a rhetorical question, "What, a foreigner (*ʿajamī*) and an Arab?," usually taken to mean, "How can a foreigner talk to an Arab?," affirming that the revelation was accomplished without the participation of non-Arabs.

The Arab responses to this varied widely, and are summarized by Kopf 1956: 40–5; Jeffery 1938: 4–11; Rippin 1981, 1983, 2002; Gilliot 1990: 95–110; and Zammit 2002: 51–5; Arabic sources include al-Ṭabarī 1969: I, 13–20; al-Rāzī 1957–8: I, 134–52; Ibn Fāris 1964: 57–62; al-Jawālīqī 1942: 3–5; al-Rāghib 1972; al-Suyūṭī 1951: I, 136–42; 1972: I, 266–8; see also al-Suyūṭī 1926; 1982, on which see Rippin 2003.

1. Abū ʿUbayda (d. 209/824–5) denied the existence of foreign words altogether in the Qurʾān; even the thought was blasphemous to him. His intention may have been to assert the linguistic and cultural independence of the Arabs from the Persians in particular, and it might also be relevant that he was a member of the Khārijī sect, which would favor an exclusive approach to the Qurʾān.

2. Al-Shāfiʿī (d. 204/820) argued that the alleged borrowings might look foreign but they are genuine Arabic, although not found in every dialect. In any case such a (supradialectal) breadth of vocabulary was beyond the powers of all but prophets. Given the fundamental role of language in al-Shāfiʿī's legal theory, his position can be seen as an attempt to eliminate non-Arabic data from the textual sources of the law.

3. Abū ʿUbayd (d. 224/838) quotes with approval several early authorities saying that there are indeed foreign words in the Qurʾān, but they were naturalized in Arabic long before the revelation, in which he was followed by, among others, Abū Ḥātim al-Rāzī (d. 322/933–4), Ibn Fāris (d. 395/1004), Abū Manṣūr al-Thaʿālibī (d. 429/1038), al-Jawālīqī (d. 539/1144), ʿAbd al-Raḥmān al-Thaʿālibī (d. 873/1468) and al-Suyūṭī (d. 911/1505; see Rippin 2003). This is essentially a philological approach (Abū ʿUbayd consciously distinguishes it from that of the lawyers), concerned mainly with the linguistic form of the words rather than the legal or theological aspects. Al-Jawālīqī, for instance, disposes of the whole question in just over a page, and freely intersperses Qurʾānic and non-Qurʾānic words in the body of his work. One effect, if not the primary aim of this position, was to refute claims that Muḥammad depended on outside informants, or that Arabic was insufficient to convey the message without the aid of loan words.

The earlier al-Thaʿālibī, a Persian by birth, represents a transitional stage (or perhaps merely an individual viewpoint) between Abū ʿUbayda and al-Ṭabarī. Chapter 29 (1861: 162–5) of his *Fiqh al-lugha* begins with a list of words "whose Persianness has been forgotten but which are still spoken and used in Arabic," a curious anthology of purely secular terms, hardly any of them looking Persian in the least. Section 2 of the chapter, entitled "Words which mostly could not exist in Persian," consists of thirty-four entirely "Islamic" neologisms of the kind we shall meet below, *muʾmin*, *kāfir*, *miḥrāb* and so forth, or uniquely Qurʾānic words such as *jibt*, *sijjīn*, and *salsabīl*. Section 3 identifies seven words which are the same in Persian and Arabic: *tannūr*, "oven," *khamīr*, "leavened dough," *zamān*, "time," *dīn*, "religion," *kanz*, "treasure," *dīnār*, "dinar" and *dirham* "dirham," and the two concluding sections describe words which the Arabs were "obliged" to borrow from Persian and Greek, with Qur'ānic items in both, but, significantly, only of a religiously neutral character, for example, *ibrīq, yāqūt, zanjabīl, misk, kāfūr, qisṭās, qinṭār*. If (following Kopf 1956: 29, n. 5), we replace his *zamān* and *khamīr* in section 3 (neither of them Qur'ānic) with the orthographically very similar *rummān*, "pomegranate," and *khamr*, "wine," found in the Qur'ān, we may have an attempt to limit the linguistic universality of the Qur'ān by quarantining those seven international words, and acknowledging a number of trivial borrowings, at the same time as reinforcing the wholly Arab nature of the technical Islamic vocabulary.

4. The great exegete and historian al-Ṭabarī (d. 310/923) inverted the principle that "in the Qur'ān is something of every language" into "some of the things in the Qur'ān are common to all languages." Consequently words which look foreign are really native Arabic and the resemblance is coincidental. A word like *tannūr* (Q 11:42; 23:27), "oven," is found in all languages, and there is no way of telling which one may have been derived from another. It was necessary for al-Ṭabarī's concept of history that Arabic should be seen as independent of other languages; even more than al-Shāfiʿī, he recognized that Islam was founded on the written record of its past, a much wider ambition than al-Shāfiʿī's juridical focus.

5. A modification of this view is credited to one of al-Suyūṭī's informants (accepting the correction by Kopf 1956: 30, n. 3, of the reading in Jeffery 1938: 9 of al-Suyūṭī 1951: I, 137) where it is stated that when there is an identical form in another language it might well have been used before Arabic, because Arabic is the most copious and accommodating of all languages.

6. Al-Juwaynī (presumably the teacher of al-Ghazālī who died 478/1085) offers a sociological justification for foreign words. In order to make the message more persuasive God had to promise great luxuries such as the silks and brocades mentioned in the Qur'ān, which only became known to the Arabs through their contact with other nations.

7. An anonymous source in al-Suyūṭī argues that a few loan words in the Qur'ān do not make it foreign any more than a Persian poem ceases to be Persian just because it has Arabic words in it. Al-Jāḥiẓ (d. 255/868–9) produced the idiosyncratic theory that the presence of loan words was intended to heighten the contrast between the native (i.e. pagan) tradition of poetry and the revealed religion, and they were one of the signs of inimitability (*iʿjāz*, cf. Hamzaoui in Zammit 2002: 52, n. 113).

The situation today probably ranges over the same spectrum. In Jeffery's time al-Ṭabarī's position was "seriously defended at the present day by the ultra-orthodox" (1938: 8), and some sixty years later it is reported that modern Islamists firmly oppose the idea of foreign words (Zammit 2002: 54). The Egyptian editor of al-Jawālīqī (first published 1942) makes a point of stating in his footnotes for every Qur'ānic word that its mere presence in the Qur'ān proves that it is not foreign! But this extreme position is not universal. One randomly sampled Internet discussion of "foreign words in the Qur'an" simply reproduces Abū ʿUbayd's opinion.

Consideration should also be given (Jeffery 1938: 9, n 3 dismisses it as irrelevant) to the fact that dialect words in the Qurʾān posed a similar problem, since there was an obvious inconsistency in the appearance of words from up to fifty dialects (the highest estimate, which included foreign languages) in a revelation delivered to a Qurayshī dialect speaker. In fact, our sources usually do not turn to the problem of foreign languages until they have dealt with the dialects, and among the examples are words classified as foreign by Jeffery, e.g., *arīka*, "couch," and *masṭūr*, "written," suggesting that there was indeed something exotic about these items.

The procedures for detecting non-Qurayshī features were similar to those applied to foreign words: the tell-tale loss of the glottal stop, and unassimilated verb forms such as *yuḍlil* for *yuḍilla*, "lead astray," were seen as indicators of the Ḥijāzī (= Qurayshī) dialect (al-Suyūṭī 1951: I, 136, *naw*ʿ38).

Bibliographical Resources

The single most influential treatise on foreign words remains the great synthesis of Jeffery (1938), whose bibliography is an almost complete repertoire of previous scholarship. Additions to his work have been relatively few and insubstantial, though some of his etymologies have been disputed (notably the Persian; see Widengren 1955) and the inventory of borrowings modified.

General reviews of the topic are in Schall (1982), Gilliot (1990), Gilliot and Larcher (2003), Rippin (2002), and Zammit (2002). It goes without saying that the *Encyclopaedia of Islām* (*EI2* 2004) and the *Encyclopaedia of the Qurʾān* have articles on many individual words, though they seldom go far beyond Jeffery.

For tracing the entire Qurʾānic vocabulary there are now CD and on-line concordances (see Rippin 1999–2000). The old *Dictionary and Glossary of the Koran* by Penrice (1873) is still useful, as its many reprints testify, but the best traditional resource remains the *Muʿjam al-mufahras* of ʿAbd al-Bāqī (1945), which quotes the words in context. However, consistency is not always achieved with proper names which are morphologically obscure. Thus Yaḥyā, "John," Sulaymān, "Solomon," and Isḥāq, "Isaac," are entered under "Arabic" roots *ḥ-y-w*, *s-l-m*, and *s-ḥ-q* respectively, while Yaʿqūb, "Jacob," Ilyās, "Elijah," and others are listed strictly alphabetically, even though Yaʿqūb has a recognized Arabic pattern.

The Scope of Jeffery and Supplementary Studies

Zammit (2002: 55ff.) has counted 322 words in Jeffery's *Foreign Vocabulary*. He calculates that of the 256 borrowed common nouns and adjectives in the Qurʾān 75 percent are of Northwest Semitic origin (Hebrew, Aramaic, Syriac), and of the 66 proper names, 80 percent are from Northwest Semitic. A further 13 percent of the common words and 12 percent of the proper names have a South Arabian origin, leaving 12 percent of common words unclassified. The residual proper names are: one North Arabian (*al-raqīm*), three Greek (*rūm*, "Byzantium," *shiʿrā*, "Sirius," *Quraysh*, "shark") and two problematical items, *tasnīm* and *al-jūdī*; further below on all these. However, this arithmetical precision is compromised by the fact that in about half the cases it is impossible to determine whether the loan is from Aramaic or Syriac. These figures also mark for us the limit of the relevance of Zammit's book to the present article, as he excludes all borrowed words from his lexical corpus (2002: 57).

Additions to Jeffery are dispersed, and not all of them will have been caught here. Margoliouth (1939) proffered eight new words: *minsaʾa* (Q 34:14), "scepter," a transformation from the Hebrew *mishʿeneth*, "staff, scepter"; *lam yatasanna(h)* (Q 2:259), "has not changed," from the Hebrew root *sh-n-y*, "to change"; *nataqnā* (Q 7:171), "we shook," from Hebrew or Aramaic *n-t-q* with the sense of pulling up roots; *ḥusbān* in one of its appearances (Q 18:40) has a Hebrew sense of a device or machine (cf. 2 Chronicles 26:15), that is, a *ḥusbān* from heaven which will render the land more fertile. Four of the words are said to be of Ethiopian origin: *asbāb* in Q 40:38, meaning "guardhouses" (but see Paret 1971: note on Q 18:84 for an alternative explanation); *rahwan* (Q 44:23) in the sense of "open" for the crossing of the Red Sea; *taʿālaw* (Q 44:18, also 27:30), "to disobey, revolt against"; and *salaqa* (Q 33:19), "to throw down," connected with the old Arabic causative *salqā* (= *alqā*), "to throw down." Two of these, *minsaʾa* and *rahw*, had already raised suspicions among the Arabs (but Jeffery 1938: 34f., calls them "obviously Arabic"), while Luxenberg (2000: 178) arrived independently at the same derivation for *yatasanna(h)*, another word which the Muslims found difficult.

Other nominated loans are *muṣayṭir* (Q 88:22) "having power over," which Ahrens (1930: 20) connects with Hebrew *sōṭer*, "overseer, officer" (cognate with the word for writing which underlies Qurʾānic *saṭara* and derivatives, see Jeffery 1938: 169f.); *ghurāb* (Q 5:31, twice), "crow," perhaps connected with Latin *corvus* (*EI2* 2004: "Ghurāb"); *qawārīr* (Q 27:44; 76:15, 16) "glass [vessels]," from Ethiopic according to Schall (1982: 147) (collocated in Q 27:44 with another Ethiopic loan, *ṣarḥ* "tower," see below); *saqar* (Q 54:48; 74:26, 27, 42) "hell," from Syriac *shegārā*, the "raging fire," in the Daniel story (O'Shaughnessy 1961: 463); *sijn* (several times in *sūra* 12, once elsewhere, Q 26:29), "prison," has been traced to Latin *signum*, either via Greek *signon* (according to *EI2* 2004: "Si͟djn") or else through Greek to Coptic (Schall 1982: 148, with references); *akhlada* (Q 7:176), very obscure, is connected by Schub with Hebrew *ḥeled* denoting the (limited) duration of life, the world as transient, as in Psalms 39:6 and 49:2; [*lan*] *yaḥūra* (Q 81:14), "it will [not] return," was listed as foreign in medieval sources (but not by Jeffery 1938: 116), and may be related to the South Arabian *ḥawrāwu* "immigrant" or the Ethiopic root *ḥ-w-r*, denoting "settle"; Penrice (1873) remarks that *sarmad* (Q 28:71, 72), "eternal," is a combination of Persian and Arabic.

Further candidates are *miḥrāb* (used five times, see Paret 1971: on Q 3:37), "niche in a mosque," which has strong links with South Arabia, especially considering that the non-Qurʾānic *minbar*, "pulpit," has also been put forward as a possible loan from Ethiopic; for *ghassāq* (Q 38:57; 78:25), "purulent, foetid," a connection with Hebrew *ʿashoq* and Syriac *ʿashoqa* denoting torture is proposed (Schreiner 1977). This word defeated Muslim attempts at explanation and, with something approaching desperation, it was said to be of Tokharian (Gilliot 1990: 107, n. 1), Coptic or Turkish origin

(Jeffery 1938: 29, and see below). Rippin (1990) adds *ʿarim* (Q 34:16, cf. also Paret 1971 on this verse), "dam," as a South Arabian borrowing.

The history of some loan words has been revised. *Zabāniya* (Q 96:18), a name of the guardians of hell, is from Syriac according to Jeffery (1938), but has since been given an Iranian etymology, *zendānbān*, "prison warder," superior to an earlier conjecture reported by Jeffery, *zabāna*, "tongue of flame" (see *EI2* 2004: "al-Zabāniya," for reference to Eilers). Iranian precedents are claimed for *falak*, "heavenly sphere," by Pagliari (1956) (Jeffery 1938 is unhelpful on *falak*, but see *EI2* 2004: "Falak," for the complex history of this word, which is not related to *fulk* "ship," on which see below).

With *ʿilliyyūn* (Q 83:18), Margoliouth (1939) reads the first letter as *gh*, corresponding to Syriac *gelayūnā*, a sort of tablet (cf. Isaiah 8:1), which would render the sense of the register of good deeds usually ascribed to this word. For a long time it was assumed that *tawrāt*, "Torah," (eighteen times) is a direct Hebrew loan, with only spelling problems to explain away. But this has been rejected (see *EI2* 2004: "Tawrāt") in favor of the view that it is some kind of hybrid of Hebrew *Torah* and Aramaic *Oriyyah*. Luxenberg (2000: 88ff.) nevertheless revives the original etymology with the inventive theory that what looks like a *yāʾ* in the consonantal spelling *twryh* is merely a tick to mark that the stress falls on that syllable.

Luxenberg offers many other ingenious explanations, mostly based on textual emendations. A typical specimen is *muzjāt* (Q 12:88), "not worth much," explained (2000: 72ff.) as a misreading of the Syriac root *raggī*, "to moisten," that is, "fresh, moist [fruit]" after Genesis 43:11. To presume such a degree of orthographical confusion is out of keeping with what is known about the general level of accuracy in Muslim scholarship, though in this he has Bellamy (1991–2002) on his side, see below, also Margoliouth (1939), who amends *bi-ḥusbān*, "with a reckoning," in Q 55:4, to *yusabbiḥāni*, "they [two] praise." However, Luxenberg does offer (2000: 36–42) an attractive explanation for the appearance of words like *ḥanīf*, "primitive monotheist," with a terminal *alif* implying the dependent case where that is not syntactically plausible; such words, he suggests, were originally borrowed with their Syriac definite article still attached, so *ibrāhīm ḥanīf^{an}* reproduces Syriac *abrahām ḥanpā*, "Abraham, the Ḥanīf."

Some words in Jeffery are no longer classified as loans, notably *ʿifrīt* (Q 27:39), "demon" (see Fischer 1904: 871f., overlooked by Jeffery 1938); *munāfiq*, of frequent use, "hypocrite" (Adang 2002 has a very different explanation which would deny that it is a foreign word at all); *mathānī* (Q 15:87, 39:24), obscure but referring to some part of the revelation (Rubin 2003b states that it is not a loan word). Tritton (1939–42) was not convinced that *ḥabl*, (used seven times), "rope," is ultimately a borrowing from Akkadian, as it seemed to him unlikely that the camel-driving bedouin would lack a word of their own for this. Boneschi (1945), with no reference to Jeffery, argues that *malak* (frequent use), "angel," is a native Arab word from the metathesized root *ʾ-l-k*, "send" (*EI2* 2004: "Malāʾika," prefers Jeffery and adds a Ugaritic cognate *mlʾk*).

A number of other words will be dealt with below, including disputed proper names such as *jibt* and *al-raqīm*, which have since been demoted to common nouns, and others which have been accounted for as textual corruptions or arbitrary coinages.

The too hard basket: it is greatly to Jeffery's credit that words which he was unable to account for are on the whole still unexplained, e.g., *abābīl* (Q 105:3) "flocks of birds?";

al-sāhira (Q 79:14), meaning unknown; *sundus* (Q 18:30, 44:53, 76:21), glossed as "fine silk" (three etymologies offered for this ancient borrowing); *qaswara* (Q 74:51), "lion?" (but explained by Bellamy 1996: 198 as a misspelling of Syriac *pantorā*, from Greek *panther*); *qiṭṭ* (Q 38:15), "judge's decision"; *muhl* (Q 18:29; 44:45; 70:8), "fused brass" or "dregs of oil."

Brunschvig draws attention to a number of words and roots which are not found at all in the Qur'ān. Perhaps the most useful result of this lipographical exercise is the discovery that the commonest verb for "to praise" is *sabbaḥa* and its derivatives (a Syriac borrowing, see below), which outnumbers the better known *ḥamida* (as in *al-ḥamdu li-llāhi*, "praise be to God" and the names Aḥmad and Muḥammad), while other synonyms are lacking altogether (*madaḥa*, *athnā*, and there are just four instances of *majīd*, "glorious, praiseworthy," only two as epithets of God). This may reflect some influence from Jewish or Christian liturgies (Jeffery 1938 favors the Christians).

In a similarly negative vein it has been observed that God is never called by the Christian and Jewish titles of "Rock" (Köbert 1961a: 204–5) or "Shepherd" (Künstlinger 1928–30). Köbert (1961a) however sees the enigmatic word *ṣamad*, applied to God in Q 112:2, as implying the sense of a solid rock expressed in the cognate *ṣamda*. This is probably incompatible with Schall (1984–6: 313) that *ṣamad* is related to *ṣindīd* < **ṣimdīd*, "a noble chief."

A Classified Presentation of Jeffery's Data

The aim here is to give an overall impression of the extent and diversity of the borrowings and the equally extensive and diverse range of opinions about them. The inevitable parade of words (and it is only a selection) will be a panoramic review of the whole army rather than a personal inspection of individual soldiers, and the reader may well end up with no more knowledge of the specifics than a field marshall has of his troops.

Barr's warning (1968: chapter 7) against the dictionary-hunting kind of etymology is still valid: apparent lexical equivalences are unreliable, and he provides figures showing how related languages can vary widely in their shared vocabulary, including a list of some quite common words which are different in all the Semitic languages. The risk of misinterpretation is at its greatest with roots in one language which have the opposite meaning in another (Barr 1968: 173), so Arabic *'-b-y*, "to refuse," but Hebrew "to be willing," Arabic *w-th-b*, "to jump," Hebrew and others "to sit down" (a legendary isogloss which led an Arab from the North to jump off a cliff when asked by his South Arabian host to take a seat).

Loan words may be categorized in three ways: by etymology, by date of borrowing or by theme. The last will be left to the reader to extract from the lists below. Jeffery (1938: 39ff.) sets out his own etymological classification:

1 Words with no Arabic connection, e.g., *istabraq*, "silk brocade"; *zanjabīl*, "ginger"; *firdaws*, "Paradise"; *namāriq*, "cushions" etc. Such words rarely assimilate and so fail to become productive roots.

2 Words for which there are Arabic roots but not in the Qurʾānic meaning, e.g., *bāraka*, "to bless"; *subḥān*, "praise"; *ṣawāmiʿ*, "cloisters"; *fāṭir*, "creator," etc. These may assimilate and become productive, e.g., *sabbaḥa*, "to praise," denominative from *subḥān*, "praise," which also has a regular verbal noun *tasbīḥ*, "act of praising" and participle *musabbiḥ*, "praising."
3 Words which have had their natural Arabic meanings extended, e.g., *nūr* "[spiritual] light"; *kalima* "word, logos."
4 Words which defy explanation, e.g., *abābīl*, "flock of birds?," *qaswara*, "lion?"

From this point the Qurʾānic locations will be indicated only in special cases (they are all given in Jeffery 1938). Translations are either *ad hoc* or taken from Jeffery (1938), as is the alphabetical order, in which he follows al-Suyūṭī, doubtless for the same reason, namely that foreign words cannot always be arranged by roots in the Arab manner.

The following chronological arrangement groups the words into (1) ancient borrowings; (2) pre-Islamic borrowings; and (3) borrowings made during Muḥammad's lifetime. This division is implicit in Schall (1982) and Zammit (2002: 57f.), who isolates ten of the words in Jeffery's list as ancient and 124 as attested before Islam. The dating is often subjective, and all we can do here is to follow Jeffery's judgment, leaving several scores of words unclassifiable where he pronounces no verdict. Common nouns and adjectives will be dealt with first, then proper names.

Ancient Borrowings

It is well known that the Arabs had contacts with the surrounding civilizations as traders, subjects, and mercenaries. The first reference to "Arabs" occurs in a cuneiform inscription of the ninth century BCE, and a small number of borrowings can safely be attributed to this ancient period. Zimmern found as many as forty-five words in the Qurʾān of Akkadian origin which had passed through Aramaic (Zammit 2002: 57, n. 140), nearly all of which are mentioned by Jeffery, though not always with acceptance. The following are those which seem to be authentic old loans, in some cases directly from Sumerian or Akkadian or, less precisely, "Mesopotamia," or from unknown languages:

> *abb*, "herbage" (Akk.); *umma*, "community" (Sum.); *bāb*, "door, gate" (Mesopot.); *tannūr*, "oven"; *dirham* (Mesopot. area), the silver coin; *sullam*, "ladder" (Mesopot.); *siwār*, "bracelet" (Akk.); *ṭabaq*, "stage or degree" Akk.); *mawākhir*, "(ships) plowing the waves" (direct from Mesopotamia, but rejected by Luxenberg [2000: 213f.] in favor of a Syriac origin); *nuḥās*, "brass" (non-Semitic, direct or via Aramaic); *yam*, "sea" (non-Semitic source).

Other Qurʾānic words which may be very early borrowings, if not already common Semitic, are *ajr*, "reward, wage"; *baraʾa*, "create"; *bashshara*, "bring good news"; *banā*, "build"; *tijāra*, "commerce"; *rummān*, "pomegranate"; *zayt*, "oil" (possibly non-Semitic);

sūq, "street, market"; *sakar*, "intoxicating drink"; *malik*, "king" (Jeffery is noncommittal on this). The word *baʿl*, "husband, master," also "Baal," is found in all the Semitic languages, and appears in pre-Islamic poetry, but there is no way of telling whether it is a native word or came into Arabic from its northern relatives. Since it is recorded in South Arabian inscriptions it must have been in circulation long before Islam.

Though rather limited, this group of words gives some impression of the cultural influence upon the Arabs. We have the notion of a community, *umma*, some seafaring terms, signs of commercial relations (*tijāra*, *sūq*) and some metal-working and construction activity.

Pre-Islamic Borrowings

Jeffery frequently asserts with confidence that a word came into Arabic well before Islam. In the lists below words are grouped by the language of origin favored by Jeffery.

There were close contacts in the Christian era between Arabs, Greeks, Romans, Copts, Ethiopians, South Arabians, and Persians, and Mecca lay at the heart of a polyglot commercial network involving all these nations. In al-Ḥijr, one of the dominant trading centers of Arabia (and mentioned in Q 15:80, after which the *sūra* is named), inscriptions dating to the third century CE have been preserved in Hebrew, Aramaic, Nabataean, Greek, Latin, all the major varieties of Old North Arabian and one, from the third century CE, which is claimed to be the oldest dated inscription in Classical Arabic.

From Ethiopic:

bighāl, "mules"; *jalābīb*, "outer garments"; *ḥizb*, "group, party"; *khubz*, "bread"; *khayma*, "tent"; *ribḥ*, "profit" (if not S. Arabian); *raqq*, "scroll of parchment"; *mishkāt*, "niche"; *ṣarḥ*, "tower"; *qalam*, "pen" (ultimately an Indo-European word); *qamīṣ*, "shirt" (ultimately Gk.); *malak*, "angel" (rejected by Boneschi, see above).

From South Arabian:

tubbaʿ, royal title; *raḥmān*, "merciful"; *shirk*, "polytheism"; *ṣuḥuf*, "pages, leaves"; *ṣalawāt*, "places of worship"; *ṣawāmiʿ*, "cloisters, cells"; *ṣūra*, "image"; *wathan*, "idol".

Since Ethiopians and South Arabians were always in close contact, their loans will be taken together. There are terms for writing and commerce and some basic religious concepts, all of which are assumed to be familiar to the Arabs long before Muḥammad started preaching. It may seem strange that a word for "tent" has to be borrowed (Tritton is skeptical that it is a borrowing at all), but it might have denoted a different kind of shelter from the *bayt shaʿr*, "house of hair," in which the bedouin had lived for centuries. The word *ribḥ*, "profit," may belong here too, as a borrowing from the south, though Jeffery himself makes no judgment about a date.

One word from this region which later became prominent is *ḥizb*, "group, party," borrowed from Ethiopic and found also in South Arabian inscriptions. It was revived in the nineteenth century as the term for a political party but it never lost its other, pejorative meaning of a splinter group or faction.

From Persian:

ibrīq, "water jug"; *arā'ik*, "couches [in paradise]"; *istabraq*, "silk brocade"; *junāḥ*, "sin, crime"; *ḥūr*, "black-eyed (Houri)" (Luxenberg 2000: 221ff. disagrees); *rawḍa*, "garden"; *zūr*, "falsehood"; *surādiq*, "awning, tent cover"; *sard*, "chain mail"; *fīl*, "elephant"; *kanz*, "treasure"; *misk*, "musk"; *namāriq*, "cushions"; *wazīr*, "minister, counselor".

These terms hint at an acquaintance with higher political systems and a degree of luxury; the words for "sin" and "falsehood" probably have a political rather than a religious connotation.

From Greek or Latin (all via Syriac):

balad, "country" (*palatium* or *palation*); *fulk*, "ship" (*epholkion*); *quraysh*, "shark" (*karkharias*).

The proper name *al-rūm*, "Byzantine Empire," (see below) confirms what we already know, that the Arabs were a border phenomenon in a very large empire. It is only the word *quraysh*, "shark," which is traced to Greek, of course, not the Arab tribe Quraysh which took that totemic name.

From Aramaic, often as the intermediary for other languages such as Hebrew, Persian and Greek, as indicated below:

aḥbār, "learned doctors" (Heb.); *burūj*, "towers" (Gk.); *bunyān*, "building"; *tawwāb*, "the relenting one," i.e. God (Akk.); *jund*, "army" (Pers.); *khinzīr*, "pig"; *sajada*, "to worship"; *sirbāl*, "garment" (Pers.); *saṭara*, "to write"; *sikkīn*, "knife"; *salām*, "peace" (Heb.); *silsila*, "chain"; *sunbul*, "ear of corn"; *shahr*, "month"; *ṣanam*, "idol"; *ʿatīq*, "ancient"; *ʿarūb*, "pleasing" (Heb.); *ʿankabūt*, "spider"; *qaṣr*, "castle" (Gk. from Lat.); *kāhin*, "soothsayer" (Heb.); *kataba* "to write" (Heb.); *masjid* "place of worship" (borrowed independently of *sajada*); *miskīn*, "poor" (Akk.); *manfūsh*, "teased, carded (wool)" (Akk.); *nabī*, "prophet"; *warda*, "rose" (Pers.).

From Syriac, also an intermediary for other languages:

amshāj, "mingled" (plur., cf. *mizāj*); *buhtān*, "slander, calumny"; *biyaʿ*, "places of worship"; *jābiya*, "cistern"; *ḥiṣn*, "fortress; *khaṭi'a*, "to sin, do wrong"; *khamr*, "wine"; *dīnār*, "gold coin" (Pers. from Gk.); *ribbiyyūn*, "myriads"; *raḥīq*, "strong [wine]"; *rizq*, "bounty" (Pers.); *zanjabīl*, "ginger" (Pers.); *zawj*, "[one of] a pair" (Gk.); *zayt*, "oil" (pre-Semitic); *sabbaḥa*, "to praise"; *sabīl*, "way"; *sulṭān*, "authority"; *sūq*, "street" (Akk.);

shīʿa, "sect, party"; *tīn*, "fig" (North Sem); *fājir*, "wicked"; *fakhkhār*, "clay"; *firdaws*, "paradise" (Gk. from Pers.); *qudus*, "holiness"(North Sem); *qarya*, "village"; *qisṭās*, "balance, scale" (Gk.); *qissīs*, "priest"; *kāfūr*, "camphor" (Pers.); *kayl*, "measure"; *mizāj*, "tempering"(a variant of *amshāj*, "mingled," see above); *nūn*, "fish"; *yāqūt*, "ruby".

The Aramaic and the Syriac borrowings jointly testify to a long-standing cultural interaction: material terms are frequent, but it is the religious terms which now begin to stand out. Many other pre-Islamic words are attributed to Jewish or Christian sources, though not conclusively to either, including:

āya, "verse (of the Qurʾān)"; *janna*, "garden (of Eden)"; *ḥanān*, "grace"; *ḥikma*, "wisdom"; *khātam*, "seal"; *rabb*, "lord, master"; *rujz*, "wrath"; *zabūr*, "the Psalter"; *zujāja*, "glass vessel"; *sāʿa*, "hour [of judgment]"; *sifr*, "book"; *safara*, "scribes"; *ṣalaba*, "to crucify"; *ṣallā*, "to pray"; *ṣawm*, "fasting"; *ʿabd*, "servant (of God)"; *ʿālam*, "world, universe"; *ʿīd*, "festival"; *qurbān*, "sacrifice, offering"; *madīna*, "city"; *yaqīn*, "certain".

The source of the word *allāh*, "god," says Jeffery (1938: 66) "must be found in one of the older religions." His explanation of the unique vocative *allāhumma*, "O God," can now be corrected. It was once thought to be connected with Hebrew *elohīm* (Jeffery 1938: 67, from Margoliouth); however, in Old North Arabian inscriptions (eighth century BCE to third century CE) the form *ʾlhm* occurs at the beginning of prayers, and this would seem to represent the same suffix as we find in *allāhumma* (*EI2* 2004: "Thamūdic").

Contemporary Borrowings

These are words which are not attested before Islam and can best be explained as direct borrowings during the period of Muḥammad's mission. There was intimate contact with other religious communities in the decades surrounding the Islamic revelation. Arabs mixed with Jews, with Christians of all kinds (including Ethiopians and Copts) and with Zoroastrians and others in Mesopotamia, and Muslim sources do not deny that Muḥammad may have received information from members of these religions, some of whom are personally identified (see Gilliot 2002).

Ethiopic and/or South Arabian:

aʿrāf, "al-Aʿrāf" (obscure name, but see Bellamy below); *āmana*, "to believe"; *injīl*, "the Gospel"; *burhān*, "proof"; *jahannam*, "hell"; *ḥawāriyyūn*, "disciples"; *rajīm*, "stoned, cursed"; *ṣuwāʿ*, "drinking cup"; *fāṭir*, "creator"; *fatḥ*, "judgment, decision"; *kibriyāʾ*, "glory"; *māʾida*, "table"; *mursā*, "harbor"; *munāfiq*, "hypocrite".

Important religious terms are now making their appearance. The form *injīl* can only be accounted for by assuming that the Greek *euangelion* had passed through Ethiopic. The hapax legomenon, *ṣuwāʿ*, "drinking cup," occurs in the Joseph story (*sūra* 12), and is one of several Ethiopic borrowings in the same *sūra* (*burhān*, *fāṭir* and the much earlier loan word, *qamīṣ*, "shirt").

Persian:

barzakh, "barrier, partition".

Greek:

iblīs, "the devil" (questionable: see below).

Aramaic:

ussisa, "was founded"; *bahīma*, "animal"; *tāba*, "to repent"; *tatbīr*, "destruction"; *darasa*, "to study" (Heb.); *zakkā*, "to purify"; *zakāt*, "alms"; *sabt*, "sabbath"; *ṭahara*, "to purify"; *ʿazzara*, "to help"; *minhāj*, "way" (Heb.); *nubuwwa*, "prophethood" (Heb.).

Syriac:

asbāṭ, "the tribes (of Israel)" (Heb.); *aslama*, "to devote oneself (to God)"; *baṭala*, "to be false"; *tajallā*, "to appear in glory"; *rabbānī*, "rabbi, teacher"; *sijill*, "seal"(Gk.); *suḥt*, "unlawful"; *sirāj*, "lamp"(Pers.); *salwā*, "quail"; *sūra*, "chapter of Qurʾān"; *sīmā*, "mark, sign"(Gk.); *shuhadāʾ*, "martyrs"; *ṣibgha*, "baptism" (but see Bellamy below); *ṭabaʿa*, "to seal"; *ṭūbā*, "good fortune"; *ṭūr*, "mountain"; *falaq*, "to split"; *qurʾān*, "recitation"; *qiyāma*, "resurrection"; *maʿīn*, "flowing water" (Heb.); *maqālīd*, "keys"(Gk.); *milla*, "religion"; *mann*, "manna".

Uncertain (Jewish or Christian) and undated:

amr, "command, affair"; *ṣadaqa*, "alms"; *ʿadn*, "Eden"; *kafara*, "to atone"; *kursī*, "throne"; *malakūt*, "kingdom, dominion".

By this stage the terminology of the Islamic revelation is approaching maturity, and to complete the process the vocabulary will be supplemented by neologisms created within Arabic itself.

New Meanings

Jeffery's (1938: 39f.) third category comprises native roots which have acquired a new religious sense, for example, *nūr*, "light"; *rūḥ*, "spirit"; *umm*, "metropolis" (Q 6:92 *umm al-qurā*, "mother of the towns"); *nafs*, "soul"; *kalima*, "word" (= Jesus); *rasūl*, "messenger"; *yawm*, "day (of judgment)" and *sāʿa*, "hour (of judgment)," all of them attributed to Christian usage (the last item is out of place here, as Jeffery lists it again later as a pure loan word). *Mathal*, "parable," may belong here, as the root is undoubtedly common Semitic, but the usage is biblical and Jeffery inclines to a Syriac inspiration. Jewish influence is credited for *zakāt*, "alms" (from a root denoting purity, unless Muḥammad himself coined it, see below); *ṭahara*, "make clean"; *sakīna*, "the Shekina" (possibly mediated by Syriac); *ṣiddīq*, "person of integrity"; it has also been suggested

(*EI2* 2004: "Khalḳ") that *khalaqa*, "to create," owes this sense to the Jewish usage of its Hebrew cognate. Perhaps *qibla*, "direction of prayer," belongs here too, as it would surely have been associated with the Jewish practice of praying towards Jerusalem.

It should not be overlooked that the pagan vocabulary was also a source of terms, among them *ḥajja*, "to perform a pilgimage"; *ṭawāf*, "circumambulation of the Kaʿba" (the name of the Kaʿba is itself pre-Islamic); *ṣawm*, "fasting" (a native word according to Tritton 1939–42, against Jeffery 1938: 201f.); *dhabaḥa*, "to sacrifice"; *dahr*, "time, eternity"; *ajal*, "term, predestined end"; *ḥasra*, "sorrow, regret"; and *ijāra/istijāra*, "giving or seeking protection," all of them expressions of a pagan view of life which was absorbed into the Islamic paradigm.

The result was a fusion of vocabularies, pagan, Jewish, Christian, and new coinages, which eventually achieved recognition as technical terms, variously called *kalimāt islāmiyya ʿarabiyya*, "Arabic Islamic words," (al-Rāzī), *alfāẓ islāmiyya* "Islamic expressions" (al-Suyūṭī 1972: I, 294–303 = *nawʿ* 20) or *asbāb islāmiyya*, "Islamic matters" (Ibn Fāris 1964: 78–80). Though not regarded as foreign by the Arabs, they do include words which Jeffery classified as such, e.g., *muʾmin*, "believer"; *munāfiq*, "hypocrite"; *kafara*, "to deny God"; *sujūd*, "prostrating in prayer"; *zakāt*, "alms," etc., all of them used in senses previously unknown to the Arabs.

The religious vocabulary is now fully established, and the study of individual terms and concepts becomes part of the history of Islam rather than of A[illegible] the scope of this chapter to examine particular words any further, b[illegible] ing articles will be mentioned as a guide to future studies. Faris and [illegible] *ḥanīf*, "primitive monotheist" (1939), remains a model of detailed h[illegible] tion, and is now counterbalanced by Rippin's 1991 warning agains[illegible] the early manifestations of Arab monotheism. *Dīn*, "religion," h[illegible] history, and Waardenburg's nuanced account (1981) of its meanin[illegible] period of revelation can be applied to other terms, among them *islā*[illegible] 1971). O'Shaughnessy (1961) sheds light on the evolution of religi[illegible] his review of the words for "Hell" in their approximate chronologi[illegible] natives: *saʿīr* (eighteeen times), *ḥuṭama* (Q 104:4, 5, evidently a bo[illegible]) *hāwiya* (Q 101:9) and *laẓā* (Q 92:14), and three are loan words: *jahannam* (seventy-seven times), *saqar* (Q 54:48, 74:26, 27, 42) and *jaḥīm* (twenty[illegible] Zammit (2002: 595) disagrees on this last. Finally, Denny's 1977 s[illegible] key Islamic terms includes several of the neologisms mentioned a[illegible] that they should not be taken in isolation.

Proper Names and Problem Words

Proper names (Zammit 2002: 55 counts sixty-six of them) are diff[illegible] biblical ones. Their Arabic forms can make it impossible to determin[illegible] came directly from the Bible or via Jewish or Christian oral source[illegible] original might have been in the first place. The name of Gabriel appears in eleven different forms; others, such as Āzar and Aṣḥāb al-Rass, have never been satisfactorily explained.

Arab personal names need little discussion, for example Abū Lahab (Q 111:1), Aḥmad (Q 61:6), Muḥammad (Q 3:144, 33:40, 47,2, 48:29), and the legendary Luqmān (Q 31). There are some historical, but no formal problems with the names of the "Arab" prophets Hūd (also a collective term for Jews, see below), Ṣāliḥ (a rare name before Islām and possibly a coinage of Muḥammad's time, *EI2* 2004: "Ṣāliḥ") and Shuʾayb (see below) and their tribes ʿĀd and Thamūd. The same is true of the compound names with *dhū*, e.g., Dhū ʾl-Nūn (Q 21:87, i.e. Jonah, with *nūn* "fish" an early borrowing from Syriac), Dhū ʾl-Ayd (David, Q 38:17), Dhū ʾl-Awtād (Pharaoh, 38:12), Dhū ʾl-Qarnayn (Alexander the Great, Q 18:83), and Dhū ʾl-Kifl (Q 21:85, 38:48), this last respelled by Bellamy (1996: 199) as Dhū ʾl-Ṭifl to give "the man with the child"; for other interpretations, e.g. "Job," see *EI2* 2004: "Dhū ʾl-Kifl."

A chronological classification of proper names is not very informative, as only a few of them can be reliably considered pre-Islamic, namely:

yahūd, "Jews" (S. Arabian); *ādam*, "Adam" (Heb.); *shiʿrā*, "Dog Star" (Gk. Seirios); *majūs*, "Magians" (Pers. or Syr.); and (all via Syriac) *isrāʾīl*, "Israel"; *ilyās*, "Elijah"; *jibrāʾīl*, "Gabriel"; *zakariyyā*, "Zachariah"; *sulaymān*, "Solomon"; *al-masīḥ*, "Messiah"; *nūḥ*, "Noah"; *hārūn*, "Aaron"; *yājūj*, *mājūj*, "Gog, Magog"; *yūnus*, "Jonah".

The following are dated to Muḥammad's time.

Hebrew or Aramaic:

jālūt, "Goliath" (Heb.); *dāwūd*, "David" (Heb.); *hāmān*, "Haman"; *yūsuf*, "Joseph".

Syriac:

ibrāhīm, "Abraham" (by analogy with *ismāʿīl*, *isrāʾīl*); *ismāʿīl*, "Ishmael"; *alyasaʿ*, "Elisha"; *ayyūb*, "Job"; *firʿawn*, "Pharaoh" (if not Eth.); *lūṭ*, "Lot"; *mālik*, "Moloch"; *maryam*, "Mary"; *mūsā*, "Moses"; *mīkāl*, "Michael"; *naṣārā*, "Christians"; *yaḥyā*, "John the Baptist"; *yaʿqūb*, "Jacob".

Greek:

iblīs, "devil," see below.

Obscure or disputed names (see further below):

āzar, "Āzar"; *jibt* and *ṭāghūt*, understood as two idols; *al-sāmirī*, "the Samaritan" (Aram. or Syr.); *al-ṣābiʾūn*, "the Sabians"; *ṭālūt*, "Saul"; *ʿuzayr*, "Ezra"; *ʿimrān*, the father of Moses; *ʿīsā*, "Jesus"; *qārūn*, "Korah"; *hārūt wa-mārūt*, names of two fallen angels; *yaghūth*, the idol "Yaghūth" (Eth. or S. Arabian).

Place names (cf. Neuwirth 2002) are infrequent; there are a few pre-Islamic Arab names, such as al-Ḥijr (Q 15:80), Mecca (Q 48:24, alternative name Bakka, Q 3:96), al-Kaʿba, (Q 5:95, 97), *al-bayt al-ḥarām* (Q 5:97) "the sacred house," *al-bayt al-ʿatīq*, "the ancient house" (Q 22:29, 33, with *ʿatīq* a loan from Aramaic).

Ancient names:

bābil, "Babel" (Akk.); *furāt* (Q 25:55, 35:13, 77:27), "sweet river water" from the Akk. name of the Euphrates.

Others:

iram, "Iram" (S. Arab.); *al-rūm*, "Byzantium" (Gk.), *sabaʾ*, "Sheba" (S. Arabian); *ṭūr saynāʾ*, "Mt. Sinai" (Syr.); *madyan*, "Midian" (Syr.); *miṣr*, "Egypt" (S. Arabian, and see *EI2*, 2004: "Miṣr, B" for additional information on its general sense and Semitic background).

Obscure:

tasnīm, *jūdī*, *al-raqīm*, see below.

It is evident that there are no personal names from Ethiopia or South Arabia except the royal title *tubbaʿ* (and perhaps *firʿawn*, "Pharaoh," though the Joseph story, which probably came from an Ethiopian source, curiously does not mention the name *firʾawn*). Only a handful of divine epithets are listed as borrowings by Jeffery (1938; e.g., *tawwāb*, *rabb*, *raḥmān*, *fāṭir*, *qayyūm*, *muṣawwir*, *mālik*, *muhaymin*), and Moubarac's extensive collection (1955) of the names of God should be consulted for the many expressions common to the Qurʾān and the divinities of South Arabia, pagan and otherwise.

Forms implying a Christian source do appear to predominate, but Jeffery is sometimes rather arbitrary and there is often a contradictory opinion buried in a footnote.

The unfamiliar form of a number of biblical names is a problem for both Muslim and Western scholars, and the latter have not shrunk from offering psychological explanations. Dvořák (1884, a, b, 1885; reported in Jeffery 1938: 39, n. 1), was of the mind that Muḥammad was trying to bamboozle his listeners with strange and mysterious words. This we can ignore, but we do have to accept that modifications may have been caused by misunderstandings in the transmission or a pressure to make the names conform to certain preferred patterns, and the possibility of textual corruption cannot be ruled out.

Textual corruption is significant because the proposed emendations may produce a word which ceases to be a borrowing and should then be withdrawn from Jeffery's list, e.g., *al-raqīm* (Q 18:8) = *al-ruqūd*, "sleeping," hence no longer an obscure place name (Bellamy 1991; Luxenberg 2000: 65f., reads *al-ruqād*, "sleep"). Bellamy (1993) also proposes *abb* (Q 80:31) = *lubb*, "kernel, i.e. nuts"; *al-aʿrāf* (Q 7:44, 46) = *al-ajrāf*, "banks of a wadi" or *al-aḥrāf*, "mountain ledges"; *ḥiṭṭa* (Q 2:55, 7:161) = *khiṭṭa*, from *khiṭʾa*, "sin"; *sijill* (Q 21:104) = *musajjil* or *musjil*, "one who registers"; *ṣibghat allāh* (Q 2:132) = *ṣanīʾat allāh*, "the favor of God" or *kifāyat allāh*, "the sufficiency of God"; *sabʿan min al-mathānī* (Q 15:87) = *shayʾan min al-matālī*, "some recitations". Others include *jibt*

(Q 4:54) = *jinnat*, "*jinn*" (Bellamy 2001, see further below); *ṭuwan* (Q 20:12), an unanalyzable place name, is simply *ṭawā*, "it rolled," used descriptively along the same lines as Gilgāl (Joshua 5:9) for a place which "rolls," Hebrew *glgl* (Bellamy 2001).

The name *āzar* (Q 6:74) has never been explained, but for Bellamy (1996) it is simply a misreading of *izrāʾan*, "contemptuously"; *idrīs* (Q 19:57, 21:85) has also defied identification (to confuse matters it appears as a variant of Ilyās, see Paret 1971: Nachträge 552 to p. 418), but Bellamy (1996) lumps it together with two other enigmatic names, *ʿuzayr* (Q 9:30) and [*aṣḥāb*] *al-rass* (Q 25:37, 38; 50:12), and makes them all corruptions of Esdras; *shuʿayb* (Q 26:177) = Shaʿyā, "Isaiah" (Bellamy 1996, hence no longer the "Arab" prophet Shuʿayb); *ʿīsā* (frequent), "Jesus" is a misreading of *al-masīḥ* (Bellamy 2002, revoking an earlier explanation of his).

Misunderstandings and allegedly deliberate corruptions must be noted here in the same spirit in which al-Suyūṭī and others recorded every viewpoint in case one of them may be right. At least since Nöldeke (1910) there has been a readiness to assume that some obscure words were errors or arbitrary creations by Muḥammad. The following are some of the explanations offered, including foreign words which have been radically transformed, and possible coinages from native resources: *al-aʿrāf* (Q 44:46), name of a wall separating paradise from hell, is a misunderstanding by Muḥammad (Jeffery 1938: 65, but see Bellamy's emendations above); *jūdī* (Q 11:46), the mountain where the Ark rested, is so called from Muḥammad's mistaken belief that Noah was an inhabitant of Arabia, where a Mt. Jūdī exists; *zukhruf* (Q 6:112; 10:25; 17:95; 43:34), "something highly embellished" seems to Jeffery (1938: 150) to be "a deformation from the Syr. *zkhūrīthā*," connected with necromancy; *furqān* (Q 2:50, 181; 3:2; 8:29, 42; 21:49; 25:1), "discrimination," is "probably a coining of Muḥammad himself" (Fleischer *apud* Jeffery 1938: 226). The connection of *iblīs* (eleven times), "devil," with Greek *diabolos* is still very speculative, but has yet to be improved on: Künstlinger (1928) (reported by Jeffery 1938: 48, n. 3), "proposes the somewhat far-fetched theory that *Iblīs* is derived from the Jewish *Belial* by deliberate transformation." *ʿIlliyyūn* (Q 83:18, 19), "upper heavens" is seen as a misunderstanding of Heb. *ʿelyon*, "the highest" (*EI2* 2004: "ʿIlliyyūn," but see also above for a Syriac etymology from Margoliouth).

Other obscure words that Muḥammad is said to have coined are *ghassāq* (Q 38:57; 78:25), "purulent?"; *tasnīm* (Q 83:27), glossed as the name of a fountain in paradise; and *salsabīl* (Q 76:18) supposedly the name of a river in paradise (Jeffery 1938: 39, from Nöldeke, who has, however, *ghislīn* (Q 69:36), "purulent?", as another unexplained Qurʾānic word). Nöldeke is in good company: Abū Ḥātim al-Rāzī (d. 606/1209; 1957–8: I, 134f.) mentions *tasnīm*, *salsabīl*, *ghislīn*, *sijjīn*, *al-raqīm* "and others" (!) as words introduced by Muḥammad and "unknown to the Arabs and other nations."

When Muḥammad uses the Aramaic pattern *tabār* (Q 71:28), "destruction," in preference to the native verbal noun pattern *tatbīr* of the newly Arabicized root *tabbara* "to destroy" (Q 17:7; 25:41), he may deliberately have chosen it to influence his Jewish listeners (Schall 1984–6: 372). Compare this with Künstlinger (1928–30) on *rāʿinā* (Q 2:98; 4:48): it is the echo of a Jewish mealtime prayer *rāʿēnū*, "pasture us," addressed to a God who is thought of as a shepherd, an idea which Künstlinger shows was repugnant to Muslims and therefore, in his interpretation, was intended to have a negative effect here (other theories in Jeffery 1938: 136). Perhaps we may include here the denominative *hāda*, "to be Jewish" (Q 2:59; 4:48), and the collective *hūd*, "Jews" (Q 2:105, 129, 134; it is also the name of "Arab" prophet Hūd), from the Aramaic loan *yahūd*, "Jews," as they seem to involve a play on *hāda*, used eleven times elsewhere in its native sense of "to repent."

Conspicuous in the Qur'ān are the rhyming pairs of the type Hārūt and Mārūt (Q 2:96) and Yājūj and Mājūj (Q 18:93; 21:96). It has been conjectured, with some plausibility, that other names have been formed on a similar principle, so Ibrāhīm, "Abraham," is modeled on Ismāʿīl and Isrāʾīl, Qārūn on Hārūn, and perhaps Iblīs and Idrīs are echoes of each other. Whether Ṭālūt (Q 2:248, 259), the name of Saul, is a deliberate echo of Jālūt "Goliath," will never be known. Margoliouth (1939: 61) links Mārūt with Ethiopic *mārīt*, glossed as *divina, fatidica*, with the *ī* converted to *ū* in keeping with the Qurʾānic preference for words ending in *-ūt*, no doubt influenced by such forms as *malakūt* (Q 6:75; 7:184; 23:90; 36:83), "kingdom, dominion," borrowed from Aramaic or Syriac.

Ṭāghūt, an unexplained name paired with *jibt* (Q 4:54), probably belongs here. If we accept Bellamy's proposition (2001) that *jibt* is simply a misspelt *jinnat* "jinn" then half the problem disappears, but he says nothing about *ṭāghūt*. The latter is of Ethiopian origin according to Jeffery (1938), but Atallah (1970) takes *jibt* and *ṭāghūt* together as meaning "Egyptian" (cf. "gypsy," hence a sorcerer) and "Thoth," lord of magic and wisdom. Some years earlier Köbert (1961b: 415–16) had suggested that *ṭāghūt* might be connected with Syriac *kawkbhe d-ṭāʾen*, "planets," i.e. wandering stars, denoting some sort of planet god, leaving *jibt* unexplained.

In a few cases the ending of a word seems to have been adapted to create a rhyme, thus *saynāʾ*, "Sinai," occurs also as *sīnīn* (Q 95:2); the name Ilyās appears as Il-Yāsīn (Q 37:130); *ghislīn* (Q 69:36), already referred to above can be added, also *yaqṭīn*, "gourd" (Q 37:146; garbled Hebrew, according to Jeffery 1938), and two new candidates are *jabīn* (Q 37:103), ordinarily glossed as "forehead" but now explained as "hill" (Calder 1986, so no longer a foreign word, *pace* Jeffery 1938: 101) and *jaḥīm* (twenty-six times) "hell" (an arbitrary distortion of *jahannam*, O'Shaughnessy 1961). There is also a variant *ismāʿīn* of the name Ismāʿīl in some readings. It is remarkable that *jabīn, jaḥīm, yāsīn*, and *yaqṭīn* all occur in the same *sūra* (Q 37), and it is not irrelevant that such games with words were a feature of *rajaz* poetry, which has been linked with the pre-metrical rhyming prose favored by the soothsayers for their oracles.

One final example will illustrate how the foreign vocabulary of the Qurʾān still challenges our philological ingenuity, namely the trio *sijill* (Q 20:104), usually treated as having something to do with documents, *sijjīl* (Q 11:82; 15:74; 105:4), thought to refer to lumps of hard clay and *sijjīn* (Q 83:7, 8), connected with writing, or else an attribute or name of hell. Of these only *sijill* is relatively securely derived (perhaps directly) from Greek *sigillon*, "an imperial edict," hence "seal." The accepted etymology for *sijjīl* used to be the Persian *sang* + *gil*, "stone + clay" (Jeffery 1938: 164) until it was replaced by Leemhuis' theory (1982) that *sijjīl* is related to the Aramaic *sgyl*, "smooth altar stone," giving a Qurʾānic sense of "stones of flint." *Sijjīn* has defied explanation, and Nöldeke (1910, agreeing with Abū Ḥātim al-Rāzī above) decided it must have been invented by Muḥammad, perhaps for the sake of the rhyme, as it is accompanied by what looks like a gloss: *kitāb marqūm*, "a written book" (*marqūm* is also a problem, and may mean "dotted," as some Semitic scripts are). In Marglliouth's amendments (1939: 58) to Jeffery, *sijjīn* is said to be simply a variant of a word borrowed from the Syriac *sīgīliyon* "seal, diploma," itself from the Greek *sigillon*, the shift of *l* > *n* being attested in other words, such as *jibrīl* and *jibrīn*, "Gabriel."

However, all this is now refuted by de Blois (1999: 62, n. 6 with acknowledgments to Sima) who has reinstated the Persian etymology for *sijjīl* but in an older form, now *sag+gil*, with an adjectival derivative *sagēn*, "of stone," which accounts for *sijjīn* as well, eliminating not only Nöldeke, al-Rāzī and Margoliouth but also O'Shaughnessy (1961: 444), who thought *sijjīn* could be cognate with *sijn*, "prison," and "might possibly refer to a place of eternal imprisonment." De Blois goes further, and invokes a god of Hatra named *shnjlʾ* in his conjecture that *ḥijārat*[an] *min sijjīl* (usually seen as explanatory: "stones consisting of hard clay") echoes a biblical formula in the story of Sodom and Gomorrah (cf. Genesis 19:24) and really means "stones from a supernatural being called Sijjīl." This was no longer understood, and so the third word, *sijill*, came into play: its association with edicts and seals led naturally to the assumption that it was connected with clay and writing, and this was then applied to the interpretation of the mysterious *sijjīl* as "clay" and *sijjīn* as "writing."

This is a unusually complex reconstruction, which is cited here at some length because it seems just as convincing as Leemhuis' once did, and as Jeffery's explanation did before him.

Conclusion

The picture is one of confusion on both sides. Muslims were (and are still) faced with the task of reconciling the declared Arabness of the revelation with the presence of non-Arabic words in the Qurʾān, while Western scholars continue to disagree about the origins of many of these words and the historical implications for Islām. Rippin (2003) offers a new interpretive approach to escape from the purely lexical or legendary. Noting that the putative Coptic and Greek etymologies sometimes had little to do with the context of the words as used in the Qurʾānic narrative, he surmises that the attribution of Coptic origins (which sometimes involved taking words in an opposite sense) was a reflection of Muslim feelings towards Coptic at the time as "a language of deception for Arabic speakers," and, similarly, the attribution of Greek origins arose from the anachronistic association of the Greeks with commerce. Seen thus, medieval Muslim and modern Western exegesis run parallel, each driven by its own sectarian and cultural preconceptions.

We remain dependent on Jeffery, and the data will continue to support all kinds of constructions, though it is difficult to go as far as Luxenberg (2000: 299) and claim that the Arabic spoken in Mecca was a "hybrid of Aramaic and Arabic." The most eirenic and impartial verdict is probably that of Kronholm (1982–3: 65), who concludes that the terminological precedents and borrowings perceived by Western scholars in the emergence of Islam, "are not to be interpreted as tokens of a spiritual dependence. Rather they are employed and transformed by Muhammad into obedient servants of his prophetic originality."

Further reading

Baalbaki, R. (1983) Early Arabic lexicographers and the use of Semitic languages. *Berytus* 31, 117–27.

Faris, N. A., and Glidden, H. (1939) The development of the meaning of Koranic *ḥanīf*. *Journal of the Palestine Oriental Society* 19, 1–13.

Gilliot, C. (1990) *Exégèse, langue et théologie en Islam. L! exégèse coranique de Tabari (m. 311/923).* J. Vrin, Paris, chapter 4, pp. 95–110.

Gilliot, C., and Larcher, P. (2003) Language and style of the Qurʾān. In: McAuliffe, Jane Dammen (ed.) *Encyclopaedia of the Qurʾān*. Brill, Leiden, vol. III, pp. 109–35.

Jeffery, Arthur (1938) *The Foreign Vocabulary of the Qurʾān*. Oriental Institute, Baroda.

Kopf, L. (1956) Religious influences on medieval Arabic philology. *Studia Islamica* 5, 33–59; reprinted in Kopf, L. (1976): 19–45; also reprinted in Rippin (1999): 215–41.

Kopf, L. (1961) The treatment of foreign words in medieval Arabic lexicology. *Scripta Hierosolymitana* 9, 191–205; reprinted in Kopf, L. (1976): 247–61.

Kronholm, T. (1982–3) Dependence and prophetic originality in the Koran. *Orientalia Suecana* 31–32, 47–70.

Luxenberg, C. (2000) *Die Syro-aramäische Lesart des Koran*. Das Arabische Buch, Berlin.

Rippin, Andrew (2003) The designation of "foreign" languages in the exegesis of the Qurʾān. In: McAuliffe, J. D., Walfish, B. D., and Goering, J. W. (eds.) *With Reverence for the Word: Medieval Scriptural Exegesis in Judaism, Christianity and Islam*, Oxford University Press, New York, pp. 437–44.

Zammit, M. R. (2002) *A Comparative Lexical Study of Qurʾānic Arabic*. Brill, Leiden.

CHAPTER 9

Structure and the Emergence of Community

Angelika Neuwirth

Three Self-designations of the Qur'ān: *Muṣḥaf–Qur'ān–Kitāb*

Qur'ānic scholarship over the last decades has generally focused on the Qur'ānic text as transmitted to readers in the canonized codex, rather than exploring its oral "pre-history," the sequence of messages pronounced by the prophet Muḥammad in the process of his addressing his emerging community. The primary scholarly concern was with the codified text in its given literary shape, not with the Qur'ān as a collection of prophetic communications that document the emergence of a community and thus, for their full understanding, need to be rearranged chronologically.

This preference of the *textus receptus* was not least due to a justified desire to overcome the earlier prevailing philological-historical search for an *ur-text.* John Wansbrough (1977) to whom the shift of focus from textual history to form history is substantially due, was to induce a veritable revolution in reading the Qur'ān. He radically revised and redefined the relationship between the Qur'ānic text and the Islamic grand narrative about its origins as presented in the biography of the prophet, the historicity of which had until then all too readily been accepted. Wansbrough's hyper-skeptical *Quranic Studies* (1977), which demanded a wholesale dismissal of the factual data of Islamic tradition, caused, however, the Qur'ānic text as a literary artifact and thus a source for the earliest history of Islam, to be swept aside, along with the rest of the traditional narrative. His claim that the Qur'ān must have originated from a later period and a different cultural milieu than traditionally assumed, violently rid the Qur'ānic text of its historical coordinates, thus disqualifying it as a subject of historical investigation.

It is not overly surprising that this approach that projected the Qur'ān into a totally new chronological (eighth century, not seventh) and geographical (Fertile Crescent, not Arabia) framework, ascribing the Qur'ānic text to anonymous compilers from a monotheist sectarian background, had the result of discouraging micro-structural literary research in the Qur'ānic text for several decades. Approaching the problem from a historical vantage-point, Patricia Crone and Michael Cook (1977) supported Wansbrough's revision of the traditional image of early Islam. Basing their discussion on non-Arabic writings, they excluded not only Arabic-Islamic sources from their material, but also, and paradoxically, the major object of investigation, the Qurʾānic text itself, whose origins they projected into yet another temporal and spatial framework. Earlier, speculations about a Christian original underlying the Qurʾān had been presented by Günter Lüling (1974; 2003), who was followed by Christoph Luxenberg (2000), both of whom argued for an overall revision of our understanding of the Qurʾān, proposing radical emendations of selected text units without, however, ever submitting the Qurʾān *in toto* to a micro-structural reading. Meanwhile, evidence of old Qurʾān codices (see Puin 1996) as well as new philological (De Blois 2002) and historical (Ammann 2001, Donner 1998; Dostal 1991; Krone 1992) studies have provided strong arguments in favor of the Qurʾān's emergence from an Arabian environment and of an early date of the Qurʾānic redaction, thus advocating for the fixation of the text in the shape transmitted to us.

On the basis of our current knowledge about the transmission process (Böwering 2001) and about the spectrum of rivaling text traditions (Jeffery 1937, Leemhuis 2001), the most plausible hypothesis is that the texts assembled in the transmitted Qurʾānic corpus do reflect the wording of communications that were actually pronounced by Muḥammad, though we have no decisive evidence as to the exact phonetic shape of the language spoken by sedentary communities at the time (Vollers 1906).

Whereas Qurʾānic stylistics from a grammatical point of view have been the object of several studies (Nöldeke 1910: 1–30; Bloch 1946, Neuwirth 1981), the impact of Qurʾānic narration on its listeners and readers has only been investigated recently (Kermani 2000). This chapter is not intended to describe Qurʾānic techniques of narration extensively, but to give an overview of major Qurʾānic sub-genres and their communicational function in the process of the emergence of the earliest community. We will first attempt to contrast the dramatic structure of the Qurʾānic communication (*qurʾān*) with the static character of the canonized text (*muṣḥaf*), starting with a description of the *muṣḥaf*. Subsequently, the literary character of the early and later Meccan *sūras* and finally the Medinan *sūras* will be discussed.

Structure of the Codex: Shape

The Qurʾānic text transmitted to us (*EI2* 2004: "Ḳurʾān"; for the history of the text see Nöldeke 1909–38) betrays a peculiar composition, essentially different than that of the Hebrew Bible, which pursues salvation history through a roughly chronological sequence of events, and equally different from the Gospels, which narrate the essential stages of the founding history of the Christian faith. It does not present a continuous narrative of the past, but in its early texts conjures the future, the imminent judgment day, before entering into a debate with various interlocutors about the implementation of monotheist religious ideas in the present. In terms of form, the Qurʾān is not a coherent book either – one for instance made up of subunits that build on each other – but is rather a collection of 114 independent text units, *sūras* (*sūra*; plural *suwar*) with no evident external link to each other. A *sūra* is marked by a headline giving its name, and by an introductory invocation, the so-called *basmala*, that is, the formula *bismi ʾllāh al-raḥmān al-raḥīm* ("In the name of God, the Compassionate and Merciful"). The term *sūra* goes back to Qurʾānic use, though originally referring to undetermined text units, smaller than the eventually fixed *sūras* (the origin of the term is obscure; see Jeffery 1938). Whereas the names of the *sūras* in some cases are controversial, several *sūras* being known under more than one name, the introductory formula most probably stems from the recitation practice of the prophet's community itself. The *sūras* vary in length from two-sentence miniature statements to lengthy polythematic communications. They are arranged in the corpus roughly according to their length: the longest *sūras* are placed first, the shorter ones following in a generally descending order. The vast majority of the *sūras* are neatly composed texts that may be viewed as constituting their own literary genre, as will be explored below. Although a great number of *sūras* appear to have been extended through later additions in the course of their oral communication, in their complemented version they still seem to follow particular rules of composition (Neuwirth 1981). Only some of the long *sūras* appear as later compilations assembled from isolated text passages; their final shape may be due to the redaction process itself.

Sūras are composed of verses (*āya*; plural *āyāt*), varying in size from one single word to an entire, complex segment. The term *āya*, which corresponds to Syriac *āthā* and Hebrew *ōth* and means a "visible sign of a transcendental reality," is first used in the Qurʾān to denote signs of divine omnipotence, such as are manifest in nature or in history. The notion developed in the course of the communication process to designate a miraculous sign apt to prove the truth of the prophetic message and was, eventually, conferred on the Qurʾānic verse. The numbering of the verses goes back to early traditions (Spitaler 1935). The early short *sūras*, assembled in the last section of the codex, are styled in a kind of rhymed prose, labeled *sajʿ* in Arabic philological theory, known as the medium of the ancient Arabian soothsayers (*kahana*; singular *kāhin*). It is a particularly succinct rhythmic diction where single phrases are marked by prose-rhyme, *fāṣila*. This pattern of phonetic correspondence between the verse endings is at once more loose than poetic rhyme (*qāfiya*) and more flexible, and thus allows semantically related verses to be bracketed by a rhyme of their own and mark off clearly distinct verse-groups.

The highly sophisticated phonetic structures produced by this style have been evaluated in the work of Michael Sells (1990; 1993). Though the *sajʿ* style will give way at a later stage of development to a more smoothly flowing prose allowing for complex segments to form a single verse, closed by only a phonetically stereotypical rhyming syllable, the unit of the verse as the smallest compositional entity is an essential element of Qurʾānic literary structure. It not only facilitates the act of memorizing but also constitutes the backbone of Qurʾānic recitation or chant (*tartīl, tajwīd*; see Nelson 1985), that is the essential self-manifestation of the Muslim scripture. The numbering of Qurʾānic verses is a modern phenomenon, whereas other technical subdivisions, like that dividing the entire text into seven *manāzil* (singular *manzila*, "station"), or into thirty *ajzāʾ* (singular *juzʾ*, "part"), which in turn are divided into two *aḥzāb* (singular *ḥizb*, "part") that are merely governed by quantitative criteria without concern for the rhetorical and semantic disposition of the *sūras*, stem from the early post-redactional period and were introduced to facilitate memorizing and reciting (for the early codices, see Jeffery 1937; Leemhuis 2001).

The sequence of the Qur'ānic *sūras*, which does not follow any logical, let alone theological guideline, betrays at once a conservative and a theologically disinterested attitude on the side of the redactors. It suggests that the redaction was carried out in an extremely cautious way, without elaborate planning, perhaps in a hurry, at a stage of development prior to the emergence of the elaborate prophetological conceptions underlying the *sīra*, the biography of Muḥammad, which was fixed around 150 AH. Furthermore, the stabilization of the text must have occurred before the great conquests, since a unification of various textual traditions dispersed over the ever-extending territories would have been difficult to implement (Donner 1991). The traditional scenario of the ʿUthmānic redaction, the hypothesis that the texts of the prophet's recitations were collected and published some twenty-five years after his death by the third caliph ʿUthmān to form the corpus we have before us, is thus not entirely implausible, though the ascription of the first official publication of the Qur'ān to the Umayyad caliph ʿAbd al-Malik (r. 685–705) whose contribution to the masoretic fixation of the text is well documented (Hamdan 2006) is perhaps more realistic (De Prémare 2005).

Place, Time and Agents of the *Muṣḥaf*

The *muṣḥaf*, being the fixed corpus, is addressed to the believers in general and is meant to be read as well as recited. Its due place is the learned circle of religious specialists, *ʿulamāʾ*, where it constitutes the basis of religious learning. Since in traditional Islam Qur'ān reading in communal (and private) worship is a recital by heart, the *muṣḥaf*'s place physically spoken is not primarily the cultic space of the mosque. Nor is the use of the *muṣḥaf* as such bound to particular sacred time periods of the day; it is unrelated to the five binding ritual prayers that demand Qur'ānic recitations performed without textual support. Aside from its purpose as a source of learning, the *muṣḥaf* is, of course, primarily a scripture, that is, a codex endowed with the symbolic power of creating social coherence and the identity of its community, the agents involved in the communication of the *muṣḥaf* being the readers over the ages (for the implications of canonicity, see Assmann and Assmann 1987).

As a product of its particular time, however, the *muṣḥaf* addresses the expectations hedged in the community about the shape of a scripture in late antiquity, a highly dignified corpus of the word of God that, of course, should have a particularly expressive beginning and end. Indeed, one realizes that the Qur'ān is embedded in a ceremonial framework clearly marked as such: the introductory text, *al-fātiḥa*, "the opening," is an exceptional text, not a *sūra* in the strict sense, not being speech conferred by God on man, but a prayer to be uttered by the community, indeed the central common prayer of Islam, comparable to the Christian "Our Father" (Neuwirth and Neuwirth 1991).

The *fātiḥa* in the beginning of the Qur'ānic corpus serves as a prayer for the divine blessing required to protect the sacred book. Analogically, the two final apotropaeic *sūras*, *al-muʿawwidhatān*, "the two by which one seeks refuge," though formally introduced by a divine command *qul*, "speak (the following text)" and thus featuring as divine speech, are equally formulae that substantially belong to humans. Invoking divine protection, these *sūras* are apotropaeic texts to shield the Qur'ān from the intervention of demons. Thus, the positioning of *sūras* 1, 113 and 114 – texts that are missing from the Qur'ānic text collections preceding the canonical edition, presumably not being acknowledged as *sūras* (see Jeffery 1937) – obviously goes back to concepts developed by the redactors of the so-called ʿUthmānic text, who were charged with the task to construct a *textus ne varietur*, a codex with a claim to canonicity. It is no coincidence that the apotropaeic formula to be used before starting Qur'ān recitation – *aʿūdhu bi-llāh min al-shayṭān al-rajīm* ("I take refuge to God from Satan who is to be stoned") – is reflective of the two final *sūras*.

Once one separates these framing parts from the text embedded in them, a text emerges that starts (Q 2:2) with identifying itself with "the book" dedicated to those readers who, as believers and practitioners of the basic religious duties of Islam, are obviously Muslims: *dhālika 'l-kitābu*, "That is the book – no doubt about it – a guide to the pious, who have faith in the unseen and are steadfast in prayer: who bestow in charity a part of what We give them: who trust in what has been revealed to you and to others before you, and firmly believe in the life to come." The text of the Qur'ānic codex ends with the perhaps most frequently recited Islamic confession of faith, which emphatically pronounces the focal truth of Islam, the oneness of God: *Qul: huwa 'llāhu aḥad*, "Speak: God is one, the eternal God, He begot none, nor was He begotten. None is equal to Him" (Q 112:1–4). These arrangements of texts are signs sent by the redactors to the readers of the codex, who are identified indirectly by their religious duties (Q 2:2–3) and directly by their belief in the oneness of God (Q 112:1–4).

The term *muṣḥaf* ("codex") itself is not Qur'ānic, since it is the receptacle of a scripture that did not yet exist throughout the Qur'ānic communication process. The Qur'ān became "the book" only after the death of Muḥammad, when the divine voice was no longer to be heard. Only then could the form of the – until then virtual – book, a transcendent text communicated in excerpts to the community, be imagined as a real, clearly defined corpus. What is comprised in the *muṣḥaf* is "the book" in its new understanding as the legacy of its transmitter; *kitāb* after the end of the process of revelation no longer designates the virtual, heavenly book – originally referred to by *kitāb* in verses like Q 2:2 – with its diverse earthly manifestations, but the real book *kat' exochen*, the Muslim scripture.

The *muṣḥaf*, then, is the reified *kitāb*, whose codification follows particular rules. At later stages it therefore identifies itself on its interior cover page as being made up of historically different layers, the oldest being the *rasm ʿuthmānī* (the graphic skeleton of consonantal signs that are claimed to go back to the ʿUthmānic redaction itself), followed by the vocalizing strokes as well as the points added to consonants to distinguish their diverse phonetic realizations – additional signs inserted systematically only some decades later (Leemhuis 2001).

These attempts at unification and at making the text unambiguous, however, never achieved a total communal consensus, but rather resulted in a diversity of traditions concerning the reading and thus the understanding of particular words, though without causing (as far as we can judge from the remnants) theologically relevant divergences. These traditions, *riwāyāt*, also used to be documented on the interior cover page of the *muṣḥaf*, where the reader usually will find the wording *bi'l-rasm al-ʿUthmānī bi-riwāyat Ḥafṣ ʿan ʿĀṣim* (or: *Warsh ʿan Nāfiʿ*), since only two from an earlier multiplicity of traditions are still in use, in the East the tradition of Ḥafṣ (d. 180/796), transmitting from ʿĀṣim (d. 128/745), in the West that of Warsh (d. 197/812) transmitting from Nāfiʿ (d. 169/785), both dating from the eighth/ninth century, though fixed as closed traditions (*qirā'āt*) only in the 9th/10th century by Ibn Mujāhid (Melchert 2000).

The Oral *Qur'ān*: The Message and its Communication Process

Yet, though the text transmitted to us may be considered a reliable source for the study of the Qur'ān as received by the Muslim community from the eighth century onward, when it was definitely fixed through an orthographic reform (Hamdan 2006), it does not immediately reflect the sequence of communications conveyed by Muḥammad. The transmitted text is presented as a fixed, "frozen" text, a codex (*muṣḥaf*), whereas the prophet's communications are oral texts, in the Qur'ān itself termed *qur'ān*, "recitation" or "text to be recited." Whereas the single text units (*sūras*) collected in the *muṣḥaf* are not interrelated but juxtaposed unconnected to each other, the oral communications dynamically build on each other, later ones often expressing a re-thinking of earlier ones, sometimes even inscribing themselves into earlier texts.

There is, thus, ample reason to assume intertextuality between single communications of the oral *qur'ān*, one that no longer exerts an effect in the *muṣḥaf*, where the temporal sequence of the *sūras* plays no role, all texts being considered equally divine and eternal. By their definition as communications, these Qur'ānic texts must also refer to issues and incidents "external" to the text itself, to an accompanying unspoken text thus embodied in the discourses that were debated in the circles of the listeners. The oral Qur'ān – to use a simplifying metaphor – structurally may be compared to a telephone conversation where the speech of only one party is audible, yet the (unheard) speech of the other is in no way totally absent, but roughly deducible from the audible part of the exchange. Indeed, the social concerns and theological debates of the listeners of the Qur'ān are widely reflected in the text pronounced through the prophet's voice.

In terms of genre it thus appears problematic to describe Qur'ānic speech as prose speech, let alone as narrative. With reference to the linguistic theory proposed by Karl Bühler (1965) who differentiates between information, presentation, and appeal, one might hold that most Qur'ānic speech falls under the category of appeal addressed, often explicitly, sometimes implicitly, to listeners. The listeners, again, are present in the text itself, being addressed, exhorted, encouraged, or reprimanded. In order to do justice to the Qur'ān as a communication to listeners, one would therefore be best to speak of a dramatic text, when referring to the period of its oral communication to the listeners during the life time of Muḥammad. It is thus necessary to differentiate between the Qur'ān as it was communicated by the prophet to the first listeners who were still in the process of becoming his community, and the Qur'ān as a codex, that, after the death of Muḥammad became the scripture of a community of believers. Both readings of the Qur'ān, though relying on the same material basis, presuppose a diverse scenario of reception and thus follow different hermeneutics.

Considering the oral Qur'ān one has to distinguish – borrowing theoretically from the literary genre of drama (Pfister 1994), which generically comes closest to the Qur'ānic communication process – between an exterior and an interior "level of communication." On the exterior level, the divine voice – mediated through the address of the prophet and fixed in a sequence of communications determined to a great extent by the redactors of the text – confronts the readers of the written Qur'ān. In contrast, on the interior level of communication, the speaker, Muḥammad, and his listeners are interacting. There is a third agent, the divine voice, who on the interior level continuously speaks to the prophet, but only rarely directly to the listeners. The divine voice, through his speech, stages the entire scenario, thus acting as both a protagonist and the stage director at the same time. On the exterior level of communication, the divine voice has merged with that of the prophet; the entire drama no longer matters since the book is received as God's immediate speech. The former listeners have disappeared from the stage, reduced to mere objects of the sole divine speaker's speech. Their active role in the communication process has been shifted to the readers of the *muṣḥaf*. The scenarios of the Qur'ān as a communication process and as a scripture are, thus, essentially diverse.

However complicated and perhaps ultimately unsatisfactory any endeavor to reconstruct the Qur'ānic communication process may be, it is an indispensable scholarly task to shed light on the founding event of Islam, the orally performed drama between the messenger and his listeners. Two achievements are due to this communication process: the emergence of the Muslim scripture and the constitution of a community. Qur'ānic studies should therefore not remain limited to the exterior level of communication, to the codex addressing the readers, but – in order to do justice to the multi-layered text of the Qur'ān – try and unearth instances of the communication process underlying the canonical text.

In the following, the changing self-designations of the Qur'ān, *qur'ān* and *kitāb*, will be taken as a guideline for exploring traces of the communication process. Each of them stands for a phase in the development of text structure in the Qur'ān's successive increase in authority, and, at the same time, in the emergence of the community. We will proceed historically, trying to reconstruct some aspects of its earliest (i.e. early Meccan) self-image, the recited text, termed *qur'ān*. The next stage to be analyzed will be the turn from the Qur'ānic self-understanding as a recitation, to that of an ensemble of both *qur'ān* and *kitāb*, the earthly manifestation of the heavenly book – a turn in reference that occurs in the middle to late Meccan period. At a still later stage, that of the Medinan texts, the Qur'ān itself becomes a manifestation of the book, *kitāb*. The codex, *muṣḥaf*, as we saw, marks the final stage where the Qur'ān has become "the Book" itself. All of these stages will be discussed as to the overall structure of the textual manifestation behind the self-designation in question, the place and time coordinates that govern the agents involved in the communication, and, finally, some characteristic key concepts that mark the four diverse discourses through the Qur'ānic development.

The Oral *Qur'ān*: The Early Meccan Texts and their Structure

During the communication process itself, the most frequent self-designation of the text is *qur'ān*, "recitation," or "text to be recited," for example, Q 85:21; 84:21; 73:4, 20; 72:1. The *sūras* commonly considered the oldest, i.e. those that display *saj*ʿ, rhymed prose, in the strict sense – short speech units rhyming in frequently changing sound patterns reiterating the last consonant and based on a common rhythm – are made up of mono-partite verses containing one phrase each, for example, Q 70:8–9: *yawma takūnu 'l-samā'u ka'l-muhl / wa-takūnu 'l-jibālu ka'l-ʿihn* ("On the day heaven will be like dispersed wool / and the mountains be like molten brass"). The longer compositions of later times, their style too complex to be pressed into short *saj*ʿ phrases, usually display a bi-partite (consisting of two phrases) structure, for example, Q 54:42, or even pluri-partite (more than two phrases) verse, for example, Q 37:102. The relative length of the verses should not be dismissed as simply conditioned by a more or less complex content. Rather, the transition from *saj*ʿ speech to a more ordinarily flowing though still poetically tinted articulation attests to the transformation of an adherence to the standard pre-Islamic tradition into a novel literary paradigm of astistic prose, one that may be considered as a genuine Qur'ānic development marking a new stage in the history of the Arabic literary language.

Ever since the sensational hypothesis presented by D.H. Müller (1896), claiming a strophic composition for the *sūras*, was dismissed without further scrutiny by subsequent scholarship, the possibility that "a firm hand was in full control" of the composition and structure of individual *sūras* has been virtually excluded. Countering this view, I hold that, when subjected to micro-structural analysis,[1] clearly discernible structures emerge in the Qur'ān from beneath the surface. These structures mirror a historical development. The crucial procedures demanded for achieving a valid periodization are, however, extremely complex, having to proceed from a thorough investigation of Qur'ānic rhyme to that of the verse and then to that of paragraph structure in relation to the diverse semantic units, a work that is still in progress.

Particularly in the short *sūras*, distinctive verse groups can be isolated that often form part of a clear-cut pattern of proportions. Thus, Q 75 is built on the following balanced verse groups: 6 + 6 + 6 + 6 + 5 + 5 + 5; Q 70 is made up of 6 + 7 + 7 + 7 + 7 + 9; Q 79 entails two groups of nine verses, its proportions being strikingly balanced, 5 + 9 / 6 + 6 + 6 / 9 + 5; and Q 51 is made up of groups of 9 + 14 + 14 + 9 + 7 + 7 verses. Similar cases are found in many of those early Meccan *sūras* that exceed some ten verses, proportions being obviously a mnemonic device required in a situation where memorizing without written support was demanded from the listeners.

What is true for Meccan *sūras* in general applies to the early Meccan texts in particular. In their final compositions they are intentional units that reflect a natural growth, not a haphazard combination of diverse elements. The following list comprises only the main types of early Meccan structural elements or *enjeux*: (1) introductory oaths and oath clusters; or (2) clusters of *idhā*-(when) phrases conjuring the last day (see below). Very prominent are (3) sections about signs (*āyāt*) of divine omnipotence as attested in nature (e.g., Q 76:6–16; 77:25–7; 79:27–32; 80:24–32; 82:6–8; 88:17–20). From early times onward, there are (4) sections of debate, both apologetic and polemic (e.g., Q 96:9–10; 53:59–60). Signs of divine power manifest in history take the shape of very short narratives – the invasion of Mecca Q 105, the Thamūd myth Q 101:11–15, the story of Pharaoh and Moses Q 79:15–26 or ensembles of similar narratives like Q 51 (which includes Abraham and Lot, Q 51:34–7; Moses and Pharaoh, Q 51:38–40; ʿĀd, Q 51:41–2; Thamūd, Q 51:34–7; Noah, Q 51:46) or evocations of stories (*sūras* 51; 53; 69; 73; 85; 89). The latter sometimes form lists: Q 51; 53; 69; 89. It is noteworthy that the longer narratives which occur in the first Meccan period are split into two equal halves exactly after the peripetia of the story, thus forming proportionate structures: Q 79:15–26, six plus six verses; Q 51:24–37, seven plus seven verses; and Q 68:17–34, nine plus nine verses.

Early Meccan *sūras* not only contain clues as to their oral composition, they also in some cases explicitly refer to their genesis out of their public performance. It is interesting to notice that the recitation of verses certainly intended to edify a believing public, such as the lengthy hymn on divine omnipotence in Q 53:59–62, is continued by a reproachful address to those among the listeners who did not show themselves impressed by the pious text, but obviously ridiculed the prophet: *a-fa-min hādhā ʾl-ḥadīthi taʿjabūn / wa-tashḥakūna wa-lā tabkūn / wa antum sāmidūn / fa-sjudū li-llāhi wa-ʿbudū* ("Do you marvel at this discourse? Do you laugh and do you not cry while you make merry? Prostrate yourselves before God and serve Him"). These verses are an immediate response to the poor reactions the recitation had received.

In other instances, for example Q 70:36–7, the stage director's comment singles out particular listeners from an otherwise obviously well-behaving public. After the recitation of a catalogue of virtues ascribed to the God-fearing that certainly was meant to address a more general public, the behavior of the unbelieving listeners is criticized: *Fa-mā li-lladhīna kafarū min qibalika muhtiʿīn/ ʿan al-yamīni wa ʿani l-shimāli ʿizzīn* ("What ails the unbelievers, running with their outstretched necks towards you? On the right and on the left hand in knots"). The immediacy of the reaction to their behavior allows us to conclude that entire sections of the early *sūras* originated in the very situation of performance.

Further instances of Qurʾānic verses critical of the behavior of unbelievers (e.g., Q 96:8f.; 77:48; 107:4f.) suggest that the recitations took place in close context with liturgical gatherings (Neuwirth 1996). Cases like the ones presented depict a lively scenario of the performance of the recitation where the prophetical mediator of the Qurʾānic speech is shown to be well aware of the process of its reception.

Place, time and agents in the early Meccan sūras

The pre-Islamic literary paradigm implies a perception of space as a challenge to humans because nature is not at their disposal. It is embattled space, demanding to be recovered by the Bedouin hero. Nor does the picture of nature that the ancient poets design for framing their poems express an enjoyment of nature or esthetic delight; rather, what is portrayed is the search for the reconstruction of the lost shape of that space (Hamori 1979), a space formerly replete with fulfilling social interaction but meanwhile decayed and disfigured through climatic influences. In contrast to such a heroic attitude of man towards space, the early Qurʾānic revelations in their *āyāt*-sections present earthly space as particularly inspiring of confidence. They present it as a locus of pleasure and enjoyment, as a venue for the reception of divine bounty and as a site of ethically charged social interaction. An early and dominant image is that of a well-preserved tent, allowing man to repose, to enjoy matrimonial life, as well as to pursue his daily activities in a peaceful and self-confident way. Q 78:6–16 strongly reminds one of some psalms of praise which interpret worldly space as a secure housing for the created beings. Worldly space, then, is a divine grace demanding gratitude, which, in turn, will enhance the coherence of the relationship between God and humankind. There is a whole Qurʾānic genre of hymnic praises of divine omnipotence, labeled in the Qurʾān itself as *āyāt* (Graham 1995).

The real space of the Qurʾānic event is, however, not nature, but the city. Its ideal image (see *sūrat al-balad*, "The city," Q 90) is presented in the Qurʾān as being governed by an ethical code which aims at a fair distribution of goods achieved in an unheroic manner (Rippin 1996). It is the experience of the city as a structured space that in the Qurʾān provides the metaphors to communicate that code. In reality, however, the hometown of the prophet and the early community was a locus of communal strife. The stubborn opposition of the Meccan elite, epitomized by their refusal to accept Muḥammad's message, appeared as a late re-staging of the frequent historical catastrophes that had befallen earlier communities of city dwellers throughout the Arabian peninsula (Horovitz 1926).

The early *sūras* often point to deserted sites formerly inhabited by prosperous communities which have disintegrated and passed away through the collapse, sudden or cumulative, of their earthworks and irrigation systems or the destruction of their buildings, events imagined as punishments for their disbelief and rejecting earlier messengers. The significance of the stories about the Arabian messengers lies in their endurance (*ṣabr*) and obedience in calling humans to accept divine guidance: every community should have been warned through a revelation in order to be spared temporary or eschatological punishment. It is noteworthy that the Qurʾānic virtue of patience is no mere endurance but presupposes triumph.

> It is an outlasting of evil, rather than its transmuting. Its task is to outstay all opposition so that the good of prophecy is not overcome by the enmity of unbelief. Its endurance keeps the cause from capitulation, so that it may anticipate the victory that other factors will achieve. It is not, broadly, a suffering which in itself and of itself makes the fabric of the triumph that is to be. This calls for other forms whose opportunity tenacity ensures. (Cragg 1971: 158)

The sites of these events are, from the beginning, presented as collective *lieux de mémoire*. Contrary to the notion of deserted space in poetry, which is not due to any historical event relevant to the present but to the seasonal practices of the camel breeding tribes who, with the beginning of the drought, would retreat to their own permanent sources of water, the deserted places in the Qurʾān are replete with meaning, assuring the listeners of a divinely endorsed order in which equilibrium between human action and welfare is achieved.

Not only ethical behavior counts in early Meccan *sūras* but ritual observance as well. Day and night are structured by the sacred time periods required for prayer, which are often evoked in introductory sections of *sūras*. The most crucial innovation as to the understanding of time is, however, the introduction of eschatological prophecies. They abound in early Meccan *sūras*, most frequently figuring in the beginning. They may be introduced by oath clusters conjuring apocalyptic scenarios (e.g., Q 77:1–6; 79:1–7) with the most expressive being Q 100:1–5.

These oaths, contrary to biblical oath formulae, do not function as invocations of a supra-natural authority external to the text. The early *sūras*ʾ claim to validity is not anchored in something beyond the text. One might speak of a poetic, rather than a theological truth-claim of the early texts (Neuwirth 1993). Apocalyptic prophecies may equally be introduced by *idhā* ("when") phrase clusters (e.g., Q 56:1–6; 81:1–13; 82:1–4; 84:1–5; 99:1–3), equally predicting the events of the "last day." Both types of clusters build up a pronouncedly rhythmical beginning to the *sūra*. In some cases the *idhā*-phrases are not confined to natural and cosmic phenomena but proceed to depict the preparations for the final judgment, such as the blowing of the trumpet, the positioning of the throne, the opening of the account books and so forth. They are followed by a "then"-phrase, focusing the behavior of people in the apocalyptic setting (e.g., Q 69:15; 79:8; 99:4, 6) and their separation into the groups of the blessed and the condemned.

The ensuing descriptions of the hereafter are strictly divided into two counterparts. Introduced by phrases like *ammā . . . fa-, wa-ammā . . . fa-*, "as to those who . . . , they will . . . , but as to those who . . . , they will" (Q 101:6–9), or *wujūh*^{un} . . . *wujūh*^{un}, "faces (will that day look) . . . and other faces (will look) . . ." (Q 80:38–42), they juxtapose the situation of the believers in the paradisiacal garden with that of the unbelievers or evildoers in the tribulations to be suffered in the fires of hell. It is noteworthy that both depictions are particularly rich in imagery and together form a double image, consisting of either an equal number of verses, or of two verse groups displaying a proportional relation to each other. As such, they remind us of the closely juxtaposed pictorial representations of both sections of the hereafter depicted in Church iconography, thus suggesting the designation of "diptychs." Not infrequently, diptychs comprise recollections of the particular behavior of the inmates of the two abodes during their worldly life, serving to justify their eschatological fate. These flashbacks are sometimes interspersed with direct speech, some of them merging into a catalogue of virtues to be emulated or vices to be avoided.

Who are the listeners of the early *sūras*? Islamic tradition presents them as chiefly pagans, admitting the exception of some individuals imprinted by Christian beliefs and knowledge. Certainly the observance of the rites at the Kaʿba occasionally documented in the early *sūras* points to a public that was not strictly monotheistic. Still, the linguistic situation of the Qurʾān attests a close vicinity of the speakers of the language reflected in the Qurʾān to Christian culture (see Griffith 2001; 2002). Although the hypotheses proffered by Lüling (1974) and Luxenberg (2000), who claim a Christian origin of the

Qurʾānic texts, are methodologically and historically unfounded, they alert us anew to the often underestimated part that Christian thinking would have played in urban centers of the peninsula like Mecca. A mass of Christian loan words already existing in the urban language of Mecca (Jeffery 1938) – not coined for the Qurʾān – attests to the close contacts entertained by the adherents of the cultus of the Kaʿba to Christians. We may thus assume that the early listeners were syncretistic in their beliefs, at least in part adhering to the rites of the Kaʿba and, at the same time, familiar with some monotheist thinking, many inclined to accept monotheism, but with a strong group, the Meccan elite, still unwilling to share the belief in the last day, let alone its imminence.

What characterizes the early Qurʾānic texts is a plethora of designations for "the last day": "the day of judgment," *yawm al-dīn*, (Q 51:12), "the hour," *al-sāʿa* (Q 79:42), "the day of separation," *yawm al-faṣl* (Q 77:13), "the day of resurrection," *yawm al-qiyāma* (Q 75:6) and its harbingers, designated by particular Qurʾānic coinages, without exception in the grammatical form of feminine participles, chosen to sound enigmatic and often threatening, such as *al-qāriʿa*, "the knocking one" (Q 104:1); "the quake," *al-rājifa* (Q 79:6); *al-ḥāqqa*, "the inevitable" (Q 69:1f.); *al-āzifa*, "the one coming close" (Q 53:57); and the like. The striking predominance of feminine morphology in eschatological contexts (Sells 1999) still awaits systematic investigation.

Eschatological sections are certainly most characteristic for the early *sūras*. It is all the more striking that there are other texts equally phrased in *sajʿ* prose that display a no less prominent, but different and complex, set of expressions betraying a close relation to the biblical psalms: liturgical words and phrases such as the invitation to hold liturgy, *sabbiḥ*, "praise" (Q 87:1), *rattil al-qurʾān*, "recite" (Q 73:4), *kabbir (rabbaka)*, "magnify your Lord" (Q 74:3), *iqraʾ bi-smi rabbika*, "pronounce the name of your Lord" (96:1) and the doxology *tabāraka*, "praise be to" (Q 67:1) (Baumstark 1947).

Obviously, in the Qurʾān elements familiar from otherwise separately transmitted traditions merge to form an ensemble: on the one hand, enigmatic speech heavily relying on sound with resonances, echoes, and undertones, such as were used by ancient Arabian soothsayers (*kahana*), creating a linguistic medium apt for arousing anxiety and tension in the minds of the listeners. On the other hand, the long established tradition of monotheistic hymnal speech relying on syntactic stratagems such as parallelisms rather than phonetic and equally fit to arouse emotions, is not foreign to Qurʾānic speech either. Both together serve to generate the "distinctive Qurʾānic combination of awe and intimacy" (Sells 1999: 204).

Structure of the Later Meccan Texts

The composition of the *sūras* substantially changes in later Meccan times. Although initially embedded in catalogues of narratives of partly extra-biblical tradition, stories about major biblical figures, like Moses, Jesus and a number of patriarchs known from Genesis, gain a function of their own. They become the stock inventory of the central part of longer Meccan *sūras*, most of them re-narrated more than once. The phenomenon of recurring narratives retold in slightly diverging fashions has often been interpreted as mere repetition and thus as a deficiency. These forms deserve, however, to be studied as testimonies to the consecutive emergence of a community and thus reflective of the process of canonization, their divergence then pointing to a successively changing narrative pact, to a continuing education of the listeners, and to the development of a moral consensus that is reflected in the texts.

In contrast to the meticulous shaping of personages and the sophisticated coding and de-coding of their motives (which are characteristic of biblical narrative: Alter 1981), Qurʾānic narrating pursues complex "para-narrative" aims. Narratives, at least in so far as they are unfolded to some extent and recall plots already known from biblical literature, are presented as excerpts or messages from the heavenly book, which is understood as a corpus of knowledge apart from the extra-biblical lore circulating through oral tradition at the time. This remoteness of "*kitāb*-generated" narrative has a strong bearing on the style of the stories presented as "*kitāb*" readings. The transcendent origin imprints them with a distinct linguistic code that, on the one hand, confers on the diction a highly stylized form (rhymed prose resulting in somewhat unusual syntactic structures); on the other hand, this code implants these narratives with the new message of the imminent eschatological catastrophe, bringing the narrative close to an exhortative appeal, or later, a sermon. It is precisely the discursive elements which are so marginal in biblical narrative that matter primarily in the Qurʾānic narrative, the explicit presentation of the moral or theological implications for the community that can be deduced from the narrated facts of speeches. To fulfill this purpose, in the later *sūras* a stylistic device unknown to the Bible is introduced to accommodate the particular moral or theological deductions from the Qurʾānic discourse, the *clausula* (Neuwirth 1981: 157–70). This stylistic device consists in a particular closure of the long verses of late Meccan and Medinan times; the last sentence of a verse often does not partake in the main strand of communication but presents a comment on its contents, indicating divine approval or disregard of the fact reported: "Truly, you were among the sinners" (*innaki kunti min al-khāṭiʾīn*, Q 12:29). It may also refer to one of God's attributes, as in "Truly, He is the hearer the seer" (*innahu huwa ʾl-samīʿu al-baṣīr* Q 17:1), which in the later stages of Qurʾānic development became parameters of ideal human behavior.

It is noteworthy that the more complex later *sūras* refer to scripture both through their transmission of scriptural texts and through their dependence on the mnemonic technicalities of writing for ensuring their conservation. Though clear-cut proportions still occur between major sections of the later *sūras*, in view of the stylistic form – later verses are filled by complex, lengthy segments – it seems most probable that the transmission of the text at this stage involved writing. At the same time, structures gradually become looser; the distinct tripartite composition prevailing in middle Meccan times comprising a discursive introduction, a narration and a discursive concluding section, often becomes blurred, with narratives being replaced by discursive sections. Many compositions also display secondary expansions, a phenomenon that still needs further investigation. Yet, for the bulk of the middle and late Meccan *sūras*, the claim to a tripartite composition can be sustained.

From Ritual to Textual Coherence

As to the function of Qurʾānic stories, we may localize a turn with the middle Meccan Q 15, where, for the first time, an allusion is made to the existence of a particular form of service in which scripture functions as the cardinal section. In the same text there is also mention of the existence of a communal prayer, the *fātiḥa* (see Q 15:37; Neuwirth and Neuwirth 1991, Neuwirth 2000). Since the middle Meccan *sūras* are obviously recited as part of worship, they have acquired a strictly liturgical function. In these *sūras* the reference to the Meccan sacred area (*ḥaram*) as the central warrant of the social coherence of the community has been replaced by new symbols. Instead of introductory allusions to liturgical times and sacred space that evoked the Meccan sanctuary and its rites (Neuwirth 1993), we encounter an evocation of the book, be it clad in an oath (Q 36:2; 37:3; 38:1; 43:2; 44:2; 50:1) or through a deictic affirmation of its presence (Q 2:2; 10:1; 12:1; 13:1 etc.). In view of the increasing interest of the community in the biblical heritage as part of their own emerging monotheistic identity, it comes as no surprise that the bulk of the middle and late Meccan *sūras*, which by now had developed into long prosaic texts, seem to mirror a monotheistic service, starting with an initial dialogical section (hymnal, apologetic, polemic, paraenetic) and closing with a generically related section, most frequently an affirmation of the Qurʾānic revelation. These framing sections have been compared to the ecclesiastic forms of worship, particularly the initial and concluding *responsoria* recited by the priest or deacon with the community. The center of the monotheistic service, and similarly of the fully developed *sūra* of the middle and late Meccan period, is frequently occupied by a biblical reminiscence – in the case of the ecclesiastic service, a *lectio*, a reading from the Bible, in the case of the *sūra*, a narrative focusing on biblical protagonists. A religious tradition, essentially dependent on written texts – the positioning of biblical pericopes in the center of the service – has thus made its way into the structure of the community's emerging identity (Neuwirth 2005). Using a category set up by the religious anthropologist Jan Assmann (1992), one might describe this change in orientation, shifting from the focusing of local sacred traditions to that of the sacred history located in the Holy Land, *al-arsh allatī bāraknā fīhā* (Q 21:71, 81) as a transition of the community "from ritual coherence to textual coherence."

In these middle and late Meccan texts, polemic and apologetic sections frequently appear as framing parts of a *sūra*. From early Meccan *sūras* onward they mostly serve to affirm the rank of the Qurʾān as a divine revelation, usually constituting the nucleus of concluding sections (Q 74:54–5). In later *sūras* these concluding affirmations of the revelation tend to merge into exhortations of the prophet (Q 11:109–23).

Stories in the later *sūras* are often explicitly referred to as elements of the transcendent book, *al-kitāb* (Madigan 2001). Indeed, some *sūras* identify themselves as drawing on a pre-existing, more extensive text; that is, they are seen as excerpts from a heavenly scripture. Such a book, obviously imagined as being unchangeable and comprehensive, presupposes a stream of tradition that has come to a standstill and become "frozen," constituting a store of warranted knowledge. Qurʾānic reference to scripture, therefore, presupposes a certain stock of narratives existing in a previously fixed form and dispatched by the divine sender in single portions to form neatly composed pericopes to be inserted into a more extensive Qurʾānic recital that also contains less universal elements, such as the debate about ephemeral issues of the community. This ceremonial function of the biblically inspired narrative is underlined by introductory formulas, for example, *wa-dhkur fī'l-kitāb*, "mention in (the excerpt of) the book" (Q 19:16). At a later stage, in Medina, as the particular form of revelation communicated to the Muslim community is regarded as constituting a scripture of its own, meaning that community matters are acknowledged as part of salvation history, whole *sūras* figure as manifestations of *al-kitāb*.

Place, time, and agents in the later Meccan sūras

In the middle and late Meccan *sūras*, a new framework of the message in terms of space is realizable. These texts, which abound in accounts of biblical narratives, have broadened the scope for the listeners, who are led away from their local surroundings to a distant landscape, the Holy Land, familiar as the scenery where the history of the community's spiritual forebears has taken place. The introduction of the orientation in prayer, *qibla*, towards Jerusalem is an unequivocal testimony of this general change in spatial orientation. It was adopted during a phase of development when, through the new focus on biblical lore, a remarkable widening of the young community's horizons was taking place, in terms of time as well as of space. One might dare to hypothesize that the Jerusalem *qibla* came about as a gestural expression of the deeply felt experience of having gained new spiritual horizons. Together, two essential novelties – the newly attained convergence of the Qurʾānic revelations with the scriptures of the two other monotheistic religions and the simultaneous adoption of the *topographia sacra* of the earlier religions – marked a new self-consciousness for the young Islamic community. The new self-awareness was no longer based primarily on the rites practiced at the Kaʿba, but on a new source of authority, the consciousness of being among the receivers and bearers of a scripture, and as such, having a share in the memory of salvation history, transported by the medium of writing.

By its very gesture, the *qibla*, oriented toward Jerusalem, points to this new connection between the emerging Islamic community and the older religions. It is not surprising then that the Qurʾānic allusion to the Meccan sanctuary and its rites as the previous guarantors of social coherence – allusions, up until that point, so numerous in the introductory sections of the Meccan *sūras* – were soon replaced by a stereotypical introductory evocation of the book, *al-kitāb*, now recognized as the most significant common spiritual possession, a spiritual space replacing the real space.

In the earliest *sūras*, up to the point of the emigration, there had been few places considered worth evoking with the exception of Mecca and some deserted sites in Arabia; after that point, however, one does not find any further reference to Mecca (with the exception of Q 17:1). Instead, the "Blessed Land" is introduced as a space in which the oppressed believer may take refuge and where most of the prophets had worked; the *sūras* culminate in an oft-repeated appeal to examples reaching far back into the history of the spiritual forebears. Jerusalem, represented through its temple, is the center of the space marked by the Banū Isrāʾīl's scripture and, thus, by writing. All prayers gravitate in the direction of Jerusalem as their natural destination (Neuwirth 2003).

The vast majority of these *sūras* start with an evocation of the book, *kitāb*, and are often introduced by a chiffre, a single letter from the Arabic alphabet or a set of such letters which serves to underscore divine authorship but which is missing in the early *sūras*. This beginning seems to hint at a newly achieved cultic function of the recited text which is no longer understood as the immediate communication of an inspired message to the community, but as a recital from a heavenly Scripture assumed as preexisting and only reproduced through recitation. With the innovation of the orientation in prayer, *qibla*, towards a new sacred space, the "more remote temple" (*al-masjid al-aqṣā*), prayer gained new momentum. Through replacing the local "sacred sanctuary" (*al-masjid al-ḥarām*), by an imagined other, the rites of *ṣalāt*, which themselves had previously been part of the syncretistic cultus centered around the Kaʿba, became a rite filled with salvific historical significance. Through the *fātiḥa*, the communal prayer, institutionalized in middle Meccan times, the expression "Lord of the worlds" (*rabb al-ʿālamīn*), becomes prominent. It occurs already in some very early *sūras* (Q 81:29; 83:6) to express a particularly comprehensive divine predicate. The Arabic *rabb al-ʿālamīn*, contrary to the Hebrew cognate, *ribbōn ʿōlām* (in the sense of "Lord of eternity"), does not denote a temporal relation, but rather refers to God as the Lord of the inhabited earthly world that is represented by humans. While the case demonstrates the closeness of Qurʾānic diction to that of other monotheist traditions, at the same time it also highlights a peculiar Qurʾānic new reading of those traditions.

Becoming a Representation of the "Book": Medinan Texts

In Medina *sūras* have not only given up their tripartite scheme but they also display much less sophistication in the patterns of their composition. One type may be summarily termed the "rhetorical" *sūra* or sermon (Q 22; 24; 33; 47; 48; 49; 57 to 66); they consist of an address to the community whose members are called upon directly by formulas such as *yā ayyuhā ʾl-nās* (Q 22:1, "O people"). In these *sūras*, which in some cases (59; 61; 62; 64) are stereotypically introduced by initial hymnal formulas strongly reminiscent of the biblical psalms, the prophet, now designated as *al-nabī*, appears no longer as a mere transmitter of the message but as a salvific historical protagonist personally addressed by God in the formula *yā ayyuhā ʾl-nabī*, "O prophet" (Q 33:22), or as an agent acting in synergy with the divine *persona* and appearing as *Allāhu wa-rasūluhu*, "God and his prophet" (Q 33:22). With the inclusion of texts about – sometimes ephemeral – community matters into the category of divine rulings, *qurʾān*, "recitation," has become identical with *kitāb*, the excerpts from the heavenly book. In contrast to the widely monothematic, medium-sized Medinan *sūras* that come close to sermons, the bulk of the Medinan texts are quite complex. Most of the so-called "long *sūras*" (Q 2–5; 8; 9) cease to be neatly structured compositions but appear to be the result of a process of collection that we cannot yet reconstruct. A systematic study of these *sūras* remains an urgent desideratum in the field.

With few exceptions, in the Medinan *sūras* we once more encounter the Meccan "*enjeux*," though the eschatological sections and the *āyāt*, the signs of divine omnipotence derived from nature, are no longer unfolded at length, but are rather summarily evoked. This should not be taken as a decisive shift in spiritual interest. Although new topics which occupy the focus of the community's attention do emerge, the earlier topics remain present, since it is the partial corpus of the early *sūras*, later assembled in the final part of the codex, which the believers know by heart and which serves as the textual basis for the emerging ritual prayers.

Although occasional regulations – mostly concerning cultic matters – do occur in Meccan *sūras* (e.g., Q 73:1–3, addressed to the prophet, revised for the community in Q 73:20), more elaborate regulations concerning not only cultic but also communal affairs figure in the Medinan context. Their binding force is sometimes underlined by a reference to the transcendent source, such as "it is prescribed for you," *kutiba alaykum* (Q 2:183–7), or "a duty imposed by God," *farīḍatun mina 'llāh*, (Q 9:60). Medinan regulations do not display any structured composition nor do they participate in neatly composed units; rather, they suggest a redaction of originally isolated texts.

A new element appearing in Medinan *sūras* is the report of contemporary events experienced or enacted by the community, for instance the battle of Badr in the year 2/624 (Q 3:123), the battle of Uḥud in 3/625 (Q 3:155–74), the expulsion of the Banū Naḍīr in 3/625 (Q 59:2–5), the siege of Khaybar in 7/628 (Q 48:15), the expedition to Tābūk in 9/630 (Q 9:29–35), or the farewell sermon of the prophet in 10/631 (Q 5:1–3). It is noteworthy that these reports do not display a particularly artistic literary rendering. Nor do they betray any particular pathos. It does not come as a surprise then that, unlike the situation in Judaism and Christianity where biblical history has been fused to form a mythical drama of salvation, no such great narrative has arisen from the Qur'ān itself. A metahistorical blueprint of the genesis of Islam was constructed only later, and through the inclusion of a great amount of non-Qur'ānic material, through the *sīra*, the biography of the prophet. The Qur'ān itself admits mythopoiesis only in one respect: to celebrate the process of revelation itself.

Place, time, and agents in the Medinan sūras

In early Medinan times, a new group of listeners, if not always real, at least virtual, appears on stage: the Medinan Jews. Jews appear as believers (Q 2:62; 5:69; 22:17), sometimes on the condition that they believe in the concrete Islamic message as in Q 4:162. In some other passages they appear as included among the People of the Book (Q 3:113–14) and are, as such, even assured to be rewarded twice over, thanks to their belief in their own revealed scriptures as well as in the Qur'ān (Q 28:52–4; see Rubin 2002: 21–34). In later Medinan texts, however, they turn into the target of fierce Qur'ānic polemics.

Apart from the Medinan *sūras* as such, there are a number of Meccan *sūras* that have been extended through Medinan additions or re-reads with a new religious-political dimension of meaning (Neuwirth forthcoming). Although additions are acknowledged in Islamic tradition (Nagel 1995) and were marked as such in earlier Qur'ānic scholarship (Nöldeke 1909–38), these texts have not yet been systematically studied (for a first attempt see Neuwirth 2004). The term "Medinan additions" is, of course, not to be understood in the sense of textual interpolations inserted into the *sūras* after their codification. They should rather be considered as additions entailing specifications or modifications (see Q 74:30 modifying 74:1) that were communicated together with their respective Meccan basis texts on the occasion of a later recitation of those Meccan *sūras* during the prophet's activity. Though we may assume that the long Medinan *sūras*, in view of the mnemotechnical challenges posed by their prosaic verse structure, should have been preserved through writing, their primary social setting, and thus the site of their reception and debate, will not have changed but will have remained a public performance.

Medinan *sūras* reflect a retrograde movement in comparison to that observed in the later Meccan texts: from the Holy Land, the realm of the history of the earlier People of the Book, back to the peninsula, in particular Mecca. Not only is the orientation of prayer shifted from Jerusalem to the Meccan sanctuary, the image of the exodus of Moses and his people is equally banished from its scope. We see the emergence of the figure of Abraham as the new role model of the prophet Muḥammad whose act of founding the Meccan sanctuary and initiating its rites establishes a new salvific paradigm. The prophet Muḥammad completes the work started by Abraham by furnishing Mecca with the essential merit of being the original site of revelation (Q 2:127), which had, until then, been the prerogative of Jerusalem (Isaiah 2:3).

Thus, in Medina the honorific name of the Kaʿba, "the sacred sanctuary" (*al-masjid al-ḥarām*), acquired new momentum. It is the center of the pilgrimage (*ḥajj*), an institution founded by Abraham. Abraham, who historically precedes the rest of the prophets, is a pure monotheist, a *ḥanīf*. The Arabic word is a cognate of Syriac *ḥanpā*, meaning people not belonging to the Church, perceived as pagans (De Blois 2002) and, in the Bible, credited with the introduction of circumcision (Hebrew *millah*) as a token of his covenant with God; the concept reappears in the Qurʾān as the warrant of a covenantal creed, called *millat Ibrāhīm*. The new community that follows the Abrahamic creed is portrayed as now having a religion of its own, expressed by the word *dīn*, a homonym of the earlier-employed *dīn* in the sense of reckoning, or divine judgment to be held on the "last day." A visible symbol of this new religion is not least the fast (*ṣawm*) of Ramaḍān that commemorates the crucial privilege of the community to be receivers of a scripture of their own (Ammann 2001).

Note

1 The task has been carried out for the Meccan *sūras* by Neuwirth (1981). In view of newly developed additional criteria the work needs to be revised and complemented.

Further reading

Cragg, Kenneth (1971) *The Event of the Qurʾān: Islam in its Scripture*. Allen & Unwin, London.
Donner, Fred (1998) *Narratives of Islamic Origins: The Beginnings of Islamic Historical Writing*. Darwin Press, Princeton.

Graham, William (1995) "The winds to herald His mercy" and other "Signs for those of certain faith." Nature as token of God's sovereignty and grace in the Qur'ān. In: Lee, Sang Hyun, Proudfoot, Wayne, and Blackwell, Albert L. (eds.) *Faithful Imagining: Essays in Honor of Richard R. Niebuhr.* Scholars Press, Atlanta, pp. 18–38.

Madigan, Daniel A. (2001) *The Qur'ān's Self-image. Writing and Authority in Islam's Scripture.* Princeton University Press, Princeton.

Neuwirth, Angelika (1993) Images and metaphors in the introductory sections of the Makkan *sūras*. In: Hawting, G. R. and Shareef, A.-K. (eds.) *Approaches to the Qur'an.* Routledge, London, pp. 3–36.

Neuwirth, Angelika (2003) From the sacred mosque to the remote temple. Sūrat al-Isrā' between text and commentary. In: McAuliffe, J., Walfish, B., and Goering, J. (eds.) *With Reverence for the Word: Medieval Scriptural Exegesis in Judaism, Christianity, and Islam.* Oxford University Press, New York, pp. 376–407.

Sells, Michael (1990) Sound, spirit and gender in Sūrat al-Qadr. *Journal of the American Oriental Society* 11, 101–39.

Sells, Michael (1993) Sound and meaning in Sūrat al-Qāriʿa. *Arabica* 40, 403–30.

Sells, Michael (1999) *Approaching the Qur'ān: The Early Revelations.* White Cloud Press, Ashland OR.

Wansbrough, J. (1977) *Quranic Studies: Sources and Methods of Scriptural Interpretation.* Oxford University Press, Oxford.

CHAPTER 10

Sacrality and Collection

Aliza Shnizer

The foundations for the Qur'ān's sacredness and standing as the major mainstay of Islamic religion and culture are to be found already in the book itself. The very fact that the word of God is expressed in direct speech and frequently in the first person plural bears witness to the book's divine character and places it within the domain of what may be defined as holy scripture *par excellence*: a book revealed by God or inspired by the holy spirit.

To the Qur'ān's divine nature testify also descriptions of its revelation, based on a heavenly source, as well as the various titles and metaphors used to describe it, such as the "book of God" (*kitāb Allāh*), "revelation" (*waḥy* or *tanzīl*), "light," as well as "precious book," "blessed book," "wise book," "tremendous book," "glorious," "honorable," and many other similar titles, epithets, and metaphors which serve to describe holy scriptures. The various descriptions of the revelation of the Qur'ān, its titles and descriptive appellations, appear inside the text next to tales of the prophets, commandments and laws, ethical sayings, and the other sundry topics we expect to find in a scripture. However, the sheer number of titles, descriptions, and metaphors used by the Qur'ān to describe its own nature as a divine book revealed by God Himself, is quite unique.

Early Islamic tradition (*ḥadīth* in Arabic), which reflects major landmarks in the history of Islam and Islamic civilization, added to these titles and metaphors, and provided profuse descriptions of the Qur'ān's divine origin, the mode of its revelation to the prophet Muḥammad, and the way in which it was cast into a single text. An examination of the traditions of this type which were disseminated during the first two centuries of Islam, a time when *ḥadīth* was taking shape, sheds light on the process by which the Qur'ān's standing within the Muslim community was established, until it became the supreme focus of sanctity in Islam. On the basis of such early Islamic traditions one may conclude that consolidation of the Qur'ān's status went hand-in-hand with the development of Muslims' perception of their religion, which had undergone various transformations during the first centuries of Islam. These transformations and their relation to the process by which the Qur'ān's status as scripture became consolidated are reflected not only in the *ḥadīth* texts, but also in the writings of Muslim scholars in the centuries that followed, where an attempt was made to cope with the many nuances, contradictions, and difficulties which they had inherited from earlier Muslims, the creators of the *ḥadīth*. In this chapter *ḥadīth* texts will be utilized as a window into the thoughts of its creators, Muslim believers who lived many decades after the prophet's death and whose religious ideas were reflected in the way they chose to describe the divine nature of the Qur'ān.

The Qur'ān's Divine Origin and Nature

The Qur'ān itself was the major source which shaped the Islamic tradition. Early Muslims based their ideas about the Qur'ān's divine nature first and foremost on the verses of the Qur'ān. It was the Qur'ān from which they adopted the terms the "preserved tablet" (*lawḥ maḥfūẓ*, Q 85:21–2), the "mother of the book" (*umm al-kitāb*, Q 43:4), the "concealed book" (*kitāb maknūn*, Q 56:78) and the "reminder" (*al-dhikr*, Q 21:105), which became synonymous in Islamic tradition with the original heavenly copy of the Qur'ān, the celestial archetype from which revelations were sent down to the prophet (see also Jeffery 1952: 15–17; Wansbrough 1977: 83). The term "heavenly books" (*al-zubur*, Q 54:52) was also perceived as relating to the Qur'ān's origins, and understood as referring to the divine originals from which the Qur'ān was revealed (see al-Ṭabarī 1972: XXVII, 66).

The concept of a heavenly Qur'ān symbolizes in early traditions the intimate relationship between God Himself and the actual, "earthly" Qur'ān, and also the idea that the heavenly and earthly copies are identical. In one tradition, for example, the relationship between God and the Qur'ān is expressed as follows: "The glorious Qur'ān is inscribed on a preserved tablet near God" (al-Ṭabarī 1972: XXX, 90). In the same spirit another tradition maintains that the preserved tablet is inscribed on the forehead of Isrāfīl, the most senior of the angels of revelation, who stands by the divine throne (see al-Ṭabarī 1972: XXX, 90; Ibn Abī Ḥātim 1997: X, 3414). The relation between the heavenly and earthly copies of the Qur'ān is clearly explained in a tradition which claims that the Qur'ān possessed by Muslims is identical to its heavenly counterpart. "The Qur'ān is found in the mother of the book near God," the tradition says, "from which it was copied" (al-Ṭabarī 1972: XXV, 30). The idea that the heavenly and earthly Qur'āns are identical is linked in some other traditions with the claim that all scripture (meaning the Jewish and Christian Bibles as well) have their origin in the divine book located in heaven. "The mother of the book is the source of all scripture" says the tradition (Ibn Abī Ḥatīm 1997: II, 593). Later Muslim scholars reiterated the idea that all scripture is of divine origin, making explicit the claim that the Qur'ān and the other holy scriptures were all copied from the mother of the book (see, for example, al-Qurṭubī 1987: XIX, 298; see also Graham 1987: 84).

The various appellations given to the divine copy of the Qur'ān are embedded within descriptions of its revelation to the prophet. The dominant view in these descriptions is that the Qur'ān was revealed in two stages. First, the Qur'ān was sent down in its entirety in a single occasion from the highest heaven, where the original copy is stored, to the lowest heaven. Then, it was sent down to Muḥammad in segments over a period of many years. An example of this view is a tradition quoting Ibn ʿAbbās, a well-known Qurʾānic commentator (cousin of Muḥammad, d. ca. 68/687), as saying that the Qurʾān was sent down "as a single utterance" (*jumla wāḥida*) from the heavenly books to the lowest heaven, whence its contents concerning commands, prohibitions, and wars were revealed at a moderate pace (al-Ṭabarī 1972: II, 84–5). The distinction made here between two separate stages of revelation is typical of descriptions of the Qurʾān's revelation in general.

The formulation of these descriptions was influenced by the fact that the Qurʾān provides no clear and unambiguous explanation of the method by which the Qurʾānic text as it exists in the divine original was revealed to Muḥammad (see also Wansbrough 1977: 36–8). From these descriptions it is clear that early Muslims' main motivation was the desire to resolve difficulties within that text; on the one hand, the Qurʾān describes its own revelation as a single occasion in the month of Ramaḍān (Q 2:185), or on a blessed night (Q 44:3), or on the night of divine decree (Q 97:1), but, on the other hand, as a multiple continuing occurrence (Q 25:32). The latter verse confirms the claim made by the unbelievers that the Qurʾān was not revealed as a "single utterance" but rather gradually, one segment at a time. Early Muslims were aware of the problematic nature of the description of the Qurʾān's revelation having occurred in a single night or even in a single month. Such a description is in direct conflict not only with certain other Qurʾānic verses (and especially with Q 25:32) but also with numerous very ancient traditions that had grown around the "occasions of revelation" (*asbāb al-nuzūl*) of numerous verses. These traditions, which expand the meaning of the Qurʾānic text and anchor many verses within a narrative background, have become a major feature of the genre known as "Biography of the prophet" (*al-sīra al-nabawiyya*) and of early Qurʾānic commentaries (on the function of these traditions, see Rippin 1988; see also Rubin 1995: 226–33). They also clearly see revelation as a continuous and on-going process, a fact reflected in countless traditions in which various Qurʾānic verses are said to have been revealed over the years in reaction to various episodes in the prophet's life.

The attempts of the early Muslim community to cope with the contradictions and occasional obscurity in the Qurʾān on this matter show clear signs of a desire to integrate the Qurʾānic view of revelation as a continuous, repetitive act (in particular according to Q 25:32), with the other Qurʾānic view, of a one-time revelation of the entire Qurʾān (mainly in Q 2:185 and Q 97:1). This latter view in the Qurʾān was probably influenced by the biblical account of the law handed down to Moses on Mt. Sinai, i.e. on a single occasion (see Wansbrough 1977: 37). The desire to find a compromise between these two mutually contradictory views of the revelation brought about the formulation of a harmonizing approach according to which the Qurʾān was indeed sent down in one step in the heavenly stage, and was subsequently revealed to Muḥammad piecemeal over many years in the second, earthly stage. All the harmonizing descriptions make use of the Qurʾānic phrase "as a single utterance" (Q 25:32) to refer to the first stage of the revelation. In fact, the impression one gets from all the traditions dealing with the revelation of the Qurʾān is that they wish to emphasize the fact that it was sent down in its entirety at least in one of the stages of revelation. This is true in particular of a group of traditions which limit themselves to describing only the first stage of revelation (see al-Ṭabarī 1972: II, 85).

Using the harmonizing technique also solved the problem of the different accounts given in the Qurʾān for the time of the revelation: the night of divine decree, a "blessed night," is claimed to have occurred in the month of Ramaḍān, thus resolving another potential contradiction. In fact, the opinion that in the first stage of revelation the Qurʾān was sent down in its entirety in the night of divine decree in the month of Ramaḍān has become generally accepted in Islamic tradition (There is some disagreement among early traditions concerning the exact date of the night of divine decree, on which the Qurʾān was revealed. Various dates, all in the latter third of the month of Ramaḍān, are given; see al-Suyūṭī 1985: VI, 416–18). The various verses on the matter were harmonized in an effort to introduce an unambiguous conception of the Qurʾān's revelation which would preserve the Qurʾān's own inner integrity and its status as a perfect, consistent, and coherent holy text.

In many of the harmonizing descriptions the question of God's relation to the prophet arises. Two views predominate. On the one hand, the sending down of the Qurʾān is described as direct divine revelation, with no mediation between God and the prophet. In one typical tradition Ibn ʿAbbās says that "God has sent down the Qurʾān to the lowest heaven on the night of divine decree, and whenever He wanted to reveal anything of it He revealed it" (al-Ṭabarī 1972: II, 84–5; see also Ibn Abī Shayba 1989: VII, 191). In another quite similar tradition, God is not just the source of revelation, but also compiles the messages in Muḥammad's lifetime after they had been revealed. "The Qurʾān in its entirety was sent down in one piece, on the night of divine decree in the month of Ramaḍān, to the lowest heaven," this tradition says, "and when God wanted to cause something to happen on earth He sent down parts of it, until He collected [all of] it together" (Ibn al-Ḍurays 1987: 71–2; the term "collected" is frequently used in descriptions of the compilation of the Qurʾānic text by the caliphs after the prophet's death). However, on the other hand, there is also a tendency to introduce an angel, Gabriel, as an intermediary between God and the prophet. The angel Gabriel's role as an intermediary is based on Q 2:97, where he is represented as the angel in charge of revealing the Qurʾān to the prophet. It is this tendency which has received general acceptance; it is reflected in traditions, for example, with an identical chain of authorities as the traditions quoted above, but in which the angel Gabriel has replaced God as the agent of revelation. "The Qurʾān was sent down in one piece from the preserved tablet to the lowest heaven," Ibn ʿAbbās says in such tradition, "and then Gabriel revealed it to Muḥammad; it contained what was said by the polytheists and its answer to them" (Ibn Manda 1996: II, 705). The motivation behind ascribing the act of revelation to Gabriel was likely the desire of some early Muslims to refrain from describing God in anthropomorphic terms. But others, who wished to stress God's closeness to the Qurʾān, did not recoil from such metaphors and did indeed attribute the act of revelation to God.

Considerable emphasis is also laid in traditions on where in the lowest heaven the Qurʾān was placed before it was revealed to the prophet. In a manner similar to descriptions of the Qurʾān's starting point on the course to revelation on earth in the highest heaven, traditions also tend to describe its intermediate resting place as a temple of the angels in heaven, named the "temple of glory" (*bayt al-ʿizza*). One tradition, for example, quotes Ibn ʿAbbās as saying: "The Qurʾān was separated from the reminder (*al-dhikr*) and placed in the temple of glory in the lowest heaven. Then Gabriel began revealing it to the prophet by portions" (al-Ḥākim al-Nīsābūrī 1990: II, 223). Later Islamic *ḥadīth* scholars explained the non-Qurʾānic term *bayt al-ʿizza* in the spirit of such traditions as a temple of the angels which was the model for the earthly Kaʿba (see Ibn Kathīr 1952: IV, 298). The non-Qurʾānic term *bayt al-ʿizza* is replaced in other versions by the Qurʾānic phrase "the inhabited house" (*al-bayt al-maʿmūr*) (Q 52:4) which, in Qurʾānic commentaries, has come to refer to the heavenly Kaʿba (see al-Ṭabarī 1972: II, 84–5). Qurʾānic expressions are also used in a tradition according to which additional angels played a part in sending down the Qurʾān. In this tradition Ibn ʿAbbās says that the Qurʾān was sent down in one piece from God, from the preserved tablet to the honorable scribes (an expression taken from Q 80:15–16, commonly taken to refer to the angels) who write in the lowest heaven. Then the scribes gave the Qurʾān to Gabriel in segments over twenty nights and Gabriel gave it to Muḥammad piece by piece over twenty years (al-Qurṭubī 1987: XVII, 224).

The symmetry between the twenty nights during which Gabriel received the Qurʾān from the angels and the twenty years it took him to reveal it, is based on the common belief that the Qurʾān was revealed to Muḥammad during the twenty years of his prophetic mission. This belief is anchored in a very widely accepted canonical tradition according to which the Qurʾān was revealed to Muḥammad for ten years in Mecca (his first period of activity) and for another ten years in Medina (see Rubin 1995: 196–7). Traditions differ with respect to the amount of revealed text at different stages in the prophet's life. The texts in question are at times described in general terms as "segments" or "parts," but at times they are also characterized more specifically as containing a certain number of verses, one, two, four, five, and so on up to ten verses, which were revealed to the prophet at any one time (al-Suyūṭī 1991: I, 97; Nöldeke 1909–38: I, 29).

The piecemeal revelation of the Qurʾān, verse by verse over a period of many years, had the advantage of providing Muḥammad with ready-made solutions to the various challenges he faced throughout his life. According to the traditions, one major challenge he had to face was the arguments which polytheists used in an attempt to refute Islam and its prophet. Numerous traditions express this concern, as reflected in the tradition quoted above, according to which revealed Qurʾānic segments contained "what was said by the polytheists and its [i.e., the Qurʾān's] response to them." In another tradition the reaction contained in the earthly phase of the revelation to Muḥammad is phrased as constituting "an answer to what people said." This tradition describes the act of revelation as follows: "The Qurʾān was sent down in one piece on the night of divine decree in the month of Ramaḍān and was placed in the temple of glory. Then for twenty years it was revealed to the prophet as an answer to what people said" (Ibn al-Ḍurays 1987: 72; cf. Madigan 2001: 63–4). The literary starting point of these traditions is the style of the Qurʾān itself; the motif of "rebuttal" in the traditions reflects the polemical style which the Qurʾān uses when attacking its opponents. Often such polemical statements in the Qurʾān open with the imperative form "Say!". This type of verse (see also Watt and Bell 1970: 75–7) contains God's answer to a question addressed to Muḥammad or a statement, a provocative declaration or an act (usually on the part of polytheists). This very common Qurʾānic literary structure was the fertile soil on which grew the many traditions of the "occasion of revelation" type, which constitute a significant element in the conception of the multi-stage, continuous revelation of the Qurʾān. As their name implies, such traditions consist of a typical answering formula: "Then God revealed the verse" in reaction to a certain event, situation, question, etc. In a broader context the concept of the piecemeal revelation of the Qurʾān has played a major role in shaping a view of human history in its entirety. Revelation in this view is not limited to the Islamic sphere, but encompasses the entire universe, as we have seen in some traditions in which the revelation of the Qurʾān is seen as part of a continuous cosmic event that has affected the course of human history ("and when God wanted to cause something to happen on earth He sent down parts of it"), as a result of God's desire to cause certain events to happen in the history of all peoples.

As part of the concept of the piecemeal revelation some traditions highlight the difference between the way in which the Qurʾān and previous scriptures were revealed. The different modes of revelation are to be found in traditions of the "occasion of revelation" type, whose justification is Q 25:32–3. In these traditions the prophet is described as engaged in a debate with the Jews or with his polytheist opponents from the Meccan tribe of Quraysh, concerning the Qurʾān's mode of revelation. Again and again it is emphasized that the Qurʾān was revealed in segments, in contrast to the books of the Jews and Christians, which were sent down in their entirety in a single revelation (see also Wansbrough 1977: 36). Thus, for example, it is related in the name of Ibn ʿAbbās that when the Jews saw that the Qurʾān was being revealed in segments, they asked: "Why was the Qurʾān not revealed to him in one utterance as the Torah was revealed to Moses, the Gospels to Jesus and the Book of Psalms to David?" It was in response to what they said that God revealed Q 25:32–3: "And the infidels said: 'Why was the Qurʾān not revealed to him in one utterance?' This [We have done] in order to strengthen with it your heart" (al-Qurṭubī 1987: XIII, 28; see also Ibn Abī Ḥātim 1997: VIII, 2689–90). Another tradition quotes the nonbelieving members of the tribe Quraysh as uttering blasphemous words and expressions of doubt in the prophet's veracity, due to the fact that revelation came to him piecemeal and not all at once. Ibn ʿAbbās says in this tradition that the polytheists in Mecca said: "If Muḥammad is a prophet, as he claims to be, why does his Lord punish him and not reveal the Qurʾān to him in one utterance, instead of sending down to him a single verse, or two verses, or a single chapter (*sūra*) at a time?" Then God revealed Q 25: 33 (Ibn Abī Ḥātim 1997: VIII, 2689).

Most later Muslim scholars adopted these views of the early traditions and discussed the possible logic in the divine decision to reveal the Qurʾān piecemeal in contrast to Jewish and Christian scripture. Their discussions reflect a concern lest this mode of revelation may be construed as a drawback or defect in the Qurʾān. However, they hasten to clarify that this supposed defect is, in fact, an expression of God's grace toward the prophet and his nation and an indication of the prophet's merit and the merit of the Islamic nation over that of all others. The gradual revelation of the Qurʾān, they explain, made it easier to learn and accept, unlike the other scriptures, which were not easy for their people to accept. As an example these later scholars bring the Jews whose Torah was revealed to them "in one utterance" and which they considered to be quite difficult to accept. In fact they refused it until God forced it upon them (al-Suyūṭī 1991: I, 94).

Some Muslim scholars tried to find a common denominator between all scripture. According to their view the Jewish and Christian scriptures were revealed in the same manner as the Qurʾān, namely in segments and at different times (see al-Suyūṭī 1991: I, 93–4). Indeed, this argument does have a basis in Jewish sources, as pointed out by Wansbrough, who mentions a Mishnaic parallel to the Muslim idea of piecemeal revelation: "The Torah was revealed scroll by scroll" (see Wansbrough 1977: 37).

The Distinction Between the Actual Qurʾān and the Heavenly Qurʾān

Early Muslims stressed the Qurʾān's divine origin and nature and praised its mode of revelation in comparison to that of previous scriptures, but they made a distinction between the heavenly Qurʾān and the actual, "earthly" text possessed by the believers. In fact, they considered the Qurʾānic text in their possession, known as the "ʿUthmānic codex," as "flawed" and incomplete. The ʿUthmānic codex was compiled and fixed, according to the most commonly accepted view in Islamic tradition, thirty years after Muḥammad's death. The codex was compiled and edited on the orders of the third Caliph, ʿUthmān b. ʿAffān (d. 35/656). The task of compilation was given to the companion Zayd b. Thābit (d. 45/663–4) who served as the prophet's "scribe of revelations."

The distinction between the two versions of the Qurʾān, one in heaven and the other the ʿUthmānic codex, is made quite clearly in a group of traditions dealing with the history of the Qurʾānic text, which describe the way Qurʾānic revelations were compiled into a complete version of the Qurʾān in the prophet's lifetime. According to these traditions the various revelations were brought together toward the end of the period of prophetic activity, and the task of putting together the entire book was completed after considerable time had elapsed. The process began with the formulation of an annual version of revelations in the month of Ramaḍān, and ended with the formulation of a final and complete version not long before Muḥammad's death (cf. Burton 1977: 192–5). The annual and final versions are described in a pair of mutually complementary traditions, both from Ibn ʿAbbās. One tradition reports on the formulation of the annual version, stressing the status of Ramaḍān as the month of revelation (based on Q 2:185): "God has sent down the Qurʾān throughout the entire year. When the month of Ramaḍān arrived Gabriel compared the Qurʾānic revelations with the prophet, and then God abrogated what was meant to be abrogated, wrote down what was meant to be written down, gave a decision on what was meant to be decided, and caused to abandon what was meant to be abandoned" (Ibn al-Ḍurays 1987: 75; see also ʿAbd al-Razzāq 1983: XI, 338; Ibn Ḥajar 1959: IX, 43). The second tradition goes on to describe the way in which the final version of the Qurʾān was fixed. In it Ibn ʿAbbās says: "The prophet recited the book before Gabriel every year in the month of Ramaḍān, and in the month in which he died he recited it before him twice" (*ʿarḍatayni*;

see Ibn Abī Shayba 1989: VII, 204; Ibn Ḥajar 1959: IX, 43). The term "reciting the Qurʾān twice" means compiling all the Qurʾānic revelations into a complete and final version. In other words, these traditions claim that toward the end of the prophet's life a special act of revelation occurred in which a final and complete version of the Qurʾān was created. The terms "recite" (*ʿarḍ*) and "recital" (*ʿarḍa*) which are here used in the context of the compilation of the Qurʾān during the prophet's lifetime are taken from the domain of learning the Qurʾān. They refer to the custom whereby a Qurʾānic scholar recites the entire Qurʾān from beginning to end a number of times before a more senior scholar. (For examples of this custom, see Ibn Abī Shayba 1989: VII, 203; Abū ʿUbayd 1995: II, 191; for the meaning of the term *ʿarḍ* as referring to a critical recital of the Qurʾānic text, see also Melchert 2000: 11). This kind of critical recital, which had become customary among Muslims, thus became the model for the description of how the Qurʾānic version was compiled in the prophet's lifetime. It also explains why the act of recital according to these traditions was performed by the prophet, with the angel Gabriel playing the role of superior authority.

However, the final version of the Qurʾān, critically reviewed by the angel of revelation, was not destined to become the text possessed by the believers, to wit the official canonical version edited according to accepted tradition in the days of the caliph ʿUthmān by the companion of the prophet, Zayd b. Thābit. Rather, branching traditions created a continuous link between the intact revealed version dating from the times of the prophet and the "pre-ʿUthmānic" version of the companion ʿAbd Allāh b. Masʿūd (d. 32/652–3), a highly respected early Islamic personality and an unimpeachable authority on the Qurʾān. The claim that ʿAbd Allāh b. Masʿūd's version is identical to the original revealed text is articulated in Kufan traditions according to which ʿAbd Allāh b. Masʿūd was actually present when the final version of the Qurʾān was revealed to the prophet. In one such tradition Ibn ʿAbbās says: "The Qurʾān was recited before the prophet every year once, in the month of Ramaḍān, until the year in which he died. Then it was recited before him twice, in the presence of ʿAbd Allāh, who witnessed the abrogations and amendments made in it" (Ibn Abī Shayba 1989: VII, 204). Another Kufan tradition goes so far as to reject the notion that the authority of Ibn Masʿūd's version was ever replaced by that of a "second" version, an allusion to the ʿUthmānic codex. In this tradition Ibn ʿAbbās is quoted as asking: "Which of the two versions do you consider to be the first?" When he was told that ʿAbd Allāh's version was the first, he replied: "No. Indeed, this is the later version." This tradition ends by saying that ʿAbd Allāh witnessed the abrogations and amendments made in the revealed version from the times of the prophet (Ibn Ḥanbal 1895: I, 362; Burton 1977: 195).

These traditions thus posit an opposition between Ibn Masʿūd's pre-ʿUthmānic complete version with its stamp of revelation, and the ʿUthmānic codex, here referred to indirectly as the "other" version. In another tradition the latter is explicitly called "the version of Zayd," an expression referring to the ʿUthmānic codex (see also Burton 1977: 194), so called after Zayd b. Thābit. According to this tradition the question asked by Ibn ʿAbbās was: "Which of the two versions do you consider to be the later?" and the answer he received was: "The version of Zayd." To this Ibn ʿAbbās replied: "No, the prophet recited the Qurʾān before Gabriel every year, and in the year of his death he recited it before him twice. Therefore, Ibn Masʿūd's version is the later" (al-Ḥākim al-Nīsābūrī 1990: II, 250; see also Burton 1977: 195).

The motivation behind these mainly Kufan traditions is quite clear: their aim is to replace the ʿUthmānic codex with an alternative version of the Qurʾān, namely Ibn Masʿūd's, which represented the original and authentic text going back to the days of the prophet. Surprisingly enough this position, which casts doubt on the ʿUthmānic codex's reliability and sacredness, was not rejected out of hand. Indeed, it was accepted by certain circles at the early stages of Islam, who went so far as to disseminate a tradition in which the prophet himself appears to undermine the status of the ʿUthmānic codex as representing the pure revealed text. The prophet is quoted as saying: "Whosoever wishes to read the Qurʾān pure as when it was revealed, let him read the version of Ibn Umm ʿAbd," i.e. Ibn Masʿūd's version (Ibn Abī Shayba 1989: VII, 184; Abū ʿUbayd 1995: II, 209; Burton 1977: 193).

Kufan preference for ʿAbd Allāh b. Masʿūd's version as the only authentic Qurʾānic text sanctioned by revelation was accompanied by strong expressions of disapproval toward Zayd b. Thābit, who was considered unfit to compile and edit the Qurʾān, both because he was younger than Ibn Masʿūd and because of his humble origins (see also Goldziher 1920: 10; cf. Jeffery 1937: 20; Lecker 1997: 261–2). The traditions in question point out that Ibn Masʿūd had learned seventy or more chapters of the Qurʾān from the prophet when Zayd b. Thābit was still a boy with two sidelocks, or even just a seed in the loins of his infidel father. Thus, in one tradition, it is related that ʿAbd Allāh b. Masʿūd gave a sermon in which he said: "I learned from the mouth of the prophet seventy-some *sūras* when Zayd b. Thābit was still a youth with two sidelocks and played with the youngsters" (Ibn Ḥanbal 1895: I, 411). In another tradition Zayd is not mentioned by name but ʿAbd Allāh b. Masʿūd is reported to have asked: "Why don't you read [the Qurʾān] according to the version of so-and-so?" to which he answered: "I recited seventy *sūras* before the prophet and he told me I did well, at a time when the one whose version you would like me to recite was still a seed in the loins of an infidel" (Ibn Shabba 1979: III, 1006). The sharpest expression of opposition to Zayd b. Thābit and the version of the Qurʾān which he edited is to be found in a single tradition in which Ibn Masʿūd rejects the ʿUthmānic codex because of Zayd's Jewish origins. According to this tradition ʿAbd Allāh b. Masʿūd was asked: "Do you not read [the Qurʾān] according to Zayd's version?" to which he answered: "Why should I have anything to do with Zayd or his version? I learned seventy *sūras* from the prophet when Zayd was still a Jew with two sidelocks" (Ibn Shabba 1979: III, 1008; Lecker 1997: 260).

The opposition to Zayd b. Thābit was not to defend Ibn Masʿūd's prestige among Muslims against that of Zayd, but rather to point out that there exists an alternative version of the Qurʾān, more complete and earlier than the ʿUthmānic codex, in the form of Ibn Masʿūd's version. The claim in the pro-Ibn Masʿūd traditions that the ʿUthmānic codex is incomplete, is based on what canonical traditions say concerning how the Qurʾān was compiled. These traditions, known by the name of "the collection of the Qurʾān" (*jamʿ al-Qurʾān*), have been analyzed extensively, by Nöldeke (1909–38: II, 11–27, 47–62; cf. Burton 1977: 141–2, 225–40) and many subsequent scholars, who attempted to reconstruct the history of the Qurʾānic text using the available materials.

According to these traditions, when Muḥammad died, no complete, compiled, and edited version of the Qurʾān was in existence; instead there were only scattered revelations, some of which had been put in writing but most were only remembered by heart. A typical feature of these traditions is the chronological gap between the prophet's lifetime and the period in which the Qurʾānic text was compiled, and the exclusion of the prophet from the compilation and the editing of the Qurʾān (see Burton 1977: 126–7, 230–40). As a result, doubt has been cast on the authenticity of the codex and its integrity. It would therefore appear that it was these traditions which paved the way to the formation of the Kufan traditions whose aim was to present an earlier version of the Qurʾān, dating back to the days of the prophet himself, a version which was later rejected and replaced by another one, i.e. the ʿUthmānic codex.

The claim that the version of the Qurʾān which is in the actual possession of Muslims is incomplete and even flawed can be found in related group of traditions in which specific arguments against the Qurʾān's completeness are advanced. The basic claim of these traditions is that certain verses which had been part of the Qurʾān were later lost or omitted. These "lost verses" contained laws, sayings, ethical teachings, and merits of the prophet which do not appear in the version possessed by the believers. Occasionally we meet with the claim that entire paragraphs are missing, without any details being given as to their content, merely as an abstract argument against the book's completeness. The terms used in these traditions to refer to the loss of a verse are: "raised to heaven" (*rufiʿa*), a term which minimizes the damage to the book's integrity since the verse was abrogated by the will of God; a second term used in the connection is "omitted" (*usqiṭa*), which implies purposeful erasure. The charge of omitting parts of the Qurʾān is occasionally leveled at the caliph ʿUthmān. Western scholars have cast doubt on the veracity of these traditions, or have demonstrated that the verses in question could not have been part of the Qurʾān (see Nöldeke 1909–38: I, 255; Watt and Bell 1970: 54–5; Burton 1990: 49, 54).

The dominant tendency in Islamic tradition to ascribe incompleteness and flaws to the Qurʾān is contradicted by a pair of traditions preserved in Ibn Shabba's (d. 262/876) *Taʾrīkh al-madīna al-munawwara*, although they do not represent the commonly accepted Muslim account of how the ʿUthmānic codex came into being. One of these traditions, with a Basran-Kufan chain of transmission, quotes ʿAbd Allāh b. Zubayr (d. 73/692) as claiming that the prophet had written down the entire Qurʾān on scrolls (*ṣuḥuf*), which were then used by ʿUthmān for creating the official version of the Qurʾān. Ibn Zubayr relates that since in that caliph's time different versions of Qurʾānic texts abounded (a very common motif in traditions about ʿUthmān's compilation, which provides the motivation behind the creation of a single, uniform text), ʿUthmān collected the "pre-ʿUthmānic" versions and sent Ibn Zubayr to ʿĀʾisha, Muḥammad's wife. "I brought [from ʿĀʾisha] the scrolls in which the prophet had written the Qurʾān," relates Ibn Zubayr, "and, after we read them and polished them, ʿUthmān commanded that the other versions be torn up." The second tradition claims that the entire Qurʾān was written down on parchment from the mouth of the prophet. This tradition possesses a Syrian chain of transmission and quotes a person by the name of Abū Muḥammad al-Qurashī as saying that ʿUthmān had written to the provinces that in order to prevent disputes about the text of the Qurʾān he had asked

ʿĀʾisha to send him the parchment "on which is to be found the Qurʾān that was written down from the mouth of the prophet when God revealed it to Gabriel and Gabriel revealed it to Muḥammad. And it (i.e. the text) was pure." After that ʿUthmān gave the task of editing the Qurʾān to Zayd b. Thābit and other scribes from Medina (Ibn Shabba 1979: III, 997–8).

These solitary traditions with their tendency to link the ʿUthmānic text to the prophet and to stress the chain of revelation of the text (Allāh → Gabriel → Muḥammad) prove that in early Islam there were those who wanted to represent the actual text possessed by Muslims as identical with the complete, pure, divine original. However, this trend did not win widespread acceptance. Instead, preference was given to the tendency to present the Qurʾānic texts as incomplete. This is the trend that is reflected in the traditions according to which the earlier and more authentic version was the one preserved by Ibn Masʿūd, and in the traditions of the "collection of the Qurʾān" type and their attendant claims about omitted verses.

From these latter kinds of tradition, taken together, we can conclude that in early Islam the believers considered the Qurʾān which they possessed to be an incomplete version to which additions were possible. For this reason early Muslims granted the status of Qurʾānic revelation to various laws, sayings, ethical teachings and merits of the prophet which they believed were worthy of being part of the Qurʾān (cf. Burton 1977: 225–40). This approach then affected how "collection" traditions and traditions about specific omissions from the text were formulated. It seems that there was a sense among early Muslims that the Qurʾān was lacking some necessary elements, and as a result the boundary between what were actual Qurʾānic verses and what were utterances which deserved to be in the Qurʾān became blurred. The sense of incompleteness is most clearly seen in the formulation of the Kufan traditions which ascribe antiquity, completeness, and authenticity to Ibn Masʿūd's version. These traditions, too, challenge the ʿUthmānic version of the Qurʾān and, in fact, present Ibn Masʿūd's "pre-ʿUthmānic" version as the ideal Qurʾān. Traditions dealing with variant readings of the Qurʾān go as far as claiming that the ʿUthmānic text is also in need of linguistic and semantic corrections. In fact, they even claim that the ʿUthmānic version contains texts which should not be in it; according to these traditions Ibn Masʿūd omitted *sūrat al-fātiḥa* and *sūras* 113 and 114 from his version (see Nöldeke 1909–38: II, 34–5; Jeffery 1937: 21; see also Madigan 2001: 36). Both this view as well as the approach denying the completeness of the Qurʾān can be said to express a kind of early "textual criticism" of the Qurʾān.

It did not take long, however, before a reaction set in to the claim that Ibn Masʿūd's version was superior to the ʿUthmānic codex, whose sacredness and unique status were being undermined. As part of a description of the revelation in which the final version of the Qurʾān was fixed in the prophet's lifetime, the Kufan ʿUbayda b. ʿAmr (d. 74/693) is quoted as saying that the version recited to the prophet in the year in which he died is the version which the people read today (Ibn Abī Shayba 1989: VII, 204). Other traditions do express doubt as to the precise identity of the final version which was revealed to the prophet at the end of his life, but in any case they tend to identify that version with the ʿUthmānic codex, clearly with the intention of protecting its sacredness. Thus, for example, the Basran Muḥammad b. Sīrīn (d. 110/728) says that in the year of the prophet's death Gabriel recited the Qur'ān before the prophet twice "and I hope that our reading [the ʿUthmānic version] is identical with the final recital" (Ibn Saʿd 1957: II, 195; see also Ibn Shabba 1979: III, 994).

A substantial change in attitude toward the Qur'ānic text occurred during the subsequent centuries. Later Muslim scholars rejected the position taken by earlier generations concerning the ʿUthmānic text and insisted that the latter is, in fact, identical with the prophet's text. Al-Baghawī (d. 510/1117), for example, claims that the ʿUthmānic codex is "the final recital" read to Muḥammad before his death, and that this recital was witnessed by no other than Zayd b. Thābit, and not by Ibn Masʿūd. "It is said that Zayd b. Thābit witnessed the final recital, in which it was made clear what was abrogated and what was allowed to stand," says al-Baghawī, adding that the "final recital" is the text as it was written by the prophet and recited by him to Zayd b. Thābit. This written version of the Qur'ān was, so he claimed, the one used in public readings of the Qur'ān until the prophet's death (see al-Suyūṭī 1991: I, 110). Ibn Ḥazm (d. 456/1064) also takes a stand definitely in favor of the ʿUthmānic codex, but unlike al-Baghawī he ascribes the fixing of the Qur'ānic text which the believers possess to God alone. According to him, God collected the Qur'ān and established the order of its chapters and in the year of the prophet's death Gabriel taught him twice how to read it. "No one but God collected it," adds Ibn Ḥazm (1987: VI, 266). Although they differ from each other, both Ibn Ḥazm and al-Baghawī represent, each in his own way, the attempts of later Muslim scholars to remove the faults and drawbacks which earlier Muslims had found in the Qur'ānic text which they possessed, to wit the ʿUthmānic codex. Their intent was to represent this text as the pure and complete revealed version of the Qur'ān, *contra* traditions which viewed Ibn Masʿūd's version as superior (see also Goldziher 1920: 10), as well as "collection" traditions whose descriptions of the history of the ʿUthmānic codex opened the door to aspersions on its authenticity and sacredness.

Later Muslim scholars usually took great care when faced with the difficulties posed by such traditions not to reject overtly and out of hand ancient traditions whose authenticity was considered beyond doubt. Instead, they looked for ways to settle the difficulties they presented. Thus, al-Baghawī circumvented the difficulty by creating a harmonizing link between the canonical "collection" traditions and the traditions which report the creation of a final version of the Qur'ān in the lifetime of the prophet. Ibn Ḥazm, however, did not hesitate to reject the "collection" traditions outright. A third approach to the ʿUthmānic codex is represented by the scholar Ibn Ḥajar (d. 852/1449) who refrained, here as elsewhere, from casting doubt on the authenticity of the traditions in question. He does not reject the claim of a continuous link between the final revealed version of the Qur'ān in the prophet's lifetime and the pre-ʿUthmānic version of Ibn Masʿūd, but he tries to find an identical link also between the version made in the prophet's lifetime and the ʿUthmānic codex. He points out that it is possible to combine the "two final recitals" (the "two recitals" of the Qur'ān in the prophet's final year) and to maintain that one is in fact the version of Ibn Masʿūd and the other that of Zayd (Ibn Ḥajar 1959: IX, 45).

When we compare the approaches of earlier and later Muslims we find that the two groups differ with respect to their views as to the quality of the Qur'ānic text which they possessed. Earlier Muslims tended to the view that the Qur'ānic text was incomplete and flawed. In fact, they considered the ʿUthmānic text inferior to Ibn Masʿūd's "pre-ʿUthmānic" version. Later Muslim scholars, in contrast, represent the ʿUthmānic codex as a pure text of revelation, written entirely in the prophet's lifetime. True, this view can be found already in early times, as in the traditions preserved in Ibn Shabba quoted above, but at the time it remained in the margins of Islamic tradition.

The difference in the views of earlier and later Muslims reflects changing attitudes toward the text of the Qurʾān during the first centuries of Islam and provides us with a glimpse into the complex and gradual process by which the Qurʾān developed into a sanctified text, perfect and flawless. Early comments on the Qurʾān's incompleteness and flaws were later replaced by a diametrically opposed approach that accepts without question the actual text possessed by the believers. This approach of later Muslim scholars, which views the extant text as complete and authentic, has not only replaced the other, earlier view, but has in fact come to represent the view which the Muslim community deems normative with respect to its holy scripture.

Further reading

Cook, M. (2000) *The Koran: A Very Short Introduction.* Oxford University Press, Oxford.

Kohlberg, E. (1972) Some notes on the Imāmi attitude to the Qurʾān. In: Stern, S. M., Hourani, Albert, and Brown, Vivian (eds.) *Islamic Philosophy and the Classical Tradition: Essays Presented by his Friends and Pupils to Richard Walzer.* University of South Carolina Press, Columbia; Cassirer, Oxford, pp. 209–24.

Modarressi, H. (1993) Early debates on the integrity of the Qurʾān: A brief survey. *Studia Islamica* 77, 5–39.

Motzki, H. (2001) The collection of the Qurʾān: A reconsideration of Western views in light of recent methodological developments. *Der Islam* 78, 1–34.

Puin, G. R. (1996) Observations on early Qurʾān manuscripts in Sanʿaʾ. In: Stefan Wild (ed.), *The Qurʾān as Text.* E. J. Brill, Leiden, pp. 107–12.

Smith, W. C. (1993) *What Is Scripture?* Fortress Press, Minneapolis.

CHAPTER 11

Written Transmission

François Déroche

Translated by Melanie Hersey

While English uses the same word for both a manuscript of the Qurʾān (*a Qurʾān*) and the revelation (*the Qurʾān*), Arabic distinguishes between the two; a copy of the Qurʾān is commonly known as a *muṣḥaf*. Far from being fortuitous, this precise distinction demonstrates the simultaneous existence of two realities: transmission in written form and transmission in spoken form. Islam strongly emphasizes the oral nature of the Qurʾān and the particular importance of this feature should not be overlooked (Graham 1987). The role of the written word cannot, however, be ignored. Calligraphy is traditionally held in high esteem, particularly in relation to the Qurʾān, and the *muṣḥaf*s hold a special place in Muslim piety; indeed, the Muslim tradition of writing down the Qurʾān largely reflects a suspicion that oral transmissions may not be entirely accurate. Furthermore, as will become evident, the development of the Qurʾān in manuscript form during the first four centuries of Islam focused upon progressively perfecting the notation, indicating without a doubt that this was of great importance to the community.

The Qurʾān is the most copied text in the Islamic world. Until printing began to play a part in the distribution of texts in the nineteenth century, transcriptions were completed by hand. There are, therefore, a considerable number of manuscripts of the Qurʾān in existence across the world, most of which are very late in date. Which period do the earliest copies date from? Copies of the Qurʾān, linked to prominent figures from the beginnings of Islam, have been identified: several have notably been associated with the caliph ʿUthmān (who ruled from 23–35/644–55). These attributions appear either in a colophon,[1] note, or even a tradition. In the city of Istanbul alone, there are no fewer than six copies of the Qurʾān, all more or less complete, which fall into this category.[2] However, historians are not convinced by any of these manuscripts (al-Munajjid 1972), some of which show signs of being very poor forgeries. It is, therefore, impossible to use them to better our understanding of the written transmission of the Qurʾān. The earliest copies which can be dated or which have been dated using reliable evidence are known to originate from the second quarter of the third/ninth century.

What is known about the preceding era? Do any sections of Qur'ān manuscripts remain from the first two centuries after the *hijra*?

The First Qur'ān Manuscripts

According to the classical Muslim tradition, written transcriptions of the Qur'ān began in the 20s/640s, upon the instruction of the caliph Abū Bakr and then ʿUthmān, to guarantee the survival and integrity of the Qur'ān. In fact, copies have been preserved which date from the second half of the first/seventh century; none of these copies is complete and, in many cases, only fragments remain. Identification of these documents was not based on direct dating in the form of a colophon, however. Instead, a range of clues from different sources were applied, such as codicology (the study of the materials used and the history of the manuscript codex), palaeography (the study of ancient writing) and philology (the study of language through text analysis). In terms of codicology, parchment has been used to write on in the vast majority of cases, with a few fragments being copied onto papyrus, as documented by A. Grohmann (1958). However, the limited scope of the latter makes it impossible to determine whether they are the remains of codices[3] which once contained the entire text of the Qur'ān or whether they are extracts, copied out perhaps by pupils or to be carried as an amulet. It is useful to note that paper was not produced in the Islamic world until after 132/750, with the earliest paper transcriptions of the Qur'ān dating from the fourth/tenth century.

These early manuscripts are normally written in vertical format. In terms of palaeography, writing is of the Arabic *ḥijāzī*[4] type script, which was succinctly defined by an Arabic author from the fourth/tenth century (Ibn al-Nadīm 1970). The script shares striking similarities with that used in letters and documents written in Arabic dating from the first/seventh century. However, the script does vary considerably between manuscripts and in cases where two copyists have collaborated on a *muṣḥaf*, their individual styles can easily be identified. These differences are due to a lack of script standardization, something which did not happen until some time later during the Umayyad dynasty (after 65/685). Finally, in terms of philology, the orthography of these early copies is very distinctive: it is defective in the sense that certain long vowels recorded in classical Arabic do not feature systematically in its "consonant skeleton" or *rasm*: thus the verb *qāla* ("He said"), which is now spelt *qāf* + *alif* + *lām*, appears as *qāf* + *lām*, like the second person singular imperative form of the same verb, *qul* ("Say!"). Two additional comments are relevant to this observation. The first is in regard to the use of diacritics,[5] which are used with varying frequency by the copyists; it is not clear whether they made this choice themselves or they were following orders from their patrons. The purpose of the decision itself is also unclear. Was it to leave open the possibility of reading the text in different ways, thus perhaps having the potential to suit greater numbers of Muslim users/readers? Second, there was no system in place at this time for recording short vowels. The various deficiencies noted in the *ḥijāzī*-style manuscripts mean that it was not, in fact, possible to adequately preserve the integrity of the Qur'ān through writing as the caliph

ʿUthmān intended when, according to the tradition, he decided to document the revelation.

The *ḥijāzī*-style manuscripts nevertheless confirm that transmission of the Qurʾān in writing began at an early stage. Various trends in that transmission have also been identified. Muslims initially chose the *codex*, a type of book which became the predominant format of the day, all but replacing the scroll or *volumen*[6] of Classical Antiquity, which remained in very restricted use as, for example, in copies of the Torah. A slightly later text, a polemical Christian piece against Islam, does, however, indicate that scrolls were used by the first Muslims following the Jewish example (al-Kindī 1885). Scrolls were subsequently used from time to time, but based upon a very different set of principles from the classic *volumen*; this will be discussed later in this chapter. Traditions mention various materials upon which texts were written (scraps of leather, palm leaf stalks, animal scapula bones, etc.), none of which remained in use for very long, having been replaced by the codex.

Manuscripts were copied out in long lines not columns from the start, a decision which proved to be a determining factor in the subsequent development of the Arabic-Muslim manuscript tradition (see facsimiles published in Déroche and Noja 1998; 2001). The spaces between words cannot be differentiated from the spaces which occur within words, where the word contains one or more letters which are not linked to the following letter, as with *dāl* which does not join to the following letter when used within a word; this may be an indication that the writing was influenced by the *scriptio continua* style used during antiquity.[7] This influence may also explain why copyists would often divide a word comprising two or more segments (four, for example, in *darajāt*: *da* + *ra* + *jā* + *t*) upon reaching the end of the line, a practice which was later strictly forbidden. The end of a verse is indicated consistently by ink strokes which are grouped together in various arrangements; markers to indicate the conclusion of five or ten verses, where they occur in the manuscripts at all, have been added in later. The *sūras* are separated from one another by blank spaces which are a whole line long in some of the more meticulously transcribed copies; the titles of the *sūras* which are sometimes included have been added later. In the case of a few *muṣḥafs*, the title area was decorated with ink, sometimes in shades of red. Some manuscripts leave a whole line for the introductory *basmala*, but this practice was not unanimously adopted. The tradition of dividing the text into sections of equal length does not seem to have been adopted during this period when copies of the Qurʾān were transcribed using the *ḥijāzī* script; in the London BL Or. 2165 manuscript, markers for such divisions of the text were inserted later and are thus found between the lines (Déroche and Noja 2001). Since the beginning and end of the manuscripts were exposed to continual wear and tear and repetitive handling, the pages have often disappeared at these points. We therefore know next to nothing about "title pages" since only one such initial page has been found to date and this is merely a fragment, the recto of which is blank.

Experimentation During the First Centuries

Some of the features which characterized the Qurʾān manuscripts of the first/seventh century have stood the test of time, but the majority were subject to significant change over the following three to four centuries. In fact, far from retaining the solutions demonstrated by the earliest copies, a desire to perfect the codex form quickly emerged among the Muslim community. This is reflected partly by the greater degree of accuracy adopted in transcriptions of the text: techniques essential to attaining ʿUthmān's alleged objectives were gradually introduced. The initial *scriptio defectiva* script was replaced by *scriptio plena* – a development which may possibly be documented in one account which tells of an Umayyad governor adding two thousand *ḥarf* (probably meaning "letters") to the Qurʾān (Jeffery 1937). The first vocalization system then emerged, probably around the end of the Umayyad period and was based on the use of red dots; gradually *hamza* and orthoepic indicators (*sukūn, shadda*) were marked down, albeit irregularly. The system as we know it today seems to have been introduced towards the end of the third/ninth century.

Considerable effort went into the appearance of a *muṣḥaf*. The script itself was subject to a process of ensuring uniformity, perhaps inspired by the efforts of the Umayyad officials: the caliphs of this period initiated reforms in the administration of the empire with the aim of establishing the Arabic language and script as official forms of communication. In the case of the script, this required considerable care to be taken over handwriting, perhaps influencing those who were assigned the task of transcribing the text of the revelation. The notion of Qurʾānic scripts, that is, specific styles adopted in copies of the Qurʾān, undoubtedly emerged during this period; the *Fihrist* by Ibn al-Nadīm shows that, by the fourth/tenth century, the notion of a Qurʾān script was standard (Ibn al-Nadīm 1970). The first script to appear in a significant number of manuscripts dates from the Umayyad period and is essentially an elaborate form of the early *ḥijāzī* script, retaining the same slender appearance; the script is written on a vertically formatted page (Déroche 2002).

A further development of this period was the inclusion of decoration in the Qurʾān codex. The most impressive example is a copy of the Qurʾān discovered in Sanaa in the Yemen (Dār al-Makhṭūṭāt 20–33.1), with an initial double-spread page depicting two buildings, assumed to be mosques (von Bothmer 1987). Other fragments from the Umayyad period reveal that the illuminators who worked on these manuscripts were familiar with Christian iconography and with the iconography of the type most spectacularly displayed at the Dome of the Rock. Other, less skillful attempts may reflect the approach adopted in those areas which were further away from the government center. Living beings are absent from these illuminations, which instead feature geometric designs and vegetation-based imagery alongside occasional architectural images. The decoration mainly occurs where there is a break in the text, either within the block of writing itself or at the edge. The latter category also includes full-page decorations placed at the start and sometimes also at the end of a volume, as well as decorative borders at the beginning and end of the text.

Scripts soon began to feature thicker strokes; they are traditionally known as "Kufic" scripts but are perhaps more accurately described by the term "early Abbasid scripts" (Déroche 1983; 1992). On the basis of the classifications proposed, it is possible for the palaeographer to identify the rules of working practice in operation for certain groups of copies (Déroche 1989). The complexity of the most remarkable of these scripts demonstrates the various levels of execution in existence, ranging from copies written in calligraphy to more clumsy attempts at imitating these skillful copies. The scripts were primarily associated with parchment manuscripts of a specific format.

The Qurʾān codex underwent significant alteration around the start of the second/eighth century: the original vertical format was replaced by an oblong format. The reasons behind this modification have not been recorded in any existing documentation and thus several hypotheses have emerged; two of these theories are very similar and are not necessarily mutually exclusive. According to the first, the decision indicates a desire to clearly distinguish the Qurʾān from the Christian codex and from the Jewish Torah scrolls. The second theory considers this modification to relate to the initial writing down of the *ḥadīth* and the resultant desire to distinguish the book of God from all other texts. It is also possible that a particular type of binding would have been developed around this time or shortly after; this would have been a closable case, serving both to protect the Qurʾān codex as well as to provide a means of identifying the document within (Déroche 2000). This case was thus part of a set of material means which would have provided the *muṣḥaf* with a strong visual identity.

It is difficult to determine the exact point in time at which the early ʿAbbāsid scripts developed. The first definite indications of a date do not feature in copies of the Qurʾān until the third/ninth century, with the exception of the pious forgeries discussed above. Establishing a date for the earliest copies is thus dependent upon palaeographic studies, dating the decorations or, in rare cases, upon scientific methods such as Carbon-14 dating. Using this technique, the Sanaa Qurʾān mentioned above is thought to date from between 657 and 690 (von Bothmer et al. 1999); the script which appears in this Umayyad manuscript already demonstrates certain traits which subsequently developed over the second/eighth and third/ninth centuries. As a whole, these scripts are defined by their thick lettering, as mentioned above, with emphasis being placed on the baseline; the copyists used pronounced horizontal strokes to create a balanced layout, punctuated by shorter vertical strokes and identical spacing between groups of letters.

One consequence of this graphic work with the script was that copyists were able to alter the volume of the text. In fact, the number of pages included in a transcription of the Qurʾān could be markedly increased, if the copyist so desired, by significantly increasing the dimensions of the characters while still maintaining a suitable appearance. Copies with approximately six hundred leaves began to appear, each leave made from a whole animal skin. One group of large *muṣḥafs* from the second/eighth century, written in this same script and often containing twelve lines per page, documents this solution; their dimensions classify them alongside the largest parchment manuscripts, marking the beginning of a trend in large-format transcriptions of the Qurʾān, initially indicated by the Sanaa Qurʾān. Preference then switched to producing series of seven to thirty parts, forming an overall volume of considerable size; the first series was produced during this period, as confirmed by Malik b. Anas' condemnation of this innovation (Fierro 1992). Given how quickly the number of such series increased during the third/ninth century, it would seem that they were produced to meet requirements. Each part was relatively close to the average size of contemparary copies, which probably facilitated manufacture. The fact that the parts were produced as series also meant that they had to be kept together in specific cases, a practice which was to remain popular throughout the Muslim world.

From the end of the third/ninth century, a new development began to take place: a script very different in appearance from the early ʿAbbāsid scripts began to appear in copies of the Qurʾān. This "new style,"[8] despite many variations in its appearance, is defined by breaks and angular forms and by extreme contrasts between the thick and thin strokes (Déroche 1983; 1992). The script was initially used in administrative and legal documents; it replaced earlier scripts, yet there is no satisfactory explanation for its apparent success. It is possible that it was easier to read than the early ʿAbbāsid scripts which differ greatly from current writing practice. Economic factors may also have played a part: one cannot fail to acknowledge the relatively simultaneous occurrence of both the "new style" being introduced and the use of paper spreading throughout the Muslim world; the decrease in the price of books triggered by the introduction of this new material seems to have led to an increase in demand. As a result, it would probably have been essential to raise productivity levels. Earlier scripts would therefore have been abandoned either because they took too long to produce or because increasing numbers of copyists (who likely had not mastered these particular scripts or who could not produce them to an acceptable level) would have been required to transcribe the Qurʾān; they would therefore have chosen simpler styles for these copies. During this same era, the vertical format gradually re-established itself as standard in these *muṣḥafs*; this was perhaps another consequence of paper being introduced. The "new style" was the last script to spread throughout the Muslim world before the introduction of printing; it remained in use until the seventh/thirteenth century, at which point it was restricted to titles only.

Around the middle of the fourth/tenth century, one final development led to scripts similar to those used in everyday life being adopted in the Qurʾān. The strong visual identity assigned to the *muṣḥaf* by previous generations was reduced. Instead, the overall presentation remained constant for several centuries, with the notable exception of the decorations, which changed in style over time.

Written Copies of the Qurʾān from the Fifth/Eleventh Century Onwards

The text of the Qurʾān was copied out both in parts in order to form a collection of extracts, and in its entirety; in the majority of cases, these copies take the form of a codex written in vertical format but copies have also been made for specific purposes, usually for use as a talisman and are produced in scroll form (*rotulus*[9] type), shirts, etc. The codices either comprise one complete volume or a series of parts, ranging from two to sixty sections. These divisions into parts are based on the number of letters which form the entire text as a result of an initiative which dates back to the Umayyad period and was allegedly ordered by al-Ḥajjāj b. Yūsuf (d. 95/714); the number found then was divided by two, three, four, and so on, and the end of the nearest verse is taken to be the waypoint which was at the half, third, or quarter (and so on) point.

The modern reader opening a manuscript of the Qurʾān cannot fail to be struck by the lack of a title at the beginning of the volume, especially given that titles have featured at the beginning of works, even taking up a full page on occasion, since the very start of the non-Qur'ān related Arabic manuscript tradition. The *muṣḥaf* is thus an exception to the rule. Many strategies have therefore been adopted to compensate for the absence of a title. As discussed above, developing a strong, instantly recognizable visual identity was one of the first steps taken to compensate for this deficiency. In the most meticulously transcribed copies, illuminations were used for this purpose. The original decorations had no writing (anepigraph); later, pious expressions or a list of the sections which comprise the Qur'ān (*sūras*, verses, letters, etc.) were included. At the end of the fourth/tenth century, quotations from the Qur'ān were introduced: the citations chosen contain the word "*Qur'ān*" or another such direct reference to the text. Verses 77–80 of *sūra* 56 were undoubtedly the most frequently used in this context, but other sections were also used, such as Q 17:88, 41:41–2, and 85:21–2. The size of the decoration affected the artist's decision regarding the length of the quotation: the illumination marking the start of a volume and relating to the citation can form one page, a double page spread, a border surrounding the *incipit* (the first words of a text) or a separate prelude to the *incipit*.

The double page which contains the *incipit* is characterized by a very particular text layout. In copies of the Qur'ān comprising one volume, *sūra* 1 or *sūra* 1 and the first verses of *sūra* 2, are arranged in a particular way; the carefully produced copies include an illumination at this point which takes the form of a border and contains one or several of these quotations from the Qur'ān. Each *sūra* is preceded by its title which may be followed by the number of verses it contains and its place in the revelation; it is much less common for an indication of its position in the chronology of the revelation to appear (that is, whether it is a Meccan or a Medinan chapter). The *sūras* are identified by title, not by number; the titles can vary from manuscript to manuscript. The *basmala* which is featured at the beginning of each *sūra* (with the exception of *sūra* 9) appears on its own on the first line. Verses are usually separated from one another by a marker or small decoration; it is rare for their number in the sequence to appear. Larger illuminations, placed either at the end of the verse concerned or in the marginal area, with the corresponding decoration, mark groups of five or ten verses; the number, if included, is written either all in letters or using the numerical value of the letters of the alphabet (*abjad*); in the more modest copies, the words "five" (*khams*) and "ten" (*ʿashr*) are written in the margin. The numbering of each of these elements is placed at its end.

A series of additional markers are also featured in the margin. The prostrations which must occur when reading the text are indicated by the word *sajda* which appears either on its own or as part of a decoration. Segments of the text are also indicated in the margin: thirtieths (*juz'*), sixtieths (*ḥizb*) and also, on occasion, further subdivisions of these sections into quarters and halves. Some of the more meticulous copies contain borders in the form of illuminations to mark these points in the text; usually there is just one, at the halfway point, but sometimes there are thirty, one for each *juz'*.

The text itself is normally written all in the same ink for both the consonant skeleton (*rasm*) and vocalization system; only in the Muslim West was the early system of using colour to mark the short vowels, *hamzas*, *sukūns* and *shaddas* retained. Despite objections from jurists, gilded ink was used, sometimes throughout the text, sometimes for certain words, most notably "Allāh;" different colors of ink appear in some copies according to the specific page layout. Where the *muṣḥafs* contain translations written between the lines for the benefit of non-Arabic-speaking Muslims, these take the form of smaller and distinct characters, often written in red ink. In some copies, symbols above the text clarify the rules of recitation, indicating in particular where pauses must and must not occur. From this period onwards, the between-word space was larger than the space which separated individual, non-joining letters within a word; splitting a word at the end of a line was no longer acceptable.

The styles of writing employed were primarily the *naskhī*, *muḥaqqaq*, *rayḥānī* and on rarer occasions the *thuluth* script, to use traditional terminology. The latter three scripts are of medium and large stature, while the first – which was in very widespread use – is small, though still larger than the *ghubār* script, employed in miniature copies. In practice, there are evident stylistic variations which relate to different periods and locations; our knowledge of this is, however, largely empirical. There exist a great many copies written in calligraphy, most of which use the same script from start to finish. During the tenth/sixteenth and eleventh/seventeenth centuries, copyists sometimes chose to employ two or even three styles of different height with two or three lines in taller script (*muḥaqqaq* or *thuluth*) separated from the others by blocks of *naskhī* script; the latter were transcribed in black ink, the others in colour. There are also regional particularities: this will be discussed in greater detail below.

Some manuscripts also contain additional appended texts, invocations (*duʿāʾ*) to be recited after reading the Qurʾān, tables for predicting the future with the aid of the text, tracts relating to the Qurʾān, etc. Individuals would sometimes note down particular family events (births and deaths) or larger-scale events in their copies.

The bindings of the Qurʾān are the same as that of other manuscripts, having a book jacket and jacket flaps (except in Central Asia). The outside of the jacket flap often bears an inscription of verse 79 of *sūra* 56 ("None but the pure may touch"), thus enabling the manuscript to be identified as a *muṣḥaf*. Special tracts state that copies of the Qurʾān must be treated with particular respect; they must be placed above all other books which are stored flat in accordance with Eastern tradition. It is also recommended that the *muṣḥaf* be kept in a protective cover. Many coverings of this type remain; the leather covers of sub-Saharan Africa are particularly important in that they prevent the leaves of the manuscript from dispersing.

Up until the fourth/tenth century, regional characteristics do not seem to have strongly influenced the Qurʾān manuscript tradition, aside, of course, from the variant readings. The situation changed with the introduction of so-called "cursive" scripts in copies of the revelation. In the Western part of the Muslim world (North Africa and Spain), the *maghribī*[10] script gradually established itself as the norm from the end of the fourth/tenth century and remained so until the arrival of the computer age. Parchment continued to be used in the production of these manuscripts which were typically square in format. Colors (red, green, yellow, and blue) were also employed over a long period to indicate vocalization and orthoepic markers. In sub-Saharan Africa, a variant form of *maghribī* developed; as mentioned above, these copies of the Qurʾān sometimes comprised a pile of separate sheets which had to be kept together with their binding in a special protective pouch.

Elsewhere, differences between the various scripts were less clearly defined. There were many variants of the classic styles from the central area of the Muslim world, as demonstrated by copies of the Qur'ān made in China (Bayani et al. 1999). More distinct is the *biḥārī* script which was used solely in the north of India between the seventh/thirteenth and tenth/sixteenth centuries. *Muṣḥafs* written in the *nasta'līq* script are comparatively rare since this style, so characteristic of the Persian world, does not have Qur'ān-script status. The illuminations often bear the mark of the region where they were completed.

The Qur'ān Manuscripts in Muslim Societies

The alleged etymological similarities between the words "Qur'ān" and the Syriac *qeryana* (liturgical reading) could lead one to conclude that the book of the Qur'ān was intended for liturgical purposes; however, this was not the case and manuscripts of the Qur'ān played no part in the religious practice established by Muḥammad who, let us not forget, died before the text was recorded in writing, according to Muslim tradition. This is not to say that the Qur'ān is never associated with devout practices. Indeed, the energy which went into multiplying copies of the book and the considerable effort invested in some of the more lavish and impressive copies indicate that the *muṣḥaf* did play a part in Muslim societies. On the other hand, developments in notation during the first centuries undoubtedly influenced the emergence of the variant readings. Unfortunately, very little is known about these different issues and studies into the matter are only just beginning.

It is important to emphasize that manuscripts of the Qur'ān are held in great esteem; this also applies to the printed versions. The basic interpretation of the verse of *sūra* 56 mentioned above is that the *muṣḥaf* may only be touched by those in a state of purity. This applies to Muslims only and prohibits non-Muslims from touching a copy of the Qur'ān. When a copy deteriorated to such an extent that it could no longer be used, Muslim law proposed various methods of protecting such copies from desecration (Sadan 1986); deposits of old manuscripts discovered in various locations across the Muslim world represent one solution to this problem. Worn pages could also be transformed into cardboard for use as a cover in binding another copy of the Qur'ān.

The history of Qur'ānic manuscripts begins in earnest with the decision of the caliph 'Uthmān to send the copies of the text, produced on his command, to the large urban centers in his empire. The significance of the overall circulation of *muṣḥafs* during the manuscript period is difficult to determine due to a lack of precise numbers. Since it would have been too costly for most Muslims to purchase a manuscript, copies of the Qur'ān were held in mortmain or *waqf* in order to make them accessible to as many people as possible. Copies have been preserved from the third/ninth century which contain a deed recording such a gift made by a devout believer to a mosque or oratory; these copies frequently took the form of a series of thirty *juz'*. More is known about the history of these copies intended for public use than about the *muṣḥafs* which belonged to individuals. Later documents only, from the twelfth/eighteenth and thirteenth/nineteenth centuries, have established that the Qur'ān was the only book possessed by most households (Anastassiadou 1999). Even then, this information relates primarily to urban areas; it is not known whether Muslims living in rural areas had access to copies of the text of the revelation during this same period. The price of the books seems to have fallen significantly as soon as paper became widely established in around the fourth/tenth century, though it is not possible to quantify this change; more is known about a second development – the spread of printing – which occurred during the second half of the nineteenth century and enabled more people to acquire a copy of the Qurʾān.

A great many pocket-sized copies of the Qurʾān have been preserved, dating from the eleventh/seventeenth century. The Ottoman world provides the best example of this development. A standard format was developed which linked the material composition of the manuscript with the structure of the text. Each *juzʾ* comprised a quire of ten leaves so that these copies all had three hundred leaves in total (usually a bit more, in fact); the text of each *juzʾ* was divided into twenty fixed sections each corresponding to one copied page with fifteen lines per page, starting with the beginning of a verse and finishing with the end of a verse (Stanley 2003; Witkam 2002). As a result, it is theoretically possible to swap two pages bearing the same pagination from two different *muṣḥafs*, produced in accordance with these rules, without omitting or duplicating any of the text. Subsequent elaboration of the text enabled the presentation to be used for specific purposes: to highlight a certain element of the text, to demonstrate the sacrality of the Qurʾān or even to suggest a deeper significance. The most striking examples are revealed by a group of manuscripts in which copyists have stretched out or compressed the script within the closed unit of each page in order to move words or groups of words so that they appear on the same line and in the same relative position as on the page opposite, where similar techniques have been applied; these words are written in red to highlight the textual symmetry, the most impressive examples of which appear in *sūra* 26 where whole passages resemble one another in this way (Déroche 2000; Stanley 2003).

Were these standardized copies intended to facilitate learning the Qurʾān by heart (Stanley 2003)? While this cannot be ruled out completely, what we know of the methods used would seem to suggest otherwise. The extensive standardization process demonstrated by these *muṣḥafs* and the impressive productivity of the Ottoman copyists indicate that the aim of these manuscripts was to respond to a very widespread demand within society, while at the same time taking into account the limited resources of potential purchasers; the influence of printing or at least what the Muslim copyists knew about printing may also have played a part in this development.

Reading the text is an act of piety and the development of the *waqf* for the *muṣḥafs*, as we have seen, provided the literate with the opportunity to read the Qurʾān in mosques or in other religious buildings. From the sixth/twelfth century onwards, rituals emerged which involved reading the Qurʾān aloud, requiring the use of copies of the Qurʾān in thirty volumes. Income from a *waqf* enabled the readers and any staff associated with this ritual to be paid; several examples have been identified in preserved manuscripts and in the *waqf* acts themselves dating most notably from the Mamluk period (James 1988). These readings sometimes took place at a burial site to benefit the deceased; at other times, they were dedicated to believers within a mosque or even to passers-by in neighboring streets. Readings were also held under more modest conditions. Sessions were organized during the month of Ramaḍān; copies of the Qur'ān from the Maghreb region contain special markers in the margin for this purpose, dividing the text into twenty-nine sections to match the number of days in the month.

Readings were sometimes focused upon particular extracts. During the seventh/fourteenth century, Ibn Baṭṭūṭa (d. 770/1368–9 or 779/1377; 1992) assisted at a gathering held daily in Tabriz in the courtyard of the mosque. During this gathering, which was following the *ʿaṣr*[11] prayer, *sūras* 36, 48, and 78 were read. There can be no doubt that the development of this practice explains the emergence of copies featuring just these *sūras*, as well as certain others from the end of the Qur'ān. These thin volumes also enabled the less affluent to obtain a partial copy of the scripture at a lower cost. These copies seem to belong to a category of manuscripts intended for private use in the same way as those copies bearing either a *juz'* or a *ḥizb* on each double page (i.e., the verso of one leaf and recto of the following); a very small script is used. This latter type of *muṣḥaf* seems to have been highly successful in the Iranian world and in India; extracts, on the other hand, may have been more popular in Turkish-speaking areas.

For non-Arabic-speaking Muslims, certain copies contained a translation written in smaller characters between the lines of the Arabic text, following the order of the Arabic word-for-word. Others provided a commentary (*tafsīr*) written in the margin, sometimes in the form of a translation. It is, of course, essential to distinguish those copies in which the elements in question are later additions from those where the copyist intended them to be inserted. The earliest examples in Persian date from the sixth/twelfth century, while those in Turkish postdate them by almost two centuries. In more recent times, the twelfth/eighteenth and thirteenth/nineteenth centuries, such copies seem to have increased in number.

Copies associated with the memory of some of the great figures of early Islam hold a special place in the evocation of piety which developed around the *muṣḥaf*. From the fifth/eleventh century onwards, sources identify a "Qur'ān of ʿUthmān" or a "Qur'ān of ʿAlī" at specific sites and describe the practices which surrounded them (Mouton 1993). The presumed absolute authenticity of these copies as well as their *baraka* explains why reading from these copies carried particular value, with believers seeking to establish physical contact with the manuscript; copies were sometimes protected by a cover or stored in a cabinet. In Cordoba where several leaves from such a copy were stored for a time, an elaborate ritual developed involving processions and candles; the relic was then transferred to Marrakech where it was protected with a silver-plated binding and stored in a special piece of furniture (Dessus Lamare 1938).

In Damascus, where a "Qur'ān of ʿUthmān" was held in the Middle Ages, important figures were entitled to read the manuscript and to contribute to the funds raised for the weaving of the veil which covered it. Copies of the Qur'ān were also integrated into strategies devised to demonstrate power. One such example is the ʿAbbāsid court ceremonial where, on special occasions, the caliph would appear seated on his throne with a copy of the Qur'ān, wearing a cloak and carrying a baton which are both said to have belonged to Muḥammad. The large parchment copies of the Qur'ān mentioned above, which were also made during this period, were very expensive to produce and costs could only be met by important figures. In the third/ninth century, three Turkish officers serving the ʿAbbāsid caliphs donated three such copies of the Qurʾān comprising thirty *juzʾ*. These copies were intended to be seen even before being read; they reflected the central character of the revelation as well as the gesture made by the donators and their position within the community. This tradition of producing large copies of the Qurʾān continued through the ages. The development of paper manufacturing techniques enabled even larger copies to be created, since parchment copies were restricted to the size of the animal skin used. Two examples reveal that the format of the manuscripts was considered important by the princes: the largest Qurʾān offered to the al-Aqṣā mosque in Jerusalem was a gift from the Mamluk sultan Barsbāy (ruled 825/1422 to 841/1438); according to another tale, Timur scorned a miniature *muṣḥaf* made for him by one calligrapher but subsequently walked to the door of his palace to accept willingly another copy produced by the same artist which was so large it had to be transported by cart (Huart 1908). Just as the etiquette of the chancery dictated that the sovereigns' letters be written in large format, so the copies of the Qurʾān they commissioned had to reflect the special requirements of their rank. Manuscripts of the Qurʾān were also readily given as presents by one sovereign to another, although they were not necessarily of such large proportions.

Copies which can be described as scholarly editions have also been identified; their more modest appearance suggests that they had no ceremonial function. They provide the reader with a text containing markers which refer to the variant readings (*qirāʾāt*): this information is not normally included since any given *muṣḥaf* is limited, in principle, to following one reading. These "erudite" copies also often contained short tracts on the technical aspects, such as the different ways of dividing the Qurʾānic text and the relative chronological positioning of the *sūras* within the text of the revelation (Bobzin 1995; Bayani et al. 1999). Such information would only have been of interest to specialists in the field, whether they were engaged in teaching or learning.

From Printed Editions to the Qurʾān Online

Printed copies of the Qurʾān originated in the West where printing with movable type was introduced towards the middle of the fifteenth century. The first attempt at printing this Arabic text took place in Venice in around 1537 or 1538. The Paganini Press printed a copy of the Qurʾān which was probably intended for sale in the East but contained so many errors that the print run was destroyed; only one copy has been preserved (Nuovo 1987). This episode occurred shortly before the first translation of the Qurʾān was published in Basel in 1543; this was a copy of an old translation completed by Robert of Ketton (Bobzin 1995). The end of the seventeenth century saw the emergence of two editions of the Qurʾān, in addition to several works containing extracts of various lengths (Bobzin 2002); the edition produced by the pastor Abraham Hinckelmann in Hamburg in 1694 contained only the Arabic text, while that published by Italian priest Ludovico Maracci in Padua in 1698 was accompanied by a translation and detailed commentary. These various editions demonstrate the development of Arabic studies in Europe. However, they were not suitable for a Muslim readership as they did not adhere to the specific rules governing the orthography of the Qurʾān and did not follow any one of the variant readings in a coherent manner.

In 1787 in Saint Petersburg, the first Qur'ān to be printed by a Muslim, Mollāh Osmān Ismāʿīl, was published, intended for fellow Muslims. It preceded the first Kazan editions (from 1803) by several years, which themselves pre-dated editions published in the East from the first half of the nineteenth century: Tehran (from 1244/1828), Shiraz (1830?), Calcutta (1831), Serampore (1833), Tabriz (1248/1833), and so forth. These editions were lithographs, a process which enabled distinctive traits of Qur'ānic manuscripts to be retained which the earlier letterpress copies from the West had disregarded. When letterpress editions are produced in Muslim countries, they will only be accepted if additional efforts are made within this long-standing tradition of written transmission to respect the traditional layout of the text, including even its catchwords.[12] In the first half of the nineteenth century, Gustav Flügel published an edition of the Qur'ān in 1834 in Leipzig; this became an important date in the history of Arabic-Islamic studies in Europe. Despite its faults (dividing up the verses and failing to follow any one set of variant readings), this edition nevertheless provided a large number of readers with access to a reliable text; Western scientific studies referred to its verse numbering for a long time thereafter. Some years later, Flügel published a concordance of the Qur'ān which was an invaluable contribution to Islamic studies.

The most significant event remains, however, the publication of an edition of the Qur'ān in Cairo in 1342/1924 which was the result of a long preparation process by scholars from al-Azhar; these scholars focused upon one variant reading, that of Ḥafṣ *ʿan* ʿĀṣim (Bergsträsser 1930). The text was based on the oral aspect of transmission, possibly aided by technical texts on recitation, the variant readings (*qirā'āt*), and so forth. Early manuscripts of the Qur'ān were not taken into account, but then few experts at this time were aware of the existence of the *ḥijāzī* style. This edition gained widespread popularity across the Muslim world and gradually replaced the Flügel edition among academic researchers. In fact, this one reading eventually began to dominate over all other ones, with the result that this text can be considered something of a vulgate, without ever having been officially sanctioned except by the *shaykhs* of al-Azhar in Cairo.

The possibilities offered by analogue disks and tapes have been exploited for making recordings of traditional recitations. In Cairo at the beginning of the 1960s, the supreme authority of al-Azhar made a recording of the entire text; there can be no doubt that this initiative influenced the Islamic world. Indeed, it may well have prepared the way for information technologies and computer-based techniques. As these techniques spread, the Qur'ān discovered a new medium and new possibilities which traditional methods of transmission had failed to offer. The text became available on CD-ROM; such storage capacity enables access to a translation, commentary, or recitation along with the passage being displayed on the screen in Arabic. It is also possible to conduct research into the recorded texts. Similarly, this method has been used to provide access to the text of the earliest copies of the Qur'ān in order to facilitate research into the history of the text (Déroche and Noja 1998, 2001).

The Internet offers the same possibilities, with websites fulfilling the same function. The text can be consulted along with a translation or commentary; Internet users can even choose between different recitations. These developments have triggered discussion among Muslims consulting these Internet resources; the immateriality of the various different electronic versions may well tie in with the concerns over purity expressed in verse 79 of *sūra* 56, yet Q 96:4 ("God instructs man by means of the pens") raises questions over the position of this new medium in relation to the revelation.

Translated by Melanie Hersey.

Notes

1 Text, generally found at the end of a manuscript, in which the copyist records details of his identity and his work: his name, the date, the location, his sponsor, etc. are all details which the copyist may (or may not) choose to include. Fake colophons may be added to an existing manuscript or may accompany a copy, causing it to be considered a forgery.
2 These are the manuscripts from Istanbul, Topkapı Sarayı HS 194, A 1, EH 1 and YY 749 (formerly 4567), and the Museum of Turkish and Islamic Art, MSS 457 and 553.
3 Singular form: codex; type of book made from sheets folded in half and assembled in one or several quires which are then stitched along the length of the fold.
4 Literally: "from Ḥijāz," a region to the North West of the Arabian Peninsula where the towns of Mecca and Medina are situated.
5 These marks are placed in varying quantities above or below certain letters to identify homographs; an unmarked set of characters within a word can have five, even six different meanings. This ambiguity is eradicated if the copyist has taken care to mark down all diacritics correctly.
6 Roll on which a text is written in columns of the same width, perpendicular to the direction of rolling.
7 Letters of the text were written next to each other, with no significant spaces left between words.
8 Also known as Eastern or Persian Kufic, Naskhi Kufic, or broken cursive.
9 A scroll on which the text is written in lines, parallel to the direction of rolling. On some scrolls of the Qur'ān, the text is arranged so as to resemble various forms or figures.
10 Script specific to the Muslim West or Maghreb region.
11 One of the five daily prayers which takes place in the middle of the afternoon.
12 In a manuscript, the first word written on the recto of one leaf is repeated at the bottom of the verso of the preceding leaf; this process helps to keep pages of the manuscript in the correct order.

Further reading

Bayani, M., Contadini, A., and Stanley, T. (1999) *The Decorated Word: Qur'ans of the 17th to 19th Centuries*. Oxford University Press, London [The Nasser D. Khalili collection of Islamic art, 4].
Déroche, François (1992) *The Abbasid Tradition: Qur'ans of the 8th to the 10th Centuries AD*. Oxford University Press, London [The Nasser D. Khalili collection of Islamic art, 1].
Déroche, François (2003) Manuscripts of the Qur'ān. In: McAuliffe, Jane Dammen (ed.) *Encyclopaedia of the Qur'ān*, Brill, Leiden, Vol. III, pp. 254–75 (with bibliography).
Grohmann, A. (1958) The problem of dating early Qur'āns. *Der Islam* 33, 213–31.

James, David (1992a) *Master Scribes: Qur'ans from the 11th to the 14th Centuries*. Azimuth editions, London [The Nasser D. Khalili collection of Islamic art, 2].
James, David (1992b) *After Timur: Qur'ans of the 15th and 16th Centuries*. Azimuth editions, London [The Nasser D. Khalili collection of Islamic art, 3].
Lings, Martin (1976) *The Quranic Art of Calligraphy and Illumination*. World of Islam Festival Trust, London.
Rezvan, Efim (2004) *"The Qur'ān of 'Uthmān" (St. Petersburg, Katta-Langar, Bukhara, Tashkent*. St. Petersburg Centre for Oriental Studies, St. Petersburg.
Sadan, J. (1986) Genizah and genizah-like practices in Islamic and Jewish traditions, Customs concerning the disposal of worn-out sacred books in the Middle Ages, according to an Ottoman source. *Bibliotheca Orientalis* 43, 1–2, col. 36–58.

CHAPTER 12

Context: Muḥammad

Herbert Berg

For many scholars the connections between Muḥammad and the Qurʾān are so obvious and intimate that they need no examination. For Muslims, the passages of the Qurʾān were revealed at specific times and places, and though they are understood to be "eternal," they were relevant to the situation of Muḥammad and his community in Mecca and Medina. Furthermore, Muḥammad, as God's chosen messenger, best understood the Qurʾān and best exemplified its teachings. Therefore, the context of the Qurʾān is the life of Muḥammad. Even for many secular scholars,[1] because they claim that the biography of Muḥammad was produced much later, the Qurʾān serves as the sole trustworthy source for gleaning details of Muḥammad's biography. All the important and critical moments in Muḥammad's life are addressed or alluded to within the Qurʾān. Consequently, to understand Muḥammad you must understand the Qurʾān and vice versa. While the trust in the extant sources varies, Muslim and most secular scholars, it will be seen, largely agree on the intimate nature of the relationship between Muḥammad and the Qurʾān.

This intimacy is seemingly supported by a wealth of material. The Qurʾān addresses itself directly to the "messenger," at times even using the name "Muḥammad." The biography of Muḥammad, the *sīra*, not only provides a context for many revelations, but also describes the process of revelation – particularly for the first revelation. Naturally, the *sunna* of the prophet, the conduct or example of Muḥammad, also contains many *ḥadīths* (reports) in which Muḥammad references the Qurʾān. As well, there is a genre of *ḥadīths* known as the *asbāb al-nuzūl* that purport to provide the exact circumstances under which specific revelations came to Muḥammad. Furthermore, some *ḥadīths* also contain Muḥammad's own exegesis of the Qurʾān (*tafsīr*). Thus, to raise doubts about Muḥammad's relationship with the Qurʾān is considered absurd by many scholars, Muslim and non-Muslim alike.

While this chapter will not dispute that the figure of Muḥammad and the text of the Qurʾān are intimately connected, it will suggest that the nature of that connection is much more complex than either the traditional Muslim view (that sees Muḥammad as the pure vessel through which God conveyed His message to the rest of humanity) or the more secular view (that usually sees Muḥammad as the conscious or unconscious source of the revelations). A third, far more skeptical view presents a radically different understanding of the connection between Muḥammad and the Qur'ān. In all cases, however, the way one views that connection dictates and is dictated by one's basic approach to the sources, that is, to what extent (or even, whether) the purportedly historical material is to be trusted. Thus, what Muslim scholars and the most sanguine and the most skeptical secular scholars share is that their arguments seem circular to those who disagree with them.

To navigate through these complexities, I will examine what the Qur'ān and early Muslim sources such as the *sīra* say about the process of revelation of the Qur'ān to Muḥammad, what the Qur'ān specifically says about Muḥammad, and then what Muḥammad says about the Qur'ān. This will lead to a discussion of Muḥammad's role in the production of the Qur'ān, particularly the various theories proposed by some secular scholars. Finally, the nature of the connection will be re-examined in light of more radical scholarship on the Qur'ān and on Muḥammad. It will be impossible to discuss all the research and hypotheses developed about Muḥammad and the Qur'ān in the last 1,400 years (or even the last 100 years). Therefore, I will select only a few typical representatives from each of the three major approaches, but they will adequately highlight the methodologies involved and the obstacles encountered in trying to make a definitive statement about the relationship between Muḥammad and the Qur'ān.

The Revelation(s) of the Qur'ān to Muḥammad

There are two ways of approaching the subject of how revelations of the Qur'ān came to Muḥammad. While the Muslim understanding and the secular scholarly theories differ somewhat, ultimately they are not that different in their approach and sources, and so their descriptions are not as divergent as it first appears.

The formulation of al-Suyūṭī (d. 911/1505) is an example of a typical Muslim account. This approach takes into account material from the Qur'ān, the *sunna*, and the *sīra*, and attempts to create a consistent whole out of them. Al-Suyūṭī states that the Qur'ān was revealed in two phases. In the first, it descended from the preserved tablet (*lawḥ al-maḥfūẓ*) to the lowest heavens on the night of power (*laylat al-qadr*). From there it was revealed to Muḥammad via Gabriel in stages starting in 610 CE and ending shortly before his death in 632 (al-Suyūṭī 1951: I, 89–92). This explains or harmonizes passages such as Q 17:106, 25:32, 76:23, and 87:6–7 with 2:185 and 97:1–5.

As for the means of revelation, this oft-cited *ḥadīth* explains:

> ʿĀ'isha related that al-Ḥārith b. Hishām asked the messenger of God, "Messenger of God, how does the revelation (*waḥy*) come to you?" The Messenger of God replied, "Sometimes it comes like the ringing of a bell; it is the hardest on me. Then it passes from me after I have grasped what it said. Sometimes the angel appears to me as a man. He speaks to me and I grasp what he says." (al-Bukhārī 1987: I, 58–9, no. 2).

The *ḥadīth* concurs with the various processes of revelation that seem to be outlined in Q 42:51, "It is not fitting for a man that God should speak to him except by *waḥy*, or from behind a veil, or by the sending of a messenger to reveal (*yūḥiya*), with His permission what He wills." The *sunna* and *sīra* consistently identify the "messenger" as Gabriel, and this conforms to Q 2:97, "Gabriel . . . brings down the [revelation] to your heart by God's will."

The accounts of the first revelation provide the longest description of the revelation process. The information comes primarily from the biography of Muḥammad as recorded in al-Ṭabarī's (d. 310/923) *Ta'rīkh* and the *Sīra* of Ibn Hisham (d. 218/833) (both of which, especially the latter, rely on the accounts transmitted by Ibn Isḥāq [d. 150/767]). These accounts are, at first glance, quite straightforward, but far more complex upon closer examination.

Muḥammad was forty (or forty-three) when he received his first revelation. He is said to have engaged in an annual devotional practice that involved remaining for a month in a cave on nearby Mt. Ḥirā'. On one such occasion in the year 610 CE, the angel Gabriel appeared and said, "Muḥammad, recite (*iqra'*)!" Muḥammad replied, "I cannot recite (or read)." Gabriel repeats his command and Muḥammad repeats that he is unable to read. Then, Gabriel accosts Muḥammad and again repeats, "Muḥammad, recite!" Now, Muḥammad responds, "What shall I recite?" With this, the first passage from the Qur'ān is revealed:

> Recite in the name of the Lord who creates. He creates man from a clot of blood. Recite: And you Lord is the Most Bountiful, He who teaches by the pen, teaches man what he knew not. (Q 96:1–5)

When Muḥammad recited it, Gabriel left.[2]

According to the most detailed account of this event, Muḥammad had this vision while he was asleep, for after Gabriel's departure, he woke up. Therefore, this vision seems to have been a dream, but one which left the recited words "written on his heart." In the more detailed version of al-Ṭabarī (1879–1901), Muḥammad feared the experience, thinking that he might be a poet or a man possessed by *jinn* (i.e., a madman). And, since he despised these, he considered throwing himself down the mountain. But he was reassured by a voice from heaven, "Muḥammad you are the messenger of God, and I am Gabriel." He looked up and saw Gabriel in the form of a man with his feet on the horizon. This encounter was apparently not convincing, since Muḥammad later told Khadīja his wife that he was either a poet or a madman, and remained anxious until reassured that he was not by his wife's Christian cousin, Waraqa.

W. Montgomery Watt, who would be a representative of a secularist view on these matters, accepts much of this account. He suggests, however, that originally Muḥammad thought his visions to be of God, not Gabriel – a view that contradicts orthodox Muslim teaching. Citing the visions in Q 53:1–18, which contains the sentence "And suggested to his servant," Watt argues that "his servant" must mean "God's servant," not "Gabriel's servant," and the grammar of the whole passage confirms his reading. Gabriel, Watt points out, is not even mentioned in the Qur'ān until Medinan passages. Following Richard Bell, he also suggests that *iqra'* and *Qur'ān* come from the

Syriac *qeryāna*, which denotes reciting sacred texts and came to mean "read" only later, perhaps in an effort to prove that Muḥammad was illiterate and thus that the Qur'ān was a miracle (Watt 1953: 46).[3]

Watt also accepts that Muḥammad was afraid, for "[t]he fear of the near approach of the Divine has deep roots in Semitic consciousness" (Watt 1953: 51). Muḥammad's despair is also "real information about Muḥammad," though his purported thoughts of suicide seem unlikely (Watt 1953: 50). Watt concludes:

> There is thus much uncertainty about the circumstances surrounding Muḥammad's call. Yet careful sifting of the earliest traditions leads to a general picture in which we may have a fair degree of confidence, even though many details, and especially the relative dates of the different features, must remain somewhat uncertain. (Watt 1953: 52)

As for the means of revelation in general, Watt again sifts the Qur'ān and *ḥadīths* to ascertain a general picture. Using Q 42:51 as an (auto)biographical and partially chronological account of Muḥammad's prophetic experience, Watt (again following Bell) suggests that *waḥy* in this passage does not mean direct verbal communication or that Muḥammad heard the passages. Rather they were suggested, prompted, or inspired, which was the work of the spirit (mentioned in Q 26:192–4). The method accords with the first description given in the *ḥadīth* related by ʿĀ'isha. However, the second method, speaking from behind a veil, suggests a voice is heard, but there is no vision. The third method, which involves a messenger, accords with the second description given in the *ḥadīth* related by ʿĀ'isha. That "man" of course came to be understood as Gabriel. Watt suggests this method involved both a voice and a vision. From his reading of the Qur'ān, Watt states that the first method was common in the Meccan period and the third in the Medinan period (though this later conception was read back onto earlier passages).

Thus the critical, but ultimately sanguine approach of which Watt is just one of many representatives, suggests that the relationship between Muḥammad and the Qur'ān are very close: Muḥammad's "prophetic consciousness" can be understood as (1) entirely of divine origin (the Muslim position), (2) as a part of Muḥammad's personality of which he was not conscious (the secular position), or (3) "the work of Divine activity, but produced through the personality of Muḥammad" (the tolerant Christian position) (Watt 1953: 53). In each case, Muḥammad is intimately involved in the revelation of the Qur'ān. Thus, while Watt and al-Suyūṭī would obviously disagree on the source of the "prophetic consciousness," ultimately if they both believe the truth is to be found within the textual sources, then it is hardly surprising that that "truth" is so similar.

The Qur'ān on Muḥammad

The close relationship between Muḥammad and the Qur'ān seems to be confirmed when one reads the Qur'ān. Although direct references to Muḥammad in the Qur'ān are very few, that is, his name is used only four times, five times if one includes the variation, Aḥmad – Q 3:144; 33:40; 47:2; 48:29, and Q 61:6, respectively – there are about two hundred references to "the messenger" in the Qur'ān and about thirty to "the prophet." Thus, a significant portion of the Qur'ān is devoted to defining and defending Muḥammad's position and authority and some addressed directly to Muḥammad.

Watt points out that there is a development in what the Qur'ān says about Muḥammad. He is first conceived of as a warner (*nadhīr*) in Meccan passages, with one of the earliest passages telling Muḥammad to "rise and warn" (Q 74:2; Watt 1953: 71). Muḥammad is also described as a messenger (*rasūl*), one in a long line of messengers sent by God. The term *nabī*, or prophet, however, was likely introduced later through Muslim contacts with Jews in Medina since the term is used primarily for prophets of the Jewish and Christian traditions of whom Muḥammad is a continuation (Watt and Bell 1970: 28–9). In another Meccan passage (Q 88:21–2) the Qur'ān states that Muḥammad is an admonisher, not one who has control over people. Once in Medina, the Qur'ān refers to Muḥammad's authority, telling believers to obey God and his messenger.[4] Even more strongly stated is "Whoever obeys the messenger, obeys God" (Q 4:80). Muḥammad is also a judge: "We have sent down the book to you in truth so that can judge between the people on the basis of what God has shown you" (Q 4:105; Watt and Bell 1970: 29).

Even from these few examples, it certainly seems that the biography of Muḥammad had a significant impact on the content of the Qur'ān. At times, the Qur'ān's rulings even appear to fit nicely with the desires of Muḥammad.[5] However, a more general example of the Qur'ān's response to events surrounding Muḥammad can be seen in the opposition Muḥammad faced before the *hijra*. The Qur'ān repeatedly declares that Muḥammad is not a soothsayer (*kāhin*), sorcerer (*sāḥir*), possessed (by a *jinn*), or a poet (*shāʿir*).[6] For Muslim scholars, that these claims were made by the pagan Meccans is obvious. It is referred to in the *sīra*. In fact, the accuser is the enemy of Muḥammad, identified as al-Walīd b. al-Mughīra who plots to discredit Muḥammad. He considers all of these accusations, but deems the charge of sorcerer to be most applicable. Then God revealed Q 74:11–25, and concerning the men with him, Q 15:90 (Ibn Hishām n.d.: I, 270–2). Muslim scholars would see this as confirmation of the purpose of serial revelation (that is, its parts were revealed when appropriate). Therefore, Muḥammad's biography and the circumstances of a revelation are useful tools for understanding the Qur'ān. For Watt, too, this is part of a larger strategy of the Meccans to discredit Muḥammad. The Meccans did not deny the divine source of Muḥammad's revelations, since each charge suggests a supernatural source for the revelations, but not God as the source (Watt 1953: 127–9). The fact that the Qur'ān describes similar charges being leveled at Moses and Jesus by their enemies (as, for example, in Q 10:76 and 61:6) only shows how even revelations with no mention of Muḥammad are frequently tied to Muḥammad.

What this brief discussion of the Qur'ān's development of Muḥammad's authority and the example of the connection between the contents of the Qur'ān and Muḥammad's life seem to reveal is that the Qur'ān serves as a reliable source for understanding Muḥammad. This position is succinctly stated by Alford T. Welch:

> A distinctive feature of the Qur'ān that cannot be ignored if the Muslim scripture is to be understood fully is its close relationship to the life of Muḥammad and his contemporaries. . . . [T]he Qur'ān is a historical document that reflects the prophetic career of Muḥammad

> and responds constantly to the specific needs and problems of the emerging Muslim community. It abounds in references and allusions to historical events that occurred during the last twenty or so years of Muḥammad's lifetime. (Welch 1980a: 626)

Again, the relationship between Muḥammad and the Qur'ān as understood by scholars such as Watt or Welch is not that different than those of Muslim scholars such as al-Suyūṭī. Where they differ is on the source of the Qur'ān: God versus a product of a mystical experience (Watt 1953: 57). However, while certainly more critical and less monolithic in their understanding, the overall conclusions of the scholars differs surprisingly little.

Muḥammad's Role in Shaping the Qur'ān

Traditional Muslim accounts provide several descriptions of the canonization of the Qur'ān, which can be categorized in two ways. The first suggests that Muḥammad's successors Abū Bakr, ʿUmar, and/or ʿUthmān ordered the collation and canonization of the Qur'ān. In this way Muḥammad stands apart from the collection process. The second suggests that not only the content, but the form of the Qur'ān was determined by God. Even the order of the *sūras* was divinely determined. In fact, towards the end of his life Muḥammad is reported to have said that Gabriel came to review the Qur'ān with him once a year.[7] Presumably, Muḥammad then essentially left a final version of the Qur'ān behind which later Muslims needed only to commit to writing and preserve. Several secular scholars agree that Muḥammad had a much more hands-on role in the production of the form and content of the Qur'ān.

Chronology of the *sūras* has long been an important matter for Muslim scholars, particularly for legal and theological reasons. The traditional Muslim dating relied primarily on the *asbāb al-nuzūl*, the "occasions of revelation" (see below), and on statements made by later Muslim scholars of the Qur'ān. European scholars have also attempted chronological orders for the Qur'ān. These scholars (e.g., Theodor Nöldeke [1909–38: I, 58–234]), unlike their Muslim counterparts, have examined the internal evidence of the Qur'ān, subjecting it to the scrutiny of historical and literary criticism.[8] The result of this work has won wide acceptance in Western academia and, perhaps not so surprisingly, also differs only in minor respects from Muslim chronologies.

The traditional Muslim chronologies and the conventional European ones also share one major flaw; both regard the *sūras* as whole entities (with only a few minor exceptions). Even though some Muslim scholars accept the idea that the Qur'ān was originally revealed only as short pericopes, they then go on to assume that all, or at least most, of the pericopes of one *sūra* were revealed at about the same time.

In the 1930s, Richard Bell set about correcting these particular oversights, thereby developing his own chronology and with it, a far more complex hypothesis on Muḥammad's role in constructing the Qur'ān. He began with an exacting analysis of each *sūra*, and its dissection into its component parts. Shifts in the grammatical construction, rhyming scheme, or content of a passage were an indication of some sort of discontinuity in the passage. Bell describes part of his process as follows:

> [The passages of the Qur'ān] begin by stating their occasion; a question is asked, the unbelievers have said or done something, something has happened, or some situation has arisen. The matter is dealt with shortly, in usually not more than three of four verses; at the end comes a general statement, often about Allah, which rounds off the passage. Once we have caught the lilt of Qur'ān style it becomes fairly easy to separate the surahs into separate pieces of which they have been built up. (Watt and Bell 1970: 73)

This method suggested to Bell that almost all *sūras* originally consisted of numerous separate passages and only rarely was there evidence of a unified composition of any great length.[9] Just as there may be no connection of subject between these passages of one *sūra*, so too no connection of time may be assumed.

Bell (1937–9: I, vi) further suggested "that the Qur'ān was in written form when the redactors [Zayd b. Thābit et al.] started their work, whether actually written by Muḥammad himself, as I personally believe, or by others at his dictation."[10] Thus Bell also considered all the possibilities for confusion in written documents, including corrections, interlinear additions, additions on the margin, deletions, substitutions, pieces cut off from a passage and wrongly placed, and unrelated passages written on the back of others but read continuously. It is due to this process (and to the fact that revelations were received on the whole as short pieces that were later put together), rather than confusion in Muḥammad's (or God's) thought and style, that resulted in what Bell calls the "dreary welter of the Qur'ān" (Bell 1937–9: I, vi).

Bell also considered content, style, and vocabulary as a guide, recognizing (like Nöldeke) that certain words and phrases belonged to certain periods of teaching or controversy. For instance, Bell made a resolute attempt not to read into any passage or word more than it actually said, setting aside the views of Muslim commentators, which appeared to have been influenced by later theological developments. Bell recognized that once a word had been introduced, it tended to persist. Thus only words and phrases that could be linked to definite events could be used as indications of date. With these techniques alone, Bell would still have been unable to date much of the Qur'ān; he could have only dated a few passages relative to one another, while categorizing the vast majority simply as Meccan or Medinan. However, Bell used one more criterion for dating passages of the Qur'ān – the sequence of ideas in the Qur'ān.

Briefly, this sequence is as follows: Muḥammad's mission began with the limited purpose of urging the local Meccans to recognize God's bounties in creation and to worship Him alone. However, the resistance and indifference of the Meccans led to the incorporation of the notion of temporal punishment. With the acquisition of information about the other monotheistic traditions, the idea of eschatological punishment was introduced along with a stricter monotheism. This resistance developed into open opposition and persecution until Muḥammad and his followers emigrated to Medina. Once there, the revelations to Muḥammad also appealed to the People of the Book to accept Muḥammad as a messenger of God. With their opposition came a turning point; the People of the Book were rejected and the religion of *islām*, the surrender to God, was introduced with its accompanying vocabulary (e.g., *ḥanīf*, *muslim*, and so forth). With these major events and ideas as guides, Bell was able to place most passages in and around them.

Thus understood, Bell felt that the Qur'ān must be final authority in all questions regarding Muḥammad. The *sunna* and *sīra* regarding his doings and sayings are so profuse with pious legend that it is impossible to distinguish the historical from the spurious. (Yet, Bell still connected the passages of the Qur'ān with events in Muḥammad's life – a method which obviously employs the chronological framework of Muḥammad's life provided by the *sīra*.) The historical authority of the Qur'ān derives from the fact that for Bell the revelations to Muḥammad were a natural outcome of the culture, mind, and life of Muḥammad, who given his situation, happened to interpret them as being sent down from God. Bell saw the Qur'ān not only as created by Muḥammad, but he also felt Muḥammad had a great deal to do with the compiling and editing of the *sūras*.[11]

Bell argues that the composition of the Qur'ān fell into three main periods:

1 an early period from which only fragments survive consisting mainly of lists of "signs" and exhortations to the worship of God;
2 the Qur'ān period, covering the latter part of Muḥammad's activity in Mecca, and the first year or two of his residence in Medina, during which he was attempting to produce a *qur'ān* (that is, a "recitation") in Arabic containing the gist of previous revelations;
3 the Book period, beginning somewhere near the end of the second year in Medina, during which Muḥammad is definitely producing a *kitāb* (that is, a "book" that would be an independent revelation) (Bell 1937–9: I, vi).

W. Montgomery Watt continued much of Bell's work, including re-editing and adapting Bell's *Introduction to the Qur'ān* (1970). His analysis of Muḥammad's biography and "prophetic consciousness" as depicted in the Qur'ān is based on similar principles (even if he disagrees with Bell on some of the details).

As radical as the hypotheses of Bell seem, they still assume the overall historicity of the Muslim account of Muḥammad's life and the development of the Muslim community. That is to say, scholars such as Bell certainly disagree with the traditional view and present hypotheses that some Muslims might find offensive by suggesting that the illiterate prophet had a hand in writing the Qur'ān. However, he still accepts that the historical kernel buried within the conflicting reports can be discovered. Thus, whether one accepts the traditional depiction(s) of the canonization of the Qur'ān, or one accepts Bell's variation (or something like it: see e.g., Burton 1977: 225–32), once again the conclusion seems to be that Muḥammad had an intimate role in producing the text of the Qur'ān.

Muḥammad on the Qur'ān

If the early sources can be trusted, even in part, then we should have a wealth of information that can shed even more light on the relationship between Muḥammad and the Qur'ān. The most likely source of that information should be the *sunna* of the prophet, or the example or conduct of Muḥammad. A frequent command in the Qur'ān is "Obey

God and his messenger." To obey God, is to obey His words as preserved in the Qur'ān. To obey the messenger, at least since his death, is to obey Muḥammad's example and words as preserved in the *sunna*. The *sunna*, at least since the end of the formative period of Islam, is preserved in the form of *ḥadīths* or short reports or anecdotes of what Muḥammad said or did. Each "authentic" *ḥadīth* normally has two parts, a *matn* (the actual report) preceded by an *isnād* (a chain of transmitters linking the person who ultimately recorded the report to Muḥammad). It is this *isnād* that guarantees its authenticity.[12] As we shall see below, it is one's trust in the *isnād*-system that determines one's approach to the early sources on Muḥammad and the Qur'ān. And that approach is absolutely critical to one's understanding of the relationship between Muḥammad and the Qur'ān.

As it turns out, the *sunna* is not a very useful source for information on this relationship. When one considers the function of the *sunna*, the reason for this becomes apparent. The two most important sources for Islamic law, the *sharīʿa*, are the Qur'ān and the *sunna*. The Qur'ān contains relatively little strictly legal material. Thus, in terms of quantity, the *sunna* is the main source of Islamic law.[13] It is also a source of law that is largely independent of the Qur'ān.

There are two types of *sunna* that are important exceptions to this principle. One is *tafsīr* (or Qur'ānic exegesis) by Muḥammad, and another is *asbāb al-nuzūl* which purport to provide the circumstances under which certain passages were revealed to Muḥammad. Although not part of the *sunna*, the *sīra* or biography of Muḥammad, also often comes in the form of *ḥadīths*. It is the *sīra*, from which the description of the first revelation and Bell's framework are drawn. Surprisingly, therefore, neither *tafsīr*, *asbāb al-nuzūl*, nor *sīra* yields much useful information either.

The *Tafsīr* of Muḥammad

The most authoritative *tafsīr*, or commentary of the Qur'ān, is that of Muḥammad. For instance, it is reported about the most prolific early exegete ʿAbd Allāh b. ʿAbbās (d. ca. 68/687):

> When asked about something concerning the Qur'ān, if it was in the Qur'ān, he reported it. If it was not in the Qur'ān, but there was [something relevant] from the messenger of God, he reported it. And if there was nothing in the Qur'ān or from the messenger of God [concerning it], but there was from Abū Bakr and ʿUmar, he reported it. And if there was nothing from them, he offered [*ijtahada*] his opinion. (Ibn Saʿd 1975: II, 266)

Therefore, it seems that this material would be the most obvious place to start looking for Muḥammad's understanding of, and relationship to, the Qur'ān.

However, as is clear from even a cursory examination of collections of exegesis, such as al-Ṭabarī's *Tafsīr*, or al-Bukhārī's (d. 256/870) section on *tafsīr* in his *Ṣaḥīḥ*, Muḥammad is not particularly important to the Qur'ān's exegesis. There are just under 500 *ḥadīths* listed in the latter. Many of these 500 cite an authority other than Muḥammad, such as Ibn ʿAbbās and many others are simply *asbāb al-nuzūl* (see below) which provide a context but do not contain any explanation of the verse by Muḥammad (see, e.g., al-Bukhārī 1987: VI, 431, with *ḥadīths* on Q 15:90–1). With over 6,000 verses in the Qur'ān, clearly the *tafsīr* of Muḥammad is a meager resource – despite the purported practice of Ibn ʿAbbās. This fact is also confirmed in al-Ṭabarī's collection of exegetical *ḥadīths*. Of his 38,397 *ḥadīths*, less than 10 percent cite Muḥammad, and those that do rarely contain an explanation by Muḥammad. Rather, these *ḥadīths* are often *asbāb al-nuzūl* or even material drawn from the *sīra*.

As a result, if we wish to understand Muḥammad and his understanding of the Qur'ān's passages, then we must turn to other sources, to those which specifically claim to explain the circumstances of Muḥammad when a certain passage was revealed or to the biography of Muḥammad.

Asbāb al-nuzūl

Asbāb al-nuzūl or, causes or occasions of revelation, are a type of *ḥadīth* which purport to provide the situation which provoked a particular passage of the Qur'ān to be revealed. Since Muḥammad must have been involved in most of these situations or at the very least aware of them, in theory the *asbāb al-nuzūl* should provide insights into how revelations came to Muḥammad. Often according to the evidence of the *asbāb al-nuzūl*, revelations came in response to questions addressed to Muḥammad. Whether events surrounding Muḥammad or specific questions addressed to Muḥammad, *asbāb al-nuzūl* presuppose a close relationship between the events of Muḥammad's life and the revelation of the Qur'ān.

In theory, especially as suggested by al-Suyūṭī, *asbāb al-nuzūl* can clarify legal issues: for example, whether a ruling is general or specific (to a person or event) or possibly the abrogation of one Qur'ānic verse by another (al-Suyūṭī 1951: I, 61–72; Rippin 1985). John Wansbrough suggests that the purpose of *asbāb al-nuzūl* is, therefore, primarily to provide "a chronology of revelation" (Wansbrough 1977: 141–2 and 177–85). In other words, their function is to provide a chronological framework for apparently related Qur'ānic passages (though not a systematic one incorporating the whole of the Qur'ān).

There are, however, several problems with this. First, it is possible for several passages from different *sūras* of the Qur'ān to be revealed in response to the same event or question. How these passages subsequently became separated into *sūras* with different contexts and theoretically revealed at different times is problematic. Second, it is also common for several *asbāb al-nuzūl* to be adduced for a single Qur'ānic passage. Third, *asbāb al-nuzūl* suggest that many Qur'ānic passages were revealed as small units, even as isolated single verses. These isolated verses, however, now appear in the Qur'ān within larger contexts, the rest of which does not seem applicable to the situation. The example noted above of the revelation of Q 74:11–25 and 15:90 in response to al-Walīd b. al-Mughīra's plot to discredit Muḥammad demonstrates some of these problems. The material certainly seems contradictory, and at the very least makes discerning Muḥammad's role(s) in fashioning a particular passage of the Qur'ān extremely difficult.

A more plausible explanation for the complexity of the *asbāb al-nuzūl* material comes from Andrew Rippin, who investigated the literary techniques used within *asbāb al-nuzūl* in hopes of discerning their function. He asserts:

> [T]he essential role of the material is found in haggadic exegesis; that is, the *sabab* functions to provide an interpretation of the verse within a basic narrative framework. I would tentatively trace the origins of this material to the context of the *quṣṣāṣ*, the wandering story-tellers, and pious preachers and to a basically popular religious worship situation where such stories would prove both enjoyable and edifying. (Rippin 1988: 19)

Although Rippin focuses primarily on the exegetical techniques employed in the *asbāb al-nuzūl* (such as, lexical clarification usually with glosses, masoretic clarification including variant readings, narrative expansion including *ta'yīn al-mubham* or identifying the unknown, and contextual definition to ameliorate what has been called the Qur'ān's "referential style"), his conclusions also neatly explain the vastness and unsystematic nature of the *asbāb al-nuzūl*. As such, these *asbāb al-nuzūl* tell us very little about Muḥammad or even the Qur'ān in Muḥammad's time. Rather, they merely indicate how later Muslims, particularly the *qurrā'*, understood or worked with Qur'ānic verses.

The *Sīra* of Muḥammad

Although not considered *asbāb al-nuzūl*, the biography of Muḥammad, the *sīra*, seems to fulfill many of the same functions and often comes in the same form. In other words, it comes in the form of *ḥadīths* – reports preceded with *isnāds*. But more importantly, the *sīra*, like the *asbāb al-nuzūl*, provides information about when particular passages were revealed. Again there is inconsistency.

The *sīra* of Muḥammad contains surprisingly little material from which to discover Muḥammad's revelatory experiences or interpretation of the Qur'ān. The most significant passages which do are the descriptions of the first revelation on Mt. Ḥirā'. As noted above, there is some inconsistency about that event. However, the problems with the descriptions are far greater than those noted by Watt.

Gregor Schoeler represents scholars who maintain that historical materials can be discerned within the *sīra* and the *sunna*. Schoeler has argued that the second generation of Muslims were the first Muslims to concern themselves with gathering reports about the prophet, which they did, naturally, from the first generation of Muslims. 'Urwa b. Zubayr (d. ca. 93/711) best exemplifies this activity and though he recited his material from memory, he possessed at least some written materials. In the second half of the first *hijrī* century, there was still a timidity about recording in writing any religious material other than the Qur'ān. The most important student in 'Urwa b. Zubayr's Medinan historical school was al-Zuhrī (d. 124/742). Schoeler suggests that al-Zuhrī used notes as mnemonic aids and notebooks for his students to copy. Only in the next generation of scholars, such as Ibn Isḥāq, were biographical reports about Muḥammad regularly committed to writing. Ibn Isḥāq, of course, collected accounts of Muḥammad's life and produced a structured narrative, a *sīra*. His book is lost, but his students further redacted it and preserved it in several forms. By comparing the various extant forms, Schoeler believes he can reconstruct earlier versions of the reports. Schoeler's method involves the comparison of traditions that share an early transmitter and searching for similarities in wording, meanings, and ordering of motifs in hopes of discerning the transmitter's recension. Having applied this technique, Schoeler suggests that at least the main features of some reports of about Muḥammad's time in Medina are accurate and correctly transmitted (Schoeler 1996: 166). In so doing, Schoeler has simply developed a far more sophisticated and rigorous methodology to do what Bell and Watt had attempted to do.

It is in his attempt to support his argument, however, that Schoeler deals with an issue critical to the understanding of Muḥammad's relationship to the Qur'ān. Schoeler examines the reports about Muḥammad's first revelation to trace their transmission from the (probable) first reporter to their final redaction in extant works. By comparing the relevant traditions in various extant collections by Ibn Hishām, al-Ṭabarī, ʿAbd al-Razzāq (d. 211/827), Ibn Saʿd (d. 230/845), al-Bukhārī, Muslim (d. 261/875) and al-Tirmidhī (d. 279/892) whose *isnād*s list al-Zuhrī as transmitter, Schoeler attempts to discover the original archetype of the report circulated by al-Zuhrī. Similar comparisons are attempted for his informant, ʿUrwa, and the latter's informant, ʿĀʾisha. Schoeler suggests that an al-Zuhrī archetype can be postulated for some, but not all *ḥadīth*s. ʿUrwa is the likely source of the report, but his son Hishām transmitted a complete version while his student al-Zuhrī redacted it. However, though it is not impossible that ʿĀʾisha would have spoken to her nephew about such matters, her absence from some *isnād*s implies that these traditions reached ʿUrwa from another source, and later transmitters repaired the *isnād* (that is, extended it back to someone who actually knew Muḥammad). Schoeler also examines another subset of traditions, those which are transmitted by Ibn Isḥāq from Wahb b. Kaysān from ʿUbayd b. ʿUmayr. Despite some significant variations, Schoeler again sees a uniform text as the source for the three extant versions, and so the original by Ibn Isḥāq can be reconstructed. A comparison of the Ibn Isḥāq traditions with those of al-Zuhrī reveals that certain motifs have different details and some motifs are unique to al-Zuhrī, whereas Ibn Isḥāq's are distinguished by the presence of more detail and narrative accessories. But since the two sets of traditions strongly resemble each other in their main motifs and sequence, Schoeler argues that both originally had the same source. The motifs were likely combined in the first *hijrī* century and emerged within the Zubayrid family. ʿUrwa cleansed the report of its story-teller (*qāṣṣ*) elements, reworking it into *ḥadīth*-format. Based on the biographical information and the *isnād*s, the original report is that of the *qāṣṣ*, ʿUbayd b. ʿUmayr who built the story out of various components while with the Zubayrid court. Significant changes were still introduced afterward: it was paraphrased, shortened, adorned, and rearranged. These changes decreased as time progressed, but came to an end with the redactions of Ibn Hishām and al-Ṭabarī (Schoeler 1996: 59–117).

More skeptical scholars might question the validity of Schoeler's attempt to reconstruct hypothetical early sources from later extant texts – a project predicated on the assumption that the *isnād* contains historically reliable information. Nevertheless, Schoeler's own example shows that for even the most critical report about Muḥammad and the Qur'ān, that is, the first revelation of the Qur'ān, we cannot be certain that any part of it is accurate – despite its production during (or close to) the lifetime of people who had lived with Muḥammad.

The Qur'ān's Role in Shaping the Biography of Muḥammad

What the depictions of Muḥammad and the Qur'ān by Bell, Watt and others share is that they ultimately see a close and intimate relationship between Muḥammad and the revelation. The Qur'ān can only be understood in light of the biography of Muḥammad. However, since the beginning of the twentieth century many Western scholars have doubted the authenticity of the biographical traditions about Muḥammad's life found in the *sīra*. At least some of the *sīra* may be a product of speculation on apparently biographical references in the Qur'ān. The most skeptical (and thus far still considered the most radical) understanding of the relationship between Muḥammad and the Qur'ān is that of John Wansbrough.

After examining the structure of the Qur'ān, Wansbrough suggested that the Qur'ān is not a product of "deliberate edition." That is, the various Muslim and secular accounts of the canonization process are incorrect. He argues:

> Particularly in the *exempla* of salvation history, characterized by variant traditions, but also in passages of exclusively paraenetic or eschatological content, ellipses and repetition are such as to suggest not the carefully executed project of one or many men, but rather the product of an organic development from originally independent traditions during a long period of transmission. (Wansbrough 1977: 47)

Wansbrough terms these independent pericopes "prophetical *logia*" which came to be seen as direct utterances of God (via Gabriel and Muḥammad) but outside the canon of the Qur'ān are reports about direct utterances from God. He proposes that these *logia* originated as separate collections with communities "essentially sectarian but within the mainstream of oriental monotheism," that is, within a Judeo-Christian sectarian milieu (Wansbrough 1977: 50). In other words, not only is the traditional depiction of the collection of the Qur'ān in the first two decades after Muḥammad's death incorrect, but also the origin of those materials with a figure called Muḥammad seems improbable.

If Wansbrough's hypothesis is correct, it would seem to sever the connection between Muḥammad and the Qur'ān. The "Arabian prophet" (to use Wansbrough's term) had no connection to the contents of the Qur'ān, for they originated in another milieu. However, that does not mean the connection is severed; rather, he has reversed the connection. As evidenced by the use of *asbāb al-nuzūl* and the *sīra*, the traditional Muslim understanding has the Qur'ān as rooted in the life and situation of their prophet. Western scholars such as Bell see the Qur'ān as so connected to Muḥammad that it is the only reliable source for the biographical details about his life. Wansbrough, on the other hand, argues that the biography of Muḥammad (the "Muhammadan *evangelium*" as he calls it) represents a historicization of the *logia*. That is, essentially anonymous material of the Qur'ān is linked to the independent Arabian prophet.

Lest one be tempted to think that Wansbrough presents merely a revised form of Bell's claim that the Qur'ān is a historical source, Wansbrough states: "The historical value of the Muslim scripture lies, it seems to me, not in its role as a source for the biography of Muhammad, but rather as source for the concepts eventually applied to composition of the Muslim theology of prophethood" (Wansbrough 1977: 56).

The relationship between the *evangelium* and the *logia* is ambivalent. At times the former serves as a narrative exegesis of the *logia*, but at other times the exegesis seems independent of the latter with Qur'ānic verses arbitrarily assigned to narrative accounts. In general, the narrative exegesis uses connected or isolated Qur'ānic passages as an outline for the narrative, or simply employs the diction and imagery of passages from the Qur'ān, or the passages are simply paraphrased (Wansbrough 1978: 1–49). In this way the Qur'ān was a source of concepts, but not historical facts. Not surprisingly, therefore, the Qur'ān does *seem* to confirm the biographical details of Muḥammad's life. And, the Qur'ān and Muḥammad (at least his biography – the *sunna* is another matter) are intimately connected.

Thus, the apparently overwhelming evidence of the close connections between Muḥammad and the Qur'ān is not what it appears to be. For instance, the accusations of soothsaying, sorcery, poetry, and possession leveled at Muḥammad reveal the arbitrariness of the dating system. Q 74 is one of the earliest Meccan *sūras*, Q 15 one of the latest. The story in the *sīra* simply connects keywords from the Qur'ān and historicizes them in a narrative account. Note also that these keywords were incorporated into the story of the first revelation – not as an accusation, but as part of Muḥammad's own doubts. (And so the Qur'ān's verses were read by the inventor of that account as reassurance to Muḥammad that he was not a poet or possessed.) As these two examples seem to show, "[t]hematic and exemplary treatment of prophethood in the Qur'ān was reformulated in the *evangelium* (*sunna*/*sīra*) as the personal history of Muḥammad" (Wansbrough 1977: 65). The fact that messengers of God are often accused of such supernatural influences, demonstrates that Ibn Isḥāq's key concern was not historicity, but faithfulness to the traditional Judeo-Christian concept of prophethood.

What of the ubiquitous references to Muḥammad and the messenger of God in the Qur'ān? Wansbrough suggests, "That Q 33:40 contains one of four occurrences in scripture of the name Muḥammad suggests a particular polemic, in which not only the credentials but also the identity of the Arabian prophet was in dispute" (Wansbrough 1977: 64).

Conclusions

The descriptions of the relationship between Muḥammad and the Qur'ān put forth by Muslim and sanguine secular scholars is clearly at odds with that put forth by skeptical scholars. The issue centers on how much the sources for the formative period of Islam, primarily the Qur'ān, *sīra*, and *sunna* can be relied upon for historical information, that is to say, "what really happened." While clearly there is as much disagreement among secular scholars as there is between the traditional Muslim accounts and these scholars, one thing is clear. Even scholars such as Schoeler, who tried to demonstrate that the *sīra* contains a discernible authentic kernel, finds that some of the most key passages about the revelation of the Qur'ān to Muḥammad are problematic.

So, while at first glance there may seem to be a wealth of material from which to reconstruct Muḥammad's relationship with the Qur'ān, none of that material is as certain as it appears. Much depends on one's faith in the *isnād*. If one believes that *isnāds* contain (some) historical information, then *sunna* (especially, prophetic *tafsīr* and *asbāb al-nuzūl ḥadīths*) and the *sīra* can yield much, as the work of Bell and Watt, for example, tries to demonstrate. However, to the more skeptical scholars, these more sanguine scholars are hardly more historiographically sophisticated than the theologically motivated Muslim scholars. Both assume that the literary sources reflect actual events, or "what really happened." The Muslim position generally assumes that the sources are an unselfconscious and transparent reflection of the events, whereas the secular position sees them as tendentially shaped and translucent. The similarity of the conclusions drawn by both should not be thought of as an emerging consensus about what really happened, but rather an emerging convergence based upon similar approaches to the sources (which *claim* to state what really happened).

If one does not trust the sources, the *isnāds*, the entire edifice begins to collapse. What we are left with is not so much a wealth of material describing (or at least providing evidence from which we can reconstruct) Muḥammad's relationship with the Qur'ān. Instead, we have a wealth of material from which we can reconstruct what Muslims (particularly those Muslims who a century or so later preserved the material) believed Muḥammad's relationship with the Qur'ān to have been. This, of course, is historically valuable too. However, for many it is frustrating, for it does not allow us to fall into that comfortable genetic fallacy that scholars share with fundamentalists: that the origins provide "essence" or "purity" and so matter far more than the development.

What all three groups of scholars (i.e., the Muslim theological, the secular but sanguine, and the secular but skeptical) share is a kind of tautology. The sources do not evince evidence of God's revelation of the Qur'ān to Muḥammad until one has assumed it; the sources do not evince evidence of Muḥammad's role in the production of the Qur'ān until one has assumed it; and the sources do not evince the Qur'ān's role in the construction of the figure of Muḥammad until one has assumed it. Obviously, these three positions are mutually exclusive and so it would be extremely useful to be able to discern which one is the correct position. The question is, "how?" The difficulty remains with the nature of our sources. The Qur'ān, the *sīra*, the *sunna* are documents:

> Documents grow in worlds and are part of those worlds; they do not materialize out of the ether. The significance and function of the document – at least as conceived by those initially responsible for it – is as a piece of a functional contribution to the world of which it is a part. And that world, while partially constituted by the document itself, cannot simply be extracted from . . . [it] by inference. (Arnal 2001: 97)

What is missing then is the concrete political, societal, and economic context(s) in which these documents developed. This kind of information must come from sources other than the Qur'ān, the *sīra*, the *sunna* – archeology, for instance. Thus, the advantage of the skeptical, secular approach to Islamic origins and to the more specific question of the relationship of the figure of Muḥammad (as presented in various documents) to the (document of) the Qur'ān is not that it is more convincing or produces more "facts." Compared with the other two approaches, not only does it produce less "facts," but it even seems to destroy "facts." Rather, the unique advantage of the skeptical approach is that it recognizes documents for what they are and so employs methods of analysis appropriate for documents.[14]

Notes

1 The use of the term "secular" is not meant to suggest that these scholars are devoid of theological agendas. Rather, a "secular" scholar is one whose research is not guided by Muslim theological motivations. The term, therefore, can include Western, non-Western, Muslim, and/or non-Muslim scholars.

2 An alternate version of the first revelation states that after coming down from Mt. Ḥirā', Muḥammad heard a voice calling him but could see nothing. Terror-stricken, he returned to Khadīja who wrapped him in a cloak. Then "O you enveloped in your cloak, rise and warn!" (Q 74:1) was revealed to him. According to al-Suyūṭī (1951: I, 52–3), others claim that *Sūrat al-faṭīha* was revealed first, and yet others that it was the *basmala*.

3 Furthermore, the Qur'ān mentions Gabriel in only two passages Q 2:97–98 and 66:4, with only the former mentioning his role as messenger. As Stefan Wild (1996: 147) points out, in the *sīra* even Gabriel acting as the mediator between God and Muḥammad is not consistent, and more direct speech may be implied with the expression *qāla Allāhu li-Muḥammadin*, "God said to Muḥammad." For problems with Q 42:51 and the concept of serial revelation see Wansbrough 1977: 34 and 38, respectively. Another gray area is the *ḥadīth al-qudsī*. These *ḥadīths* in the *sunna* purport to be revelations to Muḥammad, but are not in the Qur'ān. They are understood not to be God's words, but Muḥammad's wording of inspiration from God and not necessarily mediated by Gabriel.

4 For example, Q 3:32, 3:132, 4:13, 4:59, 4:64, 4:69, 5:92, 8:20, 8:46, and 9:71. There are many variations on this theme too, such as that in Q 4:136, which says to believe in God and his Messenger.

5 See for example, the Qur'ānic ruling which permits a person to marry the divorced wife of an adopted son, thus allowing Muḥammad to marry Zaynab, the divorced wife of Zayd b. Ḥāritha (Q 33:37). See also Q 66:3–5 in which the prophet's wives are divinely reprimanded.

6 Q 6:7, 11:7, 15:6, 21:5, 26:27, 26:224, 34:43, 37:15, 37:36; 43:30, 44:14, 46:7, 51:39; 51:52; 52:29–30, 54:2, 54:9, 68:2, 68:51, 69:41–42, 74:24, and 81:22.

7 However, that year Muḥammad was visited twice by Gabriel, which suggested to him that he would die soon. Al-Ṭabarī 1879-1901: I, 1140.

8 This method included using references to known public events and, the vocabulary and style of the passages in order to date the *sūras*. To give simple illustrations of how these three criteria were used to date passages, we need only look at some of the general distinctions between Meccan and Medinan passages: the *qibla* (that is, direction of prayer) controversy

is an event which is *known* to have occurred after Muḥammad's prophetic claims had been rejected by the Jewish tribes of Medina; the introduction of words such as *muhājir* (that is, emigrant) occurred only after Muḥammad and his Meccan community had emigrated to Medina; and the early Meccan style of short, crisp, poetic revelations gave way to longer, more prosaic passages in Medina, especially in those dealing with the day-to-day rules and regulations of the Muslim community. The key word in this paragraph is "known." We must ask, "How is it known?"

9 Even Muslim tradition, which assigns *asbāb al-nuzūl* for passages consisting of only a few verses, seems to support the assumption that the unit of revelation to Muḥammad was indeed quite short.

10 This assumption on the part of Bell has some support in both the Qur'ān and in the *sunna*. The Qur'ān indicates in Q 6:7 that the idea of producing a book on papyrus did at least enter Muḥammad's mind. In addition, *ṣuḥuf* (that is, separate, unbound sheets used for writing) are connected with revelation in Q 20:133; 53:37; 80:13; 87:18, and 98:2. Finally, when the Qur'ān replies to the accusation of being written down in Q 25:6–7, it does not deny the charge. There is also evidence that Muḥammad kept some sort of written record and that some editing took place. ʿAbd Allāh b. Saʿd b. Abī Sarḥ is said to have been writing down a Meccan revelation (Q 23:12ff.) at Medina at Muḥammad's dictation. When he reached the end, Muḥammad paused, the scribe interjected, "Blessed be God, the best of creators." Apparently when Muḥammad adopted this interjection as the needed rhyme-phrase, the scribe became suspicious and later gave up Islam and returned to Mecca. For further details on these arguments see Watt and Bell 1970: 16–19.

11 However, Bell certainly felt that Muḥammad was sincere in his belief that the revelations to him were of a divine nature, and that Muḥammad had no sinister motivations, nor any mental or medical deficiencies. Also, Bell assumed that the Qur'ān essentially contained all of Muḥammad's revelations and that the later compilers were quite assiduous in their collecting (or copying) of the Qur'ān. This assumption is borne out by the varying and even contradictory passages preserved in the Qur'ān.

12 *Sunna* is a far more complex term. For a summary of the various theories about the development of the *sunna* and *ḥadīth*, see Berg 2000: 6–64.

13 Once again the reality is much more complex than this, but a discussion of the development of the *sharīʿa* goes well beyond the scope of this chapter.

14 Wansbrough (1987) cautions us about reading literature as history or treating texts as archeological sites.

Further reading

Berg, Herbert (2000) *The Development of Exegesis in Early Islam: The Authenticity of Muslim Literature from the Formative Period*. Curzon, Richmond.

Berg, Herbert (ed.) (2003) *Method and Theory in the Study of Islamic Origins*. E. J. Brill, Leiden.

Burton, John (1977) *The Collection of the Qur'ān*. Cambridge University Press, Cambridge.

Rippin, Andrew (1985a) Al-Zarkashī and al-Suyūṭī on the function of "occasion of revelation" material. *Islamic Culture* 59, 243–58.

Rippin, Andrew (1988) The function of *asbāb al-nuzūl* in Qur'ānic exegesis. *Bulletin of the School of Oriental and African Studies* 51, 1–20.

Wansbrough, John (1977) *Quranic Studies: Sources and Methods of Scriptural Interpretation*. Oxford University Press, Oxford.

Watt, W. Montgomery (1953) *Muḥammad at Mecca*. Clarendon Press, Oxford.
Watt, W. Montgomery, and Bell, Richard (1970) *Bell's Introduction to the Qur'ān*. Edinburgh University Press, Edinburgh.
Welch, Alfred T. (1980) Qur'ānic studies – problems and prospects. *Journal of the American Academy of Religion* 47, 620–34.
Wild, Stefan (1996) "We have sent down to thee the book with the truth . . .": Spatial and temporal implications of the Qur'anic concepts of *nuzūl, tanzīl,* and *'inzāl.* In: Wild, Stefan (ed.) *The Qur'ān as Text*. E. J. Brill, Leiden, pp. 137–53.

CHAPTER 13

Context: ʿUmar b. al-Khaṭṭāb

Avraham Hakim

The basic foundations of Islamic law are the Qurʾān, the holy book that formulates the written law, and the *sunna*, the oral law. Both are believed to originate from the prophet Muḥammad, the Qurʾān having been revealed to him by the angel Gabriel and the *sunna* having been formulated on his authority.

Our knowledge on these issues derives mainly from the Islamic traditions. For our purposes, these traditions are considered not as accounts of historical events but as texts that reflect the ideas, beliefs, and predilections of the scholars who produced and circulated them in the first era of Islam, roughly towards the turn of the first *hijrī* century, the seventh/eighth century CE. These texts were provided with chains of transmitters that projected them backwards to the times of the founding fathers of Islam, Muḥammad and his companions, considered to be the highest authorities on all Islamic issues.

As regards the *sunna*, traditions sometimes attribute a law not only to Muḥammad but also to one of his companions, resulting thus in a possible conflict of authority, since the companion's law may contradict that of the prophet (Hakim 2003). As for the revelation of the Qurʾān, it is believed that it is the privilege of Muḥammad, and his alone. Only he, in his capacity as the prophet, can be addressed by God's messenger, Gabriel, and given the book.

However, a number of traditions pertaining to the excellence of the second "rightly-guided" caliph, ʿUmar b. al-Khaṭṭāb (ruled 13–23/634–644), describe him as an active partner in the revelation of the Qurʾān. The circulation of such traditions may indicate that in early Islam there was an attempt to involve the head of the Islamic community in the revelation of the book, probably in order to magnify his image as a leader. Consequently, the image of the caliph came to be opposed to that of the prophet. This chapter is devoted to the description of several of these traditions, in which the images of the prophet and the caliph join in the issue of Qurʾānic revelation.

Aiming at God's Mind

In several traditions ʿUmar's involvement in Qurʾānic revelation is illustrated by his ability to formulate a rule or take a position on a certain issue according to the Qurʾān before the revelation on this same issue occurs. In other words, ʿUmar was granted the sublime ability to read God's mind. In this context, the prophet is supposed to have said that when people spoke their mind on a matter and ʿUmar spoke his on that same matter, the Qurʾān was revealed according to ʿUmar's mind (Ibn Ḥanbal 1983: I, 339–40, no. 488). Similarly, the famous early Qurʾānic commentator Mujāhid b. Jabr (d. ca. 104/723) is said to have stated that "when ʿUmar speaks his mind on a certain issue, the Qurʾān is revealed accordingly" (Ibn Abī Shayba 1995: VI, 357, no. 31971). Another tradition attributes to ʿAlī b. Abī Ṭālib, the following impressive statement: "Indeed the Qurʾān includes many of ʿUmar's views" (Abū Nuʿaym 1994: 296–7, no. 98). All these statements imply that several Qurʾānic rulings, some of which will be described below, were fashioned on the basis of ʿUmar's views, ideas, or utterances.

The above statement by ʿAlī in praise of ʿUmar is by no means incidental and it is in need of some clarification. These two great companions of the prophet were fierce opponents: traditions report that ʿAlī was denied the caliphate after the death of the prophet at ʿUmar's instigation, and that the latter did his utmost in electing Abū Bakr to the highest office. The enmity that ensued between the two is well known (Madelung 1997: 28–56). By having ʿAlī utter such a statement praising his bitter opponent, Sunnī tradition gives greater credibility to ʿUmar's role in Qurʾānic revelation, as if claiming: "If your enemy praises you so much, then it must be true."

Mutual Agreement

The concept of a mutual understanding or agreement between ʿUmar and Qurʾānic revelation is best expressed in a widely circulated utterance attributed to ʿUmar himself: "I agreed *(wāfaqtu)* with God on three matters" (Ibn Ḥanbal n.d.: I, 23; Abū Dāwūd n.d.: 9). The verb *wāfaqa*, "to agree with," can also be rendered as "to accord with," "to consent with" or "to be of one mind or opinion with someone" (Lane 1863: s.v. *w-f-q*). In other words ʿUmar is stating that he was of one mind with God on these matters.

In a rare opposite version, ʿUmar is supposed to have said: "God agreed with me (*wāfaqanī*) on three matters" (Ibn Ḥanbal 1983: I, 343 no. 495). Read for its fullest implications, one might suggest that this bold statement infers that it is God who reads ʿUmar's mind and not the other way around. One may assume that this latter version belongs to an earlier layer of traditions than the one described above. The previous version, it can be postulated, was circulated in order to mitigate the theological difficulty inherent in this latter version, which poses the difficulty of subordinating God's revelation to human will. Nevertheless, both versions were quoted in the most revered canonical collection of Islamic traditions, that of al-Bukhārī (d. 256/870). This means that, from the Muslim point of view, these versions were taken to be trustworthy and authentic (Ibn Ḥajar 1996: IX, 20, no. 4483). Yet, the theological difficulty did not go unnoticed by Muslim scholars who strove to provide it with an explanation befitting the Muslim creed (Ibn Ḥajar 1996: II, 64)

The Jewish Sources: Moses

The concept that there can be an interaction between a human being and God's revelation is expressed already in the *Babylonian Talmud*, where two different and conflicting statements describe Moses in this context. On the one hand, it is stated: "Three things did Moses upon his own authority, and his view agreed with that of God" (Yebamot 62b). On the other hand it is stated: "Three things did Moses upon his own authority, and God agreed thereto" (Shabbat 87a). The only difference between these two versions is that the subject of the verb "to agree" varies. In the first version, it is Moses who agrees in advance with God, while in the second, it is God who agrees, *a posteriori*, with Moses.

There is a distinct similarity between the two conflicting statements about Moses in the Talmud and the two conflicting statements uttered by ʿUmar as discussed above. In both sets of statements we are told about three matters that the two did on their own authority and God either agrees with them on these matters or each one of the two men agrees with God. In both sets of traditions the verb "to agree" can be rendered as to be of the same mind as someone. This similarity more than suggests that Islamic tradition fashioned a part of ʿUmar's image after that of Moses, and ascribed to the former virtues attributed in early Jewish sources to the latter. The matters that Moses did on his own were revealed as verses in the Torah later on, just as the matters ʿUmar did on his own were revealed as verses in the Qurʾān. Moreover, the same theological issue that confronted the Muslim scholars also puzzled the Jewish scholars: they, too, debated the issue of whether it is conceivable that God agrees *a posteriori* to the matters that Moses did on his own authority.

It is difficult to determine how and by what means these early Jewish concepts would have been introduced to the Islamic tradition. However, a thorough examination of traditions in praise of ʿUmar indicates that the model of Moses served in more than one instance for the fashioning of Umar's image as an ideal leader. Thus, Muḥammad is supposed to have drawn a comparison between some of his companions and the biblical prophets, and to have compared ʿUmar to Moses (al-Daylamī 1986: VI, 40, no. 6124).

Beyond the general concept of the similarity between ʿUmar and Moses, the Islamic tradition provides a description of specific incidents where this similarity is demonstrated. These incidents occur in traditions of the *asbāb al-nuzūl* type, that is, traditions that describe the circumstances of the revelation of certain verses of the Qurʾān (Rubin 1995: 226–33). It is noteworthy that although the model of Moses relates to only three matters that he did on his own authority, the Islamic tradition describes far more than three Qurʾānic verses which are supposed to have been revealed according to ʿUmar's mind. This in itself indicates that the Islamic tradition developed with a dynamic of its own. These verses, about thirty, are known in the sources as *Muwāfaqāt ʿUmar*, that is, the agreements of ʿUmar (with God), and they were gathered by scholars in specific chapters bearing that title, in their books (al-Suyūṭī 1988: 142–6) or in independent books and epistles (Ibn al-Naqīb; al-ʿImādī 1996). In the following pages a few such typical verses will be described and textually analyzed.

Anticipating God's Revelation

One kind of mutual agreement between ʿUmar and God occurs when the former anticipates the latter and duplicates His words. This is the case with the revelation of verses Q 23:12–14 in which God describes the creation of Adam.

In the early exegesis of Muqātil b. Sulaymān (d. 150/767), it is reported that these verses were revealed to the prophet in the presence of ʿUmar: "We created the man of an extraction of clay, then We set him, a drop, in a receptacle secure, then We created of the drop a clot, then We created of the clot a tissue, then We created of the tissue bones, then We garmented the bones in flesh, then We produced him as another creature." Upon hearing this detailed description of God's creation, ʿUmar is supposed to have exclaimed: "So blessed be God, the fairest of creators!" And the prophet said: "This is the way it was revealed, O ʿUmar!" (Muqātil 1989: III, 153; al-Suyūṭī 1985: V, 7)

In this tradition, ʿUmar marvels at the sublime event of the creation of man and at the details God provided in His description. His utterance on this occasion reflects his ability to read God's mind, and God repeats word by word ʿUmar's exclamation, thus completing verse Q 23:14.

The Case of the *Ḥijāb* Verse

The name *ḥijāb* verse is given in Islamic tradition to Q 33:53 in which God addresses the Muslim believers and commands them regarding the wives of the prophet: "And when you ask his wives for any object, ask them from behind a curtain (*ḥijāb*)." This verse prohibits the wives of Muḥammad from appearing in the presence of male Muslim believers (except close family members).

According to Islamic traditions this verse was revealed after the intervention of ʿUmar who did not look favorably on the fact that the wives of the prophet used to appear in public unveiled. He uttered his opinion on the matter by saying to the prophet that men, good and bad, were accustomed to approaching his wives freely and that he, Muḥammad, should order them to take cover behind a veil. The prophet did not answer, but soon enough, God gave backing to ʿUmar's opinion by revealing the verse of the *ḥijāb* (Ibn Shabba 1979: III, 860). In some tradition collections, the canonical ones included, this verse represents one of the three matters that ʿUmar and God agreed upon (Ibn Ḥajar 1996: IX, 483, no. 4790).

Other traditions provide more details as to the circumstances and the identity of the wives of the prophet who caused ʿUmar's intervention and, consequently, the revelation of the verse. Three different versions dealing with three different wives are quoted in the sources.

ʿĀʾisha

A widely circulated version mentions an incident of physical contact between ʿĀʾisha and ʿUmar. She relates that while she was eating a big bowl of dates mixed with butter (*ḥays*) with her husband Muḥammad, ʿUmar passed by and Muḥammad invited him to share their meal. As ʿUmar was reaching for the bowl, his finger touched that of ʿĀʾisha. He shouted his objection saying: "If only I could be obeyed in what concerns you [i.e., the prophet's wives], you would remain unseen [literally: No eye would look at you]." He was obeyed indeed, and God revealed the *ḥijāb* verse according to his wish (Ibn Abī Ḥātim 1997: X, 3148, no. 17756; Ibn Abī Shayba 1995: III, 361, no. 32008).

Sawda

However, other versions describe ʿUmar as confronting the prophet directly on this issue. The circumstances of the revelation of this verse are most embarrassing from the standpoint of later Muslim behavior, which might be the reason why the circulation of these versions is quite limited and why they were left outside the canonical collections of the Islamic tradition.

The following version relates to another wife of Muḥammad, Sawda, daughter of Zamʿa, who used to appear unveiled in public. Her behavior brought about ʿUmar's intervention and consequently caused the revelation of the *ḥijāb* verse.

> ʿĀʾisha relates that the wives of the prophet used to go out by night to al-Manāṣiʿ, a large open field near Medina, to relieve themselves. ʿUmar approached the prophet more than once requesting him to put the veil on his wives. [The tradition points out that ʿUmar used to address Muḥammad in the imperative form: "Cover your wives," he used to say to him]. But the prophet did not pay heed to this request. One night Sawda, a distinctively tall woman, went out to relieve herself. ʿUmar, who had been watching, shouted at her: "O Sawda we recognize you." ʿUmar did so, hoping a verse concerning the *ḥijāb* would be revealed, and indeed God revealed the veil verse. (Ibn Ḥanbal n.d.: VI, 223; Ibn Shabba 1979: III, 860)

In this version, ʿUmar meddles in the prophet's private life. By addressing Muḥammad in the imperative ("Cover your wives"), ʿUmar seems to be patronizing the prophet of Islam, and thus shaming him. When ʿUmar realized that the prophet did not pay heed to his demands, he turned to a higher instance, to God, in the hope that He would prove him right by revealing a Qurʿānic verse. From the wording of the tradition, it seems that in order to compel God to intervene in the matter of the veil, ʿUmar goes to extreme measures, even shaming one of the prophet's wives. God grants ʿUmar's wish and reveals the verse imposing the veil. Such a course of events gives the impression that ʿUmar can summon God's intervention at will, and in this manner, his moral and religious presence as a leader is felt in its utmost intensity, as opposed to the prophet's apparent unwillingness to do "the right thing."

Zaynab

In the following version the prophet's wife who causes the verse of the veil to be revealed according to ʿUmar's wish is Zaynab, daughter of Jaḥsh. It is related that ʿUmar ordered the wives of the prophet to cover themselves with a veil. Zaynab resented this behavior and admonished ʿUmar saying: "O Ibn al-Khaṭṭāb, you are jealous for us even though the revelation (of the Qurʾān) occurs in our homes." So God revealed verse Q 33:53 (Ibn Shabba 1979: III, 860; al-Ṭabarānī n.d.: IX, 184–5, no. 8828).

Here also, ʿUmar is portrayed as offending the prophet: he addresses Muḥammad's wives behind his back and gives them orders regarding how to behave, which is unacceptable to any man in Arabian society, let alone the prophet. Zaynab reprimands him harshly for his rude behavior, alluding to the fact that he is not supposed to show jealousy regarding somebody else's wife, and that he is meddling in the private life of no less than the prophet, her husband, who lives in the house where God's revelation occurs. Yet, in spite of ʿUmar's rude behavior and its implications for Muḥammad's honor both as a prophet and as a husband, God backs up ʿUmar and reveals the verse. Once more, ʿUmar is described as blessed with God's grace, and his image serves as the most sublime source of the religious and moral laws, even at the expense of the prophet.

The Shīʿī position

The Shīʿites never acknowledged ʿUmar's virtues, mainly because of his predominant role in depriving ʿAlī of the privilege of succeeding the prophet as leader of the Muslim community. They did not miss any opportunity to slander ʿUmar, and the various stories about the revelation of the *ḥijāb* verse served them well. In particular, they focused on Sawda's story; they scorned ʿUmar for exposing in public a wife of the prophet, thus shaming her and her husband and invading the privacy of the most revered leader of Islam (Ibn Ṭāwūs 1999: II, 154).

Muḥammad causes the revelation of the verse

Sunnī scholars soon became aware of the predominant role of ʿUmar in these stories and its impact on the image of Muḥammad. For example, the commentator al-Qurṭubī (d. 671/1272) claimed that the story in which ʿUmar orders the wives of the prophet to put on the veil is totally unreliable and should be rejected (al-Qurṭubī 1965: XIV, 224).

For this reason, other versions were put into circulation, which conflicted with the versions described above. In them, ʿUmar is totally absent from the scene and the initiator of the revelation of Q 33:53 is the prophet himself. In one of these versions, the story of the prophet's meal with ʿĀʾisha is retold without mentioning ʿUmar's name. It is reported that the prophet was having lunch with ʿĀʾisha and several of his companions. The hand of one of them touched his wife's hand and Muḥammad disapproved strongly. Consequently, the *ḥijāb* verse was revealed in response to the prophet's wish (al-Ṭabarī 1987: XXII, 28)

By omitting the names of the companions present at the lunch, the tradition focuses on the prophet alone. His disapproval of any physical contact with his wife is the cause of the revelation of the verse. Thus, his image is rehabilitated vis-à-vis that of ʿUmar, and he becomes the ultimate source of authority and moral values.

The Case of the Prohibition Against Wine

A different moral aspect of ʿUmar's image as a leader blessed with God's grace is linked to the Qurʾānic prohibition against drinking wine. Here also ʿUmar is endowed with the ability to "dictate" the revelation of verses according to his wishes.

The prohibition against drinking wine is one of the fundamental beliefs that separate Islam from the two other monotheistic religions, Judaism and Christianity. It should be remembered that in the latter religions, wine is not only allowed, it is indeed a symbol of faith; in Judaism it serves as the drink of the *Kiddush*, the traditional benediction sanctifying the Sabbath and the festivals, while in Christianity wine serves also as a means of communion of the believer with Jesus Christ. Linking ʿUmar to the prohibition against wine is one of the greatest virtues attributed to him by the Islamic tradition. It is noteworthy that the ban on drinking wine in the Qurʾān is not decisive, and its finality varies from verse to verse. The revelation of the verses that seem to prohibit the drinking of wine in the clearest sense is attributed to ʿUmar.

Several versions are quoted in the sources. The one recounted below is probably from a very early layer of traditions, which explains its rarity.

> ʿUmar addressed God saying: "O God, give us a clear commandment regarding the wine." So verse Q 4:43 was revealed: "O believers, draw not near to prayer when you are drunken until you know what you are saying." The prophet [to whom the verse was revealed] summoned ʿUmar and recited it to him. It seems that this verse did not conform to what ʿUmar had in mind. So he addressed God again: "O God, give us a clear commandment regarding the wine." And verse Q 2:219 was revealed: "They will question thee concerning wine and arrow-shuffling. Say: 'In both is heinous sin, and uses for men, but the sin in them is more heinous than the usefulness." The prophet summoned ʿUmar and recited it to him. It seems that this verse (too) did not conform to what ʿUmar had in mind. So he addressed God again: "O God, give us a clear commandment regarding the wine." And verses Q 5:90–1 were revealed: "O believers, wine and arrow-shuffling, idols and divining-arrows are an abomination, some of Satan's work; so avoid it; haply so you will prosper. Satan only desires to precipitate enmity and hatred between you in regard to wine and arrow-shuffling, and to bar you from the remembrance of God, and from prayer. Will you then desist"? The prophet summoned ʿUmar and recited it to him. Upon hearing the verse ʿUmar exclaimed: "O God, indeed we desist." (al-Ḥākim al-Nīsābūrī 1990: IV, 159–60)

The wording of this tradition calls for comment. One should note that it is ʿUmar and not Muḥammad who addresses God regarding the revelation of a clear commandment regarding wine. This means that it is ʿUmar himself who initiated the prohibition of wine in the first place. As he addresses God again and again the verses revealed become clearer and more decisive. Were it not for ʿUmar's initiative the Qurʾānic prohibition would have remained indecisive as it was when the first verse was revealed. As the story develops, the reader senses the passivity of the prophet as opposed to the activity of ʿUmar concerning this issue. The main role of the prophet is to serve as the recipient of the revelation while it is ʿUmar who holds a direct dialogue with God. The role of ʿUmar in this story is astonishing and hardly conceivable in Muslim terms: he is portrayed as the one who regulates the revelation of the verses according to his own understanding. It is as if he is summoning God Almighty to reveal the "right" verse that prohibits wine according to his own views and understanding. In the words of the tradition: "It seems that the verse did not conform to what ʿUmar had in mind." And since he feels that the verse revealed is not clear enough, he demands another and another until he is satisfied, until the verse revealed prohibits wine in the way he understands it. Only then does he yield.

This tradition portrays ʿUmar's image as the true formulator of the Islamic law for the nascent Muslim community, while the prophet's image in this respect is dimmed. Ultimately, the Muslim community rallied around its prophet and not around a caliph, not even ʿUmar. This is reflected in other traditions, probably from a later layer than the one above, where Muḥammad plays the major role in the prohibition of wine. Such is the case of a tradition circulated on the authority of ʿUmar's son, ʿAbd Allāh, according to which the revelation of the different verses that prohibit wine drinking is at the exclusive initiative of the prophet, after Muslim believers differed on the status of wine. In this tradition, ʿUmar is not mentioned (Abū Dāwūd n.d.: 264, no. 1957). In other versions where ʿUmar is mentioned, he is portrayed as playing a minor role, (al-Ṭabarī 1969: IV, 332–4, no. 4145) or as accepting enthusiastically the prohibition of wine initiated by the prophet (al-Ṭabarī 1969: IV, 330, no. 4142).

The Ransom of the Prisoners of the Battle of Badr

Another aspect of the mutual agreement between ʿUmar and God is expressed in some versions of the interpretation of Q 8:67–9. According to many scholars, these verses were revealed after Muḥammad's victory over the unbelievers from Quraysh at Badr in the year 2/624 and the ransom the Muslims demanded in order to release the prisoners they had captured during the battle. The Qurʾān states:

> Q 8:67 It is not for any prophet to have prisoners until he make wide slaughter in the land. You desire the chance goods of the present world, and God desires the world to come; and God is All-mighty, All-wise.
>
> Q 8:68 Had it not been for a prior prescription from God, there had afflicted you, for what you took, a mighty chastisement.
>
> Q 8:69 Eat of what you had taken as booty, such as is lawful and good; and fear you God; surely God is All-forgiving, All-compassionate.

Some scholars read verse 67 above as a command to kill the defeated unbelievers on the battleground, before they are taken prisoner; these scholars found a direct link between this verse and the eagerness of the Muslims to enjoy the spoils of the great victory of Badr and the ransom for the prisoners of war they captured. As verses 68–9 describe, the Muslims should have been chastised for their misconduct, their craving for the pleasures of this world and because they neglected the principles of a war of extermination against the unbelievers. However, because of His preordination to show them mercy and to allow them to enjoy the spoils of wars, God deferred His chastisement. Actually, several scholars agree that the Muslims were ultimately allowed to take ransom for prisoners of war who were unbelievers according to another verse revealed in the Qurʾān (Q 4:47), and thus the above verse was abrogated.

ʿUmar's involvement in the revelation of these verses, as described below, reflects the divine grace bestowed on him. However, in this particular case, the laws that could have been formulated according to these verses and to ʿUmar's view were not put into effect and are not part of the Islamic law because of their harsh implications.

Only ʿUmar objects to the ransom and demands to kill unbelievers

Several traditions report that before the revelation of the verses that command the killing of defeated unbelievers and prohibit ransoming them, the prophet and his companions had preferred to accept the ransom and not to kill the prisoners who were the blood relatives of several companions. Only ʿUmar held the opposite view, demanding that unbelievers be killed regardless of their status. In the ensuing controversy between ʿUmar and all the other Muslim believers, including the prophet, the above verses Q 8:67–9 were revealed, vindicating ʿUmar and stating that God agreed with his view to the detriment of everybody else. The story is quoted in Muqātil b. Sulaymān's exegesis.

> The prophet consulted with his companions regarding the prisoners taken at Badr. ʿUmar b. al-Khaṭṭāb advised: "Put them all to death, for they are the heads of unbelief and the leaders of the deviation from the right path." Abū Bakr argued: "Don't put them to death, for God helped us achieve our vengeance, killed the polytheists and defeated them. It is preferable to let them redeem themselves for the ransom they pay will strengthen Islam and help finance the war against them. Maybe God will turn them to supporters of Islam and they will convert."
>
> Abū Bakr's argument pleased the prophet, for he was merciful, just like Abū Bakr, while ʿUmar was sharp and unflinching. The prophet agreed with Abū Bakr's view and demanded a ransom from the prisoners. However, God revealed a verse agreeing with ʿUmar's view, stating: "It is not for any prophet to have prisoners. . . ." Then the prophet addressed ʿUmar and said to him: "Bless God, for your God agreed with you (*wātāka*). ʿUmar said: "Bless God who agreed with me regarding the prisoners of Badr." And the prophet added: "If a chastisement were to descend from heaven none of us would be saved except for ʿUmar b. al-Khaṭṭāb; indeed he forbade me and I did not pay heed." (Muqātil 1989: II, 129)

In this story, it is Muḥammad himself who admits that he was wrong for not taking ʿUmar's advice, and he even states that only ʿUmar would have been saved had the Muslims been punished from heaven, as alluded to in the Qurʾānic verse. Moreover, the prophet understands God's agreement with ʿUmar, demonstrated by the revelation of the verse backing the latter's view, as God's compliance with ʿUmar. This is reflected in the use of the verb *wātā*, "to comply with." It is as if the prophet was saying to ʿUmar: "God obeyed you on that matter."

In a different version of this tradition, the prophet and ʿUmar are portrayed in direct confrontation over the issue of the ransom. While ʿUmar suggests putting the prisoners to death, the prophet rejects his advice on the grounds that the prisoners are blood brothers of the Muslims and prefers Abū Bakr's advice to ransom them. Then God revealed the verses justifying ʿUmar (Ibn Ḥanbal n.d.: III, 243).

In this last version the prophet and Abū Bakr are portrayed as abiding by the old principle of loyalty to the tribe, held dear in the pre-Islamic era, the *jāhiliyya*, while ʿUmar represents the true spirit of the new religion, Islam, and abides by one of its fundamental principles, the war against unbelievers. The verses revealed subsequently reflect God's accord with ʿUmar, while the prophet is described as someone who could have been punished by God for not putting the prisoners to death.

Only ʿUmar refuses a share of the booty

ʿUmar is portrayed not only as the sole companion of the prophet who opposes the ransoming of the prisoners but also as the only one who refuses to take a share of the booty. While the Muslim believers yearned for the booty in the aftermath of the battle, ʿUmar ignored it and went on slaying every prisoner he met. He said to the prophet: "What do we care about booty? We are people who set out to fight a holy war for God's religion until He is worshipped (everywhere)." The prophet commented: "O ʿUmar, if we were to be punished for what we did, you are the only one who would have been saved; God said: 'It is unlawful to take (booty and ransom) on your own will before I permit them to you. Do not do it again' " (al-Ṭabarī 1969: XIV, 71, no. 16319). ʿUmar is portrayed here as the only Muslim who cared for the war for the glory of God, *jihād*. Indeed, when addressing the prophet about fighting for God, he is made to use the word *nujāhid*, that is, "we fight a holy war."

Only ʿUmar would have been saved from God's punishment

Several versions focus on the idea that ʿUmar would have been the only survivor of the harsh punishment that would have been inflicted on the Muslims, were it not for God's predestination to forgive them. In one version, Muḥammad addresses ʿUmar, saying: "We were almost stricken by evil because we differed from you" (Abū Nuʿaym n.d.: I, 43). In a different version, the prophet states, "Because we differed from ʿUmar's opinion we were almost doomed, and if chastisement were to be sent down from heaven, none of us would have been spared except ʿUmar" (al-Suyūṭī 1985: III, 203).

The prophet, in his own words, includes himself among those who could have been punished. Consequently, he admits ʿUmar's superiority over all other Muslims. By abiding solely by the principles of holy war against unbelievers, ʿUmar is the only one whose view accords with God's view as it is revealed in the Qurʾān.

The canonical version: The prophet excluded from punishment

However, the version that was accepted by the Muslims as authoritative and reliable is more balanced, and precludes the possibility for any Muslim to be superior to the prophet himself. The following version is quoted by Muslim (d. 261/875) in the chapter dealing with *jihād* in his famous canonical collection of traditions.

It is reported that, contrary to Abū Bakr, ʿUmar suggested putting all the prisoners to death. Since the captured unbelievers were blood brothers of the Muslims, he devised a scheme according to which each Muslim would slay a relative of his (thus preventing Quraysh from seeking revenge or blood money from the Muslims). The prophet rejected this suggestion on the grounds that blood relatives should be spared (even though they are unbelievers). The next day, when ʿUmar came to meet the prophet and Abū Bakr, he saw them crying. He sympathized with them, comforted them and asked them what it was all about. The prophet said, "I am crying because your brethren suggested to me to take the ransom, and now I can see their punishment coming close, as close as this tree," and he pointed towards a tree nearby. Then God revealed the verses quoted above that deal with the duty to slay the unbelievers before they are taken prisoners, and the verses revealed after that which condone the taking of the booty (Muslim 1983: III, 1385, no. 1763).

This version does not mention the utterance according to which ʿUmar was the only Muslim who would be saved if a punishment were to be sent down from heaven. Therefore, the prophet is not threatened with any chastisement. Moreover, this tradition emphasizes that ultimately God allowed Muslims to take the ransom, and thus the dignity of the prophet and his companions is preserved. Yet even in this balanced version, ʿUmar is still the only companion who suggests to the prophet to abstain from taking ransom, and the subsequent revelation proves him right.

The Shīʿī position

The Shīʿī sources are very much aware of the impact of such traditions on the Muslim community, and they strive to diminish ʿUmar's image. Shīʿī scholars reject the above-described traditions and totally ignore ʿUmar's role in the prisoners of Badr affair (Abū ʾl-Qāsim al-Kūfī n.d.: 184). For example, the ninth Shīʿīte Imām, Muḥammad b. ʿAlī al-Jawād (d. 220/835), was asked in the presence of the ʿAbbāsid caliph al-Maʾmūn (d. 218/834) about several traditions in praise of ʿUmar, including the one that exempted him from the punishment that could have been inflicted on the Muslims for taking the ransom at Badr. Al-Jawād refuted the tradition, basing himself on Q 8:33, according to which God will never punish the Muslims as long as Muḥammad lives among them, and therefore the story about ʿUmar is nothing but a fiction since no Muslim was supposed to be punished in the first place (al-Ṭabrisī 1989: 449).

ʿUmar and the Hypocrites

ʿUmar's involvement in the revelation of the Qurʾān reflects not only his harsh attitude towards unbelievers outside the Muslim community, but also his attitude towards the hypocrites, *munāfiqūn*, who claim to profess Islam while in truth they conceal hatred towards it. Qurʾānic exegesis creates a close affinity between three different verses pertaining to these people and ascribes to ʿUmar a central role in their revelation. These are the verses in question:

> Q 9:80 Ask pardon for them, or ask not pardon for them; if thou askest pardon for them seventy times, God will not pardon them; that, because they disbelieved in God and His messenger. God guides not the people of the ungodly.
>
> Q 9:84 And pray thou never over any one of them when he is dead, nor stand over his grave; they disbelieved in God and His messenger, and died when they were ungodly.
>
> Q 63:6 Equal it is for them, whether thou askest forgiveness for them or thou askest not forgiveness for them; God will never forgive them. God guides not the people of the ungodly.

A difference in interpretation

The attitude towards the hypocrites in these verses is not uniform, especially in Q 9:80. In its first part, the prophet is supposedly given free choice to decide whether to pray for the sinners or not. This permission does not conform to the final decree stated in the other verses, a decree that rules out *a priori* any option of forgiveness for the hypocrites. Muslim scholars were well aware of the exegetical difficulty that stems from the supposed authorization given to the prophet to ask forgiveness for the hypocrites in his prayers. They are almost unanimous in their claim that the verses that deny the option of forgiveness, Q 9:84 and Q 63:6, were revealed later than the one that allows it, Q 9:80, and consequently these are the verses that formulate the final Muslim attitude towards the hypocrites in Islam. This view is expressed in exegetical traditions dealing with the circumstances of the revelation of the verses above. All traditions focus on the image of ʿAbd Allāh b. Ubayy, a leader among the Anṣār, the hypocrite par excellence in the Islamic tradition and the Muslim collective memory. The pardoning of his sins, thanks to the prophet's prayers, is the issue debated in the traditions, and the interdiction to pray for him is conveyed to Muḥammad in several ways.

The angel Gabriel

First, mention should be made of the version according to which it is the angel Gabriel who reveals to the prophet the total interdiction. According to this version, the prophet, basing himself on the permission embedded in Q 9:80, intended to pray for Ibn Ubayy who had just died. Gabriel seized him by his cloth and stopped him abruptly. He then revealed to Muḥammad Q 9:84 stating the total interdiction (al-Ṭabarī 1969: XIV, 407, no. 17053).

The prophet and ʿUmar confront

Other versions mention ʿUmar as the one who prevents the prophet from praying for Ibn Ubayy in the same manner the angel Gabriel did. This indicates ʿUmar's sublime virtue as the one who guides the prophet towards God's will, and in this case, he guides the prophet to the right interpretation of God's intention as revealed in the Qurʾān. He is also responsible for further Qurʾānic revelations that render the interdiction to pray for Ibn Ubayy more decisive.

In one version, ʿUmar guides Muḥammad to what he believes is the right interpretation of Q 9:80 that had already been revealed. He relates that, as a Muslim, he made an almost unforgivable mistake. The prophet intended to pray for Ibn Ubayy, but he, ʿUmar, seized him by his cloth while reciting the verse quoted above and prevented him from carrying on. Muḥammad countered that this verse gave him a choice to pray for forgiveness for Ibn Ubayy or not to pray. Then Muḥammad approached the grave to pray for the deceased (Ibn Abī Ḥātim 1997: VI, 1853–4, no. 10508).

In this version, ʿUmar, just like the angel Gabriel in the above version, is portrayed as seizing the prophet by his cloth to prevent him from approaching the grave of the hypocrite and offering the prayer. It is true that he deplored the use of force, which offended the prophet, but, to his mind, this lapse was necessary because the prophet intended to offer a forbidden prayer. The tradition offers no clue as to whether the prophet prayed or not. In any case, ʿUmar interpreted the verse rigorously while the prophet was more lenient in his interpretation. ʿUmar based his interpretation on the second part of the verse that states that God will never forgive the hypocrites, while Muḥammad focused on the beginning of the verse that gave him the option to choose whether to pray or not. Indeed, in another version it is reported that when verse Q 9:80 was revealed to him, he declared, "I hear my God allowing me to pray for them" (al-Suyūṭī 1985: III, 264). However, the fact that a Muslim, even ʿUmar, opposed the prophet on a point of interpretation of the Qurʾān is unforgivable by later Muslim standards: no one knows the true meaning of the God's revealed verses better than the prophet.

The controversy between the prophet and ʿUmar over the interpretation of that verse is described in yet another version. When Muḥammad expressed his wish to pray for Ibn Ubayy, ʿUmar asked him: "Did not God forbid you to pray for the hypocrites?" The prophet replied, "No, he gave me a choice to ask forgiveness for them or not to ask" (al-Ṭabarī 1969: XIV, 406–7, no. 17050–1; Ibn Ḥanbal n.d.: II, 18).

In one more version, ʿUmar not only interprets the verse rigorously but also causes the revelation of another verse, Q 9:84, thus validating his opinion against that of the prophet:

> ʿAbd Allāh b. Ubayy said to his son (named also ʿAbd Allāh): "Go to the prophet and ask him to give me a cloth of his to use it for my shroud." ʿAbd Allāh (the son) approached the prophet and said to him: "Messenger of God, you surely recognize ʿAbd Allāh (the father) standing among his tribe. He ordered me to ask for one of your cloths to use it as his shroud and also to pray for him." The prophet gave him one of his cloths and intended to pray for him. But ʿUmar said to him: "You know ʿAbd Allāh and his hypocrisy, will you still pray

> for him even when God had forbidden you to do so?" The prophet asked him: "Where?" And ʿUmar quoted (Q 9:80): "If thou askest pardon for them seventy times, God will not pardon them." The prophet said: "I will offer more (than seventy)." And then God revealed (Q 9:84): "And pray thou never over any one of them when he is dead, nor stand over his grave." (al-Ṭabarānī n.d.: XI, 438, no. 12244)

In this version, the prophet attempts to impose his moderate interpretation also on the second part of Q 9:80, where it is stated that even seventy prayers will not help the hypocrites obtain forgiveness. He intends to pray more than seventy prayers. But it is ʿUmar who understands the meaning of the verse to be that the number seventy is only typological. As corroboration to his view God reveals Q 9:84 which expresses the interdiction with more finality. God agrees with ʿUmar's symbolic and broad understanding of the verse and rejects the prophet's concrete and narrow interpretation.

An even more blatant approach of ʿUmar towards the prophet is described in a different version. ʿUmar reports:

> When ʿAbd Allāh b. Ubayy died the prophet was asked to pray for him. He stood over his grave to begin the prayer, but I confronted him, face to face, and said: "Messenger of God, will you pray for ʿAbd Allāh b. Ubayy? The same Ibn Ubayy who said this and that on the day so and so?" And I started enumerating the days. The prophet smiled, but when I persisted, he said: "Back off! I was given a choice and I chose. It was revealed to me (Q 9:80): 'Ask pardon for them, or ask not pardon for them; if thou askest pardon for them seventy times, God will not pardon them;' If need be, I will pray more than seventy times to obtain forgiveness for their sins." Then he prayed for him, went to his funeral and stood over his grave until the end. ʿUmar added: "I was amazed from what I did and from my boldness towards the prophet who knew better than I did. But I swear by God, soon enough this verse was revealed (Q 9:84), 'And pray thou never over any one of them when he is dead, nor stand over his grave; they disbelieved in God and His messenger, and died when they were ungodly.' " (Ibn Hishām 1995: IV, 151; Ibn Ḥanbal n.d.: I, 16)

In this version ʿUmar behaves rudely towards the prophet who is supposed to have more knowledge on the matter. And yet, it appears that ʿUmar's rigorous understanding accords with that of God: a verse that ends the controversy and proves ʿUmar right is revealed.

ʿUmar not mentioned

Unlike these versions which describe a confrontation between the prophet and ʿUmar over a point of interpretation of God's revelation, other versions do not mention ʿUmar at all, and consequently the affront to the prophet's image as the highest authority on the interpretation and application of Qurʾānic precepts is removed. It is probable that these versions belong to a later layer than the ones quoted above and that they were put into circulation in order to rehabilitate the prophet's image. In one of these versions, the prophet is described as praying for Ibn Ubayy and standing over his grave;

then Q 9:84 is revealed that forbids this course of action (al-Ṭabarī 1969: XIV, 407, no. 17052). From this version it is obvious that the prophet never erred by taking a course of action opposing the revelation, since the verse that forbade it was revealed only after he finished praying for the hypocrite.

The Shīʿī position

Here also, the Shīʿī scholars go to extreme measures in order to refute any virtue attributed to ʿUmar. The versions describing the incident of the prayer for Ibn Ubayy, as quoted in Shīʿī sources, have a different ending that puts ʿUmar to ridicule. One version circulated on the authority of the sixth Imām, Jaʿfar al-Ṣādiq (d. 148/765), reports that ʿUmar attempted to stop the prophet from praying for Ibn Ubayy; however, the prophet told him that he never intended to pray for him but to curse him and wish for him a destiny in hell (al-ʿAyyāshī 1991: II, 107, no. 94). In this way, ʿUmar is described as a hardheaded man who reacts unnecessarily because he has no confidence in the prophet's judgment.

In another version, also circulated on the authority of al-Ṣādiq, the prophet answers ʿUmar, who stands in his way, that it was not his intention to pray for Ibn Ubayy nor to stand over his grave, but to honor his son who was a good Muslim. ʿUmar expresses his regrets and asks forgiveness for having angered God or His prophet (al-ʿAyyāshī 1991: II, 107–8, no. 95).

Conclusion

The agreements with God suggest that ʿUmar was an active partner in the revelation of several verses in the Qurʾān and consequently define his image as opposing that of the prophet. It is probable that the traditions describing these events were put into circulation at an early stage of the crystallization of the Islamic law, a stage where the ideal leader was the caliph. These traditions were never intended to damage the prophet's image, for it is unconceivable that a Muslim in any era would do so. But at a later stage, Muslim scholars became aware of the damage to the prophet's image and they put into circulation versions rehabilitating the prophet's image and minimizing that of ʿUmar. Ultimately, the Muslim community rallied behind its prophet and not any of its caliphs.

Author note

This chapter is condensed from a chapter of my Tel Aviv PhD dissertation entitled "ʿUmar b. al-Khaṭṭāb and the Image of the Ideal Leader in the Islamic Tradition," under the supervision of Professor Uri Rubin, September 2003 (in Hebrew).

Further reading

Hakim, Avraham (2003) Conflicting images of lawgivers: The caliph and the prophet. In: Berg, Herbert (ed.) *Method and Theory in the Study of Islamic Origins*. Brill, Leiden, pp. 159–77.
Madelung, Wilferd (1997) *The Succession to Muḥammad*. Cambridge University Press, Cambridge.
Rubin, Uri (1995) *The Eye of the Beholder*. Darwin Press, Princeton.

PART III

Content

CHAPTER 14

God

Andrew Rippin

As might be assumed to be so in the case of a religious text, the figure of God is an overwhelming and overarching presence in the Qurʾān. Understanding the nature of the figure of God as He is presented in the foundational text is manifestly a central task of anyone who wishes to achieve an understanding of the nature and outlook of Islam itself. Such a task is, given the quantity of theological reflection which already exists on the text, not a straightforward matter. In approaching the subject, we are immediately confronted by the challenge of the nature of language itself and the context in which talk about God is found. The challenge for the interested reader in coming to terms with the topic is substantial, for so many different tacks have been taken in the past in order to deal with the issue; some assistance may be provided here by a clear statement of perspective and approach at the outset.

Assessing the "poetic" (or "mythical" or "religious") nature of the Qurʾān commences with an understanding that the text of scripture is an expression, distilled at a particular historical point in time, of human religious experience located within the broad context of the Near East. The Qurʾān participates within this context but does not depict all of it. It presents arguments and positions from within the overall context but it does not provide the reader with the full vision of that religious ethos. This is part of the dimension of what has been spoken of as the "referential" character of the Qurʾān (Wansbrough 1978: 1) but it may go further, since the possibility must be entertained that the Qurʾān is silent on some points of common religious assumption and makes no explicit reference to them as such. The establishment of a fixed text of scripture implies a moment in time into which a tradition of thinking puts itself, resulting in an enunciation of its understanding at that time, limited by the extent of its own self-reflection. This limitation implied by this distillation of the text into a fixed canon does not mean that the project of struggling with the text must be renounced. But it does indicate that it is a project which must proceed with considerable deliberation and appropriate modesty in expectations of one's accomplishments.

Fundamentally the issue which must be confronted focuses on the language of the Qur'ān. Our task becomes one of looking at the symbolic language used in speaking of God. In dealing with expressions related to the divine, the subject of study becomes not a matter of one "thing" being "symbolized" as another in the manner of a literary figure. Rather, what is at stake is the way in which "things" are "captured" in language in a form which is necessarily symbolic due to the use of language itself. It is here that Paul Ricoeur's maxim "metaphor gives rise to thought" has its meaning: in expressing something in language, thinking about that "thing" becomes possible. Metaphor, or symbol as I use that word here, creates new possibilities of imagination and thought. Such symbols work within systems of narrative to create new alignments which structure existence on a personal and social level.

As Mohammed Arkoun has observed, God did not prove problematic in classical Arabic or Islamic thinking: for Muslims of the classical period, God is well known and well presented in the Qur'ān. However, God has become problematic as an element of thought in the contemporary period, although that fact has not yet been widely perceived in the Muslim world. One example of a Muslim thinker who has broached the subject and taken up the challenge is Shabbir Akhtar (1990). Akhtar does not follow Arkoun into his "genuine religious issues like the consciousness of culpability, the eschatological perspective, or revelation as a springboard for mythical, or symbolic thinking" (Arkoun 1987: 23) but rather concerns himself with the defensibility of philosophical arguments for the existence of God and the possibility of revelation. However, the fundamental problem is more than simply an issue of the "unthinkable" in relation to contemporary paganism or secularism: it is also a recognition of the relationship of language to the divine. The result is that there is a need to rethink God today "in light of the new knowledge of language, mind, logic, and history" (Arkoun 1987: 15).

Now, what might that mean when it comes to speaking of God? Contemporary thought has come to recognize that, in considering the application of language to God, "either to equate human words with the divine reality or to see no relationship between them is inappropriate" (McFague 1982: 7). For example, the statement "God is king" does not suggest that God is literally a king as humans use that word to apply to other humans, but neither does it suggest that God is king by virtue of metaphor, thereby suggesting that God is, in fact, something other than a king in reality. That is, in defining metaphor, it is common to suggest that an identity between the word used metaphorically and the object referred to is not present; when we say "Zayd is a lion," we understand that Zayd is not a lion but has taken on some sense of the characteristics of a lion. In the case of God, on the other hand, it may well be asserted that He is both a king and not a king: it might be suggested that He encompasses both aspects. "God is king" is perhaps best spoken of as symbolic, conveying a sense that God is somehow beyond language in that the words which are used dissolve into their opposites. It is here, then, that we enter into the mythological world of Near Eastern monotheism.

The language used to speak of the divine in the Qur'ān may necessarily be thought of as symbolic: the finitude of language must confront the infinitude of the godhead. How can there be any other way of speaking of God? Only within the concept of God's name may there be said to be a suggestion that language "fits", but, even then, only in the magical sense of language (that is, within the first stage of language as described by Northrup Frye 1982: 6–7). It might be argued that God remains "nameless" in the Qur'ān, at least to the extent that he is not given a personal or proper name, although the status of the word Allāh is certainly debated (see Anawati 1967; Gimaret 1988). However, the use of oaths in His name and the idea of Him "having the most beautiful names" (Q 7:180; 17:110; 20:8) are clearly significant. The repetitions of *bismi-llāh*, "in the name of God," throughout the text suggest that, through God's name, the reality of God may be invoked; this is magical language which at the same time (or even, thereby, perhaps) suggests that the word reaches the object named. Be that as it may, the Qur'ān employs a wide range of symbolic vocabulary in order to describe God, and the Qur'ān holds much of this range in common with the Near Eastern monotheistic world stemming back to ancient times. The distinctiveness of the Qur'ānic contribution to this discourse about God may be viewed by comparing its emphases and ranges with other (both earlier and later) manifestations of monotheist discourse. The sum of such an investigation is to see how the monotheistic spirit expressed itself in seventh century Arabic. It is, at its basis, a comparative question as well as a conceptual one.

The images of God in relation to humanity as used in the Qur'ān have an ancient heritage. In asserting that fact we must be clear about how to separate these insights from those of the philological. The tendency is to see the assertion of a past usage as meaning that the past represents the original and true usage and that all later usages are derivative. Such are the pitfalls into which many studies of the Qur'ān have fallen. C. C. Torrey (1892) provides a classic example of this tendency in the way that his observations on Qur'ānic terminology and its parallels in the Bible led him only to the conclusion that Muḥammad was unoriginal. This is the historicist frame of mind at work.

One example adduced by Torrey regarding the word *kitāb* may be considered to illustrate the point. Torrey (1892: 9) acknowledges the Jewish and Christian usages of the symbol of the "book" (and speaks of it as being "borrowed" by Muḥammad) and knows of the image of the "divine book of reckoning" which "was common even before Mohammed." He connects this latter usage to a bill of sale which "was, of course, familiar enough among the Arabs." The leap from the monotheist imagery of the Near East to the historical reality of the Arabs of Mecca and Medina is the key to the historicist mode of thinking. The reality of mythical, symbolic discourse has been subsumed and rendered banal under the weight of establishing the reality of history in its atomistic elements. This, of course, is precisely the same process which the Muslim juridical tradition followed in its own way in order to establish a normative set of rules for conduct in society during the development of the Islamic ethos.

A comparative approach can be of some significance if the aims and the limitations of the method are clearly kept in mind. A successful (that is, meaningful) comparative methodology involves analogical comparisons in terms of systems, not in terms of isolated "bits and pieces," always keeping in mind the suspicion that analogous processes within parallel cultural situations are likely to produce similar results. Comparisons need not involve the question of "origins" of particular items: the focus of interest moves to cultural patterns and symbolic systems. There is, it must be admitted, still a decision to be made regarding the general frameworks which are brought into any comparison – in the case of the Qur'ān, for example, whether one pursues a context of Arabia (however the society of the Arabs be defined: bedouin and/or urban) or a context broadly conceived as the ancient Near Eastern religious world which is developed by Arkoun (2002: 114–25) into a notion of the "societies of the book." It is the latter which makes good sense of the data and which acknowledges most profoundly the fundamental human religious impulse.

God as King

The expression of ideology through symbolism in the ancient world extended to mechanisms whereby human standards were supported, enhanced and promoted. Such is the common background to the statement "God is King" for which we see analogous developments throughout the ancient Near East and beyond. A statement such as "God is King" legitimizes kingship as a human endeavor and sets the bounds for acceptable behavior by the human king – with the constant recognition that a mere mortal king will not necessarily reach the level of divine perfection (although, in some societies, the elevation of the king to divine status implied just that possibility, of course). The description of God being king (or queen, on some occasions) is found throughout ancient Near Eastern literature. Amon, Anu, Ashur, Ea, El, the Hittite gods, Ishtar, Marduk, and Nanna are all named as royalty. In the non-biblical ancient Near East, "Kingship belongs primarily to heaven. 'King' may be first and foremost the title of a ruling deity" (Eaton 1990: 379).

What does it mean to suggest that somebody is a king? That is, what is the semantic field and the associated imagery which goes along with "kingship"? Just what is meant by kingship? Power, authority, and justice are all linked in the concept. Kingship establishes a relationship between the king himself and the people of his territory, often with words such as subjects, servants, slaves, or citizens (the latter suggesting a sense of belonging and allegiance).

The Bible presents, like the Qur'ān, a (relatively) static tradition of the expression of Near Eastern monotheism. The Bible cannot be presumed to define the range of the symbolism said to be analogical to a text such as the Qur'ān, even less to provide the normative example by which all others may be compared. It does, however, furnish a convenient textual source from which comparative insights may begin. Thus, for our purposes here, we may observe that the image of a king within biblical vocabulary provides the following as being royal characteristics considered desirable for a king: wisdom, long life, wealth, strength, majesty, and beauty. Royal trappings spoken of include a crown, bracelet, clothing, scepter, throne, platform, palace, and a royal court.

Furthermore, in terms of symbolism of the language of the Bible, we must keep in mind that the primary focus suggests the qualities of relationship, for the relational quality of a symbol – the sense in which one "thing" relates to another through metaphor – underlies the entire structure. In that light, G. B. Caird (1980: 177) observes that "in the Bible the five metaphors in most common use to express God's relationship with his worshipers are king:subject, judge:litigant, husband:wife, father:child, and master:servant." It is important to remember that, in such analyses, we are looking at a whole range of vocabulary which is interlocked into a metaphorical whole. Each of the individual elements themselves may not be significant (or may be thought to be given a significance beyond what is called for); however, the point remains that when one looks at the vocabulary as a whole, the metaphorical picture emerges.

There are, according to my reading of the Qurʾān, three major ranges of symbolism used in talking of God in the Qurʾān: the divine warrior-king, the divine judge, and the divine covenantor: that is, in Caird's terms, king:subject, judge:litigant, and master:servant. These three are clearly inter-related and a good deal of overlap may be seen between them. Furthermore, such ranges of vocabulary bring us directly into the discussion of other central parts of monotheistic symbolism: eschatology, cosmology, personal responsibility, and the creation of community. Such a point only emphasizes the fact that "king" (*malik*) as a word is not being used simply as a metaphor but rather that it conveys an entire symbolic universe conveniently summarized as monotheism. Much traditional scholarship has not viewed matters this way; the absence of virtually all of the following vocabulary from the "standard" scholarly works on metaphor in the Qur'ān (see, e.g., Sabbagh 1943; Sister 1931) indicates the limited view of language that previous scholarship has labored under. The language of which we speak here has been taken as "mere anthropomorphism" for scholarship up to this point and is (thus) conceived of as something separate from "metaphor."

God is King

> Say: "I find refuge with the Lord of the people, the King of the people, the god of the people, from the evil of the slinkering whisperer who whispers in the breasts of the people, of jinn and people." (Q 114:1–6)

God is king, *malik* (Q 20:114; 23:116; 59:23; 114:2; in Q 3:36 *mālik* is used). Q 114:1–3 states, "Say: 'I take refuge with the Lord of men, the King of men, the God of men.' "[1] He possesses (always *li-llāh*; God is generally not described as "ruling" His kingdom) a kingdom (*mulk*) "of the heavens and the earth": see Q 2:107; 3:189; 5:17, 18, 40, 120; 7:158; 9:116; 24:42; 25:2 etc. Note should also be made of Q 3:26 where God is *mālik al-mulk*, and Q 6:73, 17:111, and 22:56 which speak of His kingdom, which He holds in His hand according to Q 67:1: "Blessed is He in whose hand is the *mulk*." He sits upon a throne, *kursī* (Q 2:255 – the throne is "the heavens and the earth"; cf. Q 38:34 in reference to Solomon's throne) and *ʿarsh* (Q 7:54; 9:129; 10:3; 11:7; 13:2; 17:42; 20:5; 21:22; 23:86, 116; 25:59; 27:26; 32:4; 39:75; 40:7, 15; 43:82; 57:4; 69:17; 81:20; 85:15). Eight of those passages are in the context of the creation story (O'Shaughnessy 1973), which perhaps suggests we are encountering a remnant of an enthronement ritual; most of the others speak of "the Lord of the throne" indicating the close connection between kingship and having a throne. The throne of kingship is surrounded by the king's retinue of angels (Q 39:75; 40:7; and 69:17; in the latter two verses the angels bear the throne). The image is reinforced in Q 89:22 in which the troops of angels are under the king's command: "Your Lord comes with the angels row by row." The king sits in charge of his treasuries, *khazāʾin* (Q 6:50; 11:31), and places His adornments, *zīna*, within His kingdom (Q 7:32; also Q 37:6 where the stars are the adornments of heaven). He uses His seal, *khatama*, to confirm his actions (Q 2:7). The same image appears in sealing, *ḍabaʿa* (Q 4:155; 9:93; 16:108; 30:59; 40:35; 47:16). He can also designate *ātā*, subsidiary kingships, (Q 2:247–58), and give authority, *sulṭān* (e.g., Q 3:151; 11:96; 17:80; 23:45; 40:23).

The main characteristic of the king is found in the exercise of power, *qūwa*, (Q 2:165; 18:39; 51:58) echoed in the notion of strength, *qawā* (Q 8:52; 11:66; 22:40 etc.). He uses this strength to render His kingdom subservient, *sakhkhara*, for the benefit of His citizens (e.g., Q 22:65; 31:20; 45:12). His citizens are His servants, *ʿibād* (Q 3:182; 8:51; 37:40 etc.), who serve Him, *ʿabada* (Q 2:83; 3:64; 4:36 etc.), and who are protected, *walī*, *mawlā*, by their relationship to the king (Q 2:107, 120; 3:150; 8:40; 18:44 etc.). His citizens are also those who submit, *aslama* (e.g., Q 2:112; 3:20; 4:125; 27:44; 31:22 – one always submits one's *wajh*, perhaps invoking an image of not gazing upon the king [see also Rippin 2000]; also Q 16:87, *salam*), as well as simply his people, *nās*. In controlling the population, the king gives permission, *idhn*, for certain actions (Q 10:59; 20:109; 24:36; 34:23; 42:21; 53:26; 78:38 and the phrase *bi-idhn allāh*, passim, e.g., Q 2:97, 102, 249, 251), can make a proclamation, *adhān* (Q 9:3; verbally in Q 7:167; 14:7; 41:47), and charges his citizens, *kallafa*, with responsibilities (Q 2:233, 286; 6:152; 7:42; 23:62; 65:7).

The king also manifests His power as a warrior. He has enemies, *aʿdūʾ* (Q 2:98; 8:60; 9:114; 41:19, 28; 60:1), and He is an enemy of others (Q 2:98; 20:39). Opponents can be overthrown, *arkasa* (Q 4:88), however. In His actions as warrior, He initiates war, *ḥaraba* (Q 2:279), is able to destroy His opponents, *dammara* (Q 47:10) and *ahlaka* (Q 7:164; 28:78; 67:28); He can seize them, *akhadha* (Q 3:11; 6:46; 8:52; 40:21–2; 79:25), and distribute the spoils of war, *afāʾa* (Q 33:50; 59:6; 59:7). People are unable to defend themselves, *manaʿa* (Q 59:2), against His onslaught. He assails, *qātala* (Q 9:30; 63:4), and kills, *qatala* (Q 8:17), and throws things, *ramā* (Q 8:17), against the enemy.

God as Judge

As king, God also sets the law: He commands, *amara* (Q 2:27, 67, 222; 4:58; 7:28; 13:21, 25; 16:90), He rules, *ḥakama* (Q 2:113; 4:141; 5:1; 7:87; 10:109; 12:80; 13:41; 22:69; 39:3; 40:48; and uses of *ḥukm*, *ḥākim* and *ḥakīm*), He declares things forbidden, *ḥarrama* (Q 5:72; 6:150, 151; 9:29, 37; 17:33; 25:68) and *nahā* (Q 7:20; 60:8, 9), and permitted, *aḥalla* (Q 2:275; 5:87; 66:1). His citizens must obey His commands, *aṭāʿa* (Q 4:13, 69, 80, etc.): "These are the limits set by God and whoever obeys God and His messenger will enter paradise under which rivers flow, abiding therein forever."

This imagery of God, the king, then moves quite easily into God, the judge. God stands in relationship to his people – his servants, slaves, submitters – not only as king but also as judge. This, too, is a symbol of ancient heritage, most powerfully, but by no means solely, used within eschatology. The role of reward and punishment in this life is linked to God making decisions on this subject and those people subject to His decisions implore him, via whatever means are available to them, to be merciful. The king is the one who is viewed as responsible for establishing, promulgating and enforcing the entire judicial system, although in ancient society, as today, lesser officials are actually responsible for the administration of the law.

The Qur'ān displays an extensive vocabulary which speaks of God in his relationship to humanity within the terms of the judiciary. God decides *qaḍā* (Q 40:20, God decides with truth, eschatological; Q 15:66 context of Lot; Q 17:4, 23; 33:36; 40:20 etc.), judges people innocent, *barra'a* (Q 33:69, context of Moses; also 9:1 but disputed as to meaning), pronounces judgment, *afatā* (Q 4:127, 176, both in a legal context), forgives, *ghafara* (for example, Q 3:135; 4:48; 48:2 etc.; God is *al-ghafūr*), gives charges, (Q 4:12, where the word puns with *waṣīya* as an inheritance; that is, God's *waṣīya* is a legacy which people must implement and it is a requirement with which we are charged; the verbal use of the second form [*waṣṣā*] in Q 6:144 and of the fourth form [*yūṣiya*] in Q 4:11 make this clearer), grants pardons, *ʿafā* (Q 3:155; 5:95, 101; 9:43; God is *al-ʿafū*, the All-pardoning). One makes a complaint to God in His role as judge, *ishtakā* (Q 58:1; note the use of the first verbal form, to complain to God, Q 12:86) and one argues one's case before Him, *jādala* (Q 4:109; 11:74; 16:111 eschatological setting). God is the reckoner in regard to the decisions He makes, *ḥasīb* (Q 4:6, 86, 33:39 and God calculates the account, *ḥisāb*, Q 2:202; 3:19, 199; 5:4; 14:51; 24:39; 40:17). God is the one who decides what is just, deeming things *aqsaṭ*, more just (Q 33:5). He has a measure by which He does this, *qadr* (Q 6:91; 22:74; 39:67). Interceding, *shafaʿ*, is at the discretion of God (Q 10:18; 39:43–4). A judicial context is suggested by God bearing witness, *shahida* (Q 2:140, 204; 3:18, 4:166; 5:106; 9:107; 11:54; 59:11; 63:1; God is also *al-shahīd*) although the question of to whom God bears witness (i.e., who is the judge in such statements) is left open. God also gives testimonies *shahāda* (Q 2:140; 5:106).

The greatest manifestation of God as judge occurs, of course, in the realm of the eschaton about which much has been written (see, e.g., Rippin 1996). Suffice it to mention that God rules over the record books and the balance, and makes the final decision on the fate of the individual. The dimensions of God writing, teaching, blotting out and annulling all add to this.

God and His Covenant

The imagery of the covenantal aspect of the divine does not clearly separate itself from either the kingly aspect or the judging character of God. There is a contractual nature underlying the idea of God as the judge such that there is an agreement between God and His citizens according to which God will judge. This is the basis of a covenant. Likewise, the acceptance of God as king is based upon a covenant agreement of protection and honor. Some of the further extensions of the image of covenanting, however, move into domestic symbolism for example, suggesting a conceptual range that is distinct.

The covenants of God, *mīthāq* and *ʿahd*, describe a prominent theme in the Qur'ān, being mentioned some seventy-five times in total. The covenants are agreements which God (primarily, although the words are also used in secular contexts: see below) sets up and to which people respond, but which implement an obligation on both sides: in Q 2:40 God says to the Children of Israel, "fulfill My covenant and I shall fulfill your covenant" (*ʿahd* in both cases). Elements often connected to the idea of a covenant, especially if such are understood within the context of treaty agreements are to be found in the Qur'ānic presentation of God, but one would not want to push the connection too far since such aspects do not form into one cohesive picture of a treaty-covenant but are rather scattered: God swears by things, *aqsama* (Q 56:75; 69:38; 70:40; 75:1, 2; 81:15; 84:16; 90:1) and curses, *laʿana*, those who violate His commands – that is, those who are unbelievers and thus remain outside His covenant (Q 2:88, 159; 4:46, 52, 118; 5:60; 9:68; 33:57; 47:23 and also seven times nominally). Making a breach in the covenant, *shāqqa*, incurs God's wrath (Q 8:13; 59:4). For those who follow God's will, He is their protector, *awlā* and *walī*, as well as a guardian, *wakīl* and *ḥafīẓ*. The imagery here is of a group of people brought together for mutual protection and benefit. It has been suggested in previous scholarship that the Qur'ān also pictures the primary covenant as being between the prophet and God, and through the prophet, the community is brought into the bond, as in Q 3:81 and 33:7.

God of the House

These people exist under the covenant within a domestic arrangement with God: God is master, *rabb*, within God's house. God's house, *bayt*, has been provided for humanity in this life: the heavens are the roof, *bināʾ* (Q 40:64), and the earth a mattress, *firāsh* (Q 2:22) such that all of creation is God's handiwork, *ṣunʿ* (Q 27:88); God's abode, *dār*, will be provided to his servants in the hereafter (e.g., Q. 2:94; 6:32, 135). The term *dār al-islām*, while not found in the Qur'ān as such, is an extension of the Qur'ānic sense of domestic space under God's rule. *Dār al-salām* is found in the Qur'ān (Q 10:25), and may refer to the life of a Muslim in the here and now. God is the light, *nūr*, in this domain (Q 5:15; 9:32; 24:35; 61:8).

Within His covenantal relationship in his house, God is the provider of sustinence, *rizq* (e.g., Q 2:212; 3:37) the absence of which he lets the disobedient taste, *adhāqa* (Q 16:112; 39:26). All the world provides the bounties of God, *ālāʾ* (Q 7:69, 74), the sacred things, *ḥurumāt* (Q 22:30), and the bounds, *ḥudūd* (Q 2:187, 229, 230; 4:13; 9:112; 58:4; 65:1). There is, therefore, manifested within such language, a fatherly image of the old man who takes care of his household by providing what is required. But this is as far as the fatherly image goes: it remains within a range that may be associated with the provider of a covenant without suggesting the establishment of a family bond. Finally, it may be noted that God is lord, *rabb* (used twenty times), but He is not shepherd, a fact which emphasizes the urban orientation of much of the Qur'ānic symbolism, as illustrated more fully by the commercial symbolism associated with eschatology (Rippin 1996).

The Meaning of the Symbolic God

It may be seen that the symbolism of "God is king" stretches widely in the Qur'ān with an emphasis on the role of the king as warrior but extending into the other dimensions of the judge and the covenantor. These three ranges do not, of course, exhaust the Qur'ānic language of speaking of God: God talks, calls, answers, sees, hears, lives, blesses, helps, gives life, creates – all elements which could be argued to combine to say that God lives a moral life although this is a life which is *not* our human life because it is "up there" from where things must be sent down, *nazzala, anzala*, and to where they must be raised up, *rafaʿa*. As G. B. Caird (1980: 178; also see McFague 1982: 149–50) has said, "the application of these terms [of human existence] to God establishes ideal and absolute standards which can be used as instruments for the remaking of man in God's likeness."

As humans, we wish to think of God – and language is used in such a way as to express our wishes – through the most powerful symbols available. The figure of God, the "king," presents the ultimate vision of kingship, fulfilling every human expectation and going beyond them. God is the ideal king; God is the enactment of the moral stance to which human kings may aspire but which they will never attain. In speaking of the biblical usage of image for God, Caird (1980: 19) suggests that,

> [w]hen the Bible calls God judge, king, father or husband it is, in the first instance, using the human known to throw light on the divine unknown, and particularly God's attitude to his worshippers. But no sooner has the metaphor travelled from earth to heaven than it begins the return journey to earth, bearing with it an ideal standard by which the conduct of human judges, kings, fathers and husbands is to be assessed.

Underlying this is a point that is the central teaching of the Near Eastern monotheist tradition: that we are, as individuals, responsible for our fate both in this world and the next. There is no special power which is going to make us into what we are not; not even kings are excluded from this reality. The empowering and explanatory power of this myth comes in its provision of a resolution of human despair and alienation, by putting off that resolution until the hereafter, in which God, as King, will enact the fullest and most moral rule, enacting fully what it means to be a king. But the point would seem to be more, for the symbolism also conveys an ethic for practice. The stress falls, symbolically, on fairness: God deals with us fairly in His role as a king (and thus the emphasis on judgeship also); so, too, should we deal fairly with our fellow humans. This is an element of the teaching regarding personal responsibility. The symbolism not only makes the reader aware of a dimension of life beyond the mundane and her responsibility in regards to it, but also of the significance of this life as a reflection of the divine realm.

Such observations apply to all language about God. But the question remains of the Qur'ān's special contribution to the discussion. There are a few remarkable areas of absence of symbolism related to God, although they need more exploration and documentation than the present context allows. Enthronement, a central motif of biblical kingship in speaking of God, is present only to the extent of the central part played by the throne itself. There is no liturgical invocation of the process of becoming king, so crucial in the biblical picture (Eaton 1990: 381). The linking of this process in the Bible to "anointing" (a particularly Christian notion in which Jesus as God is the kingly David, not a motif of the Hebrew Bible), however, may well provide the clue as to the "truncated" nature of this reference. This is especially so when the other major range of symbolism which is absent is noted: the fact that there is hardly any family imagery for God in the Qur'ān is unmistakable. Certainly God loves, *aḥabba* (also *ḥubb*), and shows compassion, *raḥma* etc., towards His people to whom He also extends a bond, *ḥabl* (Q 3:103, 112) and he is the guardian, *ḥafīẓ* (Q 42:6; also *ḥāfiẓ*, Q 12:64) and also Lord (*rabb*), but God is *not* the father, He is *not* married to his people, His sons do *not* populate the earth. The Qur'ān, it must be concluded, speaks from a "sectarian milieu," as Wansbrough has felicitously put it, within the Arkounian "societies of the book": the avoidance of ranges of symbolism in talking of God that resound powerfully within Christian circles is conspicuous.

It is at this point that we must deal with the argument that history must play a role in interpretation: the suggestion may be put forth that kingship was a concept familiar to the seventh-century Arabs, having at least been known from South Arabia. Thus, it might be said, the image of kingship should not be contextualized with the ancient Near East but within seventh-century Arabia and the absence of certain themes such as enthronement and family relations reflects a historical situation familiar to the Arabs at the time of revelation. Such, of course, may be true but, as a reading strategy, it isolates one factor without taking into account a sufficiently broad vision of what the Qur'ān is about. Once again, this is also a situation which the Muslim interpretive tradition has encouraged in its historicization of the text of the Qur'ān, most fully embedded in the *sīra* material and the concept of the *asbāb al-nuzūl* ("occasions of revelation").

The issue of what to make of all this must be taken much further, however. Understanding the nature of metaphor and symbol, especially in relationship to speaking of God, has a number of implications. Metaphors come and go in language and in culture, reflecting the priorities and principles of a historical age. In discussing these issues in the context of Christianity, Sallie McFague (1987) raises the point of whether these metaphors are appropriate to today's world. Speaking from an ecological and feminist position, McFague argues that models of God based upon male, kingly domination of the world and of women are destructive, not only to the potential of one-half of the human population but also to the earth as a place of human habitation. "[I]n the monarchical model, God is distant from the world, related only to the human world, and controls that world through domination and benevolence" (McFague 1987: 65). She suggests that the process of deconstructing the metaphors which we have inherited from the ancient Near East is essential to human survival. But, what is more, we must re-mythologize in a manner appropriate to today's ethos and ethic. She proposes the profoundly appropriate metaphor – within the Christian context certainly – of "the world as God's body" and of "God the mother." To what extent such metaphors would be productive within an Islamic context is a matter for continued discussion and debate.

Note

1 The isolation of the vocabulary treated in this essay is facilitated by the concordance constructed by Kassis (1983: 3–99) which separates out all the verbal roots used in association with God.

Further reading

Brettler, Marc Zvi (1989) *God is King: Understanding an Israelite Metaphor.* JSOT Press, Sheffield.

Chabbi, Jacqueline (1997) *Le seigneur des tribus. L'Islam de Mahomet.* Éditions Noêsis, Paris (chapter 9, "Les mots de la seigneurie tribale").

Hooke, S. H. ed. (1958) *Myth, Ritual and Kingship: Essays on the Theory and Practice of Kingship in the Ancient Near East and Israel.* Oxford University Press, Oxford.

Izutsu, T. (1964) *God and Man in the Koran: Semantics of the Koranic Weltanschauung.* The Keio Institute of Cultural and Linguistic Studies, Tokyo.

Khir, Bustami (2005) Sovereignty. In: McAuliffe, Jane Dammen (ed.) *Encyclopaedia of the Qurʾān.* Brill, Leiden, vol. V, pp. 102–4.

Marlow, Louise (2003) Kings and rulers. In: McAuliffe, Jane Dammen (ed.) *Encyclopaedia of the Qurʾān.* Brill, Leiden, vol. III, pp. 90–5.

O'Shaughnessy, Thomas J. (1973) God's throne and the biblical symbolism of the Qurʾān, *Numen* 20, 202–21 (also in his *Eschatological Themes in the Qurʾān* Manila: Cardinal Bea Institute, Loyola School of Theology, 1986).

CHAPTER 15

Prophets and Prophethood

Uri Rubin

Stories about the Prophets

The Qur'ān abounds with stories about prophets who have been sent by God before Muḥammad. The reports about them, it is asserted, are being related to Muḥammad by God (Q 7:101; 11:100, 120; 18:13; 20:99). They are sometimes described as "stories of the unseen," because they happened long ago and the prophet did not witness them in person (Q 3:44 [of Maryam]; Q 11:49 [of Noah]; Q 12:102 [of Joseph]). The information about the prophets is imparted to Muḥammad "to strengthen" his heart therewith (Q 11:120), as well as to teach the audience the bitter lesson of disobedience which already led ancient towns to destruction (Q 7:101; 9:70).

Many of the stories draw on biblical themes. Some appear in a condensed form, while other stories, such as those of Abraham, Moses, and Jesus, are given in elaborate detail and even with subtle revisions of the biblical accounts. Elements not known from the Bible appear mainly in stories about the non-biblical prophets Hūd and Ṣāliḥ.

The Qur'ān is aware of the affinity between the stories about the prophets and biblical literature, for which reason the Jews and the Christians are called upon to testify to the truth of the Qur'ānic allusions to the previous prophets. This is, at least, how Muslim exegetes explain the meaning of Q 16:43 (see also Q 21:7) which says: "And We did not send before you any but humans to whom We sent revelation: so ask the people of the reminder if you do not know." The exegetes (e.g., Ibn al-Jawzī 1984: IV, 449; al-Qurṭubī 1967: X, 108) say that the "people of the reminder" (*ahl al-dhikr*) are believers from the People of the Book, that is, Jews and Christians well versed in the Torah and the Gospel, which means that they know the history of the prophets from their own scriptures, and can confirm the truth of the Qur'ānic allusions to them.

The list of prophets mentioned in the Qur'ān is not complete, in the sense that some of them were left out on purpose. This is stated in Q 40:78 (see also Q 4:164): "And certainly We sent apostles before you: there are some of them of whom We related to you and there are others of whom We have not related to you." Some exegetes explain that the prophets were too many to mention, and according to some, there were 124,000 prophets (al-Bayḍāwī 1988: II, 346). Others suggest that some prophets were not distinguished enough to be mentioned, as in the case of a prophet who was an Ethiopian slave (al-Suyūṭī 1985: V, 357).

Status of the Prophets

The prophets emerge in succession. The Qur'ān says that they were sent "one after another (Q 2:87), or "one by one" (Q 23:44). Moreover, the prophets belong to the same genealogical descent. Thus Q 19:58 reads: "These are the prophets on whom God bestowed favors, of the seed of Adam, and of those whom We carried with Noah, and of the seed of Abraham and Israel." The same idea is conveyed in Q 6:84, in which it is stated about Abraham: "And We gave to him Isaac and Jacob; each did We guide, and Noah We guided before, and of his descendants David and Solomon and Job and Joseph and Aaron."

The fact that the prophets are said to have been "guided" by God means that they represent a divinely chosen pedigree, as is indicated, for example, in Q 3:33–4: "Surely God chose (*iṣṭafā*) Adam and Noah and the house of Abraham and the house of ʿImrān above all beings. (They are) the offspring one of the other." The chosen prophetic lineage begins here with Adam, which indicates that he too is considered a prophet. The house of ʿImrān stands for Moses (the son of the biblical Amram), but can also refer to Jesus whose mother Mary is considered a member of that house.

The verb *iṣṭafā*, which signifies here divine election, recurs in more verses dealing with prophets, as well as with angels. Thus in Q 22:75 it is stated that God chooses (*yaṣṭafī*) messengers from among the angels and from among the people. The same verb is used to describe election of individual prophets, such as Abraham (Q 2:130), Moses (Q 7:144) and Mary (Q 3:42), as well as of kings, namely Saul (*Ṭālūt*) (Q 2:247).

Another verb, *ijtabā*, also denotes divine election of prophets, such as Adam (Q 20:122), Abraham (Q 16:121), Joseph (Q 12:6) and Jonah (Q 68:50). Less frequent is the verb *ikhtāra* which denotes the same type of divine election (Q 44:32), and describes the election of Moses (Q 20:13). The latter's election is also conveyed by the verb *iṣṭanaʿa* (Q 20:41).

The divine election of the prophets provides them with abilities not shared by ordinary humans. This pertains mainly to knowledge of the unseen. Thus in Q 72:26–7 it is stated that God knows the unseen, and He does not reveal His secrets to anyone, except to an apostle with whom He is well pleased. In Q 3:179 we are told again that God does not make people acquainted with the unseen, but He "chooses (*yajtabī*) of His apostles whom He pleases."

Virtues of Individual Prophets

Some prophets possess unique traits that mark their singular status among the rest of the prophets. Abraham is described in Q 4:125 as one whom God took as a friend (*khalīl*). Moses is described as "pure" (Q 19:51), and as one whom God brought near in communion (Q 19:52), and with whom God spoke (*kallama*) (Q 4:164). This is the origin of Moses' title, *kalīm Allāh*, by which he is known in Islamic tradition. Tradition also elaborates on Moses' communion with God.

Later tradition has provided Muḥammad with a title of his own, namely, *ḥabīb Allāh* ("God's beloved"), which together with the previous prophets, completes the unique group of prophets having an intimate relationship with God. In fact, Muslim tradition has elaborated on Muḥammad's honorific titles and produced long lists of them.

The guided and divinely chosen prophets possess moral virtues that render them immune to misbehavior of any kind. Thus in Q 3:161 it is stated that it is not attributable to a prophet that he should act unfaithfully. The election of the prophets has made them belong to the righteous, a fact stated regarding several of them, for example Zechariah, John, Jesus, Elias (Q 6:85), and others. John is described in Q 3:39 as honorable and chaste and a prophet from among the righteous. Some of them are also described as truthful, as are Abraham (Q 19:41) and Idrīs (Q 19:56). Ishmael is described in Q 19:54 as "truthful in his promise."

Ranks of Prophets

The existence of distinguished groups among the prophets is a fact which the Qur'ān declares openly. Q 17:55 states that God has made some of the prophets to excel others, and in Q 2:253 the same statement is repeated, alongside names of some of the excelling prophets: "We have made some of these apostles to excel the others, among them are they to whom God spoke (*kallama*), and some of them He exalted by (many degrees of) rank; and We gave clear arguments to Jesus son of Mary, and strengthened him with the Holy Spirit."

A special group of God's messengers is mentioned in Q 46:35, being called "those endowed with constancy (*ūlū 'l-ʿazm*)." The Qur'ān says that they have borne patiently (the hardships of their mission), and Muslim exegetes are not unanimous as to who they were. Some say that they were those who established a law (*sharīʿa*) among their nations, like Noah, Abraham, Moses, Jesus, as well as Muḥammad. Others hold that they were those who suffered the hardest trials, or the deepest remorse. In the latter case, they include Jacob, Joseph, Job, and David, in addition to the five prophets already mentioned. But still others contend that all the prophets were *ūlū 'l-ʿazm* (for the various views see al-Qurṭubī 1967: XVI, 220–1).

Modes of Prophetic Revelation

Various verbs convey the idea of prophetic revelation, the most frequent being those derived from the root *n-z-l*, namely, *nazzala* and *anzala*. They denote an act of bringing down, which means that the prophetic revelation is perceived as being sent down from heaven. Occasionally, the revelation itself is described as descending (*nazala, tanazzala*), without specifying the agent that causes it to come down. A common name of the

Qurʾānic revelation is *tanzīl* (e.g., Q 20:4; 26:192; 32:2, etc.), that is, "bringing down." A less common name is *amr* ("affair"), which in Q 65:12 is said to have been descending (*yatanazzalu*) through the seven heavens. Some exegetes explain that the "affair" stands here for divine revelation that is being brought down from heaven to earth (Muqātil 1989: IV, 367).

Revelation originates in God, as is indicated in verses in which God speaks in the first person: "I have sent down (the Qur'ān)" (Q 2:41), and more often: "We have sent down (the Qur'ān)" (e.g., Q 44:3; 76:23; 97:1). But revelation does not come down directly to the prophets. The intermediate agents are the angels. God sends them down with the revelations, as is implied in Q 16:2: "He sends down (*yunazzilu*) the angels with the spirit by His commandment on whom He pleases of His servants . . ." Muslim exegetes hold, however, that only Gabriel is meant here, the angel who was commissioned to bring down prophetic revelations, or the "spirit," to Muḥammad (e.g., Ibn al-Jawzī 1984: IV, 428). In Q 16:102 the agent bringing down (*nazzalahu*) the Qurʾānic revelation is himself called "the holy spirit (*rūḥ al-qudus*), which is again interpreted as an epithet of Gabriel (e.g., Ibn al-Jawzī 1984: IV, 491). The same applies to Q 26:193, in which the revelation is brought down (*nazala bihi*) by the "faithful spirit" (*al-rūḥ al-amīn*; e.g., Ibn al-Jawzī 1984: VI, 144). Similarly, the exegetes say that it is Gabriel who says to the prophet in Q 19:64: "We do not descend (with revelations) but by the command of your Lord" (e.g., Ibn al-Jawzī 1984: V, 248–9).

As far as Muḥammad's own prophetic experience is concerned, the process of sending down revelations ends at the prophet's heart, and Gabriel is mentioned explicitly as the one who brings it down to him (Q 2:97). The Qur'ān provides specific, though not entirely coherent, details of the time when the revelation began coming down to Muḥammad. This took place either on a "blessed night" (Q 44:3), or on *laylat al-qadr*, the "night of power" (Q 97:1), or during the month of Ramaḍān (Q 2:185). Most exegetes explain that all passages refer to one and the same night, namely *laylat al-qadr* which falls in Ramaḍān (e.g., Ibn al-Jawzī 1984: VII, 336 [on Q 44:3]; I, 187 [on Q 2:185]).

There are various terms denoting the actual revelation that is being brought down. Most often it is called "signs" (*āyāt*, e.g., Q 57:9, etc.), which commentators of the Qur'ān have identified with the Qurʾānic verses (Ibn al-Jawzī 1984: VIII, 163). Elsewhere, what God sends down is called *sūra* (Q 9:86 etc.), which term came to be identified with the Qurʾānic chapters, and most obviously, the term Qur'ān, too, stands for something which God sends down (Q 76:23). Another locution standing for a whole unit of revelations being sent down is *kitāb*, a "book," or "scripture" (e.g., Q 7:2). Specific scriptures, namely "the Torah and the Gospel," are also described as being sent down by God (Q 3:3–4), which implies that all monotheistic scriptures represent the same divine revelation. Metaphorical terms are also used to describe a descending revelation, one of which being the somewhat obscure title *furqān* (Q 3:4). Some exegetes have explained it in the sense of a scripture distinguishing between truth and falsehood (Ibn al-Jawzī 1984: I, 350). "Light" (*nūr*) is also a name for the guiding revelation that God has sent down (Q 64:8).

Another widely current verb denoting the act of providing revelation is *awḥā*, with *waḥy* as the noun denoting the revelation itself. The verb means to "prompt," "inspire," or "suggest," but it is not confined to prophetic revelations. Occasionally it simply means to "instruct," or "command," as in Q 8:12 in which God instructs (*yūḥī*) the angels to support the believers. In Q 99:5 God instructs (*awḥā*) earth to tell its story on the day of resurrection, and in Q 16:68 He instructs (*awḥā*) the bee to make hives in the mountains, etc. Even when prophets are addressed, the verb *awḥā* can be a request to act rather than imparting a text for recitation. Thus in Q 23:27 God instructs (*awḥaynā*) Noah to make the Ark, and in Q 7:117 God prompts (*awḥaynā*) Moses to cast his rod. An act designated as *awḥā* can also be performed by humans. In Q 19:11, for example, Zechariah signals (*awḥā*) to his people that they should glorify God morning and evening. In most cases, however, *awḥā* stands for an act performed by God Himself, as in Q 41:12. Here God reveals (*awḥā*) the "affair" (*amr*) of the seven heavens, that is, enjoins His commandment on the heavens. But what God reveals mostly as *waḥy* is the prophetic inspiration itself. This is the case in Q 42:52 in which God reveals (*awḥaynā*) a "spirit" to His prophet. The spirit has been interpreted here as standing for the Qur'ānic revelation (Ibn al-Jawzī 1984: VII, 298). This accords with Q 53:4–5 in which the Qur'ān is explicitly described as a revelation (*waḥy*) that is revealed (*yūḥā*). In Q 35:31 it is the "book" that has been revealed as *waḥy*.

The revelation (*waḥy*) of a given Qur'ānic passage can be a prolonged process, as is the case with the revelation to Muḥammad. He is advised not to make haste before the process is completed (Q 20:114). When the reception of the *waḥy* is completed the prophet is supposed to recite it in public (Q 29:45). The same process of *waḥy* was experienced also by previous prophets, as is stated in Q 4:163: "Surely We have revealed (*awḥaynā*) to you as We revealed to Noah, and the prophets after him, and We revealed to Abraham and Ishmael and Isaac and Jacob and the tribes, and Jesus and Job and Jonah and Aaron and Solomon."

The *waḥy* does not always come directly from God to the prophets. An angel acting as God's messenger may deliver the divine *waḥy* to them. This comes out in Q 42:51, in which it is stated: "It is not for any mortal that God should speak to them, except by inspiration (*waḥy*) or from behind a veil (*ḥijāb*), or by sending a messenger (*rasūl*), to reveal (*fa-yūḥiya*) by His permission what he will." The exegetes say that the messenger delivering the *waḥy* is Gabriel (Ibn al-Jawzī 1984: VII, 297).

As for the contents of what is being revealed as *waḥy*, in some cases it consists of the sheer idea of monotheism. Thus in Q 21:108 it is stated: "Say: It is only revealed (*yūḥā*) to me that your God is one God." In other cases the *waḥy* revolves around specific legal obligations. God reveals (*awḥaynā*) to the previous prophets "the doing of good and the keeping up of prayer and the giving of alms" (Q 21:73). The Qur'ān repeats several times the injunction given to the prophet to follow what has been revealed (*yūḥā*) to him (e.g., Q 10:109; 33:2, etc.).

In Q 17:39 the content of the *waḥy* is defined as "wisdom," which seems to refer to moral lessons which must be derived from the history of past generations. This is confirmed by the fact that in Q 11:49 the *waḥy* consists of "accounts of the unseen," i.e. stories of the history of past generations which are now being revealed to the prophet. The stories deal with sinful nations which God punished and destroyed because they had rejected their prophets.

There are also other, less frequent, terms of prophetic revelation, one of which being to "cast" (*alqā*), as in Q 40:15. Here God is said to have cast "the inspiration by His command upon whom He pleases of His servants." In Q 28:86 it is the Book that has been cast unto the prophet, while in Q 77:5 some unspecified persons are mentioned who are described as "casting the reminder" (*fa'l-mulqiyāt dhikr*). The exegetes say that the "reminder" signifies the prophetic inspiration, and that those who cast it are the angels who deliver it to God's prophets and messengers (Ibn al-Jawzī 1984: VIII, 446).

"To give" (*ātā*), may also signal prophetic revelation, as is the case in Q 2:87, in which God "gives" Moses "the book." Another verb, *alhama* (root: *l-h-m*), also denotes divine inspiration, but not specifically prophetic. Thus in Q 91:8 it is indicated that God has inspired (*fa-alhamahā*) the human soul to understand what is right and wrong for it.

Dreams (*ru'yā*) may also function as prophetic visions. Abraham found out by such a dream that he had to sacrifice his son (Q 37:105), and Muḥammad knew from his own dream that he was about to enter Mecca safely (Q 48:27). Another vision of the prophet, which is mentioned in Q 17:60, was interpreted by some exegetes as referring to his nocturnal journey and ascension, while others explained that it was the same dream that foretold Muḥammad's conquest of Mecca (Ibn al-Jawzī 1984: V, 53–4).

The Qur'ān is also aware of false revelations which seem prophetic but come from Satan, which means that only a thin line separates genuine divine inspiration from satanic temptation. This is demonstrated in the fact that the Qur'ān uses the same vocabulary for the Godly as well as the Satanic spheres. Thus satans (*shayāṭīn*), like God, can deliver *waḥy* (Q 6:112, 121) which is deceiving in its varnished outward appearance. But the more common verb denoting satanic inspiration is *waswasa*, to "whisper" (e.g., Q 7:20; 20:120.). Satan also casts (*alqā*) his own verses into genuine revelations received by every prophet, "but God annuls that which Satan casts" (Q 22:52). Moreover, the satans can be God's messengers, but He sends (*yursilu*) them against the unbelievers (Q 19:83).

The distinction between a true prophet and other persons endowed with unique spiritual powers is also stated very clearly, in passages stressing that Muḥammad's prophetic message is not the words of a *kāhin* ("soothsayer"), neither of a poet nor a *majnūn*, that is, a madman possessed by demons (Q 52:29; 69:41–2; 81:22).

Imposters are severely denounced. Q 6:93 states: "And who is more unjust than he who forges a lie against God, or says: 'It has been revealed (*ūḥiya*) to me;' while nothing has been revealed to him, and he who says: I can bring down (*sa-unzilu*) the like of what God has brought down (*anzala*)?" The exegetes say that this passage refers to persons like Musaylima and others who pretended to receive revelations similar to those of Muḥammad (Ibn al-Jawzī 1984: III, 86).

Revealed Scriptures

The core of the prophetic revelation consists in revealed scriptures which are sometimes (e.g., Q 3:184) referred to as *zubur* (singular *zabūr*), or *ṣuḥuf* (singular *ṣaḥīfa*). The latter term signifies "scrolls," as, for example, in Q 87:19 in which the scrolls of Abraham and Moses are mentioned.

The most frequent name for a revealed scripture is *kitāb*, namely, something which has been written down, or simply a "book." A *kitāb* is always of high solemnity. It may stand for the written list of deeds which determines the destiny of all people on the day of resurrection (e.g., Q 39:69), or the pre-existent divine Book in which the preordained law of God has been recorded. This is, at least, how Muslim exegetes explain the locution "book of God" in Q 33:6 (also Q 30:56), which, so they hold, is identical with the "guarded tablet" (*lawḥ maḥfūẓ*) mentioned in Q 85:22 (Ibn al-Jawzī 1984: VI, 354). The Qur'ān is said to have formed part of this tablet (Q 85:21), so that this revealed book is actually a reflection of a celestial text. Another locution which is taken to refer to the original celestial version of the universal book is *umm al-kitāb* mentioned in Q 43:4. Here it is stated that the Qur'ān is in the *umm al-kitāb* "with Us, truly elevated, full of wisdom." The exegetes maintain that it is another name for the tablet, the origin of all revealed books (Ibn al-Jawzī 1984: VII, 302).

The divine origin of the Qur'ānic revelation comes out in the idea that no one can alter God's words as revealed to Muḥammad: "Recite what has been revealed to you of the book of your Lord; there is none who can alter His words . . ." (Q 18:27). God sent down the book to Muḥammad without any "crookedness" (Q 18:1), so that the revealed Qur'ān has remained faithful to the original message of the divine book. In other words, the book was sent down to Muḥammad "with the truth" (e.g., Q 39:2, etc.). It has also been sent down as a "blessed" (*mubārak*) book (e.g., Q 6:155; 38:29), and as a book "conformable" in its various parts (Q 39:23).

Not just the Qur'ān but any other revealed book is of the same divine origin, for which reason the Qur'ān recognizes the authenticity of previous revelations, saying that previous messengers, too, brought their peoples "clear arguments, scriptures, and the illuminating book" (Q 35:25, see also Q 3:184; 57:25).

Being an essential component of the prophetic message, the term *kitāb* often appears side by side with the term *nubuwwa* ("prophethood"), and both are perceived as components of a divine legacy that runs in a genealogical line of a chosen pedigree. Thus in Q 29:27, prophethood and the book are said to have remained in the seed of Abraham, Isaac, and Jacob. The same is said of the offspring of Noah and Abraham (Q 57:26). The book is therefore a divine legacy which God has bequeathed to whom he chose of his servants (Q 35:32).

Of the previous prophets, Moses in particular is mentioned as one whom God gave the book (Q 2:87). His book is described as "a light and a guidance to the people" (Q 6:91).

Apart from the term *kitāb*, previous scriptures are also mentioned by their individual titles, such as the Torah (*tawrāt*) of the Israelite prophets (Q 5:44), David's *Zabūr* (Psalms) (Q 4:163; 17:55) and Jesus' Gospel (*Injīl*). About the latter it is stated that it was full of guidance and light (Q 5:46).

Prophets and Messengers

Two major terms that describe the mission of the Qur'ānic prophets are *nabī*, "a prophet," and *rasūl*, "a messenger" or "apostle." As in the New Testament, in which apostles seem to rank higher than prophets (e.g., 1 Corinthians 12:28–31; cf. Ephesians 3:5; 4:11), in the Qur'ān, too, *rasūl* seems to be somewhat more elevated than *nabī*.

This is indicated, to begin with, in the fact that whenever both titles appear together, *rasūl* comes first, which may suggest that a messenger is more important than a prophet. Thus Q 22:52 describes Satan's attempts to lead astray any apostle (*rasūl*) or prophet (*nabī*) who was sent before Muḥammad. The Muslim commentators say that in this verse *rasūl* stands for a prophet having a message that must be delivered, whereas *nabī* has no such message. More specifically, al-Bayḍāwī (d. 685–716/1282–1316) says that *rasūl* is a prophet who establishes a new *sharīʿa* (religious law), whereas *nabī* is he who continues an old one. This means, al-Bayḍāwī says, that *rasūl* is more distinguished than *nabī*, and therefore there were more *anbiyāʾ* ("prophets") than *rusul* ("messengers"). Or, he adds, a *rasūl* receives his revelation from an angel, whereas a prophet experiences revelation only in dreams (al-Bayḍāwī 1988: II, 92–3 [on Q 22:52]).

The titles *rasūl* and *nabī* may also overlap and even refer to one and the same person, in which case, *rasūl* again comes first. This applies to Moses, about whom it is stated in Q 19:51 that he was "an apostle, a prophet." The same is stated about Ishmael (Q 19:54), as well as about Muḥammad (Q 7:157). The combination of the two in one person is perhaps designed to indicate that this person belongs to the messengers among the prophets.

But not every messenger of God is also a prophet. God is said to have made the angels "messengers flying on wings, two, and three, and four" (Q 35:1). As God's messengers, the angels bring good tidings to Abraham about the birth of Isaac and Jacob, and they also destroy the people of Lot (e.g., Q 11:69–81, etc.). God also sends angels to guard people as well as to receive their souls at the moment of death (Q 6:61, 7:37). Their primary role as God's messengers is to inspect and write down the deeds of every human being (Q 10:21; 43:80).

The Qurʾān is careful to draw a clear line between God's immortal and mortal messengers. Prophets can only be mortal, because angels, the Qurʾān says (Q 17:95), do not walk about on earth as ordinary dwellers, for which reason people cannot grasp their physical presence. Therefore, God does not send down angels to be His sent prophets.

Angels do, however, bring down prophetic revelations in their capacity as God's messengers, but they do not deliver them directly to the people, only to single human prophets. The Qurʾān mentions the "word" (*qawl*), i.e. prophetic message, of one particular "honored messenger" (Q 69:40; 81:19). Some exegetes have identified this messenger with the angel Gabriel whose mission was to reveal the Qurʾān to Muḥammad (Muqātil 1989: IV, 425). But Gabriel's task as God's messenger is not confined to prophetic revelations. He is also said to have been referred to in Q 19:19, in which God's messenger comes to Mary to give her a son (Jesus). Even the *rasūl* mentioned in the story of the golden calf (Q 20:96) was said to have been Gabriel (al-Qurṭubī 1967: XI, 239).

God started sending prophets after humankind became separated, when the initial state of righteousness was replaced by moral corruption. This is at least how some exegetes explain Q 2:213 in which it is stated: "The people were (united in) one nation, then (they became divided, and) God sent the prophets to bear good tidings and to warn" (Ibn al-Jawzī 1984: I, 229).

Scope of the Prophetic Mission

In Q 33:7 God makes a special covenant (*mīthāq*) with the prophets: "And when We made a covenant with the prophets and with you [= Muḥammad], and with Noah and Abraham and Moses and Jesus son of Mary, and We made with them a firm covenant." According to the commentators (e.g., al-Qurṭubī 1967: XIV, 127), the prophets undertook in this covenant to fulfill their mission faithfully.

The prophets are sent each to his own nation (*umma*) or people (*qawm*). This comes out in verses asserting that each nation has its own prophets sent to it (Q 10:47; 16:36), and that every apostle was only sent "with the language of his people" (Q 14:4). Thus Moses, for example, says to his people that he is God's messenger to them (Q 61:5). Moreover, some prophets are described as the "brothers" of the peoples to whom they were sent (Q 26:106, 161, etc.). This is again an appropriate precedent for Muḥammad, the Arabian prophet who has brought to his nation an Arabic Qur'ān (e.g., Q 12:2). His Arabic Qur'ān was revealed to him that he may warn "the mother of cities" (*umm al-qurā*) (Q 42:7; see also Q 6:92), which is Mecca, according to the exegetes (Ibn al-Jawzī 1984: VII, 273).

But unlike the previous prophets, Muḥammad appears in some other passages as a universal prophet whose mission goes beyond ethnic boundaries. In Q 4:79 he is said to have been sent "to mankind as an apostle," and in Q 21:107 he is sent with mercy "to the worlds." His audience includes the *jinn* (Q 46:30), to whom messengers of their own kind were also sent (Q 6:130).

Aims of the Prophetic Mission

The purpose for which the Qur'ānic prophet has been sent is to make God's religion, i.e. Islam, prevail over all religions (Q 9:33; 48:28; 61:9). This may involve waging war on the infidels, as is stated about the preceding prophets in Q 3:146: "And how many a prophet has fought, and with them were many worshippers of the Lord; so the (prophets) did not become weak-hearted on account of what befell them in God's way, nor did they weaken, nor did they abase themselves; and God loves the patient."

In other Qur'ānic passages, however, the religious campaign is based on preaching and is focused on the mere idea of monotheism and on the refutation of polytheism (*shirk*). Several times the previous prophets are described as imploring their respective peoples to "serve nothing but God" (e.g., Q 41:14). God also tells Muḥammad himself that this was the main mission of the prophets who were sent before him (Q 21:25, etc.), and he himself says to his audience: "I am only a mortal like you; it is revealed to me that your God is one God, therefore follow the right way to Him and ask His forgiveness; and woe to the polytheists (*mushrikūn*)" (Q 41:6; see also Q18:110).

On the other hand, the mission of the prophets has also a grimmer aspect, namely, to warn stubborn unbelievers of their fate in hell, in case they do not repent. But the warning usually goes hand in hand with good tidings for those who believe (in paradise). Thus Q 6:48, for example, asserts that God's messengers were sent as "announcers of good news and givers of warning, then whoever believes and acts aright, they shall have no fear, nor shall they grieve" (see also Q 4:165; 18:56, etc.). The same twofold message was entrusted with Muḥammad (Q 33:45, 48:8).

The messengers are responsible neither for the success nor failure of their message, and the Qur'ān repeatedly asserts that nothing is incumbent upon the apostles except a plain delivery (e.g., Q 16:35, etc.). Furthermore, the apostles are not even capable of changing the fate awaiting the unbelievers: "It is not (fit) for the prophet and those who believe that they should ask forgiveness for the polytheists, even though they should be near relatives, after it has become clear to them that they are inmates of the flaming fire" (Q 9:113; cf. Q 9:80, 84).

At the last judgment, believers and unbelievers will realize that the apostles had spoken the truth about their respective fate in paradise or hell (Q 7:43, 53; 36:52). The prophets themselves will be present on the scene of judgment and will act as witnesses as to who is righteous and who is a sinner (e.g., Q 4:41; 7:6; 16:84, 89). But according to Q 5:109, the messengers will not dare testify, and God Himself will know what the people were doing. But mercy is also a significant component of the prophetic message, and emanates mainly from the guidance that is inherent in the revealed book. This is stated in Q 16:89: "We have revealed the book to you explaining clearly everything, and a guidance and mercy and good news for those who are Muslims."

Being the ultimate source of guidance, some prophets are occasionally described as *imāms* who guide the people by God's command (Q 21:73), and their revealed book, too, is called "*imām* and mercy" (Q 11:17; 46:12). Guidance is achieved by the actual teaching of the book, and therefore Muḥammad is often described as a messenger teaching "the book and the wisdom" (Q 2:129, 151; 3:164, etc.).

A prophet is not only a spiritual guide but a judge too, whose adjudication is based on the revealed book. This was the case among the Jews for whom the prophets judged according to the revealed Torah (Q 5:44; 2:213), and the same is said about Muḥammad to whom God revealed the book "that you may judge between people by means of that which God has taught you" (Q 4:105).

Signs and Miracles

God not only provides His messengers with the prophetic inspiration but He also stays with them when they deliver His message. As is formulated in Q 72:27–8: "For surely He makes a guard to march before (His messenger) and after him, so that He may know that they have truly delivered the messages of their Lord." The "guards" accompanying the prophets are said to be the angels, and elsewhere it is asserted that God is always aware of what His apostles are doing (Q 23:51). God's presence renders His apostles immune to dangers (Q 27:10), and His help is always ensured for them (Q 12:110; 40:51).

God also provides His prophets with concrete means designed to increase their power of persuasion. These are called *bayyināt*, that is, clear "proofs" or "arguments." Sometimes they are represented by miracles. For example, in Q 2:87 (see also Q 2:253), God provides Jesus with *bayyināt* and strengthens him with the Holy Spirit. The exegetes say that the latter stands for Gabriel, and that the *bayyināt* are the "proofs" which Jesus brought, such as are described in Q 3:49 (al-Qurṭubī 1967: II, 24). Here Jesus says to the Children of Israel: "I have come to you with a sign from your Lord, that I create for you out of dust like the form of a bird, then I breathe into it and it becomes a bird with God's permission, and I heal the blind and the leprous, and bring the dead to life with God's permission, and I shall inform you of what you eat and what you have stored in your houses."

But miracles do not render the prophets divine, as is stressed especially with respect to Jesus. The Qur'ān insists that he is "only an apostle of God and His word which He cast unto Mary, and a spirit from Him. Believe therefore in God and His apostles, and say not: 'Three.'" (Q 4:171).

Other prophets also brought such *bayyināt* to their own nations, alongside revealed scriptures, but they were rejected (Q 3:184; 35:25). Muḥammad, too, has brought (unspecified) *bayyināt* to his people, but they have discarded them as sheer magic (Q 61:6). The term *burhān* ("proof") is also used to signal what Muḥammad has brought to his audience (Q 4:174).

The listeners, however, not only reject the *bayyināt* but demand to receive a "sign" (*āya*) of their own choice (Q 2:118; 21:5, etc.). Often they request to see an angel being sent down with Muḥammad (Q 23:24, 25:7, etc.), or a treasure descending upon him (Q 11:12), or a fountain being made to gush forth from the earth for them (Q 17:90), and so forth. The Qur'ān responds to such demands by asserting that God's messengers can only produce signs with God's permission (Q 40:78), and that they are just mortals (Q 14:11). They may even have wives and children (Q 13:38). Elsewhere it is stressed that they are merely humans receiving revelation (e.g., Q 12:109; 16:43, etc.), and that they eat food and go about in the markets (Q 25:20).

But God may at times send a sign in response to a specific request. This was the case with the prophet Ṣāliḥ who was sent as warner to Thamūd. They asked him for a sign, and he produced a she-camel. They were ordered to share their water with her on appointed intervals (Q 26:154–5), or according to another version (Q 11:64), to leave her to pasture on God's earth and not harm her. But Thamūd killed the she-camel (Q 11:65), for which reason, God no longer sends signs on demand (Q 17:59).

Nevertheless, Moses too brought a sign in response to the demand of the Pharaoh (Q 7:106; 26:31). The sign was that the rod of Moses was turned into a serpent, and his hand became "white to the beholders." The audience denied the double sign as evident magic (Q 7:107–9; 26:31–4). But these two signs were given to Moses in advance, upon his first encounter with God (Q 20:17–23; 27:10–12; 28:31–2). They formed part of nine (not ten, as in the Old Testament) signs which God gave to Moses, and they are therefore not just *āyāt* but rather *āyāt bayyināt* (Q 17:101; 28:36), as well as *burhān* ("proof") (Q 28:32). Elsewhere a list of all the signs, i.e. the calamities, is provided (Q 7:130–5).

Reception of the Prophets

The nations to whom prophets have been sent are expected to receive them with consent and obedience. As Q 4:64 puts it: "And We did not send any apostle but that he should be obeyed by God's permission." But the prophets were received with anything but obedience. They were mocked (Q 15:11, etc.) and called liars (e.g., Q 3:184; 22:42; 23:44; 35:25, etc.), and their message was denied (Q 11:59), and denounced as "medleys of dreams" (Q 21:5). The prophets were rejected mainly on account of their being ordinary human beings (e.g., Q 14:10; 17:94; 36:15; 64:6), and were accused of being mere poets, magicians (*sāḥir*) and madmen (*majnūn*) (e.g., Q 21:5; 51:52). Some of them were received with skeptic questions (Q 2:108), and above all, their audience expressed devotion to the pagan tradition of the ancestors (Q 43:23).

The prophets have also suffered actual persecution, such as the threat of expulsion (e.g., Q 14:13), and also death at the hand of their own peoples, as was the fate of the Israelite prophets (e.g., Q 2:61, 91, etc.). The sufferings of the previous prophets are recounted to comfort Muḥammad in his own distress which resembles that of his precursors. As stated in Q 41:43: "Nothing is said to you but what was said indeed to the apostles before you." Not only humankind but also the satans rose as enemies to the prophets. In Q 6:112, God says: "And thus did We make for every prophet an enemy, the satans from among humans and *jinn* . . ." Satan's enmity is seen in that he makes rebellion look attractive to nations to whom apostles were sent (Q 16:63).

Rejection is met with retribution. Time and again the Qur'ān describes how nations that disobeyed their prophets were punished by severe calamities. Such calamities are described mainly in what is known in modern scholarship as "the punishment stories." They contain the stories of the peoples of Noah, Hūd, Ṣāliḥ, Shuʿayb, Loth, and others. Rejection of messengers renders retribution inevitable, as stated in Q 7:94: "And We did not send a prophet in a town but We overtook its people with distress and affliction in order that they might humble themselves." The divine logic that comes out here is that God is enemy to anyone who is "the enemy of God and His angels and His apostles and Gabriel and Michael" (Q 2:98). Retribution is the direct result of the fact that God has promised to protect the prophets (Q 14:47), and it is defined as God's *sunna* with respect to those who persecute the prophets (Q 17:76–7). Destruction is never arbitrary or unjust, and is only inflicted on towns that have been warned in advance by their prophets (Q 17:15; 28:59). The prophets and their close entourage are always saved from the collective disaster (Q 10:103, etc.).

Polemics

The main axis around which the Qur'ānic allusions to the prophets revolves is anti-Jewish and anti-Christian polemics. The Qur'ān claims to have exclusive right to interpret the religious and moral legacy of the biblical prophets, and accuses the Jews and the Christians of a deliberate distortion of that legacy. The legacy of the prophets, according to the Qur'ān, is clearly an Islamic one. Each and every prophet was a Muslim, as stated for example in Q 5:44, which says that the Torah was revealed to the prophets "who were Muslims." Likewise, the religion that was enjoined upon the prophets was the same as the one given to the Muslims, a fact stated in Q 42:13: "He has enjoined upon you (*sharaʿa*) for religion what He prescribed to Noah and that which We have revealed to you and that which We enjoined upon Abraham and Moses and Jesus." Therefore, true Muslims are only those who believe in all the prophets with no exception (Q 2:136).

In fact, the prophets formed a "nation" of their own, as stated in Q 2:134, 141. These verses address the Jews and the Christians saying that these communities shall be judged on their own account, just as the prophets shall be judged on their own account. In other words, the prophets were neither Jews nor Christians (Q 2:140).

The religious and moral exclusion of the Jews and the Christians from the legacy of the prophets comes out most clearly in passages dealing with Abraham. The Qurʾān denies the Jews and the Christians of any right to argue with the Muslims about his religion, insisting that Abraham had lived long before the revelation of the Torah and the Gospels, and that he had neither been a Jew, nor Christian (Q 3:65–7). This means that the Muslims are no less entitled to his legacy than the Jews and the Christians, and in fact, Muḥammad's followers, more than anyone else, preserve Abraham's genuine legacy (Q 3:68).

Apart from the "Islamization" of the biblical prophets, the Qurʾān also defends Muḥammad's own position as God's prophet. The Qurʾān declares that Muḥammad is "one of the apostles" (Q 2:252), and that he is the "seal of the prophets" (Q 33:40). Moreover, the previous prophets are said to have been commanded by God in a solemn covenant to believe in Muḥammad. In Q 3:81 we read: "And when God made a covenant with the prophets: Surely, the book and the wisdom that I have given you – then an apostle comes to you verifying that which is with you, you must believe in him, and you must aid him. (God) said: 'Do you affirm and accept My compact in this (matter)?' The (prophets) said: 'We do affirm.' (God) said: 'Then bear witness, and I (too) am of the bearers of witness with you.'" The exegetes explain that the apostle in whom the prophets are demanded to believe is Muḥammad (e.g., al-Qurṭubī 1967: IV, 125).

The prophets were not only requested to believe in Muḥammad, but some of them were familiar with his titles, which were included in their own revealed scriptures. Thus in Q 7:157 it is stated that Muḥammad was mentioned as a "Gentile" in the Torah and the Gospel. Jesus, it is said in Q 61:6, annunciated the appearance of an apostle who will come after him, his name being Aḥmad. The allusions to Muḥammad in the scriptures are verified in the Qurʾān. For example, Q 2:41 addresses the Children of Israel, requesting of them to believe "in what I have revealed, verifying that which is with you." The exegetes say that this verse requests of the Jews to believe in the Qurʾān which concurs with Muḥammad's descriptions that are found in the Torah and the Gospels (Ibn al-Jawzī 1984: I, 73).

Further reading

Bell, R. (1934) Muhammad and previous messengers. *The Moslem World* 24, 330–40.

Rosenthal, F. (1962) The influence of the biblical tradition on Muslim historiography. In: Lewis B. et al. (eds.) *Historians of the Middle East*. Oxford University Press, London, pp. 35–45.

Rubin, U. (1975) Pre-existence and light – aspects of the concept of *Nūr Muḥammad*. *Israel Oriental Studies* 5, 62–119.

Rubin, U. (1979) Prophets and progenitors in the early Shīʿa tradition. *Jerusalem Studies in Arabic and Islam* 1, 41–65.
Tottoli, R. (2002) *Biblical Prophets in the Qurʾān and Muslim Literature*. Curzon, Richmond.
Wensinck, A. J. (1998) Muḥammad and the prophets. In: Rubin, U. (ed.) *The Life of Muḥammad*. Ashgate, Aldershot, pp. 319–43.
Wheeler, B. M. (2002) *Moses in the Quran and Islamic Exegesis*. RoutledgeCurzon, London and New York.
Wild, S. (1996) "We have sent down to thee the book with truth . . .": Spatial and temporal implications of the Qurʾānic concepts of *nuzūl, tanzīl* and *ʾinzāl*. In: Wild, S. (ed.) *The Qurʾān as Text*. E. J. Brill, Leiden, pp. 137–56.

CHAPTER 16

Moses

Brannon Wheeler

The significance of Moses in the Qur'ān, especially as Muslim exegesis understands his relationship to the prophet Muḥammad as the ideal prophet-conqueror, can hardly be underestimated. In Q 19:51 Moses is described as "pure, a messenger, a prophet." Elsewhere, God speaks directly to Moses (Q 4:164), and Moses sees God in the crashing of a mountain (Q 7:143). To Moses is revealed the "book" (*kitāb*), the "*furqān*" (Q 2:53), the "tablets" (*alwāḥ*) (Q 7:150–4), the "Torah", and the "first scriptures" (*al-ṣuḥuf al-ūlā*) (Q 87:18–19). Moses is given his brother Aaron as a prophet (Q 19:53) and meets with a mysterious servant of God (Q 18:60–82), later identified as the prophet Khiḍr.

Unlike the short segments of stories and odd episodes scattered in different *sūras* associated with many of the other prophetic figures in the Qur'ān, relatively long and connected narratives featuring Moses are to be found throughout the Qur'ān. Of all the prophets mentioned by name in the Qur'ān, Moses is by far the most frequent, his name occurring 137 times compared with sixty-nine occurrences of Abraham, forty-three of Noah, and twenty-five of Jesus. Most of the passages in the Qur'ān featuring Moses fall into two general categories: Moses in Egypt, and Moses with the Israelites. Close parallels to all of these passages can be found in the Bible and in Jewish and Christian exegetical traditions. It is important to keep in mind that Muslim exegetes are not only aware of these biblical parallels, but purposefully draw attention to them in their own interpretation of the Qur'ān narrative. Muslim exegesis uses a wide variety of non-Qur'ānic and non-Arabic sources in demonstrating the significance of Moses to the origins and authority of the mission of the prophet Muḥammad.

Moses in Egypt

The narrative describing the life of Moses in Egypt and his relationship to the Israelites enslaved there is found in a number of passages in the Qur'ān which may be subdivided into episodes: birth and childhood of Moses, flight to Midian, revelation, Moses and Pharaoh, and exodus from Egypt.

Birth and childhood of Moses

According to Muslim exegetes,[1] Moses was the son of Imran, a Levite descendant of Jacob, also known as Israel. Q 28:1–6 describes how the Israelites were enslaved by the Pharaoh and Haman. Muslim exegesis adds that the Pharaoh ordered the killing of all Israelite males because his advisers, on information obtained from Abraham's earlier visit to Egypt, told him of a boy who would cause the destruction of his state. Echoing a motif also found in Jewish exegesis, some Muslim exegetes mention that the Egyptians only killed the male Israelite babies every other year so that they would not extinguish their working force. This also helps to explain the existence of Moses' brother Aaron later in the narrative.

Q 20:38–41 and 28:7–13 narrate how God caused Moses to be adopted into the house of Pharaoh by being cast into the sea, later rescued by the wife of Pharaoh, and ultimately nursed by his own mother. The exegesis of these verses makes clear that the Pharaoh and his wife knew Moses was an Israelite, and perhaps the very child against which they were attempting to protect themselves. This awareness of the part of Pharaoh and his wife builds an additional dramatic tension into the story, making the Pharaoh unable to defend against his own actions in raising the child who would eventually lead to his ruin. The early authority Ibn ʿAbbās (d. 68/687) states that the wife of Pharaoh was named Āsiya, and that she asked the mother of Moses to live with her, but she declined. The exegete al-Thaʿlabī (d. 427/1035) reports that some claim that Āsiya was an Israelite and worshiped God in secret despite being married to the Pharaoh.

Flight to Midian

According to the exegesis of Q 28:14, Moses was given prophethood when he reached maturity, and Q 28:15–21 describes how he killed a man, blamed it on Satan, and then fled to Midian. Al-Thaʿlabī explains that the man who warned Moses about the Pharaoh plotting to kill him for the murder was Ḥizqīl, the Egyptian who is later credited with being one of only a couple of people from among the Egyptians who believed in Moses (Q 40:28).

Q 28:20–8 describes the flight of Moses to Midian, his saving of two daughters at a well, a vow he made with God, and his agreement to work for a number of years for his future father-in-law. Muslim exegesis casts the entire episode in terms paralleling the flight of Jacob to Laban as described in Genesis 28–32, emphasizing common elements such as the well, the vow, working for the marriage of the daughters, and the episode of the speckled sheep.

Revelation

Upon leaving Midian, Moses receives his commission from God, as recorded in Q 20:9–24, 27:7–12, 28:29–35, and 79:15–19. Ibn Kathīr (d. 774/1373) explains that it was during a cold and rainy night that Moses spotted a tree burning in the distance. When he approached the place he received instructions from God about prophesying before the Pharaoh. According to Muqātil b. Sulaymān (d. 150/767), the tree Moses found was a boxthorn surrounded by other boxthorns and olive trees, relating the location to contemporary Jewish and Christian exegesis on the burning bush in Exodus.

Al-Thaʿlabī reports that God told Moses to remove his shoes because his feet were touching ground made twice holy. The authority Saʿīd b. Jubayr (d. ca. 95/712) relates the instructions for Moses to remove his shoes with the prohibition against wearing shoes in the Kaʿba in Mecca, thereby comparing the two locations. The naming of the place as the "valley of Ṭuwā" (Q 20:12; 79:16) is also understood by some Muslim exegetes as a reference to a valley near Mecca where the prophet Muḥammad received revelations.

In Q 20:14 God states to Moses: "I am God. There is no God other than I. Worship me and establish prayer to remember me." Q 27:9 has God state: "Moses, I am God, the Mighty, the Wise." And in Q 28:30, God says: "Moses, I am God, Lord of the worlds." These expressions are understood as God's pronouncement of Himself to Moses, and may parallel the announcement of God's name in Exodus 3:14.

God gives two signs to Moses. In Q 20:17–22, 27:10, and 28:31 Moses throws down his rod which moves as if it were a snake. In Q 20:22, 27:12, and 28:32, God commands Moses to put his hand in and out of his clothes, finding his hand white but unharmed, perhaps a reference to leprosy. Q 27:12 also states that Moses' white hand is among the "nine signs" to Pharaoh and his people, and Q 28:32 describes the rod and the hand as "two proofs" from God to Pharaoh. In Q 28:33–5 Moses responds that he is afraid because of the person he killed, and describes his brother Aaron as "more eloquent in tongue," asking God to send Aaron with him as a helper.

Moses and Pharaoh

The confrontation between Moses and Pharaoh is narrated in a number of different places, each with slightly different details. Q 7:103–26 contains an account of the contest between Moses and Aaron and the Pharaoh's magicians. In Q 7:120–6 and 26:46–51, the defeated magicians profess belief in the God of Moses and Aaron though the Pharaoh threatens to crucify them all for believing without his permission. Q 10:83 states that after the contest only a "few" people believed because of their fear of Pharaoh.

Q 17:101–3, 20:49–63, and 26:10–29 recount dialogues between Moses and Pharaoh. In each of these Moses represents the God of the Israelites against Pharaoh who claims that he himself is God. Among the arguments Moses uses with Pharaoh are that God created the earth and placed Pharaoh in it with authority. In Q 26:17–19 Moses demands that Pharaoh free the Israelites, but Pharaoh counters by accusing Moses of having lived under his protection for many years, and having killed a man.

In Q 26:16 Moses says he is sent by the "Lord of the worlds" an epithet of God which is further specified in verse 24 as "Lord of the heavens and the earth and what is between them" and in verse 28 as "Lord of the east, the west, and what is between them." Q 79:20 refers to "the great sign" Moses shows Pharaoh which was rejected. Q 7:127–36 describes a number of afflictions visited upon the Pharaoh and his people including flood, locusts, pestilence, frogs, and blood. According to Mujāhid b. Jabr (d. ca. 104/722), the locusts ate the nails from the doors of the Egyptians and the insides of the wood. Saʿīd b. Jubayr says the pestilence was worms which ruined all the dry stores of grain. Muḥammad's biographer Ibn Isḥāq (d. 150/767) reports that Moses caused the pestilence to come out of a great mound of sand by hitting it with his rod.

In Q 79:24, Pharaoh proclaims "I am your Lord, most high." Muslim exegetes understand this proclamation as an epitome not only of Pharaoh's disobedience but of all human refusal to acknowledge God. Rejecting God is equivalent to claiming to be God. Q 28:36–42 describes how Pharaoh ordered Haman to build a tower out of baked brick so he could prove there was no god other than himself, perhaps recalling the Tower of Babel from Genesis. Saʿīd b. Jubayr says it took seven years and 50,000 people to build the tower, and that God made it easy for Pharaoh so that his arrogance would be even more evident. According to al-Ḍaḥḥāk (d. 105/723 or 106/724), when the tower was destroyed by the archangel Gabriel the pieces were flung as far as India.

Al-Thaʿlabī explains that God filled the house of Pharaoh with kingship, authority, wealth, and pleasure, and gave him a kingdom so great that his people worshiped him. He was given a long life, great strength, and a powerful army. Pharaoh could go for forty days with no food and water, never got sick, and did not need sleep. Saʿīd b. Jubayr mentions that Pharaoh had a certain castle with thousands of stairs for which God provided a special animal to transport Pharaoh up and down from the castle. These blessings were given to him to stress how great his sin was in rejecting God.

Egyptian who believed

Q 40:23–46 describes the encounter between Moses and Pharaoh, Haman, and Korah. Moses is given a long dialogue in which he refers to past prophets such as Noah, and the people of ʿĀd and Thamūd. Moses also refers to Joseph, and again Pharaoh orders Haman to build a tower like the Tower of Babel. During the exchange, one of the Egyptians speaks up in support of Moses. Verse 38 simply refers to the speaker as "the one who believed" though he is identified by Muslim exegesis as the son of Pharaoh's paternal uncle or a secret Israelite. Al-Thaʿlabī states that his name was Ḥizqīl, that he was one of the carpenters of Pharaoh, and that he was the one who had made the ark into which Moses had been placed and put into the sea after his birth. Ibn ʿAbbās states that the wife of Pharaoh also believed in Moses.

Exodus

Q 26:52–68 and 44:17–33 describe the exodus of the Israelites from Egypt. In Q 26:63–6 God commands Moses to strike the sea with his rod causing it to divide and saving the Israelites while drowning the pursuing Egyptians. Q 44:24 mentions God's command to Moses to return the sea to its calm in order to drown the Egyptian army. Ibn Kathīr records an account in which Gabriel appears and drags Pharaoh into the sea.

Several passages describe the punishment of Pharaoh and his people including Q 10:90–2 in which Pharaoh attempts to repent and proclaim that he believes in God. Ibn ʿAbbās relates that Muḥammad heard Gabriel say that he took a wall of the sea and shoved it into the mouth of Pharaoh so that he could not repent. God also ordered the sea to exhume the body of Pharaoh so that the Israelites would know that he had perished.

The traditionist al-Bukhārī (d. 256/870) preserves a *ḥadīth* report in which Muḥammad asks the Jews of Medina why they fasted on the tenth day of Muḥarram. The Jews of Medina replied that it was the day Moses was victorious over the Pharaoh. In the *ḥadīth* report, Muḥammad agrees and orders his followers also to fast on this day.

Moses and the Israelites

Muslim exegetes emphasize the parallels between many of the themes and motifs associated with Moses and to the Israelites in the Qurʾān. The Qurʾān does not provide a single coherent narrative of the Israelites' wandering in the wilderness but recounts key episodes from that time, most of which are closely related to the narratives found in Exodus, Numbers, and Deuteronomy.

Wilderness of wandering

Q 2:47–61 outlines a number of incidents and blessings related to the Israelites in Egypt and after their exodus. Muslim exegetes do not agree, however, on the chronology of the events mentioned. In each case, the blessing or gift given to the Israelites is followed by a statement concerning the disobedience of the Israelites, in particular their lack of thankfulness for God's generosity. The passage begins, in verse 48 with a warning of the day when the Israelites will be punished for their sins, a day when no one, including Moses, will be allowed to intercede on their behalf. The passage ends with the claim that the Israelites rejected the signs of God and killed his prophets without cause, rebelled and transgressed against God's commands.

Q 2:51–6 refers to the forty nights Moses left the Israelites in the wilderness when he was given the "book" and the *furqān* while the Israelites worshiped the golden calf. Q 2:57 refers to God's gifts of the cloud, the manna, and the quail. Q 2:58 includes God's command that the Israelites enter a particular city, entering by a gate saying "*Ḥiṭṭa*," and in verse 59 the Israelites are said to have changed the wording of what God required and were thus punished by a plague from God. Q 2:60 refers to Moses striking the rock and producing twelve springs of water for the Israelites. In Q 2:61 the Israelites complain about not having pot-herbs, cucumbers, garlic, lentils, and onions. Moses offers the option of returning to Egypt, but the Israelites recognize their sin of complaint and ungratefulness.

According to Muslim exegesis, among the other blessings given to the Israelites, throughout their history, were kings, prophets, and books. Abū ʾl-Qāsim al-Balkhī (d. 319/931) states that it was the Israelites in the wilderness whom God made like kings, providing them all the luxuries they could want: clouds to shade them by day, fire to light their way by night, bread and meat from heaven, and water from rocks. According to al-Suddī (d. 128/745) the Israelites' clothes also grew on their bodies from the time they were born so that they had no need for producing or replacing them. Some authorities compare the manna with honey and the quail with special birds that lived only in the garden of Eden.

Moses on the mountain

Q 7:142–7 describes Moses' sojourn of forty days and nights on the mountain to receive the Torah. It was during this time that Moses requested to see God, and God revealed himself to the mountain which then crashed down to the ground causing Moses to faint. According to Ibn ʿAbbās, no one was able to look at the face of Moses after this so he wore a piece of silk over his face.

Golden calf

Q 7:148–58 and 20:80–98 depict the Israelites' worship of the golden calf during the absence of Moses. In Q 20:85 and 87 someone named the "Sāmirī," perhaps a reference to the perceived division between the Jews and Samaritans, is held responsible for the golden calf, though in Q 7:150 and 20:93 it is Aaron whom Moses drags by the hair and accuses of having instigated the sin. In Q 20:96, the Sāmirī claims to have thrown a "handful from the footprint of the messenger," which Muslim exegetes claim was dirt from the ground where the horse of Gabriel alighted. According to Ibn ʿAbbās, the Sāmirī was a man from the people of Bajarma, from a people who worshiped cows. It was the love for the worship of cows that made him cause the Israelites to worship the golden calf.

Muslim exegetes state that God punished the Israelites by commanding them to kill themselves. Ibn ʿAbbās describes a scene where certain Israelites innocent of the sin of worshiping the golden calf were given daggers to kill the guilty in a supernatural darkness that resulted in the death of 70,000 Israelites. According to Ibn Isḥāq, God struck dead a group of Israelites with thunder, then raised them back to life so they could watch another group be struck dead with thunder. In another tradition, the Israelites are forced to drink from the sea into which Moses had filed down and flung the remains of the golden calf.

In Q 7:150, out of anger for the worship of the golden calf, Moses throws the tablets, and one reading of verse 154 refers to the guidance and mercy that was abrogated from the tablets at this time. Ibn ʿAbbās states that when Moses threw down the tablets, God recalled six of the seven parts and left only one seventh for the Israelites. Early Christian exegesis of Exodus likewise argues that God imposed the Torah upon the Israelites as a curse and punishment for their worship of the golden calf.

Seventy chosen

Some exegetes preserve traditions regarding a special group of Israelites whom Moses chose to go with him to the mountain. According to Ibn Isḥāq, it was this seventy chosen Israelites who asked to see God (Q 2:55) when he went up onto the mountain, and whom God struck dead with thunder and raised back to life again. Al-Suddī reports that Moses was upset at the death of the seventy chosen because he claimed that if God felt the best of the Israelites should be destroyed, what of the others back at the camp who were not chosen.

ʿAbd al-Raḥmān b. Zayd b. Aslam (d. 182/799) reports that the seventy chosen were punished by God because they refused to believe what Moses told them without being able to see God themselves. After killing the seventy with thunder and resurrecting them, God asked them again to accept his revealed book. When the seventy again refused God sent an angel to lift Mount Sinai over their heads until they repented, which they eventually did.

Water from the rock

According to Muslim exegesis, the water from the rock described in Q 7:160 came from a special square rock which the Israelites used to carry around with them during their wanderings. ʿAṭiyya al-ʿAwfī (d. 111/729) states that this rock was given to the Israelites by God and was carried around on a bull. ʿUthmān b. ʿAṭāʾ al-Khurasānī (d. second/eighth century) reports that Aaron would hold the rock while Moses would strike it with his rod. Qatāda (d. 118/736) says that it was a piece of Mount Sinai. Al-Zamakhsharī (d. 538/1144) states that the rock was about the size of a person's head, and that it came from the garden of Eden. The rock is said to have originally descended to earth in the time of Adam along with the rod which belonged to Moses, and both the rod and the rock were passed down through the prophets until Shuʿayb gave them to Moses.

Entering the promised land

Q 5:20–5 recounts God's command that the Israelites enter the "holy land" which he had promised to them. In verse 22, the people protest to Moses that the land is full of giants, and in verse 24 they refuse to enter. In verse 25, Moses renounces responsibility for the Israelites and asks God to separate him and his brother Aaron from the sinners. In verse 26, God curses the Israelites with forty years of wandering because of their refusal to enter the land.

Muslim exegetes preserve different reports regarding the meaning of the term "holy land" as it is used in this passage. According to some, it refers only to Jerusalem. Others claim that the "holy land" includes Damascus, Palestine, and part of Jordan. Mujāhid states that the "holy land" is Mount Sinai and the land which surrounds it.

Al-Ṭabarsī (d. ca. 548/1153) includes a long account of how the Israelites sent representatives from each of their twelve tribes into the land, including Joshua b. Nūn and Caleb. He also reports that there is disagreement among exegetes concerning who was responsible for conquering the land. Some traditions hold that it was Moses himself who conquered the land, being responsible for slaying the leading giant of the people there named Og b. ʿAnaq who had survived since before the time of Noah's flood. Others report that it was Joshua who conquered the land, at one time calling upon God to keep the sun up in the sky until the Israelites took the city of Jericho.

Sin of Israelites and Moses

Moses' request to God that he separate him and his brother from the sinful Israelites in Q 5:25 is understood by Muslim exegetes as his refusal to intercede on behalf of his people. Al-Ṭabarsī says that the request was equivalent to Moses asking God to take him and his brother to Heaven while the Israelites were damned to Hell. According to al-Zajjāj (d. ca. 337/949), Moses and Aaron enjoyed special privileges in the wilderness so that they suffered little while the Israelites were punished for forty years.

People of Moses

Another tradition related to Moses and the Israelites and highlighted by Muslim exegesis is the reference to the "people of Moses" (*awlād Mūsā*) in Q 7:159. According to this verse, the "people of Moses" were a group of Israelites who were guided by the truth and acted justly. Numerous exegetical traditions refer to this group of people who are said to have been taken by God to the ends of the earth where they are later visited by different kings and prophets including Alexander the Great and Muḥammad.

The historian Yāqūt (d. 626/1229) explains that the people of Moses live in the city of Jabars at the eastern extreme of the world. Ibn ʿAbbās claims that the people of Moses live in Jabars and in the city of Jabalq, a city at the western extreme of the world. Al-Qurṭubī (d. 671/1272) preserves a tradition that the people of Moses live in a land beyond China, on the other side of a river of flowing sand. God is said to have taken them to the edge of the earth by way of a subterranean passage in which they walked for over a year. According to Ibn Jurayj (d. 150/767), the people of Moses were righteous Israelites who were removed from the sinful Israelites when they were killing their prophets and disbelieving. Others report that the people of Moses live in a city beyond Spain, in the extreme west, surrounded by mountains of gold and silver.

Sacrifice of the red cow

Q 2:67–73 describes what appears to be an isolated episode from Israelite history. In verse 67, Moses relates that God commands the Israelites to sacrifice a cow. The Israelites do not obey but instead keep asking God for further specifications, such as the age, color, and type of cow to be sacrificed. Verse 71 states that the Israelites "almost did not" do the sacrifice because the cow thus described was so difficult to find.

Muslim exegetes argue that this episode epitomizes the sinfulness of the Israelites. Instead of following God's instructions, the Israelites attempted to circumvent their obligation by making the command impossible to do. With each question posed by the Israelites, though, God imposed upon them a more difficult task. What began as a simple sacrifice became the sacrifice of a specially raised red cow with no blemishes, almost unique. Other exegetes relate this account to a special ritual designed to determine the culprit in the murder of an unclaimed corpse, perhaps related to the ritual mentioned in Numbers 19:17–22.

City by the sea

Closely related to the red cow sacrifice is the story of the city by the sea found in Q 7:163–6. This short passage describes a city in which the people are not allowed to fish on the Sabbath. According to Mālik b. Anas (d. 179/796), the fish in the sea used to come out only on the Sabbath, so after some time one person in the city devised a method for snaring the fish on the Sabbath and then removing and eating the fish on another day. In this way, the people tried to circumvent the prohibition of the Sabbath. Q 7:165 states, however, that God punished the people who violated the law, and verse 166 refers to God's turning them into apes. Q 2:65 also refers to those who transgressed the Sabbath being turned into apes, and Q 5:78 refers to the Israelites cursed by David and Jesus, turned into apes and pigs.

Muslim exegetes tend to identify the city mentioned in Q 7:163–6 as Eilat or another city somewhere between Eilat and Mount Sinai. According to Qatāda, some of the people were changed into apes and some into pigs, and that is why the Israelites broke into two sects. Ibn ʿAbbās explains that it was the Israelites themselves who made the Sabbath holy, against the wishes of Moses, but because of this, God imposed upon them the obligation of keeping the Sabbath, which included a prohibition on fishing. Al-Bukhārī records a report which states that ʿAmr b. Maymūn once saw a group of primates stoning other primates who had fornicated, so he joined in the administration of the punishment.

Mythology and Intertextuality of the Islamic Moses

Given the frequency of references to Moses in the text of the Qur'ān, the importance of his character, and his historical role in the leadership of the Israelites, it is not surprising that Muslim exegetes devote so much to the development of an elaborate typology of Moses in relationship to Muḥammad. Muslim scholars rely upon non-Qur'ānic sources to craft an exegetical picture of Moses that contrasts in important ways with the model prophethood of Muḥammad. In adapting this picture, Muslim exegetes draw upon but also distinguish their own views of Moses from contemporaneous Jewish and Christian views largely based on a reading of the Bible.

Two of the most telling examples of this exegetical picture can be found in the Muslim exegesis of Q 28:22–8 and Q 18:60–82. The first is the episode of Midian which takes place just shortly after Moses reaches maturity and is granted prophethood. The second is the encounter between Moses and the mysterious servant of God, identified by Muslim exegetes as the immortal prophet Khiḍr. In both episodes, the Muslim exegetical picture shares many details with the biblical image of Moses but is distinct in its focus upon a prophet who failed to attribute his knowledge to God and intercede on behalf of his people.

Moses and Jacob

Q 28:22–8 describes Moses' flight to and residence in Midian, and these verses form the basis for a number of rich mythological associations between Moses and other prophetic figures. Muslim exegesis casts the entire episode in terms familiar from the story of Isaac found in Genesis 28:10–31:21. According to a *ḥadīth* report given on the authority of the second caliph ʿUmar b. al-Khaṭṭāb, when Moses arrived at the well of Midian he moved from its mouth a rock which could only be moved by ten men. Al-Zamakhsharī reports that the rock moved by Moses alone could only be moved by a hundred men. This parallels Jacob's feat of moving the rock from the well in Genesis 29:1–14 with the exception that Jacob's "rolling" of the rock is replaced by the more fantastic "lifting" of the rock by Moses. Jewish exegesis, such as that found in the Hellenistic Jewish sources like Philo, and medieval rabbinic sources such as the *Abot de Rabbi Nathan* and the *Midrash Rabba* on Exodus 2:17, also report that Moses performed a miraculous or heroic feat at the well of Midian.

Oaths

An important element from the Jacob story linked to Moses in Midian is the oath made between God and Jacob in Genesis 28:20–1. Q 28:24 mentions that Moses asks God for something, a request which is interpreted by Muslim exegesis as Moses asking for protection from his enemies. This parallels the situation of Jacob who, having left the protection of his father, enters into the protection of God in Genesis 28. Jacob promised that Yahweh would be his God upon his safe return to his father's house. This also parallels the oath Jacob later makes with Laban for marriage to his daughters and, after that, for receiving the speckled sheep. Moses also makes an oath with God in Q 28:24 that parallels the agreement with his future father-in-law in Q 28:27–8. Just as the oath between Jacob and God results in Jacob's return from Laban with wives, sons, sheep, and becoming Israel the father of the twelve tribes, so the oath between God and Moses foreshadows Moses' commission to lead the Israelites out of Egypt. Some Muslim exegetes also relate this oath with Moses' reception of revelation at the mountain in Q 20:10–33.

Two daughters

Muslim exegetes also link the Midian episode with Jacob by the names given to the two daughters Moses meets in Midian: Zipporah and Leah. The exegete al-Ṭabarī (d. 310/923) gives these two names, along with providing a close translation of Exodus 2:16. Zipporah is reported to be the wife of Moses in Exodus 2:21, and Leah is the name of the wife that Jacob marries first in Genesis 29:15–30 although he had intended to marry Rachel. Some Muslim exegetes claim that Moses married Leah along with Zipporah just as Jacob married both the daughters of Laban.

Speckled sheep

Muslim exegesis associates the account of the speckled sheep from the story of Jacob in Genesis with Moses and his stay in Midian. In a close parallel to Genesis 30:25–43, al-Zamakhsharī states that Moses' father-in-law agreed to give to him all the sheep born speckled in a given year, and God instructed Moses to hit each sheep with his rod at the water trough so that all of the sheep that year were born speckled. In Genesis 30, God instructs Jacob to take rods from different trees and place them in front of the water trough of the sheep while they are in heat to produce the speckled offspring.

God's attack upon Moses and Jacob

Moses and Jacob are also compared in their similar episodes of fighting with God. Al-Zamakhsharī records an account of Moses fighting with a supernatural being when he leaves Midian and being saved only by the miraculous actions of his rod. Exodus 4:24–6 also contains an account of God attacking Moses when taking leave from his father-in-law, and Moses is saved by Zipporah who cuts the foreskin of her son and rubs it on the genitals of Moses. The rod of Moses, rich in its symbolic representation of Moses' own fertility, especially when associated with the story of Jacob's rods and the speckled sheep, is in the account of al-Zamakhsharī found bloody upon defeat of the supernatural being, perhaps suggesting the circumcision of Moses.

This interpretation is explicitly linked to God's attack upon Jacob in Genesis 32:23–32 and the Muslim exegesis of Q 3:93. In Genesis 32 Jacob is said to come upon a pass where he is attacked by a supernatural being later identified as God, and is wounded in the hollow of his thigh, also understood to be his genitals, just as Moses was attacked while moving his sheep in the account of al-Zamakhsharī. Indeed, the same term, *kaff*, is used in both the Hebrew and Arabic to designate the location of the danger to Moses and Jacob. Jewish exegetes also stress the relationship between the attack on Moses and Jacob and the rite of circumcision which was representative of the oath made with God.

In the Muslim exegesis of Q 3:93 there are accounts which report that Jacob fought with God because he had not fulfilled the earlier oath he had made with God to sacrifice the last of his sons. In Genesis 28:20–2, Jacob does vow to give God a tithe of everything God gives to him if he returns safely to his father, though there is no indication of any tithe of the livestock and sons that Jacob acquires in the course of Genesis 29–32. Rabbinic exegesis in the *Pirqe de Rabbi Eliezer* and the *Targum Yerushalmi* also appears to interpret the attack upon Jacob as being due to his not fulfilling his vow to make a tithe to God of his livestock and sons. The *Midrash Tanhuma* and the *Midrash Rabba* on Genesis 32:21 both stress that Jacob refers to his brother Esau as "lord" and gives to him the tithe he should have been giving to God though Jacob had promised to call Yahweh his "Lord" in Genesis 28:20–2.

It is not likely that Muslim exegesis draws upon this parallel to put Moses in the role of redeeming his son, who is not mentioned by name in the Qur'ān or Muslim exegesis. In Exodus 4:24–6 and in al-Zamakhsharī's account of the rod defeating the supernatural being, Moses has no part in his own salvation. In addition, it is the Israelites, the people of Moses, rather than his own sons, with whom Moses is most closely associated by Muslim exegetes. The conflation of Moses and Jacob emphasizes Moses' symbolic association with Jacob/Israel, and the Israelites as his sons. What happens to the Israelites in the wilderness also parallels what happens to Moses in Egypt. Muslim exegetes indicate how the journey of the Israelites from Egypt to Mount Sinai and God's attacks upon them parallel the events of Moses and his flight from Egypt to Midian.

Jethro and Shuʿayb

Perhaps even more significant for the Muslim exegesis of the Midian episode is the identification of Moses' father-in-law as the Arab prophet Shuʿayb (see Q 7:85–93; 11:84–95; 29:36–7). Although a number of Muslim exegetes point out the historical problems associated with such an identification (see Q 11:89), several reasons are given in its support. One of these is the tradition that Moses' father-in-law was the "priest" of Midian, not found in Q 28:21–8 but in Exodus 2:16. Rabbinic tradition goes to great lengths to explain how a non-Israelite could be designated with the title "kohen" normally reserved only for priests of Yahweh. This is further complicated by the fact that the name "Jethro" does not occur in Exodus 2:15–21, and that Moses' father-in-law is also referred to as Reuel and Hobab in other contexts though Muslim exegetes also know the name of Jethro (Yatrūn or Thayrūn). A report from Muḥammad explicitly states the identity of Jethro and Shuʿayb.

Some Muslim exegetes appear to make this identification linked to the close association between the prophet Shuʿayb and the prophet Khiḍr whom Moses is said to meet according to the exegesis of Q 18:60–82. Khiḍr challenges Moses' concept of justice in Q 18:60–82 just as Jethro challenges Moses' dispensing of justice in Exodus 18. In both Q 28:24 and 18:63 Moses takes refuge in the dark after being guided to the location of the prophetic figure by supernatural means. In both Q 28:21–8 and 18:60–82, Moses undertakes a long journey and ends up at a miraculous water source. In one report, the color of Moses' stomach is described as being green, which is representative of the name "Khiḍr" which means "green" and symbolizes immortality and fertility.

Muslim exegetes also include elements familiar from late antiquity accounts of the hairy anchorites and ascetics journeying in search of Elijah or other gnostic masters. The changes affecting Moses also compare with the transformations attributed by Ambrose and other Christian authors to Jacob in his time with Laban.

The rod of Moses itself is explicitly linked with the prophet Shuʿayb and the prophethood of Moses. According to a *ḥadīth* report preserved in al-Ṭabarī, it was this rod which Adam brought down from the garden of Eden and was eventually passed down through the prophets to Shuʿayb. Numerous accounts exist in Muslim exegesis about how the rod was passed down, as a mantle of prophethood, from Shuʿayb to Moses. In many of these, the acquisition of the rod is linked with Moses' marriage to Zipporah and his assuming of the prophethood. In Jewish sources such as the late pseudepigraphic *Book of Jasher* Moses finds this rod, made out of sapphire, planted in the garden behind the house of his future father-in-law. According to rabbinic sources, the rod is supposed to be inscribed with the name of God, and because Moses was able to read this name he was able to take the rod from the ground and win Zipporah in marriage although all the other people of Midian could not move the rod from the ground.

Moses and Alexander

Q 18:60–82 stands out among all the Moses stories in the Qurʾān for a number of reasons. In this passage, Moses and his unnamed companion set out to the ends of the earth, lose a fish that disappears through a tunnel in the water, and meet another unnamed servant of God at which point Moses' original companion disappears. This is followed by Q 18:83–102 which describes the exploits of Dhū ʾl-Qarnayn, an epithet usually assigned to Alexander the Great but also attributed to Moses by Muslim as well as Jewish and Christian exegetes.

Lost fish

Muslim exegetes explain that the fish mentioned in Q 18:60–5 was dead and was brought back to life when it was washed in the water of life by Moses and his companion, who is identified as Joshua b. Nūn. This is a motif found in earlier Greek and Syriac recensions of the *Alexander Romance*, themselves based upon literary motifs and themes taken from the *Epic of Gilgamesh*. In the *Epic of Gilgamesh*, Gilgamesh searches for and finds Utnapishtim, an immortal being who lives at the mouth of the rivers, whereas Moses finds Khiḍr at the "junction of the two waters" (*majmaʿ al-baḥrayn*) mentioned in Q 18:60 and 61.

Muslim exegetes link Q 18:60–82 with Alexander and Gilgamesh stories through the motif of the fish. Al-Ṭabarī records a number of reports in which the fish escapes through a rock passage, swims away leaving dry land in its wake, and is discovered whole after having been eaten. Fakhr al-Dīn al-Rāzī (d. 606/1209) states that the fish's resurrection was intended as a sign to Moses that he had reached the meeting place of the two waters and the secret location of the prophet Khiḍr.

The Syriac sermon on Alexander by Jacob of Serugh also describes how an old man tells Alexander to command his cook to take a salted fish and wash it in every spring until the fish comes back to life. The *Babylonian Talmud*, Tamid 32a–b, contains an account of Alexander washing salted fish in a well that he then discovers contains the water of life coming from the Garden of Eden. Several Greek versions of the Alexander stories include the fish episode, and in some the cook who discovers the water of life drinks the water and becomes immortal himself.

Dhū ʾl-Qarnayn

In part, the association of Q 18:60–102 with the Alexander stories was due to the Muslim exegetical identification of Dhū ʾl-Qarnayn with Alexander the Great. Although many early Muslim exegetes propose different identifications for Dhū ʾl-Qarnayn, it is likely that an exegetical consensus emerged surrounding the character's affiliation with both Alexander and Moses. A large bulk of the motifs associated with Dhū ʾl-Qarnayn may have come from traditions linked to the pre-Islamic South Arabian king called by the same name, and circulated under the name of the early Muslim exegete Wahb b. Munabbih (d. ca. 110/728).

Many of the elements in the stories of this South Arabian Dhū ʾl-Qarnayn can be found in Greek, Syriac, Perisan, and Ethiopic recensions of the *Alexander Romance* including the mention of al-Khiḍr, the rubies in the land of darkness, and the angel's gift of the heavy stone and the bunch of grapes. The fuller versions of the stories of Dhū ʾl-Qarnayn, drawing upon the *Alexander Romance* and South Arabian traditions seems to have emerged as the dominant exegesis of Q 18:60–102 as early as the eleventh century. This included the Persian *Iskandarnamah*, Firdawsi's *Shahnamah*, and the Ethiopic recensions of the thirteenth century.

Gilgamesh and Alexander

In the *Epic of Gilgamesh*, the immediate cause of Gilgamesh's journey in search of Utnapishtim is the death of Gilgamesh's companion Enkidu. Gilgamesh travels through the gate at the Mashu mountains, and for twelve leagues through the land of darkness, until he arrives at a garden in which gems grow, by the edge of the sea. In the garden, Gilgamesh meets the young woman Sidduri who tells him about Urshanabi who might ferry Gilgamesh across the sea to Utnapishtim. The two travel together for three days until arriving at Dilmun where Utnapishtim and his wife live. Utnapishtim tells Gilgamesh two secrets of the gods: the story of the flood, and about the existence of a plant at the bottom of the sea which restores men to their youth. Gilgamesh retrieves the plant but, on his return to his home in Uruk to share the plant with his companions, a snake comes and eats the plant.

Several of the elements in this section of the epic parallel episodes from the various Alexander stories, such as the Mashu mountains, the land of darkness, gems, and the long ocean journey. There is little doubt that, on this episode in particular, the

Alexander stories are drawing upon themes earlier associated with Gilgamesh. Unlike the immediate pretext in the Alexander stories, Gilgamesh is not seeking only or even primarily immortality, but rather is seeking the justice of Enkidu's and his own impending death. In this sense, Gilgamesh's questioning of Utnapishtim recalls Moses' questioning of Khiḍr in the exegesis of Q 18:60–82. Muslim exegesis appears to draw a parallel between the failures of Gilgamesh and Alexander. Both Gilgamesh and Alexander fail to gain immortality either for themselves or their people. But, more important is that Gilgamesh fails to find a satisfactory answer to his friend's death other than fate, and Alexander is not able to conquer the world, whether by means of obtaining his own immortality, ascending to heaven, or with the force of his army.

By interpreting Q 18:60–102 in light of these extra-Qur'ānic stories, Muslim exegesis is able to show how the Qur'ān is inclusive of earlier stories and revelations. It allows the exegetes to contend that these earlier stories are part of the revelation already contained in the Qur'ān and can only be shown to be such from the privileged position of the exegetes. It also enables the exegetes to build intertextual links between different verses relative to Moses in their larger design to evaluate his character and compare it with the prophet Muḥammad.

Meeting place of the two waters

Muslim exegesis uses the unusual term "meeting place of the two waters" from Q 18:60 and 61 to emphasize the link between Gilgamesh, Alexander, and Moses. Although there are no clear parallels between this expression and elements from earlier stories, it seems to be used to signify the garden of Eden from which the water of life flows in the Alexander stories, and the "mouth of the waters" at which Gilgamesh discovers Utnapishtim. Muslim exegesis also compares Moses' journey to the meeting place of the two waters with the "water" of Midian mentioned in Q 28:24 to which Moses also travels. All of the associations of Moses with fertility, strength, and prophethood can be associated with his parallel journey and meeting with the prophet Shuʿayb.

Muslim exegetes make this connection explicit by explaining that the meeting place of the two waters is where the Persian Sea and Roman Sea meet. Al-Zamakhsharī, Fakhr al-Dīn al-Rāzī, and Ibn Kathīr indicate that the Roman Sea, normally identified as the Mediterranean Sea, and the Persian Sea, identified as the Indian Ocean, only meet at the ends of the earth where the waters of the oceans flow together and surround the continents. Qatāda pinpoints this location as the place where the Persian Sea is the farthest East and the Roman Sea is the farthest West. Other exegetes locate the place at the western or eastern extreme of the world, and Fakhr al-Dīn al-Rāzī says the water of the meeting place is from the garden of Eden.

Dhū 'l-Qarnayn as Moses

Muslim exegetes also make a direct connection between Moses and Alexander through the epithet Dhū 'l-Qarnayn. According to Wahb b. Munabbih, some say that both

Alexander and Moses had horns on their heads. In Jewish and Christian literature, both Alexander and Moses are portrayed as having actual horns on their heads. Jerome's Latin translation of Moses being horned in Exodus 34:29 is one example of this, later rendered into Anglo-Saxon vernacular translations of the Bible in fourteenth-century Europe. In his commentary on Exodus 34:29, Rashi states that Moses' face looked as though it was horned. Muslim exegesis also regards Moses' face as having changed after he spoke directly with God on Mount Sinai so that his face had to be covered with a piece of silk when he appeared before the Israelites.

Even more integral to the purposes of the Muslim exegetes is the explanation that *dhū 'l-qarnayn* refers to the one who reached the two points (*qarns*) of the sun, the place of its rising and the place of its setting. In Q 18:60–1 Moses sets off to the meeting place of the two waters which is understood as being located at the ends of the earth. In Q 18:86 and 18:90 Dhū 'l-Qarnayn reaches the place where the sun rises and where the sun sets in the extreme east and west. Muslim exegesis uses this conflation of motifs to draw upon the major theme of the *Alexander Romance*, which is Alexander's quest to the ends of the earth to find immortality. Dhū 'l-Qarnayn is the one who goes to the end of the earth, whether Moses or Alexander, in both cases in search of personal immortality and fame.

Muslim exegesis thus suggests a clear biblical precedent for Moses' challenges to God's authority in Q 18:60–82 and in other passages such as Q 28:33–4 and 20:25–32. Ubayy b. Kaʿb reports that Moses stood up in the midst of the Israelites and stated that he was the most knowledgeable of people, thus claiming God's revelation as his own. This parallels Exodus 18:17–27 in which Moses is chided by his Midianite father-in-law for judging the Israelites on his own, a passage which the rabbis also took as an indictment of Moses' self-importance.

Moses in Q 18 and 28

What the Muslim exegetes emphasize with all of these connections is an exegetical image of Moses who is like Alexander the Great but unlike the prophet Muḥammad. Q 18:60–82 portrays a Moses like Alexander in that Moses refuses to attribute his knowledge to God and boasts that he will travel to the ends of the earth to prove this. The humiliation Moses experiences because of his ignorance of the reasons behind Khiḍr's actions shows that Moses' own knowledge is not of the same type as the divine knowledge that he was given by God.

The details of Q 18:60–102 were such that Muslim exegetes could and did see in them reflections of popular late antique motifs which they could use to build certain exegetical images supportive of their own authority. Muslim exegesis is able to draw together disparate motifs to the features of the Qur'ān passages on Moses, including a strong Jewish tradition about Alexander's pride and attempts to enter the garden of Eden as reflected in the Latin *Iter ad Paradisum*, the Hebrew *Sefer Aleksandros Moqdon*, and the *Babylonian Talmud*.

Muslim exegesis draws from this image the full "lesson" of Q 18:60–102, a lesson that both contrasts Moses with the prophet Muḥammad and legitimates the authority of the exegesis itself. Muḥammad was illiterate and did not enjoy the special education of Moses in the house of Pharaoh. Muslim exegetes refer to Muḥammad as a "servant-prophet" as opposed to the "king-prophet" model exemplified by Moses. The prophet Muḥammad based his authority only on the knowledge he received as revelation, not on his own learning. His position was as messenger of God, not as king among his people.

Conclusions

The Muslim exegetes owe their own position and authority to their transmission and continuation of the prophetic knowledge originating with Muḥammad. The exegetical lesson of Moses is that Islam and Muḥammad demand a simple obedience, not a questioning of the reasons for God's instructions. The exegetes show that it is only with knowledge from the prophet Muḥammad that the Qur'ān can be understood properly, and that this understanding reinforces the structure of authority upon which the exegesis is based. It is reinforced by the understanding of the Qur'ān as stressing not the abstract qualities of good and evil, but rather the distinction between right and wrong, legal and illegal. The archetypal act of disobedience by Moses is his claim that he himself, without the aid of God, knows what is right and wrong. Throughout the Qur'ān, acknowledging God and his role as creator is defined as obedience to the revealed message of the prophets, the message to focus and direct oneself to God alone.

The exegesis of the Moses story in the Qur'ān demonstrates how Muslim exegetes drew upon non-Qur'ānic sources to legitimate their own authority. This exegesis thus preserves a wealth of information on Moses including oral sources not put into writing before the Islamic period, direct influences from Jewish and Christian groups, and an exchange of ideas among people interested in using biblical stories to formulate their self-identity.

Note

1 Because the aim of this chapter is to explore the Qur'ānic Moses and the way that has been developed in Islamic tradition in general, explicit exegetical references are not provided in this chapter. Much of the material which is cited is repeated in various works of Muslim exegesis. More complete references are found in Wheeler (2002) for readers who wish to pursue the details.

Further reading

Bienaimé, Germain (1984) *Moïse et le don de l'eau dans la tradition juive ancienne: targum et midrash.* Biblical Institute Press, Rome.
Coats, George W. (1985) *Moses: Heroic Man, Man of God.* JSOT Press, Sheffield.

Lévi, Israel (1881) La légende d'Alexandre dans le Talmud. *Revue des Etudes Juives* 2, 293–300.
Meeks, Wayne (1967) *The Prophet-king: Moses Traditions and the Johannine Christology*. Brill, Leiden.
Milgrom, J. (1983) Magic, monotheism and the sin of Moses. In: Hoffman H. B. et al. (eds.) *The Quest for the Kingdom of God*. Eisenbrauns, Winona Lake, pp. 251–65.
Schwarzbaum, Haim (1959) The Jewish and Moslem versions of some theodicy legends. *Fabula* 3, 119–69.
Smola, Leivy and Aberbach, Moshe (1968) The golden calf episode in post-biblical literature. *Hebrew Union College Annual* 39, 91–116.
Vollers, Karl (1909) Chidher. *Archiv für Religionswissenschaft* 12, 234–84.
Wasserstrom, Steven (1995) *Between Muslim and Jew: The Problem of Symbiosis under Early Islam*. Princeton University Press, Princeton.
Wheeler, Brannon (2002) *Moses in the Quran and Islamic Exegesis*. Curzon, Richmond.

CHAPTER 17

Argumentation

Kate Zebiri

Argumentation is a very prominent aspect of the Qurʾān, and an inherent part of its discourse; any reader will quickly notice how frequently the text addresses protagonists, whether real or imagined. This reflects the original circumstances in which the Qurʾān came into existence: Muḥammad encountered extensive opposition over the course of his mission, not just from the pagans in Mecca but from the Jews and "hypocrites" (nominal, opportunistic converts to Islam who often sought to undermine Muḥammad), mainly in Medina. The Qurʾān describes in some detail the arguments of those who oppose its message, both from the time of Muḥammad and from earlier times when previous prophets encountered opposition; it also provides counterarguments. There are also numerous scenes of debate, not just between prophets and their peoples but also, for example, between Moses and Pharaoh and between God and Satan.

The degree to which the Qurʾān interacts with its environment over the period of revelation (approximately twenty-three years according to majority scholarly opinion) can scarcely be overstated; one can even find within the text answers to specific questions which were put to Muḥammad by his contemporaries. In fact the Qurʾān is unique among scriptures in the extent to which it engages its audience and addresses them directly. The dynamic, interactive quality of the Qurʾān can be further appreciated when one bears in mind its oral character; while the present-day reader is likely to encounter it as a written text, it should be borne in mind that it was originally proclaimed orally and it continues to be memorized and recited by Muslims down to the present. Direct speech is not uncommon in the Qurʾān and the imperative: "Say . . .", whereby God instructs Muḥammad to say something to his followers or opponents, occurs over 300 times (see Radscheit 1997).

One striking feature of the Qurʾān is the pervasive sense of contrast or dualism. Izutsu (1964: 74) points out that "the Koranic Weltanschauung is . . . a system built on the principle of conceptual opposition", and that this contributes to its "intense atmosphere of spiritual strain and tension"; furthermore the basic dichotomy between belief and unbelief is "the very keynote of the whole ethical system of Islam" (Izutsu 1966:

187). This striking tendency towards polarization can be observed throughout the Qur'ān, in the binary opposition between good and evil, heaven and hell, this world and the next, belief and unbelief, truth and falsehood, and so forth. The structure of Qur'ānic arguments often reflects this dualism, as the audience is constantly challenged to choose between alternatives, and notably between belief and unbelief. The preponderance of (often rhetorical) questions to which the answer would be a simple yes or no provides another example of this phenomenon: "Are the blind equal to the seeing, or the darkness to the light?" (Q 13:16); "Do you know best or does God?" (Q 2:140). The Qur'ān is replete with antonyms, antitheses, and comparisons.

Such Qur'ānic argumentation does not occur in a vacuum, but in the context of certain underlying assumptions. The larger frame of reference is a metaphysical order which includes God's creation of humankind, the latter's primordial acknowledgment of Him as Lord (Q 7:172), God's subsequent communications via chosen messengers, and the future reckoning on the day of judgment. Gwynne (2004: 1) argues convincingly that these things constitute the covenant between God and humans, and that this is "the logical key to the entire structure of Qur'ānic argument", since "virtually every argument in the Qur'ān expresses or implies one or more of the covenantal provisions."

The Qur'ān assumes that humans are rational beings who are capable of critical thought, and open to persuasion. This is evident from the lengths to which it goes to appeal to people and persuade them. Furthermore, commands are rarely issued to the believers without giving the reason or underlying wisdom, and the Qur'ān frequently exhorts people to consider and reflect, especially on the wonders of the natural world which are presented as signs of God's power and beneficence; interestingly there seems to be a reciprocal relationship between faith on the one hand and understanding or intelligence on the other (Waardenburg 1980: 620ff.).

Very often, God Himself is the progenitor of an argument in the Qur'ān and thus the argument becomes an argument from authority *par excellence*, or an argument from the absolute, as Waardenburg (1980: 625) terms it. The authorial voice of the Qur'ān is privileged because it is omniscient, and is able to speak with authority not just on opponents' arguments but on their inner thoughts and motives: "Do they not know that God knows what they conceal and what they reveal?" (Q 2:77); "Fear God, for God knows what is in your hearts" (Q 5:7). There are numerous places in the Qur'ān where God reveals peoples' hidden motives or thoughts (e.g., Q 2:76; 9:107); He is also able to predict the future, as in the future projections of eschatological scenes which relate in detail conversations or interactions which have yet to take place (e.g., Q 7:44–53).

It is clear from the Qur'ān that God is utterly independent, and on a completely different level from human beings: "O humankind! It is you who need God; God is free of all need, worthy of praise" (Q 35:15; cf. 29:6; 39:7); "Nothing is like him!" (Q 42:11). Although in His mercy He very often gives reasons for his commandments (as we have just observed), He is not accountable to human beings: "He is not to be asked about what He does" (Q 21:23). In view of God's transcendence and uniqueness, the frequent authoritative proclamations and assertive affirmations contained in the Qur'ān almost acquire the force of argument in their own right, or at the very least significantly reinforce any argument that is being made, as will be seen in the following sections.

In the classical Islamic scholarly tradition, Qurʾānic argumentation did not become one of the branches of the Qurʾānic sciences; a possible explanation for this is that "reasoning and argument are so integral to the content of the Qurʾān and so inseparable from its structure that they in many ways shaped the very consciousness of Qurʾānic scholars" (Gwynne 2004: 203); thus the forms and idiom of Qurʾānic arguments were internalized rather than objectively studied. Only a relatively small number of works treated this as a subject in its own right, though it did attract the attention of a few prominent scholars such as al-Ghazālī (d. 505/1111), al-Ṭūfī (d. 716/1316), al-Zarkashī (d. 794/1392) and al-Suyūṭī (d. 911/1501) (McAuliffe 1999: 177ff.; Gwynne 2004: xiii–xiv, chapters 8–9). During recent decades, however, Arabic-speaking Muslim scholars have shown renewed interest in Qurʾānic argumentation, and several monographs have appeared on the subject (see McAuliffe 1999: 164, fn. 4).

Until recently modern Western scholarship has paid relatively little attention to the actual content and message of the Qurʾān in general, let alone argumentation in particular. Several scholars such as Cragg (especially 1994), Welch (1980; 1983), Marshall (1999) and Rahman (1980) have shown an interest in the subject but only a handful have undertaken any focused study, and that has generally been brief: Waardenburg (1980), Jomier (1997: chapter 9), and Urvoy (2002) have each devoted a chapter or an article to argumentation and persuasion. This has changed, however, with the appearance of Gwynne's *Logic, Rhetoric and Legal Reasoning in the Qurʾān: God's Arguments* (2004), which constitutes an impressive and sustained analysis of Qurʾānic argumentation, organized not thematically (as in this chapter), but on the basis of the types of argument used.

A fairly broad definition of argumentation is followed here, which includes practical as well as theoretical reasoning, and logical as well as non-rigorous persuasive reasoning (e.g., arguments from analogy, *a fortiori* arguments etc.). The Qurʾān is deliberately couched in natural language: "We sent no messenger save with the tongue of his people so that he could make things clear to them" (Q 14:4), and although it contains many different types of argument these are not set out schematically, and are far from abstract; in fact they are often expressed in highly emotive or even polemical language, as we shall see. In view of this a useful working definition of argumentation for the purposes of this chapter would be: providing reasons to the listener or reader for believing something to be the case, or for doing (or not doing) something. It will be helpful to bear in mind the classical distinction between logic and rhetoric: while logic concerns itself with the validity of arguments, in the sphere of rhetoric a good argument is one which is effective in convincing the audience, regardless of its deductive validity. It should also be borne in mind that a valid argument is not necessarily true, nor a fallacious one necessarily untrue.

At times it will be necessary and relevant to refer to the chronology of the Qurʾānic revelations. For example, the element of argumentation is particularly prominent from the middle to the end of the Meccan period of revelation which was a time when the early Muslims were struggling to survive, in contrast to the Medinan period when they became empowered and were able to fight their opponents physically and not just verbally. On the whole, however, this chapter will take a synchronic approach, which takes the Qurʾān as a unified entity without reference to the chronological order of the revelations, and observes its internal dynamics; this is the approach of the ordinary religious believer who seeks guidance from the Qur'ān and who is more concerned with its content than its chronology.

Argumentation is often inseparable from other elements in the Qur'ān. Polemic is a particularly pervasive aspect of the Qur'ānic discourse (Zebiri 2004), which is full of rebukes, criticisms, threats and warnings, declarations of woe, curses, satire, irony, rhetorical questions, challenges etc. In addition to these, the vivid use of metaphor, imagery, and parable all make a contribution to the argumentation contained in the Qur'ān; an attempt will be made here to describe and analyze some of these stylistic elements as an intrinsic part of our subject. It would, of course, be impossible to do full justice to the theme of argumentation in the Qur'ān in a chapter of this length; readers seeking more extensive coverage should consult Gwynne (2004). Here, in order to make the material more manageable and accessible, a thematic and non-technical approach is employed, selecting those themes where argumentation is particularly explicit and developed. These tend to be the more theological/doctrinal areas, which for the purposes of this essay are treated under the following headings: the unity of God, the authenticity of Muḥammad's prophethood, and the resurrection. Obviously this is not a comprehensive treatment but it will at least give a flavor of the Qur'ānic argumentation. First, however, we will briefly review the Qur'ān's attitude to dispute and argumentation.

Qur'ānic Attitude to Argumentation

The prevailing tone of the Qur'ān is often authoritarian in a way that does not encourage dissent. The reader who starts from the beginning of the Qur'ān will encounter this quality very quickly, as the second *sūra* opens with the words: "This is a book which is not to be doubted!" (Q 2:2). This type of self-attestation is extremely common, and often appears at the beginnings of *sūras*. The Qur'ān contains a number of terms that are semantically related to the concept of argumentation, such as disputation, evidence, proof, argument, authority, and so forth. In fact, the references to argumentation or disputation are overwhelmingly negative: "None dispute concerning the signs of God except those who disbelieve" (Q 40:4; cf. 2:197; 6:25; 8:6; see McAuliffe 1999), and the activity of disputing, or wrangling, is most often attributed to Muḥammad's opponents. Very often, as in the above example, they are portrayed as disputing over God or His signs, and those who engage in such disputation are characterized as perverse, stubborn, arrogant, and unreceptive to God's word. While one Qur'ānic verse simply laments that "man is the most contentious of creatures!" (Q 18:54), it is clear that the unbelievers are especially guilty of contentiousness, willfully wrangling over God's revealed truths. Thus has it always been, for the adversaries of former prophets behaved in exactly the same way, as is evident throughout the Qur'ān. One commentator observes that "there is little doubt for the Qur'ān that whereas there is such a thing as an *honest* difference of opinion, there is nevertheless very little of it" (Rahman 1980: 116; italics in original); in other words, ulterior motives often prevail.

Alongside the condemnation of disputation and wrangling one also finds, perhaps paradoxically, a certain acceptance of human disagreement and disunity as an inevitable feature of life which is not just allowed but even willed by God: "If your Lord had so willed, He could have made humankind one people; but they do not cease to differ" (Q 11:118; cf. 10:19; 16:93). Furthermore the extent to which the Qur'ān itself resorts to argument rules out any blanket condemnation of argumentation *per se*; so we may assume that it is only when arguments are employed in dishonest or inappropriate ways, or when they are not employed in the service of truth, that they are condemned. In fact, the Qur'ān prescribes a certain protocol for Muslims engaged in calling non-Muslims to the faith: "Call to the way of your Lord with wisdom and beautiful preaching and debate with them in the better way" (Q 16:125; cf. 29:46). Partly inspired by this verse, classical Muslim scholars occupied themselves with distinguishing between recommended and reprehensible debate (McAuliffe 1999: 170ff.).

God's Unity (*Tawhīd*)

The Qur'ān frequently refers to the "unbelievers" (*kāfirūn*), but this generally denotes those who disbelieve in Muḥammad's mission rather than in God *per se*. Given that even Muḥammad's pagan opponents generally believed in a high God called Allāh (see, e.g., Q 10:31; 43:87), the Qur'ān mostly assumes rather than argues for the existence of God. Disbelief in God is treated as something almost incomprehensible: "How can you disbelieve in God when you were without life and He gave you life?" (Q 2:28; cf. 3:101). We have already mentioned the reciprocal relationship between faith and understanding; there is a corresponding relationship between disbelief and stupidity: "Who turns away from the religion of Abraham except the stupid?" (Q 2:130).

Although the Qur'ān generally assumes God's existence, it is concerned to point out His uniqueness and pre-eminence, and to that end highlights His power, majesty, omniscience, and beneficence in many passages. As a result, the Qur'ān contains arguments from creation, from signs, and from providence – witness the countless references to natural phenomena: the alternation of night and day, and the sun and moon in their orbits are evidence not just of God's existence and power but also of His mercy and beneficence. One typically lyrical passage runs as follows:

> In the creation of the heavens and the earth; in the alternation of night and day; in the ships that sail on the ocean for the benefit of humankind; in the water which God sends down from the sky to revivify the earth when it is barren, scattering creatures of all kinds over it; in the change of the winds, and the clouds that run their appointed courses between the sky and the earth; here indeed are signs for a people who understand. (Q 2:164)

Much has been written on the subject of the beliefs of the Arabs of Muḥammad's day (see, e.g., Peters 1999), and the picture seems to have been quite complex; doubts have been expressed as to how seriously the pagans really took their religion. The Qur'ān tends to refer in general terms to "deities" or "that which you call on besides God," while the polytheistic pagans are referred to as "those who ascribe partners to God," and it has much to say on the subject of those partners, or deities. A common theme is their ineffectiveness: they can neither help nor harm (e.g., Q 22:12); worse, they cannot even help or harm themselves (e.g., Q 13:16); and they cannot create but are themselves created (e.g., Q 7:191). The latter verse is, of course, drawing an implicit contrast with God, a theme which is taken up elsewhere: they have no power over life or death (e.g., Q 25:3), they cannot guide to truth (Q 10:35), or answer prayer (e.g., Q 13:14).

The aforementioned implicit comparisons between the idols and God amount to an argument from the absolute. Another example of this is provided by the following:

> They worship, besides God, that which can neither harm nor benefit them, and they say: "These are our intercessors with God." Say: "Are you informing God of something he doesn't know in the heavens or the earth? Glory be to Him! Far is He above the partners they ascribe to him!" (Q 10:18)

Sometimes this type of argument is used to reinforce arguments, but often, as here, it is felt to carry sufficient weight to stand alone.

The oft-repeated criticism of the pagans for preferring sons themselves while attributing daughters to God (a reference to three goddesses whom they considered to be the daughters of Allāh: al-Lāt, al-ʿUzzā, and Manāt), sheds light on certain aspects of the Qurʾānic argumentation. The very idea that God could have offspring is denied outright (e.g., Q 37:151–2). Yet sometimes the opponents' premises may be conceded for the sake of argument, in this case producing an implicit hypothetical argument: supposing He were to have offspring, it is unreasonable of you to attribute daughters to Him and sons to yourselves. After naming the three aforementioned goddesses, the Qurʾān continues: "For you the male and for Him the female? What an unfair division!" (Q 53:21–2), reflecting the general preference for sons which was prevalent in Arabia at the time. On a superficial reading at least, the Qurʾān appears to go along with this cultural preference, but other verses seem to contain an implicit criticism of the pagans on this matter: "When news is brought to one of them of the birth of a female child, his face darkens, and he is filled with gloom" (Q 16:58; cf. 43:17). The ascription of daughters to God is deemed even more inappropriate in view of the female being "one brought up among trinkets and unclear in dispute" (Q 43:18), no doubt a reference to the fact that females of the time were less versed in the art of debating than males. Here again the Qurʾānic argument is embedded in the local culture and appeals to its audience on their own grounds, accepting (at least for the sake of argument) some of their premises.

The apparent ambiguity over the status of the rival deities or partners ascribed to God provides another example of the Qurʾān's multi-pronged approach. Some verses depict the deities as conscious, living beings with the power of speech. They are portrayed, for example, as disowning their former followers on the day of judgment (e.g., Q 19:82; 10:28), and it is asserted that they have no power of intercession (e.g., Q 43:86). Other verses highlight their malignity: Abraham refers to them as "enemies" (Q 26:77), and it is stated that they will go to hell along with those who worshiped them (Q 37:22–3). Reference has already been made to verses citing their ineffectiveness and powerlessness as compared to God; they are also portrayed as having no feet, hands, eyes, or ears (Q 7:195), no doubt in order to emphasize their inferiority to human beings; the same passage describes them as "servants like you" (Q 7:194). All this still gives the impression that they are living beings of some kind. Elsewhere, however, the deities are described as "names you have invented, you and your forefathers, and for which God has sent down no authority" (Q 7:71; 12:40; 53:23); and their former worshipers are depicted on the day of judgment as realizing that what they worshiped was "nothing" (Q 40:74), giving the impression that the deities or partners have no objective reality.

A chronological view of the verses in question seems to show a progression in the portrayal of the deities in the direction of increasing powerlessness and ultimately non-existence (Welch 1980b: 739–43); this suggests a gradual, evolutionary approach which mirrors the Qurʾānic approach to legislation (e.g., the progressive restrictions on the use of alcohol). The aim would be to make the argument (or the law) more easily acceptable, on the basis that it is easier to take several small steps than one huge leap. It would be theoretically possible to reconcile these various statements by postulating that in some cases the deities were angels or *jinn*, both of which do exist in the Qurʾānic cosmology. On balance, however, it seems more likely that not all statements are intended as objective descriptions and that they serve a rhetorical purpose; the aim is not to instruct the pagans in theology but a much more concrete and practical one: that they should be convinced of the ineffectiveness and relative inferiority of their deities or idols so that they will cease to call on them and turn instead to God.

Sometimes the Qurʾān appeals to common sense or uses logical or quasi-logical arguments. A number of hypothetical arguments are of this type, for example those that draw an analogy between God's unity and earthly kingship, and point to the need for a single unified authority to ensure order: "If there were in them [the heavens and the earth] other gods besides God, there would be ruin in both" (Q 21:22; cf. 12:39). This argument is developed elsewhere: had there been other gods, "each god would have taken away what he had created, and each would have tried to overcome the others" (Q 23:91; cf. 17:42). The deductive reasoning in these verses leads to the conclusion that since the universe is not in chaos, it must have a single Lord. Elsewhere there is an appeal to the individual, along the lines that it is better to serve one master than many who are at variance with one another (Q 39:29).

The pagans do not seem to have any reasoned defense of polytheism (with the possible exception of the appeal to God's will as in Q 6:148 – see next paragraph), but merely repeat that they are following the way of their forefathers. They even concede the argument at times, their appeal to the forefathers sounding decidedly lame; when asked concerning their idols: "Do they hear you when you call, or do you good or harm?", Abraham's contemporaries are depicted as replying: "No, but we found our forefathers doing that" (Q 26:72–4; cf. 21:53).

Not infrequently there is an *ad hominem* element to the arguments employed against Muḥammad's opponents. The pagans are depicted as fickle and irrational: when they are lost at sea, they call upon God, but when they are safe on dry land they revert to their idols (Q 29:65; cf. 6:63–4; 17:67). The attribution of daughters to God and sons to themselves is further evidence of their inconsistency and unreasonableness, while their insistence on sticking to the ways of their forefathers makes them appear stubborn and mindlessly conservative. One particular argument employed by the pagans is simply condemned as false and baseless, while the pagans themselves are depicted as dishonest and disingenuous:

> Those who ascribe partners to God will say: "If God had willed, we would not have ascribed partners to him nor would our forefathers. . . ." In this way their ancestors denied the truth, until they tasted our wrath. Say: "Have you any knowledge? If so, produce it for us. You follow nothing but conjecture; you do nothing but lie." (Q 6:148; cf. 16:35; 43:20).

Elsewhere the pagans are simply called "liars" (e.g., Q 37:152).

The tone of the Qurʾān on the subject of the "partners" ascribed to God is often cajoling or challenging, with frequent rhetorical questions and imperatives: "Do they have feet to walk with or hands to strike with, or eyes to see with or ears to hear with? Say: 'Call upon your partners and scheme against me, and give me no respite!' " (Q 7:195). At other times the tone is heavy with irony, if not sarcasm:

> Those on whom you call besides God cannot create a fly, even if they were to all collaborate, and if the fly should take something away from them they would have no power to get it back. (Q 22:73)
>
> Or do they ascribe to God partners who have created as He has created, so that the creation seemed to them similar? Say: "God is the Creator of all things." (Q 13:16)

It was not just the pagans who were guilty of associating partners with God; the Muslims also came into contact with Christians, some of whose beliefs were felt to violate the divine unity. Christian doctrines such as the sonship of Jesus, which are seen as detracting from God's unity, are given fairly short shrift. It should be mentioned here that although some of the arguments against God having a son were probably originally directed at pagans, they were subsequently used in anti-Christian polemic. The rhetorical question: "How can He have a son when He has no spouse?" (Q 6:101) provides a good illustration of the Qurʾān's preference for the concrete over the abstract. Elsewhere Muḥammad is told to say: "If the Most Merciful had a son, I'd be the first to worship him" (Q 43:81); if we add the implied conclusion: I am not worshiping him, therefore the Most Merciful does not have a son, this is recognizable as a form of argument acknowledged as valid by logicians (denying the consequent, or *modus tollens*). Attributing a son to God is portrayed as not only baseless ("a mere saying from their mouth") but also an unthinking imitation of the unbelievers of old (Q 9:30, which interestingly attributes this characteristic not just to Christians but also to Jews). As is frequently the case, the argument from the absolute is much in evidence: "Far be it from Him to have a son!" (Q 4:171; cf. 2:116).

On the subject of Jesus' alleged divinity, the Qurʾān states that he and his mother "used to eat food" (Q 5:75), an argument which, like the consort argument mentioned above, would be unlikely to appeal to Christians, almost none of whom have denied the fact of Jesus' humanity. Yet from the point of view of Islamic belief, which holds humanity and divinity to be mutually exclusive, the argument is conclusive. One verse (Q 3:59) refutes the idea that Jesus' creation through extraordinary means (the virgin birth is acknowledged in the Qurʾān) constitutes evidence of his suprahuman status, by pointing out the parallel with Adam, who also came into being without a human father. Unlike the previous argument, this one is based on premises accepted by Christians; however, it only establishes the possibility as opposed to the necessity of the non-divinity of Jesus, and Christians have other premises on which they base the argument for Jesus' divinity. As far as the Trinity is concerned, scholars have differed as to whether the Qur'ān refutes the Trinity as such or a perversion of it that may have been current in Muḥammad's day (Zebiri 1997: 17). Whatever the case, the portrayal of Christian belief by the words: "God is the third of three" (Q 5:73) may well be polemical (and thus a straw man) rather than an accurate portrayal of what Muḥammad's contemporaries actually believed. As usual the Qur'ān is less concerned with theological niceties than with making the point that Trinitarian belief (probably of any variety) is incompatible with God's majesty and pre-eminence.

Authenticity of Muḥammad's Prophethood

This is possibly the richest of the three chosen themes in terms of argument and counter-argument due to the multiplicity of accusations and challenges that were directed at Muḥammad by his adversaries. Here it should be noted that the stories of past prophets (material which accounts for approximately one quarter of the Qur'ān) are pertinent; although these stories ostensibly refer to events in the distant past, the arguments which took place between former prophets and their peoples are very much an integrated part of the Qur'ānic discourse and are usually of direct relevance to Muḥammad's own situation (see, e.g., Robinson 1996: 156).

Muḥammad seems to have been bombarded with accusations, particularly in Mecca but also in the early Medinan phase: that, far from being a prophet, he was a poet, a sorcerer, a soothsayer, or he was mad or possessed by *jinn* (see respectively Q 52:30; 43:30; 69:42; 23:25). As for the revelation, it was a forgery, and nothing but old stories or fairy tales, or confused dreams (see respectively Q 42:24; 25:5; 21:5). Muḥammad was also accused of having human informants who dictated or taught this material to him (Q 16:103; 25:4–5).

The replies to these accusations often take the form of simple denials, or affirmations of Muḥammad's true status. Some of the earliest responses incorporate oaths: "I swear by what you see and by what you do not see, truly this is the word of a noble messenger, it is not the word of a poet . . . nor is it the word of a soothsayer . . . but a message sent down from the Lord of the worlds" (Q 69:38–43). Alternatively, there may be counteraccusations: "In truth it is they who have put forward an iniquity and a falsehood" (Q 25:4), condemnation: "They have gone astray, and they will never be able to find a way!" (Q 25:9), or threats, such as the frequent reminders of the destruction that was visited on unbelievers of old (e.g., Q 21:6).

Some of the opponents' arguments are more personal, or *ad hominem*: Muḥammad's relative lack of social status is held against him ("Why was this Qur'ān not sent down on some important man from the two cities [i.e. Mecca and Medina]?" Q 43:31). Similar charges were made against former prophets: Moses was impugned for being unclear of speech (Q 43:52), and for being from a dispossessed minority (Q 23:47), and the objection of Noah's opponents, that his followers were from the lowest strata of society (Q 11:27), could easily have been directed against Muḥammad. The Qur'ān counters by appealing to Muḥammad's good character, as where he is instructed to say:

"A whole lifetime before this have I been among you: will you not then understand?" (Q 10:16).

One of the common objections both to Muḥammad and to former prophets was the fact of his humanity; the Qurʾān portrays the unbelievers as asking: "Is this more than a man like yourselves?" (Q 21:3), or: "What sort of messenger is this, who eats food, and walks about in the market places?" (Q 25:7). Muḥammad, for his part, is instructed at various times to say: "I am only a human being like you" (Q 18:110, 41:6), or "I don't say that I have treasures, nor do I claim to know the unseen, or that I'm an angel. I only follow what is revealed to me" (Q 6:50; cf. 11:31). The Qurʾān points out that the same objection was raised with former prophets, who replied: "We are only human like you . . . we come with no authority save by the leave of God" (Q 14:11). In effect, the opponents' arguments are undermined by the fact that Muḥammad never claims to be more than a human being. In similar vein the unbelievers ask why an angel is not sent down, presumably with the revelation (e.g., Q 6:8; 25:7), to which the Qurʾān gives a commonsense reply: that an angel would be sent only if the message were directed at angels (Q 17:95), or that an angel would have been sent in the form of a man anyway (Q 6:9) – presumably in order to be visible and comprehensible to humans.

In the late Meccan and early Medinan periods in particular, Muḥammad's detractors repeatedly ask for a miracle or "sign" to substantiate his prophetic status. One extended passage gives a flavor of these demands:

> They say: "We shall not believe in you until you make a spring gush forth for us out of the earth, or until you have a garden of date trees and vines, and cause rivers to gush forth in their midst, or you cause the sky to fall in pieces . . . or you bring God and the angels before us face to face, or you have a house made of gold, or you rise up into the sky, and we won't believe in your ascension until you send down to us a book that we can read." [To this, Muḥammad is told to reply:] "Glory be to my Lord! Am I anything but a man, a messenger?" (Q 17:90–3).

As with the fact of Muḥammad's humanity, his opponents' arguments are met with a simple disclaimer or disavowal.

The Qurʾān describes a number of supernatural events in connection with past prophets, and both Jesus and Moses are depicted as performing miracles in the Qurʾān (e.g., Q 3:49; 7:107–8), although it is made clear that this was only with God's permission (Q 13:38). While the Qurʾān is clear that God is able to do all things, it seems that He declines to effect miracles through Muḥammad for various reasons: because the opponents still would not believe (e.g., Q 6:7; 6:109; 54:2); because their punishment would be hastened if they still disbelieved after receiving such a sign (Q 6:8); in order to emphasize Muḥammad's human status (e.g., Q 17:93); and because the Qurʾān should be sufficient for them – in fact, it is hinted that the Qurʾān itself is such a sign (Q 29:50–1). Muslims have traditionally linked the latter theme with the phenomenon of the "challenge" contained in several Qurʾānic passages (e.g., Q 2:23–4; 10:38) which call on Muḥammad's critics to produce something comparable to the Qurʾān. Their apparent failure to do so has been taken as evidence of the Qurʾān's miraculous nature, or inimitability (*iʿjāz*).

One aspect of the Qur'ānic discourse which emerges particularly clearly in this context is the triangular dynamic between God, Muḥammad and the unbelievers. This illustrates the fluidity and multivocality of the Qur'ān; although God is the ostensible author throughout, there are frequent shifts in operative voice and addressee. Often, particularly in the Meccan revelations, God addresses Muḥammad, sometimes offering reassurance: "You are not, by the grace of your Lord, a soothsayer, nor are you possessed" (Q 52:29; cf. 68:2). At other times He seems to admonish Muḥammad: "If their rejection is difficult for you, if you can, seek to make a tunnel in the earth or a ladder to the sky and bring them a sign. If God willed, he could bring them together to guidance; so be not among the ignorant" (Q 6:35).

On the occasions when God tells Muḥammad what to say, sometimes the recommended speech or dictum takes the form of a disclaimer: "Say: 'If I've forged it, I'll pay for my crime; but I'm innocent of the crimes you commit' " (Q 11:35). God is to be called upon as witness or arbiter: "Say: 'If I had forged it, you would have no power to help me against God . . . He is sufficient as a witness between me and you' " (Q 46:8). When the pagans ask Muḥammad to change the revelation, he is instructed to say: "If I disobey God, I fear the punishment of a great day" (Q 10:15). The frequent references to the possibility of Muḥammad's punishment have a certain persuasive effect which is brought out more clearly in another Qur'ānic passage. A secret believer seeks to persuade Pharaoh to believe in Moses by pointing out that he has nothing to lose and something to gain by so doing: if Moses is lying, then he bears the responsibility for (and presumably will suffer the consequences of) his own lie, but if he is telling the truth, then Pharaoh can expect to be punished himself if he disbelieves it (Q 40:28). This sets up what the classical logicians called a false dilemma (reducing the options to two, diametrically opposed alternatives): either Muḥammad will be punished or his adversaries will be.

Not infrequently the unbelievers are addressed directly, and Muḥammad is spoken of in the third person: "Your companion is neither astray nor deluded; nor does he speak from his own desire" (Q 53:2–3). In what seems to be a paradoxical twist, in the face of the unbelievers' accusations the threat occasionally appears to be directed at Muḥammad rather than at the unbelievers: "Had he invented against us any sayings, we would have seized him by the right hand, then we would have cut his life-vein and none of you could have defended him" (Q 69:44–7). This powerful image constitutes an appeal to force, engaging the emotions rather than the rational faculties. Yet the argument is not ineffective: the fact that Muḥammad remains unharmed is a silent testimony to his authenticity.

The effect of these rhetorical elements is quite striking. A dramatic tension is set up between the various parties – in this case God, Muḥammad and the unbelievers, which has the effect of presenting God as a real presence and an effective actor. He appears in many guises/roles: as comforter and supporter of Muḥammad; as witness and arbiter; as admonisher of Muḥammad; and, perhaps most often, as potential chastiser of Muḥammad's opponents. The objectification of Muḥammad when he is spoken of in the third person conveys a sense of detachment and objectivity, enhancing Muḥammad's credibility as conveyor of a transcendent message. The dissociation between God and Muḥammad has the same effect, as do the frequent disclaimers which in effect refer the detractors to a higher authority. Interestingly this dissociation becomes much less marked in the later Medinan years, when Muḥammad becomes more powerful; for example, in that phase the Qurʾān frequently exhorts people to obey or believe in both God and His messenger (Welch 1983: 38).

Resurrection

One element of the new message seems to have drawn much scorn from the Meccan pagans, namely the idea of the final reckoning in general and bodily resurrection in particular. They especially focused on the latter which they found quite incredible; there are literally dozens of verses devoted to this subject, with the pagans expressing their objections and the Qurʾān often furnishing a reply.

The incredulity of the Meccans is often graphically depicted, focusing on the physical aspects: "Who will make these bones live when they're decayed?" (Q 36:78). "What! When we die and become dust and bones will we be raised up again, and also our forefathers?" (Q 37:16–17). At other times they are more philosophical: "There is only our life in this world . . . nothing but time can destroy us" (Q 45:24). The Qurʾānic replies to the pagan objections combine various elements: appeals to reason, arguments from nature, assertive affirmations, appeals to God's power, impugning the opposition, and threats.

By far the most common response in the Qurʾān is that since God was able to create the earth and all that is in it in the first place, then he must have the power to recreate it if He so desires. This constitutes an *a fortiori* argument to the effect that if God can create something out of nothing, then it should be even easier for Him to create something out of something. This would be a particularly effective argument given that the pagans seem to have believed that God (i.e. Allāh) was in fact the creator (see, e.g., Q 29:61). The following is a characteristically eloquent passage:

> O people! If you are in doubt concerning the resurrection, consider that We created you out of dust, then out of a drop of fluid, then out of a clot, then out of a piece of flesh, partly formed and partly unformed. (Q 22:5)

The many passages in the Qurʾān which draw attention to the marvels of nature often come in connection with this theme (e.g., Q 50:3–11). At times there is a lyrical, rhythmical quality which comes across even in translation: "Out of it [the earth] We created you and into it We shall make you return and from it We will bring you out another time" (Q 20:55; cf. 71:17–18); despite the fact that technically speaking this amounts to nothing more than an assertion, the cyclical element conveys a sense of inevitability which is highly persuasive.

Added force is given to the argument when God insists that the initial act of creation did not tire Him: "Were we wearied by the first creation? Yet they are in doubt about a new creation" (Q 50:15; cf. 46:33). Furthermore, it is implied that the second creation is even easier than the first (Q 29:19; 30:27), and one verse which responds to the pagans' incredulity makes the *a fortiori* argument even more explicit: "Say: 'Even if you were stones or iron, or any created matter which in your minds is hard [to be raised up]' " (Q 17:50–1). As is common in the Qur'ān, it is left to the listener to complete the thought; letting the opponent draw his or her own conclusions can be quite an effective strategy in argument.

It is not only the physical act of resurrection which the pagans find unbelievable but also the final reckoning which is promised, or threatened, in the Qur'ān. The two themes – resurrection and accountability – are closely related. Since the resurrection is a prerequisite for the accounting in the Qur'ānic order, to argue for the accounting is in effect to argue for the resurrection. The Qur'ān contains many future projections of dramatic eschatological scenes, and in some of them there is reference to the first-second creation topos, as where God addresses the assembled ranks of the resurrected: "You have come to Us as We created you the first time, though you claimed that We had not made this appointment with you" (Q 18:48; cf. 6:94). Other verses simply allude to the purposiveness of the creation as an argument in support of the resurrection: "Did you think We had created you in vain and that you would not be returned to Us?" (Q 23:115; cf. 75:36).

Apart from their incredulity the pagans do not bring forth any serious arguments against the resurrection, but place the burden of proof on Muḥammad. The Qur'ān is not impressed by their arguments: "And when our clear signs are related to them, their only argument is: 'Bring back our forefathers, if you are telling the truth!' " (Q 45:25; cf. 44:36). The Qur'ān's reply to this challenge is a simple but powerful assertion: "Say: 'It is God who gives you life, then causes you to die; then He will gather you together for the day of resurrection about which there is no doubt,' but most people do not know" (Q 45:26). Frequently the Qur'ān simply dismisses Muḥammad's adversaries with a laconic phrase such as: "They have no knowledge of that, they are only guessing" (Q 45:24).

The Qur'ān often urges its listeners to test its claims through their own observation, as in the arguments from nature. For example, an analogy is made between resurrection and the quickening or revivification of the earth by the rain:

> You see the earth lifeless, but when We pour down rain on it, it is stirred to life, it swells, and it produces every kind of beautiful growth . . . It is He who gives life to the dead, and it is He who has power over all things." (Q 22:5–6; cf. 30:50)

While such verses appear to constitute an appeal to empirical evidence, they are perhaps more accurately to be understood as metaphors; the same could be said of some of the many verses beginning: "Travel through the land and see. . . ." One passage draws attention to the way in which nature is constantly renewed:

> Do they not see how God originates creation, then repeats it; truly that is easy for God. Say: "Travel through the land and see how He originated creation; so will God produce a later creation, for God has power over all things." (Q 29:19–20)

More generally, however, the command to "travel through the land and see" is part of an appeal to force, alluding to the fate that awaits the pagans if they continue to disbelieve in the message that is being conveyed to them. In these cases the intention presumably is indeed to cite empirical evidence (thus constituting an argument from demonstration), for the unbelievers are being asked to witness the ruins of the towns and cities of peoples who were destroyed in the past for their disobedience and recalcitrance (e.g., Q 27:67–9; such passages are often warning against unbelief in general rather than disbelief in the resurrection in particular). It is frequently pointed out that those earlier nations were more powerful than the Meccans (e.g., Q 19:74; 44:37; 50:36), constituting an *a fortiori* argument to the effect that if God could destroy them, it would be even easier for Him to destroy the Meccans.

Threats are a prominent element of the Qurʾānic rhetoric, and are much in evidence on this subject. When the Meccans ask: "When will this promise come true?" the succinct reply is: "They'll only have to wait for a single blast!" (Q 36:48–9). In one passage the person who expresses incredulity about being raised up is quickly and graphically reminded of the punishment of hell (Q 19:66–71); in another a doubter asks rhetorically: "Shall we be raised up, and also our forefathers?", and Muḥammad is told to retort: "Yes, and you will be humiliated!" (Q 37:16–18).

Ultimately, God is able to do anything, and the theme of God's power is closely interwoven with arguments for the resurrection: "If He wills, He can remove you all and replace you with a new creation" (Q 14:19; 35:16). In reply to the question: "Who can give life to decayed bones?" (Q 36:78), the Qurʾān answers with a passage referring to the first creation and to God's power to produce fire from trees, and concludes: "Indeed when He intends a thing He only has to say 'Be' and it is! So glory be to Him in whose hands is the dominion of all things; and to Him you will all be returned" (Q 36:82–3). In a sense, the resurrection is the ultimate manifestation of God's power in nature.

Conclusion

It is clear that the Qurʾān has a rich repertoire of forms and types of argument, though the preference for the concrete and the practical over the abstract and the theoretical is everywhere in evidence. Generally speaking the Qurʾānic argumentation falls within the domain of rhetoric and persuasion rather than strict logic (although it does contain some logical arguments, as we have seen). Aristotle himself acknowledged the limitations of rational discourse, and maintained that effective communication required not just an ability to argue logically but also an understanding of human character and emotions (Edmondson 1984: 18, fn. 47). The Qurʾānic arguments are enhanced by many elements which are not considered valid in terms of pure logic, such as appeals to emotion and the appeal to the absolute. One would not expect it to be otherwise in a book which speaks in the natural language of everyday speech, the more so when we consider that this is scripture. In a religious context, one could argue that an appeal to the heart is as important as the appeal to the mind, if not more so.

If persuasion is much more than a matter of mere logic, one needs to go beyond logic in order to fully appreciate the Qurʾānic argumentation, and one needs to acknowledge that what the Qurʾān says is inseparable from how it says it. For example, when reporting the arguments of its opponents, the Qurʾān may simultaneously discredit those opponents by (sometimes quite casually) referring to them as "wrongdoers" (Q 21:3) or "liars" (Q 37:152). The subtle psychological nuances can easily be missed. For example, the accusation of forgery at one time brings the response: "If God wills, He will seal up your [i.e. Muḥammad's] heart" (Q 42:24). The listener's attention is thus drawn to the possible cessation of revelation while the underlying implication that the revelation comes from God may go unnoticed, and so be the more readily accepted. Such methods, where the argumentation operates on a subliminal level, may well be a match for those contained in contemporary manuals on the art of persuasion. Muslims have long held the view that the Qurʾān is composed with a supreme eloquence in order to convey its message in the most effective possible way, and that therein lies its inimitability; the persuasive elements which are described here could easily be seen as one aspect of this (in fact the classical commentators, such as al-Zamakhsharī [d. 538/1144], did occasionally draw attention to the Qurʾān's psychological appeal).

More fundamentally, it has been suggested that the Qurʾān as a whole purveys a worldview which, in its consistency and eloquence, is quite compelling. Once the listener begins to enter into that worldview, he or she is inducted into a "thought system" which on its own terms makes perfect sense and whose various elements can be easily accepted (Waardenburg 1980: 631; the Qurʾān's gradualist approach, sometimes conceding its opponents' premises or meeting them on their own ground, would certainly help the process of induction). This may help to account for the efficacy of certain arguments even when they may appear unconvincing to unbelievers, based as they are on premises which are not yet fully accepted by them.

The arguments in the Qurʾān are overwhelmingly between the forces of good (God, Muḥammad, believers, past prophets) and the forces that – at least for the time being – set themselves up in opposition to God and His messengers (there are exceptions: at times the believers and even Muḥammad himself are the target of God's arguments). Interestingly, one often finds the same types of argument on both sides: both God and the pagans resort to *ad hominem* arguments, and periodically issue challenges. Thus accusations of lying abound on both sides, and the opponents' challenges to Muḥammad to hasten their punishment or bring back their forefathers are mirrored in the Qurʾān's challenges to them to produce a comparable piece of scripture, or to produce proof of what they say. While Muḥammad cites God's will in his arguments (e.g., Q 10:16), his adversaries do the same (e.g., Q 6:148), albeit with questionable sincerity.

However, certain types of argument apply only to the divine – the argument from the absolute being an obvious example, which may be broadly seen as incorporating assertive affirmations and denials, appeals to force, future projections (mainly of eschatological scenes) as well as any other elements requiring omniscience (such as revealing the secret thoughts of the opponents). Such arguments may seem like preaching to the converted, to those who are already convinced of God's omnipotence, and indeed they may be partly aimed at wavering or newly converted Muslims; but bearing in mind the pagans' belief in a High God called Allāh, such verses might well have a cumulative effect in reinforcing His pre-eminence. Jews and Christians, of course, already believed in a pre-eminent God, so they could be appealed to on the basis of this common ground.

Since the lines between the two opposing camps are often so clearly drawn, there is never any doubt as to the right and wrong of any argument. When it comes to argumentative techniques the arsenal available to God seems to outweigh that of Muḥammad's detractors, and an argument between two sides where one side knows the secret thoughts of the other is of course an unequal encounter. It would be fair to say that the more persuasive arguments in terms of reasoning as well as expression are those which issue from God, and the opponents' arguments often appear rather lame by comparison (although interestingly, they appear to be rather more inventive in impugning Muḥammad than on the more strictly doctrinal issues of the unity of God and the resurrection). Finally, there is no doubt as to who will eventually prevail, and who has the last word. The Qur'ān warns the listener that all disputes will be settled in the hereafter when God will decide between the contenders: "He will certainly make clear to you on the day of resurrection those things about which you disagreed" (Q 16:92).

Further reading

Jomier, J. (1959) *Bible et Coran*. Cerf, Paris.

Jomier, J. (1996) *Dieu et l'homme dans le Coran*. Cerf, Paris.

McAuliffe, J. D. (2001) Debate and disputation. In: McAuliffe, Jane Dammen (ed.) *Encyclopaedia of the Qur'ān*. Brill, Leiden, vol. I, pp. 511–14.

Scholler, M. (2003) Opposition to Muḥammad. In: McAuliffe, Jane Dammen (ed.) *Encyclopaedia of the Qur'ān*. Brill, Leiden, vol. III, pp. 576–80.

Waardenburg, J. (1972) Un débat Coranique contre les polythéistes. *Ex Orbe Religionum: Studia Geo Widengren*. E. J. Brill, Leiden, pp. 143–54.

Welch, A. (2000) Formulaic features of the punishment-stories. In: Boullata, Issa J. (ed.) *Literary Structures of Religious Meaning in the Qur'ān*. Curzon, Richmond, pp. 77–116.

Zebiri, K. (2003) Towards a rhetorical criticism of the Qur'ān. *Journal of Qur'anic Studies* 5, 95–120.

CHAPTER 18

Knowing and Thinking

A. H. Mathias Zahniser

Embossed in beautiful Arabic calligraphy on the glass doorway to the Cambridge University Divinity School, among quotations from others of the world's scriptures in their languages of revelation, is the Qur'ānic phrase, *wa-fawqa kull dhī ʿilm ʿalīm*, "and above every possessor of knowledge is a knower" (Q 12:76). Popular and classical commentators agree on the verse's meaning, "Above every creature who knows, there is someone more knowledgeable – until you end up at God" (e.g., al-Maḥallī and al-Suyūṭī 1952). In other words, God is the ultimate knower.

Divine and Human Knowledge in the Qur'ān

Franz Rosenthal (1970: 1–2), in a detailed discussion of the Qur'ānic root *ʿ-l-m*, concludes that "no other concept," not even *tawḥīd* or *dīn*, "has been operative as a determinant of Muslim civilization in all its aspects to the same extent as *ʿilm*." Words for knowledge from this root make up one percent of the words in the Qur'ān. Except for words from the roots *k-w-n*, "being," and *q-w-l*, "saying," the only words occurring more times than words for knowledge from the root *ʿ-l-m*, are *Allāh* and *Rabb*.

Divine Knowing and Teaching

ʿAlīm, meaning, "a knower," "a learned one," "a sage," occurs 161 times in the singular. In all but eight of these God is the *ʿalīm* referred to. The exceptions include Moses, according to Pharaoh's leaders (Q 7:109; 26:34); Pharaoh's sorcerers (Q 7:112; 10:79); Joseph (Q 12:55); and the unborn son of Abraham (Q 15:53; 51:28). With the exception of Abraham's son, designated *ʿalīm* by angelic prophesy, all these "knowers" have been able to do something supernatural. The plural, *ʿulamāʾ*, occurs twice:

Q 26:197 refers to "the learned of the Children of Israel," and Q 35:28 says, "Those among His servants who have knowledge fear Allāh."

God as Knower

Overwhelmingly, however, that is in 94 percent of its occurrences, the Qur'ān uses *ʿalīm* for God. Furthermore, all of the occurrences of *ʿalīm* in reference to God occur in the rhyme phrase of a verse. Angelika Neuwirth (1980: 148–52) and Neal Robinson (1996: 200–1) have demonstrated the significance of these rhyme phrases for the impact of the Qur'ān on its receptors. Rhyme phrases reinforce the content of the verse or verse groups that they climax, provide motivation for adopting the truth or duty that their verses or verse groups advocate, and reinforce the worldview of the Qur'ān in general. The rhyme phrases containing epithets of God as Knower reinforce the Qur'ānic emphasis on God as the source of true knowledge.

The divine name *ʿalīm* occurs in rhyme phrases 154 times. In a little more than half of these, it occurs in tandem with another name, sometimes also related to knowing. Other divine names, such as Hearer (47 times), Seer (42 times), Witness (16 times), and Well-informed (44 times), also occur in rhyme phrases and relate closely to Knower. According to Robinson (1996: 200), who arranges the divine names in clusters around seven divine attributes, the names clustered around God as omniscient occur 394 times. Omnipotence, the next most numerous cluster, has 133 occurrences. These rhyme phrases powerfully reinforce the Qur'ānic emphasis on God as Knower. For example, an elaborate analogy for God, called the "verse of light," climaxes with these statements: "Light upon light! Allāh guides whom He will to His light. Allāh creates parables for humankind. In everything Allāh is Knower" (Q 24:35).

All of the names of God related to knowing are either words that have to do with God's perception, for example, Seer or Hearer, or words that express the intensity and quality of God's knowledge, such as Well-informed or Wise. The many words for the processes of human knowing that we will examine below are not involved in divine knowing. God simply perceives with perfect perception and knows with depth and comprehensiveness. He does not come to knowledge; He knows. God possesses "Complete and Absolute Knowledge" (Choudhury 2001: 94), although He does not possess knowledge of all future human acts so as to determine them (Rahbar 1960: 53–66). Humans, in contrast, must consider, reflect, remember, and come to understand. Yet both divine and human knowing can be described by words from the root *ʿ-l-m*.

In 298 verses, the Qur'ān uses a word from the root *ʿ-l-m* for God's knowledge or knowing. A significant verse for God's nature and knowledge is Q 2:255:

> Allāh! There is no god but He, the Living, the Self-subsisting. No slumber can seize Him nor sleep. His are all things in the heavens and on earth. Who is there that can intercede in His presence save by His permission? He knows what lies before and after them [unbelievers]. Nor shall they encompass any of His knowledge except as He wills.

The knowledge of God is fleshed out in many verses of the Qur'ān: God knows well what people do and what they do not do (Q 16:28); what they do openly and what they do in secret (Q 2:33); when they move about and when they stay at home (Q 47:19); what the righteous do, what the unrighteous do, and who the hypocrites are (Q 29:3, 11). God knows who have gone astray and who are rightly guided, who bring right guidance and who lead others astray (Q 28:85); and, on the basis of knowledge, God leads some astray (Q 45:23). God knows the interpretation of the scripture and the interpretation of dreams (Q 3:7; 12:101). God knows all that is in heaven and on earth – including the mysteries of both – and what has been recorded (Q 22:70; 25:6). God knows the processes of non-human life (Q 34:2; 57:4). He knows the hour of judgment and its rewards and punishments (Q 7:187; 31:34). God neither errs nor forgets and at the Judgment "will tell you everything you ever did" (Q 39:7). The Qur'ān assures receptors that God knows even their doubts and misgivings: "We have created humankind, and We know what dark suggestions his soul makes to him, for We are nearer to him than the jugular vein" (Q 50:16).

Muḥammad is also assured that God's comprehensive and intimate knowledge extends to the secrets held among people. "No three persons consult secretly but He is the fourth among them, nor between five but He makes the sixth. . . . Then, on the day of judgment, He will tell them the truth of their conduct. Allāh in all things is Knower" (Q 58:7). God's knowing not only inspires respect for the judgment, designed to lead to amendment of life; it also offers comfort for the living of life:

> Allāh determines the measure of night and day. Knowing you are unable to calculate it, He has relented towards you. Read, therefore, of the Qur'ān as much as may be easy for you. He knows some of you will be sick, others traveling through the land, seeking Allāh's bounty, and others fighting in Allāh's cause. . . . (Q 73:20)

The intimacy of God's knowledge extends to the fall of a leaf or the birth of a child: "Not a leaf falls without His knowledge" (Q 6:59); "Allāh created you from dust; then from a sperm-drop; then He made you in pairs. No female conceives, or gives birth, without His knowledge" (Q 35:11; 41:47).

Does God learn? One who is omniscient could hardly learn or be taught: "What! will you teach Allāh about your religion, when Allāh *knows* all that is in the heavens and the earth?" (Q 49:16). Some verses, however, lead one to believe God learns: "What you suffered on the day the two armies met, was by Allāh's permission, in order that He might know the believers" (Q 3:166). God roused the men who had slept sealed in a cave for a very long time "in order to *know* which of the two parties best accounted for the period they had stayed" in the cave (Q 18:12). It is God who would know the best of the two parties and not the parties themselves. Similar passages include Q 3:140, 5:94, 34:21 and 57:25. Commentators consistently deny that God learns; A. Yusuf Ali (1997: 167, n. 467) comments on Q 3:154 where the word "test" is explicit, "Testing by Allāh is not in order that it may add to His knowledge, for He knows all. It is in order to help us subjectively, to mould our will, and purge us of any grosser motives, that will be searched out by calamity." If God as learner can be questioned, God as teacher cannot.

God as Teacher

At least forty-one verses indicate God teaches. One of the clearest has God teaching humans so they can teach their domestic animals. Muḥammad is told to say, "All clean things are lawful for you and what trained hunting animals take for you, as you have taught them from what Allāh taught you" (Q 5:4). God teaches knowledge (Q 18:65–6), the Qur'ān, and self-expression (Q 55:1–4).

God taught Adam as well as the angels. "And He taught Adam the names of all things; then placed them before the angels, and said: 'Tell Me the names of these if you are truthful.' They said: 'Glory to You! We have no knowledge except what You have taught us. Truly You are the Wise Knower' " (Q 2:31–2).

The Qur'ān has God teaching Lot (Q 21:74), Joseph (Q 12: 21, 101), Moses (Q 28:14), al-Khiḍr (according to the commentaries) (Q 18:65), David (Q 2:251), Solomon (Q 21:79), Jesus (Q 3:48), and Muḥammad (Q 4:113). God taught scribes to write (Q 2:282). The Qur'ān mentions those who were given knowledge (*ūtū 'l-ʿilm*) and have come to believe (Q 17:107; 22:54).

While only words from the root *ʿ-l-m* are used for divine knowing, divine "teaching" can be expressed by other roots: *adrā*, "to make known" (Q 10:16); *ʿarrafa*, "cause to recognize" (Q 66:3); *faṣṣala*, "to explain in detail" (Q 6:126); *fahhama*, "to cause to understand" (Q 21:79); and *amadda*, "to bestow" (Q 26:132). One could even justify adding to the list *ḍaraba*, "to formulate [a parable]" (Q 24:35) and *hadā* "to guide" (Q 4:175).

The thoroughness of the Qur'ānic depiction of divine knowing and teaching should prepare us for discovering that humans learn by sharing in what God knows. When we turn to what the Qur'ān has to say about human knowing, however, we find a rich vocabulary describing the processes of human learning from perception to cognition to understanding, and finally, coming full circle again, to knowledge (*ʿilm*).

Human Knowing as Perception, Cognition, and Understanding

Human thinking, reflecting, perceiving, and evaluating take place, according to the Qur'ān, in the *qalb*, the *lubb* (found only in the plural), the *ṣadr*, the *fu'ād*, and the *nafs* – all of which have been translated "heart" by standard English translations. In accordance with normative Semitic culture, the heart is "the organ of perception and understanding" (Kermani 2002: 547), and so these terms sometimes get translated "mind" (e.g., A. Yusuf Ali 1997 on Q 20:67 and 26:194). The Qur'ān never uses the word *ʿaql*, "reason, comprehension, mind, intellect." As we shall see, however, the basic verb from the same root is very fruitful for representing a dimension of human knowing.

Daniel Madigan (2001: 149–50) charts out the Qur'ān's "extraordinarily varied vocabulary" related to knowledge. He includes in a table "all those words to do with perception, knowledge, understanding, clarity, and truth," as well as their antonyms, such as, "doubt, argument, ignorance, and forgetfulness." Of the thirty words in his positive list, only sixteen receive attention in this chapter. Of his eighteen antonyms, we deal with only two, *ẓanna*, "to surmise," and *zaʿma*, "to claim."

The Qur'ān features no systematic discussion of human knowing. A grasp of its view of the subject, therefore, requires careful and thorough contextual study of its rich vocabulary. The categories established in this study – supposition, perception, cognition, and knowing – are for heuristic purposes only and do not imply that the Qur'ān itself conforms to these categories. I begin with supposition and assertion.

Supposition and Assertion

Words from the root *ẓ-n-n* normally refer to "supposition": a thought or surmise that originates with the person thinking. "Supposition" may have a positive meaning in some contexts. For example, a divorced couple wishing to remarry may do so after the woman has been remarried and divorced, as long as they both "suppose" they can keep God's laws (Q 2:230). Such thoughts or convictions originating from the person, however, normally turn out to be wrong. For example, those who give female names to angels "have no knowledge (*ʿilm*) about it. They follow only supposition and supposition cannot replace the truth" (Q 53:28).

The root *ḥ-s-b*, meaning "to consider, have an opinion, reckon, or imagine" also originates from persons in a similar way. For example, the community at Medina spread rumors about something they had no knowledge (*ʿilm*) of, considering it "a light matter, while it was most serious in the sight of Allāh" (Q 24:15). With one possible exception (Q 18:9), all forty-eight occurrences of this root refer to erroneous considerations or imaginings.

Words from the root *z-ʿ-m* refer to claims or assertions originating from persons. For example, the Qur'ān reveals that on the day of judgment God will ask those who believed in more than one God, "Where are the partners you asserted?" (Q 6:22). All fifteen occurrences refer to erroneous assertions. We turn now to a set of words for perception, another dimension of human knowing.

Perception: Seeing, Hearing, Awareness, and Recognition

Words from the roots *b-ṣ-r* and *s-m-ʿ* refer to seeing and hearing, obvious dimensions of perception. Most of the many instances of these sensory words are literal, but many are figurative and refer to openness to the truth of what is heard or – with a negative modifier – dismissal of that truth. Just as God may grant knowledge to humans, so also God may veil the seeing and hearing of individuals, preventing them from grasping the truth (Q 2:7; 6:25).

Two other roots, *sh-ʿ-r* and *ʿ-r-f*, move from seeing and hearing in the direction of knowing, but with the nuances of "awareness" and "recognition." Eliminating words from the root *sh-ʿ-r* that do not relate to knowing, we find twenty-seven occurrences. All but two are negative. That is, they refer to the subjects as unaware of something. An obvious example comes from the narrative where Moses' sister watches him from a distance while the Egyptians are unaware (Q 28:11). At least fourteen times unbelievers are unaware of what awaits them in the next life (e.g., Q 16:21, 26, 45). The root

ʿ-*r-f* carries with it the connotation of "recognition," especially of recognizing some object that one has known before. The People of the Book, for example, weep when they listen to the Qurʾān because on the basis of their scriptures "they recognize the truth" (Q 5:83). I move now from perception to cognition, the more active dimension of human knowing.

Cognition: Recollection, Reflection, and Understanding

Several roots supply words describing the many nuances of thinking or cognition, the activity of the heart (or mind) upon what one perceives, recognizes, or is aware of. The basic verb from the root *dh-k-r* means "to remember, commemorate, make mention of, bear in mind." Thus, a causative verb from this root means "to remind" or "to admonish." The reflexive verb from this root, *tadhakkar* or *idhdhakkar*, means "to receive reminding or admonition." A reflexive verb expresses "the state into which the object of the action denoted by the [causative or intensive] form is brought by that action, as its effect or result" (Wright 1967: I, 36). In the divine interrogation of unbelievers who when facing the fires of hell request a second chance, this sense of the effect or result of reminding or admonition becomes clear, "Did We not give you long enough life so that he who would could receive admonition?" (Q 35:37). Such reception of reminding or admonition relates closely to the phrase *ūlū ʾl-albāb*, "those endowed with hearts" (i.e. understanding). Of the Qurʾān's sixteen instances of this phrase, nine are connected with this root. A couple of good examples come from portions of Q 2:269, "None receive the reminder but those endowed with understanding," and Q 13:19 "Those endowed with understanding receive admonition." Because the word *dhikr* and *dhikrā* can indicate God's message or scripture, the causative verb from this root can mean "to communicate the message," giving the reflexive form the meaning "take the message to heart." The cognitive dimension of the process of recollection shows up in Mahmoud Ayoub's (1984) translation of the portion from Q 2:269, "none reflect save those who have intelligence."

Another root *f-k-r* carries the basic idea of "thinking." It occurs in the intensive (called in the case of *dhakkara* above, the causative) verbal form, *fakkara*, meaning "to think" or "to meditate" and also in the intransitive reflexive form, *tafakkara*, "to consider" or "to meditate." An early Meccan verse succinctly describes the cognition of a greedy and stubborn person "concocting" (Ibn Kathīr 1970) a response to God's word, "He thought much and plotted" (Q 74:18). Here "thought much" translates the intensive form. It is paralleled by "plotted," an intensive form of another verb meaning "to ponder." Whereas the intensive form suggests thinking something up, as in the case of the verse quoted, the reflexive form suggests intense thinking about something and requires the preposition *fī*, "about," before the object of thought, as in Q 3:191, "thinking deeply about the creation of the heavens and the earth." It is associated frequently with signs or evidence pointing to divine guidance, grace, or power: "God makes clear to you His signs in hopes you will think deeply" (Q 2:219). Thinking deeply is also a desired response to the proclaimed message, "We have sent down to you the message so you can explain clearly to people what is sent for them, so hopefully they will think deeply" (Q 16:44). Of the sixteen instances of this root, thirteen occur, like these two, in the reflexive form at the end of verses with no following prepositional phrase, merely implying what is to be thought deeply about. This formula reinforces the inner reflective dimension of the human cognitive process.

This intensity of inner cognition is also reflected in two verbal forms from the root *f-q-h*, featuring the basic idea of understanding. The basic verbal form *faqiha*, meaning "to be wise," or "to be understanding," occurs nineteen times; and the intransitive reflexive form, *tafaqqaha*, "to be assiduous in instructing one's-self" (Penrice 1873) occurs only once. The basic form occurs fifteen times in a negative context, such as, "when he reached a tract between two mountains, he found beneath them a people who scarcely understood" (Q 18:93); three times in conditional or hopeful contexts such as in the case of Moses who asks God to remove the impediment in his speech "so they may understand what I say" (Q 20:28); and once in a positive context, "We detail our speech for a people who understand" (Q 6:98). The single occurrence of the reflexive form occurs in a verse ordering a contingent from every war party to stay behind "to strive to understand religion" and then to admonish the others when they return (Q 9:122; Walker 2003: 103).

Some other roots such as *y-q-n*, *d-r-s*, and *f-h-m* can also be treated under the topic of the cognitive or active thinking dimension of human knowing. The latter root occurs only once in the causative form, *fahhama*, in a passage (Q 21:79) already mentioned in connection with divine teaching. The basic verb *darasa* from the root *d-r-s* means "to study or read attentively" and occurs five times. The related noun *dirāsa* occurs once (Q 6:156). Five of these six occurrences connect study with sacred scripture (e.g., Q 3:79).

The most significant verb describing the process of human cognition is *ʿaqala* from the root *ʿ-q-l*. It points to the process of thinking or intellection: "to understand, be ingenious, prudent, or sagacious." It occurs forty-nine times, almost always in the second or third person plural, usually in rhyme phrases of exhortation (Kermani 2002: 547) such as "Do you not understand?" or "In order that you may understand," or "For a people who understand." The colloquial English expression "to use your head" that has a near equivalent in the Qurʾān, "Do they not travel through the land and so have a heart to understand with?" (Q 22:46; cf. 7:179; 12:109), seems appropriate for interpreting this verb in forty of its occurrences. Another verse asks, "Or do you think most of them listen or use their heads (*yaʿqilūn*)? They are merely like cattle, but even more lost" (Q 25:44). The verb does not mean rational thinking in the Enlightenment sense, however, but rather thoughtful response to divine initiative. The verb occurs in positive, possibility, and negative, contexts.

Positive

This verb depicts positive cognition, understanding, or "use of the head" nine times – less than one fifth of its total occurrences. Maybe al-Ghazālī's (1967–8: I, 114–23) very positive assessment of this term stems from its rare exercise! One of these declares that only those given knowledge understand the parables God has given (Q 29:43). All eight of the other occurrences state that God gives signs in nature, culture, and history for those who "use their heads" (Q 2:164, 13:4; 16:12, 67; 29:35; 30:24, 28; 45:5).

Possibility

Nine occurrences of the verb from this root involve a possibility or hope expressed by the use of the common Qurʾānic modal particle *laʿalla*, meaning "perhaps" (Cragg 1973: 75). In most of these passages divine signs are expected, intended, or hoped to lead to understanding: "We have shown the signs plainly to you. Perhaps you will use your head" (Q 57:17; cf. 2:73, 242; 3:118; 24:61). In one of the verses in which divine signs are explicit, the conditional particle *in*, "if," plays a semantic role similar to that of *laʿalla* in the other verses: "We have made plain to you the signs, if you use your head" (Q 3:118). God's commands are also designed to lead to this understanding – in some sense, they are also signs: "Do not take life, which Allāh has forbidden, except for some just cause. This He commanded you. Perhaps you will use your head" (Q 6:151). Finally, the Qurʾān is offered "in hopes you will understand" (Q 12:2; 43:3). These possibility passages point to human responsibility in knowing (Kermani 2002: 548; Rahbar 1960: 63).

Negative

More than half (thirty-three) of all occurrences of verbs from this root are preceded by a negative particle. Seventeen of the thirty-three occur in the form of a question such as this one directed at the People of the Book: "Do you require right conduct of the people, and neglect [it] yourselves? And yet you study the scripture! Will you not use your head?" (Q 2:44). The blessings of the afterlife should lead to understanding, "The eternal home is good for those who are pious. Will you not then use your head?" (Q 6:32). Another verse asks whether the revealed Qurʾān should not lead to understanding, "We have sent down for you a book. A message for you is in it. Will you not then use your head?" (Q 21:10). Q 23:80 is one of only three of these negatively construed verses connecting signs of God with coming to understand: "He is the one who gives life and brings death. His is the alternation of night and day. Will you not then use your head?" This and the other two (Q 22:46; 29:63) do not mention the word "signs" even though they enumerate examples of them. Thus the word "signs," *āyāt*, so common among the positive and perhaps verses, does not occur among the negatively construed verses – the clear majority of the verses featuring the basic verb from the root *ʿ-q-l*.

The remaining sixteen negative instances of this root occur in declarative sentences. For example, one verse criticizes the People of the Book who reject faith, "When you [believers] proclaim your call to prayer, they take it as mockery and sport because they are a people without understanding" (Q 5:58). Two verses charge a majority with failing to understand (Q 5:103; 49:4). Another criticizes a party of people for perverting the truth "knowingly after they understood it" (Q 2:75).

A couple of instances of this verb stand out as different from those mentioned so far. When Pharaoh claims that Moses is a madman, Moses says, "Lord of the east and the west, and all between! If you only used your head!" (Q 26:28). Here we have one of the two verses featuring this verb where the conditional particle *in* occurs. The other one was cited in connection with the verbs constructed with the possibility verses above. Finally, Q 67:10 is unique among all the verses containing this verb. In it unbelievers are depicted making confession at the judgment, "Had we but listened or used our heads, we would not be among the inhabitants of the blazing fire!".

Navid Kermani (2002: 548) draws attention to four verses in the *sūra* of the Greeks (Q 30:21–4), each ending with a different phrase representing positive human responses to divine signs. In the first verse, features of God's design for human conjugal harmony are offered as "signs for a people who think deeply." The second verse identifies divine creation and human language and culture as "signs for the knowledgeable." The satisfaction of sleep and the desire for bounty represent the third set of "signs for a people who listen." The final verse holds up the startling lightning and the life-giving rain as "signs for a people who understand." Kermani notes that these responses to divine signs include the sensual, listening; the intellectual, thinking; and the understanding that embraces the other two. But the order of the culminating phrases and the presence of "the knowledgeable" in second place indicates that the Qurʾānic perspective will frequently defy any neat analysis. The first and the fourth phrases represent distinctive human ways of knowing as we have seen; the second and third represent ways of knowing that humans share with God. Listening is a perception humans share with God. Knowledge – and here the root is again *ʿ-l-m* – consists of accurate interpretation that depends on human response to divine knowledge. I turn now to the human side of this knowing.

Knowing

The Qurʾān employs four roots for various aspects of knowing, *ʿ-r-f, sh-ʿ-r* (already discussed under perception as "awareness" and "recognition"), *d-r-y* and *ʿ-l-m*. The root *d-r-y* provides the basic verb *darā*, "to know," occurring twelve times – all cast in the negative. This is the "when-where-and-how" kind of knowing. For example, in Q 4:11, believers are said not to know inheritance procedures. This root also provides a causative verb, *adrā*, "to make known," occurring seventeen times. Sixteen times the Qurʾān asks, "What will make known to you?" In fifteen of them the phrase signals some mysterious (Sells 1999: 55) feature of the day of judgment (e.g., Q 82:18). When turning to words from the root *ʿ-l-m* for human knowing, a rich array of passages can be found. In words related to knowledge as *ʿilm*, the all-important connection between divine and human knowing is revealed.

Divine Knowledge and Human Knowing

A number of the most significant words for perception, cognition, and understanding that are unique to humanity have been explored. We are now ready to look at *ʿilm* as human knowledge. According to Rosenthal (1970: 31), the "reason for the existence of divine knowledge as well as its final destination are, in a manner of speaking, man and his need and desire for knowledge."

I shall discuss this divine-human knowledge in the Qur'ān in relation to unbelievers, people of the book, believers, prophets and messengers, and specially gifted persons. I will ignore it in relation to animals (Q 5:31), angels (Q 2:30, 102; 29:32), *jinn* (Q 37:158), and demons (Q 2:102).

Unbelievers and hypocrites

Unbelievers clearly know some things. Egyptian sorcerers are knowledgeable (*ʿalīm*) (Q 7:112; 10:79). Unbelievers know the creation of God in the beginning of things, even though their knowledge does not lead them to celebrate God's praises (Q 56:62). God has created humans from what even unbelievers know (Q 70:39): dust, a sperm, a clot, and then from a piece of flesh (Q 22:5; 23:14; 40:67; 75:38). Moses reminds Pharaoh of what he knows, "You well know," he says, "that these things have been sent down by none but the Lord of the heavens and the earth as eye-opening evidence" (Q 17:102). In Q 23:83–9, the Qur'ān directs Muḥammad to respond to the unbelievers' objections with a series of questions: "Whose is the earth and all it contains?" "Who is the Lord of the seven heavens and the throne?" and "Who governs all things?" The verses containing the first and last questions conclude with the rhyme phrase, "If you know." In each case, Muḥammad is assured, their answer will be "Allāh." While they know the answer, they do not respond by accepting God's final messenger. The Qur'ān pleads with the unbelievers as it does with Muḥammad's receptors in general: "do not set up rivals for Allāh knowingly" (Q 2:20–2).

Even though unbelievers know some things of significance, they lack knowledge of such basic truths as "God sees" (Q 96:14), owns everything, and promises reliably (Q 10:55). Because they do not know better, they allow beings that "they do not know" (Q 16:56) to share God's deity (Q 6:100). They tend to think some things they know are unknown to God (Q 41:22). They do not know that God enlarges or restricts their resources according to His pleasure (Q 39:52).

They also cannot comprehend the hereafter (Q 27:66). Some of them say there is no afterlife (Q 45:24). They reveal their lack of knowledge of the unseen world by giving female names to angels and by relying on angelic intercession (Q 53:26–30). Most unbelievers do not know that the resurrection precedes the judgment (Q 45:26). Nor does anyone know "what delights of the eye" are reserved for devout persons (Q 32:17).

Because unbelievers lack knowledge, they do not curb their passions (Q 6:119). They slay their children (Q 6:140), engage in shameful acts (Q 7:28), charge Muḥammad with forgery of scripture (Q 16:101), attribute calamity to evil omens (Q 7:131), and lead others astray (Q 6:144; 31:6). They reject God's signs even though they do "not have full knowledge of them" (Q 27:84).

Several times the Qur'ān appears to long for unbelievers to know, repeating "If they only knew." If they only knew that the suffering of the next life is worse than that of this life (Q 68:33). "If only the unbelievers knew when they will not be able to ward off the fire from their faces, nor yet from their backs, and no help can reach them"

(Q 21:39). Like the spider, unbelievers are constructing a flimsy house, "if they but knew" (Q 29:41).

But unbelievers have no real knowledge of what they claim to know about God (Q 10:68). Their lack of knowledge leads to disputation (Q 22:3; 63:7–8). In the final analysis, the way of the unbeliever could be called "the path of those who do not know" (Q 10:89). They could even be called "a people who do not know" (Q 9:6).

A frequent phrase about unbelievers is "soon they will know." For example, "O my people! Do whatever you can. I will act; so you will soon know who will have the ultimate abode" (Q 6:135). Since all messages have a fixed term, those who reject the message will "soon know" (Q 6:67). Noah's detractors will "soon know" (Q 11:39); the people of Shuʿayb will "soon know" (Q 11:93). This reliance on future experience for knowledge provides evidence that *ʿilm* is knowledge of the truth about the way things truly are.

But unbelievers who resist the message of Muḥammad also suffer from all the limitations of human knowing. They persist in following their ancestors, but even they do not really know: "They say: 'Enough for us are the ways we found our fathers following.' What! even though their fathers were void of knowledge and guidance?" (Q 5:104). If they do not know, for example, that all the prophets and messengers sent to previous peoples were humans, they should consult the people who have scriptures (Q 16:43). Abraham asks his detractors to determine who is more worthy of authority: the deities they associate with God or God himself – if they "have the knowledge" (Q 6:81).

In another context where food taboos are being debunked, Muḥammad is told to say, "Inform me with knowledge if you speak the truth" (Q 6:143). In another verse knowledge is contrasted with surmise. Muḥammad is told to reply to those who blame God's decree for their polytheism, "Say: 'Have you any knowledge? Then display it for us. You follow nothing but opinion. You only conjecture'" (Q 6:148). Knowledge parallels revealed authority: "Yet they worship, besides Allāh, that for which no authority has been sent down to them, and that of which they have no knowledge" (Q 22:71).

People of the Book

That the People of the Book know the truth does not necessarily mean they will act on it in faith: "A party of them heard the word of Allāh, and, after they understood it, perverted it knowingly" (Q 2:75). The Israelites knew Moses was a messenger of God, yet they still vexed and rejected him (Q 61:5). Another passage addressing the People of the Book lays bare what they know and what they do not know:

> And when there came to them a messenger from Allāh, confirming what was with them, a party of the People of the Book threw away the book of Allāh behind their backs. As if they did not know! . . . They learned what harmed them, not what profited them. And they knew that those who bought it [magic] would have no share in the happiness of the hereafter. And vile was the price they sold their souls for, if they only knew! If they had kept their faith and guarded themselves from evil, the reward from their Lord would have been far better, if they but knew! (Q 2:101–3)

The three verses end with a rhyme phrase containing what they do not know or what they should have known, suggesting there is a knowledge these Israelites lacked, even though they had been taught knowledge. Nevertheless, the People of the Book can be termed "those with access to the message" and can be consulted by Muḥammad's audience on matters of controversy such as whether the prophets who went before him were humans who received inspiration (Q 21:7).

The People of the Book neglected the religion of surrender through envy of one another after knowledge came to them (Q 3:19). They divided only after knowledge came to them (Q 42:14). They knew full well the Qur'ān came from God (Q 6:114). But, they concealed the truth that they knew to be true (Q 3:71). They disputed about things they knew and about things they knew not – about Abraham, for example, who lived before their religious communities were organized (Q 3:66). They knew that they told lies about God (Q 3:75, 78).

Believers

In short, to believe is to know, for example, about "the hour": "Those who believe hold it in awe, and know that it is the truth" (Q 42:18). Even believers are not fully knowledgeable, however: "To those who leave their homes in the cause of Allāh, after suffering oppression, We will assuredly give a goodly home in this world: but truly the reward of the hereafter will be greater. If they only knew!" (Q 16:41). Believers in Medina are reprimanded for spreading false rumors: "You . . . said . . . things of which you had no knowledge" (Q 24:15). After instructing believers about divorce, a long verse ends with the rhyme phrase, "God knows and you do not know" (Q 2:232). Believers may not know all who will come against them in battle, but God does know (Q 8:60). Some things that are good for the believers may be counter-intuitive – such as fighting; but God knows what believers do not (Q 2:216). Some rich believers may stay home from battle claiming exemption; but because God has sealed their hearts, they are without knowledge (Q 9:93).

Just as God has longings for unbelievers to know the truth, so He has some longings for the believers also to be fully knowledgeable. When instructing the faithful in fasting, the Qur'ān still laments, "If you only knew" (Q 2:184). Dropping commercial activities to hasten off to Friday prayers is best for all, the Qur'ān reveals, "If you only knew" (Q 62:9). At any rate, the Qur'ān insists that God teaches believers what they do not know (Q 2:239).

In some verses the imperative mood of the verb "to know" is used. For example, "O you who believe! . . . know that Allāh comes in between a man and his heart, and that it is He to whom you will be gathered" (Q 8:24). The Qur'ān distinguishes between inappropriate behavior that is inadvertent on the part of believers and that done knowingly: "Do not consume your wealth . . . with intent to consume wrongfully and knowingly a part of the wealth of others" (Q 2:188; 3:135). At one stage, the Qur'ān exhorts believers not to come to prayer intoxicated, since "You should know what you are saying" (Q 4:43). A dialogue between leaders of his community and those who have come to believe in Muḥammad's message suggests a parallel between knowledge and faith. The leaders ask the powerless believers in Muḥammad's message: "Do you know that Muḥammad is a messenger from his Lord?" The believers then reply, "We believe in what he was sent with" (Q 7:75). In a Qur'ānic parable, a man from the farthest part of a city comes running to urge its citizens to accept the message of those sent to them from God. The citizens having apparently dispensed with him, this man is invited into God's paradise. But, still thinking of his people, he wishes they had the knowledge he has had (Q 36:20–6).

Specialists

Two Qur'ānic verses mention some among the believers and the People of the Book who have gone deeply into the realm of knowledge. They are called, "those who are well-grounded in knowledge" (Q 3:7; 4:162). Only God and the well-grounded in knowledge among the Muslim believers understand the "figurative" (Cragg 1973: 42) or metaphorical verses of the Qur'ān according to Q 3:7:

> Those who are twisted of mind look for figurative verses, seeking deviation and giving to them interpretations of their own; but no one *knows* their meaning except God; and those well-grounded in knowledge affirm: "We believe in them as all of them are from the Lord." (A. Ali 2001)

The other verse speaks of the well-grounded in knowledge among the Children of Israel. They believe in what God revealed to Muḥammad and in the earlier revelations as well (Q 4:162). Maybe these are the knowledgeable of Israel whose acknowledgment of the Qur'ān should have provided evidence for the truth of Muḥammad's message (Q 26:197). A person with "knowledge from the book" competes successfully against "a crafty jinni" (A. Ali 2001) by getting the throne of the Queen of Sheba to Solomon in an instant. This suggests some esoteric knowledge connected with God's book. The commentators generally think the person knew a divine name that could cause distant objects to be brought near (Q 27:39–40). God taught another specialist knowledge, and he in turn taught Moses (Q 18:65–6).

The Qur'ān in ten places mentions "those given knowledge" or "those who have access to divine knowledge through God's initiative in addressing humanity through the prophets" (Madigan 2001: 8): "Among them are men who listen to you, but in the end, when they leave you, they say to those given knowledge, "What is it he said just then?" (Q 47:16); "God will raise those of you who believe, and those given knowledge, in position. God is aware of what you do" (Q 58:11).

Messengers

God's messengers recognize their limits. When God gathers them on the judgment day to give an account of their mission, they will confess, "We have no knowledge, You are the Knower of the unseen" (Q 5:109). Jesus in such a scenario says, "You know what is in my heart, I do not know what is in Yours. For You know in full all that is hidden" (Q 5:116). What messengers do know comes from God. Noah says to his people, "My advice to you is sincere, I know from Allāh something you do not know" (Q 7:62). In a similar vein Abraham addresses his father, "O my father! knowledge has come to me that has not reached you. So follow me" (Q 19:43). God sends Muḥammad to bring people new knowledge (Q 2:151), but he does not have knowledge of the unseen: "As to the knowledge of the time, it is Allāh's alone. I am only to warn plainly in public" (Q 67:25–6). He is not privy to the counsel of the angels (Q 38:69), and he does not have the ability to read the intentions of others (Q 9:101). Obviously, all human knowing has limits.

Limits of Human Knowing

Human knowing, as represented by words from the root *ʿ-l-m*, has limits. The Qurʾān makes clear that "God has created things of which you know nothing" (Q 16:8). As we have seen, one of the main things humans do not know – not even God's messengers – is the time of the judgment (e.g., Q 33:63). In fact, only a little knowledge is given to ordinary humans (Q 17:85). Although they should not pursue what they have no knowledge of (Q 17:36), people tend to dispute in areas where they lack knowledge (Q 3:66). They indeed tend to exaggerate the effect of what they know. For example, when trouble comes, people cry to God, but when God shows them favor, they attribute the good things that happen to their own knowledge (Q 39:49; 40:83). Indeed some things defy any knowledge except God's: "none can know the forces [angels] of your Lord except He" (Q 74:31). Yet the Qurʾān insists on the necessity of knowledge.

Necessity of Divine Knowledge

Knowledge appears to be a requisite for a number of things. Knowledge opens people to the Qurʾān as God's truth: "That those given knowledge may know that it is the truth from your Lord, and so believe in it, and so their hearts will become humble before it" (Q 22:54; 17:107). Signs can be self-evident for those given knowledge (Q 29:49), and people who know will receive explanations of God's signs (Q 6:97). God makes plain his ordinances to those with knowledge (Q 2:230). Knowledge prevents people from being misled (Q 30:29). Only those who have knowledge understand the parables (Q 29:43). People of knowledge and faith will be ready for the day of judgment (Q 30:56). Without knowledge, hearts may be sealed (Q 30:59). Knowledge, along with guidance and scripture, reduces disputes about God (Q 31:20). The gift of knowledge is a reward for goodness: "When he [Moses] reached full age, and was firmly established, We bestowed on him wisdom and knowledge. Thus We reward those who do good" (Q 28:14). We turn now to some overall conclusions from this study.

Conclusions

We observed that although the Qur'ān clearly presents some people as endowed with knowledge and understanding and frequently refers to those who know, more verses occur that speak of those who do not properly exercise their intellectual powers, who do not know, "but their hearts are divided because they are a people who do not use their heads" (*qawm lā ya'qilūn*) (Q 59:14). Furthermore, all of the sixty-five instances of *akthar*, "most," combined with various verbs such as "know," "believe," and "understand" turn up negative. For example, "Allāh never departs from His promise, but most of humanity does not know" (*lā ya'lamūn*) (Q 30:6). In other words, lack of knowledge (twenty-seven times), faith (fifteen times), and even gratitude (six times) seem to characterize the majority of humankind.

As essentially divine knowledge, *'ilm* represents accurate appraisal of the way things really are. For example, according to the following verse, God knows the true state of affairs and the community can discern it:

> O you who believe! When there comes to you believing women refugees, examine them. Allāh knows best about their faith. If you come to know that they are believers, then do not send them back to the unbelievers. (Q 60:10)

This special character of *'ilm* finds confirmation in the fact that the major processes of coming to know, such as remembering, thinking, and understanding, find elaborate application to humans in the Qur'ān, but are never attributed to God. In other words, God knows, but does not need to exercise recollection, reflection, or thinking, nor does he need to come to understand. God perceives and knows all things as they actually are.

As human knowledge, *'ilm* has this same character. Even unbelievers will "soon know" when they actually experience the final accounting (Q 6:135). Congruent with this, as human knowledge, *'ilm* represents more a state of mind or heart and a divine endowment "equated with religious insight" (Rosenthal 1970: 29). Certain passages equate knowledge and faith through parallelism (e.g., Q 30:56). A verse cluster sets knowing, intellectual perception (*yafqahūn*), and believing in obvious parallel (Q 6:97–9; cf., Q 45:3–6). In fact, "those who believe know" (Q 2:26). Such knowledge is bound up with reverence for God, "Those . . . who truly fear God have knowledge" (Q 35:28). Thus, a tradition attributed to the companion of the prophet Ibn Mas'ūd (d. 32/652–3) must contain at least a grain of truth, "Knowledge is not acquired through much sharing of information. It is a light cast in the heart" (cited in al-Ghazālī 1967–8: I, 71).

Further reading

Arberry, A. J. (1957) *Revelation and Reason in Islam*. George Allen & Unwin, Macmillan, London, New York.

Al-Ghazali (1970) *The Book of Knowledge. Being a Translation with Notes of the* Kitāb al-ʿIlm *of al-Gazzālī's* Iḥyāʾ ʿulūm al-dīn, trans. N. A. Faris, 2nd edn. Sh. Muhammad Ashraf, Lahore.

Kermani, N. (2002) Intellect. In: McAuliffe, Jane Dammen (ed.) *Encyclopaedia of the Qur'ān.* Brill, Leiden, vol. II, pp. 547–9.

Madigan, D. A. (2001) *The Qurʾān's Self-image.* Princeton University Press, Princeton.

Rahbar, D. (1960) *God of Justice: A Study in the Ethical Doctrine of the Qurʾān.* E. J. Brill, Leiden, especially pp. 51–66, 261–322.

Rosenthal, F. (1970) *Knowledge Triumphant.* E. J. Brill, Leiden.

Walker, P. E. (2003) Knowledge and learning. In: McAuliffe, Jane Dammen (ed.) *Encyclopedia of the Qur'ān.* Brill, Leiden, vol. III, pp. 100–4.

CHAPTER 19

Sex, Sexuality, and the Family

Khaleel Mohammed

The Qur'ān did not create an entirely new set of norms for the Arabian milieu to which it was initially addressed. Rather, Islam's main document concerned itself with improving the standards governing the prevailing practices, and thus reformed but never completely replaced all of Arabian patriarchal tribal values and customary laws. This is especially evident in the case of sex, sexuality, and family where such amelioration remained strictly within the parameters reflecting the values and realities of patriarchal society. The Qur'ān claims to be a continuation of the Abrahamic message and, as such, contains much of what can be determined to be biblical in precedent and parallel, thus underlining a patriarchal value-system. Females therefore remained, for all the amelioration of their status, subordinate to the males of their family.

Prior to Islam, the tribal society of Arabia regarded the family as the basic social unit, and the tribe merely as an extended family. This can be seen in the Arabic term for tribe, *banū*, meaning literally "sons;" the idea was that all the members of a tribe could be traced to a common forefather. Humankind is referred to in the Qur'ān collectively as *banū Ādam*, the sons of Adam, and the Israelites are often referred to as *banū Isrā'īl*, the sons of Israel.

It has been pointed out that the number of Qur'ānic verses on legal issues is only about 500, in comparison to that document's total 6,236 verses (according to a common counting), and that many of the issues covered in positive law rely on the *ḥadīth* as source material. On sex, sexuality, and family, however, the Qur'ān contains detailed accounts. Islam's source document clearly sees itself as inimitable (Q 2:23; 10:38; 4:82); by the fourth/tenth century, however, the jurists had conflated inimitability to include immutability. It is this concept that underlines the idea of timelessness of the Qur'ān and which presents one of the greatest hurdles to change in traditional scriptural edicts according to many modernists today.

Medieval exegetes saw no problem in reconciling the concept of timelessness of the Qur'ān with the fact that they studied and recorded the chronology and particulars of occasions of revelation of various verses. This study, rather than put the entire Qur'ān into historical context, was primarily to defend the concept of abrogation (*naskh*) wherein it was necessary to identify which the earlier and later verses were, in order to know which was abrogating and which was being abrogated. Modern discourses on the Qurʾān, however, tend to focus less on chronology since this would give the impression that the Qurʾān is a temporal document; the following discussion eschews the issue and instead details the concepts of sex, sexuality, and family as found in the text, dealing only secondarily with exegetical and *ḥadīth* interpretations.

In the Qurʾān, the connection between sex and family can be seen in the fact that the term *nikāḥ* is interchangeably used to refer to sexual intercourse, and sometimes to the marital union (see, for example, Q 2:221; 2:230; 4:22, 25, 126; 60:10; in its various grammatical forms, the word is found twenty-three times in the Qurʾān). Premarital sex is prohibited (Q 4:25 etc.), and legal intercourse can only occur within heterosexual marriage, or between a man and his female slave (but not between a mistress and her male slave). The following discussion will deal with family issues first, and then focus on sex and sexuality.

For present purposes, the term "sexuality" is not limited to the understanding of carnal and sensual gratification and expression only. Rather, it deals with the religious significance associated with such sexuality, and the practices that such significance brings about, such as the sharply defined roles of masculine and feminine behavior within patriarchal society, where men are to provide, lead, and dominate, and women are to care for children, nurture, and be dominated.

Male dominance is reflected in the issue of nomenclature, where the Qurʾān clearly points to a patrilineal system. Q 33:5 states: "Call them by [the names] of their fathers." In such a society, it was the male who was perceived to be in charge of providing for the family, and it was for this reason that the Qurʾān makes him the protector and manager of his wife's affairs: "Men are the protectors and maintainers of women because of that which God has favored one above the other, and because they support them from their means" (Q 4:34). It is for this reason that sons receive twice as much as daughters in inheritance, and the two-to-one ratio applies to male beneficiaries over their female counterparts in general (Q 4:11).

The role of the male as protector is also mirrored in the Qurʾānic imagery where the females are generally referred in terms of their relationship to a male, rather than by name, for example the "wife of Lot" and the "wife of Noah." Mary, mother of Jesus, is the only woman mentioned by name in the Qurʾān, and her uniqueness is underlined by her departure from the expected role of a female.

According to the Qurʾānic narrative (Q 3:35ff.), while Mary was yet in her mother's womb, her mother consecrated her to the service of the Lord. This seems to be following the Hebrew Nazarite custom of temple service, and al-Ṭabarī's (d. 310/923; 1969: VI, 330–3) exegesis outlines it in detail. Having made this vow, the mother felt assured that her child would be a male, since the rigid purity requirements of the temple seemed to favor males. When Mary was born, her mother was therefore disappointed, since she felt her vow had been rejected. Q 3:36 puts the matter in perspective: "She said: 'I have given birth to a female.' But God knew better what she had brought forth." The Qurʾān goes on to state that Mary was purified and the best of women (Q 3:42). Many exegetes have written copiously on this verse, seeking to explain that her purity meant freedom from menses. (There are also detailed discussions on the temporality of her exalted status as the best of women: although the Qur'ān never suggests such status was temporary, exegetes have tried to show that Fāṭima or Khadīja replaced Mary as the chosen of God.) Some exegetes have gone as far as attributing the miraculous birth of Jesus to a hermaphroditic quality of Mary.

The woman's role as mother and housekeeper has made it difficult for the general body of exegetes to accept that women could be prophets, since such office would mean interaction with society at large, an image seemingly at odds with the Arab tribal concept. The Qur'ān does not even hint at female prophets, and many use Q 21:7 to insist on maleness as a prerequisite for prophethood, since the verse states, "We did not send before you but men to whom we revealed." Others, and they are the minority, have rebutted this to state that, since Mary was spoken to by the angels, and commissioned with specific rituals, she did receive the gift of prophethood. Others have relied on Q 16:43 and 21:7 to state that even though the Qur'ān does not specifically mention female prophets, the directive to ask the Jewish scholars about the history of prophets entails the accepting of Hebrew scriptural historiography, which includes female prophets.

With the coming of Islam, wives were no longer seen as chattels and viewed rather as partners in whom husbands could find tranquility and completeness. This is reflected in the Qur'ānic verse:

> And among His signs is this that He created for you mates from among yourselves that ye may dwell in tranquility with them and He has put love and mercy between your (hearts); verily in that are signs for those who reflect. (Q 30:21)

The Qur'ān specifies that a woman has rights as well as obligations, and that a husband should not seek to force her to live with him in order to maltreat her (Q 2:228, 231). Instead of the limitless polygyny of pre-Islamic Arabia, the number of wives a man may have is limited to four. Modernist interpreters focus on the fact that this was not incipient legislation, but was rather a form of gradualism, seeking to curb the practice of polygyny. They cite the Qur'ānic advice: "And if you fear that you cannot deal with them (the wives) justly, then (marry) one" (Q 4:3). By reading Q 4:3 and 4:129, they seek to show that the Qur'ān in fact, exhorts to monogamy: "And if you cannot deal with them justly – and you will never be able to deal with them justly – then marry one." However, the traditional exegesis has been, as follows clearly from the text (Q 4:129), to counsel that overt preferential treatment for one wife at the discomfort of the others should not be done, even though one may indeed love her above the others. While there are some Muslim countries that permit polygyny, government restrictions and societal conventions have contributed to the decline of the practice.

How does the family start? Since men are the protectors of women, a marriage is generally done under the authority of males, and the female is represented by a guardian. Qur'ānic language suggests that this practice is a continuation of a pre-Islamic custom, as is evident from the normative readings of Q 2:221; the translation of the verse wherein marriage is prohibited with polytheists is addressed to the men as "do not marry polytheist women," *lā tankihū al-muskhrikāt*. The women are not addressed directly, however, and the proscription may be translated as "do not give your females in marriage," *lā tunkihū al-mushrikīn*. The Qur'ān does not detail how a marriage ceremony is to be performed, but mentions *ṣadāq/mahr*, the property that is to be given to the bride (Q 4:4). Jurists have interpreted marriage to be a contractual association, wherein there is an exchange of benefits or commodities. In exchange for the *ṣadāq/mahr*, the bride agrees to sexual fidelity to the husband and he agrees to maintain and provide for her. The Qur'ānic reading gives the impression that the *ṣadāq/mahr* is tangible property, but Muslim jurists have relied on the *ḥadīth* to show that tangible property could be replaced by a service, such as the teaching of the Qur'ān to the bride (Muslim 1992: II, 700–53). The *ṣadāq/mahr* need not be given in full at the time of the marriage agreement, and can be paid in installments.

The Qur'ān does not insist on the permanency of the marriage bond, and, as such, contains detailed instructions on dissolution of marriage by divorce. In doing so, it prohibits or severely restricts certain pre-Islamic practices that were oppressive towards women. A man would say to his wife that she was like his mother to him (*ẓihār*): this pronouncement effectively denied her conjugal rights but did not set her free from the marriage (Q 33:4). In some cases, a man would utter an oath of sexual abstinence from his wife (*īlā'*), and continue such oath indefinitely. The Qur'ān restricted such separation to a maximum of four months; after such time, the husband had to choose between reconciliation and divorce (Q 2:226).

Males have authority in divorce, and the Qur'ān outlines the process by which such divorce is to be sought. Usually, after three pronouncements, followed by an *ʿidda*, a waiting period, a divorce is irrevocable (Q 2:229–30). This does not have to be done with the agreement of the wife and can therefore be a unilateral undertaking. Although the Qur'ān allows for divorce, *khulʿ*, initiated by a female (Q 2:229), the majority position is that such divorce must be done under the supervision of a judge and with the agreement of the husband.

Since the Qur'ānic directive is addressed to a primarily male audience and mirrors the realities of a seventh-century environment, some of its counsel on the solution of marital discord has been the subject of vehement contemporary debate. Q 4:34 advises that a good wife is she who is obedient to God and guards her chastity in her husband's absence. The verse goes on to instruct that if husbands fear *nushūz* (often explained as rebellion against the husband's authority) from their wives, they should first admonish them, and then ostracize them in bed, and then finally, beat them (*wa-'ḍribūhunna*). This last instruction has been seen as promoting violence against women. Some thinkers have pointed out that there is no instruction regarding how a guilty husband is to be treated; it would seem that the Qur'ān assumes that since the man is in charge, then he cannot be guilty of *nushūz*.

In response, modern Muslims have launched several arguments, among them that the Qur'ān is not incipiently prescribing beating, but rather, seeking to make it the last resort to a situation that was, and still is, all too common in spousal relationships. Through the process of gradualism, where one inculcates the meaning of the Qur'ān increasingly, it would be realized that beating is against the Islamic philosophy and should not be resorted to. Others have relied on the medieval exegeses that, with *ḥadīth* support, propound that such beating should be done with a toothstick (*miswāk*) or similar object, held in a particular way so as not to cause discoloration or the breaking of the skin. Yet others, such as Amina Wadud (1999: 76) have argued, from an examination of Qurʾānic usage of certain terms, that the word normally taken to mean "beating" also means "to give an example." Her argument is that the idea is to reason with the wife rather than resort to physical violence. Often omitted from such discussion, however, is the fact that the Qurʾān is the first of the Abrahamic scriptures to treat wife beating as an issue of seriousness. Previous scriptures did not acknowledge it, and this certainly could not mean that it was not present. It would seem that, whatever the original meaning of *wa-ʾḍribūhunna*, the textual directive is aimed at ameliorating a particular practice.

The preceding material on dealing with marital problems should not be taken as evidence that the Qurʾān makes the issue of divorce an easy one. Within the Qurʾānic framework, the maintenance of strong family ties is seen as part of righteousness, and, in many places of the text, the Muslims are exhorted to be kind and charitable towards parents and kinsfolk (Q 2:177; 4:136; 17:23). Indeed, once the marriage bond has been established, the Qurʾān exhorts towards good treatment and the maintaining of such a bond, unless in the case of clear sexual infidelity (Q 4:19). Even in the case where there may be a certain amount of dislike, the Qurʾān advises, "If you dislike them, it is possible that you dislike something and God may cause a lot of good to come through it" (Q 4:19). Arbitration, with representatives from the kin of both parties is to be sought out when there is an issue of great discord, but in which there is the possibility of saving the marriage (Q 4:35).

In the case of a divorced woman, she is allowed spousal support until her *ʿidda* expires, and, in the case of a widow, she is supported for a year from the estate of her deceased husband, over and above that which she inherits (Q 2:240). Modernity has brought with it several attempts at reform. In many cases, such reform has been sought by a more direct textual analysis of the Qurʾānic verses, and a departure from the *ḥadīth*-influenced interpretations.

On the issue of sex and sexuality, as pointed out earlier, the Qurʾān strictly regulates the circumstances within which sexual relations can occur. It sees sex within such legal boundaries as fulfilling a human need, and not restricted only to the intent of procreation. In its narrative on the first couple's fall from grace, the Qurʾān differs from the Bible in that it does not impute blame to Eve; rather it states that Satan made them both go astray (Q 2:36). (Interestingly, the Qurʾān never mentions Eve by name, but Muslim exegetes have never had a problem with identifying Adam's mate as other than by the biblical appellation.) Any view of the woman as a temptress or tool of Satan, therefore, is not within the Qurʾānic *Weltanschauung*. The narrative, nonetheless, suggests that, even at this stage, God had ordained that the male be in charge of the female. Thus, God's order to take of the bounty of the garden is addressed primarily to Adam: "Dwell, you and your mate, in the garden" (Q 2:35). Some modern Muslim interpretations, in order to show the Qurʾān as a proto-feminist document, cite verses that seemingly impute blame to Adam rather than to Eve. Q 20:115 states, "We had already beforehand taken the covenant of Adam but he forgot: and We found on his part no firm resolve." Q 20:120 says, "But Satan whispered evil to him: he said 'O Adam! Shall I lead thee to the tree of eternity and to a kingdom that never decays?' " The verses, however, when placed into the context of other verses, seem rather to be based on the premise of establishing that the male of the primordial couple is being singled out on the presumption of his authority role. This is evidenced by Q 20:121 which says, "They both ate of the tree and so their nakedness appeared to them: they began to sew together leaves from the garden to cover themselves: thus did Adam disobey His Lord and allow himself to be led astray." They both ate, but it is Adam who is questioned. When God forgives, it is Adam who is chosen to receive the message of forgiveness and guidance. Says Q 2:37, "Then Adam received from his Lord words of inspiration and his Lord turned toward him; for He is Oft-returning Most-merciful." Q 20:122 states, "But his Lord chose him (for His grace): He turned to him and gave him guidance."

It is within this paradigm that the Qur'ānic image of sexuality is framed; certainly, for the women of seventh-century Arabian society, this new portrayal was a vast improvement over their contemporaries from other Abrahamic religions. Based on the Adam and Eve story, sexual relations, when allowed, can only be heterosexual in nature. While the Qur'ān fully acknowledges the sexual nature of human beings, it carefully outlines those with whom sexual relations are prohibited. Notably, the males are the ones addressed:

> And marry not women whom your fathers married except what is past: it was shameful and odious, an abominable custom indeed. Prohibited to you (for marriage) are: your mother, daughters, sisters, father's sisters, mother's sisters; brother's daughters, sister's daughters, foster-mothers (who suckled you), foster-sisters; your wives' mothers; your step-daughters under your guardianship born of your wives to whom ye have gone in no prohibition if ye have not gone in; (those who have been) wives of your sons proceeding from your loins; and two sisters in wedlock at one and the same time except for what is past; for God is Oft-forgiving Most-merciful. Also (prohibited are) women already married except those whom your right hands possess. Thus hath God ordained (prohibitions) against you: except for these all others are lawful provided ye seek (them in marriage) with gifts from your property desiring chastity not lust. (Q 4:22–4)

The seven references in the Qur'ān to the story of Lot and his people make it clear that divine anger and punishment was because of their deviant sexual practices (Q 7:80–4; 11:77–83; 21:74; 22:43; 26:165–75; 27:56–9; 29:27–33). The nature of such practice is explicitly stated thus:

> Of all the creatures in the world will you approach males, leaving those whom God has created for you to be your mates? Indeed, you are a people going beyond limits. They said: "O Lot! If you do not desist, you will surely be cast out. He said: I detest what you do. O my Lord! deliver me and my family from such things as they do!" So We delivered him and all of his family, except for an old woman who lingered behind. But the rest We destroyed utterly. We rained down on them a shower (of brimstone): and the shower was indeed sore upon those who had been warned. (Q 26:165–75)

In the foregoing verses, the deviation is attributed to male homosexuality and there is no clear reference to lesbian relations. Most exegetes have sought to explain away the one verse in the Qur'ān that seems to indicate a prohibition of such relations. Such exegetes suggest that certain verses were revealed at an early period when there was a difference in punishment based on gender.

> If any of your women are guilty of lewdness take the evidence of four (reliable) witnesses from amongst you against them; and if they testify confine them to houses until death do claim them or God ordain for them some (other) way. If two men among you are guilty of lewdness punish them both. If they repent and amend leave them alone, for God is Oft-returning, Most-merciful. (Q 4:14–15)

The second of the two verses, however, makes it clear that, in the case of the men, it is homosexuality rather than heterosexuality that is the offence, and suggests that the preceding verse is dealing with lesbianism. As Jim Wafer (Murray et al. 1997: 89) has observed, the mildness of the passage contrasts with other verses where severe punishments are prescribed for other crimes. In Q 24:2, where the Qurʾān mentions its most severe punishment for sexual transgression, *zīna*, the penalty is only 100 lashes, and is halved in the case of slaves. The stiffer penalties of stoning to death for married persons, or death for homosexuals, find their source in the *ḥadīth*. It would seem that in general, then, the Qurʾān is far more lenient in its treatment of sexual misconduct, heterosexual or homosexual. Even the establishment of such conduct had to be through four eyewitnesses, each testifying to actual penetration, a situation that was extremely difficult unless in a situation of absolute wantonness. Concomitant with such a stringent standard of establishing guilt, the witnesses were liable to punishment for slander if they could not establish the guilt of the accused parties (Q 24:4). Notably, although jurists have applied the law in regards to men as well, the accusation is only phrased in respect to the falsely accused being women. The consensus among exegetes is that the particular verse was revealed regarding an accusation against Muḥammad's wife, ʿĀʾisha. The verse states, "And those who accuse chaste women, and do not produce four witnesses, flog them eighty lashes, and forever reject their testimony. They are indeed mischief-mongers" (Q 24:4).

Sexual relations are prohibited during menstruation, for a period after childbirth, during the daylight hours of Ramaḍān, and while on pilgrimage. A divorced woman must remain chaste for three months after the final pronouncement, and a widow must wait four months and ten days after the demise of her spouse (Q 2:234). Exegetes have spilled much ink discussing Q 2:223, which states: "Your wives are as a field unto you, so approach your field however, wherever, and whenever you wish." The term translated as "however, wherever, and whenever" is *annā* and has given rise to debates as to whether the Qurʾān allows (heterosexual) anal intercourse. Some exegetes have opined that since the woman is referred to as a "field" and that this imagery suggests the casting of seed to produce vegetation, then the reference is to vaginal intercourse only. Others have stated that such an interpretation is incorrect; whether the intercourse is vaginal or otherwise, the woman is nonetheless like a field since it is her body in which the husband's seed germinates, and that a farmer can choose whether he leaves his field fallow or not.

This verse seems to reflect a discourse among Jews that is contained in the Talmud, and the vast majority of Muslim exegesis evidences that the early commentators were convinced of this. The traditions that they adduce in support of the explanations seem to match the following Talmudic reports:

> R. Johanan b. Dahabai said: the Ministering Angels told me four things: (1) People are born lame because they overturned the table; (2) dumb because they look at that place (3) deaf because they converse during congress (4) blind because they look at that place. This however contradicts Imma Shalom's report who was asked, Why are their children so beautiful? She replied: Because my husband neither converses with me neither at the beginning, nor at the end of night, but only at midnight, and when he converses, he uncovers only a handbreadth, and covers a handbreadth, and is as though he were compelled by a demon. . . . Rabbi Johanan said: The above is the view of Johanan b. Dahabai, but our sages said: The Halakah is not as R. Johanan b. Dahabai says, but a man may do wherever he pleases with his wife. (*Talmud*: Nedarim 20a)

> The Rabbis said: if a man has intercourse standing, he is liable to have convulsions, if sitting, spasms. If she is above and he below, he will be subject to diarrhea. (*Talmud*: Gittin 70a)

Here, it is important to note too that the Qur'ānic imagery of the woman as "field" is similar to the Halakhic presentation. Twice in *Mishnah* Ketubah, the expression "your field has been flooded" is used to refer to women in a sexual context: (1) when a bride has no physical signs of virginity, she says to her husband, "After you betrothed me, I have been raped, and your field has been ruined by a flood" (*Mishnah*: Ketubah 1:6). In the next instance, if she has a physical blemish after betrothal, she is described as a field that has been ruined by a flood (*Mishnah*: Ketubah 7:8). The *Talmud* adopts this image and in Nedarim 90b–91a, portrays the husband of the woman who has been raped as one whose field has been flooded. If she is unable to go through with a wedding because of her menses or some sickness, the man is again referred to as one whose field has been flooded (*Talmud*: Ketubah 2a–b). Of course, one may run the danger of what may be termed parallelomania here, but given the conditions and the interaction between the Jews and Muslims of Medina, as well as the Qur'ānic vocabulary, the preponderance of the evidence seems to indicate that Q 2:223 is indeed referring to a specific Judaic attitude.

The Qur'ānic view of the characteristics of the ideal man and woman has also influenced the conduct of gender interaction. If the man is strong, stubborn, and jealous, the honor of the family rests in the conduct of the nurturing, weaker woman who must always be mindful of the stronger male sex instinct. As such it is the woman who has to cover her breasts and wear a specific type of outer garment; it is she who has to speak in a manner that does not entice the male, and it is she who must walk in such a way as not to draw attention to herself (Q 24:31; 33:32, 59).

There is much contemporary disagreement regarding the aspect of women's dress, especially with regard to the head covering, *khimār*, more often and incorrectly referred to as *hijāb*. Q 24:31, it is argued, mandates the covering of the breasts, and not the head, since the term used in the verse, *juyūb*, refers to the cleft in the breasts. Those to, and among, whom a woman may adopt some laxity in respect to the sartorial requirements demanded of her are her husband, father, father-in-law, sons, stepsons, brothers, nephews, other Muslim women, old male servants who no longer have a sex-drive, or small children who are as yet not curious about the private parts of the female (Q 24:31).

The verse, "a fornicator does not marry except a fornicatress" (Q 24:3) may suggest premarital chastity on the part of both sexes. Since a man, according to the Qurʾānic imagery, could legitimately have sexual intercourse with his slave woman, the issue of virginity seems more stressed upon for the females.

The Qurʾān permits marriage with the People of the Book, and this has been taken to mean the Jews and Christians, although many jurists extended the term to include Zoroastrians. Such marriage, however, is restricted to a Muslim man contracting marriage with a woman of the People of the Book, based on the clear text of the verse: "Lawful to you are the chaste women from the believers and chaste women from those who were given the book before you" (Q 5:5). As outlined earlier, marriage with polytheists is prohibited according to Q 2:221. The only case in which marriage with a polytheist man or woman can be contracted is when the Muslim has been found guilty of adultery or fornication (Q 24:3).

Twelver Shīʿites have allowed the continuation of the pre-Islamic practice of temporary marriage, *mutʿa*, based on Q 4:24, "Give those whom you have enjoyed sexual relations their *ṣadāq* (dowry)." They argue that Muḥammad never issued a prohibition against it, and that the *ḥadīths* reporting any proscription are from unreliable Sunnī sources. They argue that it was ʿUmar b. al-Khaṭṭāb who banned it, and that such prohibition carries no legal weight since no one can ban that which is allowed in the Qurʾān. While it may have been on the decline prior to the Iranian revolution, the contemporary exhortation of many Shīʿī scholars for its practice, as well as continued conflicts and economic hardships in the Middle East have made the institution a pragmatic solution to the needs of the people and an absolutely superior one to the "free" relations between sexes in Western countries.

The Qurʾān does not hint in any way at birth control and abortion, and this has led to various differences of opinion among jurists. Since the document absolutely prohibits the killing of children due to economic circumstances (Q 6:151; 17:31), some jurists have argued against birth control and abortion. The majority opinion seems to be based on *ḥadīth* that seem to allow conditional permissibility. *Ḥadīth* that allow *coitus interruptus* (Arabic *ʿazl*) are used as the basis for rulings in favor of birth control, since Muḥammad would purportedly not have allowed the practice if he knew it was wrong. Interpretations of the Qurʾān that purport to show that in the first three months a fetus is without a soul have been used to allow abortion during that period, although there is no direct indication of such an idea in the text. Like many concepts of Islamic practice, the idea has been traced to the *ḥadīth*. This has given rise to the realization that much of what passes as the Islamic understanding on family, sex, and sexuality, is, in fact, the accumulated medieval regional and cultural imprint on the interpretation of religion. Unlike Judaism, which has had its Haskalah, and Christianity, which has had its Renaissance, the interpretation of Islam, for the most part, remains the domain faith-based scholars (*ʿulamāʾ*) who still use medieval source texts. This recognition, along with the concomitant re-examination of *ḥadīth* and legal literature, is now becoming the focus of many Muslim scholars who are seeking to achieve gender parity, or as some claim, restore the rights of women and family as outlined in the pristine message of the Qur'ān. Among such scholars are Amina Wadud (1999), Leila Ahmed (1982), Azizah al-Hibri (1982), Riffat Hassan (1991), Asma Barlas (2002), Abdullahi an-Na'im (1990) and Mohammad Arkoun (1994).

Further reading

Ahmed, Leila (1982) *Women and Gender in Islam: Historical Roots of a Modern Debate*. Yale University Press, New Haven.

An-Na'im, Abdullahi Ahmed (1990) *Towards an Islamic Reformation*. Syracuse University Press, Syracuse.

Barlas, Asma (2002) *"Believing Women" in Islam: Unreading Patriarchal Interpretations of Islam*. University of Texas Press, Austin.

Haddad, Yvonne, and Esposito, John (eds.) (1998) *Islam, Gender and Social Change*. Oxford University Press, New York.

Hassan, Riffat (1991) An Islamic perspective. In: Becher, Jeanne (ed.) *Women, Religion and Sexuality: Studies on the Impact of Religious Teachings on Women*. Trinity Press, Philadelphia.

Al-Hibri, Azizah (ed.) (1982) *Women and Islam*. Pergamon Press, Oxford.

Murray, Stephen, Roscoe, Will, Wafer, Jim, et al. (1997) *Islamic Homosexualities: Culture, History and Literature*. New York University Press, New York.

Rahman, Fazlur (1979) *Islam*. University of Chicago Press, Chicago.

Stowasser, Barbara (1994) *Women in the Qur'ān: Traditions and Interpretation*. Oxford University Press, New York.

Wadud, Amina (1999) *The Qur'ān and Woman*. Oxford University Press, New York.

CHAPTER 20

Jihād

Reuven Firestone

Jihād is a term that has come to be associated in both the Islamic world and the West with the Islamic version of "holy war" or, more accurately, divinely ordained warring. Like virtually all religions from east to west, Islam as a religious civilization allows for war under certain conditions, and like all other religions, the ultimate authority for engaging in war is the divinity. Wars may be divinely authorized beforehand or justified afterwards – or they may not. Not all wars are ordained by God, according to Islam, and there have always been battles and wars waged by factions in the Muslim world that were considered by leading religious scholars not to have been divinely justified. Elaborate discussions may be found in Islamic religious literatures over what constitutes divinely authorized war, the authority for engaging the enemy, definitions of enemy, the goal of military engagement and so forth (Morabia 1974; Peters 1996). Although the traditions of the prophet (*ḥadīth*) also serve as a source for representing divine rationale in these discussions – each of the six authoritative collections contains sections ("books") devoted to the prophet's speech and acts associated with warring usually named "The book of *jihād*," or "The book of *jihād* and expedition (*siyar*)" – it is usually the Qur'ān, the record of God's direct revelation to the prophet Muḥammad, that is cited as the ultimate authority for the determination and validation of divinely ordained war.

The range and nuances associated with the meaning of *jihād* in the Qur'ān will be explored below, but it is important to note first what the word does *not* mean. *Jihād* does not mean holy war, nor does it have any linguistic association whatsoever with the notion of warring. Two other words assume the meaning of warring and war in the Qur'ān: *qitāl*, and *ḥarb*. We shall observe how the former is the more common Qur'ānic term for warring and even for divinely authorized war, while the latter is the term for engaging in profane war.

Arabic dictionaries define the basic meaning for the root of *jihād*, *j.h.d.*, as exerting oneself and taking extraordinary pains, employing oneself vigorously and diligently. The specific form of the root from which *jihād* is derived is a verbal form that expresses mutuality of action or relates the action to another entity. *Jihād*, therefore, is exerting one's utmost efforts and abilities in relation to an "other," and that other is usually defined as "an object of disapprobation" that could range from a concrete human enemy to Satan or to the evil inclinations in one's own self (Lane 1863; Ibn Manẓūr 1375/1956). *Jihād* can thus take on a range of meanings and be applied to a number of different kinds of action. It easily becomes a religiously laden term because it represents the most basic ethical message of religion, that one must strive to do the good by overcoming the bad.

Qitāl, on the other hand, serves as a technical term in the Qur'ān for warring. The root meaning of this term is "kill," and *qitāl* occurs in the same verbal form as *jihād*, which expresses mutuality of action or relates the action to another entity. But *qitāl* is not a religious term like *jihād*. It means, simply, warring; that is, armed engagement along with a body of other comrades in hostile conflict directed against an outside group. Although *qitāl* can be activated for religious causes, it may also be employed for mundane reasons. It is not surprising, then, that the operative term in Islam for divinely authorized warring is the religiously laden *jihād*.

Contextual Meanings of *Jihād, Qitāl* and *Ḥarb*

The full range of Qur'ānic views on warring will be observed below by examining all three words that express this act in the Qur'ān, but because of the particular significance of *jihād* in contemporary discourse among both Muslims and non-Muslims, we begin with a close contextual reading of this rich term.

Although the Qur'ān is a written book, it was and continues to be known to most Muslims as an oral text. It was constructed in order to be recited and assimilated in an oral literary environment and, like all revelation, reduced to writing at a later point in its literary history. The addressee is therefore both hearer and reader. These two processes of absorption and construction of meaning are different, of course, with the latter being far more analytical than the former. But in both modes, individual words, word combinations, and word associations convey meaning in a variety of ways. It is clear that meaning is constructed largely from words and phrases in their specific contexts, but words and phrases, and especially repeated idioms, are also unconsciously and instinctively associated by the addressee with their appearance or the appearance of similar forms in other contexts. The meanings in these other contexts, therefore, have an influence on the meaning in the context in question. In order to truly understand the meaning of the word *jihād*, then, one must examine the range of its various forms and contextual associations.

Its most simple form, *jahd*, occurs four times in the Qur'ān in the idiom, *aqsamū bi-'llah jahd aymānihim*, which should be translated as "They swear (swore) to God their most powerful (strongest) oaths" (Q 6:109; 16:38; 24:53; 35:42). The reference is always to hypocritical unbelievers who claim in one way or another that, while they would follow the prophet if authentic proof came to them, they yet remain unconvinced. Contextually, *jahd* in this repeated phrase conveys the sense that these unbelievers make oaths in the name of God with what might appear to be tremendous sincerity, yet from the standpoint of the Qur'ān, they are clearly insincere because in the final analysis, they do not accept the truth of the Qur'ānic signs. The related form, *juhd*, occurs once (Q 9:79), also in a polemical context directed against deniers (*kuffār*) and dissenters (*munāfiqūn*). But the term refers to certain obedient believers with modest means who have nothing more to contribute to the community chest than their own *juhd* – that is, their own personal effort and ability.

Arabic grammatical tenses in the Qur'ān do not necessarily convey a sense of time in the same way as European languages. In the case of *jāhada*, the verb form from which *jihād* is constructed, the form typically referred to as past, or "perfect," often conveys a sense of the English present participle: "one who strives vigorously and diligently," as in Q 9:19: "Do you consider the water-givers of the *ḥajj* and the *ʿimāra* to the sacred mosque equal to one who believes in God and the last day and strives (*jāhada*) in the path of God?" I will be referring to verb tense forms typically used in English grammars of Arabic, but I use these designations to differentiate forms rather than tenses in the Qur'ān. I use the designation "past" in what follows only to refer to the form (morphology) and not as a reference to the usual sense of time.

The past form of *jāhada* in the Qur'ān almost never refers directly to fighting or even to any kind of conflict with nonbelievers (except in Q 9:88, see below). It typically occurs in one of three contexts: in reference to the afterlife (Q 2:217–18; 3:142; 16:108–10; 29:6–7, 68–9), as one reference among a number of references to sincerity in belief or sincerity in belonging to the community of believers (in all the just-cited references plus Q 8:72, 75; 9:16, 19, 20; 49:14–15), or as a reference to kinship pressure to remain outside the community of believers (Q 29:8; 31:14–15). In the first contextual category, those who strive are contrasted with those who will be destined for an afterlife in hell. The distinction becomes idiomatic: those who strive stand out against those "destined for the fire" or "the losers." In the second category, striving occurs among a number of other descriptors representing the religious integrity of the believer. In the last contextual category listed above (family pressure to associate with polytheism), God commands respect and care for one's parents (cf. Exodus 20:11; Deuteronomy 5:15) unless they "strive/strove (to influence) you to associate with Me anything of which you have no knowledge."

Jāhada, in the form of the past, is often included along with other verbal determinations of belonging: "those who believe, emigrate and strive in the path of God" (e.g., Q 2:218; 8:72, 74; 9:20; similar in Q 16:110). When referring to those who strive along with those who emigrate, the reference is to a specific group of believers defined by their emigration (*hijra*, thus *muhājirūn*) along with Muḥammad from Mecca to Medina. The verbs in this repeated verb-string occur in the form of the past tense, but their importance lies in their indicating the sincerity of the believer. The believer is thus a person who believes in God and His prophet, who supported the prophet strongly enough to leave home in Mecca for an uncertain future in Medina, and who exerts great effort in following the divinely determined path along with all that that commitment entails.

Jāhada, whether in the "past" or other forms, often occurs as part of an idiomatic phrase in which it is followed by "in the path of God" (*fī sabīl Allāh*, sometimes translated as "in the way of God" or "for religion," inevitably in reference to Islam, and conveying the sense of religious commitment). In this combination, it means to engage vigorously in religiously defined acts. "In the path of God" follows other verbs as well, the most important for this discussion being *qitāl*.[1] *Jihād* in the path of God and *qitāl* in the path of God are not synonymous. *Qitāl* in the path of God is religiously authorized war. *Jihād* in the path of God may include religiously authorized war, but it conveys a broader range of authorized or required religious acts. It might best be defined as religious activism.

In none of the three categories noted above is the past tense form of *jāhada* associated with aggression against unbelievers or enemies. The one exception is Q 9:88, which occurs in a long section (Q 9:73–89) complaining bitterly against deniers (*kuffār*) and dissenters (*munāfiqūn*), in which *jihād* occurs in all of its verbal forms found in the Qur'ān. This general tendency is not the case when the verb occurs in the imperfect and imperative forms. In these forms, *jāhada* occurs occasionally as an expression of general religious piety as striving "in the path of God" (see Q 5:35, 54), but it is more prevalent in the expression, "strive with your possessions and your souls" (*bi-amwālikum wa-anfusikum*, translated alternatively as "with your possessions and your own selves"). The latter idiom typically occurs in aggressive or militant contexts, as in Q 9:41: "Set out [for battle] lightly or heavily [armed] and strive with your possessions and your souls in the path of God" (see Q 9:41–4, 73–89 in which it occurs three times), but, in all the cases where this expression is found, it is in a context of complaint against those who prefer to remain behind while others set out on battle campaigns as in Q 9:81: "Those left behind are happy, sitting at home in opposition to the messenger of God, hating to strive with their possessions and their souls." Sometimes in the imperative, *jāhid* occurs by itself as an expression of aggression (Q 9:73, 86; 66:9). In the imperfect, it occurs once in an aggressive context with a combination of the two expressions, "in the path of God" and "with your possessions" (Q 9:81), and once again in combination but in a nonaggressive context (Q 61:11). Occasionally it occurs in the imperfect independently and in a nonaggressive context (Q 22:78; 29:6).

The noun form, *jihād*, occurs only four times in the Qur'ān. It occurs once in an aggressive context in combination with the imperative (Q 25:52): "Strive a great striving against them with it" (*jāhidhum bihi jihādan kabīran*), once again in a similar combination but not in an aggressive context (Q 22:78): "Strive in God a sincere striving," and twice in aggressive contexts with other word combinations (Q 9:24; 60:1), the latter clearly indicating military engagement with enemies. The participial form, *mujāhid(ū/īn)* occurs in two contexts, both militant (Q 4:94–6; 47:31). The former opens with an expression of raiding, "when you set out (*idhā ḍarabtum*) in the path of God," where the participial form appears three times and includes both expressions of "in the path of God" and "with possessions and souls." The latter is less obviously one of battle, though it reflects militant conflict with those who oppose Muḥammad.

Taken together, the forms of the root *j-h-d* in their various Qur'ānic contexts convey meanings that range from great personal effort to generic religious piety, to engaging in or supplying the war effort on behalf of the new community of believers. *Jihād*, then, is a nuanced term, and its meanings broadened in Qur'ān interpretation and other post-Qur'ānic religious literatures. Because of its basic notion of deep and total personal effort, *jihād*, especially "in the path of God," became the operative term for warring on behalf of Islam and the Muslim community. *Qitāl* (*qātala*) is far more prevalent in the Qur'ān as a reference to fighting, occurring some sixty-seven times. But given the range of religious meanings and contexts associated with *jihād* in the Qur'ān, it should not be surprising that engagement in war on behalf of the Muslim community, an act that often resulted in the ultimate effort of personal sacrifice in death on the battlefield, came to be identified with *jihād* rather than *qitāl*.

Another root term for warring, *ḥ-r-b*, can also be found in the Qur'ān, but it occurs far less frequently than either *qitāl* or *jihād*. Like these latter words, the word is found in the verbal form conveying mutuality of action or relating action to another entity (*ḥāraba*). In the case of *ḥāraba*, however, which occurs only twice in the Qur'ān (Q 5:33; 9:107), warring is the exact opposite of *jāhada* because it is directed against God and his prophet (*man ḥāraba 'llaha warasūlahu*). Warring as *ḥāraba*, therefore, cannot be authorized by God. It can never be "holy war." However, the noun *ḥarb* is distinct from the nouns *jihād* and *qitāl* in that it does not occur in the form expressing mutuality or transfer of action. Rather than meaning "fighting" or "battling," as do the gerunds *jihād* and *qitāl*, *ḥarb* means, simply, war, whether holy or profane as in Q 8:57: "If you come upon them in war (*fa'imma tathqafannahum fī 'l-ḥarb*), then scatter those behind them by means of them; perhaps they will take warning!" (cf. Q 2:279).

Qur'ānic Militancy in Historical Context

As in the case of the Hebrew Bible, New Testament, and other examples of divine scripture, the Qur'ān was revealed in a polemical context. One of the fundamental phenomenological aspects of divine scripture is its rarity, to which the salvation histories of the three great families of Abrahamic scriptural monotheisms attest. God may grant revelations to his creatures through a variety of means, but an official and eternal written record of revelation in the form of scripture is extraordinary. To put it differently, there must be an exceptional reason for God to break the natural course of nature by providing a particular portion of humanity with a (written) record of the divine will.

An irruption of such magnitude into the workings of human history would occur only because of exceptional circumstances, and in every case of scriptural revelation it is assumed that God connects directly with humanity in order to induce a major sea change in behavior or belief. No document is quite as revolutionary as scripture. It demands change in the name of the most powerful being in existence, more authoritative than the greatest human ruler and mightier than the most enormous army. But in every case of such revelation, the salvation history around and through which the revelation occurs emphasizes how difficult it was for the general populace to recognize the divine word. In every case of scriptural revelation, only a small elite accepts God's word unconditionally, and it becomes the task of that elite to bring the word to humanity at large.[2] Because of the natural human tendency to resist its demand for unconditional and radical change, scripture is polemical by its very nature. It chastises, cajoles, and threatens. When it meets human stubbornness under certain historical conditions, it commands war.

Those historical conditions are found quite clearly in the case of two emergent scriptures – the Hebrew Bible and the Qur'ān – but lacking in two others: the New Testament and the Talmud. The latter pair emerged in a historical environment that was dominated overwhelmingly by the political and military might of the Roman Empire. The two communities that spoke on behalf of these revealed scriptures emerged under the heel of Rome and found that they had no hope of dominating militarily the competing contemporary religious or ethnic polities. Their scriptures were most certainly highly polemical, but they tended not to advocate divinely authorized war. It was just too costly in human and political terms, though they succeeded in constructing holy war ideas for their communities later, when the historical circumstances allowed such a development.

Conversely, the Hebrew Bible and the Qur'ān emerged in environments in which tribal communities with similar military capabilities regularly battled one another on a largely equal playing field, the former during the first millennium BCE in the ancient Near East, and the latter in sixth-century CE Arabia. Fighting was a regular and normal part of tribal life in both contexts, so when a new community emerged with an independent identity, it was natural for it to engage in militant conflict with other groups. When that community defined itself against other communities in religious terms that included belief in one great God and in a divinely revealed scripture, permission and even encouragement for warring was authorized by that God and through that scripture (see Firestone 2005).

This brief schema is presented here in order to set the militant verses of the Qur'ān in context. Each of the four scriptures mentioned here contains polemical material, some of it quite virulent. In each scripture, some invective is directed against hostile outside forces while other polemics are reserved for competing factions within the larger communities of believers. It appears to be a natural phenomenon of scriptural religion to represent and articulate through scripture the anger and resentment that the newly emerging communities experienced as they battled their way to acceptance. Within the historical context of late antiquity, survival for emergent Christianity and Rabbinic Judaism required that their militancy be expressed in ways that would not actually encourage the bearing of arms. The Qur'ān, on the other hand, like the Hebrew Bible before it, seems to have emerged in a historical context that not only allowed, but required, a certain militancy for it to survive.

When reading the Qur'ān, one finds different forms of expression of conflict and polemic. The ubiquitous references and partial narratives about ancient prophets inevitably present stories in which God's messengers are confronted by unbelieving and unrelenting polytheists, who combine unethical behaviors with their denial of monotheism. Sometimes the people engage in violence among themselves; often they threaten the prophet who was sent to them with death. The inevitable result is divinely ordained punishment and destruction of the unbelievers, but survival of the prophet and any remnant believers that may have listened to his message. These are stories that depict ancient times, but they serve as allegories for the Qur'ānic present. Muḥammad is the prophet who is denied and threatened by his own people. His campaigns against his (and God's) enemies are divinely sanctioned, for without a change of heart, the Arab people are destined to meet the same fate as the many peoples who came before. Unless they accept the divine will as articulated by the prophet, they will suffer imminent and painful destruction through fire and brimstone, earthquake, and other divinely initiated disasters.

The stories of ancient prophets serve as a subtext for the Qur'ānic present, and that present is portrayed as a time for radical change from polytheism to monotheism and from wickedness and depravity to morality and justice. The world is described in binary terms, with the new prophet offering a stubborn people their one and only opportunity to emerge out of the darkness into light. This scenario is actually typical of emerging religion, where the newly emerging faith community meets vigorous opposition from establishment religion and must fight its way to success (Stark 1987; 1996).

In order to succeed, every individual in the new faith community represented by the Qur'ān must engage in *jihād*. This, as noted above, means striving to support the community of believers in a variety of ways, from demonstrating religious loyalty through certain behaviors and rituals, and providing it with material resources and political support, to engaging in military battle against its enemies. All of this is *jihād* in the path of God.

The Range of Qur'ānic Articulations of War

The Qur'ān presents a variety of positions on relations with the opponents of the emerging Muslim community, ranging from calls to ignore those who deny the truth of God and his prophet (Q 6:106) to preaching to them (Q 16:125), to killing them (Q 2:191). The many disparate verses are found in dozens of chapters and in a variety of topical and stylistic contexts. As can be observed from the tenor of the verses just cited, many appear to be in conflict with one another, and both traditional Muslim and Western scholars have found their range of meanings and the policies commanded by them worthy of study and comment. The following is a sample of some of the classic verses arranged in general categories.

Nonmilitant (nonconfrontational) verses

Q 5:13 Because of their breaking their covenant,[3] we cursed them and hardened their hearts. They change words from their contexts and forget some of what they were taught. You will continue to uncover treachery from all but a few of them, but be forgiving and pardon, for God loves the kindly.

Q 6:106 Follow what has been revealed to you from your Lord; there is no God but He; and turn away from the idolaters (*al-mushrikīn*).

Q 15:94–5 Profess openly what you have been commanded, and turn away from the idolaters, for We are sufficient for you against the scoffers.

Q 16:125 Invite (all) to the way of your Lord with wisdom and beautiful preaching; and argue with them in ways that are best and most gracious: For your Lord knows best who has strayed from His path, and who receives guidance.

Restrictions on fighting (or fighting in defense)

Q 2:190 Fight in the path of God those who fight you, but do not transgress limits (*walā ta'dadū*); for God does not love transgressors.

Q 9:36 The number of months in the sight of God is twelve [written] in God's book the day He created the heavens and the earth. Of them, four are sacred. That is the right religion, so do not wrong each other during them; but fight all the idolaters just as they fight all of you,[4] and know that God is with those who are God-fearing.

Q 22:39–40 Permission is given to those who fight[5] because they have been wronged – God is Most Powerful for their aid – those who have been unjustly expelled from their homes only because they say: "Our Lord is God."

Conflict between God's command and the response of the people

Q 2:216 Fighting is commanded you even though it is disagreeable to you. But it is possible that you dislike something that is good for you and that you love something that is bad for you. God knows, but you know not!

Q 3:156 O you who believe! Be not like the deniers who said of their brethren who went abroad in the land or went on raids: If they had been [home] with us they would not have died or been killed; that God may make it anguish in their hearts. God gives life and causes death; and God is Seer of what you do!

Q 4:75 What is wrong with you that you do not fight in the path of God when weak men, women and children are crying: "Our Lord! Bring us out of this town of evil people and give us from Your presence a protector! Oh, give us a defender!"

Q 9:42 Had the gain been nearby and the journey easy, they would have followed you, but the distance seemed too great to them. Yet they swear by God: "If we could, we would have set out with you." They destroy themselves. God knows that they are liars.

Verses strongly advocating war for God's religion (unconditional war)

Q 2:191 Kill them wherever you find them and turn them out from where they have turned you out, for *fitna*[6] is worse than killing, but do not fight them at the sacred mosque unless they fight you there. But if they fight you, kill them. Such is the reward of the unbelievers.

Q 8:39 And fight them until there is no more *fitna*, and religion becomes God's in its entirety. But if they cease, God is aware of what they do. (cf. Q 2:193)

Q 9:5 When the sacred months are past, kill the idolaters wherever you find them, and seize them, besiege them, and lie in wait for them in every place of ambush; but if they repent, pray regularly, and give the alms tax, then let them go their way, for God is Forgiving, Merciful.

Q 9:29 Fight those who do not believe in God or the Last Day, and who do not forbid what has been forbidden by God and His Messenger, nor acknowledge the religion of truth from among the People of the Book, until they pay the poll tax (*al-jizya*) out of hand, having been brought low.

Q 9:73/66:9 O prophet! Strive (*jāhid*) against the unbelievers and the dissenters (*al-munāfiqīn*), and be ruthless with them. Their refuge is Hell, a bad destination.

These verses and many others treating relations with nonbelievers occur in many different chapters and in a variety of contexts. Not only do the verses treating relations with nonbelievers show no evidence of any particular organization *in situ*, they seem inconsistent and even contradictory. The organization provided above is imposed on the verses by this writer, and, in fact, a number of distinct organizing principles could be applied to them that would result in different categories than those given here. The fact of the matter is that the great breadth of outlook expressed in the Qur'ān regarding unbelievers is problematic and difficult to decipher (Firestone 1999: 47–97). Qur'ānic regard toward unbelievers is inconsistent and even at times contradictory, suggesting perhaps that their source is inconsistent and self-contradictory, something impossible for an omniscient and omnipotent monotheistic deity.

This problem troubled early Muslim Qur'ān scholars, who found apparent contradiction in the Qur'ān intolerable. The solution that emerged was to match the revelations with an emerging biography of Muḥammad (Firestone 1999: 99–125). According to this schema, the verses legislating behaviors toward nonbelievers were considered to have been revealed according to a particular chronology. The earlier verses counseled quietism and preaching, or perhaps arguing with those who denied the prophethood of Muḥammad and the religion he represented. Very purposefully, they did not counsel militancy toward Muḥammad's enemies. Over time, however, the revelations then became increasingly aggressive. This increase in belligerency matched the increasing size and power of the community of believers.

Early on, while still in Mecca, the emerging faith community was weak and could only ignore those who railed against them and their new religion. As Muḥammad's confidence grew, they could argue against their opponents; they could begin preaching to them. But they remained a weak community and suffered both verbal and physical humiliation at the hands of their enemies in Mecca. They were powerless to defend themselves. Finally, they were expelled from their Meccan home and found refuge in the settlements of Medina.

In Medina, the community of believers was free from the immediate physical threat of their Meccan enemies. They grew in numbers and strength under Medinan protection, and at this point, the revelations began to allow fighting in defense of the community. As they continued to increase in strength and numbers, the revelations continued to evolve in response. The next stage was one in which the community of believers was permitted to initiate attack, but only against known enemies and with clear limits to the rules of engagement. Presumably, this meant the traditional restriction from fighting during certain months of the year and other pre-Islamic customs. Finally, as the community became increasingly powerful politically and militarily, it was commanded to go out and fight their opponents wherever they could be found in order to dominate the region of Arabia where they were located.

According to this representation, what looked like confusion or contradiction in the Qur'ān was actually testimony to God's great wisdom as He prudently guided His prophet and community. When aggression would have been dangerous and self-destructive, it was forbidden. As it became a successful means of building up the community, it was allowed and then commanded incrementally. This solved the problem of contradiction. The earlier verses were revealed in order to guide the prophet and his community according to the needs of the hour, but they were only intended by God to be temporary. They were superseded when later verses were revealed that articulated a more aggressive position. It was natural to assume that later verses abrogated earlier verses, and this became a general rule. The goal, therefore, was to determine the chronology of revelation.

Two literatures grew out of this need in the second–third/eighth–ninth centuries. One, called "occasions of revelation" (*asbāb al-nuzūl*), took certain verses and placed their revelation into the emerging history of Muḥammad's life (see Rippin 1985b; *EI2* 2004: "Ḳur'ān," 415–16). The other, usually called "abrogating and abrogated (Qur'ānic verses)" (*EI2* 2004: "naskh"; Burton 1977; 1990; Powers 1988), identified certain verses that appeared to contradict one another and determined which abrogated which. The study of abrogation worked well to solve problems of apparent contradiction, not only for the verses treating relations with nonbelievers, but for a number of other thorny issues such as inheritance, the consumption of alcohol, and so forth.

The problem with this solution to the problem of apparent contradiction, from the perspective of Western historiography, is that it is circular. It places Qur'ānic revelations in relation to the biography of the prophet, but the prophetic biography that we know today was constructed, in significant part, because of the very problems associated with Qur'ānic chronology. All three endeavors – determining the chronology of revelation, resolving problems of apparent contradiction through the theory of abrogation, and the writing of the prophetic biography by collecting and organizing oral traditions – were occurring around the same time. Consciously or not, they worked together to solve difficult textual and theological problems.

Now, as we return to the issue of relations with nonbelievers, we conclude with the observation that organizing principles other than prophetic biography could also be applied to the discrepant verses. Many are possible. One way to organize the verses, for example, is according to processes of group formation. As growing communities form around leadership, even charismatic leadership, they tend to form smaller sub-groups within the larger community. The breakdown naturally occurs around gender and age and other factors. In the case of emergent religious communities these factors typically include differing approaches to ritual activities or eating customs and expectations, differences in personal association with factions within the leadership, or attitudes regarding how individuals or the group as a whole should relate to people who do not belong to the group.

It is clear, for example, that a large number of verses in several chapters show evidence of disagreement over whether the believers should go out on military campaigns against nonbelievers (see above and Firestone 1999: 77–84). Verses such as Q 9:38–9 complain about the great lack of enthusiasm among some believers regarding this endeavor:

> O believers! What is the matter with you that when it is said to you: "March out in the path of God," you are weighed down to the ground?! Are you so satisfied with the life of this world over the Hereafter? The enjoyment of the life of this world is but little [when compared] to the Hereafter. If you do not march forth He will afflict you with a painful punishment and will substitute another people instead of you! You cannot harm Him at all, but God has power over everything. (See also Q 3:156; 4:72–7.)

Those not wishing to go out on campaigns are described as selfish, petty, or simply afraid and lacking faith. It is quite possible, however, that they had alternative reasons for resisting this requirement of the new religion. Perhaps some, as in the early Jesus movement, were attracted to the prophet and his religion for quietist spiritual reasons and did not consider warring to be a valid activity for the new community. Some, according to Q 3:167–8, claimed that they knew nothing of fighting.

It is quite possible, therefore, that the Qur'ān is attesting to the fact that the young community of believers simply had not settled on their communal position over how to relate to nonbelievers, and were divided into factions whose positions were articulated through the different, even conflicting, revelations. When confronted with the problem of enemies desiring to impede the success of the new community, some may have been quietist or even pacifist, others willing to fight only in defense, and others interested in transferring the warrior nature of pre-Islamic tribalism to the new trans-kinship "tribe" (*umma*) of believers. The Qur'ān certainly attests to different opinions regarding relations with nonbelievers. It is clear that however these differences were expressed during the period of emergent Islam, the militant position became dominant. The militant view then became codified during the period of empire when divine authority and justification for imperial armies was of great importance to the state (Peters 1996: 4–5).

Qur'ān and *Jihād* in the Contemporary Period

By the end of the third/ninth century when the formative period of Islam was coming to a close, a consensus developed among most Muslim religious scholars that the essential questions of Islamic law had been thoroughly discussed and finally settled. Henceforth, no one was deemed to have the necessary qualifications for independent reasoning (*ijtihād*) in law. Only explanation and application would be allowed, or at most, interpretation of doctrine as it had already been established. This consensus would be articulated to this day as the "closing of the gate of *ijtihād*" (*EI2* 2004: "*idjtihād*").

The truth of the matter, however, is that independent reasoning in Qur'ān interpretation has continued at one level or another to this day and is currently very active. The very same issues, for example, that are sources of discussion and change in the West have an impact on the Islamic world. These include the role of women, government, religion and state, economics, and, most certainly, *jihād* and relations with nonbelievers. As with the religious reformers who so radically transformed Christianity and Judaism in previous centuries, some Muslims today engage in quite independent reading of their scripture. The results of their inquiries vary, without doubt, and this is most certainly the case with regard to *jihād* and relations with nonbelievers.

Views on *jihād* have become polarized in the last decade, with the continuing attraction of modernity among a considerable segment of the Muslim world on the one hand, and the growing militant reaction of others against the threat of the West on the other. An extreme militant interpretation of the Qur'ān on relations with nonbelievers is articulated by Osama bin Laden in his famous *fatwā*, issued on February 23, 1998,[7] and in other contexts. A modernist reading of some of the same verses arrives at a radically different conclusion (Safi 2001). The process of finding, renewing and forming personal meaning from the verses of the Qur'ān will continue for as long as it exists, for constructing meaning is a part of the essentiality of being human, and applying the process to scripture is integral to the spirituality of the scriptural religions.

Notes

1 Fighting (*qitāl*) in the path of God is the most frequent verb connected with the phrase, *in the path of God*, in the Qur'ān, occurring twelve times. *Jihād* in the path of God occurs eight times, as does emigrating in the path of God. Expending personal resources occurs seven times, and being killed occurs three times. Laments or complaints about people being turned away from the path of God occur fully two dozen times.

2 This schema is the "ideal-typical" phenomenology of scriptural revelation. The narrative that tells of the giving of the Hebrew Bible (a "pre-scriptural scripture") and the response to it, is somewhat different because the Hebrew Bible emerges into the light of scripture from an earlier life as what might best be called a national literature.

3 The previous verse refers to the Children of Israel.

4 *Kāffat*^{an}. Or "fight the idolaters during all [these months] just as they fight you during all [of them]." Another reading has "engage in fighting the idolaters as a unified army, just as they engage in fighting you as a unified army. The difficulty is in determining what *kāffat* refers to.

5 Or, "those who have been fought against." The difference between the active and passive form of the verb depends on a minor change in the pointing of the text.

6 Lit. "temptation," translations of *fitna* tend to be rendered to fit the context. "Persecution" is a common translation here, though it is defined by Muslim exegetes as idolatry or dissension in other verses.

7 Published in the London-based Arabic newspaper, *Al-Quds al-ʿArabī*, February 23, 1998. URL: http://www.library.cornell.edu/colldev/mideast/fatw2.htm. English translation: http://www.fas.org/irp/world/para/docs/980223-fatwa.htm.

Further reading

Dajani-Shakeel, Hadia, and Messier, Ronald (eds.) (1991) *The Jihad and its Times*. University of Michigan, Ann Arbor.

Firestone, Reuven (1999) *Jihad: The Origin of Holy War in Islam*. Oxford University Press, New York.

Johnson, James Turner, and Kelsay, John (eds.) (1990) *Cross, Crescent, and Sword: The Justification and Limitation of War in Western and Islamic Tradition*. Greenwood Press, New York.

Kelsay, John, and Johnson, James Turner (1991) *Just War and Jihad: Historical and Theoretical Perspectives on War and Peace in Western and Islamic Traditions*. Greenwood Press, New York.

Khadduri, Majid (1955) *War and Peace in the Law of Islam*. The Johns Hopkins University Press, Baltimore.

Nardin, Terry (ed.) (1996) *The Ethics of War and Peace: Religious and Secular Perspective*. Princeton University Press, Princeton.

Peters, Rudolph (1979) *Islam and Colonialism: The Doctrine of Jihad in Modern History*. Mouton, The Hague.

Peters, Rudolph (1996) *Jihad in Classical and Modern Islam*. Marcus Weiner, Princeton.

Safi, Louay M. (2001) *Peace and the Limits of War: Transcending Classical Conception of Jihad*. International Institute of Islamic Thought, Herndon, VA.

Schleiffer, S. Abdullah (1984) Jihad: Modernist apologists, modern apologetics. *Islamic Culture* 28, 25–46.

PART IV

Interpretation

CHAPTER 21

Hermeneutics: al-Thaʿlabī

Walid Saleh

Al-Thaʿlabī (d. 427/1035) is perhaps one of the most important Qurʾān exegetes of the medieval Islamic world. The legacy of his Qurʾān commentary, *al-Kashf waʾl-bayān ʿan tafsīr al-Qurʾān* ("The Unveiling and Elucidation in Qurʾānic Interpretation;" henceforth *al-Kashf*) has only recently begun to be studied. Al-Thaʿlabī's work ushered in the high classical style of Qurʾānic commentary, and for centuries it remained the major source for later exegetes, whether explicitly acknowledged or not, through direct channels or indirectly. Moreover, *al-Kashf*, for reasons I will explain later in this chapter, would become the Sunnī work most widely utilized and abused by Shīʿī polemicists in their wars with the Sunnīs. This prompted Ibn Taymiyya (d. 728/1328) to launch a blistering critique of al-Thaʿlabī in an attempt to circumvent the Shīʿī use of his work. Eventually, Sunnī scholars downgraded the importance of *al-Kashf* and ceased to consider it mainstream. By the time Sunnī Muslim historians of Qurʾānic exegesis were writing the history of the genre, al-Thaʿlabī had become *persona non grata* in the field.

The history of *al-Kashf's* legacy thus documents the development of the genre of *tafsīr* as well as Sunnī-Shīʿī polemical wars. The recent edition and publication of *al-Kashf* by a Shīʿī scholar has only complicated the checkered history of this work. With the increased intensity of Sunnī-Shīʿī polemic in the last decades, modern Shīʿī scholars who had become aware of the significance of this work hurriedly prepared it for publication (al-Thaʿlabī 2002). The result is an abysmal edition which is useless for purposes of a close study of the work. Thus one of the major medieval Qurʾān commentaries is still unavailable in a critical edition (Saleh 2004: 229–42). Moreover, copies of this inferior edition are hard to locate.

Several features of *al-Kashf* made the prominent role it played in the history of Qurʾānic exegesis possible. First, al-Thaʿlabī did not just write a new commentary; rather he started by assessing the whole field and evaluating its salient trends. The introduction of *al-Kashf* represents an important moment in the development of the art of Qurʾānic exegesis: it adopts a self-reflective stance, and offers a detailed discussion of the field as it then stood. Readers are fully informed of what al-Thaʿlabī thought of the major figures in the field and why he excluded certain currents (namely, the Muʿtazilite *tafsīr* tradition). Moreover, he is one of a handful of medieval exegetes who listed all of his sources in detail. He utilized over a hundred books, in addition to his personal notes from the lectures of over 300 other scholars with whom he had studied. The introduction to his commentary is thus an articulate assessment of the status of the field on the eve of the fifth/eleventh century (Goldfeld 1984). The fastidiousness of his exhaustive listing of sources was never matched: not content to use one version of a certain work, he used all the available recensions – in one instance four different versions of the same work. To the degree that he collected his material independently from al-Ṭabarī (d. 310/923), we are now in a position to use *al-Kashf* in conjunction with al-Ṭabarī's work to study the early phase of Qur'ānic exegesis. Moreover, by incorporating the material made available since the publication of al-Ṭabarī's work, *al-Kashf* preserves the collective engagement of Muslim intellectuals with the Qur'ān up to the fifth century. As a source for the fourth century, *al-Kashf* is indispensable. Finally, by dropping the *isnāds* without sacrificing the content, later exegetes, who were by then less concerned with *isnāds*, preferred al-Thaʿlabī as the source for early material. *Al-Kashf* was a handy and irresistible source for these exegetes, as it contained most of al-Ṭabarī's material and more.

An abundance of sources alone, however, could hardly account for such an epoch-making work. *Al-Kashf* was influential because it offered a resolution to many of the problems facing the Sunnī hermeneutical enterprise, resolutions that proved adaptable and convincing because they were intellectually cogent. Al-Thaʿlabī's reformulation of the craft of interpretation was to transform the field and – to the degree that one can measure influence in a field where so many of the sources are still unedited – his is apparent in the whole spectrum of the medieval exegetical tradition. Al-Thaʿlabī's resolution of the hermeneutical impasse of Sunnism proved effective through six major interpretive strategies. First, he refused the temptation to effect a rupture between Sunnī hermeneutics and philology. Second, he allowed *tafsīr*, and hence the Qur'ān, to accommodate all the major trends in pietistic Sunnism. Third, he integrated a narrative style of interpretation into the philological system. Fourth, he turned exegesis into an explicitly polemical tool against the non-Sunnī camps. Fifth, he welded the prophetic corpus of *ḥadīth* to the craft of exegesis. Finally, and perhaps most importantly, he transformed *tafsīr* into a sophisticated discipline that absorbed new intellectual challenges from outside Sunnism, digested them, and rendered them mainstream and innocuous. Al-Thaʿlabī's transformation of *tafsīr* as a discipline, I believe, shows the degree to which *tafsīr* was at the center of the intellectual life of medieval Sunnī Islam; the failure of modern scholars to incorporate the study of this genre into the general intellectual history of medieval Islam is thus unfortunate. I will proceed to outline the six major interpretive strategies through which al-Thaʿlabī sought to resolve the hermeneutical impasse of Sunnism.

The Détente with Philology

The discovery of philology early on in the Arabo-Islamic tradition has rarely been accorded the revolutionary cultural significance it deserves. Philology's role in undermining any facile dogmatic interpretation of the Qurʾān was not negligible. One only need to compare the content of Muqātil b. Sulaymān's (d. 150/767) and al-Ṭabarī's commentaries to realize how professional the tone of the craft had become by al-Ṭabarī's time. The existence of a corpus of pre-Islamic literature made for a more difficult situation. One did not fear offending God or the *ʿulamāʾ* by admitting to the content of this pagan literature and its worldview: wine, hubris, debauchery, and idolatry were all there to start with, and one was spared the urge to twist the rules of philology in order to transform an abhorrent image. A philology honed on this corpus was soon to acquire an irreverence that was barely in check when confronted with any other text, even if it was divine speech. The philological geist of the age soon forced the Sunnī exegetes to postulate that Qurʾānic interpretation must be based on philology, yet they were not so naive as to let a tool so untethered take full charge of their craft. The early, pre-philological phase of the tradition was not dropped. In so far as it encapsulated a proto-Sunnī worldview, this layer was actually enshrined as canonical. As such, however, there lurked within mainstream Sunnī hermeneutics the danger of philology running amuck. Sunnī hermeneutics, by paying more than mere lip service to the role of philology in its method, was always but one step removed from theological disaster, should an exegete submit fully to the dictates of this tool at the expense of orthodoxy. While *tafsīr* forced the birth of Arabic philology, in many ways Arabic philology came back to haunt it. Philology in the last resort was not a loyal servant for it could easily show the flimsy foundations of many of the proto-Sunnī interpretations.

The fundamental claim to authority that *tafsīr* as a discipline presented to the intellectual elite was that it was a philological explanation of the Qurʾān. As such, it presupposed that any reader of the Qurʾān, who was sufficiently versed in Arabic, would reach the same conclusions that the Sunnī exegetes offered. Read philologically, the Qurʾān, Sunnī exegetes maintained, offered a Sunnī worldview. This self-presentation and assessment are, of course, easy to refute. *Tafsīr* was primarily a doctrinal enterprise that used philology as one of its tools. Sunnī hermeneutics was thus based on a paradox: philology was proclaimed the tool needed to understand the Qurʾān, yet philology was not allowed to be the final arbiter of any interpretation. Sunnī hermeneutics, in order to save its own theological reading of the Qurʾān and to present a coherent interpretation, was ultimately willing to discard any philological reading (although it had always maintained that philology was the way to understand the Qurʾān) whenever it threatened to undermine a Sunnī theological reading not supported by philology.

In his monumental exegetical work, *Jāmiʿ al-bayān*, al-Ṭabarī offered the two currents of interpretation, theological and philological, side by side, pretending that one did not negate the other. In his work, al-Thaʿlabī managed to refine the appearance of the Sunnī exegetical enterprise and to make it, through pseudo-philological methods, conform more fully to the dictates of philology. Rhetoric, a rising new discipline, was also admitted; the influence of the philologists and their new lexicons is apparent in *al-Kashf*. Far more significant was al-Thaʿlabī's willingness to discard any traditionally inherited interpretation that was blatantly unsound philologically, as long as dropping it posed no dogmatic retreat or change in the Sunnī worldview. Moreover, poetry in its form as literature (*adab*), not merely as a handmaid to philology, was also allowed to appear in the context of Qurʾānic interpretation. Poetry, the pinnacle of human creativity, was given a place inside *tafsīr* not only as a tool but as a self-contained artistic manifestation. The combined effect of these decisions was to give mainstream Qurʾānic exegesis a philological gravitas it had hitherto lacked (Saleh 2004: 130–40).

We should keep in mind that two other options were available to al-Thaʿlabī to resolve the clash between philology and theology. The first was a loosening of the bond between Sunnī hermeneutics and philology, an option that was an exceedingly attractive one for Sunnī ideologues. Shīʿī and Ṣūfī hermeneutics had done that already, showing that such a move was not only feasible, but had no apparent disadvantages. The other extreme was also tempting: a realignment of Sunnism so as to conform to a more thorough philological reading of the Qurʾān. Yet, both would have resulted in a profound intellectual loss and the desertion of two major tenets of Sunnism: conservatism and intellectual hubris. Al-Thaʿlabī was thus the architect of a major resolution to this perennial tug-of-war between philology and dogma, and his solution was and remains the happy medium that Sunnism claims. However, it should be mentioned that the two other options were also attempted within Sunnism, if only after al-Thaʿlabī. Al-Wāḥidī (d. 468/1076), al-Thaʿlabī's main student, did try in his magnum opus *al-Basīṭ* to align Sunnism with a philological reading of the Qurʾān. The attempt left him in a frenzied, albeit productive, intellectual crisis which he never seemed to have resolved. Ibn Taymiyya chose the other solution and dropped philology from his hermeneutical manifesto and thus consolidating (or possibly giving rise to) one of the major competing trends inside Sunnī hermeneutics, that I have termed radical hermeneutics (Saleh 2004: 205–27).

Tafsīr and Pietistic Sensibilities

If there is a leitmotif in al-Thaʿlabī's hermeneutics, it is the proclamation of the salvific message of the Qurʾān. Every verse is a potential herald of God's mercy and compassion towards the believers. Moreover, for him, faith entailed an ontological differentiation between the believers and the rest of humanity, and al-Thaʿlabī was determined to render this differentiation hermeneutically operative. Both of these features were also emphasized by the dogma of the intercession of Muḥammad (*shafāʿa*) on behalf of his community, which he imbedded into the meaning of the Qurʾān. *Tafsīr* left little doubt that a Muslim, no matter what, could be eternally damned. Pietistic Sunnism, meanwhile, had transformed the recitation of the Qurʾān into one of the highest forms of devotion; despite the protestations of the *ḥadīth* camp that most of the prophetic traditions that supported such a view were fabricated, the sentiment was too strong not to prevail. Al-Thaʿlabī accordingly began his exegesis of every *sūra* in the Qurʾān by recounting such traditions. Mere recitation was proclaimed salvation here. The all-engulfing salvific quality of reciting the Qurʾān, once unleashed, could not be contained, and reading parts of the Qurʾān became as efficacious as reading all of it. What the traditions cited by al-Thaʿlabī were implying was that the Qurʾān is, at once, an all-encompassing and a self-encompassing instrument of salvation, such that a part represents the whole and the whole is reducible to certain parts. The collective redemptive powers of the Qurʾān are thus attainable by reading portions of it. This synecdochic aspect of the Qurʾān can make sense only on the salvific plane: redemption comes complete to the believer (Saleh 2004: 103–8). The result of this view was to allow the Qurʾān to compete with other forms of devotion that were being developed by the likes of the Ṣūfīs.

Moreover, al-Thaʿlabī made sure that the content of the verses themselves declared an affirmation of the *najāḥ* (salvation) that awaited the faithful. Al-Thaʿlabī took pains to show this aspect of the Qurʾān where one least expected it. Here, the ability of the exegete to make the Qurʾān confirm the primary message that Sunnism wanted it to convey was supreme. The technique of achieving this was carried out in two forms: positive and negative. The positive approach was to find salvific import in an otherwise innocuously nonsalvific verse; the negative was to confine the import of harsh divine pronouncements about recalcitrant human nature to nonbelievers, hence to make sure to differentiate the believers ontologically from the nonbelievers.

I will start by giving examples of the positive approach. Q 55:19, which states, "He [God] let forth the two seas that meet together" was understood by all exegetes up to al-Thaʿlabī's time as a reference to salt and fresh water seas, and al-Thaʿlabī offers interpretations that reflect this understanding. Having disposed of the traditional interpretations, however, he offers a new meaning: "There exists between human creatures (*al-ʿabd*) and his Lord two seas. The first one is the sea of salvation (*al-najāh*) and it is the Qurʾān; whoever upholds the Qurʾān is saved. The second is the sea of perdition (*halāk*) and it is this world; whoever grasps on to it and takes it as his resort, he shall perish." Let us untangle this interpretation. First, al-Thaʿlabī was drawing on the Qurʾān's presentation of the sea as paradigmatic of human life. The many statements in the Qurʾān of human defeat in front of the mysteries of the seas has already made the sea a synonym of both God's wrath and his benevolence (Q 17:66–70). To safely journey through the seas is totally predicated on God's love and mercy. Since life itself is presented as a journey, then crossing a sea becomes part of the march of the faithful towards salvation. Moreover, the sea was used as a metonymic image of God's word in the Qurʾān (Q 18:109; 31:27). The interpretation offered by al-Thaʿlabī is thus a brilliant reconfiguration of the myriad uses of the sea in the Qurʾān and salvation becomes a journey through a sea that both is the Qurʾān and can only be traversed by the Qurʾān itself. There is also an echo here of the prophetic catechetic view of the Qurʾān as both the judge and the prosecutor. Notice how the world, hence the *terra firma*, becomes an image of a sea of perdition, for although it is firm it can still inundate and drown one in its fatal attractions (Saleh 2004: 109). The reality of salvation is thus counterintuitive. It is important to emphasize that nothing in the verse supports such an elaborate reading, apart from the word "sea."

Another example of this positive salvific interpretation is how al-Thaʿlabī understood Q 93:5, "The Lord shall give thee [Muḥammad], and thou shalt be satisfied." The verse is rhetorically cold towards the believers; this was an intimate conversation between God and Muḥammad, and the believers are nowhere in the picture. God, despite all his protestation that His face is facing all humanity, is all too focused on Muḥammad. Al-Thaʿlabī ensured that the believer intrudes into these moments of intimacy between God and Muḥammad, and so he turned the verse into nothing but a reference to the believers' salvation. Al-Thaʿlabī adduced a tradition which states that

Muḥammad can only be satisfied if none of his followers remains in hell (Saleh 2004: 124–7). This was vintage al-Thaʿlabī: God's mercy and Muḥammad's intercession were made into one here; this interpretation was also an implicit attack on a major tenet of Muʿtazilite doctrine that the grave sinner will be damned for eternity.

An example of the negative salvific interpretation is how al-Thaʿlabī dealt with Q 102:1–2, "striving for acquiring more [wealth] distracts you until you visit your graves." The whole tone of *sūra* 102 is recriminatory towards humanity. Greed blinds human beings to see that death is at hand and that the reckoning on the day of judgment would entail an account of how wealth was spent. Human beings are depicted as recalcitrant, unbending, and unimaginative. Certitude of what life is about comes only at a belated moment of recognition (Q 102:5). To leave this *sūra* as it is, is to raise questions about faith's ability to transform human nature. Al-Thaʿlabī thus offered an interpretation of the verses that limits their reference to pre-Islamic Arabs or Jews. In either case, they are not about death making human life vain, but about the greed that blinds the unfaithful. The believers are thus immune from such an assessment, and to the degree that the faithful are not implicated in this scenario, they are a different order of beings (Saleh 2004: 162–4).

The other aspect of pietistic Sunnism that al-Thaʿlabī made *tafsīr* accommodate was the admonitory sensibility and its rhetoric. In doing so, al-Thaʿlabī extended trends already present in the Qurʾān. The aim here was to transform the whole rhetoric of the Qurʾān into such a discourse. Although I have chosen the word "admonitory," I am in reality describing two complementary rhetorical stratagems: one admonitory, the other exhortatory, or what is known in Islamic pietistic literature as *tarhīb* (instilling fear) and *targhīb* (instilling hope). Moreover, woven into these two rhetorical modes of interpretation was an affirmation of the dictates of the *sharīʿa*: one is also cajoled and pushed into fulfilling the obligations imposed by God's law. This aspect of *al-Kashf* was a major factor in its popularity. The work is uncanny in its mixture of the high philological tone and the common voice of the pietistic tradition. At the moment one is drawn into reading a long list of vocabulary, gathered by philologists, about the stages of human life, one is reminded of the ephemeral quality of this life. It is mostly in these admonitory sections that pietistic poetry was cited by al-Thaʿlabī.

Narration and Exegesis

One of the remarkable features of al-Thaʿlabī's hermeneutics was his refining of methods already in existence in the tradition to suit the new tastes of his audience. Nothing shows this skill more than his transformation of narrative elements in *tafsīr* into a coherent highly developed technique. This he did in two ways: the first was to elaborate on elements already present in the narrative parts of the Qurʾān itself and turn them into artistic productions (for more on this see the chapter in this book on his "*Tales of the Prophets*"). This is what I would call the grand narrative technique, where a repeated story in the Qurʾān is developed in one instance to cover the story concerned, thus giving a full narrative of what would be a recurring story in the Qurʾān. The second was the micro narrative style, in which a narrative unit, complete in its elements, was used to explain a particular verse without it appearing in other contexts and, more importantly, without apparent connection to the verse in question. This technique I have termed fictive narrative (Saleh 2004: 161–6).

The second of these two methods can be illustrated as follows. Q 93:7, "Did he not find you erring (*ḍāllan*, literally "lost") and guide you" generated unease among Muslim commentators, for it alluded to (if it did not state) the pagan past of Muḥammad. This would have been unproblematic were it not for the development of the doctrine of the infallibility of Muḥammad, which in its more strict forms denied that Muḥammad could have been a pagan before he was called to prophecy. The ways in which commentators sought to change the meaning of this verse are varied. Most of the solutions offered to undo this verse were at odds with the meaning of the word *ḍāllan*; thus philology was always undermining these techniques even when not actively doing so. Why not defeat philology at its own game? Could it be that Muḥammad was physically lost? Why not understand the term in its original lexicographic meaning, denuding it of its acquired metaphoric meaning, and use the very method of philology to defeat it? Could it not be that Muḥammad was lost when he was a child, something that happens to every child at one time or another? Crude as this ploy sounds, it has many advantages. It is philologically sound, and if a story could be found, or invented, to support it, the story would not be implausible. Al-Thaʿlabī offers five such stories. Each tells the story of Muḥammad being lost when he was a child, then found again and reunited with his grandfather. The first represents the earliest level of the invention of this interpretation: Muḥammad was lost in the valleys of Mecca and then God guided him back to his grandfather. This is a skeletal story, whose aim is to undo the verse, and little heed was given to the narrative structure and development of the story. By the time we reach the fifth story, however, we have a long narration that weaves together various motifs to create a miraculous childhood story of the grand savior of humanity. The whole cosmos is now implicated in the drama of this prophet; the universe is alerted to the disappearance of this child; the old gods of Arabia are fearful of him being found again, and refuse to answer a quest for an oracle of his whereabouts; and a heavenly voice, no less, guides the grandfather to the hiding place of this child. He was found under a blessed tree, in a contemplative mood, eating from the blessed leaves of this tree.

The fictive narrative method employed many strategies to achieve plausibility. When necessary, the meaning of a phrase was taken literally instead of figuratively, or the opposite – a figurative use of a word was chosen and the literal discarded, even though such a reading was not supported by the rhetorical Arabic tradition. Ethnographic information, poetic citation, and detailed dramatization, including dialogues and monologues, were all employed to make the narrative coherent. It should be clear that fictive narrative interpretation was an attractive exegetical method since there were no restrictive hermeneutical rules on the exegete save coherence.

Exegesis and Theology

To state that medieval Qurʾānic interpretation was theological is to state the obvious, especially if what we mean by theology is the bolstering of a system of belief. What

I am referring to here is, however, a far more explicit articulation of the aims of exegesis as both definer and defender of a theological outlook. Al-Thaʿlabī introduced theology, or at least a more explicit theological outlook, into *tafsīr*. He rarely let an opportunity to explain how Sunnism understood a certain verse, what Sunnism thought of this or that theological point, or how others had gotten it wrong, pass him by. If there was an enemy to attack, it was Muʿtazilite theology and to a lesser degree, the Shīʿites. Al-Thaʿlabī never tired of vilifying these camps, their views and doctrines. Moreover, al-Thaʿlabī achieved the inclusion of theology in *tafsīr* without turning to the language of scholastic *kalām* in his theological discussions. Here, he showed his true colors as a brilliant cultural ideologue who, while versed in the language of theology, was willing to simplify it for an audience that lacked the training for such a discipline.

I will here give just one example of his subtle way of achieving this. Q 31:27, which reads, "Though all the trees in the earth were pens, and the sea [was ink] – seven seas after it to replenish it, yet would the words of God not be spent. God is All-hearing, All-seeing," was understood by al-Ṭabarī to refer to God's word itself, and not to its nature. Al-Thaʿlabī meanwhile achieved two things when he offered an explanation of this verse. First, he read it as an affirmation of the doctrine of the uncreatedness of the Qurʾān, and second, he saw in it a legitimizing statement for the craft of exegesis. He stated that "this verse implies that the word of God is uncreated because that which is without end to it or to what relates to it (or is connected to it), i.e., its meaning, is uncreated." Here a *kalām* concept which states that infinite things cannot be created was used to argue that God's word, since it was declared inexhaustible and thus infinite in quantity, must be uncreated. Both the *kalām* concept and its corollary were here presented in a catechetic style, easy to digest and consent to, and thus required little background in theology (Saleh 2004: 1). Al-Thaʿlabī opened the door for later exegetes to build on this approach, and to the degree that Sunnism saw the need later to turn exegesis into a "kalāmized" discipline it offered such a transformation in the work of Fakhr al-Dīn al-Rāzī (d. 606/1209).

Prophetic *Ḥadith* and *Tafsīr*

At the heart of the hermeneutical enterprise of al-Thaʿlabī lies his weaving together of two of the fundamental facets of the medieval Islamic religious traditions: the prophetic *ḥadīth* and the enterprise of Qurʾānic exegesis.[1] This fusion was in a sense the culmination of the process of integration of the different aspects of the Islamic culture in medieval times. The prophetic *ḥadīth*, an edifice that was nearing its completion both through the production of massive compilations and the elaboration of the science of *ḥadīth* (*ʿulūm al-ḥadīth*), stood apart, as it were, from Qurʾānic exegesis as it reached its first grand articulation in the commentary of al-Ṭabarī. Al-Thaʿlabī brought the two together and initiated what was to be a continuous relationship between the two streams of medieval productions. The two revelations, the written and the prophetic or oral, were reunited, thus creating in the hermeneutical event a structure resembling the character of Muḥammad, who was the only individual in whom both were once united: the Qurʾān (present as lemmas) and the *sunna* (present as exegesis) made into one. The Qurʾān, read through the prophetic *sunna*, became, like Muḥammad once was, the incarnation of that which would guide the Muslim nation. The formulation of *tafsīr* as the embodiment of both divine revelation and prophetic revelation necessarily made it a replacement of Muḥammad, his true caliph or successor who was to lead the community. The failure of the Caliphate on the religious level opened the door to a structuring of religious knowledge as Muḥammad's successor. In *tafsīr* the Sunnī community had, in effect, its immanent prophet through textual fiat.

There are here two issues that need to be addressed; the first is that most of the innovations introduced by al-Thaʿlabī were effected through the citation of prophetic *ḥadīth*. When a verse was read to declare God's mercy and offer salvation to the believers, invariably it was read in this way through the agency of a *ḥadīth* or a prophetic tradition. Thus for example, Q 93:7, which I have already presented, was read through the eyes of a *ḥadīth*, as discussed above. Moreover, the admonitory rhetorical style was already highly developed in *ḥadīth*, and al-Thaʿlabī only needed to transport this device wholesale into his work. The other issue that deserves mentioning is the consequences that this binding of the two revelations posed to Sunnī hermeneutics. If allowed supremacy, this method could overhaul the Sunnī hermeneutical project, and implicit in this method was a capitulation to the prophetic *ḥadīth* as the decipherer of divine speech. As long as the prophetic interpretive method was embedded in an encyclopedic approach that was guided by philology, it was always a controllable method. The danger was to follow through with the implicit foundation of such a method: the equating of the meaning of the word of God with the prophetic word to the exclusion of any other possible hermeneutical approach into the Qurʾān. Given the abundance of prophetic logia, it was only a matter of time before the one inundated the other. This possibility and approach are what I have termed "radical hermeneutics" and one of the most intriguing issues for *tafsīr* scholarship is to investigate the history of this hermeneutical radicalization. For the time being I am still convinced that such a method did not see its full articulation until the appearance of Ibn Taymiyya. But another candidate might well be Ibn Abī Ḥātim (d. 327/938). In either case, the significance of al-Thaʿlabī remains central. He either anticipated the trend if my assessment holds; or al-Thaʿlabī curbed it for at least four centuries, if I am wrong. His resolution, however, remains the default position of most of the encyclopedic exegetical tradition and as such ensured a heavy counterbalance to the unavoidable later prominence of radical hermeneutics.

Tafsīr as the Absorber of New Challenges to Sunnism

The main contention of my assessment of the cultural significance of medieval *tafsīr* is that *tafsīr* was the medium through which Sunnism absorbed and appropriated any new development in Islamo-Arabic culture. *Tafsīr* started with philology, which was fully put in the service of interpreting the word of God, yet without *tafsīr* fully submitting to philology's unbending rules. Theology, which could have been simply rejected through a negative theology, an option made possible through the work of the Ḥanbalites, was instead appropriated and its premises, if not its difficult language, admitted into *tafsīr*. (Of course with al-Rāzī the language of scholastic theology became the language of *tafsīr* itself, and as such *tafsīr* was willing to discard even its character in order to overcome any intellectual challenge). My contention is that *tafsīr* was making the whole world comprehensible by making an understanding of the world seem to issue from the word of God. *Tafsīr* thus was a legitimizing tool more than anything else. Nowhere else is this apparent than in al-Thaʿlabī's appropriation of Ṣūfī hermeneutics and Shīʿī pietistic sympathies with the *ahl al-bayt* (family of Muḥammad).

Al-Thaʿlabī informs us in his introduction that he was going to include the mystical level of interpretation in his commentary (Saleh 2004: 87). It is clear that he has read the work of al-Sulamī (d. 412/1021) with the author himself and included a large portion of that work in his own commentary. Far more significant to the history of mystical *tafsīr* is that al-Thaʿlabī has quoted material from other mystics that seem to have been lost and only available in his work. A more definite assessment of this aspect of *al-Kashf* awaits a more thorough study of the mystical quotations and their relationship to al-Sulamī's work. All indications suggest that al-Thaʿlabī was the first to allow mystical interpretations into mainstream Sunnī *tafsīr*, thus anticipating the work of al-Qushayrī (d. 465/1072) as well as al-Ghazālī (d. 505/1111).

The circumference of al-Thaʿlabī's exegetical circle is thus unique in Islamic history; it almost encompassed every layer, from the earliest (the Ibn ʿAbbās traditions) to that of his own contemporaries including the mystical level. Thus, at the very moment the philological approach was given primacy in Qurʾānic exegesis, the mystical approach was also admitted, creating in the Qurʾān a text that was both fully decipherable through the intellect and utterly beyond the realm of reason at the same time. The word of God was both manifestly clear (*mubīn*) and ineffable (*sirr*). As the text was being confined, it was also being set free.

Moreover, by admitting the mystical interpretation into his commentary, al-Thaʿlabī made the Qurʾān the most polyvalent text in Islamic culture: it was the only text decipherable both philologically and mystically. What is also significant about al-Thaʿlabī's polyvalent reading of the Qurʾān was his judicious refusal to accord any level of reading a preferential wink. The readings were piled atop one another and arranged (almost chronologically), and the reader was never advised to favor one over the other. Mystical interpretations were not only admitted into the commentary, a feat in itself, but they were treated equally. We have also to note the mode in which al-Thaʿlabī admitted mystical interpretations. There was no justification for their incorporation, no apologies, and no embarrassment; it is as if the mystical vision was part of the general culture and not the object of a *Kulturkampf* in early medieval Islam. His incorporation of this material is an audacious gesture and a testimony to his sagacity, for shortly after al-Thaʿlabī mysticism, as an intellectual current, would move from the periphery to the center.

What were the implications of the introduction of this new mode of interpretation into the mainstream exegetical tradition? The primary result of this infusion was to transform the prosaic in the Qurʾān into the profound. By that I mean that the language of the Qurʾān, especially when philologically clear and syntactically transparent, would become prolific with meanings, meanings which were not possible or imaginable to extract through the usual methods available hitherto to Sunnī exegetes. As a rule al-Thaʿlabī would quote mystical interpretations most copiously when interpreting the prosaic verses where quotations and interpretations from the traditional camp were scarce due to the lack of obvious problems in the text. The result was a loquacious Qurʾān, a Qurʾān profuse in meaning at every level (Saleh 2004: 151–61).

One should not think, however, that al-Thaʿlabī was simply quoting the mystical interpretations available to him without filtering the material. The mystical interpretations available in *al-Kashf* are remarkably nonmetaphysical. By that I mean they are less concerned with the question of the nature of God and more concerned with God's relationship to humanity. These remarks are the result of a preliminary survey of this material and it awaits a detailed study to compare it with al-Sulamī's Qurʾān commentary before it will be possible to supplement them.

As a paradigmatic example of al-Thaʿlabī's approach in *al-Kashf*, I will discuss here the interpretation of Q 53:10, "and He revealed to His servant that which He revealed" (*wa-awḥā ilā ʿabdihi mā awḥā*). The verse presents several problems. First there is an ambiguous reference to something revealed, the pronoun *mā*; consequently one is apt to ask about what was revealed. Second, the identity of the servant is not given. Or at least if we do know – Muḥammad is the most obvious candidate, of course – an exegete might not be willing to consent to this identification. For if it is indeed Muḥammad who was the recipient of direct revelation, then why did God need Gabriel to do his work on other occasions according to the traditional theory of Qurʾānic revelation?

Which problem in Q 53:10 an exegete decides to tackle tells us more about his approach and concerns than about the verse itself. Al-Ṭabarī, for example, was more interested in solving the riddle of the ambiguous identity of the servant. Though he quoted authorities who thought it was Muḥammad who was the recipient of the revelation, he was unwilling to grant this interpretation any validity. Al-Ṭabarī did not want to jeopardize the neat theory of revelation that had become standard by his time. Al-Thaʿlabī, on the other hand, offered a far more systematic interpretation of the verse. First, he gave two possibilities for the identity of the servant: it could be Gabriel or Muḥammad. He did not editorialize, both are valid interpretations. Neither of the two possible meanings was given more weight. Moreover, al-Thaʿlabī was also interested in the reference of the pronoun *mā*. It could mean "that which God revealed" or the verse could mean, "He revealed to his servant that which God revealed to him." The significance of this tautology would become apparent later on. It could also be that what was revealed was a whole *sūra* of the Qurʾān, *sūra* 94.

Al-Thaʿlabī then introduced an interpretation that had not been adduced before. "It has been reported that God revealed to him (Muḥammad) that paradise is barred to prophets till you enter it, and it is barred to the non-Muslim nations till your nation enters it." What God has revealed to Muḥammad was thus not a Qurʾānic *sūra* or verse, which was always claimed to be the substance of Muḥammad's revelatory experience, but a salvific message that the Muḥammadan nation will be the first to be saved. The ambiguity is now clear. The Qurʾān once more was always expressing one message, and when probed it can be revealed: Muslims are saved.

Yet there is more. Quoting al-Nūrī, an early Baghdadi mystic (d. 295/907), al-Thaʿlabī informed the reader that what was revealed to Muḥammad was a secret (*sirr*).

Two lines of poetry are quoted that stated that secrets between lovers (presumably between Muḥammad and his God) are impossible to disclose. Here is a totally different approach to the problem of the ambiguity in the verse regarding the nature of the thing revealed to Muḥammad. The very wording of the verse was, according to the mystics, indicative of its meaning. There is simply no problem in Q 53:10. God did not specify what He revealed because it was a secret that should not be made known. Clearly, the mystics were eager to claim that Muḥammad received revelations that were above and beyond the Qur'ān, a sort of esoteric knowledge that resembled theirs.

Something, however, has been divulged. Al-Thaʿlabī has already revealed to the reader what God has told Muḥammad. The secret of the Qur'ān is that it proclaims one truth: God will save the Muslim nation. By calling that which has been already disclosed a secret, al-Thaʿlabī allows the reader to experience the revelatory moment anew as an intimate conversation with God. The disparate units of interpretation as offered by al-Thaʿlabī have a cumulative effect because of the way the material has been presented. First, we are told of what was revealed; then, we are told it is a secret. The reader is already privy to the mystery that he realizes could not be disclosed either by speech or writing. The salvific message of the Qur'ān is both ineffable and resounding.

Shīʿī Traditions in *Al-Kashf*

The publication of *al-Kashf* in 2002 by a Shīʿī scholar in Beirut represents the culmination of a rather fascinating story of the reception history of the work. Unraveling this complex history has proven to be the key to understanding major developments both in the history of medieval exegesis and Sunnī-Shīʿī polemical wars. It is not only that *al-Kashf* played a foundational role in establishing the high classical style of Qur'ānic interpretation, but it was a pivotal text in the war between Sunnism and Shīʿism. Without a proper understanding of the history of this text no understanding is possible of these two issues.

Al-Thaʿlabī was active during a low point in the history of political Sunnism; both the Būyids and the Fāṭimids had shown the degree to which political Sunnism could retreat. One of the ways in which Sunnism could defang the appeal of Shīʿism was to adopt much of its pietistic language and sensibilities, most notably its love of the *ahl al-bayt*, the household of Muḥammad. If Sunnīs could show as much adoration and fervor in their love of Muḥammad's family and descendants, then surely the Shīʿī propaganda about their suffering and usurped rights could be made less appealing. This was precisely what al-Thaʿlabī set out to do in the context of *tafsīr*. The Shīʿī interpretations of the Qur'ān that claimed that certain verses were references to ʿAlī, the cousin and son-in-law of Muḥammad, were adduced in his commentary. Citing such material was, however, never allowed to become the vehicle for any justification of Shīʿī ideology. Al-Thaʿlabī is vociferous in his attacks on the Shīʿites and their political claims. He did not abandon Sunnism nor, for that matter, harbor pro-Shīʿī sympathies. There was no ambiguity in his commentary as to where he stood on this issue. His was a thoroughly Sunnī understanding of the early caliphal history. His pro-ʿAlī material was embedded in a highly intricate web of stratagems designed to rob such material of any ideological justification for Shīʿism. The aim was to make the love of Muḥammad's family as Sunnī as anything else without giving in to Shīʿī political ideology.

The introduction of Shīʿī material into the mainstream of the exegetical tradition by al-Thaʿlabī was thus not an act of subterfuge by which pro-Shīʿī sympathies were insinuated into the Sunnī worldview. It was certainly not an oversight, the result of a compulsive gathering of Shīʿī material that somehow was done inadvertently, as Ibn Taymiyya would later claim. Al-Thaʿlabī saw nothing Shīʿī in loving the family of Muḥammad and his descendants; the love of the *ahl al-bayt* constituted an act of *tazkiya*, a sort of purification and validation of one's faith. It was as Sunnī an act as any other. Thus, al-Thaʿlabī was, by incorporating Shīʿī material in his commentary, robbing it of any Shīʿī significance and making it part of the Sunnī world. The pro-Shīʿī material was declawed insofar as it need not imply a hatred for the companions of Muḥammad or an implicit hierarchization of the merits of Muḥammad's successors, with his relatives on a rank higher than that of the first three caliphs. As long as a Sunnī theologian did not subscribe to the doctrine of the imamate, then no amount of love to *ahl al-bayt*, excessive as it might be, would turn him into a Shīʿī or decrease his Sunnism (Saleh 2004: 186–7).

The danger of such an approach should be apparent. Taken out of the complex web of arguments and presentation in which al-Thaʿlabī embedded these pro-Shīʿī interpretations, they could be easily used as proof by Shīʿī polemicists that their claims for ʿAlī's supremacy were admitted to even by Sunnīs. Indeed Shīʿī polemicists found in *al-Kashf* a treasure trove of pro-Shīʿī material. Taken out of its context, it was an unbeatable argument against the Sunnīs. Indeed, the prestige of al-Thaʿlabī's work meant that the work was one of the Shīʿī polemicists' most precious finds. Soon, the situation called for a drastic answer, and Sunnism, in the person of Ibn Taymiyya, would rise to the occasion (Saleh 2004: 215–21). Ibn Taymiyya in his *Muqaddima fī uṣūl al-tafsīr* ("Introduction to the Foundations of Exegesis"; see Saleh 2004: 216–19), as well as in his *Minhāj al-sunna al-nabawiyya* ("The Path of Sunnism"; see Saleh 2004: 218–21) mounted a concerted effort to undermine the reputation of al-Thaʿlabī. To the degree that Ibn Taymiyya's assessment was eventually to prevail, it was successful. The aim of his attacks was to downgrade the significance of al-Thaʿlabī as a mainstream, trustworthy, Sunnī scholar. As such he was not part of orthodoxy, and the relevance of using him in arguments by the Shīʿī polemicists was weakened.

Al-Thaʿlabī and Medieval Qur'ānic Exegesis

The current that al-Thaʿlabī developed, what I have termed the encyclopedic exegetical tradition, would become the prevalent form of interpretation in the medieval period. Many were the challenges posed to this approach, yet its dominance and continuity endured. This has more to do with *tafsīr*'s malleability and the exegetes' own understanding of its main function: defending and defining Sunnism. Al-Thaʿlabī's enlargement of the encyclopedic approach was an attempt to resolve the cultural struggle that raged within Islamic societies all over the Muslim world during the period between the fourth and sixth century of the *hijra*. The object of this struggle was the soul of the educated man in the Arabo-Islamic synthesis. The rise of *adab* (belle lettres) and *adab* encyclopedic compilations – as the embodiment of what a learned individual was to know and cherish – was a threat to the wish of the religious-minded to make the Qurʾān the center of the learning experience. But not only was *adab* making strides in this battle, but so, too, was mysticism or Ṣūfism, with its claim both to understand human condition and proffer remedies for it. If these two strands, which were at the center of the Sunnī community, were not enough, we have to keep in mind the great danger that the Shīʿī camp posed to the Sunnī-minded communities. Shīʿism, that is, intellectual Shīʿism, was also making advances over the breadth of the Islamic world and undermining everywhere the intellectual foundations of Sunnī orientations (we need only remember the biography of Ibn Sīnā (d. 428/1037) and the works of al-Ghazālī). It is al-Thaʿlabī, I argue, whom we should credit with rising to the challenge of *adab*, Ṣūfism, and Shīʿism, to reassert the centrality of a Sunnī-interpreted Qurʾān in the lives of the educated.

Al-Thaʿlabī was also a member of a school of interpretation that I have called the Nīshāpūrī school of *tafsīr*. His student, al-Wāḥidī wrote three Qurʾān commentaries, the most important of which, *al-Basīṭ*, is still unedited and unpublished. To describe *al-Basīṭ* as revolutionary is not an exaggeration. Another author who was also heavily influenced by al-Thaʿlabī was al-Ṭībī (d. 743/1343). Nothing can be said of his work since no scholar has even investigated it. Thus, even a monographic study of an author like al-Thaʿlabī remains incomplete for we are unable to measure the full degree of his work's influence till we have the whole spectrum of the tradition accessible to us.

To explain the voluminous medieval *tafsīr* tradition as the result of a compulsive habit of medieval copying, as some modern scholars have opined, is to overlook the intellectual foundations and concerns of one of the most formidable of religious sciences of medieval Islam. While modernity has unseated most of the other medieval disciplines, *tafsīr* remains central as a discipline in fashioning an Islamic outlook even to this day. It is unfortunate that the history of the medieval exegetical tradition is the least studied of Islamic disciplines. The neglect is compounded by the fact that both Western scholars and Arab intellectuals saw little value in studying this medieval production. Arab nationalism and the intellectual movement it generated were interested in the Arabic belle lettres medieval tradition and saw little value in devoting any effort to issuing critical editions of compilations on the meaning of the Qurʾān; the result is that no major Qurʾān commentary was edited by the giants of Arab scholarship; Western scholars meanwhile were concerned with the early history of the exegetical tradition, and had only perfunctory concern for the later periods. The result is that we lack access to the complete spectrum of this tradition. Recently, however, the situation is improving, since there seems to be a concerted effort to publish this literature (due to the rise of Islamism in the Arab world and to the retreat of Arabism as the intellectual paradigm). What is needed is a change from the diachronic study of *tafsīr* to a more systematic synchronic study of *tafsīr* works in the form of monographic studies on individual scholars or works. We are still at the very early stages of outlining the history of this genre and major intellectual figures who were primarily exegetes, like al-Waḥidī, al-Baghawī (d. 516/1122), al-Zamakhsharī (d. 538/1144), al-Rāzī, al-Ṭībī, al-Bayḍāwī

(d. 685–716/1282–1316) and many others, have hardly received the attention they deserve.

Notes

1 Since research into medieval exegetical tradition is still in its infancy, assessments such as the one I am going to suggest in this subsection are unavoidably provisional. Although investigation of the exegetical works of Ibn Abī Ḥātim al-Rāzī (d. 327/938) and Ibn Mardawayh (d. 401/1010) may lead me to reverse this conclusion, I am presuming that the welding together of the non-interpretive prophetic mainstream *ḥadīth* with Qurʾānic exegesis was the work of al-Thaʿlabī. When I first published my monograph on al-Thaʿlabī, however, I was not fully aware that these two figures have to be investigated more thoroughly before one may come to the conclusions I have advanced (Saleh 2004: 226). This is much more easily said than done: Ibn Mardawayh's work is lost, and there seems to be some confusion as to how much of the commentary of Ibn Abī Ḥātim has survived. At present, I see no reason to change my conclusions, but I feel uncertain enough that I ought to voice my doubts to the reader. If anything, this caveat should summon specialists to turn their attention to these two figures in order to disentangle the history of *tafsīr*. Since the magisterial work of al-Suyūṭī (d. 911/1505), *al-Durr al-Manthūr*, is the repository of material from the above mentioned authors, a study of this work is urgently needed in order to clarify the situation further, and a study of it may be the only way out of the impasse created by our inadequate grasp of the tradition.

Further reading

Goldfeld, Isaiah (1984) *Qurʾānic Commentary in the Eastern Islamic Tradition of the First Four Centuries of the Hijra: An Annotated Edition of the Preface of al-Thaʿlabī's "Kītāb al-Kashf waʾl-Bayān ʿan Tafsīr al-Qurʾān."* Srugy Printers and Publishers, Acre.

Saleh, Walid A. (2004) *The Formation of the Classical Tafsīr Tradition: The Qurʾān Commentary of al-Thaʿlabī*. Brill, Leiden.

Al-Thaʿlabī (2002) *Al-Kashf waʾl-bayān al-maʿrūf bi-Tafsīr al-Thaʿlabī*, ed. Abī Muḥammad b. ʿAshūr. Dār Iḥyāʾ al-Turāth al-ʿArabī, Beirut.

CHAPTER 22

Stories of the Prophets

Marianna Klar

Introduction to the Text

The late tenth/early eleventh century figure Abū Isḥāq Aḥmad b. Muḥammad b. Ibrāhīm al-Thaʿlabī (d. 427/1035) was the author of five major works: a commentary on the Qurʾān (Saleh 2004), a biographical dictionary of people who died upon hearing the Qurʾān (Wiesmüller 2002), two lost books entitled *Rabīʿ al-mudhakkirīn* ("Springtime of the Admonishers") and *al-Kāmil fī ʿilm al-Qurʾān* ("The Complete Work regarding the Qurʾānic Sciences", see Saleh 2004: 51–2) and the pivotal and much imitated collection of tales of the prophets, the *ʿArāʾis al-majālis fī qiṣaṣ al-anbiyāʾ* ("Brides at (their) Weddings, Regarding the Tales of the Prophets"; Brinner 2002; Klar 2006; Nagel 1967). This latter work was written subsequent to his commentary on the Qurʾān (the *Commentary* is cited within the *Tales*) and presents a chronologically arranged description of historical events from the time of the creation of the world to the "Year of the Elephant" in 570 CE, giving the biographies of some forty-six individuals or, occasionally, peoples.[1] Many of these are routinely described as Islamic prophets – thus Adam, Noah, Abraham, Joseph, Moses, Jesus and so forth are included in the volume; others, for instance the "fallen angels" Hārūt and Mārūt, kings such as Saul and Alexander the Great, the peoples of Iram and al-Rass, are not prophets *per se* but rather historical personages or communities significant for their place in the Qurʾān or for the role they are reported to have played in religious history.

Other monographs dealing with pre-Islamic history did already exist at the time of al-Thaʿlabī; it was, however, more usual to find such material within larger scale universal histories, commentaries on the Qurʾān, or collections of *ḥadīth*, and the vast majority of our extant works of tales of the prophets post-date al-Thaʿlabī, with many of them, for example Nāṣir al-Dīn b. Burhān al-Dīn al-Rabghūzī (d. 710/1310) and Muḥammad b. Bisṭām al-Khūshābī Wānī Efendī (d. 1096/1658), openly taking al-Thaʿlabī as their model. The author alludes to his possible motivation in compiling such a volume in his introduction to the collection; among the reasons he cites for

God having told stories of past peoples to Muḥammad, al-Thaʿlabī (1985: 2–3) states that

> [God] told [Muḥammad] the stories to serve as an example of the noble traits exhibited by the messengers and prophets of old . . . and so that his community would refrain from those actions for which [previous] prophets' communities had been punished. . . . He told him the stories to confirm his [position] and prove his glory and the glory of his community. . . . God told him these stories as an education and an instruction for his community, that is to say He mentioned the prophets and their rewards, and the enemies [of God] and their punishment, then in other passages He warned the [community] against the deeds of [God's] enemies, and urged them towards the deeds of [God's] friends. God said, "In Joseph and his brethren are signs for those who ask questions" (Q 12: 7) and "In their stories is a warning for those of understanding" (Q 12: 111) and "A guide and a warning to the godfearing" (Q 5: 46) and other such verses. Shiblī said, "The common people are kept occupied [listening to] the narration of a tale, while the élite are busy learning its lesson." He told him the stories of the prophets and past friends [of God] in order to keep their memory and the memory of their deeds alive. . . . Ibn Durayd recited [the following epithet] to me, "A person leaves only a tale behind him, so strive that your tale be remembered as a beautiful one."

The work as such is presented as an exemplum, a warning, an education, an instruction, and an encouragement for its readers; al-Thaʿlabī would also appear to have believed firmly in the importance and validity of narrative. The fact of his being an established Qurʾān commentator at the time at which he compiled the collection will have given al-Thaʿlabī ample authority to attempt a work of this type. These elements are important in pointing the way one should best approach the text.

Publication History

The earliest extant manuscript of the work would appear to be in the Bibliothèque Nationale, Paris, and has been dated to the end of the eleventh century, though this manuscript is missing its final pages; the British Library has a complete but slightly later manuscript, dated 512/1119. There are a further forty extant manuscripts catalogued in Brockelmann (*GAL* I, 429; SI, 592). Brockelmann also informs us that the *Tales* in its entirety was first published in Cairo in 1282/1865, then again, by the Būlāq Press, in 1286/1869; it was printed a further ten times in Cairo between 1292/1875 and 1345/1926, once in Kashmir (1288/1871), and twice in Bombay (1295/1878 and 1306/1888); a Turkish translation appeared in the same year as the first Arabic edition, with a Tatar translation following in 1320/1903; the Joseph story was published in Cairo as an independent monograph in 1279/1862, and the Samson story in 1299/1881. The Princeton catalogue yields six different editions: the early Būlāq edition, printed by al-Maṭbaʿa al-Miṣriyya in 1286/1869; a 1297/1880 edition published in al-Azhar by al-Sharafiyya press; two further Egyptian editions, with the *Rawḍ al-rayāḥīn fī ḥikāyat al-ṣāliḥīn* of ʿAllāma al-Yāfiʿī in the margins, one printed by Maṭbaʿat al-ʿUlūm al-Adabiyya in 1344/1925 and the other by Maktabat al-Jumhuriyya al-ʿArabiyya in the 1950s; and another Egyptian edition, dated 1954 and published by Muṣṭafā ʾl-Bābī ʾl-Ḥalabī. The remaining edition is a Beirut imprint published by al-Maktaba al-Thaqafiyya in the 1970s.

It is worth pointing out that a superficial comparison of four widely available editions of the *Tales* shows little variation in the substance of the text; the printed editions moreover show surprisingly little variation of any significance when compared with the 1119 CE British Library manuscript (Supplementary Or. 1494). For instance, in the manuscript version of the Noah story, Noah is asked, "When you disembarked, how did you find your life (*ʿumraka*)?' In all four versions of the printed edition consulted for this chapter this becomes "When you disembarked, how did you find the world (*al-dunyā*)?"[2] In the Job story, where the manuscript tells us only that God forgives Job, the printed editions all inform us that God forgives Job "for what he said." In the Saul story, where the manuscript states that the king's intentions towards David improved (*ḥassan niyyātahu fīhi*), the printed editions tell us the king "felt more kindly towards him" (*aḥsan thanāʾuhu ʿalayhi*; one edition moreover gives *thanāʾ* in place of *thanāʾahu*). A random comparison yields only this level of minor textual discrepancy between editions.

However, this does not, of course, mean that the text is straightforward or lacking in textual ambiguities. A critical edition is sorely needed, not least to go some way towards setting the work in its contextual background. The dangers of a non-contextualized reading of the text are apparent in Brinner's for the most part accurate translation of the *Tales*. There he renders the events that led to the loss of Solomon's throne (Brinner 2002: 542) as "Solomon became infatuated (*uftutina*)," presumably on the assumption that the context for this anecdote is romantic: the correct context for the passage would, however, seem to be provided in al-Thaʿlabī's Qurʾān commentary, where we are told that, prior to the same events described in the *Tales*, Solomon was "tested (*uftutina*) through taking the statue into his home." An understanding of "infatuated" clearly does not work in this expanded context; the existence of an informed critical edition would be invaluable in limiting such misreadings of the text. As Jacob Lassner (1993: 64ff.) comments, "Arabic texts of the period can be extremely allusive" and this is particularly true in the relatively under-explored field of *Tales of the Prophets*. As such, care should be taken in reading the text.

Major Sources

The Qurʾān provides the framework for the tales of each figure, but hundreds of additional authorities are cited by name within the text. From these we can deduce that the major sources for the *Tales* included the Ibn ʿAbbās-based commentaries of Saʿīd b. Jubayr (d. 95/714), Mujāhid (d. 100–4/718–22), al-Ḍaḥḥāk (d. 105–6/723–4), ʿIkrima (d. 105/723–4), al-Suddī (d. 127/745), al-Kalbī (d. 146/763), and Muqātil b. Sulaymān (d. 150/767). Ibn ʿAbbās himself (d. ca. 68/687) is often cited as an authority, as are other companions of Muḥammad, notably Abū Hurayra (d. 58/678), Ibn Masʿūd (d. 32/652–3), and ʿAbd Allāh b. ʿUmar (d. 73/693). Ibn Isḥāq (d. 150/767), whose biography of Muḥammad included a section on the pre-Islamic prophets, is another frequent source for material, as are the commentaries of the famous sermonizer and preacher Ḥasan al-Baṣrī (d. 110/728) and his pupil Qatāda (d. 117/734 or 118/735). Another major source is the ubiquitous Kaʿb al-Aḥbār (d. 32/651), although the equally prolific Wahb b. Munabbih (d. ca. 114/732) is rarely cited (on all of these people see Khoury 1978; Nagel 1967).

Al-Thaʿlabī also cites his fellow commentator and historian, al-Ṭabarī (d. 310/923), and Raif Khoury (1978: 174) suggests that ʿUmāra b. Wathīma was another source for al-Thaʿlabī's *Tales* although, due perhaps to his habit of not giving full chains of transmission for his material (in the introduction to the *Commentary*, al-Thaʿlabī comments that this is a deliberate space-saving strategy; Saleh 2004: 70), ʿUmāra is never mentioned by name in the text. The inter-dependence of this type of literature is, however, clear from the fact that al-Thaʿlabī is in turn cited in the later historiographical works of Ibn ʿAsākir (d. 571/1176) and Ibn Kathīr (d. 774/1373), as well as in later commentaries and other works. Johns (1989: 225–66; cf. Saleh 2004: 127–9, 209–14 and *passim* with reference to the *Commentary*), for instance, posits a relationship between al-Thaʿlabī's *Tales* and the Qurʾān commentary of al-Zamakhsharī (d. 538/1144), stating that, with reference to the exegesis of Q 38: 21–5, the later author "at times indeed seems to be following Thaʿlabī's presentation of the David story verbatim" (Johns 1989: 237), and "It is clear how closely Zamakhsharī has followed Thaʿlabī, accepting and quoting the same mosaic of authorities, but weighting them differently" (Johns 1989: 240).

On a final note, much has been made of the supposedly Jewish or Christian origins of the bulk of this material. That there was no stigma attached to the consultation of extra-Islamic sources in this early period seems evident from *ḥadīth* reports. It is, however, generally concluded that the bulk of these sources were oral in nature and impossible to identify retrospectively; al-Thaʿlabī may well cite the amorphous "People of the Book" but he names no specific Jewish or Christian sources. As such, the extant Jewish and Christian material is not as useful as the Islamic sources in providing a contextual basis to aid our understanding of ambiguous passages. The situation is rendered particularly complex by the difficulty in accurately dating tales. The lack of manuscript versions of a tale prior to a specific date by no means rules out the possibility of that tale having nonetheless been in common circulation. It is hence almost impossible to state with any confidence whether a certain explanation of events common to both traditions entered the Islamic repertoire from that of the People of the Book and should be read in the context of that tradition, or vice versa (see Wheeler 2002: 17–19, 23–6, 39–40). As Peter Awn (1983: 9) points out, the medieval relationship between traditions was less than straightforward:

> The *qiṣaṣ* literature should not be viewed as wholly derivative from Jewish and Christian sources, for it underwent substantial Islamization at the hands of Muslim preachers and commentators. Cross-fertilization occurred, with details, nuances and embellishments traded back and forth among the various religious communities. Finally, the influence of these tales on indigenous non-Christian or Jewish pre-Islamic beliefs should not be discounted.

Construction of the Text

The *Tales of the Prophets* provides its reader with a history of the world from creation to the year of Muḥammad's birth. It opens with several chapters on the creation, divided into earth, heavens etc., closes with a description of two battles that took place shortly before the time of Muḥammad, and in between gives a chronologically arranged series of biographies; it includes the tales of all the pre-Islamic historical figures mentioned, alluded to, or suggested by the text of the Qurʾān. The vast majority of the forty-six biographies given are introduced through a Qurʾānic passage; thus Qurʾānic verses provide the framework for almost all of the tales.

Minor figures within the volume are presented over a few pages or in a single chapter, while the biographies of major figures can run to over one hundred pages and are divided into various subchapters and headings. Thus, for example, the tale of Abraham opens with a section on the prophet's birth. This is followed by a sub-chapter on his emergence from an underground hiding place and subsequent return to his people, a section on the births of Ishmael and Isaac, Ishmael's and Hagar's departure from the *ḥaram* in Mecca, and the tale of the well of Zamzam, a further section on the story of Zamzam, a fifth section on the history of the Kaʿba to the (then) present day, a sub-chapter on God's command that Abraham sacrifice his son, followed by the tale of the sacrifice itself, then a section on the destruction of Nimrod and the building of the tower of Babel, an eighth sub-chapter concerning the deaths of Sarah, Hagar, and others of Abraham's wives and their children, then a section on Abraham's death, and a concluding section listing the prophet's special characteristics.

The substantially longer Moses chapter, meanwhile, opens with a discussion of the prophet's genealogy. The second sub-chapter deals with his birth, and the next with a physical description of Moses and of Aaron. These are followed by a section on Moses' killing of the Egyptian and his subsequent move to Midian, a sub-chapter dealing with his arrival at Midian and marriage to Shuʿayb's daughter, leading into two sections concerning Moses' staff. The eighth section then describes Moses' departure from Midian and how he and his brother came to confront Pharaoh, and the ninth the arrival before Pharaoh. Then follows a sub-chapter regarding the tale of Moses, Aaron, Pharaoh, and the magicians, a section on the believer who spoke out against Pharaoh, and his family, a section on Pharaoh's wife and her death, and a sub-chapter describing how the tower was built. After sections detailing God's signs to Pharaoh, rationalizing these signs, and specifically dealing with the locusts, the narrative moves on to Moses' night flight and the parting of the sea.

The sixteenth sub-chapter of the Moses chapter then describes the prophet's encounter with God on the mountain, the tablets, and the revelation of the Torah. The "ten commandments" are discussed, followed by the matter of the worship of the golden calf and a sub-chapter on the identity of Korah and his rebellion. The Moses narrative continues with three sections describing Khiḍr, and Moses' encounter with him; a sub-chapter on the cow the people are ordered to sacrifice; and the story of the building of the temple, the ark of the covenant, the Shechina, and the sacrifice consumed by fire. A section on the journey of the Israelites to Syria is followed by the tale of Balaam, then a sub-chapter on the chiefs Moses chose to rule his people while they were away. The final five sections deal with the giant Og, God's favors to the people of Israel in the wilderness, the conquest of Jericho, and the deaths first of Aaron then of Moses.

Throughout the volume, the information in each section of al-Thaʿlabī's narrative is presented in the form of a series of individual reports. Most of these are simply ascribed to single figures, but a significant number are given fuller chains of authority. Others are ascribed to anonymous groups such as the "people of knowledge" or the "people of the book," and yet others are unascribed. These individual reports each present a facet of the topic under discussion, and it is through the accumulation of these various facets that al-Thaʿlabī constructs his narrative. The narrative therefore does not progress in a straightforward linear fashion, but rather would appear to meander its way through its presentation of historical events.

Thus if we look at the horses episode in the Solomon story, in which the prophet either slaughters or strokes his horses after they either cause him to forget to pray or remind him of God (Q 38:30–3), al-Thaʿlabī opens his description of events with an anonymous statement to the effect that God gave Arab horses exclusively to Solomon, followed by various possible descriptions of the horses referred to in Q 38:32 – one on the authority of Ḥasan, another on the authority of al-Kalbī, and a third on the authority of Muqātil. Al-Thaʿlabī then resumes the anonymous narrative voice to explain the events that caused the prophet to miss the prayer time and slaughter his horses in consequence, and follows this with Kaʿb's explanation of how many horses there were and how they were killed, coupled with the fact that God deprived the prophet of his throne for fourteen days as a result of this slaughter. This serves to move the narrative on, and the forward action is maintained in the next statement, on the authority of Ḥasan, that God in fact rewarded the prophet for his actions with command of the wind, which leads to a description of this obedient wind. The narrative then continues with the theme of the wind, and gives a lengthy anonymous report of one of the journeys Solomon took courtesy of this wind, and what he did in his hometown prior to departing on this journey. Al-Thaʿlabī cites an anonymous couplet inspired by this, which leads the narrative into a lengthy poem on the obedient wind, and other topics, supposedly found engraved on a rock and written by a friend of Solomon's.

The narrative then returns to the main story, and gives an anonymous report to the effect that Solomon did not slaughter the horses but rather branded their legs "with the brand of charity," followed by al-Zuhrī's account that Solomon wiped the dust from their legs and necks. An alternative version is then proposed, via the explanation given by ʿAlī b. Abī Ṭālib, in which God orders the angels to return the sun so that Solomon can perform his missed prayer. This leads the narrative on into another new phase: an account in which God's creation of the horse is described, statements from God and from Muḥammad about the nature and function of the horse, the angel's reaction to the creation of the horse, what the horse said when it arrived on earth, and Adam's choice of the horse among all of God's creatures.

There ends al-Thaʿlabī's description of the horses episode in the story of Solomon. Out of two full pages of narrative, there are eighteen lines directly related to the subject: thirteen stating that the horses were slaughtered, five giving other explanations. Of the thirteen lines, only one suggests that the prophet was censured for his actions, while a sum total of twenty lines are devoted to the subject of the wind the prophet was supposedly given as a reward for his actions. Sixteen lines are devoted to praise of the horse.

Thus, on the basis of narrative volume alone, the reader could assume that the "correct" reading is as follows: the horses, which were a remarkable and precious possession, were slaughtered and that God rewarded the prophet for his actions. However, it is important to stress that at no point is the reader told what he or she should think about the episode. Moreover, the nature of al-Thaʿlabī's text is such that the reader must make his or her decision about an episode based not only on the information given that directly relates to that episode, but on the strength of the chapter in its entirety. Indeed, the whole book acts as a cohesive unit. A series of complex themes runs across the tales, and it is important to view each chapter in light of those that went before. Although the text moves through the biographies of forty-six very different figures, these figures share the same basic human concerns (Klar 2006). Moreover, there are constant characters across the narrative; God, of course, and the Devil, but also prophets who continue to reappear throughout the *Tales* via the devices, both narrative and concrete, that are not confined by their actual birth and death. Thus, for instance, Adam, whose coffin is used to divide the sexes on board the Ark, who brings Moses' staff down with him when he falls from the garden, who names Joseph and is the cause of his amazing beauty, who gives sixty of his own years to prolong the future life of David, who is used, as we have seen, to add legitimacy to the horses in the story of Solomon, and so on.[3]

A further cohesive element is drawn by the constant, almost tangible presence of the voices of the prophet Muḥammad, his nephew ʿAlī b. Abī Ṭālib, the second caliph, ʿUmar b. al-Khaṭṭāb, and, of course, the Qurʾān, which all serve to remind the reader of where this apparently meandering narrative is leading. Thus while pre-Islamic figures move forwards through history, post-Islamic figures move backwards, and the end result is a narrative that is tightly woven together. Of course, the text can be utilized as a reference work to access the major opinions on a specific incident, but it is at its richest as a manual which, by wise and varied example, teaches its reader about the nuances of the human condition and the range of human experience. A similar impression of the text is apparent in Nagel's (1967: 96 – my translation) pronouncement that "Thaʿlabī's stories of the prophets are not simply history or tales as, for instance, in Ibn Qutayba's *Book of Knowledge* or Ṭabarī's *Annals*: they address themselves to the listener or the reader and require him or her to accept and to follow the insights and behaviors portrayed therein." Much like the rabbis of late antiquity, the Islamic storytellers and historiographers were engaged in an ongoing exploration of the meaning of the stories they inherited, attempting to present these stories to their readers in a convincing and communicative way, and in many ways al-Thaʿlabī's *Tales of the Prophets* is a unique expression of the desires and concerns of the ordinary medieval Muslim. The linking together of figures from the distant past, early Islamic figures, and a contemporary voice, serves to emphasize the relevance and applicability of the events described.

Social and Intellectual Context

A native of Nīshāpūr, a then bustling intellectual center several weeks' journey from the seat of the ʿAbbāsid caliphate in Baghdad, al-Thaʿlabī reflects contemporary concerns and sensibilities in his work, which is in many ways a reflection both of his person and of his times. The rising popularity of mystical thought can for instance be evidenced in his citation of Shiblī (d. 334/945) and al-Junayd (d. 298/910), and in the frequent presence of ascetic themes within the tales.[4] The thorny issue of free will versus pre-determination, at its height in the second half of the second/eighth century with the rise of the Muʿtazila, is meanwhile expressed, for instance, in the story of the phoenix which tried to cheat destiny and was duly humiliated. The question of rationalism, also brought to the forefront by the Muʿtazilī movement and much disputed over the fourth/tenth and fifth/eleventh centuries, can be seen to be expressed through al-Thaʿlabī's ongoing concern with reason (*ʿaql*), for example in the story of the Queen of Sheba where Solomon sets tests to gage the Queen's sense of reason. The infamous Qarmaṭīs of the same period are mentioned in al-Thaʿlabī's description of the history of the Kaʿba, and the fact that it was a Nīshāpūrī, described by al-Thaʿlabī as "our leader," who restored the black stone from the Kaʿba in Mecca after the failed Qarmaṭī attempt to remove it, can be taken both as evidence of the strong regional identities of the period and as an allusion to the growth of Persian nationalism. Indeed the presence of an isolated passage of Persian left untranslated in the otherwise Arabic text of the *Tales* (al-Thaʿlabī 1985: 208) can be read as something of a nod to the resurgence of Persian as a literary and scholarly language. Ibn al-Jawzī (d. 597/1200) certainly highlights the Persian aspect of al-Thaʿlabī when he mentions him (Swartz 1986: 182), making it clear that his national identity was part of how al-Thaʿlabī was later perceived.

This notwithstanding, it should be borne in mind that many of these more general features are also true of earlier works of tales of the prophets, and indeed of the genre as a whole. Moreover, at no point does al-Thaʿlabī engage with any of these theories on a sophisticated level; theological and political debate was not his purpose in compiling his text, and by concentrating on "evidence" within al-Thaʿlabī's text of the doctrinal, political, and historical issues of the times, one runs the risk of restricting medieval intellectual society, and al-Thaʿlabī's understanding of it, to a series of simple concepts. Although al-Thaʿlabī was a product of his time, his work was also a product of its genre; another element is added by the fact that al-Thaʿlabī remained throughout an individual, with his own interests and specific academic agenda: all of these factors should be considered in one's approach to the text. Furthermore, the *Tales of the Prophets* consists for the most part of citations from referenced sources rather than the author's own words. Even if adherence to a certain theological doctrine can be perceived to be implied in a report, there still remains to be decided the extent to which al-Thaʿlabī can be held to have shared such views. The situation, as such, is highly complex.

Where a relationship between al-Thaʿlabī and his medieval environment can, however, be more straightforwardly attributed is in the author's choice of sources and his methods. Later commentators who also produced a volume of pre-Islamic history tended, significantly, to utilize different criteria in selecting the sources they deemed reliable and the stories they judged to be worthy of repetition, famously rejecting many of the first generation of exegetes and traditionists as unreliable. Al-Thaʿlabī's concern was evidently not for textual criticism (though this is not to suggest that he knowingly repeated tales he suspected of being inauthentic) but for comprehensiveness (he tends to quote more variants of each episode than any other author within this genre) and narrative cohesion, as is made abundantly clear in the introduction to his *Tales*. While other collectors of tales of the prophets continued, and indeed still continue, to utilize such a methodology beyond the early medieval period, the highly traditional Sunnī scholars came to alter their perception of the function and purpose of such material. Al-Thaʿlabī, rather like al-Ghazālī (d. 505/1111) a century later, was inclusive of certain aspects of some potentially unorthodox elements of society; in al-Thaʿlabī's case these were the Ṣūfīs, the Shīʿīs, and the popular storytellers, whose customs and materials he utilized to enhance the readability and impact of his own work. As will become clear below, this decision was later to have a significant impact on his scholarly reputation, and it is in its innovative use of genre and materials that the work shows us why al-Thaʿlabī is a significant figure for this formative period of Islamic intellectual history.

Reception of the Text

Although we have no evidence of any contemporary criticisms of al-Thaʿlabī (indeed, the wide citation and dissemination of his major works implies rather that these were extremely favorably received), at a later date al-Thaʿlabī was to come under attack on several fronts. Ibn al-Jawzi mentions him as follows (Swartz 1986: 182 [Arabic 103]): "A number of Persians (*aʿājim*) have written books of a homiletic nature which they filled with incredible stories and corrupt ideas. Much of this can be found among tafsīr works of which Abū Isḥāq ath-Thaʿlabī has preserved an example."

He then goes on to single out four specific examples of the kind of material he has in mind: stories about Dhū ʾl-Kifl which evidently conflate this character with a wicked Israelite known as Kifl; reports to the effect that David wished for the death of Uriah and subsequently married his widow; the claim that Joseph loosened his belt during his encounter with Potiphar's wife; and the suggestion that Muḥammad uttered the so-called Satanic verses (with reference to Q 53:19–20).

That there was an on-going friction between the storytellers and the authorities on this issue is evident from the writings of al-Ghazālī a century earlier:

> People should guard against lies and against such stories which point to trivial faults and compromises which the common folk fail to understand, or to realize that they are nothing but trivial and unusual faults although they have been followed by atoning deeds and rectified by good works which are supposed to make up for them. (Faris 1966: 89)

Nonetheless, such material did continue to appear in later works and, as such, Ibn al-Jawzī's criticism of al-Thaʿlabī should by no means be seen as indicative of a mood of universal censure. To suggest that such anecdotes intended, or indeed were read, by those who repeated them, to imply any disrespect to the prophets in question is incorrect. Consequently, although some may have been alarmed by what they saw as the potential for misunderstandings in these stories, the tales continued to circulate in popular, scholarly, and even the most orthodox circles.

Al-Thaʿlabī was to come under criticism again under the pen of Ibn Taymiyya (d. 729/1328) who dedicates a lengthy passage in his *Minhāj al-sunna al-nabawiyya* ("The Path of Prophetic Conduct") to a refutation of aspects of al-Thaʿlabī's material and, *inter alia*, to a general critique of al-Thaʿlabī's use of *ḥadīth* (Ibn Taymiyya n.d.: IV, 2–80). Although this is with specific reference to al-Thaʿlabī's Qurʾān commentary, aspects of Ibn Taymiyya's criticism can also be perceived to have relevance for the reputation of the *Tales*; he describes al-Thaʿlabī as possessing virtue and faith, but being, in the likeness of "someone who attempts to gather firewood by night," unable to discern good *ḥadīth* from bad, or prophetic *sunna* from heretical innovation (*bidaʿ*) (Ibn Taymiyya n.d.: IV, 4).

Yet it is surely extremely significant that, despite these attacks on al-Thaʿlabī, Ibn Taymiyya's pupil, Ibn Kathīr (d. 774/1373), who is credited with carrying out his master's radical methodology in the production of his own works, cites al-Thaʿlabī repeatedly in his own history of the pre-Islamic prophets. He omits passages whose content he disputes (often albeit referring the reader instead to his Qurʾān commentary where details are provided; for the issue of *isrāʾīliyyāt* see, e.g., Calder 1993; McAuliffe 1998), and qualifies the authenticity of some *ḥadīth* taken from our author where he deems this appropriate, but al-Thaʿlabī clearly remains, for him, a substantial source. Moreover, in his entry for al-Thaʿlabī in the biographical section of his work, Ibn Kathīr (1985: XII, 43) describes al-Thaʿlabī as follows: "He knew many *ḥadīth* and had many teachers, and many marvelous things are found in his books on account of this." Ibn Kathīr would therefore appear to downplay his master's criticism of al-Thaʿlabī via his biographical entry, implying that it is merely on account of the quantity of *ḥadīth* he knows and the breadth of his learning that there are so many strange and wondrous things in his works. This can be read as a qualification of previous words of censure against our author, and indeed as something of an attempt to salvage his reputation; alternately it can be viewed, as can Ibn Taymiyya's admission of al-Thaʿlabī's religiosity and good character, as a way of criticizing the text without criticizing the man.

As for the reception of the *Tales per se*, this is difficult to gage, as the volume is not often described in classical sources. The fifteenth-century chronographer al-Sakhāwī (d. 902/1497) quotes it at length, and places the *Tales* alongside the biographies of Muḥammad by Ibn Isḥāq and al-Bukhārī, the story collections of Ibn al-Furāt (d. 807/1405) and al-Kisāʾī (fl. eleventh century), and the world histories of al-Ṭabarī, Ibn ʿAsākir, Ibn Kathīr and al-Mālikī, under the category "stories of the prophets" (al-Sakhāwī n.d.: 518), but although al-Thaʿlabī is listed in all the other appropriate biographical dictionaries and the *Tales* is usually mentioned by name, it is the Qurʾān commentary that has traditionally been the focus of scholarly attention. Similarly, we have very little documentary evidence of how collections such as al-Thaʿlabī's were used in medieval society. Nonetheless, the number of extant, catalogued manuscripts of the *Tales*, and the wide dissemination of printed editions of the work, belie any attempt to diminish its importance or popularity. From the introduction to the *Tales* we can deduce that al-Thaʿlabī believed in the importance and validity of narrative as an instructional tool. That al-Thaʿlabī also held the conviction that a work should be disparate in its sources and arranged in a reader-friendly fashion is clear from the introduction to his *Commentary*. Both of these stated methodologies place the reader firmly in pole position, and could explain why the wider success of the work may have been commercial rather than scholarly; the work's commercial success also shows itself in the number of imitative volumes that later appeared, especially in the Turkish and Persian-speaking Islamic lands.

Notes

1 This figure does not take into account personages whose biographies are provided within the tales of others, e.g., the story of Khiḍr which is contained within the tale of Moses.
2 The printed versions consulted include: al-Thaʿlabī (1985); the Azhar edition, al-Maktaba al-Saʿīdiyya, Cairo, n.d.; edition by ʿAbd al-ʿAzīz Sayyid al-Ahl, Singapore, 1962; and the edition of al-Maktaba al-Thaqafiyya, Beirut, n.d.
3 Thackston (1978: xxiii–xxiv) describes a similar phenomenon as occurring in Kisāʾī's *Tales of the Prophets*: "In Kisa'i's version . . . a sense of continuity is maintained by reintroducing 'props' throughout the tales. Adam's tābūt, for example . . . emerges at significant points in the narrative: it holds the leaves of Adam's Book and is passed down through Seth and successive generations to Noah; it contains carpentry tools used by Noah to construct his ark; it is also the Ark of the Covenant carried about by the Children of Israel. All of the articles of clothing with which Jacob invests Joseph were inherited from the former prophets. Moses' staff, which he takes from Shuʿayb/Jethro, had been brought to Adam from Paradise and passed down to Seth, Idris, Noah, Salih, and Abraham. In the Job narrative, Iblīs stands on the very rock Cain used to kill Abel. The ram that miraculously appears to be sacrificed in Isaac's stead turns out to be the very ram that Abel offered to God. And the stones which David picks up on his way to do battle with Goliath cry out that they had belonged to his fathers Abraham, Isaac and Jacob."
4 For al-Thaʿlabī's alleged Ṣūfī connections see Nagel 1967: 82. Saleh (2004: 56–65) disputes the extent to which al-Thaʿlabī can be named a Ṣūfī, yet makes it clear that he was nonetheless extremely interested in the ideas of the mystics. It is moreover evident that asceticism as a whole was a general feature of literature of this type (see Khoury 1978: 44–5, 96–7).

Further reading

Brinner, William M. (trans. and annot.) (2002) *ʿArāʾis al-Majālis fī qiṣaṣ al-anbiyāʾ or "Lives of the Prophets" as Recounted by Abū Isḥāq Aḥmad ibn Muḥammad ibn Ibrāhīm al-Thaʿlabī*. Brill, Leiden.

Johns, A. H. (1989) David and Bathsheba: A case study in the exegesis of Qurʾānic story-telling. *Mélanges de l'Institut Dominicaine d'Études Orientales du Caire* 19, 225–66.

Klar, M. O. (2004) *And we cast upon his throne a mere body*: A historiographical reading of Q 38:34. *Journal of Qurʾanic Studies* 6:1, 103–26.

Klar, M. O. (2006) *Interpreting Thaʿlabī's Tales of the Prophets: Temptation, Responsibility and Loss.* Routledge, London.

Lassner, Jacob (1993) *Demonizing the Queen of Sheba: Boundaries of Gender and Culture in Postbiblical Judaism and Medieval Islam.* University of Chicago Press, Chicago (especially pp. 64–87: A reading of al-Thaʿlabī's Solomon and the Queen of Sheba).

Saleh, Walid A. (2004) *The Formation of the Classical Tafsīr Tradition: The Qurʾān Commentary of al-Thaʿlabī (d. 427/1035).* Brill, Leiden.

Thackston, W. M. Jr. (1978) *The Tales of the Prophets of al-Kisaʾi, Translated from the Arabic with Notes.* Twayne, Boston.

Tottoli, Roberto (2002) *Biblical Prophets in the Qurʾān and Muslim Literature.* Curzon, Richmond.

Wiesmüller, Beate (2002) *Die von Koran getöteten: At̲-T̲aʿlabīs Qatlā l-Qurʾān nach der Istanbuler und den Leidener Handschriften: Edition und Kommentar.* Ergon, Wurzburg.

CHAPTER 23

Ṣūfism

Alan Godlas

Ṣūfī Qurʾān exegesis, *al-tafsīr al-ṣūfī*, *al-tafsīr al-ishārī* or *biʾl-ishāra* (Qurʾān exegesis through allusion), is a little-studied, controversial, and voluminous genre of Qurʾān commentary, the key feature of which is an "unveiling" (*kashf*) to the individual Ṣūfī commentator, an unveiling of a relationship between a Qurʾānic verse and Ṣūfī concepts. Although the only comprehensive scholarly treatment of this genre is Süleyman Ateş's work in Turkish *İşārī tefsīr okulu* ("The School of Allusive Commentary") (Ateş 1974), Paul Nwyia (1970) investigated the primacy of the individual experience of the commentator in Ṣūfī hermeneutics as well as the development of a Ṣūfī vocabulary for expressing this. Kristin Z. Sands (2005) recently completed a study in which she comparatively examined exoteric and Ṣūfī Qurʾān commentary. Because Ṣūfī commentators frequently move beyond the apparent (*ẓāhir*) point of the verses on which they are commenting and instead relate Qurʾānic verses to the inner or esoteric (*bāṭin*) and metaphysical dimensions of consciousness and existence, they have often been criticized (al-Dhahabī 1961: II, 337–78; al-Mashannī 1986: 639–50). The validity of such criticism is itself questionable, however, when it reaches the extent of conflating Ṣūfī *tafsīr* with Ismāʿīlī (*bāṭiniyya*) *taʾwīl*, which is an error that is commonly made.

Although both Ṣūfī *tafsīr* and Ismāʿīlī *taʾwīl* may share the designation of "*taʾwīl*" and are superficially similar, in fact they are two distinct kinds of hermeneutics. On the one hand, two significant features of Ismāʿīlī *taʾwīl* are as follows: first, its method derives from the foundation (*asās*) that is the Imām (as understood by Ismāʿīlīs); and second, in Ismāʿīlī *taʾwīl* the object of the verses revealed by *taʾwīl* is also often the Imām (Walker 1993: 124–33 and 1994: 120; Habil 1987: 36; Nanji 1987: 192; Corbin 1975: 523; 1983: 99; Daftary 1990: 388).

On the other hand, in Ṣūfī *tafsīr*, first of all, the method involves *kashf* (an unveiling to the heart or mind of the interpreter) – contingent not on the Imām but variously on the grace of God, the spiritual capacity and degree of understanding of the interpreter, and the degree of one's spiritual effort. Second, in Ṣūfī *tafsīr* the object revealed and linked to the verse is generally related to Ṣūfī practice or doctrines – commonly involving, for example, ontological-cosmological, anthropological, or psychological aspects or categories. Typical ontological-cosmological categories that Ṣūfī commentators relate to certain verses are various levels of reality such as the *nāsūt* (human plane), *malakūt* (the suprasensible plane), *jabarūt* (the plane of Divine compelling), and *lāhūt* (the plane of Divine unity). Examples of anthropological categories are the *ʿawāmm* (masses), *khāṣṣ* (elite), and *khāṣṣ al-khāṣṣ* (the elite of the elite); or categories such as *ʿārifūn* (gnostics), *ʿāshiqūn* (lovers), *ʿulamāʾ* (scholars), *muʾminūn* (believers), to name a few. Common psychological terms that Ṣūfīs relate to certain verses through *kashf* are faculties of consciousness such as the *nafs* (self), *qalb* (heart), *rūḥ* (spirit), and *sirr* (mystery); or states of consciousness such as *fanāʾ* (passing away in God) and *baqāʾ* (subsisting through God). By discovering through *kashf* relationships between Qurʾānic verses and various aspects of Ṣūfī practice and doctrine, Ṣūfī commentators provide a rich diversity of interpretations that contribute to producing the understanding that the Qurʾān is, as Walid Saleh expresses it, "the most polyvalent text in Islamic culture" (Saleh 2004: 154).

For the most part, in contrast to the fears of its critics, Ṣūfī *tafsīr* does not replace or invalidate the exoteric meanings of Qurʾānic verses by means of the results of *kashf* (unveiling); but rather, it adds to the exoteric meanings. In spite of the often obfuscating criticism, even Sunnī scholars such as al-Ghazālī (d. 505/1111), Ibn Qayyim al-Jawziyya (d. 751/1350), al-Shāṭibī (d. 790/1388), and Saʿd al-Dīn al-Taftazānī (d. 793/1390) accepted Ṣūfī *tafsīr* as being legitimate as long as certain conditions were met (Gätje 1976: 228–30; al-Dhahabī 1961: II, 357–8, 366–9; Qaṭṭān 1971: 309–10). One contemporary Azharī scholar even defended al-Sulamī's *Ḥaqāʾiq al-tafsīr* ("The Truths of Commentary")(see below) against the charge of being Ismāʿīlī, stating that since al-Sulamī did not deny the exoteric meaning of the Qurʾān or declare it to be invalid, the *Ḥaqāʾiq* should not be considered to be among the works of the Ismāʿīlīs (*bāṭiniyya*) (Nuqrāshī 1984: 188).

Although many Ṣūfīs wrote commentaries on individual *sūra*s such as *Sūrat Yūsuf* (Q 12) or particular verses, this survey only covers the Ṣūfī *tafsīr*s that are extant and that generally dealt with the whole of the Qurʾān (although such commentaries often omitted a significant number of verses per *sūra*). See Ateş (1974) for Ṣūfī *tafsīr*s that are outside the scope of this chapter.

Based largely upon the analysis of Gerhard Böwering (1991: 42–3) we can divide the history of Ṣūfī Qurʾān commentary into five phases. The elementary phase, lasting from the second/eighth to the fourth/tenth centuries, consists of two stages. The first of these two stages Böwering terms that of the "forebears" of Ṣūfī Qurʾān commentary. These are Ḥasan al-Baṣrī (d. 110/728), the sixth Shiʿī Imam, Jaʿfar al-Ṣādiq (d. 148/765), and Sufyān al-Thawrī (d. 161/778). Of these three commentators, the most significant was Jaʿfar al-Ṣādiq, whose commentary (as recorded by al-Sulamī [d. 412/1021]) was transmitted to his son, Imam Mūsā al-Kāzim (d. 183/799), from him to his son, Imam ʿAlī Riḍā (d. 203/818), and from him through a chain of transmission to al-Sulamī that Böwering (1991: 53–5; 1995: 18–22; also Nwyia 1968) has shown to be historically problematic.

The elementary phase in its second stage consists of al-Sulamī's commentary and the following seven Ṣūfīs who, in addition to Jaʿfar al-Ṣādiq, were al-Sulamī's primary sources: Dhū ʾl-Nūn al-Miṣrī (d. 246/861), Sahl al-Tustarī (d. 283/896), Abū Saʿīd al-Kharrāz (d. 286/899), al-Junayd (d. 298/910), Ibn ʿAṭāʾ al-Ādamī (d. 311/923), Abū Bakr al-Wāsiṭī (d. 320/932), and al-Shiblī (d. 334/946). Of these, it is possible that only al-Tustārī, Ibn ʿAṭāʾ, and al-Wāsiṭī may have been compilers of separate Ṣūfī Qurʾān commentaries (Nwyia 1973; Böwering 1991: 42). Al-Tustarī's *tafsīr*, written in Arabic and published uncritically (al-Tustarī 2001), is the only *tafsīr* of these authors to survive independently. Böwering, in his thorough study of al-Tustarī's *tafsīr* (1980: 129–30), showed that its structure is comprised of three main levels: al-Tustarī's own commentary on Qurʾānic verses, his statements and those of pre-Islamic prophets on various mystical subjects, and comments inserted into the *tafsīr* by later Ṣūfīs.

Undoubtedly the most significant author of Ṣūfī Qurʾān commentary prior to the sixth/twelfth century is al-Sulamī, without whose commentaries almost the entirety of the Qurʾān commentary of the first generations of Ṣūfīs would have been lost. Sulamī, whose full name was Abū ʿAbd al-Raḥmān Muḥammad b. Ḥusayn al-Sulamī al-Nīsābūrī, was a Shāfiʿī, who around 325/937 (or 330/942) was born in Nīsābūr, where he also died in 412/1021. Böwering has published his edition of the unique manuscript of al-Sulamī's minor commentary, *Ziyādāt Ḥaqāʾiq al-tafsīr* (1995), and is currently editing his major commentary, the *Ḥaqāʾiq al-tafsīr*, although it has recently been published uncritically (al-Sulamī 2001). These commentaries – both of which are in Arabic and consist of esoteric commentary on selected verses of the Qurʾān arranged in accordance with the Qurʾān's traditional order – are almost entirely compilations of commentaries of earlier Ṣūfīs, whose names al-Sulamī cited. Ateş briefly discussed each of al-Sulamī's seventy-four primary Ṣūfī sources (1969: 76–95). Although al-Sulamī's *tafsīrs* are essentially collections of the exegeses of other Ṣūfīs, his creative genius is evident in the fact that it is largely through his work that the Qurʾānic commentaries of the early Ṣūfīs have been preserved. Al-Sulamī himself stated that the very reason he composed his commentary was because he saw that authorities of the exoteric sciences (*al-ʿulūm al-ẓawāhir*) had written much about the exoteric implications of the Qurʾān, but that no one had collected the understanding of the Qurʾān as expressed by the "folk of the truth" (*ahl al-ḥaqīqa*), which is to say, by the Ṣūfīs. The *tafsīrs* most directly influenced by al-Sulamī are those of al-Daylamī, Rūzbihān al-Baqlī, and Gīsūdirāz, which will be discussed below. In addition, an influence of al-Sulamī's *tafsīr* upon Shiʿite literature is seen in the *Sharḥ Tawḥīd al-Ṣadūq* ("Explanation of [the book] 'Affirming Unity' of [al-Shaykh] al-Ṣadūq [Ibn Bābawayh]") of Qāḍī Saʿīd al-Qummī (d. after 1107/1696), who borrowed liberally from *Ḥaqāʾiq al-tafsīr*'s commentary on *Sūrat al-Fātiḥa* (Q 1)(al-Qummī 1994: 626–35). The overall importance of al-Sulamī's commentaries has been highlighted by Böwering, who has asserted that al-Sulamī's *Ḥaqāʾiq* is to Ṣūfīs what al-Ṭabarī's *tafsīr* is to the Sunnī community as a whole and that al-Sulamī's commentaries are as important to pre-sixth/twelfth century Ṣūfism as Ibn ʿArabī's major works are to later Ṣūfism (Böwering 1991: 56).

The second phase of Ṣūfī *tafsīr*, lasting from the fifth/eleventh to the seventh/thirteenth centuries, consists of three different forms: moderate Ṣūfī commentaries, esoteric commentaries deeply indebted to al-Sulamī, and commentaries written in Persian. Moderate commentaries are those that include esoteric Ṣūfī *tafsīr* as well as commentary based on transmissions (*riwāyāt*) from Muḥammad, companions, and early commentators as well as discussion of syntax, grammar, historical context, *fiqh*, and similar exoteric questions. One work of the "moderate" form is *al-Kashf wa'l-bayān ʿan tafsīr al-Qur'ān* ("The Unveiling and Elucidation of Commentary on the Qur'ān") of Abū Isḥāq Aḥmad b. Muḥammad b. Ibrāhīm al-Thaʿlabī (d. 427/1035) (Saleh 2004), better known for his *ʿArā'is al-majālis fī qiṣaṣ al-anbiyā'* ("The Brides of the Assemblies concerning the Tales of the Prophets"). Al-Thaʿlabī, who had read the entirety of the *Ḥaqā'iq al-tafsīr* to al-Sulamī himself, included in his commentary not only Ṣūfī *ishārāt*, but *ḥadīth*, commentaries of the early Muslim generations, *Isrā'īliyyāt*, and discussions of syntax and *fiqh*. Hence, Ateş considered it to be both an exoteric (*ẓāhir*) and a Ṣūfī esoteric (*bāṭin*) work (Ateş 1974: 97). Saleh (2004: 65, 224), more recently, convincingly argues that Thaʿlabī was not a Ṣūfī; and that his *tafsīr* should be considered an encyclopedic commentary that includes "a mystical level of interpretation" among its many other aspects.

Another example of this "moderate" form is ʿAbd al-Karīm al-Qushayrī's (d. 465/1074) *Laṭā'if al-ishārāt* ("The Subtleties of the Allusions"), written in Arabic and examined to a degree by R. Ahmad (1969: 16–69) and by its modern editor, al-Basyūnī (al-Qushayrī 1971: I, 3–37). In the *Laṭā'if*, al-Qushayrī – who was a Shāfiʿī – for the most part explicated the literal meaning of Qur'ānic verses, although at times he discussed the esoteric meanings of a verse. In spite of the fact that al-Qushayrī, unlike al-Sulamī, did not cite earlier authorities, Ateş (1974: 100) maintained that al-Qushayrī frequently utilized al-Sulamī's *tafsīr*, borrowing poetry from al-Sulamī and contemplating al-Sulamī's *tafsīr* while writing the *Laṭā'if*. In addition to the *Laṭā'if al-ishārāt*, al-Qushayrī wrote another Ṣūfī commentary which is still in manuscript, "The Great Commentary" (*al-Tafsīr al-kabīr*), and which has briefly been discussed by Böwering (1989: 571).

A final example of "moderate" commentary of this period is the Arabic *tafsīr*, *Nughbat al-bayān fī tafsīr al-Qur'ān* ("Gulps of Elucidation concerning Commentary on the Qur'ān") of Shihāb al-Dīn Abū Ḥafs ʿUmar b. Muḥammad al-Suhrawardī (d. 632/1234), the famous Shāfiʿī author of the Ṣūfī manual *ʿAwārif al-maʿārif* ("The Benefits of the Forms of Knowledge"). It is extant only in manuscripts (*GAL*: SI, 789, #4), one of which was copied with the permission (*ijāza*) of al-Suhrawardī himself (Ateş 1974: 161). According to Ateş (1974: 162), *Nughbat al-bayān* is largely an exotericly oriented *tafsīr*, although to a certain extent it does deal with asceticism (*zuhd*).

In addition to "moderate" *tafsīrs*, another subcategory of Ṣūfī *tafsīrs* of the second historical phase are those that contain primarily esoteric Ṣūfī commentary. Although these rely to a great extent on al-Sulamī, they cannot be considered to be part of a "school" of commentaries; and they were written in Arabic. *Taṣdīq al-maʿārif* ("The Confirmation of the Forms of Knowledge") or, as it is also titled, *Futūḥ al-Raḥmān fī ishārāt al-Qur'ān* ("The Openings of the Compassionate concerning the Allusions of the Qur'ān") was written by the little known Sunnī Ṣūfī, Abū Thābit ʿAbd al-Mālik al-Daylamī (d. 598/1193) and was only recently discovered by Böwering (and is still unpublished). Although commentary from al-Sulamī's authorities in the *Ḥaqā'iq al-tafsīr* comprises about half of al-Daylamī's *tafsīr*, al-Daylamī did not just directly import this material, but rather seems to have elaborated on it. The source of the remaining half of the content of the *Taṣdīq al-maʿārif* is al-Daylamī himself (Böwering 1987: 232).

The other *tafsīr* of the primarily esoteric subcategory of the second phase, *ʿArāʾis al-bayān fī ḥaqāʾiq al-Qurʾān* ("The Brides of Elucidation concerning the Truths of the Qurʾān") – written by the Shāfiʿī Ṣūfī, Abū Muḥammad Rūzbihān b. Abī Naṣr al-Baqlī al-Shīrāzī (d. 606/1209) – is similar to *Taṣdīq al-maʿārif* in a number of ways, while also exhibiting some differences. Like al-Daylamī's *tafsīr*, Rūzbihān's *ʿArāʾis al-bayān* is an esoteric Ṣūfī *tafsīr*, written in Arabic, and comprised almost equally of material from earlier *tafsīrs* and commentary from the author himself. Among the differences between the two *tafsīrs* is that (in addition to using his own commentary) Rūzbihān directly borrowed from both of al-Sulamī's two *tafsīrs*, quoting his authorities verbatim without any embellishment. Consequently, the *ʿArāʾis al-bayān* became the primary vehicle for the transmission of much of al-Sulamī's *Ziyādāt* for nine-hundred years (until Böwering's recent discovery and publication of the *Ziyādāt*); and the *ʿArāʾis* is the only major witness to the unique manuscript of the *Ziyādāt*. A second significant difference between al-Daylamī's *tafsīr* and that of Rūzbihān is that Rūzbihān included much Ṣūfī material from al-Qushayrī's *Laṭāʾif al-ishārāt* in the *ʿArāʾis*; while al-Daylamī apparently did not utilize al-Qushayrī as a source (Böwering 1987: 232). A final point concerning the *ʿArāʾis al-bayān* is that although it was published in lithograph (al-Baqlī 1884), it is rare and riddled with significant errors. Hence Ṣalāḥ al-Dīn al-Ṣāwī began an edition, which is now being followed by Godlas, who, after having located sixty-five manuscripts, is working on a critical edition, translation, and study of its entirety (Godlas 1991: 33; 1996: 31).

The entirely Persian commentaries of the second phase are those of al-Maybudī (d. 530/1135) and al-Darwājikī (d. 549/1154–5). The first of these, Abū ʾl-Faḍl Rashīd al-Dīn al-Maybūdī's published *tafsīr*, *Kashf al-asrār wa ʿuddat al-abrār* ("The Unveiling of the Secrets and the Provisioning of the Pious"), is known as the commentary of the Khwājah ʿAbdallāh al-Anṣārī (d. 481/1089), since it contains much of the esoteric commentary of al-Anṣārī, whose *madhhab* was Ḥanbalī. Nevertheless, al-Maybūdī (whose *madhhab* was Shāfiʿī) added his own esoteric commentary, extensive traditional *tafsīr bi ʾl-riwāya* (by means of transmitted material from earlier sources), and other exoteric commentary on matters such as variant readings, *fiqh*, and contexts of revelation (*asbāb al-nuzūl*), as well as a literal translation of the Qurʾānic Arabic into Persian. The literature on *Kashf al-asrār* has been surveyed by Masarrat (1995); and papers delivered at a conference on Maybūdī were edited by Pindarī (1995). The *Kashf al-asrār* has also been the subject of a study by Keeler (forthcoming).

Concerning the other Persian *tafsīr* of the second phase, there is some confusion regarding both the name of al-Darwājikī and the title of his unpublished Persian *tafsīr*, which appears to have been composed in Bukhara in the year 519/1125 (Storey 1927–39: I/1, 4). Böwering only lists the *nisba*, al-Darwājikī, along with his death date, 549/1154 (Böwering 1991: 42). Storey at first listed his name as Abū Naṣr Aḥmad b. Ḥasan b. Aḥmad Sulaymān, noted that he was "commonly called 'Zāhidī'," and in a footnote mentioned the *nisba* al-Dardājikī (Storey 1927–39: I/1, 4). Later, Storey gave a few more possibilities for his name and *nisba* (including al-Darwājikī) along with the *laqab* (honorific) Sayf al-Dīn but noted that a manuscript discussed by Ritter provided a nearly identical author's name – Abū Naṣr Aḥmad b. Ḥasan b. Aḥmad – whose *nisba* was tentatively "al-Daranī" and whose death was in 549/1154–5 (Storey 1953: I/2,

1190). Various titles given to the *tafsīr* are *Tafsīr-i Zāhidī, Tafsīr-i Sayf-al-Dīn, Laṭāʾif al-tafsīr* ("The Subtleties of Commentary") (Storey 1927–39: I/1, 4; 1953: I/2, 1190) and *Tafsīr-i Zāhid, Tafsīr-i DRwāJkī* (an upper case consonant indicating that a subsequent short vowel is unknown) and *Laṭāʾif al-tafāsīr* (Nāṣirī and Dānish' Pazhūh 1990: 218). Storey listed a number of manuscripts (most of which are partial) and also noted that a characteristic of this *tafsīr* is the recurrence of the Arabic phrase, *Qāla al-Shaykh al-imām al-zāhid* (the shaykh, the ascetic, the leader [or the ascetic leader] said) (Storey 1927–39: I/1, 1190).

The third phase of Ṣūfī commentary, written from the beginning of the seventh/thirteenth to the middle of the eighth/fourteenth century, consists of what Böwering has termed the commentaries of Ṣūfī "schools," most importantly those of Najm al-Dīn al-Kubrā (Abū 'l-Jannāb Aḥmad b. 'Umar) (d. 618/1221) and Muḥyī al-Dīn Ibn ʿArabī (d. 638/1240) (Böwering 1991: 42–3). One of the most urgent needs in the scholarship of Ṣūfī *tafsīr* is the publication of the collective *tafsīr* of the Kubrāwiyya tradition, often known as the *al-Taʾwīlāt al-najmiyya* ("The Najmī Exegeses"), commonly thought to have been so named because it was begun by Najm al-Dīn al-Kubrā. In the most recent examination of the problematic authorship of this *tafsīr*, J. Elias concluded that Najm al-Dīn al-Kubrā (a Shāfiʿī from Khwārazm) may have written the first part – from the beginning of the Qurʾān to *Sūrat al-Dhāriyāt* (Q 51), verse 19 – entirely by himself. Another possibility noted by Elias is that al-Kubrā's disciple, Najm al-Dīn al-Rāzī al-Dāya (d. 654/1256), may have written part of it. The first part – containing both exoteric and esoteric *tafsīr* – has been variously titled *ʿAyn al-ḥayāt* ("The Spring of Life"), *al-ʿAwārif* ("The Benefits"), and *Baḥr al-ḥaqāʾiq* ("The Ocean of the Truths") (al-Dhahabī 1961: II, 395; Elias 1995: 204–5). Nevertheless, *Baḥr al-haqāʾiq* also appears to have been the title of a different *tafsīr* written by Najm al-Dīn al-Rāzī (Ateş 1974: 142–4; Shpall 1981–4, regarding ms. Süleymaniye-Hasan Hüsnü MS. 37 *mukarrar*). Elias has demonstrated, however, that ʿAlāʾ al-Dawla al-Simnānī (d. 736/1336) wrote a distinct commentary, one of the names of which is *Tafsīr Najm al-Qurʾān* ("The Commentary: The Star of the Qurʾān") and which is entirely esoteric. It begins with *Sūrat al-Ṭūr* (Q 52) and covers the remainder of the Qurʾān, although it is prefaced by a long introduction and commentary on the *Fātiḥa* and in various manuscripts begins when the *tafsīr* of al-Kubrā/al-Rāzī leaves off (Elias 1995: 203–12; al-Dhahabī 1961: 395). The introduction was edited by Nwyia (1973–7: 141–57) and studied by Corbin (1978: 121–44). Elias edited various excerpts of al-Simnānī's *tafsīr*, basing his edition on two related manuscripts, one of which (Süleymaniye-Şehit Ali Paşa, Ms. 165) was collated with al-Simnānī's own copy (Elias 1991: 281–321, 1995: 203, 207). Elias also discussed al-Simnānī's understanding of the Qurʾān – explicitly expressed in his *tafsīr* – noting that according to al-Simnānī one can become transformed into a mirror for divine attributes by contemplating the Qurʾān (Elias 1995: 107–10).

Another *tafsīr* related to the Kubrawī school is that of the Shāfiʿī scholar Niẓām al-Dīn Ḥasan b. Muḥammad b. Ḥusayn al-Qummī al-Nīsābūrī (d. 728/1327, but this is problematic). Although his commentary, *Tafsīr Gharāʾib al-Qurʾān wa-raghāʾib al-furqān* ("The Commentary: Marvels of the Qurʾān and Desire of the Criterion") (1904–12), is largely a traditional exoteric *tafsīr*, it includes significant Ṣūfī commentary, most of which – as the author himself stated – came from Najm al-Dīn al-Rāzī al-Dāya (al-Nīsābūrī 1912: XXX, 223; Ayāzī 1994: 528; al-Dhahabī 1961: I, 321). Al-Zarqānī noted that after al-Nīsābūrī discussed the exoteric meaning (*ẓāhir maʿnā*) of a verse, he would write, "The people of 'allusion' (*ishāra*) say . . ." Or, he simply wrote "*al-taʾwīl*" and thereafter explicated the esoteric meaning (*al-maʿnā al-ishārī*) of the verse (Zarqānī 1943: II, 82). M. Ayoub has translated excerpts of the Ṣūfī component of al-Nīsābūrī's *tafsīr* (1984; 1992).

Ibn ʿArābī's school of Qurʾān commentary, influenced mainly by his own writings and to a lesser degree by his predecessor, Ibn Barrajān, was continued by al-Qāshānī and al-Ṣafadī (Böwering 1991: 43), although the connection of al-Ṣafadī to this school is problematic. These *tafsīrs* consist of independently composed commentaries that nevertheless are united by their common usage of Ibn ʿArabī's terms and concepts. According to Ateş (1974: 130–1) – who described various mss. of the *tafsīr* of ʿAbd al-Salām b. ʿAbd al-Raḥmān Abū ʾl-Ḥakam al-Ishbīlī, known as Ibn Barrajān (d. 536/1141) – the *tafsīr* of Ibn Barrajān greatly influenced Ibn ʿArabī. In addition, Ateş (1974: 178–9, 187–8) argued that a partial commentary – from *Sūrat Yūnus* (Q 10) to *Sūrat al-Ṭūr* (Q 52) – by Ibn ʿArabī is extant (Ms. Şehid ʿAlī Paşa 62) and that it was a model for the commentary of al-Qāshānī. If Ateş has indeed correctly identified Ibn ʿArabī as the author of this manuscript, its publication is another of the major needs of the field.

Böwering (1991: 43) noted that the *tafsīr* of al-Ṣafadī (d. 696/1296) – whose full name was Jamāl al-Dīn Yūsuf b. Hilāl b. Abī ʾl-Barakāt al-Ḥalabī al-Ḥanafī Abū ʾl-Faḍāʾil al-Ṣafadī – was influenced by Ibn ʿArabī's school of thought. Ateş (1974: 197) demonstrated that this unpublished *tafsīr*, the title of which is *Kashf al-asrār fī hatk al-astār* ("The Unveiling of the Mysteries concerning the Rending of the Veils"), had been mistakenly attributed to Ibn ʿArabī himself. Although Ateş, in the table of contents of *İşārī tefsīr okulu* (1974: 202), lists al-Ṣafadī's *tafsīr* as being among those that were influenced by the "unity of being" (*waḥdat al-wujūd*) (which is an important doctrine of Ibn ʿArabī's "school"), later, however, in his discussion of al-Ṣafadī's exegetical method, Ateş concluded by stating that al-Ṣafadī's *tafsīr* did not exhibit the characteristics of the "unity of being."

In contrast to al-Ṣafadī, the *tafsīr* of ʿAbd al-Razzāq al-Qāshānī (d. 730/1330) clearly exhibits the influence of the "unity of being." This is a major reason why even to this day al-Qāshānī's *tafsīr* (1981) is known as the "*Tafsīr* of Ibn ʿArabī." Studied by Pierre Lory (1980), excerpts of this *tafsīr* have been translated into English by Ayoub (1981; 1992). The most recent contribution to the *tafsīrs* of the "school" of Ibn ʿArabī is a contemporary collection of Ibn ʿArabī's Ṣūfī exegeses found throughout his works and compiled by M. Ghurāb (Ayāzī 1994: 464–9).

The commentaries written in India and in regions ruled by the Ottomans and Timurids, comprise the fourth phase of Ṣūfī *tafsīr*, the period from the ninth/fifteenth to the twelfth/eighteenth century. Of all the Ṣūfī *tafsīrs* written during this period, the *tafsīrs* of Gīsūdirāz, al-Kāshifī, al-Nakhjiwānī, Aziz Mahmūd Hüdāyī, and İsmail Hakkı Bursevi are the most noteworthy. Although the Naqshbandīs Khwājah Muḥammad Pārsā (d. 822/1419) and Yaʿqūb al-Charkhī (d. 851/1447) wrote *tafsīrs* that contain some Ṣūfī content, these did not cover the whole of the Qurʾān and so will not be dealt with here.

The great Chishtī shaykh, Sayyid Abū ʾl-Fatḥ Muḥammad b. Yūsuf al-Ḥusaynī, known as Khwājah Bandah'nawāz, is also commonly referred to by his ancestral name of Gīsūdirāz (longhair) (d. 825/1422). He was a Ḥanafī shaykh who spent his life in Delhi and the Deccan during the periods of Tughlaq and Bahmanid rule and wrote a still unpublished Ṣūfī *tafsīr* (almost entirely in Arabic) titled *Tafsīr-i Multaqaṭ* ("Commentary [consisting] of Unexpectedly Found Things"), that deals largely with Ṣūfī themes (in contrast to the assertion of M. Sālim al-Qidwāʾī) (Hussaini 1983: 20). It is similar in structure to but not dependent upon the *ʿArāʾis al-bayān;* which is to say that like Rūzbihān, Gīsūdirāz cited numerous verbatim passages directly from Sulamī's *Ḥaqāʾiq al-tafsīr* (which he indicated by "*Ḥaqāʾiq*") and from al-Qushayrī's *Laṭāʾif al-ishārāt* (indicated by "*Laṭāʾif*"); but he included significant commentary that is apparently his own – commentary that is preceded by the designation *al-multaqaṭ*. Hussaini (1983: 11–13) briefly discussed the *tafsīr* and the manuscripts, one nearly complete and one partial manuscript of which are extant in the India Office (#109–111), while a partial copy is held in Lucknow.

The well-known author, Kamāl al-Dīn Ḥusayn b. ʿAlī Wāʿiẓ-i Kāshifī (d. 910/1504–5 in Herat), wrote the Persian Qurʾān commentary *Mawāhib-i ʿalīya* ("The Sublime Gifts"), which is also known as the *Tafsīr-i Ḥusaynī*. Although *Mawāhib-i ʿalīya* (1938, uncritically published) is largely a translation and exoteric commentary on the Qurʾān, it has a significant and evocative Ṣūfī component. Kāshifī – who was the brother-in-law of ʿAbd al-Raḥmān Jāmī and father of Fakhr al-Dīn ʿAlī Ṣāfī (who authored the Naqshbandī hagiography *Rashaḥāt ʿayn al-ḥayāt* ["Percolations of the Spring of Life"]) – was a prominent figure in Timurid Herat and an initiate in the Sunnī Naqshbandī order. Nevertheless, the question of his *madhhab* is problematic. Some sources stated that he was a Ḥanafī, others a Shāfiʿī, and still others a Shīʿite. Whatever the case may be, his *tafsīr* (completed 899/1494) is described as being written in the style of the *ahl-i sunnat wa-jamāʿat* (i.e. the Sunnīs) and does not exhibit Shīʿī characteristics (Kāshifī 1938: 13–21, 79). There are three kinds of Ṣūfī materials that Kāshifī cites in the *Mawāhib-i ʿalīya*: earlier Ṣūfī *tafsīrs*, general Ṣūfī prose treatises, and Persian Ṣūfī poetry. Most of the Ṣūfī material in the *tafsīr* derives from the Ṣūfī comentaries of al-Sulamī, al-Qushayrī, al-Anṣārī/al-Maybudī, and the Kubrawī school, although he occasionally cites other Ṣūfī *tafsīrs* such as that of al-Qāshānī and possibly al-Darwājikī (referred to by "al-Zāhid"). Among the Persian Ṣūfī poets he frequently cites are Jalāl al-Dīn Rūmī, Sanāʾī, and Khwājah ʿAbd Allāh al-Anṣārī. He also quotes from a number of other Ṣūfī texts, among them being Ibn ʿArabī's *al-Futūḥāt al-makkiyya* and a variety of works of Jāmī.

Niʿmat Allāh b. Maḥmūd al-Nakhjiwānī (or al-Nakhjuwānī) (d. 920/1514), a Ḥanafī Naqshbandī shaykh, wrote in Arabic the Ṣūfī *tafsīr* titled *al-Fawātiḥ al-ilāhiyya waʾl-mafātiḥ al-ghaybiyya* ("Divine Openings and Unmanifest Keys") (1907, uncritically published). Originally from Nakhjiwān in Azerbaijan, Bābā Niʿmat Allāh (or Shaykh ʿAlwān, as he was also known) completed his *tafsīr* in 902/1497 in Tabriz, and from there emigrated to Akşehir in Anatolia, where he spent the last sixteen years of his life and where his grave was well known. He did not cite any other Ṣūfī *tafsīrs* and appears to have written *al-Fawātiḥ al-ilāhiyya* without consulting any sources. Although he commented on every verse of the Qurʾān, the vast majority of his exegesis consists of brief traditional exoteric commentary clarifying the meaning of words. Nevertheless, in his substantial introduction to the *tafsīr*, at the beginning and end of every *sūra*, and periodically throughout his *tafsīr*, Nakhjiwānī included Ṣūfī-oriented material involving the terminology and concepts of the school of Ibn ʿArabī (Nakhjiwānī 1907: ii (preface), 2–3; Ayāzī 1994: 563–6).

Aziz Mahmud Hüdai (1038/1628), the prolific Turkish shaykh of the Jalwatī or Celveti Ṣūfī order, who lived most of his adult life in Uskudar (across the Bosporus from Istanbul), gave discourses on the Qurʾān that after his death were composed into a *tafsīr* titled *Nafāʾis al-majālis* ("The Gems of the Assemblies"). Written in Arabic (but still unpublished), for the most part this *tafsīr* consists of exoteric commentary interspersed at times with Ṣūfī commentary dealing with aspects of the Ṣūfī path, aspects such as asceticism (*zuhd*), "consciousness of God" (*taqwā*), and "passing away in God" (*fanāʾ fī Allāh*). Although it has been asserted that Hüdai wrote his *tafsīr* without referring to any other *tafsīrs*, Ateş observed the influence of al-Sulamī on at least a part of the *Nafāʾis* (Yılmaz 1980: 111; Ateş 1974: 231).

The most extensive and comprehensive of all the Ṣūfī *tafsīrs* written during this period is the *Rūḥ al-bayān* ("The Spirit of Elucidation"), by İsmail Hakkı Bursevi (also variously written Bursavi, Bursalı, and, in Arabic, Ismāʿīl Ḥaqqī al-Burūsawī) (d. 1137/1725). Bursevi, a prolific scholar, like Hüdai was a Ṣūfī shaykh of the Celveti/Jalwatī order. A Ḥanafī, İsmail Hakkı lived most of his life in Istanbul and Bursa. *Rūḥ al-bayān* (1866?, published uncritically), written largely in Arabic, has both traditional exoteric and Ṣūfī dimensions. It includes İsmail Hakkı's own commentaries as well as quoted material from the *tafsīrs* of the Kubrawī school, in addition to material from al-Sulamī, al-Qushayrī, Ibn ʿArabī/al-Qāshānī, Rūzbihān, and Kāshifī. Furthermore, into his *tafsīr* he weaves Persian poetry from the likes of Ḥāfiẓ, Saʿdī, Rūmī, and ʿAṭṭār. *Rūḥ al-bayān* is similar to Kāshifī's *Mawāhib-i ʿaliyya*; although the Rūḥ al-bayān is more massive and has a greater emphasis on Ṣūfī *tafsīr*.

The final period in the history of Ṣūfī *tafsīr*, from the thirteenth/nineteenth century until today, includes the *tafsīrs* of Ibn ʿAjība, Pānīpatī, al-Alūsī, Sulṭān ʿAlī Shāh, Ṣafī ʿAlī Shāh, and Mullā Ḥuwaysh. First of all, Aḥmad b. ʿAjība (d. 1224/1809), a Moroccan Ṣūfī, was the author of the *tafsīr* titled *al-Baḥr al-madīd fī tafsīr al-Qurʾān al-majīd* ("The Immense Ocean concerning Commentary on the Glorious Qurʾān") (1999), which has largely been neglected by scholars of *tafsīr* outside of Morocco. Ibn ʿAjība, an initiate of the Darqāwī order, stated that he combined in his *tafsīr* "both the explanations (*ʿibāra*) of the exoterics (*ahl al-ẓāhir*) with the allusions (*ishāra*) of the esoterics (*ahl al-bāṭin*);" and hence, as we would expect, it contains significant Ṣūfī commentary (Ibn ʿAjība 1990: 38–9; Michon 1968–9: 40; 1973: 108–14, 274–5). Although most of the Ṣūfī sources of his *tafsīr* are from North Africa, Andalus, or Egypt, he also quotes from Iranian scholars such as al-Qushayrī and Rūzbihān al-Baqlī. Ibn ʿAjība's quotations from Rūzbihān have hitherto gone unnoticed because Ibn ʿAjība referred to him as "al-WRTJbī" (Ibn ʿAjība 1999 I: 67, 466, 478 and *passim*).

The *tafsīr* of Pānīpatī, titled *Tafsīr al-Maẓharī* ("The Commentary related to Maẓhar"), was written in Arabic by Qāḍī Thanāʾ Allāh ʿUthmānī Fānī Fatī (Pānīpatī) (d. 1225/1810), a Ḥanafī and Naqshbandī shaykh. The commentary has been published in ten volumes and was named after Qāḍī Thanāʾ Allāh's Naqshbandī shaykh, Mīrzā Maẓhar Jān-i Jānān (1197/1780). Both Böwering and Ayāzī regard Pānīpatī's *tafsīr* as a Ṣūfī *tafsīr*, and Ayāzī also groups it among the Ṣūfī *tafsīrs* that use the hermeneutics of allusion (*al-ishārī*) (Böwering 1991: 43; Ayāzī 1994: 833, 850). Nevertheless, Ayāzī (1994: 366) states that in spite of the fact that Qāḍī Thanāʾ Allāh (who lived most of his life in the North Indian state of Haryana) was a Naqshbandī Ṣūfī in the lineage of Aḥmad Sirhindī, his *tafsīr* consists almost entirely of exoteric commentary and only rarely deals with "esoteric matters" (*rumūz*) and "mystical allusions" (*ishārāt*).

Abū ʾl-Thanā Shihāb al-Dīn Sayyid Maḥmūd b. ʿAbd Allāh al-Ḥusaynī al-Alūsī al-Baghdādī, known commonly as Shihāb al-Dīn al-Alūsī, was one of the most important nineteenth-century Iraqi scholars and was the author of the well-known Arabic Qurʾān commentary *Rūḥ al-maʿānī fī tafsīr al-Qurʾān al-ʿaẓīm wa sabʿ al-mathānī* ("The Spirit of the Meanings concerning Commentary on the Qurʾān and the Seven Oft-repeated Verses [i.e. al-Fātiḥa (Q 1)]") (1933–4). Al-Alūsī lived most of his life in Baghdad, where he died in 1270/1854. Affiliated with the Naqshbandī *ṭarīqa* of Mawlānā Khālid al-Baghdādī (d. 1242/1827), he was the *muftī* of Baghdad for a number of years and was regarded as the shaykh of the scholars of Iraq (al-Dhahabī 1967: I, 352–3; *EI2* 2004: "Alūsī"). Some sources assert that he was a Shāfiʿī; others, however, maintain that he was a Ḥanafī (Ateş 1974: 250). Although his massive *tafsīr* deals largely with exoteric matters, it does indeed have a significant Ṣūfī component, one that is often introduced by the phrase *min bāb al-ishāra* ("from the domain of allusion"). A biographer of al-Alūsī has stated that among the Ṣūfī commentators upon whom al-Alūsī relied were Ibn ʿArabī, al-Tustarī, and Ismāʿīl Ḥaqqī (ʿAbd al-Ḥamīd 1968: 207–9). In addition, al-Alūsī relied upon Rūzbihān al-Baqlī. This, however, had gone unnoticed because al-Alūsī – on numerous occasions without attribution – quoted the *ʿArāʾis al-bayān* verbatim or creatively integrated passages from it into his *tafsīr* (al-Alūsī 1933–4: *passim*).

Ḥājjī Mīrzā Ḥasan Iṣfahānī, known as Ṣafī ʿAlī Shāh (d. 1317/1899), wrote his unique Ṣūfī *tafsīr* in Persian poetry. Titled simply *Tafsīr-i Qurʾān* ("Commentary on the Qurʾān"), it has been published in one large-size volume. Regarded as one of nineteenth-century Iran's premier poets, Ṣafī ʿAlī Shāh was a Shīʿī Ṣūfī shaykh of a branch of the Niʿmatallāhī order known as the Ṣafī ʿAlī Shāhī or Ṣafāʾiyya order, an order that was closely connected to the Qājār court (Pourjavady and Wilson 1978: 252–3). In his *tafsīr*, written in Persian rhymed couplets (*mathnawī*) but also containing the Arabic text of the Qurʾān with a Persian prose translation, Ṣafī ʿAlī Shāh dealt with conventional exoteric subjects (such as various Qurʾānic narratives) but also frequently linked the Qurʾān to explications of Ṣūfī metaphysics and the Ṣūfī path (Ṣafī ʿAlī Shāh n.d.).

Sulṭān Muḥammad b. Haydar Muḥammad b. Sulṭān Muḥammad Junābādī (Gunābādī) (d. 1327/1909), a Shīʿī Ṣūfī known as Sulṭān ʿAlī Shāh, was the author of the published Arabic Qurʾān commentary *Bayān al-saʿāda fī maqāmāt al-ʿibāda* ("The Elucidation of Felicity concerning the Stations of Worship") (Ayāzī 1994: 212). Originally from Bīdukht, a village in the vicinity of Gunābād (Iran), Sulṭān ʿAlī Shāh was a shaykh in the Gunābādī branch of the Niʿmatallāhī Ṣūfī order. In his *tafsīr*, Sulṭān ʿAlī Shāh included exoteric commentary as well as Ṣūfī commentary. Although Āghā Buzurg Tihrānī stated that Sulṭān ʿAlī Shāh had been accused of plagiarism, Ayāzī refuted these allegations (Ayāzī 1994: 214–15; Pourjavady and Wilson 1978: 252).

ʿAbd al-Qādir b. Sayyid Muḥammad Ḥuwaysh b. Maḥmūd Āl Ghāzī al-ʿĀnī, known as Mullā Ḥuwaysh, was the author of the Qurʾān commentary *Bayān al-maʿānī ʿalā ḥasab tartīb al-nuzūl* ("The Elucidation of the Meanings according to the Order of Revelation"). Mullā Ḥuwaysh, an Ashʿarī Ḥanafī, did not compose this Arabic *tafsīr* in accordance with the traditional ordering of the *sūras*. Instead, he arranged his *tafsīr* according to the chronological order of revelation. The *tafsīr*, written in 1936–7, consists of both exoteric and Ṣūfī material (although its Ṣūfī material only plays a very minor role)(Ḥuwaysh 1964–5). According to Ayāzī, among the Ṣūfī *tafsīrs* on which the author relies are those of Ibn ʿArabī/al-Qāshānī, al-Nakhjiwānī, İsmail Hakkı, and al-Alūsi. He also utilized well-known general Ṣūfī works such as al-Qushayrī's al-*Risāla* ("The Treatise"), al-Ghazāli's *Iḥyāʾ ʿulūm al-dīn* ("The Revival of the Sciences of Religion"), Abū Najīb al-Suhrawardī's *ʿAwārif al-maʿārif* ("The Benefits of the Forms of Knowledge"), and ʿAbd al-Karīm al-Jīlī's *al-Insān al-kāmil* ("The Perfect Man"). In addition, he made use of two late Naqshbandi works, Shaykh Muḥammad b. ʿAbd Allāh b. Muṣṭafā al-Khānī's (d. 1279/1862) *al-Bahja al-saniyya fī ādāb al-ṭarīqa al-Naqshbandiyya* ("Brilliant Splendor concerning the Etiquette of the Naqshbandī Path"), and Asʿad b. Maḥmūd Ṣāḥib al-Naqshbandī al-Khālidī's (d. 1347/1928) *Nūr al-hidāya wa'l-ʿirfān fī sirr al-rābiṭā wa'l-tawajjuh wa khatm al-Khwājakān* ("The Light of Guidance and Gnosis concerning the Mystery of [the Practices of] Estabishing a Connection [with one's shaykh], Turning one's Face, and Completing [the Mention of] the Masters") (Ayāzī 1994: 218–21).

Böwering (1991: 43) has stated that with the coming of the thirteenth/nineteenth century, the genre of Ṣūfī *tafsīr* began "a phase of certain decline that seems to continue today." Nevertheless, because we now know of three *tafsīrs* composed in this final phase that Böwering did not mention (those of Ibn ʿAjība, Ṣafī ʿAlī Shāh, and Mullā Ḥuwaysh, the first two of which have a strong Ṣūfī dimension), it seems prudent to abandon the assessment that this recent phase of Ṣūfī *tafsīr* is characterized by "certain decline." In addition, a number of Ṣūfī *tafsīrs* are now on the Internet (altafsir.com); and as more Ṣūfī *tafsīrs* become published and translated into various languages, this will make them available to large audiences for the first time. Hence, it is certainly possible, if not probable, that this will bring about both an increase in the appreciation of Ṣūfī *tafsīrs* as well as an increase in the production of them. One obstacle to this, however, is the current tendency in Western scholarship to minimize the importance of critical editions of texts. It is hoped that scholars will realize that without such editions, our efforts to understand Ṣūfī *tafsīr* will remain severely impaired.

Further reading

Böwering, G. (1980) *The Mystical Vision of Existence in Classical Islam: The Qurʾānic Hermeneutics of the Ṣūfī Sahl At-Tustarī (d. 283/896)*, De Gruyter, Berlin.

Böwering, G. (1991) The Qurʾān commentary of al-Sulamī. In: Hallaq, Wael and Little, Donald P. (eds.) *Islamic Studies Presented to Charles J. Adams.* E. J. Brill, Leiden, pp. 41–56.

Böwering, G. (1996) The major sources of Sulamī's minor Qurʾān commentary. *Oriens* 35: 35–56.

Godlas, A. (1996) Psychology and self-transformation in the Ṣūfī Qur'ān commentary of Rūzbihān al-Baqlī. *Sufi Illuminations* I:1, 31–62.

Habil, A. (1987) Traditional esoteric commentaries on the Quran. In: Nasr, S. H. (ed.) *Islamic Spirituality: Foundations*. Crossroads, New York, pp. 24–47.

Lory, P. (1980) *Les commentaires ésotériques du Coran d'après ʿAbd al-Razzâq al-Qâshânī*, 2nd end. Les Deux Océans, Paris.

Nwyia, Paul (1970) *Exégèse Coranique et langage mystique*. Dar el-Machreq, Beirut.

Sands, Kristin Zahra (2005) *Ṣūfī Commentaries on the Qur'ān in Classical Islam*. Routledge, London.

CHAPTER 24

Rūmī

Jawid Mojaddedi

> Mawlānā's mystic book, the *Mathnawī*,
> Is the Qur'ān in Persian poetry.[1]

The relationship between Muslim mystics and religious scholars has been remarkably harmonious for the greater part of Islamic history, especially in view of the increasing tensions in recent times. One issue of conflict which arises, perhaps inevitably, between mystics and theologians of any religion, namely the question of revelation after the cycle of prophecy, has also been debated among Muslims. However, contrary to popular belief (including among many contemporary Muslims themselves), most Muslims in the course of history have held the view that Islamic revelation is not limited to the Qur'ān. While the majority of Sunnī Muslims regard at least the prophet's normative example, or *sunna*, which was eventually compiled in *ḥadīth* collections more than 200 years after his death, as constituting a form of revelation, Shīʿī Muslims add to this the revelation received by the Imāms who succeeded Muḥammad in his role as a spiritual guide and political leader, as well as that received by his highly revered daughter Fāṭima, through whom the Imāms are his direct blood descendants. Historically, most Ṣūfīs have been affiliated to one of the Sunnī legal schools, and thus the Ṣūfī view that revelation continues to be inspired in saints (*awliyā'*), or adept mystics, of successive generations has been held by a large proportion of Sunnī Muslims. In this way, divine inspiration received by saints (*ilhām*) supplements the Qur'ān and the *sunna* as revelation for many Sunnī Muslims in a way that is comparable with the Shīʿī notion that revelation from God and communication with Him must always be possible for certain members of humanity. The Ṣūfī author Abu Naṣr al-Sarrāj (d. 377/988) refers to these different types of revelation in the introduction of his *Kitāb al-lumaʿ fī 'l-taṣawwuf* ("The Book of Flashes concerning Ṣūfism"), the oldest surviving Ṣūfī manual: "Nothing is known or comprehended other than what is present in the book of God, what has been transmitted about the messenger of God and what has been revealed to the hearts of God's saints" (al-Sarrāj 1914: 1–2).

This statement of Ṣūfī epistemology is confirmed by the structure of discourse in Ṣūfī manuals since the time of al-Sarrāj. Typically, the discussion of any topic begins with a citation from the Qur'ān and *ḥadīths*, followed by the opinions of Ṣūfī authorities. Deference is thus expressed to the Qur'ān and the *ḥadīth*. However, the reports transmitted about the opinions and actions of saints account for the vast majority of the content of Ṣūfī manuals and are not restricted to commentary on Qur'ānic verses and *ḥadīths*. They serve as an additional source of authoritative knowledge for Ṣūfism, and are arguably the most important of the three.

Rūmī

The most well-known Ṣūfī across the world today is Jalāl al-Dīn Muḥammad al-Balkhī (d. 671/1273), better known in the Middle East as Mawlānā (Turkish: Mevlana; "Our lord") and in Europe and North America as Rūmī ("the Anatolian"). Born in the province of Balkh, in what is now the border region between Afghanistan and Tajikistan, he migrated with his family as a small child and eventually settled in Konya. As an adult, Rūmī wrote a vast amount of mystical poetry, most famous among which are his collection of thousands of lyrical poems, or *ghazals*, and his *magnum opus*, the *Mathnawī*, which is a poem of some 26,000 rhyming couplets (see further Lewis 2000: 271–85). Rūmī was the rare combination of a poet recognized as being among the very best in his literary tradition, as well as a highly revered Ṣūfī master. The Mevlevi order, which was formed by his disciples, was named after him. It grew into a highly influential religious institution, especially during Ottoman times, and is today one of the most popular orders among the growing community of Ṣūfīs in North America and Europe, where its members are better known as the "whirling dervishes" because of their distinctive dance ritual.

Translations of Rūmī's poetry have topped bestseller lists in North America and Europe in recent years, after selections of it were rendered into English by contemporary poets on the basis of more literal translations made previously by orientalists. For the sake of accessibility, best-selling Rūmī translators such as Coleman Barks tend to omit culture-specific images and references which would be unfamiliar for their readership. While they have been highly successful in popularizing Rūmī, their approach has had the effect of obscuring the fact that he makes heavy use of the Qur'ān (as well as other Islamic sources). While it may not be essential for understanding Rūmī's mystical message to appreciate his use of the Qur'ān, an exploration of this aspect will help elucidate this Ṣūfī master and poet's understanding of the Qur'ān in relation to the knowledge with which he, as a Ṣūfī saint, had been inspired. Rūmī's poetry is particularly appropriate for such a study because of his remarkably frequent use of the Qur'ān, which is especially evident in his *magnum opus*, the *Mathnawī* ("The Couplets").[2]

Although the precise origins of the famous couplet presented at the beginning of this chapter, which compares Rūmī's *Mathnawī* with the Qur'ān, has remained elusive, what is known is that the *Mathnawī* has been popularly referred to as "the Qur'ān in Persian" (*Qur'ān dar zabān-i pahlawī*) since at least the beginning of the twentieth century, and possibly since as far back as the fifteenth century. As far as I am aware, no one has questioned or challenged the appropriateness of this description for Rūmī's *magnum opus*. Comparing a book to the Qur'ān is obviously meant as the highest form of praise designed to single out the work as the greatest of its kind, but it is also commonly explained that the *Mathnawī* stands out in the canon of Persian literature for its large number of exegeses of Qur'ānic passages, and even that the *Mathnawī* as a whole is some kind of commentary on the Qur'ān (e.g., Muʿīn 1992: s.v. "Mathnawī"). Such explanations suggest that the content of the *Mathnawī* is closely related to the Qur'ān, with the implication that the Qur'ān is its foundation and its immediate inspiration.

It is necessary to examine systematically the ways in which the Qur'ān is actually used in Rūmī's *Mathnawī* in order to be able to form an opinion about the relationship between the two works, particularly if one wishes to ascertain whether Rūmī's *Mathnawī* is based on the Qur'ānic text as a direct response to it. Citations of the original Arabic text of the Qur'ān constitute only a fraction of the material in Rūmī's *Mathnawī* that overlaps with the holy book in some way, or alludes to it. However, by focusing on actual citations of the Qur'ān it will be possible to make a comparison between Rūmī's *Mathnawī* and other works of the same mystical *mathnawī* (couplets) genre, and thus to reach conclusions that have taken into consideration the historical, intellectual, and literary context of his work (see De Bruijn 1997: 84–111).

The Qur'ān and the Mathnawī

Rūmī uses a number of ways to cite the actual words of the Qur'ān, the vast majority of which can be classified into a few broad types. Perhaps the most easily identifiable type of Qur'ān citation is the inclusion of parts of the original Arabic in the course of retelling a Qur'ānic story. Although a Persian poet's own rendering of a Qur'ānic story does not necessarily require the use of the actual wording of the Qur'ān, nonetheless Rūmī very often incorporates key passages from the original within his own Persian verse renditions. For instance, in the retelling of the story of God's appointment of man as vicegerent, he writes:

> *He taught the names* to Adam at the start (Q 2:31)
> Thus knowledge filled our ancestor's pure heart[3]
> (Rūmī 1990: I, v. 1243)

Like other mystical *mathnawī*s, Rūmī's work consists essentially of narratives and homilies. While there are many retellings of Qur'ānic narratives in the *Mathnawī*, most of its stories are not Qur'ānic in origin (e.g., see Lewis 2000: 288–91). Even those that are have probably been obtained from works of Qur'ānic exegesis or from the "stories of the prophets" genre (*qiṣaṣ al-anbiyā'*), which is hardly surprising in view of the scarcity of extended narratives in the Qur'ān. The majority of the Qur'ānic citations in the *Mathnawī* are embedded in the homilies, and the most celebrated way in which Rūmī uses these citations within his homilies is to corroborate an argument he has presented, often as part of a sequence of comparisons taken from the natural world, everyday life, and literary and folkloric traditions. An example of such a sequence is the following six couplets from the story about the lion who let a wolf and a fox accompany him hunting:

> The lion, though embarrassed by this pair,
> Still honored them by letting them come there,
> For such kings feel they're burdened by their troops,
> But he agreed, for blessings come from groups:
> The moon is shamed by stars, in honesty,
> It lets them near through generosity,

Was not the Prophet told "*Consult them!*" too (Q 3:159)
Though no one had as good a point of view?
On scales we pair old iron weights with gold
Though for a fraction of gold's worth they're sold;
The body is the spirit's traveling mate,
The guard dog serves the king at his court's gate.
(Rūmī 1990: I, vv. 3029–34)

In this typical example, the Qur'ānic comparison is just one member of a sequence of comparable images, all of which are designed to affirm the initial assertion that the lion was doing a favor to the fox and the wolf by letting them accompany him. It is worth noting that it is presented in the middle of the sequence rather than at the start or at the close of the sequence, and so it is not given precedence over the other images that belong to the sequence. To be precise, it follows immediately after the image of the moon accompanied by stars, an image that was already popular for describing the prophet and his disciples, those whom he had been instructed to consult in the Qur'ānic verse cited in this passage. What that Qur'ānic verse shares with the other images is that, since it originates from the Qur'ān, it would already have been familiar to the intended readers, Rūmī's students, who had a thorough knowledge of the book of Muslim revelation.

Qur'ānic citations are very often used by Rūmī in his homilies not so much as corroborating images of comparison but as alternative ways of expressing sentiments that he could quite easily have conveyed in Persian. Rūmī effectively appropriates many Qur'ānic passages for his own homilies in a way which has parallels to their use in his renditions of Qur'ānic narratives. Like those examples, the citations appropriated in this way are not necessary for the message to be conveyed. For example, Rūmī writes with regard to seeing beyond this world:

Some other clouds and rain far from your view
Exist in the unseen, and more suns too,
Just His elite see this manifestation,
The rest *feel doubt as to a new creation.* (Q 50:15)
(Rūmī 1990: I, v. 2046–7)

The appropriation of Qur'ānic passages in a text in this way is usually considered immediately with regard to its function as a weighty reinforcement of the author's sentiments. It is very common in sermons, which, in view of Rūmī's own background as a preacher, may help explain why he makes use of this method of citation so frequently. However, it is important not to overlook the fact that the majority of such citations involve word-play, which seems to be the primary reason for their use in the poem. For instance, Rūmī has quoted the Qur'ānic phrase "pleasing sowers" in the following passage, which describes the process through which a wheat grain eventually becomes part of a human, who is then annihilated in God:

If seeds are planted firmly in the ground
Wheat will eventually grow all around,

Then in the mill they grind it to make bread –
Its value soars now with it men are fed,
Next by men's teeth the bread is ground again,
Life, wisdom and intelligence they gain,
And when in love one's life becomes effaced
Sowers are pleased the seed's not gone to waste! (Q 48:29)
(Rūmī 1990: I, vv. 3178–81)

The reason why this particular citation has been used here is because it comes from a passage in the Qur'ān with agricultural imagery, albeit one with a very different message to what Rūmī is describing (see below). The same relatively long verse of the Qur'ān from which this clause has been taken is also the source of the citations in the following passage:

On fleeing death, the hare began to clap
And dance like leaves which in the breeze would flap;
Both branch and leaf like this escape earth's jail –
They lift their heads and with the wind set sail:
When leaves burst forth from branches, they ascend
Up to the tree's most high and furthest end;
Using the tongue of *its initial shoot* (Q 48:29)
God's praise is sung by every leaf and fruit:
The Giver nourished every root of ours
Until our trees *were strong and straight* like towers. (Q 48:29)
(Rūmī 1990: I, vv. 1350–4)

In the original Qur'ānic verse from which all of the last three citations have been taken (Q 48:29), believers are compared with seeds which turn into strong and tall plants thanks to the grace of God, thereby delighting sowers while at the same time enraging the infidels. It is clear that more than for any other reason, these clauses from the same Qur'ānic verse have been incorporated because they happen to have loose connections with certain images employed by Rūmī in this and the previously cited passage: one refers to the cultivation of wheat, the other to a healthy and robust tree. The citation of the Qur'ān in such instances serves as a display of Rūmī's intimate knowledge of the holy text and virtuosity as a poet, with the aim of delighting the reader and winning his admiration.

The Qur'ān citations included in the homilies of Rūmī's *Mathnawī* which are not used as appropriated speech or as an image of comparison are those embedded in the relatively few instances of Qur'ānic exegesis. While every single use of a citation inevitably structures its own interpretation through the new context in which it is presented, there are passages in the *Mathnawī* labeled as "explanations of meanings of" (e.g., *dar maʿnī-yi*), or even "Exegesis of" (*tafsīr-i*) of specific Qur'ānic verses. The first thing one notices on reading the approximately a dozen passages like this is that in most cases they do not actually constitute Qur'ānic exegesis at all, but have been inaccurately identified on the basis of the occurrence of a Qur'ānic verse towards the beginning of the passage or an association between the message of the passage and that of a verse in the Qur'ān (e.g., Rūmī 1990: I, vv. 2582–2614). This is part of a general problem with the subheadings provided in the *Mathnawī* and not something that relates exclusively to Qur'ān commentaries. They seem to have been added after the actual text of the poem, and so they often fail to represent accurately the content of the passage which they precede. In consequence, passages that have as their starting-point a verse of the Qur'ān are very rare, contrary to the impression one might gain by simply looking at the subheadings (see below for an example).

In order to evaluate what these observations may reveal about Rūmī's understanding of the Qur'ān and its relationship to his *Mathnawī*, it is important to compare his use of Qur'ān citations with that of his most well-known predecessors among the authors of Persian mystical *mathnawīs*, namely Ḥakīm Sanā'ī (d. 532/1138) and Farīd al-Dīn ʿAṭṭār (d. 616/1220). All works of the Persian mystical *mathnawī* genre, like other forms of religious literature, contain material from the Qur'ān, most obviously in the form of direct citations. Rūmī's *Mathnawī* is therefore not exceptional for containing citations of the original Arabic text of the Qur'ān, albeit with the modifications required by the meter of his Persian poem and the particular couplet's internal rhyme. However, Rūmī's use of Qur'ānic citations remains distinctive in certain aspects. First of all, a comparison with works of this genre that have relatively similar structures to the *Mathnawī* highlights the fact that Rūmī's work includes Qur'ānic citations much more frequently. For instance, while ʿAṭṭār's *Asrārnāma* contains a citation from the Qur'ān approximately every 250 couplets and Sanā'ī's *Ḥadīqat al-ḥaqīqa* every 150 couplets, Rūmī's *Mathnawī* contains a Qur'ānic citation on average every 30 couplets. Although other uses of the Qur'ān, such as retelling of Qur'ānic stories, and paraphrases of Qur'ānic verses, are not always so easy to identify and classify, one's immediate impression is that in comparison with the other works of the mystic *mathnawī* genre, Rūmī's *Mathnawī* contains more of these examples of Qur'ān usage as well.

The second most striking difference is that when Rūmī cites the Qur'ān, he invariably does so in such a way that its meaning in the context of his *Mathnawī* is transparent, either because its literal meaning makes it obvious or its new context in the *Mathnawī* determines how it is read, as the examples already cited demonstrate. While most of his predecessors often provide a mere couple of key words from a Qur'ānic passage which require reference to the Qur'ān itself for the poem to be understood, Rūmī rarely follows this convention. Although it is fair to say that medieval readers of mystical *mathnawīs* would be much more familiar with the Qur'ān than a contemporary reader, there may be more significance to this idiosyncracy than the question of accessibility – not only is Rūmī's effort to convey his message as clearly as possible to the reader indicated by this tendency to make the *Mathnawī* more self-sufficient, but in order to achieve this a considerable poetic talent is displayed, and, perhaps most significantly of all, this approach avoids implying a distance between the Qur'ān and his self-contained *Mathnawī*.

Another distinctive feature of Rūmī's use of Qur'ānic citations is his greater willingness to use citations out of their usual context. That is to say, passages are used to convey a message with which they are not usually associated in tradition, as the agricultural citations referred to above amply demonstrate. Even parts of the speech of one character in the Qur'ān are put in the mouth of another character in the *Mathnawī*, as in the case of the prophet Ṣāliḥ, who in the *Mathnawī* says "Why should I feel bad for the wicked's sake?" (Rūmī 1990: I, v. 2570), although in the Qur'ān that citation is a remark made by the prophet Shuʿayb (Q 7:93).

The *Mathnawī* in Relation to the Qur'ān

Tradition tells us that Rūmī started to compose the *Mathnawī* after being asked to do so by his deputy Ḥusām al-Dīn Chalabī, who had noticed that his disciples enjoyed reading the mystical *mathnawīs* of Sanā'ī and ʿAṭṭār more than the classical prose works of Ṣūfism. Rūmī does not himself suggest a reason for writing the *Mathnawī* although he does make it clear that Ḥusām al-Dīn had instigated it (Rūmī 1990: I, 1–2). There seems to be no reason to doubt the traditional explanation which refers to the popularity of the works of Sanā'ī and ʿAṭṭār. What it would imply is that Rūmī wrote the *Mathnawī* in order to inspire and instruct his disciples, and moreover he strove to write something they would enjoy reading more than the works of his predecessors. The ways in which Rūmī uses Qur'ān citations support this view, for Rūmī uses them in ways that make the teachings in his *Mathnawī* more immediately accessible as well as more entertaining.

The most famous tradition about the composition of the *Mathnawī* involving Ḥusām al-Dīn is that he wrote down the text as Rūmī recited whenever he became inspired with the poem. Its echoes of the biography of Muḥammad may give reason for skepticism, but there is support for this tradition in the best source of all, the text of the *Mathnawī* itself. Rūmī refers to this process on a number of occasions, including instruction to Ḥusām al-Dīn to get some paper and write down as he recites ("Ḥusām al-Dīn, please fetch a sheet or two/ And write about the guide what I tell you;" Rūmī 1990: I, v. 2947) as well as apologies for keeping him up until dawn in this activity ("It's dawn, O Refuge, who fills dawn with light/ Please make Ḥusām forgive it took all night"; Rūmī 1990: I, v. 1817). The structure of the *Mathnawī* also includes many indications that it was produced extemporaneously, albeit with clear evidence that it was edited afterwards (such as by the later insertion of subheadings, as mentioned above), which tradition also acknowledges, and that it follows a loose plan (see Baldick 1981: 125–7).

The composition method described in tradition is interesting in the context of discussing the relationship between the *Mathnawī* and the Qur'ān, as it implies that Rūmī's work was also divinely inspired rather than a calculated and logically planned poem. In fact, the *Mathnawī* contains a highly significant passage towards the end of its third volume where Rūmī not only affirms this point but also specifically compares his *Mathnawī* with the Qur'ān. This 64-couplet long passage is divided into six short sections by the subheadings provided (Rūmī 1990: III, vv. 4230–94).

The first section of this passage begins by referring to criticism that has been directed at the *Mathnawī*, mocking the poem as a trivial collection of fables. Rūmī takes solace in the observation by Sanā'ī, referred to here by his well-known title Ḥakīm-i Ghaznawī ("The Sage of Ghazna"), that even the Qur'ān was criticized in this way by ignorant contemporaries of the prophet (Rūmī 1990: III, vv. 4233–4). This discussion of criticism of the *Mathnawī* is resumed in the last of the six sections that make up this

64-couplet long passage, which includes a reference back to this specific piece of advice from Sanāʾī (Rūmī 1990: III, v. 4294). That final section in fact begins in quite extraordinary fashion with the statement:

> Deriding dog! You're barking, sense you lack!
> You're mocking the Qurʾān behind its back!
> (Rūmī 1990: III, v. 4285)

What Rūmī appears to be asserting here is that "the dog" who rudely criticizes his *Mathnawī* is in effect criticizing the Qurʾān by doing so, and he is thus deriding it behind its back. This is followed by six couplets on the virtues and status of the Qurʾān, as God's eternal speech with spiritual depth to its content, in contrast to the unworthiness of the deriding dog of a critic. Rūmī concludes this passage by returning his focus to himself (or possibly his *Mathnawī*), with the following three couplets:

> That Water of Life's fount – look here, behold!
> I free the mystic lovers from death's hold.
> If your vile greed had not caused such a smell
> God would have poured drops on your grave as well!
> No, I'll heed the advice from Sanāʾī –
> I won't let critics' comments bother me.
> (Rūmī 1990: III, vv. 4292–4)

If we take Rūmī as the speaker, which I think is the most credible interpretation, then what this verse is suggesting in this specific context is that the reason why criticizing his *Mathnawī* should be considered to be criticizing the Qurʾān behind its back is because, as different forms of divine revelation, both share common origins. What seems to be clear is that Rūmī is not suggesting that his *Mathnawī* is somehow based on the Qurʾān, but rather that it is the same in origin.

Revelation and Ṣūfī Saints

If we look briefly at the four remaining sections of the 64-couplet passage, those which separate these two parts at the beginning and the end, we can find confirmation that this final assertion by Rūmī cannot be dismissed as an isolated bold claim or poetic flight of fancy. This is because the images provided in the intervening sections structure a purposeful argument in preparation for this final assertion.

The first of these intervening sections, Section Two, expands on the criticism that has been directed at the *Mathnawī* on the basis of its outer form alone (see above), by making it clear that what counts is the inner meaning of the Qurʾān and not its form. This is a common Ṣūfī viewpoint, which is presented at length already by Sanāʾī in his *Ḥadīqat al-ḥaqīqa* (Sanāʾī 1998: 113–24, esp. 115–17).

The remaining intervening sections are, significantly, about the status of Ṣūfī saints. First of all, in Section Three saints are compared with the Qurʾān itself as having both inner and outer aspects; Rūmī makes this point in the form of a refutation of the claim that saints withdraw from society in order to hide. He argues that, just like the Qur'ān, the important aspect of a Ṣūfī saint is his inner being and that remains hidden. Therefore, they have no need to hide from people by retreating into seclusion (Rūmī 1990: III, vv. 4253–60). Section Four expands on the theme of the previous section, by comparing saints with the rod of Moses that turned into a snake and the spells of Jesus with which he revived the dead: in their outer appearance you may perceive their form as ordinary like you see a rod or hear words, but inwardly their station is extremely lofty, as vehicles through which God can act (Rūmī 1990: III, vv. 4261–70).

It is the last of these intervening sections, Section Five, which is perhaps the most significant of all because it confronts directly the question of revelation received by saints. This section is presented under the rubric of "*Tafsīr* of the Qur'ānic verse, 'O hills and birds, repeat his praise!'" (Q 34:10), and it comes as close to an extended commentary on a Qur'ānic verse as one can find in Rūmī's *Mathnawī*. This Qur'ānic verse is understood to represent God's command to the mountains and birds to repeat David's Psalms (*zabūr*), one of the four Muslim "books of revelation," in harmony with him.

> The hill joined Prophet David when he'd sing,
> Both minstrels, drunk with deep love for their king:
> When the command "*Repeat his praise!*" first came
> The two became one voice, their song the same.
> God told him, "Separation you have known,
> Cut off from good friends for my sake alone,
> A stranger with no close associate,
> In whose heart flames of longing have been lit,
> You seek companions, minstrels, singers too –
> Eternal God presents these hills to you."
> He makes them singers who can sing so well,
> He makes these hills fall drunken in a spell,
> So you'll know God can make a mere hill sing
> And saints too can experience such a thing –
> From God's creation melodies each hears:
> Their sound each moment reaches the saint's ears,
> Unheard by men in the vicinity –
> He who has faith in him lives joyfully!
> Inside his soul he hears inspired words too
> Although those sitting near him have no clue!
> (Rūmī 1990: III, vv. 4273–82)

This penultimate section of the passage under scrutiny ties together the previously explored themes concerning prophetic revelation and the lofty inner natures of saints which is kept hidden from view. More specifically, it affirms that divine revelation which prophets receive can also be received by saints, since even hills can be inspired by God to utter the Psalms of David. Rūmī explains that most people, since they judge on the basis of outward appearance alone, fail to appreciate this reality. In this context, it is clear that this homily based on exegesis of a verse of the Qur'ān, is designed to support Rūmī's subsequent comparison of his *Mathnawī* with the Qur'ān and his condemnation of the critic of his poem: the *Mathnawī* is divine inspiration which he, as a Ṣūfī saint, has received from God, even though some may be skeptical of this claim and even mock it on the basis of its form of expression.

Conclusion

In summary, Rūmī's predilections in Qur'ānic citation for the *Mathnawī* seem to serve primarily the purpose of surpassing his predecessors in presenting Ṣūfī teachings in an even more accessible, entertaining, and memorable form than their works, which his students already enjoyed reading. The high frequency of word play as the principal factor in attracting a citation, as well as the cleverness with which he forms associations with Qur'ānic verses and integrates them, contribute significantly to the fulfillment of this aim and should not be seen as contradicting or compromising it in any way. The fact that the Qur'ān is cited much more frequently by Rūmī than his predecessors can be at least partially explained as being due to his determination to convey his message in as familiar and accessible a form as possible to his readership – it is worth noting that he also stands apart from the others for his provision of so many comparisons from nature and everyday life, often in long sequences illustrating the same point. This is not, however, simply spoon-feeding his readers, but also delighting them with his sensitive imagination and poetic virtuosity. Rūmī demonstrates an intimate knowledge of the Qur'ān, which would have been for his students as familiar as natural phenomena and everyday experience.

At the same time, one can also see in Rūmī's heavy use of Qur'ān citations an indication of his perception of the relationship between the Qur'ān and the *Mathnawī*, namely that they stem from a common source. This is evident in his frequent appropriation of the words of the Qur'ān for his homilies and retellings of stories, his preference to make his use of the Qur'ān self-contained and immediately accessible, eliminating the need for reference outside of the *Mathnawī* itself, and his relatively liberal and carefree transferal of Qur'ānic citations to new, and often very different, contexts. Not only does Rūmī strive to break down the barriers in communication between himself and the reader of much lower spiritual rank and level of education, but he also downplays the distinctions between different forms of divine revelation and their bearers. This is confirmed in Rūmī's direct comments about saints and the relationship between the Qur'ān and his *Mathnawī*.

The comparison with the Qur'ān cited at the beginning of this chapter therefore need not be considered simply as extreme praise or as implying that the *Mathnawī* is a commentary on the Qur'ān. The following couplet about Rūmī, which is often presented alongside that couplet, would seem to correspond to what the Ṣūfī poet-saint himself has specifically conveyed:

> How to describe that man of lofty station?
> Though not a prophet he brought revelation.[4]

Notes

1 This couplet has appeared numerous times attributed to the fifteenth-century poet ʿAbd al-Raḥmān Jāmī (d. 1492), but never with a reference to a specific work of his. Reynold Nicholson in his edition of the *Mathnawī* (1925–40: VII, b2) refers to two more recent works where it is found: ʿĀbidīn Pasha (1887–8) *Tarjama wa sharḥ-i Mathnawī-yi sharīf* (*Translation and Commentary on the noble Mathnawī*), 6 vols., Istanbul, on the title-page, and W. Muhammad (1894) *Sharḥ-i Mathnawī* (*Commentary on the Mathnawī*), 2 vols., Lucknow, p. 3. I am indebted to Franklin Lewis for the information he shared through the Adabiyat listserve about the edition of Muhammad's work (originally written in 1728 under the title, *Makhzan al-asrār* [*Treasury of Mysteries*]) which was actually used by Nicholson.

2 While this chapter focuses exclusively on Rūmī's use of the Qurʾān for his *Mathnawī*, his lyrical poems, or *ghazals*, also reveal an extraordinarily high degree of "Qur'anicity," as demonstrated in Virani 2002. Although Rūmī is remembered primarily as a Ṣūfī master who conveyed his teachings through poetry, the content of his oral teaching sessions has also been compiled by students, including his comments on the Qurʾān and revelation received by saints (see further Keshavarz 2002).

3 The citations from the Qurʾān are presented in italics in the translations presented here. Translations of passages from Book One of the *Mathnawī* are taken from Rūmī (2004), using the same verse numbering as the edition of M. Istiʿlāmī [= Rūmī 1990], on which it is based.

4 This couplet is often found together with the couplet cited at the beginning of the chapter. Concerning its attribution and historical origins, see note 1 above.

Further reading

Banani, A., Hovannisian, R., and Sabagh, G. (eds.) (1994) *Poetry and Mysticism in Islam: The Heritage of Rumi*. Cambridge University Press, Cambridge.

Davis, R. (2000) Narrative and doctrine in the first story of Rumi's *Mathnawi*. In: Hawting, G. R., Mojaddedi, J. A., and Samely, A. (eds.) *Studies in Islamic and Middle Eastern Texts and Traditions in Memory of Norman Calder.* Oxford University Press, Oxford, pp. 93–104.

Keshavarz, F. (2002) Pregnant with God: The poetic art of mothering the sacred in Rumi's *Fihi Ma Fih*. *Comparative Studies of South Asia, Africa and the Middle East*, 22:2, 90–9.

Radtke, B., and O'Kane, J. (1996) *The Concept of Sainthood in Early Islamic Mysticism*. Curzon, Richmond.

Rūmī (1991) *Mystical Poems of Rumi*, trans. A. J. Arberry, 2 vols. University of Chicago Press, Chicago.

Rūmī (2004) *The Masnavi: Book One*, trans. J. Mojaddedi, Oxford University Press, Oxford.

Thackston, W. M. (trans.) (1994) *Signs of the Unseen*. Shambhala, Boston.

Virani, N. (2002) "I am the nightingale of the Merciful:" Rumi's use of the Qur'an and Hadith. *Comparative Studies of South Asia, Africa and the Middle East*, 22:2, 100–11.

CHAPTER 25

Twelver Shīʿī *Taʾwīl*

Diana Steigerwald

> Our cause is a secret (*sirr*) within a secret, a secret of something which remains hidden, a secret which may only be disclosed by another secret; a secret upon a secret which is supported by a secret. (Imām Jaʿfar al-Ṣādiq quoted in Corbin 1993: 37)

Shīʿism is a branch (*firqa*) of Islam in which one finds some of the most esoteric interpretations and some of the most dynamic discussions on the nature of the Qurʾān. Shīʿī interpretations of the Qurʾān concern mainly issues of authority where the concept of the imamate (*imāma*) is paramount. The issues surrounding the Shīʿī Qurʾān are multiple; they cover much more than just the history of the text and its variations. Other major subjects include exegesis (*taʾwīl*) of the text, the distinction between exoteric (*ẓāhir*) and inner (*bāṭin*) meanings. In this chapter, I will show how the Twelver Shīʿites (Ithnāʿashariyya) have interpreted the Qurʾān and developed their spiritual exegesis. This research provides a comprehensive account of the history while not pretending to be exhaustive.

Origin of Shīʿī Islam

Many verses of the Qurʾān contained statements about the notion of *imāma* which are interpreted differently by Sunnīs and Shīʿites. Here are a few verses regularly quoted by Shīʿites: "And We made them leaders (*aʾimma*, singular *imām*), guiding [men] by Our command (*amr*), and We sent them inspiration to do good deeds, to establish regular prayers and to practice regular charity; And they constantly served Us [and Us only]" (Q 21:73). The word "leaders" in this verse may refer to both prophets and Shīʿī Imāms. "Verily We shall give life to the death, and We record that which they sent before and that which they leave. Behind, and of all things have We taken account in a 'manifest Imām' (*imām mubīn*)" (Q 36:12).

For the Shīʿites, the *ahl al-bayt* ("people of the house") includes the prophet's daughter Fāṭima, his son-in-law ʿAlī, and his grandsons, Ḥasan and Ḥusayn. "And Allāh only wishes to remove all abomination from you people of the house (*ahl al-bayt*) and to make you pure and spotless" (Q 33:33). "They said: 'Dost thou wonder at Allāh's decree? The grace of Allāh and His blessings on you, O people of the house (*ahl al-bayt*)! For He is indeed worthy of all praise full of all glory!' " (Q 11:73). "That this is indeed a Qurʾān most honourable in a book well-guarded, which none touch but those who are purified (*muṭahharūn*)" (Q 56:77–9). "O you who believe! Obey God, and obey the apostle, and those charged with authority (*ūlū'l-amr*) among you" (Q 4:59). From these above verses, the Shīʿites deduced that the *muṭahharūn* designates the Shīʿī Imāms who are consequently impeccable (*maʿsūm*) and inspired, always following the divine command. "Whoever submits His whole self to God, and is doer of good, has grasped indeed the most trustworthy hand-hold (*al-ʿurwa al-wuthqā*)" (Q 31:22; see also 2:256). According to the Shīʿites, the *ʿurwa al-wuthqā* refers to the "rope of *imāma*" which is continuous till the day of resurrection and remains a permanent link between the spiritual and material worlds. Also in *sūrat al-nūr* (Q 24:35–6), the blessed olive tree is said to symbolize the Imām.

Shīʿites deduce from the following Qurʾānic verse that the *imāma* is a divine institution and that the Imām must be from the seed of Abraham: "And remember that Abraham was tried by his Lord with certain commands, which he fulfilled. He said: 'I will make thee an *imām* to the nations.' He said: 'And also [*imāms*] from my offspring!' " (Q 2:124) Based on this verse, Shīʿites maintain that the divinely appointed Imām who is an example for all mankind, must necessarily himself be impeccable (*maʿsūm*).

The origin of Shīʿī Islām goes back to the issue of succession following Muḥammad's death. There are some indications that Muḥammad may have intended for his cousin and son-in-law ʿAlī b. Abī Ṭālib to succeed him. For the Shīʿites, Muḥammad explicitly designated (*naṣṣ jalī*) ʿAlī as his successor by God's command at a place called Ghadīr Khumm. Some traditions accepted as canonical by both Sunnīs and Shīʿites give a unique status to ʿAlī in Muḥammad's eyes. For example this *ḥadīth*, which is accepted by Shīʿites, is also found in the Sunnī *ḥadīth* collection of Ibn Ḥanbal (Ibn Ḥanbal n.d.: I, 84, 118–19, 152, 331; IV, 281, 327, 370) and expressed by Muḥammad al-Bāqir al-Majlīsī (d. 1111/1699):

> When the ceremonies of the pilgrimage were completed, the prophet, attended by ʿAlī and the Muslims, left Mecca for Medina. On reaching Ghadīr Khumm, [Muḥammad] halted, although that place had never before been a halting place for caravans. The reason for the halt was that verses of the Qurʾān had come upon him, commanding him to establish ʿAlī in the caliphate. . . . The message that came from the Most High was this: "O apostle, declare all that has been sent down to thee from thy Lord. No part of it is to be withheld. God will protect you against men, for he does not guide the unbelievers" (Q 5:71). . . . When the crowd had all gathered, Muḥammad walked up on to the platform of saddles and called ʿAlī to stand at his right. After a prayer of thanks he spoke to the people, informing them that he had been forewarned of his death, and saying, "I have been summoned to the gate of God, and I shall soon depart to God, to be concealed from you, and bidding farewell to this world. I am leaving you the book of God, and if you follow this you will not go astray. And I am leaving you also the "members of the household" (*ahl al-bayt*), who are not to be separated from the book of God until they meet me at the drinking fountain of Kawthar." He then called out, "Am I not more precious to you than your own lives?" They said "Yes." Then it was that he took ʿAlī's hands and raised them so high that he showed the whites of his armpits, and said, "Whoever has me as his master (*mawlā*) has ʿAlī as his master. Be friend to his friends, O Lord, and be an enemy to his enemies. Help those who assist him and frustrate those who oppose him." (al-Majlīsī 1909: III, 339; Donaldson 1933: 5)

A verse from the Qurʾān was revealed on the same occasion: "This day have I perfected your religion for you, completed my favour upon you, and have chosen for you Islam as your religion" (Q 5: 3). The event of Ghadīr Khumm is not denied by Sunnīs but interpreted differently by them. For the Sunnīs, Muḥammad wanted only to honour ʿAlī. They understood the term *mawlā* in the sense of "friend" whereas the Shīʿites recognized ʿAlī as their master; the spiritual authority of ʿAlī was transferred afterward to his direct descendants, the rightful guides (*imāms*). The Shīʿites hold that ʿAlī and his descendants have a divine right to the caliphate (*khalīfa*). ʿAlī had received a special mandate from the prophet. Muḥammad is spoken of as having left behind him two momentous things (*thalaqayn*); the Qurʾān and the people of his household, both of which are needed in order to remain on the right path (*al-ṣirāṭ al-mustaqīm*). The Qurʾān is described as the "greater weight" (*al-thaqal al-akbar*) whereas the Imāms are called the "lesser weight" (*al-thaqal al-asghar*) (Ayoub 1988: 180).

The successor of the prophet is the inheritor (*waṣī*) of his esoteric knowledge and the interpreter, *par excellence*, of the Qurʾān. Since Muḥammad was the last prophet who closed the prophetic cycle, the Shīʿites believe that humanity still needs spiritual guidance: the cycle of *imāma* must succeed to the cycle of prophecy. The notion of *imāma* is thus a cardinal principle of Shīʿī faith since it is only through the Imām that true knowledge can be obtained. The prophet received the revelation (*tanzīl*) and established the religious law (*sharīʿa*) while ʿAlī the repository of the prophet's knowledge, provided its spiritual exegesis (*taʾwīl*). Thus the *imāma*, closely tied to ʿAlī's spiritual mission, is according to Shīʿī understanding, a rational necessity and an obligatory grace.

For Shīʿites, ʿAlī's mission is seen as the hidden and secret aspect of prophecy. This underlying idea is based on ʿAlī's declaration:

> I am the Sign of the All-Powerful. I am the Gnosis of Mysteries. I am the Companion of the Radiance of the Divine Majesty. I am the First and the Last, the Manifest (*Ẓāhir*) and the Hidden (*Bāṭin*). I am the Face of God. I am the Mirror of God, the Supreme Pen, the *Tabula secreta*. I am he who in the Gospel is called Elijah. I am he who is in possession of the Secret of God's Messenger." (Corbin 1993: 49)

There are also many other sayings attributed to ʿAlī which emphasized the necessity of an interpreter of the Qurʾān.

The Imām as successor of the prophet and spiritual leader of the community is as important as the prophet. The Shīʿites believe that God appointed prophets to guide mankind; likewise He also appointed Imāms to continue the guidance. When God selects a prophet or Imām, He chooses an individual who is impeccable – perfect on all accounts. For the Shīʿites, ordinary human beings with their own limited capacity and imperfection cannot "elect" the prophet's successor. The prophets were not elected by the people, but by God. Only Muḥammad, who possessed blessed knowledge, can appoint his successor. Similarly, only ʿAlī, who has divine inspiration (*taʾyīd*), can know who should succeed him. Even though ʿAlī eventually took his place as the fourth caliph, the Shīʿites believe he was really the first true caliph who was followed by a succession of Imāms, appointed by *naṣṣ* ("designation") by the preceding Imām. ʿAlī became the successor of the prophet by divine command as expressed through Muḥammad's will.

The concept of the Imām implies that the cycle of prophecy is succeeded by the cycle of the *walāya*, the institution of "the friends of God." The text of the Qur'ān in itself is not sufficient because it contains hidden meanings and apparent contradictions. "The knowledge of such a book cannot be grasped fully by the norms of ordinary philosophy: the text must be 'taken back' (*ta'wīl*) to the level on which its true meaning is manifest" (Corbin 1993: 45). The *bāṭin* (esoteric) and *ẓāhir* (exoteric) meanings of the Qur'ān have also been identified with the concept of *ta'wīl* (spiritual exegesis) and *tanzīl* (descent of revelation) respectively. Thus *ta'wīl* is the act of uncovering the *bāṭin* from the *ẓāhir*. Such a task is not within the competence of an ordinary human being. Its discernment requires someone who is an inspired spiritual heir possessing full knowledge of revelation. He is the *ḥujjat Allāh*, the "proof of God", and the Imām, the spiritual guide who can update the interpretation of the Qur'ān in accord with his own time. Henry Corbin observes: "Hence, the *ta'wīl* is pre-eminently the hermeneutics of symbols. . . . *Ta'wīl* presupposes the superimposition of worlds and interworlds, as the correlative basis for a plurality of meanings in the same text" (Corbin 1977: 53–4). Thus, each layer of meanings corresponds to a respective spiritual level in the hierarchy.

The Shīʿites believe in many layers of meanings hidden in the Qur'ān which they try to uncover through *ta'wīl*. The word *ta'wīl* in Arabic means to go back to the first, primary meaning. In the *tafsīr* literature of Sunnī Islam the words *tafsīr* and *ta'wīl* are used almost synonymously. But, for the Shīʿites, both have distinct meanings. *Tafsīr* refers to the manifest meaning of the Qur'ān; *ta'wīl* designates its hidden meaning. *Tafsīr* remained a term of more limited denotation while *ta'wīl*, based on intellect (*ʿaql*), connoted hermeneutical principles that sought to uncover deeper meanings.

The main principle of Shīʿī exegesis is based on the fact that "the Qur'ān has an outer dimension (*ẓāhir*) and an inner dimension (*bāṭin*); its inner dimension has yet another dimension, up to seven inner dimensions" (Ṭabāṭabā'ī 1987: 28; Ayoub 1988: 187). Thus each verse of the Qur'ān is subject to several levels of interpretation. As Imām Jaʿfar al-Ṣādiq explains, "the beginning of a verse may be sent down concerning one thing, its middle concerning another, and its end concerning yet another thing. [The Qur'ān] is constituted by speech which is closely connected and executed in various ways" (al-ʿAyyāshī n.d.: I, 11; Ayoub 1988: 187).

To the spiritual hierarchy in Shīʿism corresponds different degrees of knowledge. Hence, Imām Jaʿfar al-Ṣādiq, is reported to have said:

> The book of God contains four things: the announced expression (*ʿibāra*); the allusion (*ishāra*); the hidden meaning related to the suprasensible worlds (*laṭā'if*); and the spiritual truths (*ḥaqā'iq*). The literary expression is for the common people (*ʿawāmm*); the allusion is for the elite (*khawāṣṣ*); the hidden meaning is for the Friends of God (*awliyā'*); and the spiritual truths are for the Prophets (*anbiyā'*). (Nasr 1994: 59)

Jaʿfar al-Ṣādiq explains that the Imām is the Interpreter *par excellence* of all scriptures: "God made our authority (*walāya*) the pole (*quṭb*) of the Qur'ān and the pole of all scriptures. Around it the clear (*muḥkam*) verses of the Qurʾān revolve; through it scriptures were elucidated and through it faith becomes manifest" (al-ʿAyyāshī n.d.: I, 5; Ayoub 1988: 181). Imām Jaʿfar al-Ṣādiq is said to have declared: "We are the people of a household among whom God continues to send one who knows His book from its beginning to its ends. We possess such knowledge of God's sanctions and prohibitions as would oblige to keep its secret, not telling anyone about it" (al-ʿAyyāshī n.d.: I, 16; Ayoub 1988: 187).

Ḥaydar Āmulī, a Twelver Shīʿite of the eight/fourteenth century, uses the symbol of almond to illustrate different levels in the spiritual hierarchy. The legislative prophecy (*risāla*) is symbolized by the nutshell, the inner prophecy (*nubuwwa*) by the almond, and the institution of God's friends (*walāya*) by the almond's oil. This division in three parts corresponds to two homologous series: *sharīʿa* ("religious law"), *ṭarīqa* ("mystical path"), *ḥaqīqa* ("spiritual realization") and the second: *ẓāhir* ("exoteric meaning"), *bāṭin* ("esoteric meaning") and *bāṭin al-bāṭin* ("inner meaning of the esoteric meaning"). Thus the knowledge of the deepest meanings of the Qurʾān is the prerogative of God's friends, that is, the Imāms (Āmulī 1969: 386).

The Qurʾān is a divine revelation, but its interpretation is human, hence there have been different interpretations. The differences in interpretation began shortly after the death of Muḥammad. Different companions of the prophet began to differ from each other and with the passage of time these differences also deepened in their scope. Also, many groups came into existence in the early period of Islam and every group tried to justify its doctrine by interpreting the Qur'ān. The formation and doctrinal differences have been dealt with in various books such as *Kitāb Firaq al-Shīʿa* ("Book of Shīʿī Groups") of al-Ḥasan b. Mūsā al-Nawbakhtī (d. ca. 310/923), *Al-Farq bayn al-firaq* ("The Schism between Muslim Groups") of ʿAbd al-Qāhir b. Ṭāhir al-Baghdādī (d. 429/1037), and others. Each of these groups tried to interpret various Qurʾānic verses in their own way. The Shīʿites also subsequently divided into a number of subgroups, the main division being between Ithnā ʿashariyya (Twelver Shīʿites) and Ismāʿīlīs.

The Sunnīs differ greatly from the Shīʿites in their understanding and interpretation of the Qur'ān. This is why the Sunnī corpus of traditions (*ḥadīth*) developed separately from that of Shīʿites. The Sunnīs and Shīʿites differ on the interpretation of this verse:

> He it is who has sent down to thee the book. In it are verses basic or fundamental [of established meaning] (*muḥkamāt*); they are the "foundation of the book" (*umm al-kitāb*); others are allegorical (*mutashābihāt*). But those in whose hearts is perversity follow the part thereof that is allegorical, seeking discord, and searching for its hidden meanings, but no one knows its hidden meaning (*taʾwīl*) except God. And those who are "firmly grounded in knowledge" (*al-rāsikhūn fī ʾl-ʿilm*) say: "We believe in the book; the whole of it is from our Lord." (Q 3:7)

For Sunnīs, God alone knows the *taʾwīl*. The Shīʿites read the verse differently by not reading the text with a period after "except God" and believe that the knowledge of *taʾwīl* is possessed by God and *al-rāsikhūn fīʾl-ʿilm*, that is, the Shīʿī Imāms. Hence it is clear from the above verse that there are many passages from the Qurʾān which are subject to different interpretations.

Early Debates on the Qurʾān

This section gives a short survey on the origins of Sunnī-Shīʿī controversies on the integrity of the Qurʾānic text. The development of these debates in the first Islamic centuries represents an interesting example of how ideas evolved in the early period through disputes, as well as contacts between various schools of thought (Modarressi 1993). The major issue in these debates was whether the ʿUthmānic text comprehended all the Qurʾānic verses revealed to Muḥammad, or whether there had been further verses which are now missing from the text.

At the end of the reign of the third caliph ʿUthmān (d. 35/656), it became evident to some members of the community that there were too many variations in the memorized texts. In 12/634, many of the memorizers (*qurrāʾ*) of the Qurʾān lost their lives in a battle against a rival community at Yamāma in Arabia (al-Yaʿqūbī 1960: II, 15; al-Ṭabarī 1960: III, 296; Ibn Kathīr 1966: VII, 439). Fearing that the complete Qurʾān would be lost, the first caliph Abū Bakr asked ʿUmar and Zayd b. Thābit to record any verse or part of the revelation that at least two witnesses testified at the entrance of the mosque in Medina. All of the material gathered was recorded on sheets of paper (al-Yaʿqūbī 1960: II, 135; al-Suyūṭī 1967: I, 185, 207, 208), but was not yet compiled as a volume. These sheets were transmitted from Abū Bakr and ʿUmar to ʿUmar's daughter Ḥafṣa who gave them to ʿUthmān who had them put together in the form of a volume. ʿUthmān sent several copies of his compilation to different parts of the Muslim world and he then ordered that any other collections or verses of the Qurʾān found anywhere else be burned (al-Bukhārī 1862–1908: III, 393–4; al-Tirmidhī 1964: IV 347–8; al-Bayhaqī 1985: VII, 150–1).

According to many early transmitted reports, ʿAlī wrote his own compilation of the Qurʾān (Ibn Saʿd 1904–15: II, 338; al-Yaʿqūbī 1960: II, 135; Ibn al-Nadīm 1971: 30; al-Suyūṭī 1967: I, 204, 248; al-Kulaynī 1957–9: VIII, 18) and presented it to the companions; but they rejected it, so he took it back home (Sulaym n.d.: 72, 108; al-Kulaynī 1957–9: II, 633; al-Yaʿqūbī 1960: II, 135–6). These reports also pointed out that there were substantial differences between the various compilations of the Qurʾān. The only copy of the complete Qurʾān with verses proclaiming the exalted status of ʿAlī and the future Imāms, was in ʿAlī's possession. ʿAlī, known for his vast knowledge of the Qurʾān (Ibn Saʿd 1904–15: I, 204), preserved this original copy and passed it on his successors. In his codex of the Qurʾān he had reportedly indicated the verses which were abrogated, and those which abrogated them (al-Suyūṭī 1967: I, 204).

The Shīʿī community learned early on that to express their beliefs openly was fruitless. This only caused their community to be persecuted. Hence they started to practice *taqiyya* (religious dissimulation), which allows a Shīʿite to deny his or her faith under dangerous conditions. In doing so, believers retain their allegiance to Shīʿism while presenting an orthodox face to the oppressors. This applies to Qurʾānic interpretations as well. The Shīʿites were practicing *taqiyya* to prevent revealing esoteric interpretations to Sunnī Muslims who do not accept them. Thus *taqiyya* also means keeping the *bāṭin* secret.

The ʿUthmānic Qurʾān did not put an end to any future variations in reading. Since the science of Arabic orthography was still primitive, variations remained possible. The

ʿUthmānic text contained limited vowel markings or none at all, and the shapes of several consonants were similar, both of which allowed for a great variety of readings. These readings could lead to different interpretations. For example, the Arabic word *ʿalī*, could be taken either to be a simple adjective signifying "exalted," or to refer to the person of ʿAlī and his special role as successor of the prophet. Later in the fourth/tenth century, a limited number of variations were selected and canonized.

Unfortunately, it seems that what the variant texts were and how much they varied will most probably never be discovered. This ambiguity gave space to the most heated debate about the Shīʿī Qurʾān, both by Muslim scholars and by Western scholars. In May 1842, Garcin de Tassy edited in the *Journal Asiatique* the text and translation of an unknown chapter of the Qurʾān entitled "*Sūra* of the two lights" (*sūrat al-nūrayn*), the "two lights" referring respectively to Muḥammad and ʿAlī. Most scholars who commented on this *sūra* were uncertain of its origins (Eliash 1966: 125; 1969: 17). However this concept of "two lights" is developed by Shīʿites who distinguished between the "light of the *imāma*" and the "light of prophecy."

St. Clair Tisdall discovered a manuscript of the Qurʾān in India in 1912 that appeared to be about three hundred years old (Tisdall 1913: 228). In this manuscript he found a previously unknown *sūra* that was not part of the ʿUthmānic Qurʾān, as well as a few verses which were unique to this manuscript. The "*Sūra* of divine friendship" (*sūrat al-walāya*) contained seven verses which mentioned ʿAlī as *walī* ("friend") of God as well as the spiritual heir of the prophet, which Tisdall translated along with few "new" verses, in *The Moslem World* in 1913. Tisdall could not prove the authenticity of any of these additional chapters, and nor could von Grunebaum (1961: 80) who examined them later.

Meir M. Bar-Asher gave a complete overview of the topic in an article published in 1993 entitled "Variant Readings and Additions of the Imāmī-Shīʿī to the Qurʾān." Arthur Jeffrey had already catalogued many of variant readings in his *Materials for the History of the Text of the Qurʾān* (1937). Thus Bar-Asher decided to catalogue all of those that Jeffrey did not list and then selected only those variants that were relevant to Shīʿism (Bar-Asher 1993: 80). He examined the Shīʿī variant readings of the Qurʾān, the nature of the variations, and their difference from the ʿUthmānic compilation. Bar-Asher divided the variants into four types. First are minor alterations of words by exchanging or adding letters or vowel markings. This is the most common type of variant. Second is the exchange of one word for another, such as *imām* for *umma* (community). Third is the rearrangement of word order; this type of variant is the one most commonly accepted by Shīʿites. The Shīʿites of the first four Muslim centuries believed that ʿUthmān excised significant segments from the original Qurʾān and thus the fourth type of variant concerns some words that were omitted intentionally by ʿUthmān such as references to ʿAlī and the *imāma* (Bar-Asher 1993: 47). Today, the majority of Twelver Shīʿites affirm that the ʿUthmānic edition preserves the entire text, but in the wrong order. This, to them, explains why the narrative of the Qurʾān does not always flow smoothly.

There are two primary types of Shīʿī exegeses. First, in an analytic approach, the exegete deals with the Qurʾān verse-by-verse, in accordance with their compiled sequence. The exegete analyzes the text referring to literal meanings, traditions, or other verses in the Qurʾān that have some meaning in common with the verse under study while taking into consideration the context in which the text occurs. Analytic exegesis was the most popular approach used for many centuries by the traditionalists. In fact, *ḥadīth* remained the prime basis of exegesis for a long period of time. These traditions of the prophet and the Imāms were often replies to questions asked by the general populace. Second, a thematic approach seeks to study the Qur'ān by taking up one particular theme within the various theological, social, and cosmological contexts. It studies and discusses, for example, the doctrine of *tawḥīd* ("unicity of God"), the concept of prophethood, or the notion of creation in the Qur'ān. Both types of exegeses are complementary and may be combined. The thematic approach prevailed in jurisprudence (*fiqh*), while the analytic approach was common in Qur'ānic studies.

Some of the most sophisticated esoteric theosophy was developed during the *imāma* of Muḥammad al-Bāqir (d. ca. 114/714) and Jaʿfar al-Ṣādiq (d. 148/765) (see Nwyia 1968). It was also during this time that esoteric theories about the Qur'ān became manifest, and thus so did the assertions that the ʿUthmānic Qur'ān was incomplete. The revealed text alone is a "silent Qur'ān," in contrast with the Imāms, who were the "speaking Qur'ān" (Ayoub 1988: 184f.). It was during this time that a split occurred between Twelver Shīʿites and Ismāʿīlīs. There are many differences between Twelver Shīʿism and Ismāʿīlism even if they share a common ground; these differences were minute at the beginning but they became deeper when the twelfth Imām went into occultation (*ghayba*) in the ninth century. The Twelver theology changed gradually in the absence of the direct guidance of the Imām and developed justifications for the concept of *ghayba*.

Early Exegetes

The Ithnā ʿashariyya and the Ismāʿīlīs maintain that Jaʿfar al-Ṣādiq appointed by designation (*naṣṣ*) his eldest son Ismāʿīl as successor. But according to the Twelver Shīʿī understanding, Ismāʿīl died prematurely, so Jaʿfar designated another son, Mūsā al-Kāẓim, as Imām. In Twelver Shīʿism, the chain of *imāma* stopped with the seclusion of the twelfth Imām who will reappear at the end of time. There are mainly two theological schools within Twelver Shīʿism: the Akhbārī and the Uṣūlī. The Uṣūlī school gives more power to the *mujtahid* ("the one who exerts *ijtihād*, independent judgment") who is freer to exercise his individual reasoning. The Akhbārī school interprets the Qur'ān mainly through reliance upon traditions ascribed to the Imāms. In this respect, the sacred text is seen through the views and charisma of the prophet and the Imāms (Lawson 1993: 173–210).

The Qur'ān is maintained in a well-guarded tablet (*al-lawḥ al-maḥfūẓ*) which has a power on earth described as being beyond what a hard mountain can bear. It is a source of healing and blessing for the people. According to ʿAlī b. Ibrāhīm al-Qummī (d. ca. 307/920), the author of a Shīʿī *tafsīr*, the Imām, manifestation of God's light, shares these eternal qualities with the Qur'ān because he was with it before the creation. The Imām is seen as the purpose of creation; God created all creatures in order to worship Him. The only way to worship God is through the Imām; God has appointed him, because he is the only one who can give the right Qur'ānic interpretation. He is the source of guidance *par excellence* and can transfer the necessary knowledge to increase the faith of his disciples (al-Qummī 1386: I, 18–19; Ayoub 1988: 180).

Following the occultation of the twelfth Imām, everything changed. The Twelver Shīʿī community no longer had access to the direct guidance of their Imām, and, aside from the *abwāb* (agents of the "hidden Imām") and the *ʿulamāʾ* (religious scholars); their only source of guidance was the ʿUthmānic Qurʾān (Momen 1985: 189f.). As has been mentioned, the Twelver Shīʿites believe that the canonical recension is partly incomplete and disorganized. Imām Jaʿfar al-Ṣādiq is reported to have said: "Had the Qurʾān been read as it was sent down, you should have found us named in it" (al-ʿAyyāshī n.d.: I, 13; Ayoub 1988: 183). This saying may allude to the *ahl al-bayt* (ʿAlī, Fāṭima, Ḥasan, and Ḥusayn) who were alive during the lifetime of the prophet. But since the Twelfth Imām went into occultation, the Shīʿites seem to have relied further on the principle of *taqiyya* by accepting outwardly the ʿUthmānic Qurʾān. It seems unlikely that Shīʿites could ever fully accept the Sunnī Qurʾān, for their very affiliation with Shīʿism requires that they hold that Muḥammad had explicitly designated ʿAlī to succeed him. The Sunnī traditions and Qurʾān (according to Sunnī interpretation) do not include such proofs. Bar-Asher explains this ambivalence of Shīʿites who remain convinced of their Shīʿī faith but, because of the constant fear of persecution, decided to adopt the Sunnī Qurʾān (Bar-Asher 1993: 46).

The Imām is still among the community even while being hidden and not interacting with the world; his presence supports the very existence of the world (Amir-Moezzi 1994: 125). He and he alone is the sole being who fully understands the Qurʾān. When the twelfth Imām entered the state of occultation, the Shīʿī community lost its contact with not just the Imām but with the true Qurʾān as well. They are waiting for the Mahdī to bring the original text of the Qurʾān back when he manifests himself at the end of time.

The Shīʿī commentators in their study of a Qurʾānic verse viewed the explanations given by Muḥammad as indications of the meaning of the verse; they did not accept the companions as infallible transmitters of the sayings of Muḥammad. The Shīʿites only recognized as valid an unbroken chain of narration from the prophet through his direct descendants. Accordingly, they restricted themselves as to the use of traditions transmitted by the prophet and the Imāms. This has given rise to the following sub-groups.

The first group comprises those who have learned these traditions from the prophet and from the Imāms. Zurāra b. Aʿyūn (second/eighth century), Muḥammad b. Muslim b. Riyya al-Ṭāʾifī (second/eighth century), Maʿrūf b. Kharbūdh (second/eighth century) and Jarīr (second/eighth century) who were companions of the Imām Muḥammad al-Bāqir and Imām Jaʿfar al-Ṣādiq were part of the first group. Their original *tafsīr* works have not come down to us but their traditions were preserved by the next group.

The second group is composed of the first compilers of the commentaries such as Furāt b. Ibrāhīm al-Kūfī (third/ninth century), Abū Ḥamza al-Thumālī, Muḥammad al-ʿAyyāshī (d. ca. 319/932), ʿAlī b. Ibrāhīm al-Qummī (d. ca. 307/919–20) and Muḥammad al-Nuʿmānī (d. 360/971) all of whom lived between the second and fourth centuries after *hijra*. They avoided any kind of *ijtihād* (independent judgment). During their lifetime, the Imāms were available for questioning on matters of commentary

(Ṭabāṭabā'ī 1987: 50–1). Furāt was an authority on Shī'ī traditions during the *imāma* of Imām Muḥammad al-Jawād. Al-ʿAyyāshī was a Sunnī scholar who accepted the Jaʿfarī legal school. Al-Qummī transmitted traditions which came from his father who heard them from the Imāms' disciples. Al-Nuʿmānī was a student of al-Kulaynī (d. ca. 329/940–1) who compiled a canonical collection of Shīʿī traditions entitled *al-Kāfī fī 'ilm al-dīn* ("The Sufficient in the Science of Religion"). His work on *tafsīr* is reproduced in the *Biḥār al-anwār* ("Oceans of Lights") of Muḥammad Baqir al-Majlisī (d. 1111/1699). This second group simply compiled traditions without giving their own comments (Ayoub 1988: 184–5).

Medieval Exegetes

The third group encompasses masters of various sciences such as al-Sharīf al-Raḍī (d. 405/1015) who wrote a commentary concerned with Qur'ānic language, his brother al-Sayyid al-Murtaḍā (d. 436/1044), Abū Jaʿfar al-Ṭūsī (d. 460/1067), a student of al-Murtaḍā who composed a commentary focusing on metaphysics, his disciple who was ʿAlī 'l-Faḍl al-Ṭabarsī (d. 548/1153) who, in his *Majmaʿ al-bayān fī tafsīr al-Qur'ān* ("Collection of Elucidation in the Exegesis of the Qur'ān"), covers different fields of language, grammar, Qur'ānic recitation, traditions, death, and after-life. We may notice a shift in Twelver Shīʿī thought among members of this group who started to reject earlier Shīʿī claims about the incompleteness of the ʿUthmānic Qur'ān. Other important commentators belonging to this group are: Ṣadr al-Dīn al-Shīrāzī (d. 1050/1640) who wrote philosophic works, the gnostic commentary of al-Maybudī al-Kūnābādī and ʿAbdʿAlī al-Ḥuwayzī (d. 1112/1700) whose commentary is called *Nūr al-thaqalayn* ("Light of the Two Momentous Things"). Ḥāshim al-Baḥrānī (d. 1107/1695) composed the commentary *al-Burhān* ("The Proof") and Muḥsin al-Fayḍ al-Kāshānī (d. 1091/1680) compiled the work known as *Tafsīr al-Ṣāfī* ("Exegesis of the Sincere Friend") (Ṭabāṭabā'ī 1987: 51; Ayoub 1988: 185).

Shaykh al-Mufīd (d. 413/1022) was born in ʿUkbarā in Iraq. The Būyids were in power and there was a blossoming of Shīʿī scholarship in Baghdad where Shaykh al-Mufīd went to study. Shaykh al-Mufīd explains in *Kitāb al-irshād* ("The Book of Guidance") that God refers to ʿAlī in using the term *walī* (friend) in Q 5:55 (al-Mufīd 1981: 3). According to a *ḥadīth*, the prophet said: "You (ʿAlī) are in the same position with respect to me as Aaron was to Moses except that there is no prophet after me;" therefore, Shaykh al-Mufīd applies to ʿAlī all the Qur'ānic verses (see, e.g., Q 20:29–36) describing the function of Aaron. ʿAlī and Aaron have a share in prophecy and their role is to help the prophet deliver the message and to deputize on behalf of the prophet (al-Mufīd 1981: 3).

Then al-Mufīd enumerates numerous traditions showing the outstanding merit of ʿAlī over everybody in religious knowledge.

> The prophet said: "I am the city of knowledge and ʿAlī is its gate. Therefore whoever wants knowledge should learn it from ʿAlī." When the pledge of allegiance was made to the commander of the faithful [ʿAlī] for the caliphate, he went out to the mosque wearing the

> turban and cloak of the apostle of God. . . . Then he said: "Question me before you lose me. Question me, for I have the knowledge of those who came earlier and those who will come later. If the cushion [on which a judge sits] was folded for me [to sit on], I could give judgements to the people of the Torah by their Torah, to the people of the Gospels by their Gospels, to the people of their Psalms by their Psalms and to the people of the *Furqān* [i.e. Qur'ān] by their *Furqān*, so that each one of these books will be fulfilled and will declare, 'O Lord, indeed ʿAlī has given judgement according to Your decree.' By God, I know the Qur'ān and its interpretation [better] then anyone who claims knowledge of it. If it were not for one verse in the book of God, most High, I would be able to inform you of what will be until the day of resurrection." Then he said: "Question me before you lose me, for by Him who split the seed and brought the soul into being, if you questioned me about [it] verse-by-verse, I would tell you of the time of its revelation and why it was revealed, I would inform of the abrogating [verse] and the abrogated, of the specific and general, the clearly defined and the ambiguous, of the Meccan and the Medinan. By God, there is not a party who can lead astray or guide until the day of resurrection, without me knowing its leader, the one who drives it forward and the one who urges it on." (al-Mufīd 1981: 21–2)

Al-Mufīd concludes that there are numerous reports similar to this one but that he chooses to report only few examples.

ʿAllāma al-Hillī (d. 726/1325), known as Ibn al-Muṭahhar, was a Shīʿī theologian who lived during the Īl-khanid dynasty, the descendants of Hūlāgū. In one of his books, *al-Bāb al-ḥādī ʿashar* ("A Treatise on the Principles of Shīʿī Theology"), he explains that all the arguments proving that prophecy is necessary are relevant for the *imāma*. Since the *imāma* is the successor (*khilāfa*) of prophecy and stands in its place, the Imām must be impeccable; if that were not so, the command to do what is approved by Allāh and the prohibition against what is disapproved would cease to be obligatory, and that is impossible. Since he is the guardian of the law, the Imām must be impeccable to preserve the law from addition or loss. The Imām must be impeccable because he cannot be unjust, since God said, "My covenant embraced not the evildoers" (Q 3:112) and "O you who believe! Obey God, and obey the apostles, and those charged with authority among you" (Q 4:59). He argues that "those charged with authority among you" could be either impeccable or not; however, the second possibility must be false, since God cannot ordain obedience to one for whom error is possible. Hence the first option be true. Further, it must refer to ʿAlī and his descendants since impeccability was not claimed by anyone else (al-Hillī 1958: 64–5, 68, 76).

Modern Exegetes

The modern contemporary trend in *tafsīr* may be illustrated in the thought of Muḥammad Ḥusayn al-Ṭabāṭabāʾī (1321/1904–1402/1981) and of al-Sayyid Abū ʾl-Qāsim al-Khūʾī (1899–1992) who wrote *Bayān fī tafsīr al-Qurʾān* ("Elucidation in the Exegesis of the Qur'ān"). Al-Ṭabāṭabāʾī was one of the great masters of Qurʾānic commentary, Islamic philosophy and gnosis (*ʿirfān*). His thought gives a good illustration of the attitudes toward the Qur'ān adopted by many Twelver Shīʿites presently. He is the author of a Qurʾānic commentary entitled *al-Mīzān fī tafsīr al-Qurʾān* ("The Balance in the Exegesis of the Qur᾽ān"), which consists of some twenty-seven volumes written in Arabic. This immense commentary is based on the principle of using one part of the Qur᾽ān to elucidate other parts.

Al-Ṭabāṭabā᾽ī is also the author of another work written in Persian, entitled *Qur᾽ān dar Islām*, translated into English under the title of *The Qur᾽ān in Islām*, which gives an introduction to the study of the Qur᾽ān as traditionally understood by the mainstream of Shīʿī thought. He also discusses the Shīʿī attitude towards the Qur᾽ān in his book *Shīʿite Islām*. Al-Ṭabāṭabā᾽ī affirms that the Qur᾽ān "never uses enigmatic or puzzling methods of exposition and always expounds any subject in a language suitable for that subject" (Ṭabāṭabā᾽ī 1975: 99). According to him, the Qur᾽ān is perfect and shows man the way to realize his goal on earth in the most complete terms. It gives a way of correctly viewing the universe and a correct manner of behavior (Ṭabāṭabā᾽ī 1987: 26). The Qur᾽ān is endowed with an eternal quality, which proves that its validity is not restricted to a particular time or place; since it is perfect, it does not need anything else to be completed. This attitude toward the Qur᾽ān is not basically different from the Sunnī position.

Al-Ṭabāṭabā᾽ī refers also to Q 3:7 already quoted at the beginning of this chapter. For him, the *muḥkamāt* verses of the Qur᾽ān are explicit, clear, unambiguous, and safe from misinterpretation. The *mutashābihāt* verses are implicit and allegorical. It is the duty of all sincere Muslims to believe in and act according to the *muḥkamāt* verses. It is also their duty to believe in the *mutashābihāt* verses but they must abstain from acting upon them, because it is only those who are not sincere Muslims who follow the *mutashābihāt* verses, fabricating interpretations to deceive common people. The Shīʿites also maintain that the believer must seek knowledge of the *mutashābihāt* verses from God, the prophet, and the Imāms. There is no verse whose meaning is totally obscure since the Qur᾽ān describes itself as a light and a source of guidance for humanity. Thus, there are no verses in the Qur᾽ān which fail to reveal their meaning (Ṭabāṭabā᾽ī 1987: 33–4). According to al-Ṭabāṭabā᾽ī, all verses of the Qur᾽ān may reveal their true meaning to ordinary human beings. It is clear from the different maxims of the Imāms that there is always a way to discover the real meaning of the implicit verses. Each verse, even the ones with implicit meaning, can be explained by reference to other verses. Hence the real meaning of the allegorical verses can be found in relation to the explicit verses. ʿAlī is reported to have said that one part of the Qur᾽ān bears witness to another and clarifies the other (Ṭabāṭabā᾽ī 1987: 36–7).

Conclusion

Shīʿī interpretations of the Qur᾽ān concern mainly issues of authority within which the concept of *imāma* is paramount. For the Shīʿites, Muḥammad explicitly designated ʿAlī as his successor at Ghadīr Khumm by God's command. The prophet left behind him two momentous things: the Qur᾽ān and the people of his household; both are needed in order to remain on the right path. Since Muḥammad was the last prophet who closed the prophetic cycle, the Shīʿites believe that humanity still needs spiritual guidance: the cycle of *imāma* must succeed to the cycle of prophecy. *Imāma* is a cardinal principle of

Shīʿī faith since it is only through the Imām that true knowledge can be obtained. The Imām, the manifestation of God's light, shares these eternal qualities with the Qurʾān because he was with it before the creation. The Imām encapsulates the purpose of creation and it is only through him that it is possible to worship God. Muḥammad received the revelation and established the religious law while ʿAlī, the repository of the prophet's knowledge, provided its spiritual exegesis. The main principle of Shīʿī exegesis is based on the fact that the Qurʾān has an outer dimension and an inner dimension which has up to seven inner dimensions.

Today the majority of Twelver Shīʿites affirm that the ʿUthmānic edition preserves the entire text in the Qurʾān, but in the wrong order in some places. The Shīʿites of the first four *hijrī* centuries maintained that ʿUthmān excised significant verses from the original Qurʾān. Following the occultation of the Twelfth Imām, the Twelver Shīʿī community no longer had access to the direct guidance of their Imām, and aside from the agents of the hidden Imām and the *ʿulamāʾ*, their only source of guidance was the ʿUthmānic Qurʾān. Since the Twelfth Imām went into occultation, the Shīʿites seem to have relied on the principle of *taqiyya* to a significant extent by accepting outwardly the ʿUthmānic Qurʾān.

Further reading

Ayoub, Mahmoud (1984) *The Qurʾān and its Interpreters*. State University of New York Press, Albany.

Ayoub, Mahmoud (1988) The speaking Qurʾān and the silent Qurʾān: A study of the principles and development of Imāmī Shīʿī *tafsīr*. In Rippin, Andrew (ed.) *Approaches to the History of the Interpretation of the Qurʾān*. Oxford University Press, Oxford, pp. 177–98.

Bar-Asher, Meir (1993) Variant readings and additions of the Imāmī-Shīʿī to the Qurʾān. *Israel Oriental Studies* 13, 39–75.

Bar-Asher, Meir (1999) *Scripture and Exegesis in Early Imāmī Shiism*. E. J. Brill, Leiden.

Eliash, Joseph (1969) "The Shīʿite Qurʾān:" A reconsideration of Goldziher's interpretation. *Arabica* 16, 15–24.

Jafri, S. Husain M. (1979) *Origins and Early Development of Shīʿa Islām*. Librairie du Liban, London.

Lawson, B. Todd (1991) Note for the study of a "Shīʿī Qurʾān." *Journal of Semitic Studies* 36, 279–95.

Lawson, B. Todd (1993) Akhbārī Shīʿī approaches to *tafsīr*. In: Hawting, G. and Shareef, A.-K. (eds.) *Approaches to the Quran*. Routledge, London, pp. 173–210.

Modarressi, Hossein (1993) Early debates on the integrity of the Qurʾān: A brief survey. *Studia Islamica* 77, 4–39.

Tisdall, St. Clair W. (1913) Shiʿah additions to the Koran. *The Moslem World* 3, 227–41.

CHAPTER 26

Ismāʿīlī *Taʾwīl*

Diana Steigerwald

This chapter, surveying how the Ismāʿīlīs have interpreted the Qurʾān and developed their spiritual exegesis, provides an account of the relevant history while not pretending to be exhaustive. Even when the Ismāʿīlīs lived in difficult times, they were still the champions of *bāṭin* (the "inner meaning" of revelation) because they, especially the Nizārī Ismāʿīlīs, remain attached to the necessity of a "speaking" (*nāṭiq*) Qurʾān, accessible in this physical world and whose main function is to update the interpretation of the Qurʾān for the present time. The Ismāʿīlīs maintained the Shīʿī doctrine of *imāma* which acts as the foundation of the Ismāʿīlī theosophy; it is based on the necessity of a divinely guided and sinless (*maʿṣūm*) Imām. After the death of Muḥammad, the Imām acts on his behalf to guide the believers in their spiritual and material lives. The Imām possesses knowledge (*ʿilm*) and a perfect understanding of the Qurʾān as well as the religious law (*sharīʿa*).

In the second/eighth century, the Shīʿī communities, under the leadership of Imām Jaʿfar al-Ṣādiq, acquired notoriety. The Ismāʿīlīs separated from the rest of the Twelver Shīʿites on the death of Imām Jaʿfar al-Ṣādiq in 147/765, but the political success of the Ismāʿīlīs culminated in the establishment of the Fāṭimid dynasty in North Africa in 297/909. There was a dispute over the succession of Imām al-Mustanṣir biʾllāh, after his death in 487/1094. Mustanṣir designated Nizār, his elder son, to succeed him. But al-Afḍal, commander-in-chief of the army, at the death of al-Mustanṣir biʾllāh, placed a younger son of Mustanṣir, al-Mustaʿlī, who was married to al-Afḍal's sister, on the throne. Hence emerged the Nizārī and the Mustaʿlī branches of the Ismāʿīlīs. Al-Mustaʿlī, was recognized as Imām by the Ismāʿīlīs of Egypt, Yemen, and Western India. The Ismāʿīlīs of Persia and Iraq, under the leadership of Ḥasan-i Ṣabbāḥ (d. 518/1124), acknowledged al-Mustanṣir biʾllāh's eldest son, Nizār (d. 489/1096), as their next Imām.

The Ismāʿīlīs attempted to raise human consciousness to a higher plane; they were not at all the irreligious libertines their adversaries often represented them as. On the contrary, they were dedicated to a life of service and self-improvement. Their goal was

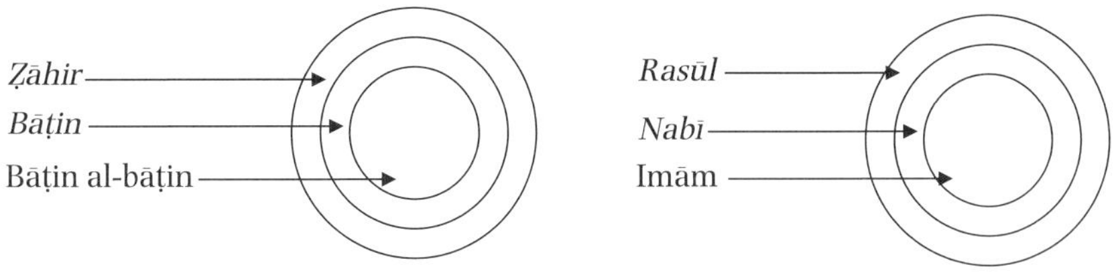

Figure 26.1 Ismāʿīlī theory of interpretation

wholly spiritual. Ismāʿīlism is neither a philosophy nor a theology, but it is a theosophy or "divine wisdom." The Ismāʿīlīs built one of the most remarkable speculative systems on the basis of the Qurʾān, the science of the cosmos, and neo-Platonism. These three elements were interwoven to give a rich and coherent worldview. The Ismāʿīlīs sought to understand the cosmos and their place within it.

Ismāʿīlī *taʾwīl* shares common ground with Ṣūfism. We need to distinguish in Ismāʿīlism two types of *taʾwīl*. First, the supreme *taʾwīl*, elucidating the *bāṭin* – the interior or hidden meaning – of the *bāṭin* meaning of the text, is the prerogative of the Imām only. Second, there is a lower level of *taʾwīl* of elucidating the *bāṭin* which is exercised by an individual member of the Ismāʿīlī mission (*daʿwa*) who will give an interpretation of the Qurʾān corresponding to his own spiritual level. This second type of *taʾwīl* resembles Ṣūfī exegesis. The method is called *kashf*, an "unveiling" to the heart of the interpreter, and is dependent upon the master (*murshid*), the grace of God, and the spiritual capacity of the interpreter (see Figure 26.1).

For Marshall Hodgson (1974: I, 394–5, 400), Ṣūfī exegesis is less allegorical or symbolic than that found in Ismāʿīlism and focused more on the personal experience that words inspire. By searching the inner meaning of the Qurʾānic words, the Ṣūfīs wanted to revive the spiritual states from which the words originated. Their exegesis was accompanied with isolation and meditation. For the Ṣūfīs, the objective is to seek nearness to God through the Qurʾān. Although Ismāʿīlīs are also mystics and they practice meditation, their method of approaching the Qurʾān seems to be more intellectual than the Ṣūfīs. The Ismāʿīlīs seek to understand the Qurʾān by penetrating to the roots, and then retrieving and disclosing that which is interior or hidden. This search engages both the intellect and the spirit (*rūḥ*) in order to discover the truths (*ḥaqāʾiq*). Their Qurʾānic exegesis is based on the word, letter order, and on calculating the numerical value of letters. Each verse of the Qurʾān has a surface meaning and several hidden meanings.

In every cycle of seven days (in the time frame of the celestial realm) an Adam is created and the chain of prophethood ends with the last prophet who is in turn succeeded by Imāms. The cycle of *imāma* ends with the *Qāʾim al-qiyāma* ("Lord of the resurrection") who will reveal the *taʾwīl* of previous revelations. The six main speaking-prophets (*nuṭaqāʾ*) were accompanied respectively by an Imām (Table 26.1).

Thus, according to this theory, these cycles will continue until there is no more matter in this universe and all matter is transformed into *laṭāfa* ("gracefulness," "kindness").

Table 26.1 The chain of prophethood

Days	Prophets	Imāms	
1	Adam	Seth	*tanzīl*
2	Noah	Shem	*taʾwīl*
3	Abraham	Ishmael	*tanzīl/taʾwīl*
4	Moses	Aaron	*tanzīl*
5	Jesus	Simon Peter	*taʾwīl*
6	Muḥammad	ʿAlī	*tanzīl/taʾwīl*
7	–	*Qāʾim al-qiyāma*	taʾwīl al-taʾwīl

Early Exegetes

The pre-Fāṭimid period runs from Imām Ismāʿīl (ca. 147/764 or later) to Imām Raḍī ʾl-Dīn ʿAbd Allāh (d. ca. 268/882). It was a period of *satr* ("concealment") in which the Imāms were *mastūr* ("hidden" from the majority) since their life was endangered. This concept of *mastūr* must be differentiated from the Twelver Shīʿī idea of occultation (*ghayba*) which means that the Mahdī is occulted until the day of resurrection. It was in this complex situation that the *Treatises* of the Ikhwān al-Ṣafāʾ (the "Brethren of Purity") were written. These works are of great importance in Ismāʿīlī literature and were composed by authors who had a vast knowledge of Hellenic literature and of the various sciences existing during that time. These treatises do not, however, present a systematic exposition of *taʾwīl*.

The Ikhwān al-Ṣafāʾ divide people in three classes. First, the common people have to follow the religious law (*sharīʿa*) to improve their character. The second class improves their comprehension of religion by studying the Qurʾān and the *sunna*, the spoken and acted example of Muḥammad. This class is gifted with discursive reasoning and is capable of *ijtihād* (independent judgment) in order to arrive at solid proofs. This category is subdivided into many spiritual levels. The third class is composed of the elite who know the inner (*bāṭin*) and hidden (*khafī*) meanings of the Qurʾān. They are the purified ones (*muṭahharūn*), that is, the prophets and the Imāms, who know the mysteries of religion (*Rasāʾil Ikhwān al-Ṣafāʾ* 1376/1957: III, 504, 511–2).

The Brethren explain that verses in the Qurʾān referring to the throne, to the sight and speech of God should not be interpreted literally. Only God and the experts of Qurʾānic interpretation can properly interpret these verses (*Rasāʾil Ikhwān al-Ṣafāʾ* 1376/1957: III, 344–5). They also attempted to speculate on the numerical value of the Arabic letters (*kāf, hāʾ, yāʾ, ʿayn,* and *ṣād*), appearing at the beginning of some Qurʾānic chapters in order to finally conclude that their meaning should remain a secret reserve to a few select servants of God (*Rasāʾil Ikhwān al-Ṣafāʾ* 1376/1957: III, 378–83). They also give a spiritual exegesis of the encounter of Moses, described as the Lord of the religious law, with al-Khiḍr, the master of secrets (*Rasāʾil Ikhwān al-Ṣafāʾ* 1376/1957: III, 509). Concerning the nature of the Qurʾān, the Brethren consider the actual sounds, words, and letters as *makhlūqa* ("created") while the ideas or meanings in the mind of God are uncreated (*Rasāʾil Ikhwān al-Ṣafāʾ* 1376/1957: III, 517).

Fāṭimid Exegetes

The Fāṭimid period started with Imām ʿUbayd Allāh (d. 322/934) and ended with Imām al-ʿĀḍid (d. 567/1171). An Ismāʿīlī state was established in Ifriqiyya (Tunisia) and later in northern Africa. The University of al-Azhar was founded around 360/970. The Ismāʿīlī theosophy was gradually structured by al-Nasafī (d. 331/942), Abū Ḥātim al-Rāzī (d. 322/933–4), Abū Yaʿqūb al-Sijistānī (fourth/tenth century), al-Qāḍī al-Nuʿmān (d. 363/974), and others. Later Ismāʿīlism received an official form through the labors of Ḥamīd al-Dīn Kirmānī (d. 412/1024) and Nāṣir-i Khusraw (d. after 465/1072). Fāṭimid theosophy is characterized by the preservation of the equilibrium between the *ẓāhir* and the *bāṭin*.

Some important books of *taʾwīl* are the *Kitāb al-shawāhid wa ʾl-bayān* ("The Book of Evidences and the Declaration") and *Kitāb al-kashf* ("The Book of Unveiling") ascribed to Manṣūr al-Yaman (d. 302/914), *Kitāb aʿlām al-nubuwwa* ("The Book of Signs of Prophecy") of Abū Ḥātim al-Rāzī, *Taʾwīl al-daʿāʾim* ("The Spiritual Exegesis of the Pillars") and *Asās al-taʾwīl* ("The Foundation of Spiritual Exegesis") of al-Qāḍī al-Nuʿmān, *Kashf al-maḥjūb* ("Unveiling of the Hidden") and *Kitāb al-yanābīʿ* ("The Book of Sources") of Abū Yaʿqūb al-Sijistānī (d. ca. 390/1000), *Rāḥat al-ʿaql* ("The Tranquility of Intellect") of Ḥamīd al-Dīn al-Kirmānī, and *Al-Majālis* ("The Assemblies") of Muʾayyad fī ʾl-dīn al-Shīrāzī (d. 470/1077).

Manṣūr al-Yaman (Ibn Ḥawshab), a famous missionary (*dāʿī*) responsible for the spread of Ismāʿīlism in Yemen, gives a spiritual exegesis of a verse from *sūra Yāʾ-Sīn* (Q 36:40), "It is not permitted to the sun to catch up the moon, nor can the night outstrip the day: each [just] swims along in [its own] orbit [according to law]." The Imām, in the Qurʾān, is symbolized by the sun while the *ḥujja* (proof of the Imām), a spiritual dignitary, is represented by the moon. The Imām usually does not overtake his *ḥujja* unless he establishes the hidden mission (*daʿwat al-bāṭin*). That night cannot outstrip the day signifies that the hidden mission does not overtake the outward mission (*daʿwat al-ẓāhir*) (Engineer 1980: 56; Engineer cites his own personal manuscript of *Kitāb al-shawāhid waʾl-bayān*).

Al-Qāḍī al-Nuʿmān, a renowned jurist who worked for the first four Fāṭimid Caliphs, in *Asās al-taʾwīl*, quotes a saying attributed to Imām Jaʿfar al-Ṣādiq: "We can speak about a word in seven different ways." When the astounded questioner responded, "Seven!" the Imām retorted: "Yes, even seventy. If you ask us more we can increase it even more." Al-Nuʿmān explains that there are many possible interpretations corresponding to different spiritual rank. The number of interpretations increases as you ascend the spiritual hierarchy (al-Nuʿmān 1960: 27; Poonawala 1988b: 221).

Al-Nuʿmān describes in his *Taʾwīl al-daʿāʾim* the hidden meanings of the seven *daʿāʾim* (pillars) (Engineer, 1980: 55; Engineer cites his own personal manuscript of the *Taʾwīl al-daʿāʾim*, 54) – see Table 26.2.

Table 26.2 Hidden meaning of the seven pillars

	Spiritual guides	Pillars of faith
1	Adam	*walāya* (love, devotion)
2	Noah	*ṭahāra* (purity)
3	Abraham	*ṣalāt* (prayer)
4	Moses	*zakāt* (almsgiving)
5	Jesus	*ṣawm* (fasting)
6	Muḥammad	*ḥajj* (pilgrimage)
7	Imām	*jihād* (exertion in the way of God)

The very first pillar for the Ismāʿīlīs is *walāya* (love, devotion) to the family of the prophet (*ahl al-bayt*). For al-Nuʿmān, each pillar represents a prophet from Adam to Muḥammad. Adam was the first prophet whose *walāya* was made obligatory for the angels who prostrate before him (Q 2:34). Adam is the first of the prophets and his *walāya* symbolizes the *walāya* of all the succeeding prophets and Imāms. In Ismāʿīlī theosophy, the second pillar, *ṭahāra* ("purity"), is associated with the second prophet Noah. Noah was sent for the purification of mankind. Whatever sins were committed after Adam's time, Noah came to purify. The floodwater during the time of Noah symbolizes purity, as water is needed to purify the body from dirt. The spiritual meaning (*bāṭin*) of water is knowledge of ultimate reality, *ʿilm*, which is necessary for spiritual purity and ascent.

The third pillar is prayer, *ṣalāt*, and al-Nuʿmān relates it to the prophet Abraham who constructed the house of Allāh in Mecca, the direction of prayers, *qibla*, for the Muslims. Moses represents *zakāt* ("almsgiving") since he is the first prophet who is said to have asked Pharaoh to purify (*tazakka*) himself (see Q 79:18). The root of *zakāt* in Arabic is related to purification; it is through *zakāt* that one purifies one's wealth by giving a part away to the poor. *Ṣawm* ("fasting") is related to the prophet Jesus. It was Mary, the mother of Jesus, who said to her people (Q 19:26), "I have vowed a fast to (God) Most Gracious, and this day will I enter into no talk with any human being." Hence the inner meaning of *ṣawm* is to keep silent about the *bāṭin*.

Since the pilgrimage (*ḥajj*) is the last of those things made obligatory by God, it is related to the last prophet Muḥammad who first required Muslims to perform the *ḥajj* to Mecca. The last of the pillars of Islām, *jihād* ("exertion in the way of God"), is related to the seventh Imām in the chain of Imāms. The seventh Imām, also called *nāṭiq* ("speaker"), reveals part of the esoteric meanings of the Qurʾān through his effort (*jihād*) to purify religion. The *Qāʾim al-qiyāma*, the last of the seventh Imāms, will reveal the esoteric truth in its entirety and through him the Muslim community (*umma*) will be unified. Thus Muḥammad excels over all other prophets by his function in the sense that two pillars of Islām – *ḥajj* and *jihād* – have been related to him and his descendants.

Abū Yaʿqūb al-Sijistānī, a *dāʿī* of Khurāsān, in his *Kitāb al-maqālīd* ("The Book of Keys") explains clearly the difference between *tanzīl* ("plain revelation") and *taʾwīl*:

> *Tanzīl* is similar to the raw materials, while the *taʾwīl* resembles the manufactured goods. For example, nature produces various types of wood, but unless a craftsman works on them and gives them a specific shape, such as a door, a chest or a chair, the wood is not worth more than fuel [to be consumed] by the fire. The wood's worth and benefit become manifest only after it receives the craftsman's craftsmanship. . . . Similarly, *tanzīl* consists of putting things together in words. Beneath those words lie the treasured meanings. It is the practitioner of the *taʾwīl* who extracts the intended meaning from each word and puts everything in its proper place. This is, then, the difference between the *tanzīl* and the *taʾwīl* (Al-Sijistānī, 52nd *iqlīd*, translated by Poonawala 1988b: 206).

The function of *taʾwīl* comes always after *tanzīl*. The prophet's role is to bring *tanzīl* and the *sharīʿa* to the people whereas the function of the successor (*waṣī*) is to reveal gradually the hidden meanings through *taʾwīl*. Only the *waṣī* has the knowledge of each thing's proper place in the hierarchy, which he reveals by the act of *taʾwīl*.

Al-Sijistānī explains that *taʾwīl* is necessary for two categories of Qurʾānic verses: one, verses with physical objects such as heaven, earth, and mountains, and two, the allegorical verses (*mutashābihāt*). In chapter 12 of *Kitāb al-iftikhār* ("The Book of Pride"), al-Sijistānī gives some examples such as Q 21:105: "Before this We wrote in the Psalms, after the message (given to Moses): 'My servants, the righteous, should inherit the earth'." This, he suggests, should not be interpreted in the literal sense since it is always the tyrants who take the land. The earth on which vegetation grows is a source of nourishment for all creatures; therefore its inner meaning is the nourishment of the soul (i.e. spiritual knowledge). In another passage, Q 21:104, "The day that We roll up the heaven like a scroll rolled up with the writings," the "heaven" signifies the *sharīʿa* which will be abrogated on the judgment day (Poonawala 1988b: 210, 214–15).

Nāṣir-i Khusraw was a *ḥujja* of Khurasān, although it should be noted that the rank of *ḥujja* during the Fāṭimid period is not equivalent to the rank of *ḥujja* in Alamūt (see below) and afterward. In his *Shish Faṣl* ("Six Chapters"), he gives some examples of spiritual exegesis (*taʾwīl*). He explains that God speaks about the believer in this verse: "Seek the forgiveness of your Lord, and turn to Him in repentance; that He may grant you enjoyment, good (and true), for a term appointed, and bestow His abounding grace on all who abound in merit! But if ye turn away, then I fear for you the penalty of a great day" (Q 11:3). Nāṣir-i Khusraw indicates that the expression "a term appointed" signifies that God will guide the believer toward the knowledge of truth when he will acknowledge the Lord of the time, that is, the Imām, who is the supreme teacher (Nāṣir-i Khusraw 1949: 36–7). The Qurʾān is presented in the form of symbols and parables which are beyond the human intellect to unravel its contradictions, if they are not clarified by the true Imām (Nāṣir-i Khusraw 1949: 49–50).

For Nāṣir-i Khusraw, the Qurʾān should be revealed by stages in order for the Imāms, in their own times, to reveal gradually to the people the inner sense by their *taʾwīl*. This is indicated in "[It is] a Qurʾan which We have divided (into parts from time to time), in order that thou might recite it to men at intervals. We have revealed it by stages" (Q 17:106; Nāṣir-i Khusraw 1949: 51–2). He further explains that the manifestation of the *Qāʾim-i qiyāmat* is the purpose of creation. All the prophets previously announced his advent and warned the people about his power, as it is said in Q 78: 1–3: "Concerning what are they disputing? Concerning the great news, about which they cannot agree" (Nāṣir-i Khusraw 1949: 59–60).

Alamūt Exegetes

The Alamūt period extended from Imām Nizār to Imām Rukn al-dīn Khurshāh. The Nizārī Ismāʿīlī state was established in Alamūt by Ḥasan-i Ṣabbāḥ (d. 518/1124). The *sharīʿa* was abolished only during the *qiyāmat-i qiyāmat* ("great resurrection") proclaimed by Imām Ḥasan ʿAlā Dhikrihi al-Salām in 559/1164. According to Henry Corbin:

> What the proclamation implied was nothing less than the coming of a pure spiritual Islām, freed from all spirit of legalism and of all enslavement to the law, a personal religion of the Resurrection which is spiritual birth, in that it makes possible the discovery and the living realisation of the spiritual meaning of the Prophetic revelations. (Corbin 1993: 95)

Alamūt theosophy enhanced the value of *bāṭin* while considering *ẓāhir* as an essential first step in the initiation. Later, during his *imāma*, Jalāl al-Dīn Ḥasan re-established the religious law. Alamūt was destroyed by the Mongol Hūlāgū in 654/1256, but Ismāʿīlism survived in Persia under the cover of Ṣūfism.

Al-Shahrastānī (d. 548/1153), an influential historian of religions and heresiographer who lived during that time, secretly adhered to Nizārī Ismāʿīlism. In his *Milal* (al-Shahrastānī 1366–75/1947–55: I, 560–2), he takes the position of *ḥunafāʾ* (plural of *ḥanīf*, those who "adhere to pure monotheism") against the Qurʾānic Sabians on the necessity of a human guide gifted with impeccability. In his *Nihāya*, he insists on the fact that the prophet confirms his predecessors while proclaiming his successor (al-Shahrastānī 1934: 486). He cites a tradition generally quoted by Shīʿites according to which "the earth will never be deprived of an Imām [acting according to] the divine command (*amr*)" (al-Shahrastānī 1934: 478–9).

In the *Mafātīḥ al-asrār* ("The Keys of Mysteries"), al-Shahrastānī asserts that

> the people and the awaiting Shīʿites (*al-Shīʿa al-muntaẓira*) do not profess anything except an absent and awaited Imām while God has on earth "Honored servants [who] speak not before He speaks, and act [in all things] by His command" (Q 21:27). "He chose the servants as heirs of His book" (Q 35:32). Whoever fights them, fights God; whoever loves them, loves God; whoever obeys them, obeys God; whoever prostrates himself before them prostrates himself before God. (al-Shahrastānī 1989: I, 121 *verso* to 122 *recto*; a similar idea is expressed by al-Nuʿmān 1956: 38.)

In most of his writings, al-Shahrastānī demonstrates his fidelity to ʿAlī and the *ahl al-bayt*. He quotes another well-known tradition, in which Muḥammad declares: "There is one among you who will fight for the [correct] interpretation (*taʾwīl*) of the Qurʾān just as I myself fought for its revelation (*tanzīl*); he is the one (ʿAlī) who sews up [my] sandal" (al-Shahrastānī 1366–75/1947–55: I, 409–10).

In the *Majlis*, al-Shahrastānī clearly distinguishes different spiritual ranks: Moses as the judge of *sharīʿa*, Khiḍr as the deputy of the judge of resurrection (*qiyāma*), and ʿAlī as the riser (*qāʾim*). Two lights were inherited from Abraham: an apparent light (*nūr-ī ẓāhir*) and a hidden one (*nūr-ī mastūr*). These two lights recall the Shīʿī concepts of *nūr al-nubuwwa* ("light of prophecy") and *nūr al-imāma* ("light of the *imāma*"). Al-Shahrastānī teaches some Ismāʿīlī concepts such as *amr* ("command") versus *khalq* ("creation"), ʿAlī at the level of the first command, and Ḥasan as the heir of the revelation. The *Majlis* lays emphasis on the necessity of a guide belonging to the spiritual and physical world. For each spiritual level there is a teacher (al-Shahrastānī 1998: 95). For al-Shahrastānī, the star, moon, and sun, mentioned in the Qurʾān, must be interpreted as referring to different ranks in the spiritual hierarchy. The *dāʿī* (the "summonser," symbolized by the star), the *ḥujja* (the "proof," represented by moon), and the Imām (symbolized by the sun) are manifest in the world. Al-Shahrastānī explains clearly that on the day of resurrection, ʿAlī will have the function of the riser (*qāʾim*) who separates those deserving paradise from those deserving hell. The description of ʿAlī as the *qāʾim* has an Ismāʿīlī imprint (more particularly Nizārī). Abū Isḥāq-i Quhistānī (d. 904/1448), a Nizārī Ismāʿīlī author, refers to a prophetic tradition describing ʿAlī as the *qāʾim*. He quotes a *ḥadīth*: "And Muṣṭafā [Muḥammad] said that ʿAlī b. Abī Ṭālib, may God beautify his countenance, will, on the day of resurrection, raise the banner of the *qiyāma* single-handed" (Abū Isḥāq-i Quhistānī 1959: 40).

In his *Majlis*, al-Shahrastānī gives a spiritual exegesis of the initiation of Moses by the servant of God as recounted in Q 18:59–82. His understanding of the dynamic evolution of humanity is similar to Ismāʿīlism in which each prophet opens a new cycle. Along with Ḥasan-i Ṣabbāh, he brings a new understanding of the Nizārī Ismāʿīlī tradition. In the Alamūt period, Moses, who is part of the ephemeral world, corresponds to the speaking-prophet at the rank of the universal soul. On the other hand, Khiḍr, the *ḥujja*, at the rank of the universal intellect, belongs to the eternal world. Al-Shahrastānī relates the spiritual evolution of Abraham in the same way as it is related by Abū Ḥātim al-Rāzī in his *Kitāb al-iṣlāḥ* ("The Book of Restoration") and by al-Qāḍī al-Nuʿmān in his *Asās al-taʾwīl*. These Ismāʿīlī authors relate the initiation of Abraham by the *dāʿī* (the star), then by the *ḥujja* (the moon) and finally by the Imām (the sun) before reaching the prophetic level (Steigerwald 1997: 294–5). Al-Shahrastānī identifies Khiḍr as the servant of God who gradually initiates Moses to esoteric truths. Khiḍr helps Moses ascend to the spiritual ranks. The figure of Khiḍr, in al-Shahrastānī's *Majlis*, is equivalent to the *ḥujjat-i Imām* ("proof of the Imām"), who is a dignitary second only in importance to the Imām in Nizārī Ismāʿīlism. Unlike the speaking-prophet, the *ḥujja* is infallible; he is similar to the "perfect man" (*al-insān al-kāmil*) of the Ṣūfīs. Khiḍr is immortal and in possession of an esoteric gnosis beyond time and space. In this passage Khiḍr rebukes Moses:

> Yesterday, today and tomorrow are all temporal: they all pertain to time. And you, of course, being a temporally-bound man, a man of "the times", you pass judgment according to "the times". But I am not a "man of the times": yesterday, tomorrow, and today to me are all one. Whatever shall come into existence in the future has already occurred for me. The tyrant who "shall come in the future" has already visited me. The infidelity of that

> child, that is bound to occur, has for me already happened. The wall that shall crumble for me has already fallen down. Therefore, I don't pass judgment according to "the times", for the judgment I pass is not a temporal one; it transcends time. You must spend an entire year wandering about to find me, whereas I can find you instantaneously, in a single moment traveling from East to West. Time and space obey my dictates. I transcend space and time, so that all the judgments I pass are not subject to temporal or spatial conditions, nor pertain to what is temporal. (al-Shahrastānī 1998: 103; unpublished partial English translation of Leonard Lewisohn)

Moses is the judge of religious law while Khiḍr is the deputy of the judge of resurrection (i.e. ʿAlī) (al-Shahrastānī 1998: 47, 94). Apparently, on the level of *ẓāhir*, the actions of Khiḍr (Khiḍr tore a ship open to drown its people and he killed a boy) seem to go against the law; but in its inner reality, it is in agreement with it because Khiḍr knows its deepest meanings.

In the *Mafātīḥ al-asrār*, al-Shahrastānī presents a spiritual exegesis of the two first Qurʾānic chapters based on the sayings attributed to the *ahl al-bayt*. Al-Shahrastānī praises ʿAlī and the *ahl al-bayt* and tells us that the prophet designated his family to assemble the Qurʾān. Therefore, only the compilation of ʿAlī was valuable and perfect. Al-Shahrastānī condemns exegeses based on personal opinions; he explains that some verses need the intervention of an authority. The interpretation of the Qurʾān belongs to ʿAlī and his sucessors. Al-Shahrastānī quotes a *ḥadīth* of the prophet which says that the Qurʾān was revealed according to seven letters (*ḥurūf*) corresponding to seven levels of interpretation. He distinguishes between *taʾwīl* and *tafsīr*. *Tafsīr* comes from *fassara* which means "to comment," but it is also close to *safara* ("unveil") in the sense of *kashafa* ("discover, unveil"). All *taʾwīl* is a *tafsīr*, but not all *tafsīr* is *taʾwīl*. *Taʾwīl* means to take back the thing to its first meaning. Al-Shahrastānī relates the allegorical verses (*mutashābihāt*) of the Qurʾān to the temporal world while the fundamental verses (*muḥkamāt*) of established meaning are referred to the spiritual world (al-Shahrastānī 1989: 307–8, 310–12; Steigerwald 1997: 70–2).

Naṣīr al-Dīn al-Ṭūsī (d. 676/1274) described his conversion into Ismāʿīlism in one of his works *Sayr wa sulūk* ("Contemplation and Action"). In another work *Taṣawwurāt*, he gives a *taʾwīl* of the seven Ismāʿīlī pillars of Islām which is complementary to the one of al-Qāḍī al-Nuʿmān. The *shahāda* ("profession of faith") means to recognize God. *Ṭahāra* ("ritual ablution") indicates that one has to dissociate himself from established religious rules. *Namāz* ("congregational prayer") implies preaching the recognition of God. *Rūza* ("fasting") signifies practicing *taqiyya* ("precautionary dissimulation"), meaning that one should not reveal esoteric meanings of the Qurʾān to those who are unable to understand them. *Zakāt* ("religious obligatory alms") means to impart to others what God has given to us. *Ḥajj* ("pilgrimage") symbolizes giving up the attachment to this material world and look for the eternal realm. The seventh pillar *jihād* ("exertion for a religious cause") means to seek annihilation of oneself in God (al-Ṭūsī 1950: 106).

Abū Isḥāq-i Quhistānī, a Nīzārī Ismāʿīlī *dāʿī* who lived during the *imāma* of Imām Mustanṣir biʾllāh II (d. 885/1480), explains that the *waṣī*, the successor of the prophet, gives knowledge to everyone according to his capacity. To those who accept only the plain revelation (*tanzīl*), he speaks in the line of *tanzīl*, and to those who accept the *taʾwīl*, he reveals its inner meanings. The function of ʿAlī was to bring his community from a state of being lost in the letter of religious law to a world of truth (Abū Isḥāq-i Quhistānī 1959: 31–2). For Abū Isḥāq-i Quhistānī, the one who understands the mysteries of the religious law has attained the truth. Those who know the Imām, have reached a state of "permanent prayer" as they are mentioned in this Qurʾānic passage: "Those who remain steadfast to their prayer" (Q 70:13). The outward injunction does not apply to them. Another verse of the Qurʾān mentioned is: "Within it shall be mercy, and outside and before it is torment" (Q 57:13). Therefore, those who know the inner meanings of the religious law (*sharīʿa*) pertain to the world of mercy. For Abū Isḥāq-i Quhistānī, the physical body is the grave and the injunctions of the *sharīʿa* are the torments of the grave reserved for those who are attached exclusively to the letter of *sharīʿa* (Abū Isḥāq-i Quhistānī 1959: 53).

Mustanṣir biʾllāh II (d. 885/1480), a Nizārī Imām, in his *Pandiyāt-i Jawān mardī* ("Advices of Manliness") gives instruction to his followers:

> If a man does not recognize the Imām of his time, does not accept him as such, treats his orders as already contained in the plain commandments of the *sharīʿa*, ascertains from the ordinary theologians the indications of the Qurʾān and the various *ḥadīths* concerning the institution of *imāma*, and if he acts according to the theologians' opinion, all his pious acts will be fruitless. . . . This is because the correct meaning of the Qurʾān and *ḥadīths* is only with the Imām. The prophet, peace be upon him, himself said that whoever accepted his progeny and the book of God as his guidance would never be lost. The expression "my progeny" refers to the Imām, according to the words of the Q 3:30: ". . . my progeny, one following the other." But the Imām can only be recognized with the help of another Imām, being the person whom the Imām appoints to that office from amongst his own progeny. Only he will be the Imām, no one else. Ordinary mortals cannot appoint any one as their Imām. (Mustanṣir biʾllāh II 1953: 48–9)

Hence Imām Mustanṣir biʾllāh II clearly states the necessity to accept the Qurʾān and the "Imām of the time" as the only one who knows the inner and deepest Qurʾānic meanings.

Ginānic Exegetes

The *Ginānic* period began with Imām Shams al-Dīn Muḥammad (d. ca. 720/1320) and ended with Imām Khalīl Allāh III (d. 1233/1818). The Pīrs started to preach in northern India around the end of the thirteenth century. The Pīr (*ḥujja*), at the spiritual level of the "universal intellect," is the second most important dignitary after the Imām in the spiritual hierarchy. The most important Pīrs were Pīr Shams (d. ca. mid-eighth/fourteenth century), Pīr Ṣadr al-Dīn (d. end eighth/fourteenth century), and Pīr Ḥasan Kābir al-Dīn (d. end ninth/fifteenth century). The Pīrs composed *Gināns* (mystical odes) which give an esoteric interpretation of the Qurʾān and contain moral and religious instructions leading to the *sat panth* ("true path" or *al-ṣirāṭ al-mustaqīm*). The *Gināns* are "anagogic" in nature because they can create a tapestry of multi-leveled meanings. According to Āghā Khān III (d. 1376/1957), those who rejected the Qur'ān of ʿAlī will remain ignorant of its real content until the judgment day (Āghā Khān III 1950: I, 63–4, guidance delivered on December 31, 1893). He describes the revealed book, the Qur'ān, as containing ten extra parts for which Pīr Ṣadr al-Dīn has given explanations in his *Ginān*s (Āghā Khān III 1950: I, 81, guidance delivered on July 1, 1899).

One of the major themes developed in the *Ginān*s is the mystical quest of spiritual knowledge through the reminiscence (*dhikr*) of the divine name. Many Qur'ānic verses (Q 29:44–5; 76:25–6; etc.) relate the importance of remembering the *logos* (divine word) in order to become closer to the One above all else (Steigerwald 1999: 175–96). Muḥammad is called the master (*guru*) of the word: he will guide each believer on the spiritual path (Imām Shāh 1972: 475; Ṣadr al-Dīn in *Collectanea* 1948: 114). The disciple is initiated into the knowledge of the *ism-i aʿẓām* ("supreme name"); in the *ginān* the equivalent technical word is *bol* or *nām* or *shabda* (Shacke and Moir 1992: 150). This quest has a Qur'ānic root: "But keep in remembrance the name of thy Lord and devote thyself to Him whole-heartedly" (Q 73:8).

> The true word (*sat shabda*) is our Master (*Guru*),
> The world does not recognize it.
> Reflect upon the true word (*sat shabda*)
> Utter *Pīr-Shāh* [Pīr = *ḥujjat al-Imām*, Shāh = Shīʿī Imām] frequently.
> (Pīr Shams 1985: 41)

Muḥammad, Fāṭima, Ḥasan, Ḥusayn, and ʿAlī are part of the "the five companions of the mantle," *panj-tan-i pāk*, in Shīʿī doctrine (Nanji 1985: 170–1). These luminous creatures were part of the initial act of divine creation. Before the physical creation, there was only God (*nārāyana*), the Originator, the Everlasting and above all Attributes. The unknowable mystery (*bāṭin*) wanted to manifest (*ẓāhir*) himself. After a while, his desire becomes a reality by originating the spiritual world of the *panj-tan-i pāk*: the light of ʿAlī, Muḥammad, Fāṭima, Ḥasan, and Ḥusayn. These five lights were the former *creatio ex-nihilo* which came out of the mouth of God (Nārāyana); this metaphor corresponds to the idea of the *kūn* of the verbal Qur'ānic command (*amr*) or word (*kalima*). The *panj-tan-i pāk* refers to the Qur'ānic *ahl al-bayt* (Q 33:33; 2:177). This Ginānic understanding goes beyond the apparent meanings of the Qur'ān and gives importance to the *ahl al-bayt* (Steigerwald 1987: 70–113).

The concept of light developed in the Qur'ān, more particularly in *sūrat al-nūr* (Q 24), was extensively commented on in Shīʿī literature. Hence the "blessed olive tree" of Q 24:35 symbolizes the Imām who is the source of light. Pīr Shams, in his *Garbī* (*Collectanea* 1948: 59), relates that the light of Imām will remain eternally present in the world. The Imām is manifest in all the spiritual levels to guide believers, but his real being is perceived differently according to each individual. This doctrine of "monorealism" previously existed in the Hindu Vaiṣnava tradition and was taken over by the Ismāʿīlī Pīrs and is associated with the necessity of the living Imām. The Imām's presence is symbolized by the sun (Imām Shāh 1972: 304, 353) that precedes the origin of humanity and will continue to exist until the end of time. As the sun is essential for the survival of all beings, the Imām is essential for the salvation of his disciples. And those "who recognize the Lord of the time acquire immortality" (*Collectanea* 1948: 65).

The Pīr must heal and shape the soul of his disciple and transmit to him the necessary *taʿlīm* ("teaching") to reach the mystical union. Every Pīr gives the *taʾwīl* of the Qurʾān in their *Ginān*s; thus, the esoteric truth can only be accessible through the Pīr, the holder of wisdom. The disciple is unable to unravel the true nature of the Imām alone; the Pīr is the link between the disciple and the Imām.

The Nizārī Pīrs presented Islam in a form that was attractive to Hindus. They tried to convey the spirit of Islam and explained its high ideals in familiar terms that would be understood by new converts from Hinduism. They presented Islam as the crowning phase of Hinduism; the Qurʾān was presented as the final Veda, completing previous revelations. In Ginānic tradition, the light of prophecy and the light of *imāma* must always be present in this world. The "light of Muḥammad" was transferred to Ḥasan b. ʿAlī and afterward through a specific line of Pīrs whereas the light of *Imāma* came from Abū Ṭālib. Pīr Ṣadr al-Dīn wrote in one of his *Ginān*s that those who possess the true knowledge of the Qurʾān (*Atharva-Veda*) know the "lord of the time" (*Imām al-zamān*) who is now unveiled (*Collectanea* 1948: 105). Sayyid Fatḥ ʿAlī Shāh in one of his *Ginān* wrote: "No one has the knowledge of the mystery of the Lord of the time, the Naklankī. Only those can recognize him who are guided by the Guru. Know the true Guru in the person of Muḥammad the Apostle of God" (*Collectanea* 1948: 111). Here Naklankī refers to Imām ʿAlī and all Imāms who will succeed until the day of resurrection.

Modern Exegetes

The current period started from the first Āghā Khān (Shāh Ḥasan ʿAlī, d. 1298/1881). Until recently, the Imāms were living in the Indian subcontinent, but they now have relocated to Europe. His Highness Prince Karīm Aghā Khān IV, the spiritual head of the Nizārī Ismāʿīlīs, today lives in France. During this period, the present Imām gives a spiritual exegesis of the Qurʾān suited for modern times. He mainly emphasizes an intellectual approach to the Qurʾān and favors the use of intellect (*ʿaql*) as a means to acquire knowledge.

Pīr Shihāb al-Dīn Shāh (d. 1302/1885), the son of the 47th Imām of the Nizārī Ismāʿīlīs Āghā Khān II (Shāh ʿAlī Shāh), also acknowledged the importance of the intellect. In his treatise *Risālat dar ḥaqīqat-i dīn* ("The True Meaning of Religion," he explains that in order to remain on the right path (*al-ṣirāṭ al-mustaqīm*) one must follow the intellect which has the capacity to discover the purpose of creation. Shihāb al-Dīn quotes some traditions: "O, Muḥammad, if not for thy sake, We would not have created this world," "If there were no ʿAlī, We would not have created thee (Muḥammad)." For Shihāb al-Dīn, the purpose of creation is to reveal to humanity both Muḥammad and ʿAlī. If the prophet did not proclaim the *walāya* of ʿAlī, his mission would have remained incomplete as it is clearly stated in the Qurʾān: "Apostle! Proclaim the (message) which has been sent to you from your Lord. If you do not, you will not have fulfilled and proclaimed His mission" (Q 5:70). Muḥammad was entrusted the outward dimension of religion while ʿAlī inherited its inward dimension (Shihāb al-Dīn Shāh 1947: 14–15, 23–4, 43). Concerning the Qur'ān, Pīr Shihāb al-Dīn wrote:

> Under ʿUthmān the authorities selected some portions, rejecting others. It would be too long to narrate this in detail. Then they seized by force all the other copies, and burnt them. Thus the knowledge of the original Qur'ān which was really left by the prophet, and which remains in the hands of his *ʿitrat*, or legitimate successors, was taken from the people. But these legitimate lieutenants of the prophet still remained. (Shihāb al-Dīn Shāh 1947: 63)

Thus, for Pīr Shihāb al-Dīn, the knowledge of the Qur'ān will always remain in the hands of the Imām of the time, who has to be physically present in this world.

The Imām Āghā Khān III (d. 1376/1957), in his *Memoirs*, gives some idea of his approach to the Qur'ān:

> To a certain extent I have found that the following verse of the Qur'ān (*sūrat al-nūr*, Q 24:35), so long as it is understood in a purely non-physical sense, has given assistance and understanding to myself and other Muslims. I must, however, warn all who read it not to allow their material critical outlook to break in with literal, verbal explanations of something that is symbolic and allegorical. (Āghā Khān III 1954: 172–3)

Āghā Khān III further expounds on how the faithful should approach the Qur'ān:

> Fortunately the Qur'ān has itself made this task easy, for it contains a number of verses which declare that Allāh speaks to man in allegory and parable. Thus the Qur'ān leaves the door open for all kinds of interpretations without any one interpreter being able to accuse another of being non-Muslim. A felicitous effect of this fundamental principle of Islam, that the Qur'ān is constantly open to allegorical interpretation, has been that our Holy Book has been able to guide and illuminate the thought of believers, century after century, in accordance with the conditions and limitations of intellectual apperception imposed by external influences in the worlds. It leads also to a greater charity among Muslims, for since there can be no cut-and-dried interpretation all schools of thought can unite in the prayer that the Almighty in His infinite mercy may forgive any mistaken interpretation of the faith whose cause is ignorance or misunderstanding. (Āghā Khān III 1954: 173)

Āghā Khān III proceeds further by explaining the task of the Shīʿī Imām who:

> is thus the Successor of the Prophet in his religious capacity; he is the man who must be obeyed and who dwells among those from whom he commands spiritual obedience. . . . The Shīʿites say that this authority is all-pervading and is concerned with spiritual matters also, that is transferred by inherited right to the Prophet's Successors of his blood. (Āghā Khān III 1954: 178–9)

Āghā Khān IV, the present living Imām, in a speech delivered at the Ismāʿīlī Centre (London) on October 19, 2003 at the opening session of "Word of God, Art of Man: The Qur'ān and its Creative Expressions," maintains a similar understanding of the Qur'ān as his grand-father (Āghā Khān III):

> The Holy Book continues to guide and illuminate the thought and conduct of Muslims belonging to different communities of interpretation and spiritual affiliation, from century to century, in diverse cultural environments. The Noble Qur'ān extends its principle of pluralism also to adherents of other faiths. It affirms that each has a direction and path to which they turn so that all should strive for good works, in the belief that, wheresoever they may be, Allāh will bring them together. . . . Scientific pursuits, philosophic inquiry and artistic endeavour are all seen as the response of the faithful to the recurring call of the Qur'ān to ponder the creation as a way to understand Allāh's benevolent majesty. As *Sūrat al-Baqara* proclaims: 'Wherever you turn, there is the face of Allāh'. Does not the Qur'ān challenge the artist, as much as the mystic, to go beyond the physical – the outward – so as to seek to unveil that which lies at the centre but gives life to the periphery? . . . The Qur'ān's is an inclusive vision of society that gives primacy to nobility of conduct. It speaks of differences of language and colour as a divine sign of mercy and a portent for people of knowledge to reflect upon. Ours is a time when knowledge and information are expanding at an accelerating and, perhaps, unsettling pace. There exists, therefore, an unprecedented capacity for improving the human condition. And yet, ills such as abject poverty and ignorance, and the conflicts these breed, continue to afflict the world. The Qur'ān addresses this challenge eloquently. The power of its message is reflected in its gracious disposition to differences of interpretation; its respect for other faiths and societies; its affirmation of the primacy of the intellect; its insistence that knowledge is worthy when it is used to serve Allāh's creation; and, above all, its emphasis on our common humanity. (Āghā Khān IV 2003: 2–3)

Thus for Āghā Khān IV, the Qur'ān, full of parables and allegories, allows for the freedom of interpretation which permits it to guide and illuminate Muslims living in different cultural environments. The Qur'ān invites Muslims to ponder creation in order to understand God. Hence it becomes a source of inspiration for many scientific, philosophic, and artistic inquiries. The holy book also inspires the development of ethical behavior, respect for other faiths, and the acquisition of knowledge to serve Allāh's creation.

Conclusion

The Ismāʿīlīs belong to the Shīʿī branch of Islām. The *imāma* is a cardinal principle of Shīʿī faith since it is only through the Imām that true knowledge can be obtained. The main principle of Shīʿī exegesis is based on the fact that the Qur'ān has an outer dimension (*ẓāhir*) and an inner dimension (*bāṭin*); its inner dimension has up to seven inner dimensions. Fāṭimid Ismāʿīlī theosophy preserves the equilibrium between the *ẓāhir* and the *bāṭin* while the Alamūt theosophy enhanced the value of *bāṭin* while considering *ẓāhir* as an essential first step in the initiation.

The Nizārī Ismāʿīlīs maintain, like the Shīʿites of the first four *hijrī* centuries, that ʿUthmān excised significant verses from the original Qur'ān. There are many differences between the Nizārī and the Mustaʿlī branches of Ismāʿīlism even if they share a common ground; these differences were minute at the beginning but they became deeper when the last Mustaʿlī Imām went into occultation (*ghayba*) in 495/1101. Following the occultation (*ghayba*) of their Imām, the Mustaʿlī Shīʿī community no longer had access to the direct guidance of their Imām, and aside from the ʿ*ulamāʾ* (religious scholars), their only source of guidance was the ʿUthmānic Qurʾān. Since there is no concept of *ghayba* in Nizārī Ismāʿīlism, they rely mainly on the living Imām to update the Qurʾān according to the times and to uncover its esoteric meanings.

Further reading

Corbin, Henry (1993) *History of Islamic Philosophy*, trans. P. Sherrard. Kegan Paul International, London.

Daftary, Farhad (1992) *The Ismāʿīlīs: Their History and Doctrines*. Cambridge University Press, Cambridge.

Engineer, Asghar Ali (1980) *The Bohras*. Vikas Publishing House, New Delhi.

Kassam, Tazim R. (1995) *Songs of Wisdom and Circles of Dance: Hymns of the Satpanth Ismāʿīlī Muslim Saint, Pīr Shams*. State University of New York Press, Albany.

Nanji, Azim (1978) *The Nizārī Ismāʿīlī Tradition in the Indo-Pakistan Subcontinent*. Caravan Books, New York.

Nanji, Azim (1985) Towards a hermeneutic of Qurʾānic and other narratives in Ismāʿīlī thought. In: Martin, R. C. (ed.) *Approaches to Islam in Religious Studies*. University of Arizona Press, Tucson, pp. 164–73.

Poonawala, Ismail (1988a) Ismāʿīlī *taʾwīl* of the Qurʾān. In Rippin, Andrew (ed.) *Approaches to the History of the Interpretation of the Qurʾān*. Oxford University Press, Oxford, pp. 199–222.

Poonawala, Ismail (1988b) An Ismāʿīlī treatise on the Iʿjāz al-Qurʾān. *Journal of the American Oriental Society* 108, 379–85.

Steigerwald, Diana (1996) The divine word (*kalima*) in Shahrastānī's *Majlis*. *Studies in Religion/Sciences Religieuses* 25, 335–52.

Walker, Paul (1993) *Early Philosophical Shiism: The Ismaili Neoplatonism of Abū Yaʿqūb al-Sijistānī*. Cambridge University Press, New York.

PART V

Application

CHAPTER 27

Exegetical Sciences

Jane Dammen McAuliffe

In the graduate program of any religious studies faculty in the Muslim world you will find students taking courses in something called "the sciences of the Qurʾān" (*ʿulūm al-Qurʾān*).[1] While that phrase sounds a bit strange to English-speaking ears, the field which these studies encompass has profound importance for Muslim belief and practice. Such classes cover the range of topics necessary for the development of an accurate and faithful understanding of the Qurʾān. Within the world of Muslim scholarship they are essential preparation for any credible teaching or research on the Qurʾān.

I have used the term "field" because the Qurʾānic sciences combine multiple subjects or disciplines and a full program of their study would involve serious work in all of the constitutive subfields (see McAuliffe 2002). While relatively few manage that, many students at Muslim universities are exposed to at least a general overview of the Qurʾānic sciences and publishers continually replenish their stock of relevant texts (Quṭb 1980; Ṣābūnī 1985; al-Ṣabbāgh 1986; al-Ṣāliḥ 1990; Abū Sinna 1995; ʿInāya 1996; Rūmī 2000). Graduate students pursue more focused studies and academic research in this field continues to flourish. To understand how this curriculum, and its associated subject, evolved requires looking back at least five centuries and initiating an effort in retrospective reconstruction.

Starting with Summation

Two works represent the classical culmination of this process of discipline building. The first of these was written in the late fourteenth century, the other about a hundred years later. The earlier text is Badr al-Dīn al-Zarkashī's (d. 794/1392; see *EI2* 2004: "al-Zarkashī") *al-Burhān fī ʿulūm al-Qurʾān* ("The Proof in the Qurʾānic Sciences"), while the later is Jalāl al-Dīn al-Suyūṭī's (d. 911/1505) *al-Itqān fī ʿulūm al-Qurʾān* ("The Perfection in the Qurʾānic Sciences"). Both are the primary citations in any contemporary textbook on this topic. The tale that ties them together proves that in late fifteenth-century Egypt academic competition was alive and well.

The connection between these two works begins with a story of academic discovery and of an author's discomfiture at seeing his own efforts surpassed. As al-Suyūṭī tells this tale in the first pages of his *Itqān*, it is easy to recognize the mixed feelings that such a discovery would prompt in any scholar. Using a formulaic introductory format, al-Suyūṭī begins the *Itqān* with a lament for the lack of any work on the Qur'ānic sciences that could compare with those available for the sciences of *ḥadīth*. With a dismissive mention of some prior efforts, he describes his own first attempt to fill this void. In 872/1467, while still a very young man, al-Suyūṭī tells us that he completed a book entitled *al-Taḥbīr fī ʿulūm al-Qur'ān*. He then provides its table of contents, numbering 102 chapters. Only after its completion, al-Suyūṭī continues, and while still enjoying a justifiable pride in his considerable accomplishment, did he learn of the existence of an earlier and more comprehensive work, that of al-Zarkashī.

Accordingly, he cites the full table of contents for the *Burhān*, expresses his delight at discovering it and promptly decides to improve upon al-Zarkashī's work. Thus is born the *Itqān*, which al-Suyūṭī promises will be better organized than its predecessor, with additional material "to please its listeners" (al-Suyūṭī 1967: I, 14).[2] A comparison of the two works reveals that at some points al-Suyūṭī acknowledges his dependence upon his predecessor and at others he draws from it without explicit acknowledgment. For present purposes, however, the links are less important than the structure and taxonomy that each of these summations conveys. (For detailed treatments of the relation between these two works see Nolin 1968; Ḥaydar 1999.)

Comparing Two Compendia

Jalāl al-Dīn al-Suyūṭī was among the most prolific scholars that Egypt has ever produced (his list of titles numbers more than 600; for the difficulties involved in establishing a secure account of all works see Sartain 1975). Although his family claimed roots in Persia and Mesopotamia, by the time of his birth, they were settled in Egypt, especially Assiut/Asyūṭ. Al-Suyūṭī himself was born and educated in Cairo and lived most of his life during the final century of Mamlūk rule.[3] Among his extant works is an extended autobiography, *al-Taḥadduth bi niʿmat Allāh*, that details, in the usual fashion, information about his studies, travels, teaching positions and other official posts (Sartain 1975; for a literary study of this autobiography see Brustad 1997). It also provides a list of his writings, which he categorizes in an idiosyncratic fashion. He classifies some of his works by length, others by quality. For example, he lists eighteen works which he deems to be unique in the quality of their scholarship and another fifty which are important but not unparalleled.[4] He also cites forty of his earlier writings that he now considers insufficient and another eighty-three that he started but, for lack of sustained interest, never completed (Sartain 1975: 46–7).

Al-Suyūṭī's predecessor, al-Zarkashī, was also an Egyptian by birth although his family's origins were Turkish. His was not a scholarly pedigree and his designation as al-Zarkashī comes from the craft of brocade embroidery (*zarkasha*), a trade in which his father may have trained him. Nevertheless, he clearly managed to assimilate an extraordinary knowledge of the Qur'ān and its relevant scholarly disciplines. Ibn al-ʿImād counts his principal teachers as Jamāl al-Dīn al-Asnawī (d. 772/1370), Sirāj al-Dīn al-Bulqīnī (d. 805/1403) and Shihāb al-Dīn al-Adhraʿī (d. 783/1381) and records his educational travels to Damascus, where he studied with Ibn Kathīr (d. 774/1373), and Aleppo. As a professional scholar, he spent his life teaching, delivering legal judgments and writing on a wide variety of topics (ʿAbd al-Ḥayy b. ʿImād 1966: V, 335). His biographers depict him as so completely engrossed in his work that the conduct of his worldly affairs was left to relatives. According to one account, he only left his house to visit the book market. There he would spend the day perusing one volume after another, taking notes to use in his writings and leaving the poor bookseller with no sale to his credit (Ibn Ḥajar 1929–32: III, 398).

Turning now to the summative works of these two scholars, it is important to note that the *Itqān* stands first on al-Suyūṭī's list of the writings on which he most prides himself. A source of that pride is surely the significant advance that he made in the *Itqān* over the work of his esteemed predecessor al-Zarkashī in matters of arrangement and classification. Comparing the structure of the *Itqān* and the *Burhān* demonstrates that the former has achieved a decided improvement in organization. Although the *Itqān* is arranged in eighty consecutive chapters (*anwāʿ*, s. *nawʿ*) with no indication of thematic groupings, it is not too difficult to discern al-Suyūṭī's organizational method. He uses what I would call an increasingly telescopic perspective, beginning with the macro and then moving in closer and closer.[5] The *Itqān* starts with the fact and process of revelation, taking the Qurʾānic event as a whole in order to analyze it both chronologically and contextually (chapters 1–16). The opening chapter, which explores the fundamental temporal-spatial categories of Meccan and Medinan, is followed by those that categorize passages revealed during the day and during the night, during the summer and during the winter, while Muḥammad was settled or on a journey or in bed.

Al-Suyūṭī then moves to a series of chapters (17–27) that deal with the collection and transmission of the Qurʾān, providing precise detail about the relative reliability of particular forms of conveyance. Having devoted more than a third of his eighty chapters to these macro matters, al-Suyūṭī next turns to the text itself, examining it from four interrelated perspectives: articulation (28–35), lexicology and morphology (36–42), rhetoric (43–58) and textual structure (59–63). The group of chapters on articulation covers the technical specifics of Qurʾānic recitation (*tajwīd*), such as points of pause and resumption (*waqf* and *ibtidāʾ*), forms of consonantal assimilation (*idghām*, *ikhfāʾ* and *iqlāb*) and vowel lengthening or shortening (*madd* and *qasr*). The chapters on lexicology and morphology delve into issues of polysemy and linguistic provenance. For example, two sequential chapters (37 and 38) treat Qurʾānic lexemes that do not occur in the language of the Ḥijāzī Arabs and those that derive from languages other than Arabic.

A long segment that can be broadly described as devoted to the rhetoric of the Qurʾān offers an extended set of semantic binaries. These constitute the most characteristic feature of *ʿulūm al-Qurʾān*, creating an exegetical taxonomy of multiple, overlapping categorizations. Although the precise significance of several of these terms is a matter of debate, I offer a brief mention of the most important combinations: clear and obscure (*muḥkam wa-mutashābih*), inversion of the natural word order (*taqdīm wa-taʾkhīr*), general and particular (*ʿāmm wa khāṣṣ*), synoptic and explicated (*mujmal wa-mubayyana*), abrogating and abrogated (*nāsikh wa mansūkh*), qualified/restricted and unqualified/unrestricted (*muṭlaq wa muqayyad*), explicit and implicit (*manṭūq wa mafhūm*), literal and figurative (*ḥaqīqa wa-majāz*), comparison and metaphor (*tashbīh wa istiʿāra*), metonymy and allusion (*kināya wa taʿrīḍ*), concision and prolixity (*ījāz wa iṭnāb*), informative and performative (*khabar wa inshāʾ*). The last grouping among the four forms of textual dynamics that I have drawn from the *Itqān* is that of textual structure. Here al-Suyūṭī details the beginnings and endings of the *sūras*, the divisions between verses and the connection (*munāsaba*) to be found between verses and between *sūras*.

Before the final four chapters (77–80) that discuss Qurʾānic commentary and commentators, al-Suyūṭī includes thirteen chapters that are not easily configured as a group (64–76). I am tempted to view this as a kind of expanding appendix to the rest of his work, a place to situate topics that did not fall easily into the groups just discussed. This miscellany ranges from the inimitability (*iʿjāz*) of the Qurʾān to its orthography (*marsūm al-khaṭṭ*). Some chapters detail the excellent qualities (*faḍāʾil*) of the Qurʾān while others treat particular genres, such as parables (*amthāl*), oaths (*aqsām*) and passages of debate or dialectic (*jadal*).

The textual architecture that I have drawn from the *Itqān* can be graphed as shown in Figure 27.1

The significance of al-Suyūṭī's organizational accomplishment can be better understood when compared to the predecessor text which he extolled in his introduction, that is, al-Zarkashī's *Burhān*. While most of the same individual topics are treated in this earlier work, no equivalent textual architecture can be discerned. Al-Zarkashī's work, which contains forty-seven chapters to al-Suyūṭī's eighty, does include some sequential groupings. For example, chapters 16–20 cover much of what al-Suyūṭī surveys in the chapters I have described as "lexicology and morphology." Another discernible grouping deals with some of the matters contained in those sections of al-Suyūṭī that I have subtitled as "rhetoric." But, for the most part, the *Burhān* presents a succession of forty-seven topics with little concern for their ordering or their connection. Of course, it should be noted that chapter titles do not constitute an automatic equivalence between the two works. In other words, some topics to which al-Suyūṭī devotes a separate section are treated as a subcategory by al-Zarkashī and vice versa.

Selecting Some Samples

While comparison of the structures of these two summative works in the sciences of the Qurʾān provides some sense of the major topics addressed in this discipline, the real flavor of the enterprise is found in the details. The range of subtopics is vast but a small selection may offer some representative examples.

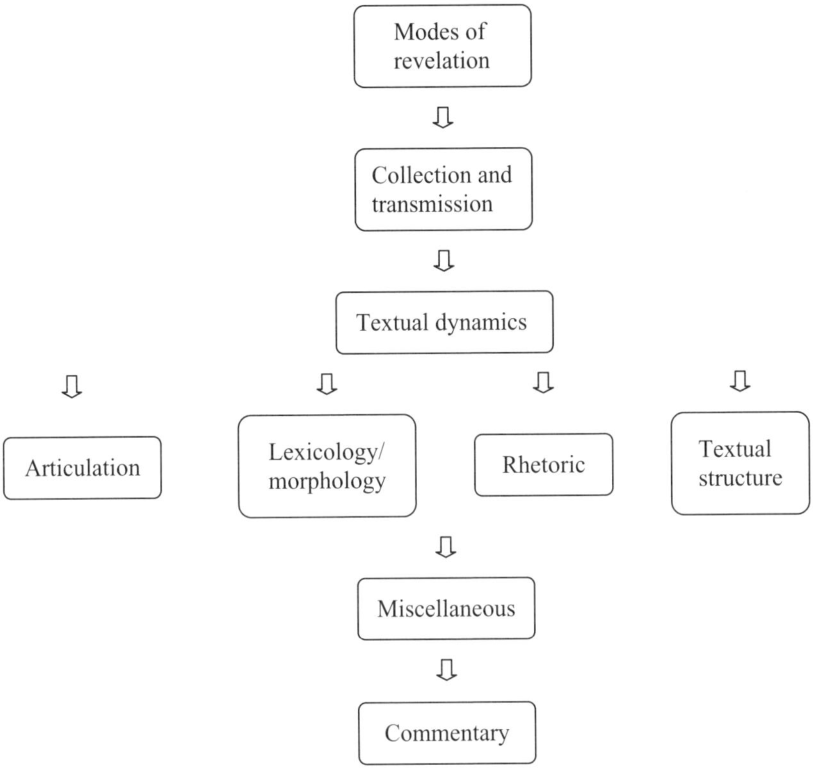

Figure 27.1 Al-Suyūṭī's textual architecture

Distributed revelation

Among al-Suyūṭī's initial sections, those that treat the modes of revelation, there is a chapter entitled "What was revealed to some of the [earlier] prophets and what was revealed to no one before the prophet [Muḥammad]." These pages of the *Itqān* collect a number of *ḥadīth*, many of which are attributed to Ibn ʿAbbās (d. 68/687), a much younger cousin of Muḥammad, who is commonly credited with a formative role in the nascent exegetical tradition. Summarizing the *ḥadīth* relevant to the second half of the chapter's title, al-Suyūṭī counts the first *sūra* (*al-Fātiḥa*), Q 2:255 (which is known as the "Throne verse") and the final verses of the second *sūra* as those revealed only to Muḥammad. The supporting *ḥadīth* that al-Suyūṭī cites differ about whether the last two or the last three verses of the second *sūra* are to be included. They also place an additional verse in the category. Al-Suyūṭī quotes Abū ʾl-Qāsim al-Ṭabarānī's (d. 360/971) conveyance of a prophetic statement transmitted by Ibn ʿAbbās, "For times of calamity my community has been given something which no other community has been given: 'To God we belong and to him will we return' (Q 2:156)" (al-Suyūṭī

1967: I, 112). From Abū ʿUbayd al-Qāsim's (d. 224/838) *Faḍāʾil al-Qurʾān*, al-Suyūṭī quotes a statement about verses that were given to Muḥammad but not to Moses and a verse that was given to Moses but not Muḥammad. The latter is: "O God, do not let Satan enter our hearts and free us from him so that to you belong the sovereignty, the authority, the power, the dominion, the praise, the earth, the heaven, time everlasting, forever and ever, amen, amen."

Turning to those Qurʾānic verses that were also revealed to earlier prophets, the cited *ḥadīth* center primarily on Q 87 and Q 53, attesting that these, or their equivalent, could be found in the scriptures (*ṣuḥuf*) of Abraham and Moses. The Qurʾānic warrant for this claim is itself drawn from Q 87:18: "This truly is in the earlier scriptures (*al-ṣuḥuf al-ūlā*)" (al-Suyūṭī 1967: I, 113–14). Additional citations point to passages from Q 9, Q 23, Q 33, and Q 70. More specifically, a connection is made between the Torah (*Tawrāt*) and several *sūras* of the Qurʾān (Q 6, Q 11 and Q 17). A *ḥadīth* on the authority of Kaʿb al-Aḥbar (d. 32/652–3), drawn from Ibn al-Ḍurays' (d. 294/906) *Faḍāʾil al-Qurʾān*, states that the Torah begins with the initial verses of Q 6, "Praise God who created the heavens and the earth and made the darknesses and light, etc." – a phrase that is clearly reminiscent of the creation narratives in Genesis – and ends with the final verse of Q 17, "Praise God who does not beget offspring and has no partner in dominion nor any protector because of weakness, so exalt him with glorification." Variants of this *ḥadīth* associate the Torah's beginning with Q 6:151–65 and its conclusion with Q 11:123 (al-Suyūṭī 1967: I, 114).

Counts and curiosities

Moving from contextual to textual considerations, there is a chapter in al-Zarkashī's *Burhān* which furnishes a fascinating example of the degree of painstaking scrutiny to which classical scholars of the Qurʾān subjected the text. Chapter 14 deals with *sūra* names and enumerations. One part of this discussion devotes itself to numbering the *sūras*, verses, words, and letters of the Qurʾān. The totals vary somewhat for rather complicated reasons but the entire effort is framed with an attractive narrative. According to this story, the renowned Umayyad governor, al-Ḥajjāj b. Yūsuf (d. 95/714), gathered the Qurʾān reciters of Baṣra and chose several from among them, including al-Ḥasan al-Baṣrī (d. 110/728), Abū ʾl-ʿĀliya (d. 90/708–9), Naṣr b. ʿĀṣim (d. 89/707), ʿĀṣim al-Jaḥdarī (d. 128/745) and Mālik b. Dīnār (d. 131/748). He then asked those selected to tally the letters of the Qurʾān and that task took them four months, counting with corns of barley. Their final reckoning was: 323,015 letters and 77,439 words (al-Zarkashī 1959: I, 249). Other accounts then go on to supply verse totals that vary from 6104 to 6236, as well as calculations for the longest *sūra* (Q 2), the longest verse (Q 2:282 at 128 words), the shortest verse (either Q 89:1 or Q 93:1, each a verse of a single word) and even the longest word (*faʾsqaynākumūhu* in Q 15:22; al-Zarkashī 1959: I, 252).

These enumerations are immediately followed by a section that describes the eight halves into which the Qurʾān can be divided. If by *sūras*, the division falls between Q 57 and Q 58; if by verses, between Q 17:45 and Q 17:46; if by words, between the final word in Q 22:20 and the first in Q 22:21; and if by letters, between the first two consonants of the word *nukran* in Q 18:74 (al-Zarkashī 1959: I, 253). Then al-Zarkashī embarked upon a discussion which can only be described as "Qur'ānic *Jeopardy*," a series of questions and answers such as: How many times does the expression "only to cause strife" (*illā ghurūran*) occur in the Qur'ān? How many verses begin with the letter *shīn*? How many end with it? What is the longest sequentially voweled segment? Additional details tell us that (1) in one *sūra* of the Qur'ān, Q 58, every verse contains the divine name; (2) there is a verse, Q 2:282, that has thirty-three *mīms*; (3) there is a *sūra* of over one hundred verses, Q 12, that makes no mention of either heaven or hell; (4) the letter *kāf* never occurs successively in a word without an intervening letter except in Q 2:200 and Q 5:42 (al-Zarkashī 1959: I, 253–5).

Repeal and revocation

Moving now to a more consequential topic among the Qur'ānic sciences, one with legal implications, both al-Zarkashī and al-Suyūṭī devote substantial attention in their respective works to the subject of Qur'ānic abrogation. In brief, the doctrine of abrogation asserts that the legal force of some Qur'ānic verses (and some *ḥadīth*) has been replaced by that of others (Burton 1977 and 2001; Rippin 1984; Powers 1988). Treatment of the topic by these two authors is interesting in itself but also offers a good example of the ways in which al-Suyūṭī appropriated material virtually wholesale from al-Zarkashī.

Both of their respective chapters begin with a list of earlier authors who have written on this topic and then characterize the subject of abrogation as utterly indispensable for anyone who would attempt interpretation of the Qur'ān (al-Zarkashī 1959: I, 28f.; al-Suyūṭī 1967: III, 59f.). Al-Suyūṭī systematically tackles such matters as (1) the different meanings of the term "abrogation" (*naskh*), (2) the question of whether the Qur'ān can be abrogated only by the Qur'ān or whether it can also be abrogated by the sunna (i.e., *ḥadīth*), (3) the kinds of Qur'ānic verses that are capable of abrogating or being abrogated and (4) different forms of abrogation. Given the penchant for categorization that these summative works display, it is not surprising to find al-Suyūṭī dividing all 114 *sūras* of the Qur'ān into four lists: (1) those that contain neither abrogating not abrogated verses – these number forty-three, (2) those that contain both – twenty-five, (3) those with only abrogating verses – six, and (4) those with only abrogated verses – forty. Further definitions and distinctions precede a listing of abrogated verses. A few samples should provide some sense of how this aspect of Qur'ānic study operates.

In some cases, such as that of Q 8:65, a verse is abrogated by a following verse in the same *sūra*. Whereas Q 8:65 urges believers to fight with the promise that twenty steadfast warriors will overcome a force of two hundred, Q 8:66 modifies the prediction to more realistic odds, that is, two to one. In another example, Q 9:41 urges believers to go forth to war whether they are physically and financially fit to do so or not. (The Arabic terms used to designate these states are "light" and "heavy," respectively.) Al-Suyūṭī then cites several verses, including Q 48:17, Q 9:91 and Q 9:122, that qualify the burden of this divine command. Finally, in a case of marriage legislation, Q 24:3

and its pronouncement that an adulterer can only marry an adultress is abrogated by Q 24:32 which offers the more general directive to marry those who are without spouses (al-Suyūṭī 1967: III, 66–8).

Cleanliness and comportment

The rules and etiquette of reciting and handling the Qur'ān provide yet another topic to which both al-Zarkashī and al-Suyūṭī devote long and detailed chapters. The subjects covered include such mundane matters as securing a clean place for recitation – ideally a mosque – and sitting in a quiet, dignified manner with head bowed facing the *qibla*. To emphasize the importance of a respectful posture al-Zarkashī cites a story about the companion Saʿīd b. al-Musayyib al-Makhzūmī (d. 94/713) who was asked, while stretched out in a reclining position, about a certain *ḥadīth*. He immediately sat up and exclaimed, "I abhor relating the *ḥadīth* of God's messenger while reclining and even more so in the case of God's speech" (al-Zarkashī 1959: I, 459). The preference for ritual ablution (*al-wuḍūʾ*) before recitation is discussed as well as the degree of ritual impurity that would preclude reciting or even touching the Qur'ān. A *ḥadīth* attributed to ʿAlī b. Abī Ṭālib even recommends oral hygiene as an additional preparation of the body that will honor God, "Indeed your mouths are pathways for the Qur'ān so use a tooth stick (*siwāk*) to make them pleasing" (al-Suyūṭī 1967: I, 296).

Both works deal with the many prescriptions and proscriptions that a session of recitation entails, such as: (1) the importance of forming the proper intention (*niyya*) and of avoiding all carelessness in recitation, (2) the commendability of reciting the Qur'ān aloud, (3) the prayer formulas with which each segment of recitation should commence, (4) the disrespect evidenced by interrupting recitation to engage in conversation, (5) the verses whose recitation is to be accompanied by physical prostration.

One interesting question that both al-Zarkashī and al-Suyūṭī raise in their respective chapters on the "etiquette" of Qur'ān recitation is whether it is better to recite the Qur'ān from memory or by looking at the written text (*muṣḥaf*). Given the importance attached to memorization of the Qur'ān and the respect accorded to those who accomplish it, the response to this question would seem obvious. Yet both authors come down strongly in favor of recitation from the *muṣḥaf*. Al-Zarkashī provides the longer treatment of this issue – it is a topic on which al-Suyūṭī acknowledges his predecessor directly – and cites a number of authorities to support his view, such as Abū Ḥāmid Muḥammad al-Ghazālī (d. 505/1111) and Muḥyī al-Dīn b. Sharaf al-Nawawī al-Shāfiʿī (d. 676/1277; author of *Kitāb al-tibyān fī ādāb ḥamalat al-Qurʾān*). The primary reason provided for this preference understands looking at the *muṣḥaf* to be an act of veneration (*ʿibāda*), one that ranks with other such acts like looking at the Kaʿba and gazing upon the faces of one's parents. He includes statements from Muḥammad that credit recitation from the *muṣḥaf* as meriting twice the divine reward that recitation from memory secures and the same idea of doubling is captured in yet another rationale: since two parts of the body are used, the mouth and the eyes, the greater effort warrants the greater reward. Respect for the physical text seems to underlie an additional reason given: "Anyone who possesses a copy of the Qur'ān should recite short verses from it every day so as not to leave it unused" (al-Zarkashī 1959: I, 463).

The *Burhān* and the *Itqān* both record the competing view, that recitation is best done from memory, but with attribution to only a single source, Abū Muḥammad b. ʿAbd al-Salām's (d. 660/1262) *Amālī*. The reason given captures a key element of Qur'ānic practice: meditative reflection (*tadabbur*). Citing Q 38:29, "so that you may reflect upon its verses," as his proof text, Ibn ʿAbd al-Salām insists that this is best accomplished when one's eyes are not engaged. Both al-Zarkashī and al-Suyūṭī, however, quote al-Nawawī who allows for the possibility that this may vary with individuals. What is important is this reflective presence to the divine word, whether that is achieved with eyes on the text or with eyes unengaged (al-Zarkashī 1959: I, 468; al-Suyūṭī 1967: I, 305).

Ranking revelation

As a final entrant in this selection of subjects that fall within the field of the Qur'ānic sciences, I turn to a topic that raises an interesting theological question, and one that generated considerable discussion and disagreement. This is the question of whether some parts of the Qur'ān are superior to others. Both authors begin their respective chapters on this subject with the views of those who would argue that the inquiry itself is ridiculous – if the entire Qur'ān is God's speech how can some parts of it be considered better than other parts? Against this argument, however, stand the hundreds of *ḥadīth* that speak to the merits and distinction of particular verses and *sūras* (al-Zarkashī 1959: I, 438–9; al-Suyūṭī 1967: IV, 117–18). Ranged in defense of this latter position are such well-known figures as al-Ghazālī – his *Jawāhir al-Qur'ān* ("Jewels of the Qur'ān") is an important source on this topic, one from which both al-Zarkashī and al-Suyūṭī quote extensively – the Khurāsānī traditionist, Isḥāq b. Rāhwayh (d. 238/853), as well as the Andalusian exegetes, Abū Bakr Muḥammad b. al-ʿArabī (d. 543/1148), and Abū ʿAbd Allāh Muḥammad al-Qurṭubī (d. 671/1272).

Representations of the argument center on matters of content and form or semantics and rhetoric. An often cited example is the contrast between Q 112:1, "Say, 'He is God, One'," and Q 111:1, "Perish the hands of Abū Lahab and perish he." Considered from the perspective of content these two verses pit an uncompromising statement of God's unicity against an especially vehement curse and many would contend that any discourse about God is inherently superior to any other discourse, particularly a curse. Seen, however, from a formal perspective, those who specialize in Qur'ānic rhetorics (*ʿilm al-bayān*) could argue that Q 111:1 is a perfectly constructed curse, just as Q 112:1 is a perfectly constructed statement of God's unicity and uniqueness (al-Zarkashī 1959: I, 440).

Among the most frequently lauded *sūras* are Q 1 (*sūrat al-fātiḥa*), Q 112 and Q 36. An example of the kinds of statements cited would be that by al-Ḥasan al-Baṣrī on the first *sūra*: "God put all the knowledge found in previous [holy] books into the Qur'ān; then he put all the knowledge in the Qur'ān into *sūrat al-fātiḥa*. So whoever knows its interpretation is like one who knows the interpretation of all the revealed books" (al-

Suyūṭī 1967: IV, 120). Individual verses are also noted, especially Q 2:255, the "Throne verse" (*āyat al-kursī*) for its proclamation that God's "throne extends over the heavens and the earth." Both al-Zarkashī and al-Suyūṭī raise the question of whether this verse is superior to Q 112 and Ibn al-ʿArabī's negative response is quoted. That response is built on two premises: (1) *sūras* are more significant than verses and (2) Q 112 managed to convey the entire teaching of God's unicity in but fifteen words while it took fifty for Q 2:255 to do so (al-Zarkashī 1959: I, 42; al-Suyūṭī 1967: IV, 122).

Al-Zarkashī concludes his chapter on this topic with statements about those Qur'ānic verses that are most hope-inspiring and those that are most fear-inspiring. Al-Suyūṭī takes this over but creates a new chapter for it. While the final quarter of his chapter replicates some of the *Burhān*'s treatment of what I have earlier called "Qur'ānic *Jeopardy*," the earlier sections offer such statements as this one from Muḥammad:

> Truly the mightiest verse in the Qur'ān is "There is no God but he, the Living, the Sustainer, etc. (Q 2:255)," the most justice-assuring verse in the Qur'ān is "Truly God commands justice and doing good, etc. (Q 16:90)," the most fear-inspiring verse[s] in the Qur'ān is "Whoever does an atom's weight of good will see it and whoever does an atom's weight of evil will see it (Q 99:7–8)," and the most hope-inspiring verse in the Qur'ān is "Say, O my worshippers who have committed excesses against themselves, do not despair of God's mercy, etc. (Q 39:53)" (al-Suyūṭī 1967: IV, 129; al-Suyūṭī cites this from Abū Dharr al-Haraqī's [d. 435/1044] *Faḍā'il al-Qur'ān*).

Al-Suyūṭī then provides fifteen entrants, drawn from a wide variety of sources, in the category of most hope-inspiring verse: Q 39:53; 2:260; 93:5; 4:48; 24:22; 9:102; 46:35; 13:6; 90:15–16; 17:84; 34:17; 20:48; 42:30; 8:38 and 2:282 (al-Suyūṭī 1967: IV, 129–31). The last-mentioned, the "verse of the debt" (*āyat al-dayn*) requires some explanation because rather than being primarily a brief reminder of God's mercy, it is a long verse about both the necessity and the procedure for recording financial obligations. What connects it to the idea of "hope" is the analogy between the divine diligence in assisting humans with their worldly goods and the great care that God exercises in forgiving them their failings (al-Suyūṭī 1967: IV, 131).

This brief discussion of but a few of the topics in the *Itqān*'s eighty chapters – and their counterparts in the *Burhān* – amounts to just a dip into the vast ocean of the Qur'ānic sciences. It does not begin to address subjects that consumed large portions of these two works, particularly those whose comprehension requires a knowledge of the Arabic language. There are carefully detailed treatments of matters such as the many phonetic variations necessary for the proper recitation of the Qur'ān, the rules for its correct representation and orthography, and the accepted range of its variant readings (*qirā'āt*). Exhaustive examinations of the Qur'ānic lexicon catalogue words of non-Arabic origin, those that are rare and obscure (*gharīb*) and those that carry multiple meanings (*wujūh wa naẓā'ir*). The doctrine of the inimitability of the Qur'ān, which is largely constructed on assertions of its rhetorical superiority, results in minute analysis of all contributing elements of Qur'ānic "eloquence" (*balāgha*). Al-Zarkashī devotes almost one-half of his *Burhān* to the many facets of rhetorical classification.

Seeking the Sources

While studying these two summative works – the two *summas* of the Qur'ānic sciences – affords a convenient entry to this vast and complex discipline, it carries the accompanying disadvantage of stepping in midstream, minus the perspective formed by a knowledge of genesis and historical development. All compendia build upon earlier efforts. So it is worth asking how and when the individual topics that eventually constituted the Qur'ānic sciences emerged. Among the questions that a more extensive treatment of this subject – one beyond the scope of this chapter – could explore are: What were some of the formative early efforts and investigations? How did the various, separate subjects within the larger discipline of the Qur'ānic sciences begin to connect? Is it possible to define a point at which the Qur'ānic sciences coalesce as a distinct discipline?

In his citation of sources, al-Suyūṭī himself provides plenty of leads. Most chapters of the *Itqān* begin with a bibliographic nod to some of those who had previously treated a particular topic and with a survey of earlier scholarly opinion about it. Many of al-Suyūṭī's sources themselves represent earlier efforts to consolidate elements of this emerging discipline. Retrospective reconstruction must take note of such works but must also push beyond them to the initial stages of all the sub-topical elaboration that eventually coalesced to form the overarching discipline of the Qur'ānic sciences. Clearly interpretation and study of the Qur'ān were co-extensive with its promulgation. For example, the early works on the life of the Prophet and on the initial expeditions and military campaigns (*sīra* and *maghāzī*) offered material pertinent to such subtopics as "occasions of revelation" (*asbāb al-nuzūl*), the designation of *sūras* and verses as Meccan or Medinan, abrogating and abrogated passages and the interpretation of the Qur'ān. (For relevant titles see *EI2* 2004: "Maghāzī" and "Sīra".)

Ḥadīth works, especially the Sunnī and Shī'ī canonical collections, are another early source for *'ulūm al-Qur'ān*. The *Ṣaḥīḥ*s of both al-Bukhārī and Muslim contain chapters on the interpretation (*tafsīr*) of the Qur'ān and on its "excellences" (*faḍā'il*). The other Sunnī collections, Abū Dāwūd, Ibn Māja, al-Tirmidhī and al-Nisā'ī, are also significant sources, as is the tenth-century compilation by the Shī'ī scholar al-Kulaynī. An additional source that pre-dates the canonical collections is 'Abd al-Razzāq al-Ṣan'ānī's (d. 211/827) *al-Muṣannaf*. The *faḍā'il* chapters or sections of these collections themselves combine aspects of the Qur'ānic sciences that would eventually receive individual treatment by later authors or be catalogued separately by al-Zarkashī and al-Suyūṭī (Afsaruddin 2002).

Jurisprudence and the formation of legal hermeneutics represent another emerging Islamic discipline that contributed to the classical elaboration of the Qur'ānic sciences. In his seminal legal treatise, *al-Risāla*, Muḥammad b. Idrīs al-Shāfi'ī (d. 204/820) contends, for example, that the Qur'ān contains nothing that is not pure Arabic, offering many Qur'ānic citations to buttress his argument (al-Shāfi'ī 1979: 41–53). He speaks of those verses that have been abrogated by others, using the example of Q 73:1–4 having been abrogated by Q 73:20 (al-Shāfi'ī 1979: 113–17), and explains how verses of general applicability differ from those that are more circumscribed (*al-'amm wa'l-khaṣṣ*; al-Shāfiʿī 1979: 53–62). To emphasize his expertise in the Qurʾānic sciences, al-Shāfiʿī's biographer recounts his interrogation by the caliph, Hārūn al-Rashīd. When asked by the caliph, "What do you know about the Book of God," al-Shāfiʿī responded with a counter-question: "About what area of knowledge [i.e. "science"] do you ask, O Commander of the Faithful?" He then proceeds to list most of the sub-topics that have already been mentioned in this chapter as the constitutive elements of the Qurʾānic sciences (al-Bayhaqī 1970: I, 131–2).

The emerging sciences of lexicography and grammar also contribute important foundational works to the developing Qurʾānic sciences and are among the sources on which the summative works of al-Zarkashī and al-Suyūṭī draw. Aspects of lexical and grammatical analysis are captured in such early works as Abū ʿUbayda's (d. 210/825) on the literary expression of the Qurʾān (*Majāz al-Qurʾān*), Ibn Qutayba's (d. 276/889) on the interpretation of difficult words and passages (*Taʾwīl mushkil al-Qurʾān*) and the work by al-Naḥḥas (d. 338/950) on the Qurʾān's morphology and grammar (*Iʿrāb al-Qurʾān*).

The final contributing category, and one that proves to be a very fruitful source, is that of exegetical works themselves, particularly their introductions (McAuliffe 1988; Markaz al-Thaqāfa waʾl-Maʿārif al-Qurʾāniyya 1995–7). An important work on the early development of Arabic grammar notes that "*in nuce* the early commentaries contain all elements found in later commentaries but what is more, they also contain the material which at a later stage became a specialized field in different Islamic sciences" (Versteegh 1993: 92). In his *Irshād*, Yāqūt b. ʿAbd Allāh al-Ḥamawī (d. 626/1229), citing Abū Bakr b. Kāmil (d. 350/961), presents a succinct description and appreciation of the most important Qurʾān commentary of the early classical period, Abū Jaʿfar b. Jarīr al-Ṭabarī's (d. 310/923) *Jāmiʿ al-bayān ʿan taʾwīl āy al-Qurʾān*.[6] Particular note is made of the "introductory topics" (*muqaddimāt*) with which this exegete prefaced his magnum opus. These include such matters as comparative lexicography/dialectology, the various aspects or modes of interpreting (*wujūh al-taʾwīl*), and *ḥadīth* conveying Muḥammad's statement about the seven *aḥruf*, a much contested term that has been interpreted to mean such diverse phenomena as dialectical differences in the Arabic of the classical period or levels of interpretative signification. Yāqūt goes on to mention additional matters that al-Ṭabarī's introduction treats: transmitted accounts that proscribe interpretation based on unformed personal opinion (*al-tafsīr biʾl-raʾy*), the praise or censure of particular early exegetes, the interpretation of the names of the Qurʾān, of its *sūras* and verses, of the prayer formulas that accompany its recitation, etc. (Yāqūt 1907–27: VI, 439–41).

But al-Ṭabarī's *Jāmiʿ al-bayān* is itself a summative work, one that attempts a comprehensive collation of earlier exegetical efforts.[7] Moving behind al-Ṭabarī, it is possible to find yet earlier examples of *tafsīr* introductions that treat topics that will eventually coalesce into the Qurʾānic sciences. For instance, the Khūrāsānī scholar, Muqātil b. Sulaymān (d. 150/767), deals in two parts of his exegetical introduction with the "modes" or "aspects" (*awjuh*) of the Qurʾān. First he cites the statement: "The Qurʾān was revealed according to five modes (*awjuh*), its command, its prohibition, its promise, its threat and the tales of ancient peoples" (Muqātil b. Sulaymān 1989: I, 26; see editor's first note on this same page where he indicates that one of the manuscripts lacks this introduction). Paul Nwyia (1970: 67–8) recognized within these five modes three fundamental modalities. The first pair, command and prohibition, represent the realm of literal exegesis while the second, promise and threat, raises eschatological concerns. Finally, the tales of ancient peoples, understood not simply as past history but as instances of divine intervention accomplished through prophetic mediation, open the anagogical level.[8] Later, Muqātil repeats an oft-cited description from Ibn ʿAbbās: "The Qurʾān has four aspects (*awjuh*): *tafsīr* which the learned know, *ʿarabiyya* [i.e., linguistic usages] which the Arabs understand, *ḥalāl* and *ḥarām* of which no one is allowed to be ignorant and *taʾwīl* which only God knows" (Muqātil b. Sulaymān 1979: I, 27).[9] It is worth pausing here, however, to note the difference between this and the previous *awjuh* citation: the earlier citation divides the Qurʾānic material by *contents*, for example into verses that contain commands and prohibitions, or eschatological expectations or axiological narratives. In the latter citation, however, the *awjuh* or "aspects" categorization is not contents but levels or capacities of comprehension. The angle of vision changes here as a focus on identifiable genre gives way to a concern for intellectual grasp.

Already with Muqātil's introduction can be found a number of the binaries that were to become such a characteristic feature of *ʿulūm al-Qurʾān* works: the particular and the general, the obscure and the clear, the explicated and the indefinite, the abrogating and the abrogated, inversion of word order, polysemous words and those of univocal significance, and so forth (for somewhat differing readings of this list see Gilliot 1990: 118–19; Goldfeld 1988: 24).

Matters of categorization also mark the partially recovered introduction of the Ibāḍī theologian and jurist, Hūd b. Muḥakkam (d. ca. 280/893 or 290/903; on this author see Gilliot 1997: 179–82). He relates a statement on the authority of Abū ʾl-Dardāʾ al-Anṣārī (d. 32/652) that divides Qurʾānic contents by verse type: "The Qurʾān was revealed according to six [kinds of] verses: a verse that announces good tidings, a verse that issues a warning, a verse [conveying God's] ordinance, a verse that commands you, a verse that forbids you, a verse of stories and accounts" (Hūd b. Muḥakkam 1990: I, 69). He, too, provides a summative statement of Qurʾānic typology: "Only those with knowledge of the following twelve items can understand the interpretation of the Qurʾān: Meccan and Medinan, abrogating and abrogated (*nāsikh* and *mansūkh*), inversion of word order (*taqdīm* and *taʾkhīr*), disconnected and connected verses (*maqṭūʿ* and *mawṣūl*), particular and general (*khāṣṣ wa ʿāmm*), ellipsis (*iḍmār*) and *ʿarabiyya*" (Hūd b. Muḥakkam 1990: I, 71). Again, as in earlier lists of this sort, the rhetorical (e.g., *taqdīm* and *taʾkhīr*), the semantic (e.g., *khāṣṣ* and *ʿāmm*), the linguistic (e.g., *ʿarabiyya*), and the legal (e.g., *nāsikh* and *mansūkh*) are intermingled.

As a final example of the way that *tafsīr* introductions function as a source for the history of the Qurʾānic sciences, I turn to that of the Ṣūfī commentator Sahl al-Tustarī (d. 283/896). Almost a century and a half separates al-Tustarī from Muqātil b. Sulaymān but their origins in the eastern part of the Islamic empire and their common place of death, Baṣra, provide points of geographical connection. The introduction to al-Tustarī's *Tafsīr* is divided into two parts but this division does not entail a strict segregation of contents. Specific terminology and particular emphases migrate back and forth between the two sections. One theme that emerges even from the initial encomium passages marks the unbreakable connection between understanding and action, between recitation and behavior (al-Tustarī 1911: 2–4). The polarity of *ẓāhir* (external or literal) and *bāṭin* (internal or esoteric) introduces a motif that marks a major hermeneutical orientation within the body of the commentary itself. It first appears amid the inaugural encomiums where the Qurʾān is characterized as that "whose *ẓāhir* is beautiful (*anīq*) and whose *bāṭin* is profound (*ʿamīq*)." Successive presentations link this polarity with the four senses (*maʿānin*) of scripture, with general or specialized comprehension and with prescription and proscription (*amr* and *nahy*).[10] Use of the Qurʾānic self-description, Q 42:52, "We have made it a light by which we guide whomever we wish of our servants," combines *ẓāhir* and *bāṭin* with another abiding emphasis within this introduction, the references to light both as an attribute of the Qurʾān and as a grace lodged within the heart of the mystic. Several "light" verses are cited and the Qurʾān as a source of illumination provides the means for distinguishing the literal (*ẓāhir*) from the hidden (*bāṭin*).

These three early commentaries, all apparently produced within about a century and a half of each other, provide an interesting sectarian spread (Sunnī, Ibāḍī, Ṣūfī) and reproduce typological concerns and classifications that had evolved during this time. Linking all three is an abiding concern for categorization, one that would emerge and re-emerge, in ever more finely detailed form as the discipline of Qurʾānic studies moved toward its summative expressions. Taken as a group, these introductions testify to the early appearance of various trajectories of Qurʾānic analysis. The first trajectory concentrates upon creating a typology of genre groups, rhetorical elements and textual properties within the Qurʾānic text, classifying textual contents from various angles of analysis. The second turns attention from the text to its recipient and assesses the receptive capacities of different classes of readers, acknowledging diversity of both linguistic and intellectual aptitude. A third trajectory recouples the text and its recipient but in a more interactive fashion. Here levels of textual meaning correspond to moral and spiritual qualities or capabilities within the listener, with each side of this polarity understood to be an active site of both engagement and reciprocity. The moral and spiritual acuity of some listeners reaches levels of meaning inaccessible to others. Conversely, the inexhaustible depths of Qurʾānic signification provoke and elicit understandings that only those thus prepared can achieve.

Evolution and Expansion

While the full textual archeology of the two summative works by al-Zarkashī and al-Suyūṭī remains to be done, a sketch of the excavation plan for such an endeavor can be drawn from the genres of early Islamic literature that I have just described. Centuries of development and consolidation contributed to the full classical formulation of the Qurʾānic sciences and that formulation, in turn, has generated its own continuing legacy. In a fashion not unlike that of the centuries-long dissemination of medieval scholastic theology and philosophy, this legacy has manifested itself as both a curriculum and a literary tradition. I have used the term *summa* to characterize the *Burhān* and the *Itqān*, a term most commonly associated with the medieval masterpiece penned by Thomas Aquinas, the *Summa theologica*.[11] Just as that work decisively influenced the church pedagogy of subsequent centuries, so too have these "*summas*" of the Qur'ānic sciences shaped the contours of all future study of the Qur'ān. A quick glance through the modern Arabic textbooks mentioned in the first paragraphs of this chapter will confirm this comment. A similar scan of their English-language counterparts (e.g., von Denffer 1983; Qadhi 1999) will serve the same function. While the structure and arrangement may vary from one to another of these books – as well as the dozens of others like them – all of them replicate significant portions of the classical formulation of the Qur'ānic sciences.

It is not, however, only the curricula of Islamic schools and universities that reproduce, from one generation to the next, the traditional compendia of the Qur'ān sciences. The foundational works of Western scholarship on the Qur'ān have also been built upon this basis. Theodor Nöldeke's *Geschichte des Qorans*, a work that remains indispensable for all critical scholarship on the Qur'ān, draws extensively on the *Itqān*, making very frequent and specific citation of it (Nöldeke 1909–38). He constructs, for example, his influential discussion of the chronology of the Qur'ānic *sūras* directly on al-Suyūṭī and his sources with, of course, extensive refinement and variation (Nöldeke 1909–38: I, 58 ff.; cf. Böwering 2001: 320–6). Both the shape and the substance of modern Western scholarship on the Qur'ān remains, in very large measure, tied to the traditional questions, concerns, and categories of its medieval Muslim antecedents (Arkoun 1982: xx–xxv). That scholarship, however, does not operate within the same theological framework as the classical Qur'ānic sciences and its understanding of history, philology, and literary genesis is consequently different. It has also brought some new topics to the table, such as the manuscript tradition of the Qur'ān, the creation of printed editions, and the centuries of translation activity, topics that have now become part of contemporary Muslim teaching and research. Finally, in an intriguing example of cultural dialectic, the work of Western scholars (Arabic *mustashriqūn*, i.e. "Orientalists") has itself become a subject within the expanded agenda of modern Muslim scholarship on the Qur'ān (McAuliffe 2003: 445–6; Ṣaghīr 1999; Banī ʿĀmir 2004).

Notes

1 The plural of "sciences" is important because this field must not be confused with the contemporary, and largely quixotic quest, by some Muslim scholars and scientists to find references in the Qur'ān to current scientific knowledge (Dallal 2004).

2 Al-Suyūṭī's teacher, Muḥammad b. Sulaymān al-Kāfiyajī (d. 879/1474), also produced a related work with the stated aim of improving upon earlier ones (al-Kāfiyajī 1990: 116–17) but this effort is dismissed by al-Suyūṭī as insufficient (al-Suyūṭī 1967: I, 4).

3 For the educational world of Mamlūk Cairo see Berkey (1992).

4 Al-Suyūṭī's penchant for self-adulation has not escaped criticism. While acknowledging the excellence of the *Itqān*, Ignace Goldziher excoriates its author for his "vanity" and "pompous style" (Goldziher 1871). A contemporary biographer, al-Sakhāwī (d. 902/1497), accused him of what amounts to plagiarism, appropriating the work of others and, with slight alteration, presenting it as his own (Meursinge 1839: 22).

5 Trying to organize the eighty chapters of the *Itqān* has tempted other colleagues (see Arkoun 1982: ix; Balhan 2001: 24–9; Gilliot 2005).

6 Apparently, al-Ṭabarī's commentary was not widely disseminated in the several centuries immediately succeeding his own and a modern editor of his *tafsīr* has lamented the lack of extant manuscripts. Yet he also points to its use by such subsequent commentators as al-Qurṭubī (d. 671/1271), Abū Hayyān al-Gharnāṭī (d. 745/1344), Ibn Kathīr (d. 774/1373), al-Suyūṭī and al-Shawkānī (d. 1250/1832) (see the introduction by M. M. Shākir and A. M. Shākir in al-Ṭabarī 1969: I, 13–14).

7 It has recently been argued that al-Thaʿlabī's (d. 427/1035) *al-Kashf wa ʾl-bayān ʿan tafsīr al-Qurʾān* was a more important conduit of this early material (Saleh 2004; also see the chapter by Saleh in this book). Many post-Ṭabarī commentaries on the Qurʾān are introduced with a discussion of multiple aspects of the Qurʾānic sciences. Of particular note are those of Ibn ʿAṭiyya (d. 541/1147) and Ibn Bisṭām (see Gilliot 2005), which are published in Jeffery (1954). In fact, al-Suyūṭī's *Itqān* was conceived as an introduction to an unfinished commentary, *Majmaʿ al-baḥrayn wa maṭlaʿ al-badrayn* (al-Suyūṭī 1967: I, 14).

8 In commenting on Nwyia's interpretation of this passage, C. Gilliot connects it with al-Ṭabarī's use of a similar statement on the authority of Ibn Masʿūd: "God revealed the Qurʾān according to five *aḥruf*: lawful and unlawful, clear and ambiguous, and parables" (Gilliot 1990: 118).

9 John Wansbrough contrasted this rendition with the later one to be found in al-Suyūṭī's *Itqān* (al-Suyūṭī 1967: IV, 188), which uses only the term *tafsīr*, not the polarity of *tafsīr/taʾwīl* (see Wansbrough 1977: 155).

10 For the relation of the polarity *ẓāhir/bāṭin* to the notion of multiple senses (*maʿānin*) see Böwering 2003: 346–65.

11 While the *Burhān* and the *Itqān* express the encyclopaedic character of a *summa*, the question and response structure of a work like the *Summa theologica* is closer to that of some Qurʾān commentaries, such as Fakhr al-Dīn al-Rāzī's (d. 606/1210) *al-Tafsīr al-kabīr (Mafātīḥ al-ghayb)*.

Further reading

Arkoun, Mohammed (1982) *Lectures du Coran*. G.-P. Maisonneuve et Larose, Paris.

Balhan, J.-M. (2001) *La révélation du Coran selon al-Suyūṭī: Traduction annotée du chapitre seizième de Ǧalāl al-Dīn al-Suyūṭī*, al-Itqān fī ʿulūm al-Qurʾān. Pontificio Istituto di Studi Arabi e d'Islamistica, Rome.

Berkey, J. (1992) *The Transmission of Knowledge in Medieval Cairo: A Social History of Islamic Education*. Princeton University Press, Princeton.

Gilliot, Claude (2005) Traditional disciplines of Qurʾānic Studies. In: McAuliffe, Jane Dammen (ed.) *Encyclopaedia of the Qurʾān*. Brill, Leiden, vol. V, pp. 318–39.

Goldfeld, Y. (1988) The development of theory on Qur'anic exegesis in Islamic scholarship. *Studia Islamica* 67, 5–27.

McAuliffe, Jane Dammen (1988) Ibn al-Jawzī's exegetical propaedeutic: Introduction and translations. *Alif: Journal of Comparative Poetics*, 8, 101–13.

McAuliffe, Jane Dammen (2002) Disparity and context: Teaching Qurʾānic studies in North America. In: Wheeler, B. (ed.) *Teaching Islam*, Oxford University Press, New York, pp. 94–107.

McAuliffe, Jane Dammen (2003) The genre boundaries of Qur'ānic commentary. In: McAuliffe, J., Walfish, B., and Goering, J. (eds.) *With Reverence for the Word: Medieval Scriptural Exegesis in Judaism, Christianity and Islam*. Oxford University Press, New York, pp. 445–61.

Nolin, K. (1968) The *Itqān* and its sources: A study of *al-Itqān fī ʿulūm al-Qur'ān* by Jalāl al-Dīn al-Suyūṭī with special reference to *al-Burhān fī ʿulūm al-Qur'ān* by Badr al-Dīn al-Zarkashī. PhD dissertation, Hartford Seminary, Hartford, CT.

Sartain E. M. (1975) *Jalāl al-Dīn al-Suyūṭī: Biography and Background.* Cambridge University Press, Cambridge.

Versteegh, C. H. M. (1993) *Arabic Grammar and Qur'ānic Exegesis in Early Islam*. E. J. Brill, Leiden.

von Denffer, A. (1983) *ʿUlūm al-Qur'ān: An Introduction to the Sciences of the Qur'ān.* The Islamic Foundation, Leicester.

CHAPTER 28

Theology

Binyamin Abrahamov

In introducing the role of the Qur'ān in Islamic theology, this chapter will mainly focus on Sunnī medieval Islam, although references to sectarian groups and Shīʿī Islam will be adduced. First, I shall examine the Qur'ān as a book containing theological ideas. Then the question of whether the Qur'ān serves as a stimulus to theological discussions will be dealt with. Approaching Islamic theology through its traditional and rational trends will serve to function as a preliminary section for discussion of the various appearances of the Qur'ān in Islamic theology. We shall see that the more rationalist a theologian is, the more he uses the Qur'ān as corroboration and not a departure for his proofs. On the other hand the traditionalist employs the Qur'ān as the basis for his theological theses, but often replaces the Qur'ān by traditions which come to the fore. The discussion here is not historical, but rather phenomenological; that is, I am outlining the place of the Qur'ān within the main streams in Muslim theology. However, one cannot escape the impression that at its beginning, Muslim theology dealt more extensively with interpretations of the Qur'ān, and in its later phases somewhat neglected the Qur'ān in favor of the *sunna* on the one hand and reason on the other. In the present chapter I have concentrated on the role of the Qur'ān in theological discussions setting aside certain issues such as the Qur'ān as a miracle (*iʿjāz al-Qur'ān*), which may testify to the theologians' estimation of the scripture but not to their true attitude to it as a theological device. Finally, the presentation here is not exhaustive; it only indicates the main directions taken by Muslim theologians regarding the use of the Qur'ān.

Theology in the Qur'ān

Prophets are not theologians; their teachings are not arranged systematically as are theological treatises (Goldziher 1981: 67). However, the Qur'ān contains many theological notions expressed both explicitly and implicitly. The main tenets of Islam are scattered throughout the Qur'ān in the long and short *sūras*. These dogmas, as a rule, are stated rather than proved. The existence of God who created the world (Q 6:1) constitutes the foundation of the theology in the Qur'ān. God is depicted, *inter alia*, as Living (*ḥayy*), Eternal (*qayyūm*), Omniscient (*ʿalīm*) and Omnipotent (*qadīr*) (Q 2:20, 29, 255). God acts for the benefit of human beings; He supplies them with sustenance and water and designs nature so that they can find their way in the earth (Q 6:95–9).[1] God's unity is stated in two ways: the positive ("He is God, the One" Q 112:4) and the negative ("There is no god but He" Q 2:163). Sometimes in the context of God's unity the Qur'ān inserts a polemic against Christianity: "Those who say that God is the third of three, whereas there is no god but He, are unbelievers" (Q 5:73).

The Qur'ān applies expressions to God which when taken literally are anthropomorphisms. God is described as sitting on the Throne (Q 20:5), as having a face (Q 55:27), hands (Q 38:75), eyes (Q 54:14), and as speaking to human beings (Q 2:253). Other verses, which contradict the anthropomorphic phrases, express the idea that there is no one equal to God (Q 112:4) and that "there is nothing like Him" (Q 42.11).

On the question of man's free choice, the literal text of the Qur'ān is equivocal in the same manner. On the one hand, man can choose his acts freely without God's intervention, while on the other, he is strictly coerced to act because of God's decree or predestination. Contrary to Q 18:29: "Whoever wills let him believe and whoever wills let him disbelieve" stands Q 76:30: "You will not unless God wills." The notion that human beings are completely subject to God's rule and power contradicts the notion of human responsibility based on man's free choice. In addition to the idea of God's omnipotence and will to which human beings are subject, the Qur'ān speaks of God's guidance (*hudā*) and leading astray (*ḍalāl*) in two different manners: Either God guides a man or leads him astray before he acts, which implies predetermination, or He does so after a man acts, meaning that He rewards or punishes him. These two terms and others, such as God's giving sustenance (*rizq*) or sealing man's heart (*khatm*) so that he cannot understand God's admonitions and as a result disbelieves, together with *ajal* (the appointed time of death – Q 6:2), *kasb* (acquisition – Q 2:286) and *ʿadl* (justice – Q 16:90) play a great role in later theological discussions about free will and predestination (Watt 1948: 12–17).

Numerous instances of the verbs *āmana* (he believed) and *kafara* (he disbelieved) and their derivatives occur in the Qur'ān. However, the Qur'ān provides us with no definition of either belief (*īmān*) or disbelief (*kufr*). Only once are we told that a difference exists between belief and *islām*:

> The Bedouins say: "We believe" (*āmannā*). Say: "You do not believe, but say: 'We surrender' (*aslamnā*), for belief has not yet entered your hearts." (Q 49:14)

Here the verb *aslamnā* seems to convey the formal acceptance of Islam, whereas *īmān* (belief) is connected with a feeling of the heart. This feeling may increase owing to God's acts (Q 3:173; 48:4; 74:31). The worst form of unbelief is to ascribe partners to God (*shirk*), which is a sin He will not pardon (Q 4:116).

The content of belief is mentioned many times. One must believe in God, His angels, His books, His messengers and the resurrection (Q 2:62, 285). According to the Qur'ān the unbelievers will enter hell and the believers will enter Paradise (Q 4:116–24). In this world, the believers must shun the unbelievers; they should not become the latter's friends and they should fight against them (Q 3:28; 9:1–5, 36).

The verb *fasaqa ʿan* means to transgress God's orders, meaning to sin. Satan was ordered to prostrate himself before Adam and "he transgressed God's command (*fasaqa ʿan amr rabbihi* – Q 18:50). The derivatives of this verb are sometimes related to belief and unbelief: "Is the believer (*muʾmin*) like the unbeliever (*fāsiq*)? They are not equal" (Q 32:18). Two types of sins are mentioned in the Qurʾān: minor sins (*ṣaghīra*; plural *ṣaghāʾir*) and grave sins (*kabīra*; plural *kabāʾir* – Q 18:49; 42:37). Also here we do not know what sins are subsumed under either *kabāʾir* or *ṣaghāʾir*. As in other theological notions and terms, this lacuna is expanded by the theologians.

The Qurʾān as Stimulus to Theological Discussions

Besides the above-mentioned list of theological ideas and terms in the Qurʾān, two additional factors have motivated the development of theology in Islam.[2] The first is the polemics between God and human beings and between prophets and their peoples. God provided Abraham with an argument so that he could refute his people. "That is our argument. We gave it to Abraham against his folk" (Q 6:83). Likewise, a debate occurred between Muḥammad and his people: "And those who argue [against the prophet] concerning God[3] after he [the prophet] has been known [as prophet], their argument is invalid in God's eyes" (Q 42:16). The notion that human beings cannot refute God after His sending of messengers to mankind is best exemplified in the following verse: "[We have sent] messengers to announce [God's reward for the believers] and to warn [them of God's punishment to the evil-doers] in order that human beings might have no argument against God after [His sending of] messengers" (Q 4:165). Moreover, Muḥammad is ordered to call people to the religion by certain means including disputation: "Call to the way of your Lord by [using] wisdom, good exhortation, and dispute with them in the better way" (Q 6:125). In like manner, he must dispute the People of the Book (Jews and Christians) in the better way (Q 29:46).

Having spoken in general of the Qurʾān's use of arguments, we now proceed to some specific arguments. One of the most repeated themes in the Qurʾān is the resurrection (called, among other names, *al-qiyāma*: see *EI2* 2004: "ḳiyāma"). The Arab pagans believed that God created the heavens and the earth (Q 29:61), but did not believe in the resurrection. They asked: "Who shall restore us to life? Say: 'He who created you at the first time' " (Q 17:51). Here the Qurʾān uses an *a fortiori* argument, namely, if the pagans believe in the greatest work of God, that being the creation of the world, then they should believe in a lesser work of God, that is, the resurrection (cf. Q 75:37–40). Similarly, a syllogism is made between God's revivification of the earth by water and the resurrection (Q 35:9).

In opposition to the pagans and Christians (according to the Qurʾān the latter believed in three divinities), the Qurʾān puts forward an argument later known as *dalīl al-tamānuʿ* (the argument from mutual hypothetical prevention – see below) to prove God's unity. It reads: "If there were in the heavens and the earth gods other than God, they [the heavens and the earth] would be ruined" (Q 21:22). In another formulation of this argument clearly directed towards the Christians, the Qurʾān states: "God has not taken to Himself any son, nor is there any god with Him, [if it were so], then each god would take off what he created and some of them would rise up over others" (Q 23:91). Thus the state of a stable world proves its being ruled and directed by the one God.

Every Muslim unquestioningly regards the Qurʾān as the realization of the absolute truth. However, contradictions in central issues discussed above, such as anthropomorphism vis-à-vis its negation, urged Muslims to find solutions to these inconsistencies which might impair the perception of the Qurʾān's perfection. The arguable condition of the Qurʾānic text has been one of the major internal stimuli for the emergence of Islamic theology and the attempt to create through interpretation and theological discussion of a coherent doctrine.

To sum up, the Qurʾān provides Muslims with theological notions, terms, forms of arguments, and models of debates. To some extent, these elements have affected the Qurʾān's position in Islamic theology.

Types of Theology

The role of the Qurʾān in Islamic theology can be best apprehended through examination of the different theological trends in Islam. The categorization of this theology as it relates to reason and the *sunna* may lead us to lucid conclusions, because Muslim theologians naturally cite Qurʾānic verses which affirm their position vis-à-vis these two sources of knowledge. Along broad lines, it is possible to differentiate between rationalist and traditionalist theologians. By rationalist theologians I mean thinkers who rely on reason as their sole argument in theological discussion and who prefer reason to the Qurʾān in cases of contradiction between the two. (In the broader context of rationalism versus traditionalism, we may add to the Qurʾān, the *sunna* and *ijmāʿ*, the consensus either of religious experts or of all Muslims). Of course, a purely rationalist theologian, that is, a theologian who employs only rational arguments without any reference to the Qurʾān, cannot be reckoned as a Muslim; therefore, when I speak of rationalist theologians I mean those who base their theological arguments, mainly but not exclusively, on reason. In Islamic theology the most radical of the rationalists were the Muʿtazila.[4] The traditionalists, on the other hand, rely first and foremost on the Qurʾān, the *sunna*, and the consensus as their basis of theology. Here we can distinguish between pure traditionalism, which means sole dependence on these sources, and other forms of traditionalism which move from the extreme towards reason. However, reason cannot serve them as a point of departure, but only as corroboration (Abrahamov 1998: vii–xi).

Traditionalist theology

Among the traditionalists a distinction is made between the speculative theologians who are called *mutakallimū*[5] *ahl al-ḥadīth* (the speculative theologians of the people of the *ḥadīth*; Ibn ʿAsākir 1984: 105), and those who do not employ speculative theology. The latter sometimes prefer the tradition (*sunna*) to the Qurʾān. I shall now introduce examples showing how the Qurʾān was utilized among these previously mentioned groups. As I have said, the materials are not arranged historically but phenomenologically. The discussion here begins with the traditionalists and ends with the rationalists.

First, it is important to realize that the traditionalists were aware of the Qurʾān's inadequacy to supply believers with both legal and theological solutions. The traditionalist theologian al-Ājurrī (d. 360/970) declares one who accepts only what is found in the Qurʾān an evil man. All God's ordinances are known only through the messenger's traditions. The Qurʾān's status is equal to that of the *sunna*, a comparison that is proved through Q 4:59: ". . . If you dispute about any matter, refer it to God and the messenger . . ." A tradition brought forward by al-Ājurrī explains that "to God" means to God's book, while "the messenger" means to the messenger's traditions. Here, a Qurʾānic verse legitimizes the equal status of the *sunna* and the Qurʾān (al-Ājurrī 1983: 49–53; cf. Abrahamov 1998: 3–4).

Notwithstanding the comparison between the Qurʾān and the *sunna*, the Qurʾān is elevated to the position of uncreated being (*al-Qurʾān ghayr makhlūq*), because it is God's speech (*kalām*) or knowledge (*ʿilm*), which are God's eternal attributes (al-Ājurrī 1983: 75–6). In the chapter dealing with this issue, most of the materials cited by al-Ājurrī are traditions, and the few Qurʾān verses he quotes are interpreted according to traditions. One of these few is Q 7:54: "Verily, to Him belong the creation and the command." The creation is interpreted to mean God's created things, and the command is the Qurʾān itself which is not reckoned among the created things.

When the Qurʾān provides verses supporting the author's thesis, he cites them all. Al-Ājurrī expresses the usual traditionalist dogma concerning the elements of faith. Faith is composed of three principal parts: (a) the belief in the heart (*al-taṣdīq biʾl-qalb*); (b) the affirmation of God's unity and Muḥammad's mission by uttering the *shahāda*; and (c) carrying out God's precepts. Al-Ājurrī refutes those who hold only the first two roots of faith,[6] by citing fifty-six verses which prove that fulfilling God's commands is a requisite for faith. The verses are quoted almost without comment, which creates the impression that the author regards the Qurʾān as a theological source which needs no interpretation. In this case, al-Ājurrī is right, for these verses connect belief with the doing of good deeds; see, for example, Q 4:57, 122; 7:42; 14:23; 18:30; and 20:82.

However, in contradistinction to his treatment of faith, when dealing with the problem of predestination and free will, al-Ājurrī is very careful to select verses which fit his doctrine of predestination which is very probably dictated by the traditions. Here (al-Ājurrī 1983: 149–68) we cannot speak of Qurʾānic theology, but rather of a theology which seeks corroboration from the Qurʾān. Thus, verses which teach that God puts a seal on one's heart, ears, and eyes so that one is unable to hear God's message and hence unable to believe are cited (Q 2:6–7; 4:155; 5:41). Likewise, the author cites verses dealing with God's guidance and leading astray (*al-hudā, al-ḍalāl* – Q 4:88; 6:39, 149; 7:186). In his view, God guides and leads human beings astray from the beginning; thus, whomever God leads astray is incapable of believing in Him. Conversely no attempt is made to interpret other verses (Q 2:26; 14:27; 40:74) which suggest God's leading astray as a punishment for man's unbelief or evil-doing. For example, Q 14:27

reads: "God leads astray the wrong-doers" which may imply that leading astray is a reaction to transgression of the laws. Like many other traditionalists, who base their theology on the Qur'ān, al-Ājurrī holds that everything depends on God's will, even man's will: "You do not will unless God wills" (Q 81:29).

Some theological dogmas are plainly dictated by the Qur'ān, and the relevant traditions are cited in support of these. This is the case with man's seeing of God regarded by all Muslims as the highest reward that God will give human beings in the hereafter (al-Ājurrī 1983: 251–76). The cornerstone of this doctrine is Q 75:22–3: "On that day (on the resurrection) faces shall be luminous looking at their Lord" (*ilā rabbihā nāẓira*). This verse is accompanied with other less lucid verses and with many traditions to the same effect. Contrary to his treatment of predestination, here, al-Ājurrī willingly refers to a verse whose plain meaning may refute the present doctrine: "The eyes [literally: the glances – *al-abṣār*] do not perceive Him, and He perceives the eyes" (Q 6:103). Rationalist thinkers, such as the Jahmites[7] and the Muʿtazilites, use this verse to claim that it is impossible to see God. Al-Ājurrī, however, interprets the verb "he perceived" to mean "he encompassed a thing by seeing" meaning "he saw the whole thing," just as one says "I saw the sea," but he did not see the whole sea (al-Ājurrī 1983: 276). Accordingly, the Qur'ān teaches us that one cannot see God as a whole, but only part of Him. Here, the author uses a lexical device to interpret a verse and hence to solve a theological problem.

Another means used by the traditionalists to understand a Qur'ānic verse is called *istinbāṭ* (literally: finding, discovery). Here, the interpretation of a verse is based on reason (al-Jurjānī 1978: 22). One of the most often cited verses in the long-running dispute over the creation of the Qur'ān[8] is Q 36:82: "His order, when He wills a thing, is only to say to it 'be' and it is." Everything is created through the creation word "be" uttered by God. Now, if this word is also created, it follows that there will be an endless chain of creations, which is an absurdity. Hence, "be," God's speech, is not created, which proves that the Qur'ān, God's speech, is uncreated (al-Lālakā'ī 1990: I, 217–18). I call this process an act of rationality, to be differentiated from rationalism, since the theological conclusion or proof is derived on the basis of the Qur'ān, but only with reasoning. In rationalism the basis is reason, and the Qur'ān, if it is involved in the process, plays only a role of corroboration.

Another theology dominated by traditions is that of the Shāfiʿite traditionalist theologian al-Lālakā'ī (d. 418/1027). Although he uses *istinbāṭ*, his theology is largely dominated by traditions. His discussion of predestination (al-Lālakā'ī 1990: II, 577–8) begins with a list of relevant verses and a few interpretive notes, but the whole section is devoted to traditions. Sometimes, for example, in the section treating the Murji'ites (al-Lālakā'ī 1990: III, 986–1007), there are no quotations from the Qur'ān, though the author could have cited some relevant verses. Thus the Qur'ān is replaced by traditions.

In his *al-Radd ʿalā al-zanādiqa wa'l-jahmiyya* ("The Refutation of the Heretics and the Jahmiyya"), Aḥmad b. Ḥanbal (d. 241/855), after whom the Ḥanbalite school is named, refutes Jahm b. Ṣafwān by using Qur'ānic verses through the method of *tafsīr al-Qur'ān bi'l-Qur'ān*, meaning the interpretation of Qur'ānic verses by other Qur'ānic verses. One may assume that this form of argumentation is employed because his adversary uses Qur'ānic verses to support his own theses. Hence, our author is forced to use the same weapon. In the above-mentioned work Ibn Ḥanbal's theology is expressed through the plain meaning of the Qur'ān. This attitude can be best summarized by Ibn Ḥanbal's sentence, which is brought after introducing certain verses (for example, Q 2:255; 7:54; 16:50) regarding God's abode: "This is God's report in which He informs us that He is in the heaven" (al-Nashshār and al-Ṭālibī 1971: 93). Also in *al-Ikhtilāf fī 'l-lafẓ wa 'l-radd ʿalā 'l-Jahmiyya wa 'l-mushabbiha* ("The Controversy Concerning the Utterance [of the Qur'ān][9] and the Refutation of the Jahmiyya and the Anthropomorphists") written by the traditionalist theologian Ibn Qutayba (d. 276/889), the dependence on the Qur'ān in the refutation is dictated by the Qur'ānic arguments of the opponent (al-Nashshār and al-Ṭālibī 1971: 233).

In his *al-Radd ʿalā al-Jahmiyya* ("The Refutation of the Jahmites"), the traditionalist theologian Abū Saʿīd al-Dārimī (d. 280/893) discusses the Qur'ānic verses in a rational way. Rejoining to the Jahmites' dogma that God is everywhere, meaning that He rules every place, al-Dārimī asks what is then the meaning of God's particularization of the throne among all other places, to which the Jahmites have no answer. This proves their doctrine to be untenable. An argument from disjunction which follows shows that al-Dārimī may be considered among the speculative theologians in the traditionalist circles (*mutakallimū ahl al-ḥadīth*). Notwithstanding, he asks the Jahmites to prove their dogma in the following order: first, proofs from the Qur'ān, then from the Tradition and then from the consensus of the Muslims. The Jahmites claim that they seek to argue on the basis of Qur'ānic verses alone without resorting to the exegetes' interpretations, to which al-Dārimī responds that they should pay attention to the whole verse and not only to phrases taken out of context. In doing so, the argument of the Qur'ān is deeper and clearer than other arguments (al-Nashshār and al-Ṭālibī 1971: 268–70). Thus al-Dārimī plainly states that the Qur'ān furnishes the best argument in theological debates. A further development of this notion considered the Qur'ān the origin of rational arguments.

The approach regarding the Qur'ān as a source of both rational arguments and theological terms was further expanded among certain later traditionalists, mainly speculative theologians. The first was Abū 'l-Ḥasan al-Ashʿarī (d. 324/935), the eponym of the Ashʿarite school of theology. Though first a Muʿtazilite thinker, he later converted to traditionalism and defended Ibn Ḥanbal's theses through speculative arguments. His *Risāla fī istiḥsān al-khawḍ fī ʿilm al-kalām* ("An Epistle Concerning the Approval of Dealing with the Science of the Speculative Theology;" al-Ashʿarī 1953: 87–97) refutes the claim that the Qur'ān and the *sunna* are devoid of speculative theology. Al-Ashʿarī sets out the principle that the Qur'ān and the *sunna* contain the roots of this kind of theology in a general way. For our purpose we shall deal only with the Qur'ān.

Al-Ashʿarī refers to the four modes of being (*kawn*; plural *akwān*): movement (*ḥaraka*), immobility (*sukūn*), combination (*ijtimāʿ*) and separation (*iftirāq*). These constitute a genus of accidents which must inhere in the substances (Peters 1976: 128–32; Gimaret 1990: 99–120). According to al-Ashʿarī, it is possible to learn about the accident of movement from the story of Abraham (Q 6:76–9) who intermittently declared the star, the moon, and the sun to be his Lord, but after seeing their disappearances and being aware of their movements from place to place, he believed in God, because it is inconceivable for God to disappear and to move from place to place (al-Ashʿarī 1953: 89).

Likewise the proof from hypothetical mutual prevention (*dalīl al-tamānuʿ* – see above) for God's unity is founded on Qurʾānic verses (Q 13:16; 21:22; 23:91) which teach that the existence of more than one god would ruin the world. The possibility of the resurrection is proved in the Qurʾān through verses (Q 7:29; 30:27; 36:79) that assert that if God was able to create the world from nothing, it is far easier for Him to vivify the dead (al-Ashʿarī 1953: 89–91).

Those who denied God's creation of the world and the second creation, namely, the resurrection, and believed in the eternity of the world, introduced a false argument against the resurrection. Basing themselves on the law of contradiction, they argued that life is characterized by humidity and heat, while death is defined by coldness and dryness. Thus how can these contradictory elements be brought together in one place? Al-Ashʿarī admitted that two opposites cannot be combined in one substrate; however, they can exist in two substrates by way of vicinity. This he learns from Q 36:80 which reads: "God created for you fire out of the green tree so that you can kindle from it." Consequently, it is proved that fire, which is characterized by heat and dryness, comes out of the green tree characterized by coldness and humidity. This further demonstrates that life may come after death (al-Ashʿarī 1953: 91). It seems that here al-Ashʿarī not only points to the fact that the Qurʾān puts forth theological arguments, but also that the Qurʾān anticipates the claims of the opponents of Islam.

Another principle, which pertains to the doctrine of atoms, states that every body has an end and that an atom (*juzʾ*)[10] cannot be divided. This is proved on the basis of Q 36:12: "We have counted every thing in a clear register." Al-Ashʿarī concludes that it is impossible to count that which is endless or that which is divisible *ad infinitum* (al-Ashʿarī 1953: 92–3).

In sum, al-Ashʿarī turned the Qurʾān into the essential foundation of theological terms and speculative arguments and in so doing paved the way towards the elaboration of the notion that there is no contradiction between reason and revelation, for revelation includes the principles of the rational arguments.

A similar approach to rational arguments and hence to the Qurʾān was advanced by Abū Manṣūr al-Māturīdī (d. 333/944), a contemporary of al-Ashʿarī and the eponym of the Māturīdite school of theology (on this school see *EI2* 2004: "al-Māturīdiyya"). He states that religion is known through rational proofs (Abrahamov 1998: 86n). For example, a man is recognized as a true prophet first by an examination of his character and then through sensual and rational proofs. For all these proofs, in al-Māturīdī's view, the Qurʾān supplies the Muslims with pieces of evidence (al-Māturīdī 1970: 202–10).

The Ẓāhirī[11] theologian, jurisprudent, and heresiographer Ibn Ḥazm (d. 456/1064) also advocates the use of reason in religious matters including theology. But this use is subject to the teachings of the Qurʾān; otherwise, rational arguments are nothing but personal preferences of theologians and philosophers. The Qurʾān explains everything which pertains to religion, as Q 16:89 testifies: "We have revealed to you the scripture explaining all things." Thus, for example, contrary to the Ashʿarites who derive some of God's names from His characteristics, Ibn Ḥazm permits only the use of the names and attributes of God which occur in the Qur'ān (*EI2* 2004: "Ibn Ḥazm"). Clearly, the Qur'ān plays a central role in Ibn Ḥazm's theology.

The Qur'ān also occupies a high place in al-Ghazālī's (d. 505/1111) Ashʿarite theology, although he introduced Greek logic into Islamic theology. How did he reconcile these two seemingly opposed sources of knowledge? Probably following al-Ashʿarī, al-Ghazālī continues to elaborate the notion that the Qur'ān is the basis of rational arguments. In al-Ghazālī's view expressed in his *al-Qisṭās al-mustaqīm* ("The Just Balance"), God is the first teacher, the second is Jibrīl (Gabriel, the conveyer of revelation), and the third is the messenger. By God and Jibrīl he means the teachings of the Qur'ān, and by the messenger, the teachings of the *sunna*. However, his treatment of the subject is more detailed, technical, and sophisticated than that of al-Ashʿarī, for he seeks to prove that the three Aristotelian figures of syllogism and the two Stoic conjunctive and disjunctive syllogisms are found in the Qur'ān (Marmura 1975: 102; Abrahamov 1993a: 145). Each syllogism is called a "balance" (*qisṭās*) because by these devices one can weigh the true knowledge.

As an example let us take the first figure of syllogism in Aristotle's *Prior Analytics*, I, 3 (McKeon 1941: 68). Al-Ghazālī calls it the "great balance of the equality balances" (*al-mīzān al-akbar min mawāzīn al-taʿādul*), and along with the middle balance (*al-mīzān al-awsaṭ*) and the small balance (*al-mīzān al-aṣghar*), they constitute the three Aristotelian figures of syllogism. According to al-Ghazālī, Abraham used this kind of syllogism when disputing with Nimrūd who declared that, like God, he gives life and causes death. Consequently, Abraham said to him: "God causes the sun to rise from the east, so bring it from the west" (Q 2:258). On the basis of this verse al-Ghazālī builds his syllogism in the following way: (a) Every being which is capable of making the sun rise is God; (b) My god is capable of making the sun rise; and the conclusion is (c) My god is God. The first premise is known through the agreement of all people that God is able to do everything, including making the sun rise. We know the second premise by seeing that Nimrūd and all other beings are incapable of making the sun rise (al-Ghazālī 1996: 184–5). Thus, the Qur'ān appears in al-Ghazālī's teaching not only as a source of arguments but also as a source of logic, as a balance through which one weighs the truth.

The famous Ḥanbalite jurist and theologian Ibn Taymiyya (d. 728/1328) expresses a similar attitude towards the Qur'ān. In his view, *ʿaqliyyāt* (proofs known through reason) can be derived from the Qur'ān and the *sunna*. The Qur'ān points at, draws one's attention to, and explains rational arguments, although some rational proofs can be known through observation (Ibn Taymiyya 1979: I, 199f.; Abrahamov 1992: 267).

Later Ashʿarite *mutakallimūn* reveal different approaches to the Qur'ān. In his *Ghāyat al-marām fī ʿilm al-kalām* ("The Utmost Aspiration in the Science of Kalām"), the Ashʿarite *mutakallim* Sayf al-Dīn al-Āmidī (d. 631/1233), being greatly influenced by philosophy, almost ignores the Qur'ān. It is highly surprising to see whole chapters dealing with religious issues such as man's seeing of God in the hereafter (al-Āmidī 1971: 159–78) or prophecy and miracles (al-Āmidī 1971: 317–40) accompanied by very few verses which serve only as support, not as a point of departure. However, in another *kalām* work, which is the basis of *Ghāyat al-marām*, entitled *Abkār al-afkār* ("The First Thoughts") he employs Qur'ānic proofs (al-Āmidī 1971: 16).

Contrary to al-Āmidī, Fakhr al-Dīn al-Rāzī (d. 606/1209), an Ashʿarite theologian also known for his command of philosophy, continues to maintain the high place of the Qurʾān in his writings. However, Qurʾānic proofs occupy the secondary place in his discussion, for example, on the issue of God's creation of man's acts,[12] while rational proofs appear foremost in this discussion (al-Rāzī 1987: IX, 19–198).

Al-Rāzī substantiates his hierarchy of proofs stating that verbal proofs, meaning those which stem from the Qurʾānic text, do not provide us with certainty, and on the issue of who creates man's acts one must have certainty. Hence, it is forbidden to base the resolution of this question on traditional proofs. He further explains that verbal proofs are based on ten matters and that each of these is probable; hence, that which is based on a probable matter is probable. The very characteristics of the language of the Qurʾān, states al-Rāzī, prevents the possibility of attaining certainty. For example, the Qurʾān is full of omissions and concealed contents, thus a positive statement may turn into a negative one and vice versa. The absence of omissions and concealed contents is also probable. Probability also results from the possibility of various meanings of words.

Special attention should be paid to the question of the contradiction between Qurʾānic verses and reason. Al-Rāzī illustrates one such contradiction by pointing to the anthropomorphic phrases in the Qurʾān.[13] In such a case, one should use reason to overcome the *sunna*. Reason is the basis of the *sunna*, because one cannot believe in the *sunna* unless one uses rational proofs. In the present issue the solution is to figuratively interpret the anthropomorphic verses.

In sum, al-Rāzī considers the Qurʾān a weak device for attaining certainty with regard to theological problems in general and on the issue of predestination in particular. However, he disapproves of the claim that the Qurʾān is defamed because of contradictory verses regarding the issue of predestination (some of which defend man's choice as opposed to others which defend God's predetermination). The Qurʾān may contain plain meaning *(ḥaqīqa)* as well as figurative speech (*majāz*), and the way to solve the problem of contradictory statements is to use *majāz* (al-Rāzī 1987: IX, 113–33). Also he defends the division of the Qurʾān into self-evident verses (*muḥkamāt*) and ambiguous verses (*mutashābihāt*) as we are informed in Q 3:7, arguing that such a division motivates learning and the use of rational proofs and supplies all ideological systems in Islam with Qurʾānic support for their tenets (al-Rāzī 1987: VII, 172).

Rationalist theology

It seems that like other later Ashʿarites, al-Rāzī adopted the rationalist approach of the philosophers or of the Muʿtazila. The latter were the first adherents of rationalism in Islam. Their rationalism is expressed by the notion that God and the world can be examined through the intellect which God creates in human beings. One can know God's existence, His unity and attributes through reason. Likewise, one is capable of understanding the creation and structure of the world and man and his actions. Consequently, they hold that the world is directed according to rational rules and that even

God is subject to these rules. Contrary to the traditionalists' perception, the rationalist approach holds it quite possible to know God without the support of the Qurʾān (Abrahamov 1998: 32).

The Muʿtazilite ʿAbd al-Jabbār (d. 414–16/1023–5) wrote a treatise entitled *Faḍl al-iʿtizāl wa-ṭabaqāt al-muʿtazila* ("The Superiority of the Muʿtazilites and their Biographies") in which he expounds the rationalist approach. Surprisingly enough, but not uncommon, as we shall see, among the Muʿtazilites, he begins his discussion of man's best way to knowledge by citing Q 6:153: "This is my straight path, so follow it and do not follow [other] paths lest they cause you to divert from His path." Since, says ʿAbd al-Jabbār, the straight path is not known through seeing, it is incumbent on man to follow proofs and to speculate on them in order to know. Following this verse, he states that there is only one way to true knowledge, while ignorance has infinite ways to express itself. Although our author is a master of rationalism, he bases his doctrine of one true path on the Qurʾān. However, the first proof in ʿAbd al-Jabbār's view is the rational proof, because through this form of reason one can distinguish between good and evil and know that the Qurʾān, the *sunna* and the consensus are proofs. We know through reason, says ʿAbd al-Jabbār, that God exists, that He is one, that He is wise and that He sent messengers to mankind with miracles. Through this knowledge we know that the Messenger's statements are proofs, meaning that the *sunna* is right, and the *sunna* in turn legitimizes the consensus (ʿAbd al-Jabbār 1986: 138–9).

Notwithstanding the placing of reason as the first proof, the Muʿtazilites did not neglect the Qurʾān as the base of their doctrines. Mānkdīm (d. 425/1034), a Zaydite[14] commentator of ʿAbd al-Jabbār's *Kitāb al-uṣūl al-khamsa* ("The Book of the Five Principles"), states in his *Sharḥ al-uṣūl al-khamsa*[15] ("The Interpretation of the Five Principles") that, concerning the issue of seeing God, it is possible to draw conclusions from both reason and revelation (*ʿaql* and *samʿ*), because the soundness of revelation does not depend on this issue. According to Mānkdīm's rule, it is allowed to prove each theological issue through revelation provided that the soundness of revelation does not depend on this issue (ʿAbd al-Jabbār 1965: 233). The soundness of prophecy (ʿAbd al-Jabbār 1965: 563–6), for example, cannot be based on revelation, because this would entail a vicious circle.

The Muʿtazilites' high estimation of the Qurʾān is further evidenced in their exhaustive treatments of the miracle of the Qurʾān (*iʿjāz al-Qurʾān*) and by their refuting of defamations of the Qurʾān (ʿAbd al-Jabbār 1960). But it is worth noting that the Muʿtazilites were blamed at times for not referring to the Qurʾān in the formulation of their theological theses. Ibn al-Rāwandī (d. 245/860 or 298/912), who was first a Muʿtazilite but later became an adversary of the Muʿtazilites (Stroumsa 1999: 37–9), censured the Muʿtazilites for not basing their arguments for the knowledge of God's existence and His attributes on the Qurʾān and the *sunna*. In his rejoinder to Ibn al-Rāwandī's accusation, the Baghdadian Muʿtazilite Abū ʾl-Ḥusayn al-Khayyāṭ (d. 300/913) plainly states that, according to the Muʿtazilites, one of God's messages is the Qurʾān, and that "it is their argument against their adversaries in the subjects of God's unity (*tawḥīd*) and justice (*ʿadl*), the promise and the threat (*al-waʿd waʾl-waʿīd*) and the order to do good and the prohibition to do evil"[16] (al-Khayyāṭ 1957: 43 of the Arabic text).

Yet, despite the above, we find elsewhere an Ashʿarite reference to the Muʿtazilite use of Qurʾānic verses in their treatment of theological matters. Fakhr al-Dīn al-Rāzī devotes some sections of his *al-Maṭālib al-ʿāliya min al-ʿilm al-ilāhī* ("The High Issues of Metaphysics") to a discussion on the use of the Qurʾān by the Muʿtazila in the question of free will and predestination, or more exactly, to the question of who creates man's acts: Is it God or man? The first possibility implies predestination. According to al-Rāzī, the Muʿtazilites draw the conclusion that the Qurʾān denies predestination not only from separate verses, which he cites and to which he responds, but also from the very structure of the Qurʾān. The Qurʾān deals with three main issues: (a) proofs for God's unity, prophecy and the hereafter; (b) commands and prohibitions, praising of the good-doers and dispraising the evil-doers; and (c) stories which urge man to obey God's commands. The gist of the Muʿtazilite argumentation here is that if God created man's acts, it would have been of no avail to bring forth the contents of the Qurʾān, for ought implies can; that is, if a man is prevented from creating his own acts, there is no benefit in teaching him obedience to God (al-Rāzī 1987: 275–354). Thus the contents of the Qurʾān prove free choice.

Conclusion

Although we have not approached our subject along historical lines, we can safely state that, generally speaking and on most issues, the beginning of Islamic theology (the first–third/seventh–ninth centuries) is characterized by discussions of Qurʾānic verses among both traditionalists and rationalists (see, for example, the treatment in Schwarz 1972). Already in the third/ninth century we can discern an early tendency towards the use of traditions instead of Qurʾānic verses on the traditionalist side, and on the rationalist side reliance on speculative arguments in place of the Qurʾān. Thus the position of the Qurʾān in Islamic theology has been impaired, that is, diluted to some extent by both tradition and reason. However, as we have seen, there are other trends. Some traditionalist theologians regarded the Qurʾān as a source of rational arguments and terms and attempted to formulate theological ideas based on both reason and the Qurʾān. But whatever their approach, the *mutakallimūn*, both rationalists and traditionalists, have continued to consider the Qurʾān as the greatest miracle God did for Muḥammad, and so defend it against all opponents' contentions.

Notes

1 The argument from design, which proves the existence of God through the wonderful design observed all over the world, is fully supported by the Qurʾān (Abrahamov 1990).
2 Naturally, other factors contributed to the development of Muslim theology, such as the influence of Christian theology and internal political tensions, but these are beyond the scope of this chapter (cf. Cook 1980).
3 They argue that God did not send Muḥammad.
4 The Muʿtazilites are the first rationalists in Islam. They are so named because their alleged founders, Wāṣil b. ʿAṭāʾ (d. 131/748) and ʿAmr b. ʿUbayd (d. 144/761), adopted ascetic

conduct (*iʿtizāl*) (Stroumsa 1990). The school of the Muʿtazila began its activity at the beginning of the second/eighth century or by the end of this century at the latest.

5 In Islam the speculative theology is named *kalām* (literally: speech or word), which means conversation, discussion, and controversy, and the practitioner of *kalām* is a *mutakallim*. The Muslim philosopher al-Fārābī (d. 339/950) considers the science of *kalām* "a science which enables a man to procure the victory of the dogmas and actions laid down by the Legislator of the religion, and to refute all opinions contradicting them." This is done through using discursive arguments (*EI2* 2004: "kalām"). The *kalām* discussion is built by a *mutakallim* on a question-answer structure in which the questioner, that is, the theological opponent, is generally fictive (van Ess 1970).

6 These are the Murjiʾites. Their name derives from the verb *arjʾa* meaning to postpone or to repel. They held the view that judgment of the grave sinner must be postponed to the hereafter. Alternatively, their name can be understood as those who refused to accept man's acts as being part of the definition of belief. See on them *EI2* 2004: "Murjiʾa."

7 This school is named after Jahm b. Ṣafwān (d. 129/746) and its members appear to be the forerunners of the Muʿtazilites on the issue of God's attributes (Abrahamov 1996: 73–5, n. 42).

8 The Qur'ān is God's speech, that is, one of His attributes. According to the Muʿtazilites, who deny the existence of God's attributes as separate entities in God, because such existence would impair God's unity and eternity, the Qurʾān was created by God (*al-Qurʾān makhlūq*). The traditionalists who affirm God's attributes as separate entities existing in God consequently claim that the Qurʾān was not created and it is eternal (al-Ashʿarī 1963: 582–600; Bouman 1959).

9 Muslim theologians also disputed about the question of whether the utterance of the Qurʾān is created or uncreated.

10 Here Al-Ashʿarī uses the term atom in a brief manner. Usually, the *mutakallimūn* designate atom by *al-juzʾ alladhī lā yatajazzaʾu* (indivisible part) or *al-jawhar al-wāḥid* (the single substance). (Pines [1936] 1997: 4). Al-Ashʿarī's statement that every body has an end is borrowed from Aristotle (Davidson 1987: 89, 409–11).

11 The Ẓāhiriyya school of law and theology was so named because they relied exclusively on the literal meaning (*ẓāhir*) of the Qurʾān and the *sunna* in their legal and theological discussions (*EI2* 2004: "Ẓāhiriyya").

12 In the context of predestination, Muslim theologians have dealt mainly with the question of who creates man's acts, God or man (Abrahamov 1990: 40).

13 If God had hands (Q 38:75) or organs such as eyes (Q 54:14), which means that He is composed of parts, He would be considered created entity, because a composition of parts is characteristic of created things. Since God is the eternal Creator, it is inconceivable for Him to be created and produced in time. Thus, rational argument contradicts anthropomorphism.

14 The Zaydites accepted the Muʿtazlite doctrines beginning in the middle of the third/ninth century (Abrahamov 1990). Also the Imāmiyya, the Shīʿites who believe in the existence of twelve imams, accepted the Muʿtazilite theology in the fourth/tenth century (Madelung 1979). For an Imāmī text influenced by the Muʿtazila see al-Ṭūsī (1986).

15 This treatise was published by ʿAbd al-Karīm ʿUthmān as a work of ʿAbd al-Jabbār (1965) (Gimaret 1979; Abrahamov 1993b: 44).

16 These are four out of the five principles of the Muʿtazila. The fifth principle is the intermediate position (*manzila bayna ʾl-manzilatayn*) of the grave sinner between belief and unbelief. See al-Khayyāṭ 1957: 93 of the Arabic text.

Further reading

Abrahamov, B. (1992) Ibn Taymiyya on the agreement of reason with tradition. *The Muslim World* 82, 256–72.

Abrahamov, B. (1993a) Al-Ghazālī's supreme way to know God. *Studia Islamica* 77, 141–68.

Abrahamov, B. (1993b) ʿAbd al-Jabbār's theory of divine assistance (*luṭf*). *Jerusalem Studies in Arabic and Islam* 16, 41–58.

Abrahamov, B. (1996) *Anthropomorphism and Interpretation of the Qur'ān in the Theology of al-Qāsim ibn Ibrāhīm, Kitāb al-Mustarshid.* E. J. Brill, Leiden.

Abrahamov, B. (1998) *Islamic Theology, Traditionalism and Rationalism.* Edinburgh University Press, Edinburgh.

van Ess, J. (1970) The logical structure of Islamic theology. In: von Grunebaum, G. E. (ed.) *Logic in Classical Islamic Culture.* O. Harrassowitz, Wiesbaden, pp. 22–50.

Goldziher, I. (1981) *Introduction to Islamic Theology and Law.* Princeton University Press, Princeton. (Translation of *Vorlesungen über den Islam*, 1910).

Peters, J. R. T. M. (1976) *God's Created Speech: A Study in the Speculative Theology of the Muʿtazilī Qāḍī l-Quḍāt Abū l-Ḥasan ʿAbd al-Jabbār ibn Aḥmad al-Hamadhānī.* E. J. Brill, Leiden.

Stroumsa, S. (1990) The beginnings of the Muʿtazila reconsidered. *Jerusalem Studies in Arabic and Islam* 13, 265–93.

Stroumsa, S. (1999) *Freethinkers of Medieval Islam, Ibn al-Rāwandī, Abū Bakr al-Rāzī, and their Impact on Islamic Thought.* Brill, Leiden.

CHAPTER 29

Jurisprudence

A. Kevin Reinhart

The Qur'ān of the legists is a different Qur'ān from the one held in the hand. It is less, and sometimes more than the book one buys from religious bookstores across the Islamic world. It has parts that are obscure and parts that are clear, figural and literal parts, parts that are explicit and parts that are implicit. On the one hand, a Qur'ānic verse has no context in the obvious sense – the meaning of a verse is not clarified by the verses that surround it. On the other hand, no verse, in principle, is self-subsistent; any verse draws its true meaning from a constellation of relevant verses throughout the Qur'ān and also from the *sunna*, from previous agreement about its meaning and from reflection upon its linguistic implications. Above all, the Qur'ān is truth and, because it is all truth, its language – Arabic – and even its very particles require the legists' study and analysis.

Questions of the historical development of legal doctrine are too complex for a single chapter – or book. By the fourth Islamic century, however, juristic theoreticians had constructed a fairly stable body of doctrine that remained the framework for legal approaches thereafter for a millennium – indeed, the framework that for many still shapes the sophisticated legal appropriation of the Qur'ān. Here we will treat the Qur'ān from the standpoint of the Islamic science of principles of jurisprudence (*uṣūl al-fiqh*).

Defining the Book

In the science of "principles of jurisprudence," one of the bases (*uṣūl*), indeed according to, for example, al-Ghazālī (d. 505/1111), *the* base for legal assessment is the book.[1] Al-Shaybānī (d. 189/805) defines the Qur'ān thus: "The book is the Qur'ān which is sent down to the messenger of God, which is written [between] covers [or leaves] of the codices, plurally transmitted to us in the seven well-known consonantal forms" (al-Sarakhsī 1372: I, 279).[2] A world of dogma and a history of scholarly compromises is summed up in this short sentence. First, there is the assertion that the Qur'ān as we have it is complete (we will see below a caveat to this) with no parts suppressed (see Burton 1977: 49ff. on the missing parts of the Qur'ān). This refutes the doctrine of some of the Shīʿa that parts of the revelation supporting ʿAlid claims were discarded by the redactors (Kohlberg 1973). It also distinguishes the Qur'ān from other statements attributed to God in other sources – for instance the so-called divine utterances (*aḥādīth al-qudsiyya*; see Graham 1977) or other scriptural books such as the *Injīl* (Gospels). At the same time, "seven variant readings" of the Qur'ān were all acceptable and equally Qur'ānic. This is because all seven are "well known" and, in what is the key point, plurally transmitted (*naql mutawātir*).[3]

Reliability (*Tawātur*)

The concept of plural-transmission is the bedrock of Qur'ānic epistemology. It is that, on the one hand, an uninterrupted string of reciters has handed on the text one-to-another over the period since the time of revelation and redaction (see As-Said 1975). On the other hand, the transmission also is, as it were, plural horizontally – so that no part of a generation's Qur'ān transmission is dependent on a single source. *Tawātur* means both horizontal and vertical plurality of transmission such that no mistake, no forgery, no lacuna could possibly be agreed upon by the transmitters (al-Sarakhsī 1372: I, 282–5).[4] Just as the indisputable details of the cultus – the number of daily acts of worship and the number of cycles (*raka'āt*) appropriate to them, the amounts due for *zakāt*-tax and bloodwit are transmitted plurally, and so, are known indisputably – so, too, the Qur'ān's text is known with indisputable certainty because of its plural transmission (al-Sarakhsī 1372: I, 282–3).

The Basmala

The boundaries of the text are, for the legist (*uṣūlī*) rather less stable than reference to the "text between the two covers" might suggest. For example, all *sūras* except the ninth *sūra* begin with the written phrase: "In the name of God, the Merciful, the Compassionate"(see *EI2* 2004: "*basmala*"). What is the status of this phrase, *uṣūlīs* asked. Is it a textual throat-clearing to signify the beginning of a *sūra* or is it an integral verse (*āya*) of the Qur'ānic text itself?[5] In short, most Sunnī schools considered the *basmala* part of the Qur'ān while some Ḥanafīs did not – they considered the *basmala* to be textual but as a sort of punctuation that could be omitted when it was contextually clear that a *sūra* was beginning (al-Bukhārī 1393/1974: I, 23). There are important ritual implications to the question of the *basmala*'s textuality. For instance, is a ritual recitation in worship (*ṣalāt*) that omits the *basmala* valid? Can worship performed behind an *imām* who omits the *basmala* be valid (see Weiss 1996)? So this quite hypothetical-sounding textual problem has important ritual consequences.

Abrogation – The Assessment but Not the Recitation

The text of the written or printed Qur'ān does not coincide completely with what we might call "the legal Qur'ān." The legal Qur'ān is, from one perspective, much smaller than the published text. By some estimates there are 350–550 legally stipulative verses, but some of these are "erased" because some verses are superseded by other scriptural sources. This supersession is known in the literature as "abrogation," *naskh* (see Burton 1990; Hallaq 1997: 68–74; Kamali 1991: 149–67; *EI2* 2004: "*naskh*"). The literature on supersession and its ramifications is voluminous, but for our purposes what matters is that, just as the Qur'ān abrogates previous scriptures such as the Torah or Injīl, parts of the Qur'ānic text are, as it were, withdrawn by other subsequent Qur'ānic texts – or even, for some legists, by subsequent acts or sayings of Muḥammad.

For instance, classically, wine, which is praised as one of God's bounties (Q 16:67), is proscribed definitively in Q 5:90–2 – the latter having superceded the assessment in the former. The supersession concept reflects or creates the genre of "occasions of revelation" (*asbāb al-nuzūl*) which details the circumstances provoking revelation of a given Qur'ānic pericope (see Rippin 1985b, 1988). To each verse the tradition attached a story of the "occasion" (*sabab*) of its revelation. These stories served two functions: first, they provided something like "legislative intent" to amplify and define the scope of the verse. Thus the verse banning wine occurred either in the context of ʿUmar's petitioning for clarification on the status of wine, or when Saʿd b. Abī Waqqāṣ reproached someone for drinking wine and the drinker split Saʿd's nose in retaliation, or, perhaps, when two of the Anṣār tribes got into a drunken boasting match, or from concerns of general disorder (al-Ṭabarī 1388/1968: VII, 32–5 ad. Q 5:92). Second, the *asbāb al-nuzūl* literature provided a putative order of verses' revelation so that, where there was conflict in the verses' legislation, the antecedent could be superceded by the latter. The whole chain of verses concerning wine – it is a bounty (Q 16:67); it has virtues but drawbacks (Q 2:219); do not come to prayer drunk (Q 4:43); wine is forbidden (Q 5:90) – is sorted out as part of the *asbāb al-nuzūl* enterprise (al-Ṭabarī 1388/1968: IV, 96 ad. Q 4:43).

In this way the Qur'ānic verse is decontextualized from its textual environs and resituated in a *Sitz im Leben* that may define the scope of the verse, but more importantly, places it in chronological order with other verses that might seem to contradict it. Determine the later verse and you have determined the effective one. As a result, the number of legally effective verses is considerably reduced while contradictions are eliminated and the legal message of the Qur'ān is clarified. In this sense, however, the legists' Qur'ān is much diminished in size from the textual Qur'ān.

Abrogating – The Recitation but Not the Assessment

The received text is further destabilized by a doctrine invoked in only a few cases, the doctrine of "superceding the assessment but not the recitation." This subversive notion was invoked to justify the legal requirement that free, married adulterators be executed by stoning. According to this notion, the uncertainty of the Qur'ānic provisions (Q 4:15–16; 24:2) for adulteresses is removed by a Qur'ānic revelation that somehow never made it into the redacted text. It was asserted – and accepted by many legists – that there had been revealed a verse ordaining this penalty which read, "The *shaykh* and the *shaykha*, when they fornicate, stone them outright as an exemplary punishment from God. God is Mighty and Wise" (Burton 1977: 78); this was considered to remain in force even though the verse was never redacted into the codex (Burton 1977: 72ff.; Burton 1990: chapter 7). Though there a very few instances of this extra-Qur'ānic efficacious verse, the notion that such a thing exists in a few cases makes the boundaries of the extant written text more porous than might at first seem to be the case.

Thus the straightforward definition of the Qur'ān as "what is between the two covers" is less straightforward than it might have seemed. There are seven "acceptable" versions of the Qur'ān, and for some, the *basmala* is part of the text, for others it is not. More importantly, some of what is in between the two covers is efficacious, but a significant amount is not. Indeed, some parts of the Qur'ān, being later, are more important than others and there are cases where a Qur'ānic verse is rendered insignificant by a Qur'ānic verse "outside the two covers."

Translation

What is it that lies between the two covers? Is it sounds, is it comprehensible words, is it meanings? The text of the Qur'ān is determined by "being between the two covers," but the *uṣūlīs* wrestled with the question of whether the Qur'ān is its utterances – sounds and locutions – or whether it included the ideas underlying the words or even the inferences drawn from these sounds and words. The *Ur*-text of the Qur'ān is, of course, in Arabic. But if the Qur'ān is its meanings, then rituals involving the Qur'ān ought to be doable in a translation – when the meanings of the Qur'ān are embodied in another language. The ritual implications were significant. Abū Ḥanīfa (d. 150/767), it was reported, allowed Muslims to perform ritual worship using Persian translations of the Qur'ān. Though other Ḥanafīs hesitated to embrace this position (see the discussion in Amīr Bādshāh 1350: III, 4), the other schools rejected it out of hand. The best his apologists could say of the esteemed Abū Ḥanīfa was that either he had come to repudiate this position, or he had allowed the use of Persian only when necessary because a Muslim was unable to learn the Qur'ān. In other than these cases, its use was prohibited, they said, and for later scholars to defend the idea amounted to active heresy (al-Zarkashī 1413/1992: I, 448; al-Sarakhsī 1372: I, 282 for a Ḥanafī defense). Linguistic specificity was understood somehow to be intrinsic to the Qur'ān: perhaps because of some features of Arabic itself – that it is "more capacious, more eloquent" (al-Zarkashī 1413/1992: I, 445). More than a utilitarian reason, there is an important dogmatic reason for the insistence on the Qur'ān as inseparably sound, structure, and meaning (al-Sarakhsī 1372: I, 281).[6] The Qur'ān's miracle is its inimitability (*iʿjāz*) – the very word translated as miracle, *muʿjiza*, means an incapacity – something one is incapable of, or prevented from doing. The Qur'ān's *iʿjāz* resides in both its expression (*iʿrāb*) and its presentational structure (*naẓm*). Consequently, "the translation of the Qur'ān into Persian (for ritual purposes) or any other [language] is not permissible; instead one must recite it in the form to which is connected its inimitability, which precludes translation from it and renders other languages incapable of the perspicuousness by which it is characterized above any other language" (al-Zarkashī

1413/1992: I, 447). As al-Qaffāl (d. 507/1113) is reported to have said: "It is possible to arrive [in commentary] to some of what God intended, while being unable [to convey] other parts. But if one wants to recite in Persian, it is impossible to come to all of what God intended" (al-Zarkashī 1413/1992: I, 447; also see Ibn Qudāma 1403/1983: I, 526 ff.).

Hermeneutics: Found Text and the Construction of Context

It is a characteristic feature of the Qur'ān for jurists that it is, in a sense, a "found" text. It must be worked with, as is; it is a closed text. There is no possibility of asking the speaker for clarification of an unclear passage or for new information when a new case arises. Faced, then, with this textual edifice, the jurist's task was to find in it as much clarity and certainty as possible and to find the means to have it address new cases.

To enable the jurist's task, they embraced three assumptions, or as we may call them, myths. These served the same function as primordial narratives inasmuch as they made assertions about the founders' time that determined later belief, practice, and orientation. These jurists' myths of the Qur'ān were (1) that the Qur'ān is language; (2) that the Qur'ān's language is Arabic, and not just haphazardly Arabic but normative and normal Arabic. As far as other Arabic texts might differ linguistically, to this extent they were deviant; (3) the Qur'ān can be understood only in context, but a verse's context is not necessarily textual but, one might say, it is socio-historical. It must be understood against whatever else has been preserved of the founding generation's practice and discourse. That supplementary knowledge must come from another restricted set of sources whose corpus amounts to a second Islamic scripture.

The Qur'ān Is Language

The Qur'ān is language: it is, as we have seen, word (*naẓm*), or utterance (*lafẓ*) and it is meaning. Jurists believed, however, that "there is no natural relationship between the utterance and what it signifies" (al-Isnawī 1993: 211). This means not merely that the word *kitāb* does not necessarily signify "book" but that even in a particular language in which *kitāb* might mean "book," it does not always or reliably signify that. They recognized whole varieties of signification and implicature apart from mere denotation. Bearing in mind the definition of the Qur'ān as "utterance," and "speech" or, in the words of al-Maḥbūbī (d. 747/1347), "eternal speech and that which is recited; an ordered thing[7] indicating meaning" (al-Maḥbūbī et al. 1996: I, 71–2). The Qur'ān irreducibly is language. For a given utterance, for instance, the jurist had to consider not just what was said (*manṭūq*) but what was understood (*mafhūm*) for a statement – locutionary meaning and illocutionary meaning, as we would say. The illocutionary might agree in thrust with the locutionary, in which case it was *mafhūm muwāfiqa*, or be contrary to the locutionary, *mafhūm mukhālifa*.[8] In short, it is meaning that the jurist seeks first from the text of the Qur'ān. "One should know that the aim is attaining the moral assessment (*ḥukm sharʿī*) but that attaining of the moral assessment awaits first the attaining of 'meaning;' one must therefore inquire into the attaining of meaning" (al-Maḥbūbī and al-Taftazānī 1998: I, 72). In this respect, the jurist's enterprise was indifferent to the particular language in which revelation appeared.

The Qur'ān Is Arabic

The Qur'ān is not itself, we have seen, in any random language, but only in Arabic. This is because the Qur'ān is understood as speech, with the written text an edited anthology of that speech. Insofar as it is language, tools that might ordinarily be applied to any language for its analysis were applied by the *uṣūlī* to the Qur'ān. Insofar as it is uniquely effective language (producing not just meaning but also the moral/legal assessment), the Qur'ān is read in ways particular to itself as *sui generis* (al-Maḥbūbī and al-Taftazānī 1998: I, 72).

As the discussion of translating the Qur'ān has shown, the Qur'ān is inadequately represented by a translation because a translation necessarily closes off some concepts that are meanings of a given Qur'ānic Arabic text. Therefore it is as Arabic that the Qur'ān has to be read, understood, and exploited. The *uṣūlī* had available a whole series of tools developed by reading Arabic prose and poetry – including the Qur'ān – by many generations of meticulous and analytically original lexicographers, grammarians, and rhetoricians.

The fact that the Qur'ān is the Qur'ān in Arabic establishes the hermeneutical tools the legist may use in reading the Qur'ān. The strong consensus that everything in the Qur'ān was in use by Arabs (whether or not it was etymologically Arabic) meant that all of the tools from the Arabic grammatical and syntactical sciences would be serviceable for the legal reader of the Qur'ān.[9]

Uṣūlīs were instructed in the instrumental use of the Qur'ān. The first level of analysis might be to see an Arabic as a kind of self-sufficient map of intended meaning. Careful study of its landmarks would tell the legist exactly where he is in the meaning of the text. As an example, every major *uṣūl* work has a section trying definitively to define the scope and implication of Arabic particles. The most elementary linguistic or hermeneutical inquiry was at the level of meaning and semantic scope.

Particles

As an example, the humble particle *wa*, a mere single consonant (written with only the equivalent of a double-u ["w"]), is very often equivalent to the English conjugation "and;" sometimes it may be translated as "while;" at other times it functions as a kind of punctuation. So the *uṣūlī* posed the question: If one says, "I saw Zayd *and* ʿAmr," is a sequence implied? Did he see Zayd *then* ʿAmr? A related problem is whether any conjunction in time is implied: Could "I saw Zayd *and* ʿAmr" possibly refer to a situation in which he saw Zayd in 2000 and ʿAmr in 2004? (al-Zarkashī 1413/1992: II, 203–4) No sequence is implied, say the Shāfiʿīs and Ḥanafīs and no temporal limitations are effected by the use of "and."

This seemingly arcane discussion bears fruit in a case where, for instance, one stipulates, "I leave my house in trust for my children and my children's children." Given what we know of the force of "and," it is clear that at the owner's death his/her children and grandchildren will jointly share in the house immediately; it is not the case that the grandchildren succeed to the house at the passing of my children (al-Zarkashī 1413/1992: II, 204).

Or consider the verses enjoining ablution on those who would perform worship: "O you who are faithful! When you rise to undertake worship, then wash your faces and (*wa*) your hands, . . . and (*wa*) rub your head and (*wa*) your feet . . . (Q 5:6)". If "and" denotes sequence, then one must wash the face before the hands, and those before the head, and those before washing the feet. But since the Ḥanafīs, for instance, believed that *wa* implied no sequencing, then the ritual ablution could, on Qur'ānic evidence alone, be done in any order (Ibn Nujaym 1355/1936: II, 5).

Also, consequently, Ibn Nujaym (d. 970/1563; 1355/1936: II, 6) states, if one says "to a woman with whom one has an as-yet unconsummated marriage, 'If you enter the house you are divorced *and* divorced *and* divorced,' she is divorced only once, according to Abū Ḥanīfa [and thus, can be remarried to the same man, without an intervening marriage to someone else]". This is because the *wa* has no temporal signification. Having declared her divorced, the rest of the utterance is void of meaning. Presumably, had he said, "I divorce you, *then* (*fa*) I divorce you, *then* I divorce you," she would be triply divorced, and so they could not remarry without her contracting an intervening marriage.

The declaration to a slave, "Give us a thousand *and/then/while* [possible meanings of *wa*] you are free," poses a problem. It cannot be that *and* simply conjoins two facts, as in "a dog *and* a cat," because no slave could have "a thousand" to give for his or her freedom. However, *wa* cannot signify temporal sequence. Understanding of context (in this case, social reality) leads one to understand that the *waw* is being used in a figurative (literally: "extended") way (*majāz*) to signify a state (*ḥāl*). The second part is not a condition but rather it is an inverted locution whose implied meaning is "Be free and you shall give me a thousand" or it implies a state of capacity: "Give me a thousand with the capacity of freedom, freedom being the state in which [the slave] does the giving" (Ibn Nujaym 1355/1936: II, 8).

This extensive discussion of the slightest of Arabic particles is simply a demonstration of the significant consequences that follow from the minute examination of the Qur'ān's Arabic locutions. The Qur'ān offers not just rules but definitive models of linguistic usage, and these norms then shape contracts, performative utterances and other forms of legal discourse.

The Qur'ān's Context

For the legist, the Qur'ānic text is not homogenous. Instead, verses have different rhetorical or pragmatic qualities which affect their efficacy. Some are self-subsistent but some call out for a rhetorical context that modifies or alters their plain meaning. The task of the *uṣūlī* is to grasp correctly the nature of the utterance and to place it in its full rhetorical context.

Uṣūlī analyses of the utterance (*lafẓ*; plural *alfāẓ*) begin with the master myth of Qurʾānic hermeneutics, one that can be traced back at least to al-Shāfiʿī (d. 204/820). Most utterances have a context of some sort that is indispensable for the listener to understand what the speaker intends. The Qurʾān's first auditors lived that context – they were aware of the totality of the Qurʾān, Muḥammad's normative acts and statements, and the linguistic and customary usage of the Arabs, especially those of the Quraysh tribe (al-Shāfiʿī 1399/1979: section 51). Afterwards, that epistemological holism was broken by time and distance and no one anymore naively knows all that any of the companions of the prophet knew almost without reflection. Al-Shāfiʿī's great creative assertion, one embraced by nearly all subsequent jurists, was that all of revelation – that is, *all* of the Qurʾān and all of the prophetic utterances and acts recorded in the *ḥadīth* – should be taken as a single expression (Ali 2000: 52 citing Ibn Ḥazm). Consequently, it is the task of the legal hermeneuticist to recover the lost wholeness, the "thick" understanding of the Qurʾānic locution that belonged to the companions. He must master the data that allow the inquirer to understand a Qurʾānic utterance properly. For every Qurʾānic utterance, then, the *uṣūlī* searches the rest of the Qurʾān, and the *ḥadīth* that record the prophet's acts, for texts to supplement the utterance in question. This includes "occasions of revelation." The supplementary datum is called *bayān* by al-Shāfiʿī, that is, "elucidation." While al-Shāfiʿī's exact terminology becomes less central over time as the hermeneutical sciences grew more elaborate, the analytic assumption – that texts are usually not self-subsistent – rules all subsequent *uṣūl* scholarship.

This attention to context both in ordinary Arabic linguistics and particularly in Qurʾānic studies gave rise to extensive attempts to categorize Qurʾānic expression in terms of its self-subsistence, its effective force, its mode of address, its clarity and its effective force.[10]

Self-subsistence: Manifest and Indeterminate, Figurative and Literal

Ẓāhir, "manifest," is a term for a text whose meaning seems initially to be, perhaps or in fact, obvious, whether through the utterance itself, or some other factor.[11] A manifest text, according to Ibn Qudāma (1378: 92) is one which "one understands first in its unrestricted sense, though the possibility exists of another [sense]." It is "when two meanings are possible, it is the most manifest . . . one may not ignore [this meaning] without reflection (*taʾwīl*)." An example could be Q 2:275 "God has permitted selling." It would take a very strong indicant to lead one to suppose that the plain sense of this utterance – "selling is permitted by God" – is not operative.

The concept of *ẓāhir* is a kind of stand-in for the master-view of the entire Qurʾān. It has an initial meaning, in most cases, that strikes the reader, and that meaning must be taken seriously. Yet the encounter with the *ẓāhir* text does not end at the first experience of it. Various cues may turn the reader to reflection upon other possible understandings of the text.

So, from one perspective, the opposite of a *ẓāhir* text is a text "reflected upon" (*muʾawwal*). A manifest text generally has at least two meanings, one straightforward and one to which one moves only because of some indicant that it is not the obvious, but some secondary meaning, that is intended. The obvious meaning is, all things being equal, the preferred meaning. But, on reflection (another meaning of the root ʾ-*w-l*), an opinion may be changed. Thus, when the Qurʾān says, "We built the sky by hand" (Q 51:47), the manifest meaning is that God used His hands to build the sky. But reflection on the doctrine of God's incorporality inclines one away from the obvious meaning to something else; that something else is the interpreted meaning. Similarly, the meaning "Do not eat of that over which the name of God has not been mentioned" (Q 6:121) would seem to allow all foods over which the name of God has been mentioned; but reflection excludes, for instance, animals sacrificed to false gods, whether or not the name of God was pronounced over it (al-Mārdīnī 1996: 172).

Taʾwīl, "reflection," is, according to Ibn Qudāma (d. 620/1223; 1378: 92), "the diversion of the utterance from the probable manifest meaning to a probability that is [in the end] preferable to its alternative; [the means] is an indicant that [the secondary meaning] is more likely than the meaning to which the manifest sense points." He adds that the secondary meaning may be quite remote from the manifest or primary meaning; in that case the indicant that prompts diversion must be proportionally powerful. The indicant may be contextual, or another manifest text, or a piece of *qiyās*-reasoning that gives rise to a preference for the unlikelier sense of the utterance.

For the student of Islamic thought, the significance of *ẓāhir* as a concept may be that unreflective "literalism" is impossible for the competent jurist. Every text, no matter how bald-faced, must be subject to reflection because of the possibility that somewhere in the revelational discourse there is a text that might be brought to bear on the manifest text so as to divert its meaning from the obvious to a more obscure, but more correct, sense.

The pragmatic opposite of the manifest text is the *mujmal* or indeterminate text. Indeterminate utterances have more than one sense and, on the face of it, there is no reason to prefer one to another (Ibn Qudāma 1378: 93). An example would be Q 2:237, "or they, in whose hand is the marriage contract, forgo [the marriage portion]." This could refer either to the bride or her guardian, and textually there is no immediate reason to prefer one sense to another. In this respect it can also be called *mushtarak* (a term that some restrict to homonyms). In addition to indeterminacy from imprecision or lexical equivalence, there are many reasons why an utterance can be indeterminate, for instance ambiguous declension: *al-mukhtār* (meaning "chosen" or "choice") can be both an active and passive participle (Ibn Qudāma 1378: 93–4). Whatever the reason, when confronted with a *mujmal* text, the jurist is obliged to withhold judgment until the speaker or speaker's intention can be clarified (also see al-Shīrāzī 1377/1957: 26–7).

Like the *mujmal*, the term *mushtarak* – more common as a Ḥanafī hermeneutical term – etymologically implies the idea of the incorporation of diversity into singularity in a confusing way. *Mushtarak* words share a single form among diverse meanings. For the Ḥanafīs, the *mushtarak* is "what includes concepts with different definitions." A classic example would be the word *ʿayn* which can mean "hard currency," "eye," and "spring." When confronted with a homonymous utterance, the jurist "must stay his judgment – with the condition that he reflect, seeking [grounds for] preference of some of its aspects so as to act upon it" (Ibn Nujaym 1355/1936: I, 109–10). The entire reflective process is one of seeking further clarification of the context, broadly speaking, of the utterance. Similar is the case of the term *qurū'*, a word used in Q 2:228 that means both "purification" and "menstruation" (al-Mārdīnī 1996: 167; al-Shīrāzī 1377/1957: 93). Words are used in the Qur'ān both in an extended sense and in their original sense, such as words derived from the root *sh-r-y* which means "to sell," but also in Q 2:227, "to impose a difficult duty on oneself." This is, at least initially, a *mushtarak* usage, since wherever the root occurs, both meanings are possible (al-Isnawī 1993: 214).

Q 2:67–71 shows the hermeneuticist a model for the "disambiguation" of an indeterminate utterance. The utterance that modifies the original unclear reference is called in some texts *bayān*, "clarification." The unclear is "that which is in need of clarification;" clarifying is "taking a thing from the domain of uncertainty (*ishkāl*) to the domain of manifestness (*al-tajallī*)" (al-Mārdīnī 1996: 166). So, when Moses is ordered to sacrifice a cow (Q 2:67), the word *baqara*, "cow," is unclear; it is generic (*mujmal al-jins*). Consequently, in Q 2:68–71, the reference to "cow" is clarified: it should be neither calf nor immature; it must be yellow, unyoked, whole, and without mark. The "disambiguated" text, or one that requires no clarification, is called *mubīn* (though the term can also be used for the clarifying text itself) (al-Mārdīnī 1996: 170). Poetically, the concept is explained:

> It is derived from the throne on which the bride is displayed which points to [the idea that] the text[12] in its clarity resembles a sitting bride on high, un-concealed from anyone. It is not possible that she be other than who she is. Likewise the text is in its manifestness which bears no possibility other than of a single meaning. (al-Mārdīnī 1996: 171)

We have already seen that one source of indeterminacy in the text is uncertainty about whether the utterance is used in its "original" (*ḥaqīqī*) or "extended" (*majāzī*) sense. The problem here is, how tethered the reader is to be to a supposed original/authentic sense of a word or phrase.

The classic example is "lion" (*asad*). When the legist encounters the term, it may mean either "beast of prey" (literal) or "man of courage" (figurative). The figurative is known by certain clues (*adilla*) among other signs, being (a) something attached to the utterance that restricts it to a figurative use like "fire of war" or "wing of kindness." Either word in the phrase can be taken literally but together they compel the hearer to understand an extended not literal sense; (b) something joined to a word or phrase that makes one hesitate to understand another thing, as in Q 3:54: "They plotted and God plotted and God is the best of plotters." The second clause – "God plotted" – makes one doubt the literalness of the first clause; (c) a negation of the obvious – as if one said of a foolish man "he is not a donkey" (al-Isnawī 1993: 217). Another *majāzī* example would be Q 5:33, "Those who make war on God and His messenger" because God cannot be defeated or battled in the ordinary sense of the term (see Kīyā al-Harrāsī n.d: III, 126).

As a legal problem, the *locus classicus* of the literal/extended text for Ḥanafīs and Shāfiʿīs (but not, e.g., for Mālikīs) is Q 4:43 (see also Q 5:6), "Or if you have touched a woman . . ." in a verse devoted to the "simulacrum ablution" (*tayammum*). The text says "if you have touched a woman" then perform *tayammum*. Is mere touching enough to require cleansing? *Tayammum* is a substitute for both the minor and major ablution.

Since it is the major ablution that is prescribed for a certain kind of contact between a man and a woman – namely intercourse – the Ḥanafīs and Shāfiʿīs infer that "touching" cannot mean here "contact" in the literal sense of the word "So," says al-Isnawī, "touching is verified as an extended usage for intercourse – since the obligation to do *tayammum* is established [only] for intercourse" (al-Isnawī 1993: 237).

Textual Force: General and Restricted

A problem with any utterance, especially an imperative one, is its scope and its force. If the Qurʾān says to fast, does that apply to everyone, even those, for instance, for whom fasting would be a harmful act? In *uṣūlī* hermeneutics this was discussed under the rubric of "general expressions" (*ʿāmm*) and "restricted (or "qualified") expressions" (*khāṣṣ*).

The general is defined as "that which indicates a plurality of individuals," that is, God or the prophet in some way require an act, and address the command to some group or class. Conceptually, general and qualified are relative terms, of course. "O men" is general; it is generic for all males. It is a qualified subset of "O humankind" however, which, in turn, can be seen to be a subset of animals and so forth (see Weiss 1992: 393). Generality can be signaled by extra-textual considerations or textual ones. *Uṣūlīs* look first to the *form* of expression to determine which, *a priori*, are general and which are qualified. There are various forms that signify the general.

One indication that a phrase is general in scope would be that the utterance contains a generic noun ("Man is superior to woman"; "The *dīnār* is better than the *dirham*").[13] Another indication of generality would be a plural definite noun, such as "men" (which has the definite article in Arabic, *al-rijāl*) or "legal scholars" (*fuqahāʾ*), or "men of Basra." Or there might be an utterance that "includes two or more things or states" (al-Mārdīnī 1996: 137 and n. 3). Not all indicators of generality are grammatical; there are also lexical indicants as in the Qurʾānic phrase "Those who make war on God" (Q 5:33). "Those who" marks the general. Indefinite prepositions are also indicators of the general, as with "whoever" (*man*), as in "whoever is rational" (*fīman yaʿqil*) or "whoever enters my house, I will give a *dirham*," because that means "anyone," whether the person be free or slave, male or female (al-Mārdīnī 1996: 138–41).

Not all Qurʾānic verses have legislative force for all Muslims in all circumstances. Verses that are not "general" in their force are qualified, restricted, specified (*khāṣṣ*). "Qualification" distinguishes some members of a set from others and "does not imply the applicability [of the utterance] to a genus, while the general does imply that," says the commentator. Qualification is envisioned as follows. Consider a phrase like "Those among you who see the [crescent moon that marks the start of the] month [of Ramaḍān], let them fast [the month] (Q 2:185)." After reflection and investigation (not a very lengthy one, most likely), one recognizes that the general injunction to fast is qualified by Q 2:184, "Whoever among you is ill or traveling then [let him fast] the number [of days he misses] on other days." This "extracts" those who are ill or traveling from the genus of those otherwise obliged to fast the month of Ramaḍān; it restricts somewhat the class of those "who see the month" and are otherwise required to fast.

We can understand something of the difference between general and qualified if we consider a controversy over whether the phrase "the men" is general in a way that is not true of "the women" (Ibn Nujaym 1355/1936: 93–4). It is a given that "the women" cannot be general in that the phrase cannot include men. It is, as linguists would say, a "marked" category, in contrast to "people." Under the rules of Arabic syntax, "the men" may or may not be general. So how should the legists read a Qurʾānic command to "men?" Does "the men" include a set larger than is stipulated by the lexical meaning of the term – masculine persons? In the end, the consensus emerges that the lexical trumps the grammatical. As al-Taftazānī (d. 792/1390) says, "the men" is not a "logical category" the way that "the horse" ("horse") is, as can be seen in the differing Qurʾānic stipulations for prophecy, leadership, witnessing and so forth since prophecy and leadership are for men, and the rules for male witness differ from those for female witness. Thus, men and women are functionally different species under the genus "humankind" and "general" terms address genii, not species or individuals (al-Maḥbūbī and al-Taftazānī 1998: 29).

Another way in which the Qurʾān qualifies general injunctions is through restrictive clauses – what al-Juwaynī (d. 478/1085) summed up as "exception, condition and restriction by quality." "Honor the legists, save Zayd" exemplifies qualification by exception. "Honor the legists if they come to you," exemplifies qualification by condition. And "honor the legists who have memorized God's book" demonstrates the meaning of "restrictive qualification by attribute or quality." There are other kinds of qualification as well (al-Mārdīnī 1996: 148).

All of the foregoing are obvious examples of qualification, in which a phrase is immediately altered by either grammatical, syntactic, or lexical considerations. But indicants of qualification may also be revelation that qualifies revelation, either directly connected with the utterance that it qualifies or separate from it (al-Mārdīnī 1996: 145–6). As we saw with the restriction of the general injunction to fast by the prior exception of the travelers or those who are ill, al-Shāfiʿī's extended notion of context means that a text far removed from the verse in question may effectively restrict it. The text may be elsewhere in the Qurʾān or even in the prophetic *sunnah*. This modification of a verse by a distant text demands more of the hermeneuticist. These "separated" qualifications are utterances affecting an utterance – however distant – when they are, in some way, juxtaposed against it. The various positive sources of law, particularly Qurʾān and *sunna*, can interact, so that Qurʾān, for example, is qualified by some command or piece of data in the *sunna*, as conveyed in the *ḥadīth* (al-Mārdīnī 1996: 159).[14]

Examples of texts of Qurʾān qualifying other Qurʾānic verses would include "Marry such women as seem good to you" (Q 4:3) which is qualified by Q 4:23, "Prohibited to you are your mothers." Likewise Q 4:11, "God charges you with provisioning [through inheritance] your children" is modified by a strong *ḥadīth*, "The killer does not inherit" (al-Mārdīnī 1996: 161). Or consider Q 2:228, "Women who are divorced shall keep themselves apart three (monthly) courses."[15] This would seem to be a general dictum for divorced women. But then there is Q 33:49: "then you divorce them before you have touched them, then there is no period that you should reckon" which qualifies Q 2:228 by making it read, in effect "Women who are divorced [whom you have touched]," that is, this reading specifies a sub-set of those mentioned in the verse to which the qualifying verse is applied.[16]

The task of the Qur'ānic hermeneuticist is to read the text correctly so that the scope of a Qur'ānic dictate is properly understood either as applying to everyone, or to some subset of Muslims. If a text appears to be indeterminate, the task is to try to find the information to resolve the utterance's indeterminacy. Even if a text appears to be general, or qualified on the face of it, the reader must continue to inquire, since some utterances seem to be general but are actually restricted, and vice versa.

Ḥanafī Rhetorical Analysis: The Sliding Scale of Clarity and Effective Force

The hermeneutic techniques just discussed are shared – with mostly small differences – among three Sunnī schools: Mālikī, Ḥanbalī, and Shāfiʿī. It is worth briefly noting the Ḥanafīs' differences because hermeneutics is so central to Ḥanafī *uṣūl* and so distinct from the other schools' methods in many respects. The Ḥanafīs were particularly inclined to linguistic taxonomy but not from analytic energy alone. They correlated the obligation to act to the possibility of disputing the force of an utterance, that is, to its clarity. The result was that they used the vocabulary of rhetoric in a distinctly Ḥanafī way.

For the Ḥanafī, a *ẓāhir*, or "manifest," text is the least certain of intelligible texts. The term is used for a text whose intention is obvious to the hearer from its form. In the Ḥanafī scheme, this kind of clarity governs one's response. One must act on the basis of what seems manifest in an utterance. A *naṣṣ*, "obvious," text is clearer than the one which is manifest (*ẓāhir*) in its meaning, though the clarity does not come from the form of the text, but from other factors, particularly context. The difference between *ẓāhir* and *naṣṣ* is explained in this way:

> If one says "I saw so-and-so when the people came to me," "came to me" is *ẓāhir* because talking about the coming of the people is not the intent toward which the speaker is driving, though it is likely that the people did [in fact] come. [This can be learned from the text.] Whereas, if one moves the clause to the central place in the sentence, as in, "The people came to me [when I saw so-and-so]," that would be *naṣṣ* because it is [more obviously] what is intended. (Ibn Nujaym 1355/1936: 112–14)

One's obligation is to act on the basis of what seems clear – with the possibility that there might be need for further reflection (*taʾwīl*). The *mufassar* ("interpreted") text is even clearer than the *naṣṣ* since it allows no possibility of an alternative interpretation, since it has an absolutely determinative indicant joined to it; one acts according to it without any uncertainty; it can, however, be abrogated. The "determinative" (*muḥkam*) is a text whose intention is clear and there is no possibility of abrogation or substitution.

This hierarchy of clarity is not, however, a hierarchy of found texts but of texts reflected upon and put in context. The text Q 4:3, "Marry of the women who seem good to you, two or three or four" is, says Ibn Nujaym, manifest in its permission to marry, but because of the augmentary text – "two, or three, or four" – it is a *naṣṣ* text in its delimitation of the number of wives allowed. There is no linguistic space to read "two or three, or four" as meaning "five, or six, or seven." Q 9:36 "Wage war on all the idolaters" closes the door of restrictions, though it is possible that the modifier "all" might have been abrogated. That is the only contestable space in the utterance. At the far end of linguistic certainty is the Qurʾānic tagline, found throughout the entire text, "God is of everything the Knower." This is a determinative text. "It is best and most suitable to action as the clearest and strongest text." This is a text with an emphatic "everything" that resists restriction and, for theological reasons, it is inconceivable that it could ever have been abrogated (Ibn Nujaym 1355/1936: 112–14). We see that in the Ḥanafī system, texts *in situ* do not signify by themselves; it is only when they are juxtaposed with other texts by an association that takes place in the mind of the legist that they acquire their effect.

Conclusion

The Qurʾān of the legists was, in some subtle and important ways, different from the "textual" Qurʾān, that is, "what is between the two covers." First, it is an atomized Qurʾān, in which each little unit of meaning, each "pericope," stands alone, with no presumptive link to verses around it. To assert that verses before or after a given verse constitute a context, the legist has to prove it; mere propinquity does not constitute context.

To atomize the Qurʾān is, oddly enough, to insert the traditional account of revelation and redaction into the text. The revelation of the Qurʾān is remembered by the community as a piecemeal affair: verses appeared in the context of situations, sometimes surprising Muḥammad, sometimes in response to his seeking guidance. The Qurʾān was not, however, the *Book of Mormon*, revealed all at once as an integral text. Thus, to deconstruct the text as legists do is to restore it to its state before the ʿUthmānic scribes stitched the Qurʾān together into a book – something between two covers. In that sense, the legists' approach to the text is truer to revelation than, say, the recitor's.

In the destabilized text of the legist, in which no verse can be presumed to mean only what is "says," without further reflection, in which, in fact, both Qurʾānic and non-Qurʾānic material must be considered in order to understand a given Qurʾānic verse, the legist finds flexibility. This combination and recombination allows the legist to extend the scope of the Qurʾān to new cases, to read the Qurʾān in new ways and, in effect, to restore the immanence of the Qurʾān to what would seem to be a transcendent, closed text. The legists' approach also makes true literalism impossible. No text is read in isolation, as an isolated dictum laying down the law. Instead, it is recognized that meaning does not inhere in expressions in a simple, one-to-one way, but what is meant by a text may lie entirely outside the terms of its locutionary thrust. This realization makes true literalism impossible, or at least, un-Islamic.

The hermeneutics of Islamic legal scholars has a great deal to teach us about scriptural hermeneutics in general. It also tells us how the Qurʾān functioned in the formation of both Islamic ideal and practice.

Notes

1 Al-Ghazālī 1995: I, 119, says: "Know that if we inquire correctly then there is only a single basis (*aṣl*) for juridical assessments (*aḥkām*), and that is the saying of God the most high. This is because the saying of the messenger [by itself] is not an assessment, nor is it compelling; rather it is information that God the most high has ruled such-and-such. Assessment is to God alone."

2 Other definitions Amīr Bādshāh 1350: III, 3: "The Book is the Qur'ān as utterance (*lafẓī*) that is, the Arabic utterance sent down that is plurally transmitted to order [humankind's affairs] and to remind [humankind of God's sovereignty, of salvation history, the apocalypse etc.];" al-Ghazālī 1995: I, 119: "The book is what is plurally transmitted to us between the two covers of the codex, in the seven well-known readings;" al-Ṭūfī 1408/1987: II, 5: "The book is His speech sent down to miraculously incapacitate [any one to produce] a chapter (*sūra*) of it – it is the Qur'ān. To define it as, 'What is plurally transmitted between the two covers of the codex' is a circular definition."

3 There are some technical differences here. The Ḥanafīs as a whole maintain that the seven readings are *mashhūr*, that is, well known, but that their transmission does not rise to the level of plurally transmitted. The Shāfiʿīs maintain that the seven readings are plurally transmitted (al-Zarkashī 1413/1992: I, 466). Al-Zarkashī (1413/1992: I, 285) suggests that later scholars differentiated between the transmission of the text from the prophet to the *imāms*, which is *mashhūr*, and the transmission of the text from the seven reporting *imāms* to later Muslims, which is *mutawātir*. This leads al-Ṭūfī (1408/1987: II, 21ff.) to the interesting suggestion that the Qur'ān (as God knows it) and the recited text are "two [different] realities."

4 There is an interesting discussion following in al-Sarakhsī's text on whether the Christian claim for the crucifixion as *mutawātir* is sound.

5 For the theological anxiety caused by the lack of the *basmala* see al-Nīsābūrī 1962–4: X, 37–8.

6 Of the three, meaning seems least important for ritual purposes, however. See the discussion of sound and order by the two Ibn Qudāmas in Ibn Qudāma 1403/1983: I, 526ff. Note that in that passage Abū ʿUmar does mention that mispronunciation to such an extent that meaning is violated makes recitation invalid.

7 *Naẓm* – literally, an utterance; see al-Maḥbūbī and al-Taftazānī 1998: I, 73. On *naẓm* see *EI2* 2004: s.v.

8 See Ḥasan 1989: chapter 3. There are also other pragmatic features discussed at length; see, e.g., al-Qarāfī 1393/1973: 270ff.

9 For a discussion of hermeneutic tools and techniques already developed early in the history of Qur'ānic exegesis, see Versteegh 1993: chapter 4.

10 What follows is summary. I know of no concise introduction to this topic. Ali (2000) is useful, but does not cover all *uṣūl* concerns, and seems more focused on the appropriation of terminology and concepts from modern pragmatics into *uṣūl*. Weiss (1992) has by far the best discussion I know of in any European language. Weiss' philosophical background enables him to grasp, and clearly explain, all of the Shāfiʿī hermeneutical discussions in eye-crossing detail. As the title suggests, however, Weiss is drawing almost entirely from the *falsafa*-oriented work of al-Āmidī, who was a Shāfiʿī. Zysow (1984) has a thorough and characteristically lucid discussion of Ḥanafī hermeneutics. It is also quite long and detailed. I have benefited from these works and also from Ḥasan (1989).

11 The concept is somewhat complicated by al-Shāfiʿī's use of the term *naṣṣ* for a similar concept. Shāfiʿīs were faced with what computer experts call "a legacy issue," and tended to retain the term in various meanings. The most common use was for an exceptionally clear *ẓāhir* text. See al-Zarkashī 1413/1992: I, 462–5. *Naṣṣ*, as we shall see, was also a technical term in Ḥanafī jurisprudence.

12 This is a pun, since bridal throne is *minaṣṣa*, and text is *naṣṣ*, from the same root.

13 A generic noun is a singular noun with the definite article; these, says the commentator, are general because the intent "is the genus . . . not some individuals [from among the class]."

14 There is dispute among the schools whether plurally transmitted Qurʾān can be qualified only by Qurʾān and plurally transmitted *sunna*, or whether suppositional (*ẓannī*) sources like consensus, analogy, or unitary (*aḥad*) *ḥadīth* can qualify the definitive sources. Shāfiʿīs intend to affirm the idea; Ḥanafīs to deny it.

15 Translated referring to Pickthall 1938.

16 Example from Ḥasan 1989: 13, but his footnote 3 cites the wrong verse, and the text he cites in the text is slightly corrupt, taking the first word from Q 2:237.

Further reading

Ali, Mohamed Mohamed Yunis (2000) *Medieval Islamic Pragmatics: Sunni Legal Theorists' Models of Textual Communication*. Curzon, Richmond.

Burton, John (1977) *The Collection of the Qurʾān*. Cambridge University Press, Cambridge.

Burton, John (1990) *The Sources of Islamic Law: Islamic Theories of Abrogation*. Edinburgh University Press, Edinburgh.

Graham, William A. (1977) *Divine Word and Prophetic Word in Early Islam: A Reconsideration of the Sources, with Special Reference to the Divine Sayings or ḥadīth qudsī*. Mouton, The Hague/Paris.

Hallaq, Wael B. (1997) *A History of Islamic Legal Theories: An Introduction to Sunnī uṣūl al-fiqh*. Cambridge University Press, Cambridge/New York.

Kamali, Mohammad Hashim (1991) *Principles of Islamic Jurisprudence*, Revised edition. Islamic Texts Society, Cambridge.

Kohlberg, Etan (1973) Some notes on the Imamite attitude to the Qur'an. In: Hourani, Albert, and Brown, Vivian (eds.) *Islamic Philosophy and the Classical Tradition*. University of South Carolina Press, Columbia, pp. 209–44.

Weiss, Bernard G. (1992) *The Search for God's Law: Islamic Jurisprudence in the Writings of Sayf al-Din al-Amidi*. University of Utah Press, Salt Lake City.

Weiss, Bernard (1996) Ibn Taymiyya on leadership in the ritual prayer. In: Masud, M. K., Messick, B. M., and Powers, D. S. (eds.) *Islamic Legal Interpretation: Muftis and Their Fatwas*. Harvard University Press, Cambridge, pp. 63–71.

Zysow, Aron (1984) The economy of certainty: An introduction to the typology of Islamic legal theory. PhD thesis, Harvard University.

CHAPTER 30

Contemporary Ethical Issues

Leah Kinberg

The Qurʾān in the Service of Contemporary Islamic Aspirations

The use of sacred script for polemic purposes is a method as ancient as the script itself. Biblical citations, which are used as a vehicle to support an ideology at stake, can be traced easily in various texts throughout history. Like Judaism and Christianity, Islam, from its earliest days, has integrated Qurʾānic verses into its writings, gradually turning the technique into a major form of expression. In the last few years, however, we have witnessed a significant increase in the number of Qurʾānic verses that are used as a source for the justification or sanction of specific current events. We often encounter citations of the divine word that are not limited to sacred texts or religious items, but are rather interwoven into the rhetoric of central figures and communicated through the general media. The present chapter is necessarily a preliminary study of this emerging and changing phenomenon.

Islam regards the Qurʾān as the word of God that was gradually revealed to Muḥammad to answer the needs and changing circumstances of the developing nascent community. Although prophecy ended with Muḥammad's death, the idea of a perfect compatibility between the revelation and current events did not stop in the first/seventh century. Instead it expanded to the next generations and became a central part of the Qurʾānic sciences (*ʿulūm al-Qurʾān*), known as the "occasions of revelation" (*asbāb al-nuzūl*). This flexibility was facilitated by the general, sometimes vague, nature of the Qurʾānic text. Most Qurʾānic verses are phrased in a style that avoids specific details, and consequently can be understood to have more than one meaning within more than one context. Islamic scholars, therefore, could use these verses as recourse for instruction, whenever and wherever needed, thus taking these verses beyond the scope of the time in which they were revealed.

This special Qurʾānic style underlies a major part of the Islamic dogma that deals with the miraculous nature of the Qurʾān (*iʿjāz*). The latter views the Qurʾān as a divine revelation that cannot be imitated by mortals, as an eternal and universal truth that can be adapted to changing circumstances, and as assistance and guidance that may be applied to any situation at any given time or place. The act of identifying a part of the Qur'ānic truth with a specific experience has always been accepted as an ultimate authorization. In other words, the ability to interpret a verse in a way that was relevant to a debatable issue always reinforced the confidence in the decisions taken.

This may explain why, from the very first days of Islam till our own time, advice has been sought from Qur'ānic verses in controversial matters. A general glance at classical Islamic literature shows that whenever there was a need to validate a custom or an idea, it was – first and foremost – attached to a Qur'ānic verse that could provide support, then to an auxiliary prophetic statement (*ḥadīth*), and only then to other material. This pattern has not changed throughout the ages, and can be widely traced in present days. Suffice it to mention the speeches of Muslim leaders, *fatwās*, Friday sermons held in mosques all over the Muslim world, official reports from Muslim countries, editorials or polemic articles, and even chats in popular forums over the Internet. Examination of this material, provided generously nowadays through the Web, allows us to say that the stronger the message is meant to be, the more Qur'ānic verses are used. As the issue becomes more equivocal, the number of Qur'ānic verses cited as sources for support increases.

To demonstrate the usage of Qur'ānic verses in contemporary material, a wide range of texts may be consulted. Radical Islam uses Qur'ānic verses to support aspects that touch upon the general idea of *jihād*, whereas other Islamic groups are more interested in emphasizing the anti-militaristic ideas elaborated in the Qur'ān, and present a moderate image of Islam; some groups are interested merely in domestic issues, whereas others are West-oriented. The present study is a compilation of moderate texts, issued in the Islamic community, that deal with both domestic and foreign policies and address both the Islamic community and the West, all using Qur'ānic verses to support their arguments. Most of the texts consulted are written in English; sometimes they are English versions of material written in languages of other parts of the Islamic world. All are adduced here as presented over the Web with no further editing. Arabic texts have been translated and summarized. These texts struggle against the association of Islam with aggression, oppression, violence, intolerance, and backwardness, and try to enhance its image by presenting it as "The" universal call for peace, equality, and pluralism.

Out of a wide variety of texts, I chose to concentrate only on excerpts that make use of a single Qur'ānic passage, verse 13 of chapter 49 (*sūrat al-ḥujurāt*). On its surface, this verse does not appear to contain any extraordinary content, and ordinarily would not draw special attention or lead to controversy. The verse reads: "O mankind, We have created you male and a female, and appointed you races (*shuʿūb*) and tribes (*qabāʾil*), that you may know one another. Surely the noblest of you in the sight of God is the most god-fearing of you. God is All-knowing, All-aware."

The verse focuses on three aspects: first, it deals with individuals, men and women, and can be understood as calling for egalitarianism of gender; second, it deals with the existence of different groups of people and can be interpreted as a call for equality; and third, it concentrates on ethico-religious aspects and advises believers to discern people by piety rather than by any other criterion.

The classical literature of the "occasions of revelation" (*asbāb al-nuzūl*) often connects the revelation of this verse with the conquest of Mecca (in the year 8/630), and recounts that when Muḥammad entered Mecca as a conqueror, he ordered Bilāl, a black slave, to summon people for prayer. Upon hearing that, several people expressed their resentment and named Bilāl "the black crow." As a reaction, a verse that teaches the equality of mankind was revealed. This was Q 49:13 (al-Wāḥidī 1388/1968: 295). Later on, the Shuʿūbiyya, the movement which proclaimed equality of non-Arabs with Arabs within Islam, adopted this verse as the source for their name: "nations," *shuʿūb*, was the word used to designate the *ʿajam*, or non-Arab peoples, while "tribes," *qabāʾil*, was commonly taken to refer to the Arab tribes.

Rather than dealing with classical commentaries of the verse, I will examine how Q 49:13 is treated by present-day texts. Hundreds of texts, either in Arabic or in English (sometimes in a translated version), choose to quote Q 49:13 to support their message. The verse is introduced either along with other Qurʾānic verses, or as a lone verse, and reference is made either to the whole verse or merely to one of its parts. In any case, the complete verse is integrated into the text and interpreted to meet the needs and intentions of the writer, whether communal, religious, or even political, addressed either to the community of believers or to the outer world.

Throughout the analysis of the texts I will show the powerful influence of this verse, especially as a source of inspiration that enables its users to present Islam as "The" religion of love and peace, where equality and human rights play a central role, "The" religion that should be embraced by non-Muslims, or, at least, be used as a model for the world to follow and adopt. Special attention will be drawn to cases in which Q 49:13 has been put in perfect compatibility with daily occurrences. No separation will be made between texts that deal with internal Islamic issues and those that deal with the world outside. Conversely, I will show that the interior and exterior topics are actually interwoven with one another, both aiming at the interaction between Islam and the West, either by emphasizing the divergence between the two cultures or by calling attention to their common features.

Human Rights and Freedom

An official document of the United Nations, which contains a report of the *International Covenant on Civil and Political Rights* (CCPR), August 27, 1993 (translated into English from French), submitted by the Government of Morocco, provides a good understanding of the centrality of Q 49:13 within the sphere of human rights, as well as the natural way in which modern aspects cooperate with the classics. Article 3, paragraph 17, reads:

> Article 3: Equal rights for men and women
>
> 17. Morocco, a Muslim country with a centuries-old tradition and culture, has a modern legal system with its roots in Islam. Human rights are not a concept alien to Islam, for the religion deals with human beings at various stages of their life from fetus to adult, and with women as mothers, wives, daughters and human beings, placing them on an equal footing with men as regards obligations and rights: "O mankind! We created you from a

> male and a female, and divided you into nations and tribes that you might come to know one another. The oldest [*sic*!] of you in the sight of God is he who fears Him most." (Arab Human Rights 2005)

Slavery and Freedom

Osama Abdallah was born 1975 and raised as a Muslim in the Middle East; he arrived in the USA in 1988. He was a typical Muslim apologist who built his own web site, www.answering-christianity.com, to counter-balance the accusations of the Christian adversary site answering-islam.org.uk, and proclaim his ideas about Islam, showing that the Bible is not necessarily the book that teaches freedom of speech and choice. With this purpose in mind, Osama Abdallah cites Q 49:13 frequently, each time to explain a different matter, with an ongoing emphasis on the distinctive qualities of Islam. While dealing with slavery, he says:

> The religion of Islam is a very beautiful religion when it comes to human equality and to liberation of slaves. When Prophet Muhammad peace be upon him brought Islam to his people from Allah Almighty, they used to practice the Judeo-Christian and Pagan slavery. They used to buy and sell slaves, abuse them, and flog them to death if slaves disobey. The Muslims had fought long and bloody battles against the Pagan Arabs to liberate slaves and women. (Answering Christianity 2005a)

His site also states:

> No human being is better than the other in Islam here on earth. Only the better ones in righteousness are considered better in the sight of Allah Almighty: "O mankind! We created you from a single (pair) of a male and a female, and made you into nations and tribes, that ye may know each other" (Answering Christianity 2005b)

Brotherhood

Salam magazine is the official magazine of the *Federation of Australian Muslim Students and Youth Inc.* (FAMSY). The March–April 2004 issue published a presentation given in Sydney by Siddiq Buckley who migrated to Australia from England in 1962 and embraced Islam in 1976; he currently serves as a Principal of al Noori Muslim Primary School. He wrote the treatise entitled "The Concept of Brotherhood in Islam" (Famsy 2005). The presentation opens with the following statement: "It is unnatural for people on this planet to live in isolation. . . . Islam has taken every necessary measure to preserve humanity from division and discord. One of these measures is the principle of brotherhood."

Analyzing the meaning of the term brotherhood, Buckley suggests three types: one, "based on biological relatedness," two, existing "between all people on account of their common humanity," and three, "based on belief and religious identity." Q 49:13 is adduced to support the second definition:

> This is the brotherhood between all the descendants of Adam . . . Allah says: "O mankind, verily We created you from a male and a female and made you nations and tribes so you could come to know one another. Verily the noblest of you in the sight of Allah is the most righteous of you". This refers to all of humanity: believers and disbelievers, people of lineage and those without, close relatives and distant ones.

Proper brotherhood relations can be maintained through mutual aid, of which charity is an important indicator. While listing the basic duties of Islam, Buckley mentions the *zakāt* (almsgiving) and explains: "Charity is highly encouraged in Islam and made obligatory for the wealthy Muslim to give a portion of their yearly savings to his poor Muslim brother."

In a totally different context, the same spirit of welfare is presented, this time through commercial terms. Issam Tlemsani, in an article entitled "Compatibility in Islamic and Western Traditions: The Case of Social Capitalism," published by the Centre for International Business Policy, Kingston Business School (Kingston Business School 2005) presents the Islamic economic system as it is reflected through the religious duty of *zakāt*. To prove his point, he uses the Qur'ān as a major source. In section III ("Zakat as Social Capital") when dealing with "universal brotherhood community," he quotes Q 49:13, and connects it to his understanding of the basic idea of *zakāt*, to foster solidarity and mutual cooperation among Muslim.

Status of Women

The status of women in Islam is one of the most popular, albeit sensitive, topics to be discussed over the Internet. Some discussions blame Islam for depriving women of their rights, but others present Islam as an enlightened religion that has always given rights to women within the restrictions of their gender. Q 49:13 plays an important role in both kinds of texts.

The site www.muslimaat.com was established by a small group of young Muslim women in the UK, "with the aim to bring about an Islamic change in society by working with other young Muslim women and the native women of Britain . . . to change the disastrous condition of the Muslim Community for the better and healthy society," all this by "responding to the call of Allah."

The site has a large collection of articles, in which citations of Qur'ānic verses play an important role. Such is the basis of the article entitled "The Women in Islam" (Muslimaat 2005). Here we find a historical survey of the situation of women before the rise of Islam, with special emphasis on the significant change that Islam brought about:

> Then Islam came, proclaiming her rights and her equality with men. It established for her all of her rights to bring her out of the miserable state that she was in and elevate her to the noble status that she deserves . . . Islam establishes the principle of equality between men and women in all aspects of life that they are equal in, because both of them are equally human. . . . Islam conclusively establishes that all human beings have a common origin. This fact is mentioned in many verses of the Qur'ân. . . . "O Mankind, verily we created you from a male and a female."

Relying on the same verse, Osama Abdallah, while dealing with the status of women in Islam, takes a different angle. In an article entitled "Females: The Cursed Gender" (Answering Christianity 2005c), he explains: "It seems that God Almighty has some sort of 'resentment' or perhaps even 'dislike' toward women, because they can easily create great wickedness on earth and in society." He nevertheless presents Qur'ānic verses that, in his words, "praise the Good Women." Here he mentions Q 49:13, and states: "A female in Islam can be more righteous than any man in her community." With this notion in mind he reaches the following conclusion:

> According to Islam it seems that most women carry a great deal of evil in them. Their ultimate destiny is Hell fire. There are however women who also carry a great deal of good in them. Allah Almighty praised them in the Noble Quran. . . . A good woman in Islam is not one who has lots of wealth, social status or even beauty. Only faith determines how beautiful and valuable a woman truly is.

A quarterly newsletter for today's Muslim woman by the name Daughters of Adam, based in Houston, Texas, supplies answers to questions of family and religious matters. In the issue of April–June 2002 (Daughters of Adam 2004) we find the following question:

> I would like to ask a question that is a common problem among many of us. How does Allah look at physical beauty? How is it discussed in Hadith and Qur'an? Many people favor some of their children over others just because of light skin color or eye color. How does the Qur'an view this?

Sheikh Muhammad Salih Al-Munajjid, a prominent Saudi scholar and author, answers citing Q 49:13:

> Physical beauty is not considered to be a measure of virtue among people in Islam; rather the standard on which distinctions are made is taqwa (piety, fear of Allah). Allah says (which means): "O mankind! We have created you from a male and a female, and made you into nations and tribes, that you may know one another Verily, the most honorable of you with Allah is that (believer) who has *taqwa* . . ." With regard to dealing with one's children, it is obligatory to treat them fairly and not to prefer some of them over others.

Ethics

A question discussed frequently touches on the Muslim code of behavior. Some texts address the Muslim communities within the Muslim countries; others aim to instruct Muslims who live in the West. In both cases, the texts present Islam as the only religion that contains paramount values. Consequently, these texts encourage Muslims to adhere to the Qur'ānic concepts and to familiarize non-Muslims with these virtues. These edifying texts often use Q 49:13 to support their call; under the title "A System for Warning Wrong-doers" (Islamic Lit 2005) we find a general call:

> This is a presentation of statements from Allah, the Exalted, which condemns the practice of arrogance, greed, murder, breaking agreements, lying, hypocrisy, vilification, ethnic cleansing and supporting injustice . . . Every time the kafir [*kāfir* = unbeliever, infidel], thalim [*ẓālim* = oppressor, evil-doer] or fasiq [*fāsiq* = sinner] opens his or her mouth or does something, they [i.e. the Muslims] should point out his lack of credibility, integrity and moral authority – past and present. They should ask him/her to repent and change his/her evil ways. When the following actions and statements occur, cite the Qur'an.

Following this comes a long list of actions of assault, verbal or physical, directed at the Muslims. With each of the hostile symptoms a Qurʾānic verse is cited that might mitigate the situation. Encountering such behavior, every Muslim is advised to read the relevant Qurʾānic verses out loud, and in so doing to let those who have gone astray see the right path. Q 49:13 is to be used to counter any sign of arrogance:

> Allah, the Exalted, condemns Arrogance. Concerning racial superiority, Allah, the Exalted has said: "Oh people, We created you from a male and a female and We made you into races and tribes so that you may recognize each other. The most honorable of you in the opinion of Allah is the most God-fearing of you."

Discussions about the moral code of Islam may often develop into general statements that present Islam as a set of norms to be emulated or even as a faith to be embraced. Such texts focus on two main aspects. The first treats Islam as a universal faith, whereas the second presents Islam as a model. Both aspects are supported by Q 49:13, and use it as a supreme authorization.

Islam as a Model

A Friday-sermon, delivered in April 2004 by Shaykh Muhammad Taher in the grand mosque of Leeds, opened with a description of the virtues of Islam and called attention to the duty of the Muslims who live in Europe to spread their religion among non-Muslims:

> Today there are approximately 15 million Muslims living in Europe, and many of them were born and raised in Europe. It is appropriate for [*sic*] that their duty be to call to Islam and to educate people about Islam. . . . Today, we urgently need to clarify for people the magnanimity of our deen [*dīn* = religion and way of life], and the greatness of its objectives, which respect human life and honor it. Indeed, our deen is one of justice, peace, brotherhood, love and righteousness for whoever is exposed to its loving care. Allah says in the Qur'an: "Oh Mankind! We created you from a male and a female, and made you into nations and tribes." (Leeds Grand Mosque 2005)

A similar message is delivered in an Australian Newsletter ("High Notes") of the Sydney Boys High School (an academically selective high school for boys conducted by the NSW Department of Education and Training, founded in 1883) in a speech given by Ali Alsamail on November 17, 2003 at a forum organized by "The Islamic Society of Sydney Boys." While explaining the purpose of the organization (ISSBH), the speaker stressed the duty of the Muslim boys: "to open up to the rest of the school with their culture and religion. The main aims of the ISSBH," he explained, "are to first teach ourselves more about Islam, and then to try to inform others about it." He goes on to quote a few Qur'ānic verses, including Q 49:13 (Sydney Boys High School 2004). Islam, he says,

> sets up a system of social ethics which is yet to be paralleled, even in today's human rights aware society. The Qur'an says: "O mankind, we created you from a male and a female, and made you into nations and tribes, so that you may know one another. Those of you who are most honorable, are those that are most pious". This means that humans should be judged by one factor alone. Not their race, gender, nationality or skin color, but the way they behave.

The speech ends with the following apologetic statement: "Islam is not a religion of terror and backwardness; it is a religion of compassion and advancement."

Islam as a Universal Faith

As we have already seen, Osama Abdallah uses Q 49:13 on several occasions. He also cites the verse to confirm the universal nature of Islam. Under the title "What is the Wisdom of Islam? And How will Allah Almighty Judge Muslims and non-Muslims?" (Answering Christianity 2005d), he says:

> Allah Almighty created all mankind with different races, mentality and beliefs; "O mankind [this includes all races and all nations], We created you from a single (pair) of a male and a female. . . ." Throughout the Noble Quran, Allah Almighty sometimes talks directly to Muslims, to non Muslims and to all mankind (both Muslims and non Muslims). This by itself means a lot to me as a human being. It tells me that Allah Almighty's Book (The Noble Quran) is not just meant for Muslims only. Anyone can reach his Creator through Islam . . . It is important to know that in the Noble Quran, Allah Almighty will admit to Paradise those from the Muslims and non-Muslims who He loves because of their righteous work and belief. Let us look at the following Noble Verses: "O mankind [this includes all races and all nations] We created you from a single (pair) of a male and a female."

The Islamic Center of Rochester (2005) treats the universality of Islam under the question "Is Islam an Arab Religion," stating:

> No! Islam is a religion for all humanity. It is the first religion, which had a universal beginning. The early followers of Prophet Muhammad (peace is upon him) came from Arabia, Africa, Iran, Asia, and the West. Racism, tribalism, and nationalism divided the world before Islam. Some people claimed to have been chosen by God and others as inferiors. The rich considered the poor as people of lower classes. Islam came with: "O people! God created you from a single pair of male and female and made you unto tribes and nations so that you may know one another (not to chastise one another). The best among you is the one who is the most conscious of God."

Sayyid Mujtaba Musavi Lari is the son of Ayatullah Sayyid Ali Asghar Lari, one of the great religious scholars and social personalities of Iran. He was born in 1925 in Lar, Iran. In 1963 he wrote *The Face of Western Civilization*, a comparative discussion of Western and Islamic civilization. In 1978, after visiting the USA, England and France he returned to Iran and began writing a series of articles on Islamic ideology, later collected in a book called *The Foundations of Islamic Doctrine*. In 1980, he established the "Office for the Diffusion of Islamic Culture Abroad" in Qum which dispatches free copies of his translated works throughout the world. While presenting the idea of equality as one of the most significant achievements of Islam, he summons the world to embrace Islam. In an article entitled "Islam, Freedom and Justice" (Lari 2005), he cites Q 49:13 and says:

> The peoples of today's world yearn for unity, justice and freedom. They long to be saved from exploitation and war. They wander lost, like sheep gone astray. Let them turn to the sunshine of Islam's regulations of life and living. Under that common sun, all – black, white, red and yellow – are at one in justice, freedom and equality. For Islam, true excellence lies not in the intellectual or manual attainments of people of differing gifts; but in the moral attainments of a pure heart. These are equally open to all, whatever their other gifts. As it is written: "O Mankind, We created you from a male and a female; and made you into tribes and nations that you may get to know each other, and verily, most honored before God is the most virtuous."

Equality and Diversity

The texts presented so far call for a better understanding of Islam. With the focus on its virtues, especially the idea of equality, these texts present the Islamic spirit as a source of edification, as the ultimate truth. Q 49:13 is treated here as the essence of Islam, as a certificate that presents all the precious features of its holder. As such, it can serve the aspiration of Islam to be the religion of the masses and not merely of the elect.

These, however, are not the only ideas attached to the verse. Another group of texts bases its arguments on Q 49:13 and focuses on the paramount qualities of Islam. Such texts avoid the comparison of Islam with other faiths but rather call for interaction. Whereas the first group treats God's creation of men and women/nations and tribes to show similarity between the creatures of God and to establish the idea of equality, the second group uses God's creation to explain the diversity of people and to promote the need for a dialogue. Instead of citing the part of the verse that describes creation, these texts focus on a single word used in Q 49:13, *li-taʿārafū* ("so that you know one another"), and argue that God's purpose was to create individuals who are different from each other in order to enable interaction between them and encourage them "to know one another."

The *Pakistan Link*, the first Pakistani newspaper on the Internet, established in 1994, published a speech that was delivered at the "Annual Banquet of Interfaith Council of Westminster," May 5, 2001, at the Latter-Day Saints Church in Westminster, California (the name of the speaker is not mentioned):

> I believe that it is possible to have unity with diversity. In the world in which we are living today, and it is rightly called "the global village", we cannot imagine having unity without diversity. It is not only that people in different parts of the world are diverse, but now we have a lot of diversity in our own cities, towns, indeed in our neighborhoods . . . Islam teaches us that diversity is a fact of nature and it makes the nature beautiful. God has created this whole universe with diversity. . . . The diversities of races, families and tribes also have a healthy and constructive purpose, viz. that "you may know each other". In the words of the Qur'an: "O people, We have created you from a male and a female and made you into races and tribes so that you may know each other. Surely the most honored of you in the sight of God is the one who is the most righteous of you." (Pakistan Link 2005)

Dialogue and Pluralism

God has created mankind the way He did to make people "know one another," (*li-taʿārafū*). Knowing each other is actually a call for unity and dialogue, meaning that any racial, tribal, and religious difference should be accepted and directed to a constructive way. Dr. Muḥammad Nimr al-Samak, a Lebanese journalist and writer, explains that dialogue "is actually tantamount to a wisdom which – if understood and applied properly – could well serve as a stepping stone for the promotion of a 'new world order', which all men of good will are dreaming of today."

Dr. Muḥammad Nimr al-Samak, presented this definition in a talk entitled "The Culture of 'Knowing One Another' in Islam" (Islam On Line 2005a). The talk was given at an international conference in Tripoli in September 2003, held by the international forum named "Lita'arafu," belonging to the World Council of the Islamic Call. The participants at the conference agreed upon:

> asserting the adherence to the culture of TA'ARUF between people on the basis of Christian and Islamic spiritual values and the exalted human principles which are in accordance with the rule of respecting man whom God has honored. (Islam On Line 2005b)

The term *taʿāruf* was chosen as a motto to show "Cooperation Towards the Attainment of a 'ta'aruf', which comprehends Allah's wisdom behind creating us of different languages and colors" (Islam On Line 2005c). From here, the idea of pluralism, still based on Q 49:13, is not distant. Dr. al-Samak in his above mentioned talk (Islam On Line 2005a) asserts:

> Accepting and respecting plurality as God created us, is in itself an expression of believing in God. . . . [E]thnic differences do not form any base for preference. . . . [T]hese differences are part of the nature of humans.

Pluralism is often put in contrast with Samuel Huntington's *Clash of Civilisation*. Talking about peace in Islam, the chairman of the United Muslim Association of Hong Kong (UMAH), Mohamed Alli Din, explained:

> God almighty made the human society, built on interconnected interest, benefits and made to promote mutual understanding and cooperation, if peaceful co-existence is to be achieved as given in the Holy Quran Chapter 49 Verse 13 . . . As religious people we should not misrepresent each other. We must wish for others what we wish for our selves. We should encourage dialogue and cooperation rather than prejudices and confrontations. As religious people it is our responsibility to live in peace with others. Instead of talking about the clash of civilization, let us talk about building bridges between civilizations. (United Muslim Association 2005)

The idea of *taʿāruf* receives a more comprehensive meaning in a speech, given upon the request of the Vatican, of the Grand Imām of al-Azhar, Shaykh Muḥammad Sayyid Ṭanṭawī who is regarded as Egypt's senior Islamic figure and one of the most respected Sunnī Muslim leaders in the world. The Vatican declared January 24, 2002 a "day of prayer for peace in the world." Representatives of different churches and other religions were invited to give "testimonies for peace." The representative of the Islamic world was Ṭanṭawī. His speech, published in the official site of the Vatican (Ṭanṭawī 2005), consisted of citations of five central Qurʾānic verses, which made five central points indicating the Muslim love for peace. Q 49:13 was cited in the third place, and was preceded by one explanatory sentence: "God has created us in this life so that we may know one another."

Sects and Ethnic Groups

The question of differences and variations often comes up in discussions concerning the issue of ethnic groups and sects in Islam. The following statement may illustrate the role of Q 49:13 in supporting the idea of diversity in Islam. It is presented as a manifesto of a Kurdish individual, addressing Turkey and the Turkish people. It opens with a full citation of Q 49:13 and continues with some elaboration on the verse:

> The diversity in human race and culture is God's creation. The purpose of such diversity, as the verse above suggests, is for human nations and tribes to know each other . . . Any effort to unify cultures and languages leads to disappearance of that diversity and against the original purpose of God of creating that diversity. I am not a Persian, Arab or Turk. I am a Kurd and I shall remain as one because that's what Allah SWT wants me to be . . . In Islam, no culture is superior or inferior to another culture and all Islamic cultures have the right to exist and co-exist with other cultures in the society (Hajir 2005)

Similar arguments were made in a dialogue between Arabs and Kurds concerning human rights, as presented in the newspaper from Bahrain, *al-Wasaṭ* (in Arabic), (June 30, 2004). Using Q 49:13 and several prophetic sayings as authorization, the text condemns the denial of the Kurds' rights and shows that Islam has always taught the importance of mutual aid among Muslims and has never accepted discrimination nor compulsion for reasons of race or nation.

Nationalism and Racism

The notion of unity characterizes great portions of the ideology of ʿAbd al-ʿAzīz b. ʿAbd Allāh b. ʿAbd al-Raḥmān b. Muḥammad b. ʿAbd Allāh b. Bāz (d. 1999). Ibn Bāz was the Grand Mufti in the kingdom of Saudi Arabia. In his book *Naqd al-Qawmiyya al-ʿArabiyya* ("A Criticism of Arab Nationalism") he unequivocally states that nationalism should be condemned in Islam, since it reflects the spirit of the *jāhiliyya*, the period prior to Islam. Trying to justify Islam's anti-nationalistic nature, Ibn Bāz quotes some prophetic sayings, such as: "Let the people stop boasting about their forefathers that have passed away," and explains, while citing Q 49:13, that this anti-nationalistic attitude is in accordance with the Qurʾān. He further analyzes the implications of the verse and says:

> So Allaah, the One free from all defects, has made it clear in this noble verse that people have been made into nations and tribes so that they may come to know one other, NOT so that they could brag and be proud over one another! And Allaah, the Most High, considers the most noblest amongst them to be the one who has the most piety and taqwaa. (Ibn Bāz 2005)

A text of a different nature is "Working in Muslim Schools" by Yahiya Emerick (Islamic Foundation 2005). It is the purpose of the article to show that secular education is not enough for Muslim children and that Islamic religious schools are a must. In establishing his theory, Emerick takes several Qurʾānic verses as his foundation. Q 49:13 helps him to establish his argument against nationalism.

> Freedom is a curious thing. In an oppressive society, people tend to keep their mouths shut and their eyes closed. In this way they hope the strong arm of the government will leave them alone. If the government of Syria or Algeria, for instance, suppresses Islamic democracy and Muslim concerns, few will challenge them because of the brutal consequences. Hence people, for the most part, grow up without much Islamic awareness. A citizen of such a country will tend to base his or her identity and sense of self on an ethnic feeling or on nationalism, which is quite common in the modern world. Islam, on the other hand, is the antithesis of racism (Qur'an 49:13) or nationalism. Thus, for those who are interested in seriously passing the teachings of Islam on to the next generation, a secular education will not suffice.

The section on "Nationalism" in the work *Rope of Allah* presented by the One Ummah Network appears under the title "The Disease of Nationalism and How it has Divided the Ummah (Global Muslim Community)." Following the definition of the term "nationalism," we find the following:

> For Muslims, separating into nations and adopting nationalism is actually denying the supremacy of the "global nation". Furthermore, believing in the sovereignty of a nation is denying the sovereignty of Allah. In an Islamic State, Allah is the absolute authority, and sovereignty rests exclusively with Him. By denying this, we are denying what Allah tells us in the Qur'an. [8 Qurʾānic verses are then cited, among which is Q 49:13]. As you

can see, splitting up the religion into sects is clearly forbidden in Islam. There is no difference in whether the divisions between Muslims are based on beliefs, race, nationality, political views, or simply dislike of each other. Differences of opinion do not make dividing the Ummah legitimate or necessary. (One Ummah Network 2005)

The above three examples, among many others, attest to the great need to eradicate any possible correlation between Islam and nationalism. Various texts would add the issue of racism to the discussion and argue that Islam, as a paramount religion that calls for equality, cannot be contaminated with nationalism, racism or any kind of discrimination.

A general Islamic site by the name of *The Islam Knowledge Site*, in a section dedicated to non-Muslims, lists some misconceptions about Islam. The first item on the list is racism and nationalism. Here we find:

Many people think that Islam preaches racism or nationalism. However one can see from the Qur'an this is not true, as it states what means, "Oh mankind, We created you from a single soul, male and female, and made you into nations and tribes." (Islam Knowledge 2005)

In his site www.answering-christianity.com, Osama Abdullah once again has issued a challenge to Jews and/or Christians. The points raised represent apologetic and polemic approaches, of which the article "Muhammad the Racist?" (Answering Christianity 2005e) is merely one example. The article opens with an explanation, followed by Q 49:13:

We must first of all know that Allah Almighty in the Noble Quran loves us because of our Righteousness and not because of our race or gender: "O mankind! We created you from a single (pair) of a male and a female."

The term "peoples and tribes" is taken here to mean "people with different cultures, races and religions," and with the exegesis of al-Qurṭubī (d. 671/1272) in mind ("peoples" are those with unknown genealogies, unlike "tribes"), Osama Abdullah draws the following conclusion:

All human collectivities, of whatever race, are included in the verse, which moreover states that ethnic identity is a natural and legitimate thing, insofar as it does not obstruct religious solidarity.

An official document of the United Nations that contains a report of the "Committee on the Elimination of Racial Discrimination," submitted by Saudi Arabia (March 5, 2003), focuses on discrimination of women in education, but has also more general articles. Article No. 9 integrates Q 49:13 in the following way:

9. The State party made use of all available educational and cultural means and the media to promote tolerance and eliminate discrimination. Religious and other academic curricula emphasized the firmly established Islamic principles prohibiting discrimination, in

> accordance with the words of the Almighty in the Koran, "People! We created you from a male and a female, and made you into nations and tribes so that you may know each other. In the sight of God, the most noble of you is he who fears Him most." (Committee on the Elimination of Racial Discrimination 2005)

Islam On Line, a formal, representative and major Islamic Internet site that covers news from the Muslim world and contains editorial and commentary sections on social issues, contributes to the issue of racism in Islam in the following provoking way:

> Islam is a way of life that transcends race and ethnicity. The Glorious Qur'an repeatedly reminds us of our common origin: (O mankind, We created you from a single (pair) of a male and a female, and made you into nations and tribes, that ye may know each other (not that ye may despise (each other). . . .') The eradication of race consciousness is one of the outstanding moral achievements of Islam. In the contemporary world there is, as it happens, a crying need for the propagation of this Islamic virtue. (Islam On Line 2005d)

Politics: Islam – The Religion of Peace, Tolerance, and Dialogue

The excerpts mentioned above use Q 49:13 to endorse the status of Islam as a moral code among Muslims and non-Muslims. They do not relate it to any significant political matter. Whether the discussion is within the Islamic community or addressed to the outer world, the general messages delivered in these texts are of a societal nature flavored with religious aspects. This ethico-religious approach fits the way Q 49:13 was treated in early Islam, both in the *asbāb al-nuzūl* literature and later on by the *Shuʿūbiyya*, always with the notion that those divine words referred to Islamic communal and spiritual life. There are, however, some contemporary texts that widen the implications of the verse to include political issues. In so doing, however, the message delivered does not lose its general edifying purpose, but merely draws attention to further likely implications of the verse.

A memo addressed to Osama bin Laden was written as a personal letter by Muqtedar Khan, the director of International Studies in Adrian College in Michigan, the Center for the Study of Islam and Democracy. It was a response to a tape recorded message by Osama bin Laden, dated February 11, 2003. The purpose of the memo is to answer the devastating image of the "Islam of B. Laden" by drawing an ideal picture of "another Islam." Q 49:13 plays an important role in this combat:

> Mr. Binladen, In the name of Allah, The Most Merciful, the Most Benevolent. I begin by reciting some important principles of Islam to remind you that there is more to Islam than just a call to arms . . . "People, We have created you from a male and a female, and made you into nations and tribes that you might know one another. The noblest of you before God is the most righteous of you." . . . I am writing this to make it clear that there are Muslims in America and in the world who despise and condemn extremists and have nothing to do with Bin Laden and those like him for whom killing constitutes worship. Islam was sent as mercy to humanity and not as an ideology of terror or hatred. . . . To use Islam as a justification to declare an Armageddon against all non-Muslims

> is inherently un-Islamic – it is a despicable distortion of a faith of peace. (Islam for Today 2005)

In December 2003, after the capture of Saddam Hussein, Tashbih Sayyed (editor-in-chief of *Pakistan Today*, a California-based weekly newspaper, and president of Council for Democracy and Tolerance) published an article entitled "The Face of the Cowardice." Here we find Q 49:13 cited to repudiate dishonesty. "Saddam Hussein's capture was important," explains the writer.

> It was needed to deprive the radical Islamists of a rallying symbol . . . There is a lesson in Saddam's capture. People who pretend to be brave and heroic by muzzling the voice of dissent are those who basically lack honor . . . Peace in this earth and love among peoples need real leaders who believe in democracy. Pretenders cannot defend a faith that preaches against hatred. Remember what Islam's holy book says, "O mankind, We created you from a single (pair) of a male and female and made you into nations and tribes that ye may know each other (not that ye may despise each other). . . ." What the world saw on Sunday, December 14, 2001 was the real Saddam Hussein – a pretender. (Pakistan Today 2005)

Two months earlier, in October 2003, the Saudi prince ʿAbd Allāh b. ʿAbd al- ʿAzīz gave a speech during a grand banquet held in his honor by the Pakistani president General Pervez Musharraf (Islamabad, October 19, 2003). The official site of the Ministry of Foreign Affairs of Saudi Arabia published the speech:

> From the land of the two holy mosques, the cradle of the true message, the site of the revelation that descended on prophet Mohammed, and the quiblah [*qibla* = direction of prayer] for all Muslims, I came to bring with me the genuine affection and friendship of your brothers in Saudi Arabia . . .
>
> Dear brothers,
>
> A small group of murderous terrorists were able to spoil our relations with non-Muslims, and distort the image of Islam and Muslims. We have to confront this deviant group and its false claims, and establish our relation with non-Muslims on a sound basis of mutual understanding. It was Allah's will to create mankind into distant individuals and individual tribes and nations, not to kill each other, but for the purpose of coming to know each other and to cooperate into glorious human enterprise, which is the creation of civilization on this planet . . . "O mankind, We have created you from a male and a female, and made you into nations and tribes, that you may know one another. Verily, the most honourable of you with Allah is that (believer) who has At-Taqwa [*taqwā* = god-fearing] Verily, Allah is All-Knowing, All-Aware." (Ministry of Foreign Affairs, Saudi Arabia 2004)

Much earlier, in the 1990s, we find Q 49:13 cited in a peace-process speech, in the "Summit of the Peacemakers," convened in Sharm el-Sheikh, Egypt, in March 1996, in order to put the Palestinian-Israeli peace process back on track after a spate of suicide bombings in Israel. In his address to the gathering, His Majesty King Hussein stressed that those who use religious justifications for terrorist acts have tarnished the image of Islam, which is a religion of peace, tolerance, and dialogue. The following is the last part of his speech:

My country will always be on the front line in the effort to protect the peace process and to maintain the gains made by ordinary people. Our commitment to human rights and democratization will remain a constant component of our national identity, and a guiding light for our actions in the Arab, Islamic and international arenas. Jordan will remain committed to combating ethnic and sectarian conflicts. We will continue working to end terror. We will direct every effort against poverty, despair and fanaticism, so that we can all live in dignity and freedom. In this, we take our guidance from the Holy Qur'an, in which God Almighty tells us: "*O mankind, we have created you male and female, and have made you nations and tribes that you may know one another. Verily, the most honored among you in the sight of Allah is the most righteous. Allah is all-knowing, all-aware.*" (King Hussein, Jordan, 2005)

Conclusion: The Media as Qur'ānic Commentary

Reading the Qur'ān without commentary (*tafsīr*) is almost impossible. The text is too general to be understood without additional explanation or detail, and these are generously supplied in the *tafsīr*. The vast *tafsīr* literature can take a variety of forms. It can take the form of a lexicon to deal with vague expressions; it can offer a syntax analysis and explain the structure of the verses, and it can also become immersed into philosophical questions or legal issues; yet, it can also be of the kind that studies the events that preceded the revelations. The latter is the kind of *tafsīr* relevant to the present study. It examines the historical/communal background, fills in missing details and identifies people or facts alluded to in the verses. We may say that this is the most elaborated and popular form of *tafsīr*, the one kind of which Islam has always been fond, with a never-ending passion to study the details. Verse-enlightening material may be found either in *tafsīr* books or in special works dedicated to "occasion of revelation", in *ḥadīth* collections and in *sīra* compilations (the biography of Muḥammad). This is the kind of *tafsīr* that underlies the idea of the Qur'ān as a source of guidance for the Muslim community to follow, the genre that supports the rationale of the gradual "descent" (*nuzūl*) of the verses.

Although the word of God has been kept above the seventh heaven on the "well-preserved tablet" (*al-lawḥ al-maḥfūẓ*), it nevertheless was not given as one unit at one time, but rather reached the people step by step. The idea of gradual revelation means constant interaction with God and provides assurance of His guidance. Revelations that result from a need can answer immediate questions, solve complicated situations and take good care of the believers. Having confidence in the universal and eternal word of God, Muslim scholars let the idea of divine guidance extend to all the following generations, and, in so doing, allowed people at any given time to find their own aspirations in the Qur'ānic text.

This background may explain the heavy usage and massive citations of Qur'ānic verses in Islamic texts of various periods of time including our own. The media in the contemporary Islamic world, as we have seen, follows the steps of classical Islam. It integrates the holy text into its communications and suggests new backgrounds to the verses. In so doing, the media actually adds a contemporary layer to Islamic exegetical literature. The present study is merely one example of the smooth adoption of the traditional techniques. As demonstrated by a variety of current texts, different meanings, ideas, values, and theories can be read into one particular verse. Thus, Q 49:13, which in its early days helped to handle new demographic facts in a rapidly growing community, has recently become a symbol of integrity, equality, peace, and piety. The great quantity of texts that seeks support in this verse attests to its special function as a central argument in the ongoing Islamic efforts to eradicate its militant image. There is no better way to penetrate the hearts and, at the same time, address your own people with the most sacred and authoritative source, while also enabling the outer world to reach the same material and be influenced by it. By incorporating Q 49:13 into media-communications, a different notion of Islam is being created: moderate rather than radical, peace loving rather than hate-mongering.

Further reading

Bunt, Gary R. (2003) *Islam in the Digital Age: E-Jihad, Online Fatwas, and Cyber Islamic Environments.* Pluto Press, London.

CHAPTER 31

Narrative Literature

Roberto Tottoli

Translated by Elizabeth Molinari

If we look at Islam and try to identify a foundational element in its tradition, one that is destined to leave an exact mark on Islamic history, we are obliged to choose between the Qur'ān and the example of the life of Muḥammad. In this chapter we will concentrate on the former and retrace evidence of the legacy of the Qur'ān, restricting our focus to the sphere of a literary legacy, or in other words, the mark left by Qur'ān narratives on Islamic Arabic literature. The Qur'ān is at the heart of Islamic history and culture, holding authority, inspiring concepts, behavior, definitions, visions, and, above all, literature, more than any other aspect in Islamic life. Every genre of Islamic literature is therefore, to a greater or lesser extent, the fruit of an acquired and elaborated Qur'ānic legacy. Be it poetry or juridical casuistry, the Qur'ān permeates nearly every page (see Zubaidi 1983: 334–9 on the Qur'ān's legacy also in profane literature). In the theological ideal, all Islamic literature is to be the fruit of a direct or indirect exegetical path, or owes at least an explicit or implicit reference to the sacred text.

Ideals, however, will remain ideal if they are unachievable models of perfection. If it is true that everything that is conceived, realized, or written must conform to the word of the sacred text, this also means finding "justification" and backing in the Qur'ān for concepts that are unrelated to it. Yet, it is of little importance that authors of the Islamic age adhere to the Qur'ān as a formal expedient to diffuse literature that in effect only refers to the Qur'ān instrumentally: the cultural model survives even when it becomes artificial or affected, if we can call affected the recourse to the word of an omnipotent God. What holds for Islam and the Qur'ān, holds also for literature: its scope – at least the scope intended by the founders of Islamic traditionalism – is life as a whole and not just a restricted cultural and ritualistic sphere.

The relationship between the Qur'ān and subsequent literature is necessarily composite. The Qur'ān can directly condition literary discourse or it can function as an unrelated point of reference to reinvigorate other concepts and ideas. Islamic literature, like any tradition of religious literature, offers cases for each of these – traditions deriving directly and logically from the sacred text, others that adhere to its contents and others still that are totally unrelated to it. This chapter will evaluate the Qur'ān on the one hand and religious literature on the other, to identify where the former has influenced the latter or where the latter has absorbed elements of the former. This relationship is obviously determined in part by the choice of individual authors in the course of the history of the literary tradition as a whole. Exploration of the literary legacy of the Qur'ān is also a question of the exegetical style and method of each author in his approach to the Qur'ān, to use it, to refer to it frequently or to completely ignore it, but either way to keep it present at all times. Nevertheless, the liberty of the author-exegete is not unlimited. To a significant extent the relationship is also determined by the nature of the Qur'ānic word on the topic under consideration. Where there is an ample supply of verses on a particular topic in the Qur'ān, reference to these becomes inevitable, and, at times, the distinctive quality of a particular author is characterized merely by the number of citations he makes.

As mentioned above, this chapter will not be looking at the legacy of the entire sacred text, but only at the legacy of Qur'ān narratives. A preliminary hurdle is one of definition. A univocal definition of Qur'ān narrative is problematic owing to the nature and style of the Qur'ānic text. Other genres, such as the juridical parts, are more easily distinguishable. It would almost be easier to proceed by elimination. An approved method is that of identifying Qur'ān narratives with verses that are historical in character.[1] Indeed, the Qur'ān relates events or issues that are true, that are factual history, and that are to be believed precisely because they took place or will occur in the history of the world (Leder 1998: 39–40). Moreover, there is no room for professedly fantastical narratives or explicative parables. The historical character is manifest in the condemnation of the *asāṭīr al-awwalīn*, the fantastical stories that the Qur'ān sets itself against. The Qur'ān narratives are thus narratives with a historical subject-matter and are related in particular to three categories – or moments – of history: the past, the present, and the future (Rosenthal 2002: 430–9). The past and the future are awarded the most space and careful attention. Of the 6,000-plus verses that make up the Qur'ān, just over 1,500 are dedicated to the past, to the stories of the patriarchs and prophets, while 1,700 mention eschatological issues (Platti 2002: 174). Reference to the present consists in allusions to the mission of Muḥammad and is less frequent than the other categories. Polemical references to unbelievers and Jews cannot be included in this category because here, for a question of style among other things, the Qur'ān does not mention them in connection with the life of Muḥammad.

In this chapter, we will try to define the relationship between the Qur'ān and post-Qur'ānic literature within each of the genres that developed from the three historical moments identified in the Qur'ān. In other words, we will explore Islamic literature that covers pre-Islamic history, the life of the prophet and the eschatological future. The aim, therefore, is to draw some general conclusions about the relationship between certain literary works written over time and the Qur'ān, and to ascertain the extent to which the sacred text influenced or determined the distinctive qualities of such literature.[2]

Past: The Stories of the Prophets

The Qur'ān mentions the past mainly by reference to the prophets that preceded the mission of Muḥammad. These figures coincide almost entirely with those from the Judeo-Christian biblical tradition, roughly from Adam to Jesus and his apostles (see Tottoli 2002: 3–79). These references cannot be described as sporadic, given that a quarter of the Qur'ān is taken up with these stories. The sheer number of references to these figures and their importance in terms of establishing the definition of prophecy in Islam has determined the considerable role assigned to them in post-Qur'ānic literature. Reference to patriarchs and prophets can thus be found in abundance and in different ways, in all the literary genres.

The most significant aspect to emerge in the literature related to the stories of the prophets is, undoubtedly, the definition of a linear chronology. The Qur'ān presents passages in open order, with frequent repetitions of the same episode in more than one *sūra*. Islamic literature, however, rapidly defined a chronological path from creation to the threshold of the advent of Muḥammad within which to arrange Qur'ānic data and narrative material of different origin. This occurs mainly in historiography, or rather, in history books and in the first books specifically dedicated to the lives of the prophets, the so-called *Qiṣaṣ al-anbiyā'*. If, in historiography, the succession of prophets constitutes the initial stage of a history based on three periods – prophets, Muḥammad, and Islamic history – the *Qiṣaṣ al-anbiyā'* represent a type of genre limited to the description of the first among these. Here, in a temporal and literary space that goes from creation to the advent of Muḥammad, medieval Islamic authors gather stories and traditions of different kinds to alternate with and link to Qur'ānic verses and passages.

The distinctive features of the genre of the stories of the prophets, and the relationship between Qur'ānic and extra-Qur'ānic material, are made explicit in what is considered to be the most significant *Qiṣaṣ al-anbiyā'* written by Abū Isḥāq al-Thaʿlabī (d. 427/1035). It was composed in the first half of the eleventh century, when the literary genres had already been defined and when some of the works destined to acquire greatest prestige had already been written. In his *Qiṣaṣ al-anbiyā'*, having met the requirement of an initial eulogy, al-Thaʿlabī dedicates a couple of pages to introducing the work and begins with the quotation of Q 11:120, "And all that We relate to thee of the tidings of the messengers is that whereby We strengthen thy hearth." There then follows a passage ascribed vaguely to some sages, according to which God had five reasons to reveal to Muḥammad the stories of the prophets that preceded him. These reasons are not explained on the basis of the content of the Qur'ān, but each of the five points contains at least one Qur'ānic passage that corroborates what has been stated (al-Thaʿlabī 1954: 2–3; Brinner 2002: 3–5). An example, taken from Brinner's translation (2002: 5), further clarifies al-Thaʿlabī's method:

> The fifth is that He told him the stories of the preceding prophets and saints to keep their memory and legacy alive, so that those who do well in keeping the saints' memory alive assure themselves thereby a speedy reward in this world, in order that the saints' good renown and legacy may remain forever, just as Abraham, the friend of God, desired

> the preservation of his good reputation and said: "And let me have a good report with posterity" (Q 26: 84). For men are tales – it is said that no man dies but mention of him revives him.

The close ties of this literary genre with the Qur'ān are thus stated from the introductory pages of the work. It is also interesting to trace the actual use of the sacred text. Al-Thaʿlabī cites the Qur'ān with a certain frequency, even though, for a work on this scale, these quotations represent only a small part of the text (Calder 1993: 15). In most cases, passages are inserted in the traditions gathered within the chapters, while at other times a chapter begins with a verse from the Qur'ān prefixed by "God Almighty said." These introductions are then followed by the quoted verse from the Qur'ān and then a story is introduced with the names of the "authorities" or "sages," "those who know the stories," "experts," or "narrators." These two uses of citations from the Qur'ān do not seem to be systematically defined in the text. For example, not all chapters dedicated to the prophets start with a citation prefixed by "God Almighty said." This formal structure appears preferential when minor prophets are discussed, in a way that suggests that a citation from the Qur'ān provides justification for the story itself and its inclusion in the work. Nonetheless, even in the biographies of Moses and Jesus, and in these particularly, a number of passages that are dedicated to individual events in their lives are introduced in this way.[3] Thus perhaps the most striking aspect of al-Thaʿlabī's *Qiṣaṣ al-anbiyā'* is the lack of any systematic treatment of citations from the Qur'ān. Also significant is the fact that chapters do not appear to be constructed on the basis of a consistent number of citations and that no individual chapter titles contain citations. Al-Thaʿlabī does not, therefore, adhere to any specific system for connecting citations from the Qur'ān with non-Qur'ānic material, but manages nonetheless to create a work that is able to alternate and combine narrative with verses from the holy text and exegesis (McAuliffe 1998: 358).

The other works belonging to the genre of the *Qiṣaṣ al-anbiyā'* follow the same pattern. In the particularly ancient work written by Isḥāq b. Bishr (d. ca. 206/821; on him see Tottoli 2002: 141–4), verses from the Qur'ān are placed after the initial eulogy to justify a collection of stories about the prophets. Again, the same arguments are used to explain why God revealed to Muḥammad the lives of the prophets and of past peoples, the favor granted him and his people, and so forth. Isḥāq b. Bishr's work is divided into chapters (*bāb*) which begin in some instances with lists of names of the "sages" (*isnād*) and not with citations from the Qur'ān. In other cases, chapters begin with passages from the Qur'ān followed by exegetical discussions. By the time Ibn Bishr was writing, therefore, non-Qur'ānic narrative material already constituted the main body of the literary work. The Qur'ān is inserted when needed in narrative outlines based primarily on non-Qur'ānic material, or is discussed where particularly problematic passages require additional interpretation. These characteristics are particularly evident in another collection of stories on the prophets, one often considered to be the work of storytellers and popular tradition rather than a work of exegetical literature: the *Qiṣaṣ al-anbiyā'* of al-Kisā'ī (d. sixth/twelfth century; see al-Kisā'ī 1922–3; cf. Tottoli 2002: 151–5). The long initial eulogy does not include Qur'ānic citations but when the Qur'ān is referred to, it offers support and almost exegetical justification. It is common to find citations introduced by formulae, such as *fa-* (or *wa-*)*dhalika qawluhu* ("These are His words") or *qāla Allāh taʿālā* ("God Almighty said") to show how the use of passages from the Qurʾān corroborates the stories. On other occasions, verses are used to dramatize certain episodes. An example is the story of Joseph and the dramatic construction of the twelfth *sūra*: literary efforts to reconstruct the dialogue between the protagonists of the story turn to the quotation of verses from the Qurʾān.

Similar is the method of another author who affirms the exegetical nature of his *Qiṣaṣ al-anbiyāʾ* in its first pages. Ibn Muṭarrif al-Ṭarafī (d. 454/1062) justifies his work precisely by stating the close ties between his collection of stories of the prophets and the Qurʾān. The work begins with the identification and quotation of those verses from the Qurʾān that suggest the utility of the stories of the prophets and their uplifting character. The essentially exegetical nature of his work is made explicit again in the introduction, where he states that he will only include stories of prophets mentioned in the Qurʾān: the twenty-four prophets mentioned by name and the seven that are merely alluded to (Tottoli 1998: 137–8). However, his work is not all that different from the models that preceded it. Long passages are cited without referring to the sacred text, although to a lesser extent than Thaʿlabī's work. Quotations from the Qurʾān are inserted in the stories where possible, or they are placed at the beginning with formulae such as *wa-qawluhu* ("And God's words are"), *wa-qāla Allāh ʿazza wa-jalla* ("God, may He be praised and glorified, said"), or again, at the beginning of a purely exegetical sequence, with no introduction (cf. Tottoli 2003a, paragraphs 26, 52, 90, 92, 93, 113, 129, 130, etc.).

On the whole, the relationship between the Qurʾān and the literature exemplified by these works is constant and homogeneous. It is clear from the earliest works that a greater volume of non-Qurʾānic material – compared to passages from the Qurʾān – is used to retrace pre-Islamic history, even though the Qurʾān dedicates so much space to the subject. In the literature we find traditions where no recourse is made to the Qurʾān, passages where reference to the Qurʾān is placed merely at the start or at the end, and passages where quotations are inserted in longer stories and constitute the main bulk of the text. Among these, the most numerous are narratives of the first kind, where the Qurʾān is not mentioned and where in any case, the stories told do not feature in the Qurʾān. That said, these narratives are still under the indirect influence of the Qurʾān, effectively filling in the gaps of a pre-defined structure set by the Qurʾān. Obviously, the authors of works, when dealing with major Qurʾānic figures such as Abraham, Moses, Joseph, or Jesus, award these tens of pages or even more. And no doubt, the structure of these biographies is based on the salient features of their lives as described by the Qurʾān, into which traditions that are non-Qurʾānic to varying degrees are inserted.

The quantity of these non-Qurʾānic traditions is determined by the nature of the reference in the Qurʾān; it is not solely an authorial decision. In the biography of Jesus, for example, the few brief verses in the Qurʾān on his miracles justify and legitimize pages upon pages of traditions on many of his other prodigious acts. Given the small number of verses in the Qurʾān on the subject (apart from the miracle of the descent of the table from Q 5:112), the narrative sequence rarely uses the Qurʾān, and if it does, only to provide initial support or as a final seal. In dealing with Mary's pregnancy and the birth of Jesus (Q 19:16–23), numerous Qurʾānic verses are quoted with exegetical insertions and alongside other traditions that are then modeled on the sacred text. The third case that was mentioned above, where passages from the Qurʾān have been inserted into traditions, brings together an explicitly exegetical intention with a narrative construction that is directly influenced by the contents of the Qurʾān. In this case, it is often the dramatic construction of the Qurʾān that makes its use possible, through the insertion of passages into narrative structures that reproduce this dramatic structure. This is a clear sign of continuity between the word of the Qurʾān and subsequent traditions, where we find the same preference for factual narrations in which the use of dialogue between the protagonists is particularly favored.

Present: The Life of Muḥammad

The Qurʾān contains very few explicit references to the life of Muḥammad, but has numerous allusions that are not placed in a concrete context (cf. Rubin 2003a: 455). References to his contemporaries and allusions to the vicissitudes of his life are, in fact, nearly always only intelligible in exegetical literature. The constant appeals to his mission and its nature, or to the vicissitudes of the first period of his career when only a few Meccans followed his preaching, are there without being tied to a precise historical reality; they take the form of evocations of episodes that are to be understood as universally valid, rather than as testifying to specific historical facts. The life of the prophet is, therefore, not revealed through the precise identification of his life in historical moments, but rather through a message of moral intent.

Passages with a precise reference are an exception. Mention of the fact that Muḥammad was an orphan, for example, can be found in Q 93:6: "Did he not find you an orphan, and shelter you?" The punishment of eternal fire given to his adversary Abū Lahab (Q 111:1–5) and to his wife is referred to briefly, with reference made merely to his name, his wealth, and the destiny that awaits him. The same goes for the numerous verses that are hurled against opponents, unbelievers and idolaters: it would be hard not to notice in these the evidence of the obstacles to Muḥammad's preaching, but how to go about connecting them to precise episodes in the absence of any precise reference? When the Qurʾān says that Muḥammad must not be identified with a soothsayer (*kāhin*, Q 52:29; 69:42) or when it rejects the accusation that his revelation was dictated to him (Q 16:103; 25:4f.; 44:14), or again when in other passages, it tells of the accusations launched against him, it does not provide any precise historical indications. Only subsequent exegetical literature is able, in some cases, to link these generic references to concrete episodes in his life (see Rubin 2003a: 455–7).

The life of the prophet is, however, the present of the prophetic revelation. The desire and then the necessity to attain a deeper knowledge of it run through the first generations of the Islamic community. The Qurʾān, appearing to allude to certain episodes, implied at least an ephemeral scriptural bond, but also the necessity to search for material to describe the life of Muḥammad outside of the sacred text. Therefore, in post-Qurʾānic literature on the life of the prophet, we find a predominant amount of non-Qurʾānic traditions that only rarely include quotations from the Qurʾān.

The relation between traditions on the life of the prophet and the Qur'ān has been subject to various interpretations. For example, it has been argued that certain supposed Qur'ānic references to the life of Muḥammad have been inserted in his biographies after the narratives themselves had evolved and that they are not to be found in the earliest attested traditions. There is debate about the question of whether this insertion of Qur'ānic passages into more developed traditions took place within the exegetical tradition or whether the biographical tradition on the prophet was defined first, and the Qur'ānic data were attached later on (Rubin 1995: 14, 224, 226; Raven 1998: 426–7). The insertion of the Qur'ān would have thus been to adorn or support. These considerations are of little relevance from a literary point of view. Regardless, the Qur'ān never discusses the life of Muḥammad in a narratively functional way and, consequently, the traditions on the life of the prophet needed to "construct" a historical biography of the prophet without reliance on the Qur'ān from the point of view of literary form. The authors of this genre did not therefore find Qur'ānic passages that could condition their work except in the most allusive terms.

An example taken from the most famous work on the life of Muḥammad, *al-Sīra al-nabawiyya* ("Life of the prophet") edited by Ibn Hishām (d. 218/833) from the work originally written by Ibn Isḥāq (d. 150/767), will be enough to illustrate the point. As mentioned earlier, one of the few names mentioned in the Qur'ān is that of Abū Lahab, enemy of the prophet, to whom the whole of *sūra* 111 is dedicated. The citation of the passage from the Qur'ān takes place at the beginning of a chapter dedicated to the persecutions and mistreatment suffered by Muḥammad during his stay in Mecca:

> His uncle [i.e. Abū Ṭālib] and the rest of B. [Banū] Hāshim gathered around him and protected him from the attacks of the Quraysh, who, when they saw that they could not get at him, mocked and laughed at him and disputed with him. The Qur'ān began to come down concerning the wickedness of Quraysh and those who showed enmity to him, some by name and some only referred to in general. Of those named are his uncle Abū Lahab and his wife Umm Jamīl, "the bearer of the wood." God called her this because she, so I am told, carried thorns and cast them in the apostle's way where he would be passing. So God sent down concerning the pair of them: "Abū Lahab and his hands, God Blast, / His wealth and gains useless at the last, / He shall roast in flames, held fast, / With his wife, the bearer of the wood, aghast, / on her neck a rope of palm-fibre cast [Q 111: 1–5]." I was told that Umm Jamīl, the bearer of the wood, when she heard what had come down about her and about her husband in the Qur'ān, came to the apostle of God, when he was sitting in the mosque by the Kaʿba with Abū Bakr, with a stone pestle in her hand, and when she stood by the pair of them God made her unable to see the apostle so that she saw only Abū Bakr and asked him where his companion was "for I have been told that he is satirising me, and by God, if I had found him I would have smashed his mouth with this stone. By God I am a poet." (Guillaume 1955: 161)

The narrative outline of the event described in this passage is entirely absent in the Qur'ān. The passage is evoked with the standard formula that establishes that God has revealed something about what is being narrated. The story is completely independent of the Qur'ānic verse, even though this determined the need for it. Furthermore, given that the passage quoted above is probably the one in which a Qur'ānic citation is provided with the greatest weight within the entire book, and that quotations of Qurʾānic verses are only found very seldom, then it is clear that the literature on the life of Muḥammad takes shape entirely independently of any structure or reference that can be ascribed to the Qurʾān. That at the origin there may be a few relevant or pertinent passages does not matter. Nor does it matter that there are stories inspired directly by Qurʾānic passages but where these passages are not quoted (Raven 1998: 432): the Qurʾān may be at the origin of such narratives, but it does not influence the literary form of the tradition. Compared to the stories of the prophets, the relationship between this narrative material and the Qurʾān is one of complete independence, and these stories are superimposed on the Qurʾānic script.

This is all the more evident in the specific genre that brings together passages from the Qurʾān with the traditions on Muḥammad, the so-called literature on the *asbāb al-nuzūl* ("occasions of revelation") in which an attempt is made to date the revelation of specific passages in the Qurʾān by connecting them to episodes in the life of Muḥammad. The material used for works of this kind and for the biographies of the prophet (*sīra*) is often shared and overlapping (Schöller 1998, 132). The principal works of this genre were written quite late and therefore cannot be of use for the analysis of the earliest periods of the literary traditions tied to the revelation of the Qurʾān. Their specifically exegetical rather than historic character is evident already in their structure, as the traditions follow the sequence of the *sūras* of the Qurʾān which provide the title of each chapter. The verses from the Qurʾān are introduced with the (*wa-*)*qawluhu taʿālā* formula ("And the words of the Almighty;" see al-Wāḥidī 1968), followed by material to place the relevant verse in an episode of the life of Muḥammad. Occasionally, the verse is repeated and introduced by a reminder of the revelation such as *fa-nazala fī* ("And on this subject it was revealed") or *fa-lammā anzala (Allāh) ʿalā rasul Allāh* ("And when God revealed to God's messenger;" al-Wāḥidī 1968: 48f.). The passage from the Qurʾān is secondary and never included in the story. For example:

> His words "Say: O God, Master of the kingdom!" (Q 3:26) and the rest of the verse. Ibn ʿAbbās and Anas b. Mālik said that when God's messenger, God bless Him and grant Him salvation, had conquered Mecca and promised His people the kingdom of Persia and of Byzantium, the hypocrites and the Jews said: "How absurd! How will he obtain the kingdom of Persia and Byzantium? They are undoubtedly stronger and more powerful. Has not Muḥammad enough with Mecca and Medina to wish for the kingdom of Persia and Byzantium?" It was thus that God revealed this verse. (al-Wāḥidī 1968: 55)

The amusing quality in this exchange between the hypocrites and the Jews is the result of significant literary elaboration. The dramatization of the discussion bears the mark of the common preference in Islamic tradition for realistic reconstruction. The Qurʾānic verse is, however, completely unrelated to the story and accessory to it. This is the case for all the traditions that appear in the literature that belongs to this genre. And this is all the more clearly expressed in the other major work of this genre (al-Suyūṭī 1954), that gathers its materials from previous works, of which it accurately and unequivocally reflects the style (cf. Rippin 1985a: 249; Radtke 2003: 39–58). What interests us here is that these are stories where the Qurʾānic reference is ephemeral and indirect, with little or no narrative function.[4]

The use of the Qur'ān in the biography of Muḥammad has been exhaustively described by Wansbrough (1978). He has shown how narratives relating to events in the biography of the prophet mentioned in the *Sīra* are accompanied by relevant Qur'ānic references connected to them by a keyword or phrase. Wansbrough (1978: 9) explicitly defines this "historicization derived from a keyword" by suggesting two narrative techniques: "history is itself generated by scriptural imagery or enhanced by scriptural reference. I have proposed designating the first style 'dynamic' and the second '*ex post facto*' or ornamental. The former exhibits a process of historicization, the latter one of exemplification" (Wansbrough 1978: 7). The nature of the two narrative techniques, as also maintained in his *Quranic Studies* (1977), is defined as "exegetical, in which extracts (serial or isolated) from scripture provided the framework for extended *narratio*; and parabolic, in which the *narratio* was itself the framework for frequent if not continuous allusion to scripture" (Wansbrough 1978: 2). The literary product is however, just one, within which the same features are evident, e.g., the secondary role of the Qur'ān in the literature on the life of Muḥammad. That verses from the Qur'ān are themselves at the origin of certain passages, or that the few Qur'ānic quotations are subsequent interpolations into texts that were previously free of such quotations, makes little difference from a literary point of view. The Qur'ān has not left any mark in the literary structure of Muḥammad's biography, nor does its word in any way influence or determine the content or tone of the biographical traditions.

Future: Heaven or Hell

In quantitative terms, using the number of verses and not their size as our measure, the space dedicated to eschatology in the Qur'ān is even greater than that awarded to the prophets. The constant reference to the destiny of man and humanity, of which certain revelations announce the end, punishment or imminent beatitude, filters through the text as a whole, and particularly the more ancient revelations. In hell, an unbearable heat will overcome the damned, who will be forced to eat from *al-zaqqūm* tree and drink scalding water and pus. Boiling water will be poured over their heads and other tortures will be inflicted under the watchful eye of the angels, whereas in heaven the blessed can enjoy all kinds of wonders, from luxurious gardens and precious clothes, and can rest in the shade and have what they wish for, food and wine will be served, they can take pleasure in the Houris (virgins) and enjoy the vision of God. The future of the community and of humanity coincides completely with the eschatological future. There is, however, a substantial difference compared to the Qur'ānic narratives on the prophets that preceded Muḥammad's advent. Even when eschatological passages go beyond the simple mention of a particular, they essentially remain simple descriptions of what awaits man in the near future. In other words, they contain descriptions of humanity's eternal resting places, and these descriptions are used as a warning to induce the correct behavior in believers and other men. The description of what will occur on the day of judgment is not, therefore, the result of a sustained presentation that is part of a linear progression in the narrative. When the Qur'ān mentions stories of Moses, Joseph, and other prophets, even though no precise temporal reference is given, the description of their exploits implicitly communicates a necessary temporal sequence. In eschatology this does not occur, for the reason that eschatological time is a "non-time" *par excellence* – a time that cannot be defined in a linear fashion, that represents a point of arrival chosen by the Qur'ān with no detailed reference to what will happen along the path that will take humanity in that direction.

These features determine the relationship between Islamic traditions and Qur'ānic data. If, on the one hand, with regard to certain elements of eschatology, the Qur'ān is consistent and cannot be ignored, on the other hand, the possibility of a narrative sequence that describes the individual eschatological fate after death and then the route towards the end of time and eternal life, cannot have the Qur'ān as its model. An example of the legacy of the Qur'ān on eschatological themes in later literature is provided by an ancient work on the description of paradise, by the Andalusian writer ʿAbd al-Malik b. Ḥabīb (d. 238/853). The quotations from the Qur'ān in the traditions are numerous and manifest different typologies. There are plenty of verses inserted at the beginning and end, signifying that the Qur'ān corroborates the story; as well, the typical exegetical definitions are also present, but there are also numerous traditions that provide the narrative outline where the Qur'ānic wording has a functional role in the narration (Monferrer Sala 1997: 29–30). For example, in a tradition that opens the chapter on the various levels of paradise, we find:

> With regard to the words of the Almighty, "And surely what the world to come has is greater in rank, greater in preferment" (Q 17:21) and with regard also to the words of the Almighty "Those in truth are the believers; they have degrees with their Lord, and forgiveness, and generous provision" (Q 8:4), ʿAbd al-Malik said that the "degrees" are the ranks and merits. The degree of paradise signifies the merit and the rank reflecting how God considers some people superior to others in reference to their acts in this world obeying Him. Does not the Almighty say "Behold, how We prefer some of them over others!" (Q 17:21), that is, in the sustenance in this world; "and surely the world to come is greater in degrees" (Q 17:21), in the merits and the ranks? Then He explained this and stated "greater in preferment" (Q 17:21) and the degrees and the ranks according to which God considers some superior to others number one hundred. The people of each degree, rank and merit become companions; this does not mean that they are companions in eating, drinking and living but only that the same merit puts them together. Have you not considered the words of the Almighty, "Whosoever obeys God and the apostle, they are with those whom God has blessed, prophets, just men, martyrs, the righteous; they are good companions!" (Q 4:69)? They are companions because they are gathered in that degree, in that merit and in that rank. (ʿAbd al-Malik b. Ḥabīb 1987: 17; cf. Monferrer Sala 1997: 63–4).

The structure of the discussion takes place around the content of the verses from the Qur'ān. The complex definition of the different ranks of the blessed in paradise is possible owing to the rich number of passages on the subject in the sacred text. This allows for the construction of a story with a coherent narrative and one that is ultimately exegetical. The "active" insertion of references from the Qur'ān is all the more evident in dealing with the benefits that the blessed enjoy in paradise, or of the tortures endured in hell, topics for which the Qur'ān is lavish with details. The Qur'ān tells us, for example, of the seven doors of hell, it describes various punishments known by the damned in a dozen or so different passages, and generically categorizes the damned, in the fragmented and evocative style that lends itself so well to further exegetical study. As far as eschatology is concerned, therefore, the exegetical path is determined by such a great number of references in the Qur'ān to be able to form a rough outline within which to insert further narratives.

The particular character of Qur'ānic data on eschatology is evident, for example, in those works that also deal with a subject about which the sacred text is on the whole silent: man's destiny after death and all that which precedes the day of judgment and the entry into paradise or hell. The narrative on the destiny of the individual, or the fate of the soul after death, the torments in the grave, the visitation of the angels and so forth are reconstructed almost exclusively through mention and apposition of the *ḥadīth* reports (sayings of Muḥammad) and of *āthār* (sayings attributed to the companions, successors or authorities of early Islam), a literary genre in which quotations from the Qur'ān have an accessory and confirming function, and are therefore not very frequent. If we consider the traditional medieval works that examine eschatology in depth, we necessarily find a different use and influence of the Qur'ān. The polygraph al-Suyūṭī (d. 911/1505) shows how the traditions inserted into his works on eschatology exhibit a different role for the Qur'ān on the basis of the topic dealt with. In long chapters on the fate of the deceased the quotations are sporadic, due also to the particular features of the traditional literature used, but the situation is very different when the discussion is dictated by numerous passages from the Qur'ān, as for example, in the chapter on the wives that a believer will find in paradise (al-Suyūṭī 1990: 436–44). This can also be seen in similar works, from the work of al-Bayhaqī (d. 458/1066; 1986) to the more famous and lengthier *Tadhkira* of al-Qurṭubī (d. 671/1273; 1992: for example, 200f., 448f.), or in those whose content is marked by more popular traditions, such as *al-Durra al-fākhira* attributed to al-Ghazālī (d. 505/1111; Gautier 1878) or the *Daqā'iq* of ʿAbd al-Raḥīm al-Qāḍī (fl. eighth/fourteenth century; al-Qāḍī 1984: 42f.).

Traditional literature necessarily absorbs the non-temporality of the sacred text. The exegete or historian must transmit the description of eschatology given in the Qur'ān, or in the sayings of the prophet, in a framework that nearly always lacks any temporal linearity. This explains how the rich traditional material is abundant but blocked by a descriptive rigidity. Such features are all the more clear when one considers the absence of any details that can be traced to the apocalyptic genre, often connected to eschatological events, and that generally provides these with a narrative outline and a historical perspective. The Qur'ān does not contain apocalyptic material, although there are certain themes of this kind connected to verses on eschatology. For example, the Qur'ān mentions Gog and Magog and the *dābba* ("beast"), but it is well known that apocalyptic literature does not make great use of the Qur'ān and when it does, references in the text are made in the usual way that denotes its unrelatedness: at the beginning or at the end of the traditions (Cook 2002: 275f.).

What has been discussed thus far denotes a different typology of use of Qur'ānic verses in post-Qur'ānic Islamic literature. The particular features of the topic (eschatology, future) and how it is treated in the numerous passages found in the Qur'ān, denote a total absence of a temporal sequence capable of providing a fixed structure for narrative. Eschatological time is a non-time and any literature that seeks to explain it must rely on traditions that deal with the fate of the individual after death that are based almost entirely on later traditions and not on the Qur'ān. When we are dealing with issues for which there is an abundance of data in the Qur'ān, the picture is altogether different. These traditions and the authors that gather them, endeavor to insert the references in a harmonious way into the narrative outline. This occurs outside of a clear and well-developed narrative framework precisely because the frequent quotations from the Qur'ān determine the subject matter and how it should be dealt with, and restrict successive literature to an exegetical discourse that must relate the numerous descriptions found in the Qur'ān.

Conclusion

The narrative references found in the Qur'ān correspond to the three historical periods described above, which look to the past, the present and the future of the community of believers. The Qur'ān, however, deals differently with each. The past is awarded a great deal of space and an implicitly historical narrative framework, while only rare allusions are made to the present and the future features in a substantial part of its verses but only for descriptions not included in sustained narratives. The subsequent tradition models itself on these features and it is here that the legacy of the Qur'ān makes its sharpest contribution. In the case of literature on the past, on the prophets, the Qur'ān affects the definition of themes and the fundamental roles, offering a narrative outline and often references to specific events. We find here all the characteristic typologies in the relation between sacred text and non-canonical tradition. With regard to the life of Muḥammad, the narrative framework is not determined by the Qur'ān, nor does the Qur'ān offer anything more than the odd sporadic reference. When it does feature, the Qur'ān is clearly unrelated to the content of the later non-Qur'ānic tradition, and when a connection is made, it appears to be the fruit of an exegetical path. With regard to eschatology, we find a third scenario. The Qur'ān provides neither narrative framework, nor a defined historical backdrop, but it does contain many verses on this subject. Subsequent literature goes on to create a sequence that goes from individual eschatology to the description of celestial dwellings, not inferred from the Qur'ān, within which to insert the necessary references to the holy text. Here we find all kinds of traditions with a prevalence of traditions connected to the Qur'ān or that pick up from it and define its contents.

The definition of a historical and narrative path based on these three moments, has, therefore, its origin in the contents of the Qur'ān, but achieves completion only in subsequent literature. The best example of this is offered by Ibn Kathīr (d. 774/1373) whose follow up to his universal historiography *al-Bidāya wa'l-nihāya* ("The Beginning and the End") was a collection of eschatological traditions entitled *Nihāyat al-bidāya* ("The End of the Beginning"). Past, Islamic present, and future are all included in a solid conception of history, fruit of a theology based on the Qur'ānic revelation and that is by all accounts a salvation history (Calder 1993; cf. Wansbourgh 1978; Gilliot 1993; 1994). This unified vision of history conceived by Ibn Kathīr emphasizes another point. The religious literature that brings together the three topics/literary genres just discussed, in so much as it is essentially historical, manifests a unity that is achieved in historiographical literature.

Such a phenomenon, as mentioned elsewhere (Tottoli 2003b), derives in part from the particular conception of history inspired by the Qur'ān, but to no lesser extent also from the form of Islamic narratives. The fragmentation and reciprocal independence of the traditions that constitute the smallest narrative units *(akhbār)* make each of these traditions a piece of an ever-expanding and more complex mosaic. In successive literature, the author's presence is less marked, and an external viewpoint is privileged that aims to respect the legacy of previous generations and emphasize verisimilitude (cf. Leder 1992: 307; Radtke 2003: 143–6). In this way, medieval works are long collections of smaller units that are chosen by authors whose intervention is minimal. Even here though, it is possible to see a generic Qur'ānic influence. The taste for factual narrations typical of the Qur'ān leaves its mark in subsequent literature that uses this technique in the formal presentation of the criteria of transmission – with the quotation of *isnād* – and even in the style. The dramatic style which is also typical of the Qur'ān is brought out in subsequent traditions that privilege the use of direct speech by the protagonists, with no additional commentary. Here, exactly as in the definition of the historical themes, we can find one of the most significant and consistent legacies of Qur'ānic narratives in Islamic literature.

Translated by Elizabeth Molinari.

Notes

1 The question of the historical character of the Qur'ān is, from our perspective, of little relevance. The Qur'ān does not have a defined conception of history, and its intent is moral rather than historical. However, the Qur'ān frequently makes use of narratives that have historical significance, in the terms described above. On this issue see Donner (1998: 80, and n. 64) who states that "the very concept of history is fundamentally irrelevant to the Qur'ān's concern" and mentions "Qur'ān's ahistorical point of view." For further information, and for arguments against this position (by Rosenthal, Obermann, and Khalidi), see the material quoted by Donner.

2 The exegetical aspect of this issue is not relevant here. On this matter, and on the narrative features of Qur'ānic exegesis, see Calder 1993; Afsaruddin 2001; Riddell 1997; McAuliffe 1998: 353f.

3 Chapters on prophets that begin with a quotation from the Qur'ān: Hūd (Brinner 2002: 105), Ṣāliḥ (Brinner 2002: 114), Yūsuf (Brinner 2002: 181, but cf. the original Arabic: al-Thaʿlabī 1954: 181), Iram (Brinner 2002: 238), Aṣḥāb al-rass (Brinner 2002: 247), Job (Brinner 2002: 254). Shuʿayb (Brinner 2002: 274), Moses (Brinner 2002: 278), in which also many paragraphs of his long biography begin with a quotation from the Qur'ān, and so also Korah (Brinner 2002: 351), al-Khiḍr (Brinner 2002: 361), Elijah (Brinner 2002: 419), Dhū 'l-Kifl (Brinner 2002: 436), Eli and Samuel (Brinner 2002, 439), Saul (Brinner 2002: 445), David (Brinner 2002: 462), David and Solomon (Brinner 2002: 482, 485), Isaiah etc. (Brinner 2002: 549), Ezra (Brinner 2002: 576), Luqmān (Brinner 2002: 586), Dhū 'l-Qarnayn (Brinner 2002: 603), Aṣḥāb al-kahf (Brinner 2002: 689), Samson (Brinner 2002: 726), Aṣḥāb al-ukhdūd (Brinner 2002: 728), Aṣḥāb al-fīl (Brinner 2002: 733).

4 There are of course different typologies. Certain traditions of *asbāb* have a legal role (Wansbrough 1977: 38), while others have mainly a "haggadically exegetical" function (Rippin 1985a: 256–7; Rippin 1988: 3, 19). Some collections of *asbāb al-nuzūl* also contain narratives on the prophets, even though they are introduced with a different terminology: *qiṣṣa* ("tale") rather than *sabab* ("occasion") (Rippin 1985b: 5–6). In this sense, the material has the function of narratively expanding a verse (Rippin 1988: 4). The issue of dating is subject to a number of interpretations (cf. Kister 1983: 352–3; Schöller 1998: 114–33).

Further reading

Brinner, W. M. (2002) *ʿArāʾis al-majālis fī qiṣaṣ al-anbiyāʾ or "Lives of the Prophets" as Recounted by Abū Isḥāq Aḥmad ibn Muḥammad ibn Ibrāhīm al-Thaʿlabī*. Brill, Leiden.

Calder, N. (1993) *Tafsīr* from Ṭabarī to Ibn Kathīr: Problems in the description of a genre, illustrated with reference to the story of Abraham. In: Hawting, G. R. and Shareef, A.-K. (eds.) *Approaches to the Qurʾān*. Routledge, London, pp. 101–40.

Donner, F. M. (1998) *Narratives of Islamic Origins: The Beginnings of Islamic Historical Writing*. Darwin Press, Princeton.

Kadi, W., and Mir, M. (2003) Literature and the Qur'ān. In: McAuliffe, Jane Dammen (ed.) *Encyclopaedia of the Qurʾān*. Brill, Leiden, vol. III, pp. 205–27.

Leder, S. (1998) Conventions of fictional narration in learned literature. In: Leder, S. (ed.) *Storytelling in the Framework of Non-fictional Arabic Literature*. Harrassowitz, Wiesbaden, pp. 34–60.

Raven, W. (1998) The biography of the prophet and its scriptural basis. In: Leder, S. (ed.) *Storytelling in the Framework of Non-fictional Arabic Literature*. Harrassowitz, Wiesbaden, pp. 421–32.

Rubin, U. (1995) *The Eye of the Beholder: The Life of Muḥammad as Viewed by the Early Muslims*. Darwin Press, Princeton.

Tottoli, R. (2002) *Biblical Prophets in the Qurʾān and Muslim Literature*. Curzon, Richmond.

Wansbrough, J. (1978) *The Sectarian Milieu: Content and Composition of Islamic Salvation History*. Oxford University Press, Oxford.

Zubaidi, A. M. (1983) The impact of the Qurʾān and *ḥadīth* on medieval Arabic literature. In: Beeston, A. F. L., Johnstone, T. M., Serjeant, R. B., and Smith, G. R. (eds.) *Arabic Literature to the End of the Umayyad Period*. Cambridge University Press, Cambridge, pp. 322–43.

CHAPTER 32

Recitation

Anna M. Gade

A unique characteristic of the recited Qur'ān is its tendency to reference itself, to discuss the effects of its recitation even as it is being read. The word Qur'ān itself is often said to be a variant of the verb *q-r-'* which means "to read" or "to recite aloud." According to Muslims, the Qur'ān's most authoritative transmission has been oral since the time of its revelation to Muḥammad. Many of the Qur'ān's names for itself also highlight the active aspects of the rendering of the Qur'ān in voice, such as its being a repeated "reminder," *dhikr*. Technical sciences for "reading" the Qur'ān have been developed in the Islamic traditions of learning and practice where they have a central place. The recitation of the Qur'ān is a central act of Islamic piety both in required practice (canonical prayer, *ṣalāt*) as well as in other supererogatory and voluntary religious expression. Today, the recited Qur'ān is the basis of Islamic revitalization in parts of the contemporary Muslim world, indicating its foundational role in collective Muslim life worldwide.

The Qur'ān and the *Sunna* on the Recited Qur'ān

Throughout the development of traditions of Qur'ān recitation and up until the present, Muslims have based the theory and practice of the recited Qur'ān on the two most authoritative sources in Islamic tradition: the Qur'ān itself and, second, material in *ḥadīth* reports. The latter comprise the *sunna* or exemplary model of comportment of Muḥammad. The ethico-legal injunctions to recite the Qur'ān and the norms for how to recite it are expanded in other authoritative material such as information on how influential early Muslims recited and other normative guidelines for the technique and practice of recitation. Within this material, however, it is the Qur'ān and the *sunna* that carry the most authoritative force because of their status in tradition.

As a highly self-referential text, the Qur'ān includes many descriptions of its own recitation and the power of hearing and voicing the text. The Qur'ān discusses its own recitation in general terms, and only somewhat less so in specific or technical terms. Because of the Qur'ān's unique authority in Islamic systems to guide Islamic thought and action, these descriptions of the recited Qur'ān function also as a kind of instruction to believers. The verses of the Qur'ān that have been said to be among the first revealed to Muḥammad, the beginning verses of *sūra* 96, *al-ʿAlaq*, are often interpreted as a command, specifically directed to the prophet while also directed to Muslims in general, to voice the Qur'ān, "Recite! In the name of your Lord who created humanity from a clot." The Qur'ān also gives guidelines about how to perform its own recitation, as in Q 73:4, "Recite the Qur'ān with *tartīl* [slowly, deliberately]." Muslims often cite Q 75:16 as instruction on Qur'ān recitation: "Do not hasten your tongue with it; it is for Us [God] to collect and to read it; when We recite it, follow then its recitation." The Qur'ān includes many recommendations about its own recitation, such as to concentrate fully, to recite as an act of supererogatory piety especially at night, and to "remember" and to "preserve" its message.

Many of the Qur'ānic directives concerning recitation found in the Qur'ān are descriptions of the effect of the recited Qur'ān on its listeners. The Qur'ān often expresses the embodied, emotive responses of believers to its own recitation. For example, the Qur'ān describes these reactions as "shivering" skin and "trembling" heart (for example Q 19:58 and 39:23). Weeping as a recognition of the message of the recited Qur'ān is a common Qur'ānic theme, as in Q 5:83, "And when they hear what has been sent down to the messenger [of the Qur'ān], you see their eyes overflow with tears because of what they have recognized of truth. They shout: 'Our Lord! We believe; so You will write us down among the witnesses to the Truth'." The Qur'ān often links such descriptions of affective response to the altered moral state of the believer who is receptive to the message. An example is Q 17:107–9, "When it [the Qur'ān] is recited to them, they fall down upon their faces, prostrating, and say: 'Glory be to our Lord. Our Lord's promise is fulfilled.' And they fall down upon their faces, weeping, and it increases them in humility."

Ḥadīth material enhances Qur'ānic prescription and description by conveying the ideal intensity of Qur'ānic engagement through the injunction to follow the model of Muḥammad. This is because the *sunna*, in the form of the sayings, actions, and tacit approvals and disapprovals of the prophet, is preserved in *ḥadīth* "traditions." *Ḥadīth* material contains many separate accounts that relate what kind of recitation Muḥammad favored, how he reacted to hearing the recited Qur'ān, as well as some information on how the prophet himself recited the Qur'ān. For example, there are many reports of statements made by Muḥammad that he valued beautiful voices in Qur'ān reading in the collection of al-Bukhārī (d. 256/870) and others, such as the following, "God has not heard anything more pleasing than listening to a prophet reciting the Qur'ān in a sweet, loud voice" (al-Bukhārī n.d.: VI, Book 61, no. 541). *Ḥadīth* literature also includes many descriptions of the prophet weeping and shedding tears when he heard recitation that was especially affecting.

In addition, *ḥadīth* accounts preserve information about how Muḥammad himself recited the Qur'ān. These traditions include detailed information about particular *sūras* that he recited, and even at what time of day he would read them. This material is a basis for later pious traditions of recitation which build on this information. In general, *ḥadīth* reports and other authoritative material from the earliest period highlight the occasions and merits of recitation instead of practical technique. Actual practice is covered in another kind of literature, treating the technical aspects of recitation determined by the "science of readings" which developed out of Qur'ān and *sunna*, and which further derives authority from practices understood to have been transmitted in an unbroken way since the earliest centuries of Islam times.

Systems for Reading the Qur'ān: *Qirā'āt* and *Tajwīd*

The recitation of the Qur'ān (*tilāwat al-Qur'ān*) is part of the fundamental branches of Qur'ānic study and learning. As such, it is a field within of the overall sciences of the "readings" (*qirā'āt*) of the Qur'ān. The term *tilāwa* appears often in the Qur'ān in both the forms of a noun and a verb. In the Qur'ān it refers, for example, to the signs of God that are "rehearsed" in the Qur'ān, the accounts of previous messengers and communities in sacred history, as well as the actual practice of rendering the Qur'ān in voice. Usually, when the word refers to the reading of the Qur'ān, *tilāwa* conveys a sense of "following" the Qur'ānic message in voice. The practice of reading the Qur'ān follows a set of guidelines known as *tajwīd*. *Tajwīd*, although not a Qur'ānic term, is the basic system for the correct pronunciation and rendition of the speech of the Qur'ān; these guidelines are understood to have been revealed to the prophet by the angel Gabriel along with the Qur'ān itself. Recitation of the Qur'ān according to the rules of *tajwīd* has many names across the Muslim-majority world. Some of these are forms of the Qur'ānic expression *tartīl*, which conveys a sense of "measuring out" the recited Qur'ān in a careful way.

Early readers and transmitters of the Qur'ān were known for their knowledge as well as their piety. There are reports that Muḥammad personally dispatched readers throughout the growing Muslim-controlled territories in order to teach the Qur'ān to others. This class of "readers" of the Qur'ān had an important place in early Islamic history. It was their loss during war in the first generations that is said to have precipitated the standardization of the Qur'ānic text. Later, concern over nonstandard readings in non-Arab lands led to the formalization of sciences of reading the Qur'ān based on the accepted text. As Frederick Denny has shown, the related Qur'ānic sciences of Arabic grammar, Qur'ānic exegesis, and recitation (including variant readings [*qirā'āt*] or vocalizations of the standard text) developed all at the same time, as a simultaneous response to prevailing conditions (Denny 1980). Like the standardization of the 'Uthmānic text, the technical guidelines for readings of the Qur'ān were systematized to guide the potential diversity of Muslim practices of recitation.

In its more technical and restricted usage, the term *qirā'āt* usually denotes the idea of the variant accepted readings of the Qur'ān. These differing readings do not relate to pitch variation nor any substantive textual variants. Instead, all of the readings pertain to minor differences in the vocalization of the same 'Uthmānic text; they all employ the same rules of sound production (*tajwīd*). There are said to be seven accepted readings in the system of *qirā'āt*. This number has been disputed at times in the past. The number seven is based on a well-known *ḥadīth* transmitted in several versions. One states that Muḥammad said, "This Qur'ān has been revealed to be recited in seven different modes [*aḥruf*], so recite of it whichever is easiest for you." (al-Bukhārī n.d.: VI, Book 61, no. 561) Some variants of this report give an "occasion of revelation" or context for the verse, which was a question about the proper reading of Q 25; another *ḥadīth* report states that Muḥammad said that the angel Gabriel would recite in different ways for him. The idea of the "seven modes" has been open to a variety of interpretations in Islamic tradition, including the possibility that the *aḥruf* may refer to differing dialects among the Arabs at the time of the revelation of the Qur'ān. The standard interpretation, however, is that the *aḥruf* refer to what became known as the "seven readings" (*qirā'āt*) of the Qur'ān. The reasons given for the diversity of these accepted readings include the idea that they afford an easier reception of the Qur'ān for learners, as well as the suggestion that they may enhance the multifaceted semantic layers of Qur'ānic meanings.

The establishment of the accepted range of variation in "readings" is credited to Abū Bakr b. Mujāhid (d. 324/936). The seven readings that were standardized in the time of Ibn Mujāhid as the accepted *qirā'āt* represented prominent traditions of reading in five centers of Muslim learning in that period: Mecca, Medina, Damascus, Basra, and Kufa. A list corresponding to this selection includes the following seven readers: Ibn Kathīr (Mecca, d. 120/737), Nāfiʿ (Medina, d. 169/785), Ibn ʿĀmir (Damascus, d. 118/736), Abū ʿAmr (Basra, d. 154/770), ʿĀṣim (Kufa, d. 128/745), Ḥamza (Kufa, d. 156/772), and al-Kisā'ī (Kufa, d. 189/804). A rationale behind this authoritative selection was to take independent lines of authoritative transmission going back to Muḥammad, and thereby minimize the possibility of error. There was, however, some controversy over the selection at the time. In addition, the "science of readings" continued to develop after this time as well; the later, influential scholar, Ibn al-Jazarī (d. 833/1429), describes ten variant readings, while other scholars have cited fourteen. Nevertheless, Ibn Mujāhid's system of seven *qirā'āt* has been accepted as the standard. Today, the most popular readings are those transmitted from ʿĀṣim by Ḥafṣ (d. 180/796), along with Nāfiʿ transmitted by Warsh (d. 197/812).

In general, when recitation of the Qur'ān is begun in one of the seven readings, the reciter must continue with that reading consistently until he or she has finished the entire selection. In other words, it is not permissible to mix up the readings within a single performance. The differences in readings are, in general, minor differences in vocalizing particular words as well as stylistic variation. An example of accepted variation among the readings is found in the first *sūra* of the Qur'ān. The first word in the third verse may be rendered either as *māliki* or *maliki*. Both versions convey the same sense of meaning, which is God's dominion over the day of judgment. In another example, one that has led to differences of opinion on ritual law for ablution, Q 5:6 may carry two meanings about how to purify the area of the feet, depending on vocalization; it may be understood as "wash" (according to Nāfiʿ and Ḥafṣ) or "wipe" (according to Ibn Kathīr and Abū ʿAmr). These parameters of diversity among the standard readings have been seen by some, including those in European traditions of textual analysis, as important sources of information about Qur'ānic expression and the history of its reception.

There are two key terms for the applied aspects of the recitation of the Qur'ān: *tartīl* and *tajwīd*. These are technical components of *tilāwa*, aspects of any reading (*qirā'a*).

Tartīl and *tajwīd* are closely related terms; for example, the Qur'ān's own instruction, "Recite the Qur'ān with *tartīl*" (Q 73:4) is often considered to mean, "Recite the Qur'ān according to the rules of *tajwīd*." *Tajwīd* refers to a rigorous system of guidelines that determine the proper vocalization of the Qur'ān and thereby shape its characteristic rhythm and specific sound. It does not pertain to pitch variation, however, which is always improvised.

The root meaning of the word *tajwīd* carries senses of "beautifying" and "making correct." *Tajwīd* is part if the wider "science of readings" (*qirā'āt*) within the classic "Qur'ānic sciences." It is often defined in Muslim sources by some variant of the expression, "giving each sound its correct weight and measure." The formal system of *tajwīd* provides instruction on the correct articulation of phonetic sounds, the assimilation of vowels and consonants in juxtaposition, and the proper rhythmic duration of vowel sounds. It also includes parameters for nonmelodic improvisational flexibility, since it governs, for example, pauses and starts in reading; these allow the reader to emphasize certain words, phrases, or sections. One of the reasons for the development of this Qur'ānic science alongside grammar and exegesis was the standardization of style and sound across the growing linguistic diversity of the Islamic world in the early period. The rules of *tajwīd* assure uniformity and consistency in the vocalization of God's speech through clear guidelines.

By determining the unique sound of Qur'ān recitation in these ways, *tajwīd* distinguishes the recited Qur'ān from ordinary Arabic speech and singing. Shaping cadences and rhythms of recitation, *tajwīd* also "musicalizes" the recited Qur'ān to some degree, although the recited Qur'ān is never to be understood in terms of a human product such as "music." It is one of the first areas of study of the Qur'ān, since children need to learn to recite the Qur'ān properly in order to fulfill one of the most basic ritual obligations, canonical prayer. For the four-fifths of the Muslim world that is not Arabic-speaking, this study also doubles as an introduction to the Arabic language. Native speakers of Arabic must study *tajwīd*, since the rules of *tajwīd* concern much more than grammatical and intelligible pronunciation. In some cases, the end of the formal study of *tajwīd* is the successful reading of the entire Qur'ān text with a teacher; known as *khatm al-Qur'ān*, this achievement is marked with a life-cycle celebration in parts of the Muslim world.

The formal system of *tajwīd* as found in these sources has two primary branches. The first of these is the correct vocalization of letters and how the sounds may blend or assimilate, and especially rules corresponding to the sounds, "m" and "n." A second important area of the science of *tajwīd* is the relative duration of vowels, which is based on where they appear. In addition, the field covers the accepted and recommended stops and starts in sectioning, along with other guidelines that may be said to relate to comportment with the Qur'ān (*adab tilāwat al-Qur'ān*). The handbooks for elementary *tajwīd* used all across the Muslim world begin with instruction on the points of articulation (*makhārij*) of the letters of the Arabic alphabet.

A first principle of *tajwīd* is that consonants with the same point of articulation will assimilate, or blend together. For example, as in spoken Arabic, *al-rasūl* ("the messenger"), is pronounced as *ar-rasūl* because *rā'* is a blending "sun" letter. In *tajwīd*, other kinds of consonantal assimilations (and partial assimilations) which are not heard in ordinary spoken Arabic also occur. Unique to Qur'ānic pronunciation are rules for particular letters (such as *mīm* and especially *nūn*). There are special conventions for nasalized pronunciation (*ghunna*) of the letters *mīm* and *nūn* when they are doubled in a word or if their doubling happens between two words. There is also a class of rules related to changes that these letters undergo based on adjacent consonants. The second major area of beginning *tajwīd* study, pertaining to the articulation of vowels, covers the three vowel sounds in Arabic ("a," "i," and "u," in long and short forms). Adjacent consonants affect not only the sound shape of these vowels (as occurs in standard spoken *fuṣḥa* Arabic) but, in Qur'ān recitation, also their duration. In the system of *tajwīd*, vowels are classified according to their duration or elongation, which is called *madd*. *Madd* is measured in terms of a basic unit or weight (called *madd aṣlī* or *madd ṭabiʿī*).

Another class of rules in the system of *tajwīd* pertains to stops and starts in sectioning or phrasing (*al-waqf wa'l-ibtidā'*) which may only occur at the end of a complete word. At certain points in the text of the Qur'ān, a range of permissible and impermissible stops are marked, ranging according to the classification of their desirability. There are seven most general forms of stop, such as the *lāzim* stop (marked with the letter *mīm*), where a stop must be made or else meaning would be distorted. For stops, there are at least five levels of preference (such as, "permissible to continue, but stopping is better" [*jā'iz*, marked with the letter *jīm*], or "permissible to stop, but it would be better to continue" [*murakhkhaṣ*, marked with the letter *ṣād*]").

Even though the term *tajwīd* does not appear in the Qur'ān, the practice of recitation according to such guidelines is understood to have been a central dimension of Islamic piety since the time of Muḥammad. According to Islamic tradition, the prophet learned the recitation of the Qur'ān and the rules for its vocalization from Gabriel when the Qur'ān was first sent down. Classical recitation manuals consolidated techniques and definitions that had certainly been long-accepted. As with the other Qur'ānic sciences like exegesis (*tafsīr*), systematic writings on the sciences of *qirā'āt* and *tajwīd* appeared in the fourth *hijrī* century and were circulated widely after that time. Most manuals and discussions after the time of Ibn al-Jazarī follow his systematization. According to such formal, established systems, the interrelated ideas of *tilāwa*, *aḥruf*, *qirā'āt* and *tajwīd* are all dimensions of reading that provide guidelines for the vocalization of the Qur'ān.

Norms of Qur'ānic Worship, Preservation, and Piety

The practice of reciting the Qur'ān is a foundational element of Islamic education, practice, and piety. During the fasting month of Ramaḍān, the Qur'ān is read throughout the course of the month in nighttime prayers called *tarāwīḥ*. One of the standard divisions of the Qur'ān is its partition into thirty equal, consecutive parts, or *juz'*; this sectioning facilitates complete recitation of the Qur'ān over the course of a month. In addition, during Ramaḍān or during the days of *ḥajj*, the whole Qur'ān may be recited through in one night by pious Muslims. Muslims read the Qur'ān frequently as an act of supererogatory piety, and recitation especially at night is performed by committed Muslims.

Reciting the Qurʾān is required as a part of one of the fundamental acts of worship in Islam, *ṣalāt* (canonical prayer). The recitation of the opening *sūra* (*al-Fātiḥa*) is carried out seventeen times a day by practicing Muslims due to its liturgical use as a component of *ṣalāt*. This chapter of the Qurʾān is also read in other contexts, such as the sealing of contractual agreements and blessings. During canonical prayer, Muslims are required to read another, unspecified part of the Qurʾān besides *surat al-fātiḥa*. When prayer is conducted individually, this is often a *sūra* selected from among the short Meccan *sūras* that are the thirtieth *juzʾ* of the Qurʾān; if the prayer is led by a prayer leader (*imām*) this reading will be according to the leader's choice. In addition, it is common in worship and other practices of Muslim piety to hear the well known "light verse" (Q 24:35) or the "throne verse" (Q 2:255). The final *juzʾ* of the Qurʾān, as well as other passages like these, are commonly memorized by Muslims. *Sūras* 49 and 67 are also often committed to memory. Other parts of the Qurʾān that are also well known and read on certain occasions include *sūra* 12 especially for life-cycle observances, and *sūra* 36, read for the deceased or dying in a sometimes controversial practice. *Sūra* 18 is often read communally as well.

The recitation of the Qurʾān is a prototype for the practice of *dhikr*, a Qurʾānic word for "reminder" and a practice associated with Ṣūfī piety. The Qurʾān is the basis for the formulae used for such recitational piety as well as the recitation of the ninety-nine names of God (*al-asmāʾ al-ḥusnā*). These "beautiful names" are mentioned in Q 17:110, part of which reads, "Say: Call on Allāh or call on al-Raḥmān. By whatever name you call [Him], His are the most beautiful names (*al-asmāʾ al-ḥusnā*)." Not all of the names are given in the Qurʾān, however. The Qurʾān's brief listing of some of the names is found in Q 59:22–4.

Differing styles of reading the Qurʾān in worship, public performance, and more private acts of piety are usually identified in terms of their relative rapidity, although the terms used may vary across the Muslim-majority and Muslim-minority worlds. Usually *ḥadr* is the expression for a rapid recitation, either performed from memory or for the purpose of reading of large portions of the text aloud; recitation of the Qurʾān in canonical worship tends to be fairly fast as well. *Tartīl* (or *murattal*) is at a slower pace, used for study and practice (sometimes called *tadarrus*). In many places, the term *tajwīd* has a non-technical meaning of cantillated recitation. The term *mujawwad* refers to a slow recitation that deploys heightened technical artistry and melodic modulation, as in public performances by trained experts.

The memorization of the complete Qurʾān, which is known as its "preservation" (*taḥfīẓ*), was encouraged ever since the earliest period of Islam. Among those known especially for memorizing and preserving the Qurʾān in the time of the prophet were his wives. There are many *ḥadīth* reports that encourage Muslims to read the Qurʾān and to know it by heart. Traditionally, formal education begins with the memorization of the Qurʾān at an early age and then branches out from there to other subjects; this institutionalized practice continues in many Muslim-majority societies. The memorization of the Qurʾān is a life-long pursuit, however, because readers must continually repeat the text so that no part of it is forgotten. The nonlinear structure of the Qurʾān demands this continual rehearsal in order to commit to memory since it is, as a *ḥadīth* on memorization transmitted from Muḥammad has it, "like a camel that is always trying to run away." Memorizers who have made the commitment to "preserving" the Qurʾān often repeat one-seventh of it each day of the week. Students who are memorizing the Qurʾān for the first time study handbooks on difficult aspects of the Qurʾān, such as verses that closely resemble one another. For Muslim men and women who do not attempt the challenge of memorizing the entire Qurʾān, and then keeping it memorized, many are able to meet the goal of having memorized the final *juzʾ* (thirtieth) of the Qurʾān.

According to Islamic ethical and legal traditions, memorization is a recommended act of piety; it is classified as an obligation that must always be observed by some members of a community on behalf of the group (*farḍ kifāya*). This means that Qurʾān memorizers are a special class of readers of the Qurʾān and they command a special respect within their communities since they "hold" the Qurʾān in memory. They have a responsibility to contribute to the ethical order of society. This is often expressed in the literature through representation of the reader's unending practice that continues both day and night: Qurʾān reading by night and constructive moral action by day. Memorizers are also expected to meet scrupulous standards of moral comportment, or *adab*, and to commit themselves to the highest of ethical standards.

Material on the proper behavior and comportment with the Qurʾān is known as *adab al-Qurʾān*. This literature continues the precedent of collecting reports about the recitational practice of Muḥammad, while it also includes further information about the recitational customs of other pious persons and other norms of practice. These include respectful silence when listening, sitting facing the *qibla* (the direction of prayer) if possible, meeting the standards of ritual purity, repeating verses, and reciting the standard opening and closing formulae. These latter formulae are the opening statement, the *taʿawwudh* ("I take refuge in God from the accursed Satan") which is followed by the *basmala* ("In the name of God, the Merciful, the Compassionate"), no matter where in the Qurʾān the reader begins. The reciter always closes a reading with the formula *ṣadaqa ʾllāh al-ʿaẓīm*, meaning "Thus God the All-mighty has spoken truly." If the reciter is interrupted by a greeting (*salām*) while reading, he or she is to stop to return the greeting; he or she is also to stop when hearing the *adhān* (call to prayer). Reciters and listeners may observe *sajdat al-tilāwa*, which is the prostration that is to be performed at fourteen or fifteen verses (according to different traditions) in the Qurʾān that refer to created beings who bow before their Creator. Only in some parts of the Muslim world is there concern over men listening to the voices of women reciting the Qurʾān; in other regions, such as Indonesia, women reciters are very popular.

The *adab* of the recited Qurʾān also includes information compiled on matters such as how quickly to recite the entire Qurʾān as well as what times of day are considered to be good to complete a reading of the entire text; it also considers common challenges that reciters may face, such as confusing pauses and starts in sectioning. In addition, much material addresses the intents of recitation, such as the problem of acquiring a worldly reward or payment for teaching or performance. In a related manner, it includes prohibitions against reciting the Qurʾān just for show, or in an ostentatious manner that draws attention to the reader instead of the reading. The latter is considered a form of hypocrisy and is condemned in accepted *ḥadīth* reports as well as other material on the *adab* of recitation. For example, one tradition reports: "Abū Saʿīd al-Khudrī narrated that he heard God's messenger saying, 'There will appear some among you whose ritual prayers will make you look down on yours, and whose (good) deeds will make you look down on yours, but they will recite the Qur'ān and it will not leave their throats [i.e. they do not act upon it]' " (al-Bukhārī n.d.: IX, Book 84, no. 67).

Material on the *adab* of *tilāwat al-Qur'ān* and on the *faḍā'il* ("excellences") of the Qur'ān, in both accepted *ḥadīth* accounts and other sources, underscores that the recitation of the Qur'ān grants rewards to individuals and to their pious communities. There is an emphasis on the idea that the recitation of the Qur'ān brings on individual and collective rewards both for persons and their communities. This is, for example, expressed in the following statement of Abū Hurayra, cited in authors such as al-Ghazālī (d. 505/1111):

> Surely the house in which the Qur'ān is recited provides easy circumstances for its people, its good increases, angels come to it [in order to listen to the Qur'ān] and satans leave it. The house in which the book of God is not recited provides difficult circumstances for its people, its good decreases, angels leave it, and satans come to it. (al-Ghazālī 1983: 24)

In addition to describing the peace and tranquility (*sakīna*) that descend when the Qur'ān is read in this world, the effects of recitation and of studying and teaching the recited Qur'ān are also described in terms of the accounting on the day of judgment and the consequences in the world to come. In an eschatological mode of piety, rewards for reciting the Qur'ān are often accounted *sūra* by *sūra* in this literature, or even letter by letter. Early traditions of ascetic and Qur'ānic piety elaborated such material within Islamic tradition, and Ṣūfīs, among the heirs to this pious tradition, developed especially the soteriological and interiorized Qur'ānic dimensions of piety. In this tradition, a close relationship to the Qur'ān is depicted as an ongoing intimacy, at times framed in terms of the key Ṣūfī concept of "friendship." Engaging the Qur'ān in practice should also conform to the reader's close and immediate experience of following (*tilāwa*) the Qur'ān in the "heart," and this pious ideal is central to the tradition of the recited Qur'ān within any pious Islamic orientation.

Qur'ānic Esthetics and Performance

Doctrine, worship, and esthetics link closely the theory and practice of Qur'ān recitation. The closeness of this linkage of theory and practice comes in part because the recited Qur'ān is understood to be the actual voicing of the speech of God. For example, early philosophical controversies that arose in the first centuries of Islam, regarding questions of temporality and the nature of the Qur'ān as created in time or being eternal, grew in part out of practical questions about human agency in following divine speech in voice. More generally, a range of theoretical and practical issues about the recited Qur'ān are seen to connect to, and their tensions are resolved through, the doctrine of *i'jāz*, which is the idea of the miraculous and inimitable nature of God's speech. This doctrine of inimitability supports the idea that the Arabic text, as divine revelation and speech, is a unique class of discourse. Many issues of worship, piety, and performance are clarified in theory and practice by connecting them to the transcendent status and experience of the recited Qurʾān.

Throughout the history of Islam, Qurʾān reciters have confronted the issue of their artistry potentially becoming confused with the transcendent power of the Qurʾān. Al-Ghazālī (1983) presents rules for recitation to resolve such an apparent tension. He does this by positing an external as well as an internal dimension to the act of voicing God's speech. In this formulation, the intents, consciousness, and sensibilities of the reciter are seen to be secondary to the act of voicing divine speech. The reciter is thus to strive to diminish the aspects of performance that are not pure amplifications of the manifestation of an idealized presence. Well-defined and specific techniques of affect and performance may be applied in order to achieve this ideal.

The appreciation of the vocal artistry of trained reciters has been part of Muslim religious and social life since the earliest times. Much of the explicit theorization and practice related to the esthetics of Qurʾān recitation relates to the key idea of spiritual audition. The term for this, *samāʿ*, is usually associated with Ṣūfī traditions, but in the case of the recited Qurʾān, multiple styles of classical piety overlap. Normative questions relating to musical practice and its application and acceptability are tied to the issue of *samāʿ*. These legal debates usually center on the intents and contexts of practice rather than the status of music as a general category. The most authoritative sources on what Kristina Nelson (1985) has termed the "*samāʿ* polemic" in Islamic traditions highlight a tension between the cultivation of experiential perceptions related to "listening" (*samāʿ*) on the one hand and the ideal of the absolute separation of transcendent revelation and human components on the other.

According to Islamic tradition, the "melodic" aspects of Qurʾān recitation may not be fixed in any one performance or in an overall system. This is in order that God's speech, in the form of the revealed Qurʾān, will not become associated with human technical artistry. It is not known what melodic structures were used in the recitation of the Qurʾān in the earliest period. It is documented, however, that practices of Qurʾān recitation developed into something resembling the highly ornamented *mujawwad* style in the ʿAbbāsid period, when reciters began to deploy the emerging modal system of music (*maqām*; plural *maqāmāt*). It is in this period that the question of "recitation with melody" (*qirāʾa biʾl-alḥān*) appears in the literature, and the melodic structures deployed in this time were apparently those of Arab art music. Today, the highly proficient style of recitation known as *mujawwad* uses melodic structures also found in contemporary Arab art music.

A *maqām* is a musical mode; the term denotes both scalar pitch class and melody type. Diversity and flexibility characterize the modal system both diachronically and synchronically. Early treatises formulated an analytical framework for the system that was followed for centuries, deploying musical characteristics in the identification of mode, such as initial and final pitch, as well as, in some cases, melody types. Not only are modes applied flexibly in practice, but the overall musical system is difficult to formalize or classify historically or geographically. In the early nineteenth century, a system for analyzing scale (based on quarter-tones) became widespread in the Middle East. An attempt was also made to codify all of the *maqāmāt* being used in Arab countries at the historic Cairo congress on Arab music in 1932. Such efforts, however, face the challenge of systematizing the diversity of the entire musical system, as well as the problems of notation and standardization.

Contemporary performers of the recited Qur'ān in the style called *mujawwad* have been increasingly popular in recent decades due to broadcast and recording technologies and other global trends. In *The Art of Reciting the Qur'ān*, Kristina Nelson (1985) studies the practices of Egyptian reciters in the 1980s, the same figures who became renowned the world over in the following decade or more because of the popularity of their recordings. Across the Muslim-majority and Muslim-minority worlds of Islam in the late twentieth century, the recitation recordings of a few of Egyptian reciters (many of whom trained in classical Arabic music) were highly influential and offered models for aspiring reciters transnationally. The singing of the great women vocalists from the Arab world, such as Fairouz, Warda, and above all Umm Kulthūm has influenced the improvizational styles of these performers as well as those who have come after them. Examples of contemporary recitation representing regions all over the world may be heard on the sound recording accompanying Sells (1999).

The Recited Qur'ān and Contemporary Islamic Revitalization

In the late twentieth century, changes in technology coupled with the global Islamic awakening have encouraged the popularity of the widespread and popular practice of the recitation of the Qur'ān. Evidence of this is a worldwide women's mosque movement that focuses on reciting the Qur'ān in mosques and improving recitation technique. Transnational connections support curricula for teaching recitation at all levels. For example, in the 1960s and 1970s, the Egyptian government sponsored many of the most renowned Egyptian reciters to travel to Southeast Asia, a region with as many Muslims as the entire Arabic-speaking world, in order to teach and to perform as a global Islamic outreach.

Da'wa is a Qur'ānic term interpreted and applied in different ways in different global contexts. Most basically, the term means a "call" to deepen one's own, or encourage others', Islamic piety. As such, it has been a crucial concept in the historical propagation of the Islamic religious tradition; this has been the case especially for certain historical traditions in specific. *Da'wa* is a key concept for how the Qur'ān is understood as a basis of contemporary Islamic revitalization movements. Qur'ānic *da'wa* supports recitational aesthetics and schooling as a primary basis for educative programs among Muslims of diverse orientations.

In the most populous Muslim-majority nation in the world, Indonesia, the recitation of the Qur'ān has been the focus of an energetic movement in Islamic revitalization since the last decades of the twentieth century. The region of Southeast Asia is well known for world-class recitation, evidenced in the popularity of the woman reciter from Jakarta, Hj. Maria Ulfah. Southeast Asia has also long been known for the production of exceedingly short, clear, and precise methods and materials for teaching and learning about Islam and the Qur'ān. In Indonesia in the 1990s, mainstream *da'wa* was viewed as an invitation to voluntary Islamic piety issued to Muslims, and much of this *da'wa* emphasized engagement with the recited Qur'ān. Examples of the energy of this movement are the massive *Baitul Qur'an* ("House of the Qur'ān") exhibit near Jakarta, as well as the promotion of a wide array of Qur'ānic arts like recitation and calligraphy.

In Indonesia in the 1990s and later, as the Qur'ān increasingly became the focus of programs to promote Islamic engagement, learning to read the Qur'ān became the basis of a widespread revitalization movement. New pedagogies blended with traditional methods of teaching and learning recitation. Popular activities ranged from basic study of *tajwīd* to performance in the highly proficient *mujawwad* style of recitation. The phenomenon of Qur'ānic learning and engagement has not been limited to young people in Indonesia; it has also included mature Muslims who labeled themselves as "learners." As part of a resurgent movement in the fundamentals of religious practice in Indonesia during the decades of the 1980s and 1990s, religiously oriented individuals actively adopted and promoted projects such as local and national Qur'ān recitation competitions, a widespread movement in Qur'ān kindergartens, revitalized efforts to memorize the Qur'ān, and lively women's mosque groups trained on the development of reading skills.

In Indonesia, virtuosic readings in the *mujawwad* style have not been appreciated most intensively in terms of inducing heightened experiential states, but instead in terms of the tendency of listeners to attempt actively and with full effort to emulate that very performance. In Indonesia, expert performances from the Arab world and by Indonesians have doubled as pedagogy for ordinary practitioners, disseminated and mediated by competition frameworks and other programs and interests. Under these educationally oriented influences, a great variety of material – including the recordings of great Egyptian reciters – has become in Indonesia, educational *kurikulum*. In Indonesia, reciters at all levels were instructed to listen avidly to these performances in order to improve their *mujawwad* Qur'ān recitation, and especially to master the modal system.

Contests for the recitation of the Qur'ān were also interpreted in Indonesia to be a form of *da'wa*. The increasing popularity of Qur'ān reciting and recitation contests, and their promotion by various organizations over several decades, has contributed to an explosion of interest, and new media and techniques, for the study and appreciation of the recited Qur'ān in Southeast Asia. Possible controversy over the voicing of the speech of God as a competition was overcome in Indonesia by recognizing the positive effects of the events for Islamic youth. Recitation tournaments, especially the National Contest for the Recitation of the Qur'ān ("Musabaqa Tilawatil Qur'an," MTQ), had come to be viewed by many in Indonesia as an avenue for *syi'ar Islam*, or the propagation and deepening of Islamic practice through an appreciation of Qur'ānic knowledge and ability, as well as an avenue for the expression of distinctive aspects of Indonesian Islamic piety within the context of the global Muslim community. Competitions, as *syi'ar Islam*, were understood to be simultaneously a form of education and an invitation to Muslim practice. They show how Qur'ān recitation, as a practice of piety, is being revitalized globally as the basis of movements of Islamic awakening in the contemporary Muslim-majority and Muslim-minority worlds.

Conclusion

The recitation of the Qur'ān is foundational to Islamic worship and piety. It is central to the Qur'ān's depiction of itself and its own reading. As a Qur'ānic science, branches of the science of reading relate to classical fields of Islamic learning such as grammar, law and exegesis, aesthetics and piety; it is now the bases of some contemporary Muslim revitalization movements. In all of these domains, Qur'ān recitation is not just a personal or individual religious act. The theme of the sociality of the recitation of the Qur'ān echoes throughout the classical literature, even interiorized systems such as that of al-Ghazālī. Al-Bukhārī and other major *ḥadīth* collections, for example, relate the report that Muḥammad said, "The best among you are those who learn the Qur'ān and teach it to others" (transmitted on the authority of ʿUthmān b. ʿAffān). This is echoed in the special status given to memorizers or those who "preserve" the Qur'ān on behalf of religious community. In the contemporary world, educative programs for Qur'ānic reading are increasingly popular, as are the recordings of proficient reciters. Teaching, learning, practicing, and appreciating the recited Qur'ān are voluntary open-ended projects, drawing inspiration from the models of others' piety. In reading the Qur'ān aloud, the Qur'ān itself states that Muslims may affect others' religiosity and thereby build religious community: "The believers are only they whose hearts tremble when God is mentioned; and, when His signs [or "verses," the Qur'ān] are recited to them, they multiply in faith and put their trust in their Lord" (Q 8:2).

Further reading

Denny, F. M. (1981) The adab of Qur'ān recitation: Text and context. In: Johns, A. H. (ed.) *International Congress for the Study of the Qur'ān*. Australian National University, Canberra, pp. 143–60.

Denny, F. M. (1989) Qur'ān recitation: A tradition of oral performance and transmission. *Oral Tradition* 4, 5–26.

Al-Faruqi, L. I. (1985) Music, musicians, and Muslim law. *Asian Music* 17, 13–36.

Al-Faruqi, L. I. (1987) The cantillation of the Qur'ān. *Asian Music* 19, 2–25.

Gade, Anna M. (2004) Recitation of the Qur'ān. In: McAuliffe, Jane Dammen (ed.) *Encyclopaedia of the Qur'ān*. Brill, Leiden, vol. IV, pp. 367–85.

Gade, Anna M. (2004) *Perfection Makes Practice: Learning, Emotion, and the Recited Qur'ān in Indonesia*. University of Hawaii Press, Honolulu.

Graham, William A. (1987) *Beyond the Written Word: Oral Aspects of Scripture in the History of Religion*. Cambridge University Press, New York.

Husaini, S. K. (1990) *Easy Tajwīd: A Text Book on Phonetics and Rules of Pronunciation and Intonation of the Glorious Qur'ān*. Khadri, trans. S. N. and Q. H. Khan. Muslim Community Center, Chicago.

Martin, R. C. (1986) Tilāwah. In: Eliade, Mircea (ed.) *The Encyclopedia of Religion*. Macmillan, New York, vol. X, pp. 526–30.

Nelson, K. (1985) *The Art of Reciting the Qur'an*. University of Texas Press, Austrin.

von Denffer, A. (1983) *ʿUlūm al-Qur'ān: An Introduction to the Sciences of the Qur'ān*. The Islamic Foundation, London.

Bibliography

Initial definite article ("al-," "the") is ignored in alphabetization.

ʿAbd al-Bāqī, Muḥammad Fuʾād (1945) *al-Muʿjam al-mufahras li-alfāẓ al-Qurʾān al-karīm*. Dār al-Kutub al-Miṣriyya, Cairo.

ʿAbd al-Ḥamīd, M. (1968) *al-Alūsī mufassirān*. Maṭbaʿat al-Maʿārif, Baghdad.

ʿAbd al-Ḥayy b. ʿImād (1966) *Shadharāt al-dhahab fī akhbār man dahab*. Al-Maktaba al-Tijārī, Beirut.

ʿAbd al-Jabbār, Abū ʾl-Ḥasan b. Aḥmad (1960) *Al-Mughnī fī abwāb al-tawḥīd waʾl-ʿadl*, part 16 (*Iʿjāz al-Qurʾān*), ed. Amīn al-Khūlī. Wizārat al-Thaqāfa waʾl-Irshād al-Qawmī, Cairo.

ʿAbd al-Jabbār, Abū ʾl-Ḥasan b. Aḥmad (1965) *Sharḥ al-uṣūl al-khamsa*, ed. ʿAbd al-Karīm ʿUthmān. Maktabat Wahba, Cairo.

ʿAbd al-Jabbār, Abū ʾl-Ḥasan b. Aḥmad (1986) *Faḍl al-Iʿtizāl wa ṭabaqāt al-muʿtazila*, ed. Fuʾād Sayyid. Al-Dār al-Tūnisiyya lil-Nashr, Tūnis.

ʿAbd al-Malik b. Ḥabīb (1987) *Kitāb wasf al-firdaws*. Dār al-Kutub al-ʿIlmiyya. Beirut.

ʿAbd al-Razzāq (1983) Al-*Muṣannaf*, ed. Ḥabīb al-Raḥmān al-Aʿẓamī, 11 vols. Al-Maktab al-Islāmī, Beirut.

Abdel Haleem, M. (2000) *Understanding the Qurʾan: Themes and Style*. I. B. Tauris, London.

Abdel-Meguid, A.-A. (1954) A survey of story literature in Arabic from before Islam to the middle of the nineteenth century. *The Islamic Quarterly* 1, 104–13.

Abrahamov, B. (1990) *Al-Ḳāsim B. Ibrāhīm on the Proof of God's Existence, Kitāb al-Dalīl al-Kabīr*. E. J. Brill, Leiden.

Abrahamov, B. (1992) Ibn Taymiyya on the agreement of reason with tradition. *The Muslim World* 82, 256–72.

Abrahamov, B. (1993a) Al-Ghazālī's supreme way to know God. *Studia Islamica* 77, 141–68.

Abrahamov, B. (1993b) ʿAbd al-Jabbār's theory of divine assistance (*luṭf*). *Jerusalem Studies in Arabic and Islam* 16, 41–58.

Abrahamov, B. (1996) *Anthropomorphism and Interpretation of the Qurʾān in the Theology of al-Qāsim ibn Ibrāhīm, Kitāb al-Mustarshid*. E. J. Brill, Leiden.

Abrahamov, B. (1998) *Islamic Theology, Traditionalism and Rationalism*. Edinburgh University Press, Edinburgh.

Abū Dāwūd, al-Ṭayālisī (n.d.) *Musnad Abū Dāwūd al-Ṭayālisī*. Dār al-Maʿrifa, Beirut (reprint).

Abu Deeb, Kamal (1979) *Al-Jurjānī's Theory of Poetic Imagery*. Aris and Phillips, Warminster.
Abū Isḥāq-i Quhistānī (1959) *Haft Bāb*, ed. and trans. Wladimir Ivanow. Ismaili Society, Bombay.
Abū ʾl-Qāsim al-Kūfī (n.d.) *Al-Istighātha fī bidaʿ al-thalātha*. Dār Nashr Iḥqāq al-Ḥaqq, Sargodha.
Abū Nuʿaym, Aḥmad b. ʿAbd Allāh (1994) *Kitāb al-Imāma waʾl-radd ʿalā ʾl-Rāfiḍa*, ed. ʿAlī b. Muḥummad al-Faqīhī. Maktabat ʿUlūm al-Ḥadīth, Medina.
Abū Nuʿaym, Aḥmad b. ʿAbd Allāh (n.d.) *Ḥilyat al-awliyāʾ wa ṭabaqāt al-aṣfiyāʾ*. Dār al-Fikr, Beirut.
Abū Sinna, ʿA. al-F. (1995) *ʿUlūm al-Qurʾān*. Dār al-Shurūq, Beirut.
Abū ʿUbayd (1995) *Faḍāʾil al-Qurʾān wa maʿālimuhu wa-ʾadābuhu*, ed. Aḥmad b. ʿAbd al-Wāḥid al-Khayyāṭī, 2 vols. Wizārat al-Awqāf waʾl-Shuʾūn al-Islāmiyya, Morocco.
Abū Zahra, Muḥammad (1970) *Al-Qurʾān, al-muʿjiza al-kubrā*. Dār al-Fikr al-ʿArabī, Cairo.
Adang, Camilla (2002) Hypocrites and hypocrisy. In: McAuliffe, Jane Dammen (ed.) *Encyclopaedia of the Qurʾān*. Brill, Leiden, vol. II, pp. 468–72.
Adonis (1985) *Al-Shiʿriyya al-ʿarabiyya*. Dār al-Ādāb, Beirut.
Adonis (1998) *Die Gesänge Mihyars des Damaszeners. Gedichte 1958–1965*, trans. Stefan Weidner. Ammann, Zürich.
Afsaruddin, Asma (2001) Constructing narratives of monition and guile: The politics of interpretation. *Arabica* 48, 315–51.
Afsaruddin, Asma (2002) The Excellences of the Qurʾān: Textual sacrality and the organization of early Islamic society. *Journal of the American Oriental Society* 122, 1–24.
Āghā Khān III (1950) *Kalām-i Imām-i mūbīn*. Ismāʿīlī Association, Bombay.
Āghā Khān III (1954) *The Memoirs of Aga Khan*. Cassell and Company, London.
Āghā Khān IV (2003) Speech at the Opening Session of "Word of God, Art of Man: The Qurʾān and its Creative Expression" (Ismaili Centre London, October 19) www.iis.ac.uk/learning/speeches_ak4/2003b.pdf.
Ahmad, R. (1969) Abū ʾl-Qāsim al-Qushayrī as a theologian and commentator. *Islamic Quarterly* 13, 16–69.
Ahmed, Leila (1982) *Women and Gender in Islam: Historical Roots of a Modern Debate*. Yale University Press, New Haven.
Ahrens, K. (1930) Christliches im Qoran. *Zeitschrift der Deutschen Morganländischen Gesellschaft* 84, 15–68.
Al-Ājurrī, Abū Bakr Muḥammad b. al-Ḥusayn (1983) *Al-Sharīʿa*, ed. Muḥammad Ḥāmid al-Fiqī. Dār al-Kutub al-ʿIlmiyya, Beirut.
Akhtar, Shabbir (1990) *A Faith for All Seasons: Islam and the Challenge of the Modern World*. Bellew, London.
ʿAlī b. Abī Ṭālib (1999) *Nahj al-Balāgha*. 12th edn., trans. Askari Jafri. Islamic Seminary Publications, New York.
Ali, A. (trans.) (2001) *Al-Qurʾān: A Contemporary Translation*. 9th edn. Princeton University Press, Princeton.
Ali, Abdullah Yusuf (1934; 1977; 1997) *The Holy Qurʾān: Text, Translation and Commentary*. Shaikh Muḥammad Ashraf, Lahore; American Trust Publication, Brentwood.
Ali, Mohamed Mohamed Yunis (2000) *Medieval Islamic Pragmatics: Sunni Legal Theorists' Models of Textual Communication*. Curzon, Richmond.
Alter, Robert (1981) *The Art of Biblical Narrative*. Basic Books, New York.
Al-Alūsī, Abū ʾl-Thanā Shihāb al-Dīn Maḥmūd (1933–4) *Rūḥ al-maʿānī fī tafsīr al-Qurʾān al-ʿaẓīm wa-sabʿ al-mathānī*, 30 vols. in 15, Idārat al-Ṭibāʿa al-Munīriyya, Cairo; reprinted 1985, Dār Iḥyāʾ al-Turāth al-ʿArabī, Beirut.
Al-Āmidī, ʿAlī b. Abī ʿAlī, Sayf al-Dīn (1971) *Ghāyat al-marām fī ʿilm al-kalām*, ed. Ḥasan Maḥmūd ʿAbd al-Laṭīf. Lajnat Iḥyāʾ al-Turāth al-Islāmī, Cairo.

Amīr Bādshāh, Muḥammad Amīn al-Ḥusaynī al-Khurasānī al-Bukhārī al-Ḥanafī (1350) *Tayasīr al-Taḥrīr*. 4 vols. in 2. Muṣṭafā ʾl-Bābī ʾl-Ḥalabī, Cairo.

Amir-Moezzi, Mohammad Ali (1994) *The Divine Guide in Early Shiʿism: The Sources of Esotericism in Islām*, trans. David Streight. State University of New York Press, Albany.

Ammann, Ludwig (2001) *Die Geburt des Islam. Historische Innovation durch Offenbarung*. Wallstein, Göttingen.

Āmulī, Ḥaydar (1969) *Jāmiʿ al-asrār.* In: Corbin, Henry, and Yahia, Osman (eds.) *La philosophie shīʿite*. Adrien-Maisonneuve, Paris.

Anastassiadou, M. (1999) Livres et "bibliothèques" dans les inventaires après décès de Salonique au XIXe siècle. *Revue du monde Musulman et de la Méditerranée* 87–8, 111–41.

Anawati, Georges C. (1967) Le nom suprême de Dieu (*ism Allāh al-Aʿẓām*). In: *Atti del terzo congresso di studi Arabi e Islamici, Ravello 1–6 settembre 1966*. Instituto Universitario Orientale, Napoli, pp. 7–58.

An-Naʾim, Abdullahi Ahmed (1990) *Towards an Islamic Reformation*. Syracuse University Press, Syracuse.

Answering Christianity (2005a) http://www.answering-christianity.com/equality.htm January 23, 2005.

Answering Christianity (2005b) http://www.answering-christianity.com/slaves_brothers.htm January 23, 2005.

Answering Christianity (2005c) http://www.answering-christianity.com/cursed_gender.htm January 23, 2005.

Answering Christianity (2005d) http://www.answering-christianity.com/islam.htm January 23, 2005.

Answering Christianity (2005e) http://www.answering-christianity.com/muhammad_not_racist.htm January 23, 2005.

Arab Human Rights (2005) http://www.arabhumanrights.org/countries/morocco/ccpr/ccpr-c-76-add3-93e.pdf January 23, 2005.

Arberry, A. J. (1983) *The Koran Interpreted*. Oxford University Press, Oxford.

Arkoun, Mohammed (1982) *Lectures du Coran*. G.-P. Maisonneuve et Larose, Paris.

Arkoun, Mohammed (1987) *Rethinking Islam Today*. Centre for Contemporary Arab Studies, Georgetown University, Washington.

Arkoun, Mohammed (1994) *Rethinking Islam: Common Questions, Uncommon Answers*, trans. R. Lee. Westview Press, Boulder.

Arkoun, Mohammed (2002) *The Unthought in Contemporary Islamic Thought*. Saqi Books, London.

Arnal, William E. (2001) *Jesus and the Village Scribes: Galilean Conflicts and the Setting of Q*. Fortress Press, Minneapolis.

Asad, Muḥammad (1980) *The Message of the Qurʾān*. Dar-al-Andalus, Gibraltar.

Asani, Ali S. (1991) *The Būjh Niranjan: An Ismaili Mystical Poem*. Harvard University Press, Cambridge.

Asani, Ali S. (2002) *Ecstasy and Enlightenment: The Ismaili Devotional Literature of South Asia*. I. B. Tauris, London.

Al-Ashʿarī, Abū ʾl-Hasan ʿAlī b. Ismāʿīl (1953) *Risālat istiḥsān al-khawḍ fī ʿilm al-kalām*. In: McCarthy, R. J. (ed.) *The Theology of al-Ashʿarī*. Al-Maṭbaʿa al-Kāthūlikiyya, Beirut.

Al-Ashʿarī, Abū ʾl-Hasan ʿAlī b. Ismāʿīl (1963) *Maqālāt al-islāmiyyīn wa-ikhtilāf al-muṣallīn*, ed. H. Ritter. Franz Steiner, Wiesbaden (reprint of the Istanbul edn. 1929–30).

As-Said, L. (1975) *The Recited Koran: A History of the First Recorded Version*, ed. and trans. B. Weiss, M. A. Rauf and M. Berger. Darwin Press, Princeton.

Assmann, Aleida, and Assmann, Jan (eds.) (1987) *Kanon und Zensur. Archäologie der literarischen Kommunikation II*. Fink, Munich.

Assmann, Jan (1992) *Das kulturelle Gedächtnis. Schrift, Erinnerung und politische Identität in frühen Hochkulturen*, C. H. Beck, Munich.

Atallah, W. (1970) Ğibt et Ṭāghūt dans le Coran. *Arabica* 17, 69–82.

Ateş, S. (1969) *Sülemī ve tasavvufī tefsīrī*. Sönmez Neşriyat, Istanbul.

Ateş, S. (1974) *İşâri tefsir okulu*. Ankara Üniversitesi, Ankara.

Awn, P. J. (1983) *Satan's Tragedy and Redemption: Iblīs in Sufi Psychology*. E. J. Brill, Leiden.

Ayāzī, M. (1994) *Al-Mufassirūn: Ḥayātuhum wa-manhajuhum*. Wizārat-i Farhang wa Irshād-i Islāmī, Tehran.

Ayoub, M. (1984, 1992) *The Qur'an and Its Interpreters*, 2 vols. State University of New York Press, Albany.

Ayoub, Mahmoud (1988) The speaking Qur'ān and the silent Qur'ān: A study of the principles and development of Imāmī Shī'ī tafsīr. In: Rippin, Andrew (ed.) *Approaches to the History of the Interpretation of the Qur'ān*. Oxford University Press, Oxford, pp. 177–98.

Al-ʿAyyāshī, Muḥammad b. Masʿūd (1991) *Tafsīr*. Mu'assasat al-Aʿlamī, Beirut.

Al-ʿAyyāshī, Muḥammad b. Masʿūd (n.d.) *Tafsīr al-ʿAyyāshī*, ed. Hāshim al-Rasūlī al-Mahallātī. Chāpkhānah-i ʿIlmīyah, Qom.

Baalbaki, R. (1983) Early Arabic lexicographers and the use of Semitic languages. *Berytus* 31, 117–27.

Baldick, Julian (1981) Persian Ṣūfī poetry up to the fifteenth century. In: Morrison, G. (ed.) *History of Persian Literature from the Beginning of the Islamic Period to the Present Day*, E. J. Brill, Leiden, pp. 111–32.

Balhan, J.-M. (2001) *La révélation du Coran selon al-Suyūṭī: Traduction annotée du chapitre seizième de Ğalāl al-Dīn al-Suyūṭī*, al-Itqān fī ʿulūm al-Qur'ān. Pontificio Istituto di Studi Arabi e d'Islamistica, Rome.

Baneth, D. Z. H. (1971) What did Muḥammad mean when he called his religion Islām? *Israel Oriental Studies* 1, 183–90 (reprinted in Rippin [2001a], pp. 85–92).

Banī ʿĀmir, M. A. (2004) *Al-Mustashriqūn wa'l-Qur'ān al-karīm*. Dār al-Amal, Irbid, Jordan.

Al-Baqlī, Rūzbihān (1884) *ʿArā'is al-bayān fī ḥaqā'iq al-Qur'ān*. Newal Kishore, Cawnpore.

Bar-Asher, Meir M. (1993) Variant readings and additions of the Imāmī-Shīʿī to the Qur'ān. *Israel Oriental Studies* 13, 39–75.

Bar-Asher, Meir M. (1999) *Scripture and Exegesis in Early Imāmī Shiism*. Brill, Leiden.

Barlas, Asma (2002) *"Believing Women" in Islam: Unreading Patriarchal Interpretations of Islam*. University of Texas Press, Austin.

Barr, James (1968) *Comparative Philology and the Text of the Old Testament*. Oxford University Press, Oxford; reprint Eisenbrauns, Winona Lake (1987) with supplement.

Baumstark, Anton (1947) Jüdischer und Christlicher Gebetstypus im Koran. *Der Islam* 16, 353–76.

Bausani, Allesandro (1974) Islam as an essential part of western culture. In: *Studies on Islam: A symposium on Islamic studies organized in cooperation with the Accademia dei Lincei in Rome, Amsterdam, 18–19 October 1973*. North-Holland Publishing Company, Amsterdam, pp. 19–36.

Bayani, M., Contadini A., and Stanley, T. (1999) *The Decorated Word: Qur'ans of the 17th to 19th Centuries*, Oxford University Press, London [The Nasser D. Khalili collection of Islamic art, 41].

Al-Bayḍāwī, ʿAbd Allāh b. ʿUmar (1988) *Anwār al-tanzīl wa-asrār al-ta'wīl*, 2 vols. Dār al-Kutub al-ʿIlmiyya, Beirut.

Al-Bayhaqī, Aḥmad b. Ḥusayn (1970–1) *Manāqib al-Shāfiʿī*, ed. A. Ṣaqr, 2 vols. Maktabat Dār al-Turāth, Cairo.

Al-Bayhaqī, Aḥmad b. Ḥusayn (1985) *Dalā'il al-Nubuwwa*, ed. A. M. Qalʿajī. Dār al-Kutub al-ʿIlmiyya, Beirut.

Al-Bayhaqī, Aḥmad b. Ḥusayn (n.d.) *Kitāb al-baʿth waʾl-nushūr*. Markaz al-Khadamāt waʾl-Abḥāth al-Thaqafiyya, Beirut.

Beeston, A. F. L. (1976) *Warfare in Ancient South Arabia*. Luzac, London.

Bell, Richard (1937–9) *The Qurʾān: Translated, with a Critical Re-arrangement of the Surahs*, 2 vols. T & T Clark, Edinburgh.

Bell, Richard (1953) *Introduction to the Qurʾān*. Edinburgh University Press, Edinburgh.

Bellamy, J. A. (1991) Al-Raqīm or al-Ruqūd? A note on sūrah 18:9. *Journal of the American Oriental Society* 111, 115–17.

Bellamy, J. A. (1992) *Fa-ummuhu hāwiyah*: A note on sūrah 101:9. *Journal of the American Oriental Society* 112, 485–7.

Bellamy, J. A. (1993) Some proposed emendations to the text of the Koran. *Journal of the American Oriental Society* 113, 562–73.

Bellamy, J. A. (1996) More proposed emendations to the text of the Koran. *Journal of the American Oriental Society* 116, 196–204.

Bellamy, J. A. (2001) Textual criticism of the Koran. *Journal of the American Oriental Society* 121, 1–6.

Bellamy, J. A. (2002) A further note on ʿĪsā. *Journal of the American Oriental Society* 122, 587–8.

Berg, Herbert (2000) *The Development of Exegesis in Early Islam: The Authenticity of Muslim Literature from the Formative Period*. Curzon, Richmond.

Bergsträsser, G. (1930) *Plan eines Apparatus Criticus zum Koran*, Sitzungsberichte der Bayerischen Akademie der Wissenschaften, Phil.-hist. Abteilung, Jahrgang 1930, Heft 7, Munich.

Berkey, J. (1992) *The Transmission of Knowledge in Medieval Cairo: A Social History of Islamic Education*. Princeton University Press, Princeton.

Blakemore, D. (1987) *Semantic Constraints on Relevance*. Blackwell, Oxford.

Bloch, Alfred (1946) *Vers und Sprache im Altarabischen. Metrische und syntaktische Untersuchungen*. Verlag für Recht und Gesellschaft, Basel.

Bobzin, H. (1995) *Der Koran im Zeitalter der Reformation, Studien zur Frühgeschichte der Arabistik und Islamkunde in Europa*. Franz Steiner, Stuttgart.

Bobzin, H. (2002) From Venice to Cairo: On the history of Arabic editions of the Koran (16th–early 20th century). In: Hanebutt-Benz, E. et al. (eds.) *Middle Eastern Languages and the Print Revolution, A Cross-cultural Encounter: A Catalogue and Companion to the Exhibition*. WVA-Verlag Skulima, Westhofen, pp. 151–76.

Boneschi, P. (1945) Is *malak* an Arabic word? *Journal of the American Oriental Society* 65, 107–11.

Boullata, Issa J. (ed.) (2000) *Literary Structures of Religious Meaning in the Qurʾān*. Curzon, Richmond.

Boullata, Issa J. (2003) Literary structures of the Qurʾān. In: McAuliffe, Jane Dammen (ed.) *Encyclopaedia of the Qurʾān*. Brill, Leiden, vol. III, pp. 192–205.

Bouman, J. (1959) *Le conflit autour du Coran et la solution d'al-Bāqillānī*. Van Campen, Amsterdam.

Böwering, G. (1980) *The Mystical Vision of Existence in Classical Islam: The Qurʾānic Hermeneutics of the Ṣūfī Sahl At-Tustarī (d. 283/896)*. De Gruyter, Berlin.

Böwering, G. (1987) The writings of Shams al-Dīn al-Daylamī. *Islamic Studies*, 26:3, 231–6.

Böwering, G. (1989) Review of Richard Gramlich, *Das Sendschreiben al-Qushayrīs über das Sufitum*. *Orientalia*, 58, 569–72.

Böwering, G. (1991) The Qurʾān commentary of al-Sulamī. In: Hallaq, Wael, and Little, Donald P. (eds.) *Islamic Studies Presented to Charles J. Adams*. E. J. Brill, Leiden, pp. 41–56.

Böwering, G. (1995)*The Minor Commentary of Abū ʿAbd ar-Raḥmān Muḥammad b. al-Ḥusayn as-Sulamī*. Dar el-Machreq, Beirut (also 1997, 2nd edn., Beirut).

Böwering, G. (1996) The major sources of Sulamī's minor Qur'ān commentary. *Oriens* 35, 35–56.

Böwering, G. (2001) Chronology and the Qur'ān. In: McAuliffe, Jane Dammen (ed.) *Encyclopaedia of the Qur'ān*. Brill, Leiden, vol. I, pp. 316–35.

Böwering, G. (2003) The scriptural "senses" in medieval Ṣūfī Qur'ān exegesis. In: McAuliffe, J., Walfish, B., and Goering, J. (eds.) *With Reverence for the Word: Medieval Scriptural Exegesis in Judaism, Christianity and Islam*, Oxford University Press, New York, pp. 346–65.

Brinner, W. M., trans. (2002) *ʿArāʾis al-majālis fī qiṣaṣ al-anbiyāʾ or "Lives of the Prophets" as Recounted by Abū Isḥāq Aḥmad ibn Muḥammad ibn Ibrāhīm al-Thaʿlabī*. Brill, Leiden.

Brunschwig, R. (1956) Simples remarques negatives sur le vocabulaire du Coran. *Studia Islamica* 5, 19–32 (translation in Rippin [2001a], pp. 285–95).

Brustad, K. (1997) Imposing order: Reading the conventions of representation in al-Suyūṭī's autobiography. *Edebiyât* 7, 327–44.

Bühler, Karl (1965) *Sprachtheorie. Die Darstellungsfunktion der Sprache*. G. Fischer, Stuttgart.

Al-Bukhārī, ʿAbd al-ʿAzīz b. Aḥmad ʿAlāʾ al-Dīn (1393/1974) *Kashf al-asrār ʿan uṣūl Fakhr al-Islām al-Bazdawī*. 4 vols. in 2. Dār al-Kitāb al-ʿArabī, Beirut.

Al-Bukhārī, Muḥammad ibn Ismāʿīl (1862–1908) *Kitāb jāmiʿ al-ṣaḥīḥ*, ed. L. Krenl and Th. W. Juynboll, 4 vols. Brill, Leiden.

Al-Bukhārī, Muḥammad b. Ismāʿīl (1987) *Ṣaḥīḥ al-Bukhārī*, ed. Qāsim al-Shammāʿī al-Rifāʿī, 9 vols. in 4. Dār al-Fikr, Beirut.

Al-Bukhārī, Muḥammad b. Ismāʿīl (n.d.) *Ṣaḥīḥ al-Bukhārī*, English trans. Muḥammad Muḥsin Khān. Dar al-Arabia, Beirut (reprint).

Bulliet, R. W. (1972) *The Patricians of Nishapur: A Study in Medieval Islamic Social History*. Harvard University Press, Cambridge.

Bulliet, R. W. (1973) The political-religious history of Nishapur in the eleventh century. In: Richards, D. S. (ed.) *Islamic Civilisation 950–1150*. Cassirer, Oxford, pp. 71–91.

Burdei, Michael (2002) Approaching the controversy: How UNC chose *Approaching the Qur'ān* and the lessons liberals and conservatives can learn from the Summer Reading Program. *Carolina Review* 10.1 (September), 5–7, online at <www.unc.edu/cr>.

Bursevi, İsmail Hakkı (1866) *Tafsīr Rūḥ al-bayān*, 10 vols. N.p., Istanbul.

Burton, John (1977) *The Collection of the Qur'ān*. Cambridge University Press, Cambridge.

Burton, John (1990) *The Sources of Islamic Law: Islamic Theories of Abrogation*. Edinburgh University Press, Edinburgh.

Burton, John (2001) Abrogation. In: McAuliffe, Jane Dammen (ed.) *Encyclopaedia of the Qur'ān*. Brill, Leiden, vol. I, pp. 11–19.

Caird, G. B. (1980) *The Language and Imagery of the Bible*. Westminster Press, Philadelphia.

Calder, Norman (1986) The *saʿy* and the *jabīn*: Some notes on Qur'ān 37:102–3. *Journal of Semitic Studies* 31, 17–26.

Calder, Norman (1993) *Tafsīr* from Ṭabarī to Ibn Kathīr: Problems in the description of a genre, illustrated with reference to the story of Abraham. In: Hawting, G. R., and Shareef, A.-K. (eds.) *Approaches to the Qur'ān*. Routledge, London, pp. 101–40.

Chejne, A. (1969) *The Arabic Language: Its Role in History*, University of Minnesota Press, Minneapolis.

Choudhury, M. A. (2001) Perspectives on the Islamization of knowledge and their implications for organization of the occupational composition: The case of Canadian Muslims in the labor market. *Journal of Muslim Minority Affairs* 21, 93–107.

Collectanea (1948) ed. Wladimir Ivanow. E. J. Brill, Leiden.

Committee on the Elimination of Racial Discrimination (2005) http://www.bayefsky.com/summary/saudiarabia_cerd_c_sr_1558_2003.pdf January 23, 2005.

Cook, D. (2002) *Studies in Muslim Apocalyptic*. Darwin Press, Princeton.

Cook, M. A. (1980) The origins of Kalam. *Bulletin of the School of Oriental and African Studies* 43, 32–43.

Corbin, Henry (1961) *Trilogie ismaélienne*. Adrien Maisonneuve, Paris.

Corbin, Henry (1971) *En Islām iranien*. 4 vols. Gallimard, Paris.

Corbin, Henry (1975) Nasir-i Khusrau and Iranian Ismāʿīlism. In: Frye, R. N. (ed.) *The Cambridge History of Iran*. Cambridge University Press, Cambridge, vol. IV, pp. 520–42.

Corbin, Henry (1977) *Spiritual Body and Celestial Earth*, trans. Nancy Pearson. Princeton University Press, Princeton.

Corbin, Henry (1978) *The Man of Light in Iranian Sufism*. Shambhala, Boulder.

Corbin, Henry (1983) *Cyclical Time and Ismaili Gnosis*. Kegan Paul, Boston.

Corbin, Henry (1993) *History of Islamic Philosophy*, trans. Philip Sherrard. Kegan Paul International, London.

Cragg, Kenneth (1971, 1994) *The Event of the Qurʾān: Islam in its Scripture*. George Allen & Unwin, London; 2nd edn., Oneworld Publications, Oxford.

Cragg, Kenneth (1973) *The Mind of the Qurʾān: Chapters in Reflection*. George Allen & Unwin, London.

Crone, Patricia, and Cook, Michael (1977) *Hagarism: The Making of the Islamic World*. Cambridge University Press, Cambridge.

Daftary, Farhad (1990) *The Ismāʿīlīs: Their History and Doctrines*. Cambridge University Press, Cambridge.

Dajani-Shakeel, Hadia, and Messier, Ronald, eds. (1991) *The Jihad and its Times*. University of Michigan, Ann Arbor.

Dallal, A. (2004). Science and the Qurʾān. In: McAuliffe, Jane Dammen (ed.) *Encyclopaedia of the Qurʾān*. Brill, Leiden, vol. IV, pp. 540–58.

Daughters of Adam (2004) http://www.daughtersofadam.org/archives/vol2issue2/fatwa.html June 15, 2004 (off line January 2005).

Davidson, H. A. (1987) *Proofs for Eternity, Creation and the Existence of God in Medieval Islamic and Jewish Philosophy*. Oxford University Press, New York and Oxford.

Al-Daylamī, Shīrawayh b. Shahradār (1986) *Al-Firdaws bi maʾthūr al-khiṭāb*. Ed. Muḥummad b. Basyūnī Zaghlūl. Dār al-Kutub al-ʿIlmiyya, Beirut.

De Blois, François (1999) *Ḥijāratun min sijjīl*. *Acta Orientalia* 60, 58–71.

De Blois, François (2002) Nasrani (nazoraios) and hanif (ethnikos): Studies on the religious vocabulary of Christianity and of Islam. *Bulletin of the School of Oriental and African Studies* 65, 1–30.

De Bruijn, J. T. P. (1997) *Persian Sufi Poetry: An Introduction to the Mystical Use of Classical Poems*. Curzon, Richmond.

De Prémare, Alfred-Louis (2005) ʿAbd al-Malik b. Marwān et le processus de constitution du Coran In: Ohlig, Karl-Heinz, Puin, Gerd-R. (eds.) *Die dunklen Anfänge Neue Forschungen zur Entstehung und frühen Geschichte des Islam*. Schiler, Berlin, pp. 179–211.

Denny, F. M. (1977) Some religio-communal terms and concepts in the Qurʾān. *Numen* 24, 26–59.

Denny, F. M. (1980) Exegesis and recitation: Their development as classical forms of Qurʾānic piety. In: Reynolds, F., and Ludwig, Th. M. (eds.) *Transitions and Transformations in the History of Religions: Essays in Honor of Joseph M. Kitagawa*. E. J. Brill, Leiden, pp. 91–123.

Déroche, F. (1983) *Catalogue des manuscrits arabes*, 2e partie, I/1. *Les manuscrits du Coran. Aux origines de la calligraphie coranique*. Bibliothèque Nationale, Paris.

Déroche, F. (1989) A propos d'une série de manuscrits coraniques anciens. In: Déroche, F. (ed.)

Les manuscrits du Moyen-Orient. L'institut Français d'études Anatoliennes d'Islanbul et la Bibliothèque Nationale, Istanbul-Paris, pp. 101–11.

Déroche, F. (1992) *The Abbasid Tradition: Qur'ans of the 8th to the 10th Centuries AD*. Oxford University Press, London [The Nasser D. Khalili collection of Islamic art, 1].

Déroche, F. (2000) The Ottoman roots of a Tunisian calligrapher's "tour de force". In: Yaman, Z. Yasa (ed.) *Sanatta Etkilesim – Interactions in Art*. Türkiye Is Bankasi Yayinlari, Ankara, pp. 106–9.

Déroche, F. (2002) New evidence about Umayyad book hands. In: *Essays in Honour of Salāh al-Dīn al-Munajjid*. Al-Furqan Islamic Heritage Foundation, London, pp. 611–42.

Déroche F., and Noja Noseda, S. (1998) *Le manuscrit Arabe 328 (a) de la Bibliothèque nationale de France*. Fondazione Ferni Noja Noseda Studi Arabo Islamici, Lesa [Sources de la transmission manuscrite du texte coranique, I. Les manuscrits de style hijāzī: 1].

Déroche, F., and Noja Noseda, S. (2001) *Le manuscrit Or. 2165 de la British Library*. Fondazione Ferni Noja Noseda Studi Arabo Islamici, Lesa [Sources de la transmission manuscrite du texte coranique, I: Les manuscrits de style hijāzī: 2, i].

Dessus Lamare, A. (1938) Le mushaf de la mosquée de Cordoue et son mobilier mécanique. *Journal Asiatique* 230, 551–75.

Al-Dhahabī, Muḥammad (1961) *Al-Tafsīr wa'l-mufassirūn*, 2 vols. Dār al-Kutub al-Ḥadītha, Beirut.

Al-Dhahabī, Muḥammad (1396/1976) *Kitāb al-kabā'ir*. Dār al-Wa'y, Aleppo.

Dininger, Johannes (1987) Revelation. In: Eliade, Mircea (ed.) *Encyclopedia of Religion*. Macmillan, New York, vol. XII, pp. 356–62.

Donaldson, Dwight (1933) *The Shi'ite Religion: A History of Islām in Persia and Irak*. Luzac, London.

Donaldson, Dwight (1938) Al-Kumayl: A companion of the secret. *The Moslem World* 28, 249–57.

Donner, F. M. (1998) *Narratives of Islamic Origins: The Beginnings of Islamic Historical Writing*. Darwin Press, Princeton.

Dostal, Walter (1991) Mecca before the time of the prophet – attempt of an anthropological interpretation. *Der Islam* 68, 193–231.

Drory, R. (1994) Three attempts to legitimize fiction in classical Arabic literature. *Jerusalem Studies in Arabic and Islam* 18, 146–64.

Dvořák, Rudolf (1884a) *Ein Beitrag zur Frage über die Fremdwörter im Koran*. O. Schulze, Munich.

Dvořák, Rudolf (1884b) Ueber "tinûru" des Assyrisch-babylonischen und die demselben entsprechenden Formen der übrigen semitischen Sprachen, *Zeitschrift für Keilschriftforschung und verwandte Gebiete*, 1, 115–50.

Dvořák, Rudolf (1885) *Über die Fremdwörter im Koran*. C. Gerold's Sohn, Vienna.

Eaton, John (1990) Kingship. In: Coggins, R. J., and Houlden, J. L. (eds.) *A Dictionary of Biblical Interpretation*. SCM Press, London, pp. 379–82.

Edmondson, R. (1984) *Rhetoric in Sociology*. Macmillan, London.

EI2 (2004) *The Encyclopaedia of Islam*, CD-ROM of the New Edition. Brill, Leiden.

El-Awa, S. M. S. (2004) Qur'ānic repetition: A relevance based explanation of the phenomenon. *Islamic Studies* 42, 577–93.

El-Awa, S. M. S. (2005) *Textual Relations in the Qur'ān: Relevance, Coherence and Structure*. Routledge, London.

Elias, J. J. (1991) Ṣūfī Thought and Practice in the Teachings of 'Alā' ad-dawla as-Simnānī. PhD dissertation, Yale University.

Elias, J. J. (1995) *The Throne Carrier of God: The Life and Thought of 'Alā' al-dawla as-Simnānī*. State University of New York Press, Albany.

Eliash, Joseph (1966) 'Alī b. Abī Ṭālib in Ithna-'Asharī Shī'ī belief. PhD thesis, University of London.

Eliash, Joseph (1969) "The Shīʿite Qurʾān:" A reconsideration of Goldziher's interpretation. *Arabica* 16, 15–24.
Engineer, Asghar Ali (1980) *The Bohras*. Vikas Publishing House, New Delhi.
EQ (2001–6) *The Encylopaedia of the Qurʾān*. 5 vols. Brill, Leiden.
Esmail, Aziz (2002) *A Scent of Sandalwood: Indo-Ismaili Religious Lyrics*. Curzon, Richmond.
Euben, Donna R. (2002) Curriculum matters. *Academe: Bulletin of the American Association of University Professors* 86 (November/December) www.aaup.org/publications/Academe/2002/02nd/02ndLW.htm.
Fabb, N. (1997) *Linguistics and Literature*. Blackwell, Oxford.
Famsy (2005) http://famsy.com/salam/Brotherhood0404.htm. January 23, 2005.
Faris, N. A. (1966) *The Book of Knowledge, being a Translation with Notes of the Kitāb al-ʿIlm of al-Ghazzālī's Iḥyāʾ ʿUlūm al-Dīn*. Ashraf Press, Lahore.
Faris, N. A., and Glidden, H. (1939) The development of the meaning of Koranic Ḥanīf. *Journal of the Palestine Oriental Society* 19, 1–13.
Al-Farrāʾ (1955–72) *Maʿānī ʾl-Qurʾān*, A. Y. Najātī and M. A. Najjār (eds.), 3 vols. Dār al-Kutub al-Miṣriyya, Cairo.
Fierro, M. (1992) The treatises against innovations (*kutub al-bidaʿ*). *Der Islam* 69, 204–46.
Firestone, Reuven (1997a) Disparity and resolution in the Qurʾānic teachings on war: A re-evaluation of a traditional problem. *Journal of Near Eastern Studies* 55, 1–19.
Firestone, Reuven (1997b) The failure of a Jewish program of public satire in the squares of Medina. *Judaism*, Winter, 438–52.
Firestone, Reuven (1999) *Jihad: The Origin of Holy War in Islam*. Oxford University Press, New York.
Firestone, Reuven (2005) A problem with monotheism: Judaism, Christianity, and Islam in dialogue and dissent. In: Hinze, Bradford (ed.) *Heirs of Abraham: The Future of Muslim, Jewish and Christian Relations*. Orbis Books, New York, pp. 20–54.
Fischer, A. (1904) Miszellen. *Zeitschrift der Deutschen Morgländischen Gesellschaft* 58, 869–76.
Friedmann, Yohanan (1986) Finality of prophethood in Islam. *Jerusalem Studies in Arabic and Islam* 7, 177–215.
Frye, Northrup (1982) *The Great Code: The Bible and Literature*. Harcourt Brace Jovanovich, New York.
Fück, J. (1950) *Arabiya. Untersuchungen zur arabischen Sprach- und Stilgeschichte*. Akademie-Verlag, Berlin.
Fyzee, Asaf A. A. (1982) *A Shīʿite Creed: A Translation of Iʿtiqādātuʾl-Imāmiyyah*. World Organization for Islamic Services, Tehran (reprint).
GAL = Brockelmann, C. (1996) *Geschichte der arabischen Litteratur*, 2nd edn. 2 vols. and 3 supp. vols. E. J. Brill, Leiden.
GAS = Sezgin, F. (1967–84) *Geschichte des arabischen Schrifttums*. E. J. Brill, Leiden.
Gätje, H. (1976) *The Qurʾān and its Exegesis*, ed. and trans. Alford Welch. Routledge and Kegan Paul, London.
Gautier, L. (1878) *La perle précieuse (ad-dourra al-fākhira) de Ghazālī, 450–505 A.H.* H. Georg, Geneva (reprint Oriental Press, Amsterdam, 1974).
Geertz, C. (1976) Art as a cultural system. *Modern Language Notes* 91, 1490–9.
Al-Ghazālī, Abū Ḥāmid Muḥammad (1967–8) *Iḥyāʾ ʿulūm al-dīn*, ed. ʿA. al-ʿIdrūs Bāʿlawi, 5 vols. Al-Ḥalabī wa-Shurakāʾ-hu, Cairo.
Al-Ghazālī, Abū Ḥāmid Muḥammad (1983) *The Recitation and Interpretation of the Qurʾān: Al-Ghazālī's Theory [Iḥyāʾ ʿUlūm al-Dīn, Book 8]*, trans. Muḥammad Abū'l Quasem. Kegan Paul International, London.

Al-Ghazālī, Abū Ḥāmid Muḥammad (1995) *Al-Mustaṣfā min ʿilm al-uṣūl*, ed. Muḥammad Yūsuf Najim, 2 vols. Dār al-Ṣādir, Beirut.

Al-Ghazālī, Abū Ḥāmid Muḥammad (1996) *Majmūʿat rasāʾil al-imām al-Ghazālī*. Dār al-Fikr, Beirut.

Gilliot, Claude (1990) *Exégèse, langue et théologie en Islam. L'exégèse coranique de Tabari (m. 311/923)*. J. Vrin, Paris.

Gilliot, Claude (1993) Récit, mythe et histoire chez Tabari. Une vision mythique de l'histoire universelle. *Mélanges de l'Institut Dominicaine d'Études Orientales du Caire* 21, 277–89.

Gilliot, Claude (1994) Mythe, récit, histoire du salut dans le commentaire du Coran de Tabari. *Journal Asiatique* 282, 237–70.

Gilliot, Claude (1997) Le commentaire coranique de Hūd b. Muḥakkam/Muḥkim. *Arabica* 44, 179–82.

Gilliot, Claude (2002) Informants. In: McAuliffe, Jane Dammen (ed.) *Encyclopaedia of the Qurʾān*. Brill, Leiden, vol. II, pp. 512–18.

Gilliot, Claude (2005) Traditional disciplines of Qurʾānic studies. In: McAuliffe, Jane Dammen (ed.) *Encyclopaedia of the Qurʾān*. Brill, Leiden, vol. V, pp. 318–39.

Gilliot, Claude, and Larcher, Pierre (2003). Language and style of the Qurʾān. In: McAuliffe, Jane Dammen (ed.) *Encyclopaedia of the Qurʾān*. Brill, Leiden, vol. III, pp. 109–35.

Gimaret, Daniel (1979) Les Uṣūl al-Khamsa du Qāḍī ʿAbd al-Ǧabbār et leurs commentaries. *Annales Islamologiques* 15, 47–96.

Gimaret, Daniel (1988) *Les noms divins en Islam: exégèse lexicographique et théologique*. Les éditions du Cerf, Paris.

Gimaret, Daniel (1990) *La doctrine d'al-Ashʿarī*. Les éditions du Cerf, Paris.

Godlas, A. (1991) The *ʿArāʾis al-bayān*, the mystical Qurʾānic exegesis of Rūzbihān al-Baqlī. PhD dissertation, University of California, Berkeley.

Godlas, A. (1996) Psychology and self-transformation in the Ṣūfī Qurʾān commentary of Rūzbihān al-Baqlī. *Sufi Illuminations* I:1, 31–62.

Goitein, S. D. (1966) *Studies in Islamic History and Institutions*. Brill, Leiden.

Goldfeld, Isaiah (1984) *Qurʾānic Commentary in the Eastern Islamic Tradition of the First Four Centuries of the Hijra: An Annotated Edition of the Preface of al-Thaʿlabī's "Kītāb al-Kashf waʾl-Bayān ʿan Tafsīr al-Qurʾān."* Srugy Printers and Publishers, Acre.

Goldfeld, Y. (1988) The development of theory on Qurʾanic exegesis in Islamic scholarship. *Studia Islamica* 67, 5–27.

Goldziher, I. (1871) Zur Charakteristik Gelâl ud-Dîn us-Sujûṭî's und seiner literarischen Thätigkeit. *Sitzungsberichte der Philosophisch-Historischen Klasse der Kaiserlichen Akademie der Wissenschaften* 69, 7–28. (trans. M. Barry, Ignaz Goldziher on Al-Suyūṭī. *The Muslim World* 68 [1978], 79–99).

Goldziher, I. (1889/90) *Muhammedanische Studien*, 2 vol. Georg Olms, Hildesheim (reprint).

Goldziher, I. (1920) *Die Richtungen der Islamichen Koranauslegung*. E. J. Brill, Leiden.

Goldziher, I. (1981) *Introduction to Islamic Theology and Law*. Princeton University Press, Princeton. (trans. of *Vorlesungen über den Islam*, 1910).

Graham, William (1977) *Divine Word and Prophetic Word in Early Islam: A Reconsideration of the Sources, with Special Reference to the Divine Sayings or ḥadīth qudsī*. Mouton, The Hague/Paris.

Graham, William (1987) *Beyond the Written Word: Oral Aspects of Scripture in the History of Religion*, Cambridge University Press, Cambridge.

Graham, William (1995) "The Winds to herald his mercy" and other "Signs for those of certain faith." Nature as token of God's sovereignty and grace in the Qurʾān. In: Lee, Sang Hyun, Proudfoot, Wayne, and Blackwell, Albert L. (eds.) *Faithful Imagining: Essays in Honor of Richard R. Niebuhr*. Scholars Press, Atlanta, pp. 18–38.

Griffith, Sidney H. (2001) Christians and Christianity. In: McAuliffe, Jane Dammen (ed.) *Encyclopaedia of the Qur'ān*. Brill, Leiden, vol. I, pp. 307–16.

Griffith, Sidney H. (2002) Gospel. In: McAuliffe, Jane Dammen (ed.) *Encyclopaedia of the Qur'ān*. Brill, Leiden, vol. II, pp. 342–3.

Grohmann, A. (1958) The problem of dating early Qur'āns. *Der Islam* 33, 213–31.

Guillaume, A. (1955, 1980) *The Life of Muhammad: A Translation of Ibn Isḥāq's Sīrat Rasūl Allāh*. Oxford University Press, Oxford/Karachi.

Gwynne, Rosalind W. (1993) The neglected sunna: sunnat Allāh (the sunna of God). *American Journal of Islamic Social Sciences*, 10, 455–63.

Gwynne, Rosalind W. (2002) Hell and hellfire. In: McAuliffe, Jane Dammen (ed.) *Encyclopaedia of the Qur'ān*. Brill, Leiden, vol. II, pp. 414–20.

Gwynne, Rosalind W. (2004) *Logic, Rhetoric, and Legal Reasoning in the Qur'ān: God's Arguments*. RoutledgeCurzon, London.

Habil, Abdurrahman (1987) Traditional esoteric commentaries on the Quran. In: Nasr, Seyyed Hossein (ed.) *Islamic Spirituality: Foundations*. Crossroad, New York, pp. 24–47.

Haddad, Yvonne, and Esposito, John (eds.) (1998) *Islam, Gender and Social Change*. Oxford University Press, New York.

Haeri, Shahla (1989) *The Law of Desire: Temporary Marriage in Iran*. I. B. Tauris, London.

Hajir (2005) http://hajirstony.blogspot.com/2004/02/kurdish-problem-and-islam.html. January 23, 2005.

Hakim, Avraham (2003) Conflicting images of lawgivers: The caliph and the prophet. In: Berg, Herbert (ed.) *Method and Theory in the Study of Islamic Origins*. Brill, Leiden, pp. 159–77.

Al-Ḥākim al-Nīsābūrī, Muḥammad (1990) *Al-Mustadrak ʿalā al-Ṣaḥīḥayn*, ed. Muṣṭafā ʿAbd al-Qādir ʿAtā. Dār al-Kutub al-ʿIlmiyya, Beirut.

Hallaq, Wael B. (1997) *A History of Islamic Legal Theories: An Introduction to Sunnī uṣūl al-fiqh*. Cambridge University Press, Cambridge.

Hamdan, Omar (2006) *Studien zur Kanonisierung des Koran Al-Ḥasan al-Baṣrī und das Koran projekt der Umayyaden*. Harrassowitz, Wiesbaden.

Hamori, Andras (1979) *On the Art of Medieval Arabic Literature*. Princeton University Press, Princeton.

Hamzaoui, R. (1978) Idéologie et langue ou l'emprunt linguistique d'après les exégètes du Coran et les théologiens: interprétation socio-linguistique. In: Fronzaroli, Pelio (ed.) *Atti del secondo congresso internazionale di linguistica Camito-Semitica, Firenze, 16–19 aprile 1974*. Instituto di Linguistica e di Lingue Orientali, Université de Florence, Florence, pp. 157–72.

Ḥasan, Khalīfa Bū Bakr (1989) *Manāhij al-uṣūliyyin fī ṭuruq dalīlāt al-alfāẓ ʿalā ʾl-aḥkām*. Maktabat Wahba, Cairo.

Hassan, Riffat (1991) An Islamic perspective. In: Becher, Jeanne (ed.) *Women, Religion and Sexuality: Studies on the Impact of Religious Teachings on Women*. Trinity Press, Philadelphia.

Ḥaydar, Ḥ. S. (1999) *ʿUlūm al-Qurʾān bayna ʾl-Burhān waʾl-Itqān: dirāsa muqārana*. Maktabat Dār al-Zaman lil-Nashr waʾl-Tawzīʿ, Medina.

Al-Hibri, Azizah (ed.) (1982) *Women and Islam*. Pergamon Press, Oxford.

Al-Hillī, ʿAllāma (1958) *Al-Bāb al-Hādī ʿAshar. A Treatise on the Principles of Shīʿite Theology*, trans. William McElwee Miller. Luzac, London.

Hodgson, Marshall G. S. (1974) *The Venture of Islam*, 3 vols. University of Chicago Press, Chicago.

Hollister, John Norman (1953) *The Shiʿa of India*. Luzac, London.

Horovitz, Josef (1926) *Koranische Untersuchungen*. Walter de Gruyter, Berlin, Leipzig.

Huart, C. (1908) *Les calligraphes et miniaturistes de l'Orient musulman*. E. Leroux, Paris (reprint Osnabrück, 1972).

Hūd b. Muḥakkam (1990) *Tafsīr kitāb Allāh al-ʿazīz*, ed. B. S. Sharīfī. Dār al-Gharb al-Islāmī, Beirut.

Hussaini, S. Sh. Kh. (1983) *Sayyid Muḥammad al-Ḥusaynī-i Gīsūdirāz (721/1321–825/1422): On Sufism.* Idārah-i Adabiyat-i Delli, Delhi.
Ḥuwaysh, Mulla ʿAbd al-Qādir b. al-Sayyid Muḥammad (1964) *Bayān al-maʿānī ʿalā ḥasab tartīb al-nuzūl,* 6 vols. Maṭbaʿat al-Taraqqī, Damascus.
Ibn ʿAbbās, ʿAbd Allāh (1978) *Al-Lughāt fī'l-Qur'ān,* ed. Ṣalāḥ al-Dīn al-Munajjid. Dār al-Kitāb al-Jadīd, Beirut.
Ibn Abī Ḥātim, ʿAbd al-Raḥmān (1997) *Tafsīr al-Qur'ān al-ʿazīm,* ed. Asʾad Muḥammad al-Ṭayyib, 9 vols. Maktabat Nazār Muṣṭafa al-Bāz, Mecca.
Ibn Abī Shayba, ʿAbd Allāh b. Muḥammad (1989) *Al-Muṣannaf fī'l-aḥādīth wa'l-āthār,* ed. Saʿīd al-Lahham, 8 vols. Dār al-Fikr, Beirut.
Ibn Abī Shayba, ʿAbd Allāh b. Muḥammad (1995) *Al-Kitāb al-muṣannaf fī'l-aḥādīth wa'l-āthār,* ed. Muḥammad ʿAbd al-Salām Shāhīn. Dār al-Kutub al-ʿIlmiyya, Beirut.
Ibn ʿAjība, Aḥmad (1990) *Al-Fahrasa,* ed. ʿA. Ḥamdān. Dār al-Ghad al-ʿArabī, Cairo.
Ibn ʿAjība, Aḥmad (1999) *Al-Baḥr al-madīd fī tafsīr al-Qur'ān al-majīd,* ed. A. ʿA al-Qurashī Raslān, 6 vols. Al-Hay'a al-Miṣriyya al-ʿĀmma lil-Kitāb, Cairo.
Ibn ʿAsākir, Abū 'l-Qāsim ʿAlī b. al-Ḥasan (1984) *Tabyīn kadhib al-muftarī fīmā nusiba ilā 'l-imām Abī 'l-Ḥasan al-Ashʿarī.* Dār al-Kitāb al-ʿArabī, Beirut.
Ibn Bābawayh, Muḥammad (1377/1957) *Kitāb al-hidāya,* ed. Mahdī al-Wāʿiz al-Khurāsānī as: *Al-muqniʿ wa'l-hidāya.* Al-Maktaba al-Islāmiyya, Tehran.
Ibn Bābawayh, Muḥammad (1385/1966) *ʿIlal al-sharāʾiʿ wa'l-ahkām.* Maktabat al-Ḥaydariyya, Najaf.
Ibn Bābawayh, Muḥammad (1387/1967) *Kitāb al-tawḥīd,* ed. Hāshim al-Ḥusaynī. Maktabat al-Ṣadūq, Tehran.
Ibn Baṭṭūta (1992)*Voyages et périples choisis,* trans. P. Charles-Dominique. Gallimard, Paris.
Ibn Bāz (2005) http://www.calgaryislam.com/imembers/Sections+index-req-viewarticle-artid-47-page-1.html (translation by Abu Rumaysah). January 23, 2005.
Ibn al-Ḍurays (1987) *Faḍā'il al-Qur'ān,* ed. Ghazwat Budayr. Dar al-Fikr, Damascus.
Ibn Fāris, Aḥmad (1964) *Kitāb al-ṣāḥibī fī fiqh al-lugha,* ed. M. Chouémi. Mu'assasat Badrān lil-Ṭabāʿa wa'l-Nashr, Beirut.
Ibn Ḥajar, al-ʿAsqalānī (1929–32) *al-Durar al-kāmina.* Majlis Dā'irat al-Maʿārif al-ʿUthmāniyya, Haydarabad.
Ibn Ḥajar, al-ʿAsqalānī (1959, 1990–3, 1996) *Fatḥ al-bārī sharḥ Ṣaḥiḥ al-Bukhārī,* ed. ʿAbd al-ʿAzīz b. ʿAbd Allāh b. Bāz, 13 vols. Dār al-Fikr, Beirut.
Ibn Ḥanbal, Aḥmad (1895; n.d.) *Al-Musnad,* 6 vols. Al-Maṭbaʿa al-Maymaniyya, Cairo; reprint Dār al-Fikr, Beirut.
Ibn Ḥanbal, Aḥmad (1983) *Kitāb faḍā'il al-Ṣaḥāba,* ed. Waṣiyy Allāh b. Muḥammad b. ʿAbbās. Mu'assasat al-Risāla, Beirut.
Ibn Ḥazm (1987) *Al-Iḥkām fi uṣūl al-aḥkām,* 2 vols. Beirut.
Ibn Ḥibbān (1988) *Al-Iḥsān fī taqrīb ṣaḥīḥ Ibn Ḥibbān,* tartīb ʿAlā' al-Dīn al-Fārisī, ed. Shuʿayb al-Arna'ūṭ, 16 vols. Mu'assasat al-Risāla, Beirut.
Ibn Hishām, ʿAbd al-Malik (1995; n.d.) *Al-Sīra al-nabawiyya,* ed. Muṣṭafā al-Saqqā, Ibrāhīm al-Abyādī, and ʿAbd al-Ḥāfiẓ Shalabī, 4 vols. in 2. Dār al-Khayr, Beirut; Dār al-Maʿrifa, Beirut.
Ibn al-Jawzī (1984) *Zād al-masīr fī ʿilm al-tafsīr,* 9 vols. Al-Maktab al-Islāmī, Beirut.
Ibn Kathīr, Ismāʿīl b. ʿUmar (1952, 1970) *Tafsīr al-Qur'ān al-ʿazīm,* 4 vols. Dār Iḥyā' al-Kutub al-ʿArabiyya, Cairo; Dār al-Fikr, Beirut.
Ibn Kathīr, Ismāʿīl b. ʿUmar (1966) *Tafsīr al-Qur'ān al-ʿaẓīm.* Dār al-Andalus lil-Ṭibāʿa wa'l-Nashr, Beirut.
Ibn Kathīr, Ismāʿīl b. ʿUmar (1985, 1990) *Al-Bidāya wa'l-nihāya,* ed. Aḥmad Abū Milḥim et al. Dār al-Kutub al-ʿIlmiyya, Beirut; Maktabat al-Maʿārif, Beirut.

Ibn Kathīr, Ismāʿīl b. ʿUmar (1987) *Al-Sīra al-nabawiyya*, ed. M. ʿAbd al-Wāḥid. Dār al-Rāʿid al-ʿArabī, Beirut.

Ibn Khālawayh (1380/1960) *Iʿrāb thalāthīn sūra min al-Qurʾān al-karīm*. Dār Ṣādir, Beirut.

Ibn Khaldūn (1967) *The Muqaddima: An Introduction to History*, trans. F. Rosenthal. Princeton University Press, Princeton.

Ibn Manda, Abū ʿAbd Allāh Muḥammad (1996) *Kitab al-īmān*, ed. ʿAli b. Muḥammad al-Faqīhī, 2 vols. Beirut.

Ibn Manẓūr, Muḥammad (1375/1956) *Lisān al-ʿArab*, 15 vols. Dar Ṣādir, Beirut.

Ibn al-Nadīm, Muḥammad b. Isḥāq (1970) *The Fihrist of al-Nadīm: A Tenth-Century Survey of Muslim Culture*, 2 vols., trans. B. Dodge. Columbia University Press, New York.

Ibn al-Nadīm, Muḥammad b. Isḥāq (1971) *Kitāb al-Fihrist*, ed. R. Tajaddud. Maktabat al-Assadī, Tehran.

Ibn al-Naqīb, Aḥmad b. ʿAlī (MS) *Kitāb al-Muwāfaqāt*. MS Staatsbibliothek zu Berlin, Wetzstein II, 1782.

Ibn Nujaym, Zayn al-Dīn b. Ibrāhīm (1355/1936) *Fatḥ al-ghaffār bi-sharḥ al-manār al-maʿrūf bi-mishkāt al-anwār fī uṣūl al-manār*. 3 vols. in 1. Muṣṭafā ʾl-Bābī ʾl-Ḥalabī, Cairo.

Ibn Qudāma, ʿAbd Allāh b. Aḥmad al-Maqdisī (1378) *Rawḍat al-nāẓir wa-jannat al-munāẓir*. Al-Maṭbaʿa al-Salafiyya, Cairo.

Ibn Qudāma, Muwaffiq al-Dīn ʿAbd Allāh b. Aḥmad (1403/1983) *al-Mughnī wa-sharḥuh al-kabīr*. 12 vols, 2 vols. indexes. Dār al-Kitāb al-ʿArabī, Beirut.

Ibn Saʿd, Muḥammad (1904–15) *Kitāb al-ṭabaqāt al-kabīr*, ed. E. Sachau. Brill, Leiden.

Ibn Saʿd, Muḥammad (1957, 1975) *Kitāb al-ṭabaqāt al-kubrā*, 8 vols. Dār Ṣādir, Beirut.

Ibn Shabba, ʿUmar (1979) *Taʾrīkh al-madīna al-munawwara*, ed. Fuhaym Muḥammad Shaltūt, 4 vols. Dār al-Turāth, Mecca.

Ibn Ṭāwūs, ʿAlī b. Mūsā (1999) *Al-Ṭarāʾif fī maʿrifat ahl al-ṭawāʾif*, ed ʿAlī ʿĀshūr. Muʾassasat al-Aʿlamī, Beirut.

Ibn Taymiyya (1392) *Muqaddima fī uṣūl al-tafsīr*, ed. Adnan Zarzour. Beirut.

Ibn Taymiyya (1979) *Darʾ taʿāruḍ al-ʿaql waʾl-naql*, ed. Rashād Sālim. Dār al-Kunūz al-Adabiyya, Riyad.

Ibn Taymiyya (n.d.) *Minhāj al-sunna al-nabawiyya*, 4 vols in 3. Maktabat al-Riyāḍ al-Ḥadītha, Riyad.

Ilkkaracan, Pinar (ed.) (2000) *Women and Sexuality in Muslim Societies*. Women for Women's Human Rights, Istanbul.

Al-ʿImādī, Ḥamīd b. ʿAlī (1996) *Al-Durr al-mustaṭāb fī muwāfaqāt ʿUmar b. al-Khaṭṭāb*. Dār al-Kutub al-ʿIlmiyya, Beirut.

Imām Shāh, Sayyid (1972) *Dasa Avatāra*, trans. Gulshan Khakee, The Das Avatāra of Satpanthi Ismailis and Imam-Shahis of Indo-Pakistan. PhD thesis, Harvard University, Cambridge.

ʿInāya, G. (1996) *Hudā ʾl-furqān fī ʿulūm al-Qurʾān*. ʿĀlim al-Kutub, Beirut.

Iṣlāḥī, Amīn Aḥsan (2000) *Tadabbur-i Qurʾān*, 9 vols. Fārān Foundation, Lahore.

Islam for Today (2005) http://www.islamfortoday.com/khan09.htm. January 23, 2005 (originally appeared in the Saudi Arabic newspaper in *Al-Sharq al-Awsat*, February 25, 2003).

Islam Knowledge (2005) http://www.islamknowledge.com/Non-Muslim/islam_and_muslims.htm. January 23, 2005.

Islam On Line (2005a) http://taarafu.islamonline.net/English/Taarafo_Conference/2003/article06.shtml. January 23, 2005.

Islam On Line (2005b) http://taarafu.islamonline.net/English/Taarafo_Conference/2003/article22.shtml. January 23, 2005.

Islam On Line (2005c) http://taarafu.islamonline.net/English/Taarafo_Conference/topic_01.shtml. January 23, 2005.

Islam On Line (2005d) http://www.islamonline.net/english/in_depth/islamintro/topic09.shtml. January 23, 2005.

Islamic Center of Rochester (2005) http://www.rochesterislamiccenter.org/INTRODUCTION %20TO%20ISLAM.pdf. January 23, 2005.

Islamic Foundation (2005) http://www.islamicedfoundation.com/bookreviews/muslimyo.htm. January 23, 2005.

Islamic Lit (2005) http://members.tripod.com/~IslamicLit/. January 23, 2005.

Al-Isnawī, ʿAbd al-Raḥīm b. al-Ḥasan (1993) *Zawāʾid al-uṣūl ʿalā minhāj al-wuṣūl ilā ʿilm al-uṣūl*, ed. Muḥammad Sinān Sayf Jalālī and ʿUmar b. ʿAbd al-ʿAzīz Muḥammad. Maktabat al-Jīl al-Jadīd, Sanaa.

Izutsu, Toshihiko (1956) *Language and Magic*. The Keio Institute of Cultural and Linguistic Studies, Tokyo.

Izutsu, Toshihiko (1964) *God and Man in the Koran: Semantics of the Koranic Weltanschauung*. The Keio Institute of Cultural and Linguistic Studies, Tokyo.

Izutsu, Toshihiko (1966, 2002) *Ethico-Religious Concepts in the Qurʾān*. McGill University Press, Montreal.

Jaʿfar b. Manṣūr al-Yaman (2001) *Kitāb al-ʿālim waʾl-ghulām*, ed. and trans. James Morris, *The Master and the Disciple: An Early Islamic Dialogue*. I. B. Tauris, London.

Jafri, S. Husain M. (1979) *Origins and Early Development of Shīʿa Islām*. Librairie du Liban, Beirut.

Jakobson, R. (1993), *Poetik. Ausgewählte Aufsätze 1921–1971*, ed. E. Holenstein and T. Schelbert (eds.), 3 vol. Suhrkamp, Frankfurt.

James, David (1988) *Qurʾāns of the Mamlūks*. Alexandria Press, London.

Al-Jawālīqī, Abū Manṣūr (1942) *Al-Muʿarrab min al-kalām al-aʿjamī ʿalā ḥurūf al-muʿjam*, ed. A. M. Shākir. Dār al-Kutub al-Miṣriyya, Cairo.

Jeffery, Arthur (1936) The Qurʾān readings of Zayd b. ʿAlī. *Rivista degli Studi Orientali* 16, 249–89.

Jeffery, Arthur (1937) *Materials for the History of the Text of the Qurʾān: The Old Codices* E. J. Brill, Leiden.

Jeffery, Arthur (1938) *Foreign Vocabulary of the Qur'an*. Oriental Institute, Baroda.

Jeffery, Arthur (1952) *The Qurʾān as Scripture*. Russell F. Moore, New York.

Jeffery, Arthur (1954) *Two Muqaddimas to the Qur'anic Sciences*. Brothers al-Khaniji, Cairo.

Johns, A. H. (1989) David and Bathsheba: A case study in the exegesis of Qurʾānic story-telling. *Mélanges de l'Institut Dominicaine d'Études Orientales du Caire* 19, 225–66.

Johnson, James Turner, and Kelsay, John (eds.) (1990) *Cross, Crescent, and Sword: The Justification and Limitation of War in Western and Islamic Tradition*. Greenwood Press, New York.

Jomier, J. (1997) *The Great Themes of the Qurʾan*. SCM Press, London.

Al-Jurjānī, ʿAbd al-Qāhir (1984) *Dalāʾil al iʿjāz fīʾl-Qurʾān*, eds. M. ʿAbduh and R. Riḍā. ʿĀlam al-kutub, Beirut.

Al-Jurjānī, ʿAlī b. Muḥammad (1978) *Kitāb al-taʿrīfāt*, ed. G. Flügel. Maktabat Lubnān, Beirut (reprint of Leipzig, 1847).

Juynboll, G. H. A. (1974) The position of Qur'an recitation in early Islam. *Journal of Semitic Studies* 19, 240–51.

Kadi (al-Qāḍī), Wadad, and Mir, Mustansir (2003) Literature and the Qurʾān. In: McAuliffe, Jane Dammen (ed.) *Encyclopaedia of the Qurʾān*. Brill, Leiden, vol. III, pp. 205–27.

Al-Kāfiyajī, Muḥammad b. Sulaymān (1990) *al-Taysīr fī qawāʿid ʿilm al-tafsīr*, ed. N. al-Maṭrūdī. Dār al-Qalam, Damascus.

Kafka, F. (1983) *Hochzeitsvorbereitungen auf dem Lande und andere Prosa aus dem Nachlaß (Gesammelte Werke in acht Bänden)*, ed. Max Brod. Fischer, Frankfurt.

Kamali, Mohammad Hashim (1991) *Principles of Islamic Jurisprudence*, revised edition. Islamic Texts Society, Cambridge.

Kāshifī, Kamāl al-Dīn Ḥusayn b. ʿAlī Wāʿiẓ (1938) *Mawāhib-i ʿalīya yā Tafsīr-i Ḥusaynī*, ed. M. Jalālī Nāʾīnī, 4 vols. Iqbāl, Tehran.

Kassam, Tazim R. (1995) *Songs of Wisdom and Circles of Dance: Hymns of the Satpanth Ismāʿīlī Muslim Saint, Pīr Shams*. State University of New York Press, Albany.

Kassis H. (1983) *A Concordance of the Qur'an*. University of California Press, Berkeley.

Keeler, Annabel (forthcoming) *Ṣūfī Hemeneutics: Maybūdī's Persian Commentary on the Qurʾān, the Kashf al-asrār*. Oxford University Press, Oxford.

Kelsay, John, and Johnson, James Turner (1991) *Just War and Jihad: Historical and Theoretical Perspectives on War and Peace in Western and Islamic Traditions*. Greenwood Press, New York.

Kermani, Navid (1996) *Offenbarung als Kommunikation. Das Konzept* waḥy *in Naṣr Hāmid Abū Zayds* Mafhūm an-naṣṣ, Peter Lang, Frankfurt.

Kermani, Navid (1999) *Gott ist schön. Das ästhetische Erleben des Koran*. C. H. Beck, Munich.

Kermani, Navid (2000) The aesthetic reception of the Qurʾān as reflected in early Muslim history. In: Boullata, I. J. (ed.) *Literary Structures of Religious Meaning in the Qurʾān*, Curzon, Richmond, pp. 255–76.

Kermani, Navid (2002) Intellect. In: McAuliffe, Jane Dammen (ed.) *Encyclopaedia of the Qurʾān*. Brill, Leiden, vol. II, pp. 547–9.

Keshavarz, F. (2002) Pregnant with God: The poetic art of mothering the sacred in Rumi's Fihi Ma Fih. *Comparative Studies of South Asia, Africa and the Middle East* 22:1, 90–9.

Khadduri, Majid (1955) *War and Peace in the Law of Islam*. Johns Hopkins University Press, Baltimore.

Al-Khayyāṭ, Abū ʾl-Ḥusayn ʿAbd al-Munʿim b. Muḥammad (1957) *Kitāb al-intiṣār waʾl-radd ʿalā ibn al-Rāwandī al-mulḥid*, ed. H.S. Nyberg, trans. A. Nader. Al-Maṭbaʿa al-Kathūlīkiyya, Beirut.

Khoury, Raif Georges (1978) *Les légendes prophètiques dans l'Islam: depuis le 1er jusqu'au IIIe siècle de l'Hégire*. Otto Harrassowitz, Wiesbaden.

Al-Khūʾī, al-Sayyid Abū ʾl-Qāsim al-Mūsawī (1394/1974) *Al-Bayān fī tafsīr al-Qurʾān*. Muʾassasat al-Aʿlamī lil-Maṭbūʿāt, Beirut.

Al-Kindī, ʿAbd al-Masīḥ (1885) *Risāla*, ed. A. Tien. London.

King Hussein, Jordan (2005) http://www.kinghussein.gov.jo/96_march13.html. January 23, 2005.

Kingston Business School (2005) http://business.kingston.ac.uk/research/intbus/coiaw.pdf. January 23, 2005.

Kirmānī, Ḥamīd al-Dīn (1953) *Rāḥat al-ʿaql*, ed. Kāmil Ḥusayn, E. J. Brill, Leiden.

Al-Kisāʾī (1922–3) *Qiṣaṣ al-anbiyāʾ*, ed. I. Eisenberg. E. J. Brill, Leiden.

Kister, M. J. (1980) *Studies in Jāhiliyya and Early Islam*. Variorum, London.

Kister, M. J. (1983) The *sīrah* literature. In: Beeston, A. F. L., Johnstone, T. M., Serjeant, R. B., and Smith, G. R. (eds.) *Arabic Literature to the End of the Umayyad Period*. Cambridge University Press, Cambridge, pp. 352–67.

Kīyā al-Harrāsī, ʿAlī b. Muḥammad (n.d.) *Aḥkām al-Qurʾān*, ed. Mūsā Muḥammad ʿAlī and ʿIzzat ʿAlī ʿAṭiyah, 4 vols. Dār al-Kutub al-Ḥadītha, Cairo.

Klar, M. O. (2004) *And We cast upon his throne a mere body*: A historiographical reading of Q 38: 34. *Journal of Qurʾanic Studies* 6:1, 103–26.

Klar, M. O. (2006) *Interpreting Thaʿlabī's Tales of the Prophets: Temptation, Responsibility and Loss*. Routledge, London.

Knappert, J. (1976) The Qisasu'l-Anbiya'i as moralistic stories. *Proceedings of the Seminar for Arabian Studies* 6, 103–16.

Köbert, R. (1961a) Das Gottesepitheton *aṣ-ṣamad* in Sure 112,2. *Orientalia* (NS) 30, 204–5.

Köbert, R. (1961b) Das koranische "tāghūt." *Orientalia* (NS) 30, 415–16.

Kohlberg, Etan (1973) Some notes on the Imamite attitude to the Qur'an. In: Hourani, Albert, and Brown, Vivian (eds.) *Islamic Philosophy and the Classical Tradition*. University of South Carolina Press, Columbia, pp. 209–44.

Kohlberg, Etan (1991) *Belief and Law in Imami Shi'ism*. Variorum, Aldershot.

Kohlberg, Etan (1992) *A Medieval Muslim Scholar at Work: Ibn Ṭāwūs and his Library*. E. J. Brill, Leiden.

Kopf, L. (1956) Religious influences on medieval Arabic philology. *Studia Islamica* 5, 33–59; reprinted in Kopf, L. (1976): 19–45; also reprinted in Rippin (1999): 215–41.

Kopf, L. (1961) The treatment of foreign words in medieval Arabic lexicology. *Scripta Hierosolymitana* 9, 191–205; reprinted in Kopf, L. (1976): 247–61.

Kopf, L. (1976) *Studies in Arabic and Hebrew Lexicography*, ed. M. Goshen-Gottstein. Magnes Press, Jerusalem.

Krone, Susanne (1992) *Die altarabische Gottheit al-Lāt*. Peter Lang, Frankfurt.

Kronholm, T. (1982–3) Dependence and prophetic originality in the Koran. *Orientalia Suecana* 31–2, 47–70.

Al-Kulaynī, Muḥammad (1377–9/1957–9) *Al-uṣūl min al-kāfī*, ed. ʿA. A. Ghaffarī. Maktabat al-Ṣudūq, Tehran.

Künstlinger, D. (1928) Die Herkunft des Wortes Iblīs im Koran. *Rocznik Orientalistyczny* 6, 76–83.

Künstlinger, D. (1928–30) Rāʿinā. *Bulletin of the School of Oriental and African Studies* 5, 877–82.

Al-Lālakāʾī, Abū ʾl-Qāsim (1990) *Sharḥ uṣūl iʿtiqād ahl al-sunna waʾl-jamāʿa min al-kitāb waʾl-sunna wa-ijmāʿ al-ṣaḥāba waʾl-tābiʿīn min baʿdihim*, ed. Aḥmad Saʿd Ḥamdān. Dār Ṭayyiba, Riyad.

Lalani, Arzina (2000) *Early Shīʿī Thought: The Teaching of Imām Muḥammad al-Bāqir*. I. B. Tauris, London.

Lane, E. (1843) *Selections of the Ḳur-án with an Interwoven Commentary*. Houghton, Osgood, London.

Lane, Edward William (1863) *An Arabic-English Lexicon*. Williams and Norgate, London.

Lari, Sayyid Mujtaba Musavi (2005) http://home.swipnet.se/islam/articles/freedom.htm. January 23, 2005.

Lassner, Jacob (1993) *Demonizing the Queen of Sheba: Boundaries of Gender and Culture in Post-biblical Judaism and Medieval Islam*. University of Chicago Press, Chicago.

Lawson, B. Todd (1988) Interpretation as revelation: The Qurʾān commentary of Sayyid ʿAlí-Muḥammad Shírází, the Báb. In: Rippin, Andrew (ed.) *Approaches to the History of the Interpretation of the Qurʾān*. Oxford University Press, Oxford, pp. 223–53.

Lawson, B. Todd (1991) Note for the study of a "Shīʿī Qurʾān". *Journal of Semitic Studies* 36, 279–95.

Lawson, B. Todd (1993) Akhbārī Shīʿī approaches to *tafsīr*. In: Hawting, G. R. and Shareef, A.-K. (eds.) *Approaches to the Quran*. Routledge, London, pp. 173–210.

Lecker, M. (1997) Zayd b. Thābit, a Jew with two sidelocks: Judaism and literacy in pre-Islamic Medina (Yathrib). *Journal of Near Eastern Studies* 56, 259–73.

Leder, S. (1992) The literary use of *khabar*: A basic form of historical writing. In: Cameron, A., and Conrad, L. I. (eds.) *The Byzantine and Early Islamic Near East. Problems in the Literary Sources Material*. Darwin Press, Princeton, pp. 277–315.

Leder, S. (1998) Conventions of fictional narration in learned literature. In: Leder, S. (ed.) *Storytelling in the Framework of Non-fictional Arabic Literature*. Harrassowitz, Wiesbaden, pp. 34–60.

Leeds Grand Mosque (2005) http://www.leedsgrandmosque.org.uk/khutbahs/khutba-20040402.asp. January 23, 2005.

Leemhuis, F. (1982) Qurʾānic siǧǧīl and Aramic sgyl. *Journal of Semitic Studies* 27, 47–56 (reprinted in Rippin 2001a: 117–26).

Leemhuis, F. (2001) Codices of the Qurʾān. In: McAuliffe, Jane Dammen (ed.) *Encyclopaedia of the Qurʾān*. Brill, Leiden, vol. I, pp. 347–51.

Lewis, F. D. (2000) *Rumi, Past and Present, East and West: The Life, Teachings and Poetry of Jalal al-Din Rumi*. Oneworld Publications, Oxford.

Lory, P. (1980) *Les commentaires ésotériques du Coran d'après ʿAbd al-Razzâq al-Qâshânī*, 2nd edn. Les deux océans, Paris.

Lüling, Günter (1974) *Über den Ur-Qurʾān. Ansätze zur Rekonstruktion vorislamiascher christlicher Strophenlieder im Qurʾān*. Lüling, Erlangen.

Lüling, Günter (2003) *A Challenge to Islam for Reformation: The Rediscovery and Reliable Reconstruction of a Comprehensive Pre-Islamic Christian Hymnal Hidden in the Koran under Earliest Islamic Reinterpretations*. Motilal Banarsidass Publishers, Delhi.

Luxenberg, Christoph (2000) *Die Syro-aramäische Lesart des Koran. Ein Beitrag zur Entschlüsselung der Koransprache*. Das Arabische Buch, Berlin.

Madelung, Wilferd (1979) Imamism and Muʿtazilite Theology. In: Fahd, T. (ed.) *Le Shīʿism imāmite*. PUF, Paris.

Madelung, Wilferd (1997) *The Succession to Muḥammad*. Cambridge University Press, Cambridge.

Madigan, Daniel A. (2001) *The Qurʾān's Self-Image: Writing and Authority in Islam's Scripture*, Princeton University Press, Princeton.

Al-Maḥallī and al-Suyūṭī (1952) *Tafsīr al-Imāmayn al-Jalālayn*. ʿAbd al-Hamīd Aḥmad Ḥanafī, Cairo.

Al-Maḥbūbī, ʿUbayd Allāh b. Masʿūd, al-Taftazānī, Masʿūd b. ʿUmar, and Umayrat, Zakariya (1996) *Al-Talwīḥ ilā kashf ḥaqāʾiq al-Tanqīḥ*. Dār al-Kutub al-ʿIlmiyya, Beirut.

Al-Maḥbūbī, ʿUbayd Allāh b. Masʿūd, and al-Taftazānī, Masʿūd b. ʿUmar (1998) *Al-Talwīḥ ilā kashf ḥaqāʾiq al-Tanqīḥ*, ed. Muhammad ʿAdnān Darwīsh. Sharīkat al-Arqam b. Abī ʾl-Arqam, Beirut.

Mahdihassan, S. (1953) Kursi or throne: A Chinese word in the Koran. *Journal of the Bombay Branch of the Royal Asiatic Society* 28, 19–21.

Maḥmūd Saʿd (1988) *Mabāḥith al-takhṣīṣ ʿinda al-uṣūliyyin wa-al-nuḥāh*. Munshaʾat al-Maʿārif, Alexandria.

Al-Majlisī, Muḥammad al-Bāqir (1301–15 SH) *Biḥār al-anwār*. Lithographed Edition, Tehran.

Al-Majlīsi, Muḥammad al-Baqīr (1909) *Hayāt al-Qulūb*. Tehran.

Al-Mārdīnī, Muḥammad b. ʿUthmān Shams al-Dīn al-Shāfiʿī (1996) *Al-Anjum al-ẓāhirāt ʿalā ḥall alfāẓ al-waraqāt fī uṣūl al-fiqh*, ed. ʿAbd al-Karīm b. ʿAlī b. Muḥammad Namla, 2nd edn. Maktabat al-Rushd, Riyad.

Margoliouth, D. S. (1939) Some additions to Professor Jeffery's *Foreign Vocabulary of the Qurʾan*. *Journal of the Royal Asiatic Society*, 53–61.

Markaz al-Thaqāfa waʾl-Maʿārif al-Qurʾāniyya (1995–7) *ʿUlūm al-Qurʾān ʿinda al-mufassirīn*, 3 vols. Maktabat al-Iʿlām al-Islāmiyya, Qom.

Marmura, M. E. (1975) Ghazali's attitude to the secular sciences and logic. In: Hourani, G. (ed.) *Essays on Islamic Philosophy and Science*. State University of New York Press, Albany, pp. 100–11.

Marshall, David (1999) *God, Muḥammad and the Unbelievers: A Qurʾānic Study*. Curzon, Richmond.

Al-Marzūqī, Abū ʿAlī Aḥmad b. Muḥammad (1951–3) *Sharḥ dīwān al-ḥamāsa*, 4 vols. Maṭbaʿat Lajnat al-Taʾlīf waʾl-Tarjama waʾl-Nashr, Cairo.

Masarrat, H. (1995) *Kitāb'shināsī-yi Abū ʾl-Faḍl Rashīd al-Dīn al-Maybūdī*. Anjuman-i Āthār wa Mafākhir-i Farhangī, Tehran.

Al-Mashannī, M. (1986) *Madrasat al-tafsīr fī ʾl-Andalūs*. Muʾassasat al-Risāla, Beirut.

Al-Māturīdī, Abū Manṣūr Muḥammad b. Muḥammad (1970) *Kitāb al-tawḥīd*, ed. Fathalla Kholeif. Dār al-Mashriq, Beirut.

Mawdudi, Sayyid Abu al-Aʿla (1988) *Towards Understanding the Qurʾān*, trans. Zafar Ishaq Ansari. Islamic Foundation, Leicester.

Al-Maybūdī, Abū ʾl-Faḍl (1982) *Kashf al-asrār wa-ʿuddat al-abrār*, ed. ʿA.-A. Ḥikmat, 10 vols. Amīr Kabīr, Tehran.

Al-Māzarī, Abū ʿAbd Allāh Muḥammad b. ʿAlī al-Tamīmī (2001) *Īḍāḥ al-maḥṣūl min burhān al-uṣūl*, ed. ʿAmmār Ṭālbī. Dar al-Gharb al-Islāmī, Beirut.

McAuliffe, Jane Dammen (1988) Ibn al-Jawzī's exegetical propaedeutic: Introduction and translations. *Alif: Journal of Comparative Poetics*, 8, 101–13.

McAuliffe, Jane Dammen (1998) Assessing the *isrāʾīliyyāt*: An exegetical conundrum. In: Leder, S. (ed.) *Story-telling in the Framework of Non-fictional Arabic Literature*. Harrassowitz, Wiesbaden, pp. 345–69.

McAuliffe, Jane Dammen (1999) "Debate with them in the better way": The construction of a Qurʾānic commonplace. In: Neuwirth, A. et al. (eds.) *Myths, Historical Archetypes and Symbolic Figures in Arabic Literature: Towards a New Hermeneutical Approach*. Steiner, Beirut, pp. 163–88.

McAuliffe, Jane Dammen (2002) Disparity and context: Teaching Qurʾānic studies in North America. In: Wheeler, B. (ed.) *Teaching Islam*, Oxford University Press, New York, pp. 94–107.

McAuliffe, Jane Dammen (2003) The genre boundaries of Qurʾānic commentary. In: McAuliffe, J., Walfish, B., and Goering, J. (eds.) *With Reverence for the Word: Medieval Scriptural Exegesis in Judaism, Christianity and Islam*, Oxford University Press, New York, pp. 445–61.

McCutcheon, Russell T. (1999) Theoretical background: Insides, outsides, and the scholar of religion. In: McCutcheon, R. T. (ed.) *The Insider/Outsider Problem in the Study of Religion: A Reader*. Continuum, London, pp. 15–22.

McDermott, Martin J. (1978) *The Theology of Shaikh al-Mufīd (d. 413/1022)*. Dar El-Machreq, Beirut.

McFague, Sallie (1982) *Metaphorical Theology: Models of God in Religious Language*. Fortress Press, Philadelphia.

McFague, Sallie (1987) *Models of God: Theology for an Ecological, Nuclear Age* Fortress Press, Philadelphia.

McKeon, R. (ed.) (1941) *The Basic Works of Aristotle*. Random House, New York.

Melchert, C. (2000) Ibn Mujāhid and the establishment of seven Qurʾānic Readings. *Studia Islamica* 91, 5–22.

Mendenhall, G., and Herion, G. (1992) Covenant. In: Freedman, D. N. (ed.) *The Anchor Bible Dictionary*. Doubleday, New York, vol. I, pp. 1179–1202.

Meursinge, A. (1839) *Specimen e litteris orientalibus exhibens sojutii Librum de Interpretibus Korani*. S. and J. Luchtmans, Lugduni Batavorum.

Michon, J.-L. (1968–9) L'autobiographie (*Fahrasa*) du Soufi Marocain Aḥmad b. ʿAgība (1747–1809) *Arabica* 15: 225–69 and 16: 25–64, 113–54, 225–68.

Michon, J.-L. (1973) *Le Soufi Marocain Aḥmad b. ʿAjība (1746–1809) et son Miʿrāj*. Vrin, Paris.

Ministry of Foreign Affairs, Saudi Arabia (2004) http://www.mofa.gov.sa/ooo/cpa-isl18-10-2003.html June 15, 2004 (not online January 2005).

Mir, Mustansir (1986) *Coherence in the Qurʾān*. American Trust Publications, Indianapolis.

Mir, Mustansir (1989a) *Verbal Idioms of the Qurʾān*. Center for Near Eastern and North African Studies, University of Michigan, Ann Arbor.

Mir, Mustansir (1989b) The Qurʾānic oaths: Farahi's interpretation. *Islamic Studies* 29:1, 5–27.

Mir, Mustansir (1992) Dialogue in the Qurʾān. *Religion and Literature* 24:1, 1–22.

Modarressi, Hossein (1993) Early debates on the integrity of the Qurʾān: A brief survey. *Studia Islamica* 77, 4–39.

Momen, Moojan (1985) *An Introduction to Shiʿi Islam: The History and Doctrines of Twelver Shiʿism*. George Ronald, Oxford; Yale University Press, New Haven.

Monferrer Sala, J.P. (trans.) (1997) *ʿAbd al-Malik b. Ḥabīb, Kitāb wasf al-firdaws (La descripción del paraíso)*. Universidad de Granada, Granada.

Morabia, Alfred (1974) *La notion de Gihad dans l'Islam medieval*, PhD thesis, Université de Lille.

Moubarac, Y. (1955) Les noms, titres et attributs divins dans le Coran et leurs correspondences en épigraphie sud-sémitique. *Le Muséon* 68, 93–135, 325–68.

Mouton, J. M. (1993) De quelques reliques conservées à Damas au Moyen Age, Stratégie politique et religiosité populaire sous les Bourides. *Annales islamologiques* 27, 247–54.

Al-Mufīd, Muḥammad (1371/1952) *Awāʾil al-maqālāt fīʾl-madhāhib waʾl-mukhtārāt*, ed. ʿAbbāsqulī Wajdī. Tabriz.

Al-Mufīd, Muḥammad (1371/1952) *Tasḥīḥ al-iʿtiqād*, ed. ʿAbbāsqulī Wajdī. Tabriz.

Al-Mufīd, Muḥammad (1981) *The Book of Guidance*, trans. I. K. A. Howard. Tahrike Tarsile Qur'an Inc., New York.

Muʿīn, M. (ed.) (1992) *Farhang-i Fārsī*, 8th printing. Amīr Kabīr Publications, Tehran.

Müller, David Heinrich (1896) *Die Propheten in ihrer ursprünglichen Form. Die Grundgesetze der ursemitischen Poesie, erschlossen und nachgewiesen in Bibel, Keilschriften und Koran, und in ihren Wirkungen erkannt in den Chören der griechischen Tragiker*, 2 vols. Alfred Hölder, Vienna.

Al-Munajjid, S. (1972) *Dirasat fī taʾrīkh al-khaṭṭ al-ʿarabī mundhu bidāyatihi ilā nihāya al-ʿasr al-umawī*. Dār al-Kitāb al-Jadīd, Beirut.

Muqātil b. Sulaymān (1989) *Tafsīr al-Qurʾān*, ed. ʿAbd Allāh Maḥmūd Shiḥāta, 5 vols. Al-Hay'a al-Miṣriyya al-Āmma lil-Kitāb, Cairo.

Murray, Stephen, Roscoe, Will, Wafer, Jim et al. (1997) *Islamic Homosexualities: Culture, History and Literature*. New York University Press, New York.

Muslim, Ibn al-Ḥajjāj (1983) *Ṣaḥīḥ Muslim*, ed. Muḥummad Fuʾād ʿAbd al-Bāqī. Dār al-Fikr, Beirut.

Muslim, Ibn al-Ḥajjāj (1992) *Ṣaḥīḥ Muslim*, trans. Abdul Hameed Siddiqui. Ashraf, Lahore.

Muslimaat (2005) http://www.muslimaat.com/live/articleDetail.php?id=16 January 23, 2005.

Mustanṣir biʾllāh II (1953) *Pandiyāt-i Jawān-Mardī*, ed. and trans., Wladimir Ivanow. E. J. Brill, Leiden.

Nagel, Tilman (1967) *Die Qisas al-Anbiyaʾ: Ein Beitrag zur Arabischen Literaturgeschichte*. Rheinische Friedrich-Wilhelm-Universität, Bonn.

Nagel, Tilman (1995) *Medinensische Einschübe in Mekkanischen Suren*. Vandenhoeck & Ruprecht, Göttingen.

Nakhjiwānī, Niʿmat Allāh b. Maḥmūd (1907) *Al-Fawātiḥ al-ilāhiyya waʾl-mafātiḥ al-ghaybiyya*, 2 vols. Al-Maṭbaʿa al-ʿUthmāniyya, Istanbul.

Nanji, Azim (1978) *The Nizārī Ismāʿīlī Tradition in the Indo-Pakistan Subcontinent*. Caravan Books, New York.

Nanji, Azim (1985) Towards a hermeneutic of Qurʾānic and other narratives in Ismāʿīlī thought. In: Martin, Richard C. (ed.) *Approaches to Islam in Religious Studies*. University of Arizona Press, Tucson, pp. 164–73.

Nanji, Azim (1987) Ismaʿīlism. In: Nasr, Seyyed Hossein (ed.) *Islamic Spirituality: Foundations*. Crossroad, New York, pp. 179–98.

Nardin, Terry (ed.) (1996) *The Ethics of War and Peace: Religious and Secular Perspectives*. Princeton University Press, Princeton.

Al-Nashshār, ʿAlī Sāmī, and al-Ṭālibī, ʿAmmār (eds) (1971) *ʿAqāʾid al-salaf*. Munsha'at al-Maʿārif, Alexandria.

Nāsirī, Ḥasan Sādāt, and Dānish'Pazhūh, M. (1990) *Hizār sāl tafsīr-i fārsī*. Nashr-i Alburz, Tehran.

Nāṣir-i Khusraw (1332/1953) *Jāmiʿ al-ḥikmatayn*, ed. Henry Corbin and Muḥammad Muʿin. Qismat-i Īrānshinsī-i Instītū-i Īrān va Firānsa, Tehran.

Nāṣir-i Khusraw (1949) *Shish Faṣl*, ed. and trans. Wladimir Ivanow. E. J. Brill, Leiden.

Nasr, Seyyed Hossein (1980) *Living Sufism*. Unwin, London.

Nasr, Seyyed Hossein (1971, 1994) *Ideals and Realities of Islam*. Unwin, London.

Nelson, K. (1985) *The Art of Reciting the Qur'an*, University of Texas Press, Austin.

Neuwirth, Angelika (1980) Zur Strukture der *Yûsuf*–Sure. In: Diem, W. and Wild, S. (eds.) *Studien aus Arabistik und Semitistic: Anton Spitaler zum siebzigsten Geburtstag von seinen Schülern überreicht*. Otto Harrossowitz, Wiesbaden, pp. 148–52.

Neuwirth, Angelika (1981) *Studien zur Komposition der mekkanischen Suren*. Walter de Gruyter, Berlin.

Neuwirth, Angelika (1983) Das islamische Dogma der "Unnachahmlichkeit des Korans" in literaturwissenschaftlicher Sicht. *Der Islam* 60, 166–183.

Neuwirth, Angelika (1993) Images and metaphors in the introductory sections of the Makkan suras. In: Hawting, G. R., and Shareef, A.-K. (eds.) *Approaches to the Qur'ān*. Routledge, London, pp. 3–36.

Neuwirth, Angelika (1996) Vom Rezitationstext über die Liturgie zum Kanon. Zu Entstehung und Wiederauflösung der Surenkomposition im Verlauf der Entwicklung eines islamischen Kultus. In: Wild, Stefan (ed.), *The Qur'ān as Text*. E. J. Brill, Leiden, pp. 69–105.

Neuwirth, Angelika (2000) Referentiality and Textuality in *Sūrat al-Ḥijr*. Some observations on the Qur'ānic "Canonical Process" and the emergence of a community. In: Boullata, Issa (ed.) (2000) *Literary Structures of Religious Meanings in the Qur'ān*. Richmond, pp. 143–172.

Neuwirth, Angelika (2002) Geography. In: McAuliffe, Jane Dammen (ed.) *Encyclopaedia of the Qur'ān*. Brill, Leiden, vol. II, pp. 293–313.

Neuwirth, Angelika (2003) From the sacred mosque to the remote temple. Sūrat al-Isrā' between text and commentary. In: McAuliffe, J. D., Walfish, B., and Goering, J. (eds.) *With Reverence for the Word: Medieval Scriptural Exegesis in Judaism, Christianity, and Islam*. Oxford University Press, New York, pp. 376–407.

Neuwirth, Angelika (2004) Meccan Texts – Medinan Additions? Politics and the re-reading of liturgical communications. In: Arnzen, R., Thielmann, J. (eds.) (2004) *Words, Texts and Concepts Cruising the Mediterranean Sea. Studies on the Sources, Contents and Influences of Islamic Civilization and Arabic Philosophy and Sciences. Dedicated to Gerhard Endress on his Sixty-fifth Birthday*. Uitgevberij Peters, Leuven, pp. 71–94.

Neuwirth, Angelika (2005) Sūra. In: McAuliffe, Jane Dammen (ed.) *Encyclopaedia of the Qur'ān*. Brill, Leiden, vol. V, forthcoming.

Neuwirth, Angelika (forthcoming) *Umm al-kitāb* and *Theotokos*. Female venues of Divine Power in the Qur'an. In: Tamer, Georges (ed.) *Jubilee volume for Bishop Georges Khodr.*

Neuwirth, Angelika, and Neuwirth, Karl (1991) Surat al-Fatiha –"Eröffnung" des Text-Corpus Koran oder "Introitus" der Gebetsliturgie? In: Gross, W. et al. (eds.) *Text, Methode und Grammatik*. St. Ottilien, pp. 331–58.

Nicholson, R. A. (ed. and trans) (1925–40) *The Mathnawi of Jalalu'ddin Rumi*, W. Gibb Memorial New Series, 8 vols. Luzac, London.

Al-Nīsābūrī, Niẓām al-Dīn (1904–12) *Tafsīr Gharā'ib al-Qur'ān wa-raghā'ib al-furqān* in margin of al-Ṭabarī, *Kitāb Jāmiʿ al-bayān fi tafsīr al-Qur'ān*. Al-Maṭbaʿa al-Kubrā al-Amīriyya, Būlāq.

Al-Nīsābūrī, Niẓām al-Dīn (1962–4) *Tafsīr gharā'ib al-qur'ān wa-raghā'ib al-furqān*, ed. Ibrāhīm ʿAṭwah ʿAwaḍ, 24 vols. Sharikat Maktabat wa-Maṭbaʿat Muṣṭafā 'l-Bābī 'l-Ḥalabī, Cairo.

Nöldeke, T. (1909–38) *Geschichte des Qorāns*, new edition by F. Schwally, G. Bergsträsser and O. Pretzl, 3 vols. Dieterich'sche Verlagsbuchhandlung, Leipzig.

Nöldeke, T. (1910) Zur Sprache des Korans. In: Nöldeke, T., *Neue Beiträge zur semitischen Sprachwissenschaft*. Karl Trübner, Strassburg, pp. 1–30; trans. G. H. Bousquet, *Remarques sur les particularités stylistiques et syntaxiques de la langue du Coran*. A. Maisoneuve, Paris, 1953.

Nöldeke, T. (1967) *Beiträge zur Kenntnis der Poesie der alten Araber*, reprint Georg Olms, Hildesheim.

Nolin, K. (1968) The Itqān and its sources: A study of *al-Itqān fī ʿulūm al-Qurʾān* by Jalāl al-Dīn al-Suyūṭī with special reference to *al-Burhān fī ʿulūm al-Qurʾān* by Badr al-Dīn al-Zarkashī. PhD dissertation, Hartford Seminary, Hartford, CT.

Al-Nuʿmān, Abū Ḥanīfā (1951) *Daʿāʾim al-Islām*, ed. and trans. by Asaf ʿAlī Fyzee. Dār al-Maʿārif, Cairo.

Al-Nuʿmān, Abū Ḥanīfa (1956) *Al-Risāla al-Mudhhiba*. In: A. Tāmir (ed.) *Khams Rasāʾil Ismāʿīliyya*. Dār al-Anṣāf, Salmiyya, Syria.

Al-Nuʿmān, Abū Ḥanīfa (1960) *Asās al-Taʾwīl*, ed. A. Tāmir. Dār al-Thaqāfa, Beirut.

Nuovo, A. (1987) Il Corano ritrovato. *La Bibliofilia* 89, 237–71.

Nuqrāshī, M. (1984 or earlier) Al-Baḥth waʾl-darāsa fī mawḍūʿ Abū ʿAbd al-Raḥmān al-Sulamī mufassiran. PhD dissertation, Jāmiʿat al-Azhar.

Nwyia, Paul (1968) Le *Tafsīr* mystique attribué à Jaʿfar al-Ṣādiq. *Mélanges de l'Université Saint-Joseph*, 43: 4, 181–230.

Nwyia, Paul (1970) *Exégèse coranique et langage mystique. Nouvel essai sur le lexique technique des mystiques musulmans*. Dar el-Machreq, Beirut.

Nwyia, Paul (1973) *Trois oeuvres inédites de mystiques musulmans* (Le Tafsīr d'Ibn. ʿAṭāʾ). Dar el-Machreq, Beirut.

Nwyia, Paul (1973–7) Muqaddimat tafsīr al-Qurʾān li-ʿAlāʾ al-Dawla Simnānī. *al-Abḥāth*, 26, 141–57.

One Ummah (2005) http://www.1ummah.org/encyclopedia/national.html January 23, 2005.

O'Shaughnessy, T. J. (1961) The seven names for Hell in the Qurʾān. *Bulletin of the School of Oriental and African Studies* 24, 444–69.

O'Shaughnessy, T. J. (1973) God's throne and the biblical symbolism of the Qurʾān. *Numen* 20, 202–21 (reprinted in his *Eschatological Themes in the Qurʾān*. Cardinal Bea Institute, Loyola School of Theology, Manila 1986, pp. 12–34).

Ott, Gil (1998) *The Yellow Floor: Poems 1978–1983*. Sun & Moon Press, Los Angeles.

Pagliari, A. (1956) I precedenti iranici di ar. *falak* 'cielo'. In: *Studi orientalici in onore di Giorgio Levi della Vida*. Rome, vol. II, pp. 252–78.

Pakistan Link (2005) http://www.pakistanlink.com/religion/2001/0518.html January 23, 2005.

Pakistan Today (2005) http://www.paktoday.com/cowardice.htm January 23, 2005.

Paret, R. (1971) *Der Koran. Kommentar und Konkordanz*. Kohlhammer, Stuttgart.

Pauliny, J. (1974) Zur Rolle der Quṣṣāṣ bei der Entstehung and Überlieferung der populären Prophetenlegenden. *Asian and African Studies* 10, 125–41.

Pauliny, J. (1992) Dependence and originality: Jewish-Arab contacts in the domain of religious folklore before and after 1000 A.D. *Graecolatina et Orientalia* 23–4, 117–23.

Paz, O. (1990) *Der Bogen und die Leier. Poetologischer Essay*, trans. Rudolf Wittkopf. Suhrkamp, Frankfurt.

Penrice, J. (1873) *A Dictionary and Glossary of the Kor-ân, with Copious Grammatical References and Explanations of the Text*. H. S. King, London; Adam Publishers, Delhi.

Peters, F. E. (ed.) (1999) *The Arabs and Arabia on the Eve of Islam*. Ashgate, Aldershot.

Peters, J. R. T. M. (1976) *God's Created Speech: A Study in the Speculative Theology of the Muʿtazilī Qāḍī l-Quḍāt Abū l-Ḥasan ʿAbd al-Jabbār ibn Aḥmad al-Hamadhānī*. E. J. Brill, Leiden.

Peters, Rudolph (1979) *Islam and Colonialism: The Doctrine of Jihad in Modern History*. Mouton, The Hague.

Peters, Rudolph (1996) *Jihad in Classical and Modern Islam*, Marcus Weiner, Princeton.

Pfister, Manfred (1994) *Das Drama: Theorie und Analyse*. Fink, Munich.

Pickthall, M. M. (1938, 1953) *The Meaning of the Glorious Koran (An Explanatory Translation).* Government Central Press, Hyderabad-Deccan; The New American Library, New York.
Pindarī, Y. (1995) *Zabān-i ahl-i ishārat.* Anjuman-i Āthār wa Mafākhir-i Farhangī, Tehran.
Pines, S. (1936, 1997) *Studies in Islamic Atomism,* trans. from German M. Schwarz; ed. T. Langermann. The Magnes Press, Jerusalem.
Platti, E. (2002) Les thèmes du Coran. In: Urvoy, M.-T. (ed.) *En hommage au père Jacques Jomier, o.p.* Les éditions du Cerf, Paris, pp. 171–83.
Poonawala, Ismail (1988a) An Ismāʿīlī Treatise on the Iʿjāz al-Qurʾān. *Journal of the American Oriental Society,* 108, 379–85.
Poonawala, Ismail (1988b) Ismāʿīlī *taʾwīl* of the Qurʾān. In: Rippin, Andrew (ed.) *Approaches to the History of the Interpretation of the Qurʾān.* Oxford University Press, Oxford, pp. 199–222.
Pourjavady, N., and Wilson, P. L. (1978) *Kings of Love.* Imperial Iranian Academy of Philosophy, Tehran.
Powers, David S. (1988) The exegetical genre *nāsikh al-Qurʾān wa mansūkhuhu.* In: Rippin, Andrew (ed.) *Approaches to the History of the Interpretation of the Qurʾān.* Oxford University Press, Oxford, pp. 117–38.
Puin, Gerd-Rüdiger (1996) Observations on early Qurʾān manuscripts in Sanʿa. In: Wild, Stefan (ed.) *The Qurʾān as Text.* E. J. Brill, Leiden, pp. 107–11.
Qadhi, Y. (1999) *An Introduction to the Sciences of the Qurʾaan.* Al-Hidaayah Publishing, Birmingham.
Al-Qāḍī (1984) *Daqāʾiq al-akhbār fī dhikr al-janna waʾl-nār.* Dār al-Kutub al-ʿIlmiyya, Beirut.
Al-Qarāfī, Abū ʾl-ʿAbbās Aḥmad b. Idrīs (1393/1973) *Sharḥ Tanqīḥ al-Fuṣūl fī ikhtiṣār al-maḥṣūl fīʾl-uṣūl,* ed. Tāhā ʿAbd al-Raʾūf Saʿīd. Maktabat al-Kuliyyāt al-Azhariyyah, Cairo.
Al-Qāshānī, ʿAbd al-Razzāq (1981) *Tafsīr al-Qurʾān al-karīm lil-shaykh al-akbar al-ʿārif bi-llāh al-ʿallāma Muḥyī ʾl-Dīn Ibn ʿArabī,* ed. M. Ghālib, 2 vols., 3rd printing. Dār al-Andalus, Beirut.
Qaṭṭān, M. (1971) *Mabāḥith fī ʿulūm al-Qurʾān.* Manshūrāt al-Dār al-Ḥadīth, Riyad.
Al-Qummī, Abū ʾl-Ḥasan ʿAlī b. Ibrāhim (1386) *Tafsīr al-Qummī,* ed. al-Sayyid al-Mūsawī al-Jazāʾirī. Maktabat al-Hadī, Najaf.
Al-Qummī, al-Qāḍī Saʿīd Muḥammad (1994) *Sharḥ Tawḥid al-Ṣadūq,* ed. N. Ḥabībī. Wizārat-i Farhang wa Irshād-i Islāmī, Tehran.
Al-Qurṭubī, Abū ʿAbd Allāh (1965) *Al-Jāmiʿ li-aḥkām al-Qurʾān.* Dār Iḥyāʾ al-Turāth al-ʿArabī, Beirut.
Al-Qurṭubī, Abū ʿAbd Allāh (1967) *al-Jāmiʿ li-aḥkām al-Qurʾān,* ed. Abū Isḥāq Ibrāhīm Iṭfīsh, 20 vols. Dār al-Kātib al-ʿArabī lil-Ṭibāʿa waʾl-Nashr, Cairo.
Al-Qurṭubī, Abū ʿAbd Allāh (1987) *Al-Jāmiʿ li-aḥkām al-Qurʾān,* 22 vols. Dār al-Fikr, Beirut.
Al-Qurṭubī, Abū ʿAbd Allāh (1992) *Al-Tadhkira fī aḥwāl al-mawtā wa-umūr al-ākhira.* Al-Maktaba al-Tawfiqiyya, Cairo.
Al-Qurṭubī, Abū ʿAbd Allāh (1997) *Al-Jāmiʿ li-aḥkām al-Qurʾān.* Dār al-Kutub al-ʿIlmiyyah, Beirut.
Al-Qushayrī, Abūʾl-Qāsim ʿAbd al-Karīm (1971) *Laṭāʾif al-ishārāt,* ed. I. Basyūnī, 3 vols. Al-Hayʾa al-Miṣriyya al-ʿĀmma lil-Kitāb, Cairo.
Quṭb, Muḥammad (1980) *Dirāsāt Qurʾāniyya.* Dār al-Shurūq, Beirut.
Quṭb, Sayyid (1967) *Fī Ẓilāl al-Qurʾān.* Dār Iḥyāʾ al-Turāth, Beirut.
Quṭb, Sayyid (1982) *Al-Taṣwīr al-fannī fīʾl-Qurʾān.* 7th reprint. Dār al-Shurūq, Beirut.
Radscheit, M. (1997) Word of God or prophetic speech? Reflections on the Quranic *qul*-statements. In: Edzard, L., and Szyska, C. (eds.) *Encounters of Words and Texts: Intercultural Studies in Honor of Stefan Wild on the Occasion of His 60th Birthday, March 2, 1997, Presented by His Pupils in Bonn.* Georg Olms, Hildesheim, pp. 33–42.
Radtke, A. (2003) *Offenbarung zwischen Gesetz und Geschichte. Quellenstudien zu den Bedingungsfaktoren frühislamischen Rechtsdenkens.* Harrassowitz, Wiesbaden.

Al-Rāghib al-Iṣfahānī, Abū ʾl-Qāsim (1972) *Muʿjam mufradāt alfāẓ al-Qurʾān*, ed. Nadīm Marʿashlī. Dār al-Kitāb al-ʿArabī, Beirut.

Rahbar, Daud (1960) *God of Justice: A Study in the Ethical Doctrine of the Qurʾān*. E. J. Brill, Leiden.

Rahbar, Daud (1961) Relation of Shīʿī theology to the Qurʾān. *The Muslim World* 51, 92–8 and 211–16.

Rahbar, Daud (1962) Relation of Shīʿī theology to the Qurʾān. *The Muslim World* 52, 17–21 and 124–8.

Rahman, Fazlur (1965) *Islamic Methodology in History*. Central Institute of Islamic Research, Karachi.

Rahman, Fazlur (1966, 1979) *Islam*. Weidenfeld & Nicolson, London; University of Chicago Press, Chicago.

Rahman, Fazlur (1980) *Major Themes of the Qurʾān*. Bibliotheca Islamica, Chicago.

Rasāʾil Ikhwān al-Ṣafāʾ (1376/1957), ed. Butrus al-Bustānī, 4 vols. Dār Ṣādir, Beirut.

Raven, W. (1998) The biography of the prophet and its scriptural basis. In: S. Leder (ed.) *Storytelling in the Framework of non-Fictional Arabic Literature*. Harrassowitz, Wiesbaden, pp. 421–32.

Al-Rāzī, Abū Ḥātim (1957–8) *Kitāb al-zīna fīʾl-kalimāt al-islāmiyya al-ʿarabiyya*, ed. Ḥusayn F. al-Hamdānī, 2 vols. Al-Maʿhad al-Hamdānī lil-Dirāsat al-Islāmiyya, Cairo.

Al-Rāzī, Fakhr al-Dīn (1981) *Tafsīr Mafātīḥ al-Ghayb*. Dār al-Fikr, Beirut.

Al-Rāzī, Fakhr al-Dīn (n.d.) *Mafātīḥ al-ghayb (al-Tafsīr al-kabīr)*. Dār Iḥyāʾ al-Turāth al-ʿArabī, Beirut.

Al-Rāzī, Fakhr al-Dīn (1987) *Al-Maṭālib al-ʿāliya min al-ʿilm al-ilāhī*, ed. Aḥmad Ḥijāzī al-Saqā. Dār al-Kitāb al-ʿArabī, Beirut.

Rescher, Nicholas (1966) *The Logic of Commands*. Routledge and Kegan Paul, London.

Riddell, P. G. (1997) The transmission of narrative-based exegesis in Islam. In: Riddell, P. G., and Street, T. (eds.) *Islam: Essays on Scripture, Thought and Society. A Festschrift in Honour of Anthony H. Johns*. E. J. Brill, Leiden, pp. 57–80.

Rippin, Andrew (1981) Ibn ʿAbbās's *Al-lughāt fi ʾl-Qurān*. *Bulletin of the School of Oriental and African Studies* 44, 15–25 (reprinted in Rippin 2001b: chapter XIII).

Rippin, Andrew (1983) Ibn ʿAbbās's *Gharīb al-Qurʾān*. *Bulletin of the School of Oriental and African Studies* 46, 332–3 (reprinted in Rippin 2001b: chapter XIV).

Rippin, Andrew (1984) Al-Zuhrī, *naskh al-Qurʾān* and the problem of early *Tafsīr* texts. *Bulletin of the School of Oriental and African Studies* 47, 22–43 (reprinted in Rippin 2001b: chapter XVI).

Rippin, Andrew (1985a) Al-Zarkashī and al-Suyūṭī on the "occasion of revelation" material. *Islamic Culture* 59, 243–58 (reprinted in Rippin 2001b: chapter XVIII).

Rippin, Andrew (1985b) The exegetical genre *asbāb al-nuzūl*: A bibliographical and terminological survey. *Bulletin of the School of Oriental and African Studies* 48, 1–15. (reprinted in Rippin 2001b: chapter XVII).

Rippin, Andrew (1988) The function of *asbāb al-nuzūl* in Qurʾānic exegesis. *Bulletin of the School of Oriental and African Studies* 51, 1–20 (reprinted in Rippin 2001b: chapter XIX).

Rippin, Andrew (1990) Epigraphical South Arabian and Qurʾanic exegesis. *Jerusalem Studies in Arabic and Islam* 13, 155–74 (reprinted in Rippin 2001b: chapter XXI).

Rippin, Andrew (1991) RḤMMN and the Ḥanīfs. In: Hallaq, W., and Little, D. P. (eds.) *Islamic Studies Presented to Charles J. Adams*, E. J. Brill, Leiden, pp. 153–68 (reprinted in Rippin 2001b: chapter III).

Rippin, Andrew (1993) Interpreting the Bible through the Qurʾān. In: Hawting, G. R., and Shareef, A.-K. (eds.) *Approaches to the Qurʾān*. Routledge, London, pp. 249–59 (reprinted in Rippin 2001b: chapter XII).

Rippin, Andrew (1996) The commerce of eschatology. In: Wild, Stefan (ed.) *The Qurʾān as Text*. E. J. Brill, Leiden, pp. 125–35.

Rippin, Andrew (ed.) (1999) *The Qur'ān: Formative Interpretation.* Aldershot, Ashgate.

Rippin, Andrew (1999–2000) The study of *tafsīr* in the 21st century: e-texts and their scholarly use. *MELA Notes 69–70 (Fall 1999–Spring 2000)* <http://www.lib.umich.edu/libhome/area/Near.East/MELANotes6970/tafsir.pdf>

Rippin, Andrew (2000) "Desiring the face of God": The Qur'ānic symbolism of personal responsibility. In: Boullata, I. J. (ed.) *Literary Structures of Religious Meaning in the Qur'ān.* Curzon, Richmond, pp. 117–24.

Rippin, Andrew (ed.) (2001a) *The Qur'ān: Style and Contents.* Aldershot, Ashgate.

Rippin, Andrew (2001b) *The Qur'ān and its Interpretative Tradition.* Aldershot, Variorum/Ashgate.

Rippin, Andrew (2002) Foreign Vocabulary. In: McAuliffe, Jane Dammen (ed.) *Encyclopaedia of the Qur'ān.* Brill, Leiden, vol. II, pp. 226–37.

Rippin, Andrew (2003) The designation of "foreign" languages in the exegesis of the Qur'ān. In: McAuliffe, J., Walfish, B., and Goering, J. (eds.) *With Reverence for the Word: Medieval Scriptural Exegesis in Judaism, Christianity and Islam.* Oxford University Press, New York, pp. 437–44.

Roberts, Alexander, and Donaldson, James (eds.) (1989–90) *Ante-Nicene Fathers, vol. 8: The Twelve Patriarchs, Excerpts and Epistles, the Clementina, Apocrypha, Decretals, Memoirs of Edessa and Syriac Documents, Remains of First Age.* Eerdmanns, Grand Rapids (reprint).

Robinson, Neal (1986) The Qur'ān as the word of God. In: Linzey, A., and Wexler, P. (eds.) *Heaven and Earth: Essex Essays in Theology and Ethics.* Churchman, Worthington, pp. 38–54.

Robinson, Neal (1996) *Discovering the Qur'an: A Contemporary Approach to a Veiled Text.* SCM Press, London.

Robinson, Neal (2000) The structure and interpretation of *Sūrat al-Mu'minūn. Journal of Qur'anic Studies* 2:1, 89–106.

Robinson, Neal (2001) Hands outstretched: Towards a re-reading of *Sūrat al-Mā'idah. Journal of Qur'anic Studies* 3:1, 1–19.

Rosenthal, F. (1970) *Knowledge Triumphant.* E. J. Brill, Leiden.

Rosenthal, F. (2002) History and the Qur'ān. In: McAuliffe, Jane Dammen (ed.) *Encyclopaedia of the Qur'ān.* Brill, Leiden, vol. II, pp. 428–42.

Rubin, Uri (1995) *The Eye of the Beholder: The Life of Muḥammad as Viewed by the Early Muslims.* Darwin Press, Princeton.

Rubin, Uri (2002) Jews and Judaism. In: McAuliffe, Jane Dammen (ed.) *Encyclopaedia of the Qur'ān.* Brill, Leiden, vol. II, pp. 21–34.

Rubin, Uri (2003a) Muḥammad. In: McAuliffe, Jane Dammen (ed.) *Encyclopaedia of the Qur'ān.* Brill, Leiden, vol. III, pp. 440–58.

Rubin, Uri (2003b) Oft-repeated. In: McAuliffe, Jane Dammen (ed.) *Encyclopaedia of the Qur'ān.* Brill, Leiden, vol. III, pp. 474–75.

Rūmī (1990) *Mathnawī*, ed. M. Isti'lāmī, 2nd edn., 7 vols. Zuwwār Publications, Tehran.

Rūmī (2004) *The Masnavi: Book One*, trans. J. Mojaddedi. Oxford University Press, Oxford.

Rūmī, F. (2000) *Dirāsāt fī 'ulūm al-Qur'ān al-karīm*, 7th edn. Maktabat al-Tawba, Riyad.

Al-Ṣabbāgh, M. (1986) *Lamaḥāt fī 'ulūm al-Qur'ān wa-ittijāhāt al-tafsīr.* Al-Maktaba al-Islāmī, Beirut.

Sabbagh, T. (1943) *Le métaphore dans le Coran.* Adrien-Maisonneuve, Paris.

Ṣābūnī, Muḥammad (1985) *Al-Tibyān fī 'ulūm al-Qur'ān.* 'Ālam al-Kutub, Beirut.

Sachedina, Abdulaziz A. (1981) *Islamic Messianism: The Idea of the Mahdi in Twelver Shi'ism.* State University of New York Press, Albany.

Sadan, J. (1986) Genizah and genizah-like practices in Islamic and Jewish traditions, Customs concerning the disposal of worn-out sacred books in the Middle Ages, according to an Ottoman source. *Bibliotheca Orientalis* 43:1–2, col. 36–58.

Ṣadrā, Mullā (1981) *Al-ḥikma al-ʿarshiyya*, trans. James Winston Morris as *The Wisdom of the Throne*. Princeton University Press, Princeton.

Ṣadrā, Mullā (1992) *Kitāb al-mashāʿir*, ed. and trans. Parviz Morewedge. Institute of Global Cultural Studies, Binghamton.

Ṣafī ʿAlī Shāh, Ḥājjī Mīrzā Ḥasan Iṣfahānī (n.d.) *Tafsīr-i Qurʾān*. N.p. (Iran?)

Safi, Louay M. (2001) *Peace and the Limits of War: Transcending Classical Conception of Jihad*. International Institute of Islamic Thought, Herndon, VA.

Ṣaghīr, M. Ḥ. (1999) *al-Mustashriqūn waʾl-dirāsāt al-Qurʾāniyya*. Dār al-Muʾarrikh al-ʿArabī, Beirut.

Al-Sakhāwī (n.d.) *Iʿlān biʾl-tawbīkh*. Dār al-Kutub, Beirut.

Saleh, Walid A. (2004) *The Formation of the Classical Tafsīr Tradition: The Qurʾān Commentary of al-Thaʿlabī (d. 427/1035)*. Brill, Leiden.

Al-Ṣālih, S. (1990) *Mabāḥith fī ʿulūm al-Qurʾān*. Dār al-ʿIlm lil-Malāyīn, Beirut.

Sanāʾī (1998) *Ḥadīqat al-ḥaqīqat*, ed. M. Rawshan. Nigāh Publications, Tehran.

Sands, Kristin Zahra (2005) *Ṣūfī Commentaries on the Qurʾān in Classical Islam*. Routledge, London.

Al-Sarakhsī, Muḥammad b. Aḥmad (1372) *Uṣūl*, ed. Abū ʾl-Wafāʾ al-Afghānī, 2 vols. Dār al-Kitāb al-ʿArabi, Cairo.

Al-Sarrāj (1914) *Kitāb al-Lumaʿ fiʾl-taṣawwuf*, ed. R. A. Nicholson. E. J. Brill, Leiden.

Sartain, E. M. (1975) *Jalāl al-Dīn al-Suyūṭī: Biography and Background*. Cambridge University Press, Cambridge.

Schall, A. (1982) Geschichte des arabischen Wortschatzes, Lehn- und Fremdwörter im Klassichen Arabisch. In: Fischer, W. (ed.) *Grundriß der Arabischen Philologie*. Harrassowitz, Wiesbaden, vol. I, pp. 142–53.

Schall, A. (1984–6) Coranica. *Orientalia Suecana* 33–35, 371–3.

Schleiffer, S. Abdullah (1984) Jihad: Modernist apologists, modern apologetics. *Islamic Culture* 28, 25–46.

Schoeler, Gregor (1996) *Charakter und Authentie der muslimischen Überlieferung über das Leben Mohammeds*. De Gruyter, Berlin.

Schöller, M. (1998) *Exegetisches Denken und Prophetenbiographie*. Harrassowitz, Wiesbaden.

Schreiner, S. (1977) Zwei Miszellen zum koranischen Wörterbuch. *Der Islam* 54, 109–11.

Schub, M. B. (1988) Two notes. *Zeitschrift für arabische Linguistik* 18, 95–7 (reprinted in Rippin 2001a: 127–8).

Schwarz, M. (1972) The letter of al-Ḥasan al-Baṣrī. *Oriens* 20, 15–30.

Sells, Michael (1990) Sound, spirit and gender in Sūrat al-Qadr. *Journal of the American Oriental Society* 11, 101–39.

Sells, Michael (1993) Sound and meaning in Sūrat al-Qāriʿa. *Arabica* 40, 403–30.

Sells, Michael (1999) *Approaching the Qurʾán: The Early Revelations*. White Cloud Press, Ashland, OR.

Shackle, Christopher, and Moir, Zawahir (1992) *Ismaili Hymns from South Asia: An Introduction to the Ginans*. School of Oriental and African Studies, University of London, London.

Al-Shāfiʿī, Muḥammad b. Idrīs (1399/1979) *Al-Risāla*, ed. Aḥmad Muḥammad Shākir. Maktabat Dār al-Turāth, Cairo.

Al-Shāfiʿī, Muḥammad b. Idrīs (1983) *Al-Risāla*, ed. M. Sayyid Kaylānī. Muṣṭafā ʾl-Bābī ʾl-Ḥalabī wa-Awlāduh, Cairo.

Al-Shahrastānī, Abū ʾl-Fatḥ (1366–75/1947–55). *Kitāb al-milal waʾl-niḥal*, ed. Muḥammad Fatḥ Allāh Badrān. Maktabat al-Anjlū al-Miṣriyya, Cairo.

Al-Shahrastānī, Abū ʾl-Fatḥ (1934) *Nihāyat al-aqdām fī ʿilm al-kalām*, ed. and partially trans. Alfred Guillaume in *The Summa Philosophiae of al-Shahrastānī*. Oxford University Press, Oxford.

Al-Shahrastānī, Abū ʾl-Fatḥ (1989) *Mafātīḥ al-asrār wa-maṣābīḥ al-abrār*. Markaz-i Instishār-i Nusakh-i Khaṭṭī, Tehran.

Al-Shahrastānī, Abū ʾl-Fatḥ (1998) *Majlis-i maktūb-i Shahrastānī-i munāqid dar Khwārazm*, ed. Muḥammad Riḍā Jalālī Nāʾīnī and trans. in French, Diane Steigerwald in *Majlis discours sur l'ordre et la création*. Les Presses de l'Université Laval, Sainte-Foy, Québec.

Shams, Pīr (1985) *Brahm Prakāsh*, trans. Hasina M. Jamani, Brahm Prakāsh, a translation and analysis. MA thesis, McGill University, Montreal.

Shihāb al-Dīn Shāh (Pīr) (1947, 1966) *True Meaning of Religion; or, Risālat dar Ḥaqīqat-i Dīn*, ed. and trans. W. Ivanow. Ismaili Society, Bombay.

Shirazi, Sayyid ʿAlí-Muḥammad (known as "the Báb") (1950) *Dalaʾil-i Sabʿih* ("The Seven Proofs") No pub., Tehran; reprinted, H-Net, Lansing, MI 1998. Available at: <http://www.h-net.org/~bahai/areprint/bab/A-F/dalail/dalail.htm>.

Al-Shīrāzī, Abū Isḥāq Ibrāhīm b. ʿAlī (1377/1957) *Al-Lumaʿ fī uṣūl al-fiqh*. Muṣṭafā ʾl-Bābī ʾl-Ḥalabī wa-Awlāduh, Cairo.

Shpall, William (1981–4) A note on Najm-al-Dīn al-Rāzī and the *Baḥr al-ḥaqāʾiq*. *Folia Orientalia* 22, 69–80.

Sībawayhi, Abū Bishr ʿAmr b. ʿUthmān (1881–5) *Al-Kitāb*, ed. H. Derenbourg, 2 vols. Paris (reprinted Hildesheim 1970).

Sībawayhi, Abū Bishr ʿAmr b. ʿUthmān (1898–1900) *Al-Kitāb*. Būlāq Press, Cairo (reprinted al-Muthanna, Baghdad, 1965).

Al-Sijistānī, Abū Yaʿqūb (n.d.) *Kitāb al-Iftikhār*, ed. Muṣṭafā Ghālib. Dār al-Andalus, Beirut.

Al-Sijistānī, Abū Yaʿqūb (MS) *Kitāb al-Maqālīd*. Hamdani Collection.

Sister, M. (1931) Metaphern und Vergleiche im Koran. *Mitteilungen des Seminars für Orientalische Sprachen*, 34, 104–54.

Smith, Wilfred Cantwell (1959) Comparative religion: Whither – and why? In: Eliade, Mircea, and Kitagawa, Joseph (eds.) *The History of Religions: Essays in Methodology*. University of Chicago Press, Chicago, pp. 31–58.

Speicher, K. (1997) Einige Bemerkungen zu al-Hūlīs Entwurf eines *tafsīr adabī*. In: Edzard, L., and Szyska, C. (eds.) *Encounters of Words and Texts: Intercultural Studies in Honor of Stefan Wild*. Georg Olms, Hildesheim, pp. 43–66.

Sperber, Dan, and Wilson, Deirdre (1995) *Relevance: Communication and Cognition*. Blackwell, Oxford.

Sperber, Dan, and Wilson, Deirdre (2004) Relevance theory. In: Horn, Laurence R., and Ward, Gregory (eds.) *The Handbook of Pragmatics*. Blackwell, Oxford, pp. 607–32.

Spitaler Anton (1935) *Die Verszählung des Koran nach islamischer Überlieferung*. München, SBAW.

Spitaler, Anton (1953) Review of Johann Fück (1950) *Arabiya. Untersuchungen zur arabischen Sprach- und Stilgeschichte. Berlin*. In: Bibliotheca Orientalis 10 (1953), 144–50.

Stanley, T. (2003) Page-setting in late Ottoman Qurʾans: An aspect of standardization. *Manuscripta Orientalia* 9, forthcoming.

Stark, Rodney (1987) How new religions succeed: A theoretical model. In: Bromley, David, and Hammond, Phillip (eds.) *The Future of New Religious Movements*. Mercer University Press, Macon, pp. 11–29.

Stark, Rodney (1996) Why religious movements succeed or fail: A revised general model, *Journal of Contemporary Religion* 11, 133–46.

Steigerwald, Diane (1987) L'Imāmologie dans la doctrine ismaélienne nizarienne. MA thesis, McGill University, Montreal.

Steigerwald, Diane (1997) *La pensée philosophique et théologique de Shahrastānī (m. 548/1153)*. Les Presses de l'Université Laval, Sainte-Foy, Quebec.

Steigerwald, Diane (1999) Le *Logos*: clef de l'ascension spirituelle dans l'ismaélisme. *Studies in Religion/Sciences religieuses* 28:2, 175–96.

Storey, C. A. (1927–39; 1953) *Persian Literature: A Bio-Bibliographical Survey*. Royal Asiatic Society of Great Britain and Ireland, London.

Stowasser, Barbara (1994) *Women in the Qur'ān: Traditions and Interpretation.* New York: Oxford University Press.

Stroumsa, S. (1990) The beginnings of the Muʿtazila reconsidered. *Jerusalem Studies in Arabic and Islam* 13, 265–93.

Stroumsa, S. (1999) *Freethinkers of Medieval Islam, Ibn al-Rāwandī, Abū Bakr al-Rāzī, and Their Impact on Islamic Thought.* Brill, Leiden.

Al-Sulamī, Abū ʿAbd al-Raḥmān Muḥammad b. al-Ḥusayn (2001) *Ḥaqāʾiq al-tafsīr*, ed. S. ʿImrān. Dār al-Kutub al-ʿIlmiyya, Beirut.

Sulaym b. Qays (n.d.) *Kitāb Sulaym ibn Qays al-Hilālī.* Al-Maṭbaʿa al-Ḥaydariyya, Najaf.

Al-Suyūṭī, Jalāl al-Dīn (1926) *The Mutawakkili of as-Suyuti*, ed. and trans. William Y. Bell. Nile Mission Press, Cairo.

Al-Suyūṭī, Jalāl al-Dīn (1951, 1991) *Al-Itqān fī ʿUlūm al-Qurʾān*, 2 vols. Muṣṭafā ʾl-Bābī ʾl-Ḥalabī, Cairo (reprint Dār al-Kutub al-ʿIlmiyya, Beirut).

Al-Suyūṭī, Jalāl al-Dīn (1954) *Lubāb al-nuqūl fī asbāb al-nuzūl.* Muṣṭafā ʾl-Bābī ʾl-Ḥalabī, Cairo.

Al-Suyūṭī, Jalāl al-Dīn (1967, 1996) *Al-Itqān fī ʿulūm al-Qurʾān*, ed. M. A. Ibrāhīm, 4 vols. Dār al-Turāth, Cairo; Maktabat Naẓār Musṭafā al-Bāz, Riyad.

Al-Suyūṭī, Jalāl al-Dīn (1972) *Al-Muzhir fī ʿulūm al-lugha wa ʿanwāʾihā*, ed. M. A. Jād al-Mawlā et al., 2 vols. Dār Iḥyāʾ al-Kutub al-ʿArabiyya, Cairo.

Al-Suyūṭī, Jalāl al-Dīn (1982) *Al-Muhadhdhab fī mā waqaʿa fīʾl-Qurʾān min al-muʿarrab*, ed. al-Tihāmī al-Rājī al-Hāshimī. In: ʿAbd Allāh al-Jubūrī (ed.) *Rasāʾil fīʾl-fiqh al-lugha.* Maṭbaʿat Faḍḍāla, Ribat.

Al-Suyūṭī, Jalāl al-Dīn (1985) *Al-Durr al-manthūr fī l-tafsīr bi-l-maʾthūr*, 6 vols. Maṭbaʿat al-Anwār al-Muḥammadiyya, Cairo (reprint Dār al-Maʿrifa, Beirut).

Al-Suyūṭī, Jalāl al-Dīn (1988) *Taʾrīkh al-kulafāʾ*, ed. Muḥammad Muḥyī al-Dīn ʿAbd al-Ḥamīd. Dār al-Jīl, Beirut.

Al-Suyūṭī, Jalāl al-Dīn (1990) *Al-Budūr al-sāfira fī umūr al-ākhira*, ed. Muṣṭafā ʿĀshūr. Maktabat al-Qurʾān, Cairo.

Swartz, Merlin (1986) *Ibn al-Jawzī's Kitāb al-quṣṣāṣ waʾl-mudhakkirīn, Including a Critical Edition, Annotated Translation and Introduction.* Dar el-Machreq Editeurs, Beirut.

Sydney Boys High School (2004) http://www.sbhs.nsw.edu.au/default.asp?pg=notes&spg=display&articleid=3588#islam June 15, 2004. (Not on line January 2005; published as High Notes, Vol. IV, No 37, 5, December 2003).

Al-Ṭabarānī, Sulaymān b. Aḥmad (n.d.) *Muʿjam al-kabīr*, ed. Ḥamdī ʿAbd al-Majīd al-Salafī. Maktabat Ibn Taymiyya, Cairo.

Al-Ṭabarī, Abū Jaʿfar Muḥammad b. Jarīr (1388/1968, 1972, 1987) *Jāmiʿ al-bayān ʿan tāʾwīl āy al-Qurʾān.* 30 vols in 12. Muṣṭafā ʾl-Bābī ʾl-Ḥalabī wa-Awlāduh, Cairo (reprints Dār al-Ḥadīth, Beirut).

Al-Ṭabarī, Abū Jaʿfar Muḥammad b. Jarīr (1879–1901) *Taʾrīkh al-rusul waʾl-mulūk*, ed. M. J. de Goeje et al. E. J. Brill, Leiden.

Al-Ṭabarī, Abū Jaʿfar Muḥammad b. Jarīr (1960) *Taʾrīkh*, ed. M. A. Ibrāhīm. Dār al-Maʿārif, Cairo.

Al-Ṭabarī, Abū Jaʿfar Muḥammad b. Jarīr (1969) *Jāmiʿ al-bayān ʿan taʾwīl āy al-Qurʾān*, ed. M. M. Shākir and A. M. Shākir, 16 vols. Dār al-Maʿārif, Cairo.

Al-Ṭabāṭabāʾī, Muḥammad Ḥusayn (1973) *Al-Mīzān fī tafsīr al-Qurʾān.* Muʾassasat al-Aʿlamī, Beirut.

Ṭabāṭabāʾī, Muhammad Husayn (1975) *Shiʿite Islām*, trans. Seyyed Hossein Nasr. State University of New York Press, Albany.

Ṭabāṭabāʾī, Muhammad Husayn (1987) *The Qurʾan in Islam: Its Impact and Influence on the Life of Muslims.* Zahra Publications, London.

Al-Ṭabrisī, Aḥmad b. ʿAlī (1989) *Al-Iḥtijāj.* Muʾassasat al-Aʿlamī, Beirut.

Taji-Farouki, S. (ed.) (2004) *Modern Muslim Intellectuals and the Qur'an*, Oxford University Press, Oxford.

The Talmud (1952) trans. Isidore Epstein. Soncino Press, London.

Ṭanṭawī, Shaykh Muḥammad Sayyid (2005) http://www.vatican.va/special/assisi-testimonianze_20020124_en.html#Geshe%20Tashi%20Tsering, January, 23, 2005.

Al-Thaʿālibī, Abū 'l-Manṣūr (1861) *Fiqh al-lugha*, ed. Rochaid Dahdah. Paris.

Thackston, W. M. Jr. (1978) *The Tales of the Prophets of al-Kisa'i, Translated from the Arabic with Notes.* Twayne, Boston.

Al-Thaʿlabī, Abū Isḥāq Aḥmad (1954) *ʿArā'is al-majālis al-musammā qiṣaṣ al-anbiyā'*. Muṣṭafā 'l-Bābī 'l-Ḥalabī, Cairo.

Al-Thaʿlabī, Abū Isḥāq Aḥmad (1985) *ʿArā'is al-majālis*. Dār al-Kutub al-ʿIlmiyya, Beirut.

Al-Thaʿlabī, Abū Isḥāq Aḥmad (2002) *Al-Kashf wa'l-bayān*. Dār Iḥyā' al-Tturāth al-ʿArabī, Beirut.

Al-Tibrīzī, Abū Zakariyyā (1964) *Sharḥ al-Qaṣā'id al-ʿAshr*. Maktabat wa-Maṭbaʿat Muḥammad ʿAlī Ṣabīḥ wa-Awlāduh, Egypt.

Al-Tirmidhī, Abū ʿĪsā Muḥammad (1964) *Sunan*. Al-Maktabat al-Salafiyya, Medina.

Tisdall, W. St. Clair (1913) Shiʿah additions to the Koran. *The Moslem World* 3, 227–41.

Torrey, C. C. (1892) *The Commercial-theological Terms in the Koran.* E. J. Brill, Leiden.

Tottoli, R. (1998) The *Qiṣaṣ al-anbiyā'* of Ibn Muṭarrif al-Ṭarafī (d. 454/1062): Stories of the prophets from al-Andalus. *Al-Qanṭara* 19, 131–60.

Tottoli, R. (1999) Origin and use of the term *isrā'īliyyāt* in Muslim literature. *Arabica* 46, 193–210.

Tottoli, R. (2002) *Biblical Prophets in the Qur'ān and Muslim Literature.* Curzon, Richmond.

Tottoli, R. (ed.) (2003a) *The Stories of the Prophets by Ibn Muṭarrif al-Ṭarafī.* Klaus Schwarz Verlag, Berlin.

Tottoli, R. (2003b) Motivi narrativi e cornici dalla storia universale alle storie dei profeti nella letteratura araba musulmana. In: G. Carbonaro, E. Creazzo, and N.L. Tornesello (eds.) *Macrotesto fra Oriente e Occidente. Atti del IV Colloquio Internazionale Medioevo Romanzo e Orientale*, Rubbettino Editore, Soveria Mannelli, pp. 155–69.

Tritton, A. S. (1939–42) Review of Arthur Jeffery, *Foreign Vocabulary of the Qur'an. Bulletin of the School of Oriental and African Studies* 10, 1009–11.

Al-Ṭūfī, Abū Rabīʿ Sulaymān b. ʿAbd al-Qawwī 'l-Ḥanbalī (1408/1987) *Sharḥ Mukhtaṣar al-rawḍa*, ed. ʿAbd Allāh al-Turkī, 4 vols. Mu'asasat al-Risāla, Beirut.

Al-Ṭūsī, Muḥammad b. al-Ḥasan (1986) *Al-Iqtiṣād fīmā yataʿllaqu bi'l-iʿtiqād.* Dār al-Aḍwā', Beirut.

Al-Ṭūsī, Naṣīr al-dīn (1950) *Taṣawwurāt*, ed. Wladimir Ivanow. E. J. Brill, Leiden.

Al-Ṭūsī, Naṣīr al-dīn (1998) *Sayr wa Sulūk*, ed. and trans. Jalal Badakhchani in *Contemplation and Action.* I. B. Tauris, London.

Al-Tustarī, Sahl b. ʿAbd Allāh (1911) *Tafsīr al-Qur'ān al-ʿaẓīm.* Muṣṭafā 'l-Bābī 'l-Ḥalabī, Cairo.

Al-Tustarī, Sahl b. ʿAbd Allāh (2001) *Tafsīr al-Qur'ān al-ʿaẓīm*, ed. Maḥmūd Jīrat Allāh. Al-Dār al-Thaqāfiyya lil-Nashr, Cairo.

United Muslim Association of Hong Kong (2005) http://www.geocities.com/umahweb/acts.html#speech January 23, 2005 (written by Yahiya Emerick; originally appeared in *Religion and Education* Winter 1998).

Urvoy, M. (2002) De quelques procédés de persuasion dans le Coran. *Arabica* 49, 456–76.

van Ess, J. (1970) The logical structure of Islamic theology. In: von Grunebaum, G. E. (ed.) *Logic in Classical Islamic Culture.* O. Harrassowitz, Wiesbaden, pp. 22–50.

Versteegh, C. H. M. (1993) *Arabic Grammar and Qur'ānic Exegesis in Early Islam.* E. J. Brill, Leiden.

Versteegh, K. (1997) *The Arabic Language*, Edinburgh University Press, Edinburgh.

Virani, N. (2002), "I am the Nightingale of the Merciful": Rumi's use of the Qur'ān and Hadith. *Comparative Studies of South Asia, Africa and the Middle East* 22:2, 100–111.

Vollers, Karl (1906) *Volkssprache und Schriftsprache im alten Arabien*. Trübner, Strassburg.

von Bothmer, H.-C. (1987) Architekturbilder im Koran, Eine Prachthandschrift der Umayyadenzeit aus dem Yemen. *Pantheon* 45, 4–20.

von Bothmer, H.-C., Ohlig, K.-H., and Puin, G.-R. (1999) Neue Wege der Koranforschung. *Magazin Forschung, Universität des Saarlandes* 1, 33–46.

von Denffer, A. (1983) *ʿUlūm al-Qurʾān: An Introduction to the Sciences of the Qurʾān*. The Islamic Foundation, Leicester.

von Grunebaum, G. E. (1961) *Islam: Essays in the Growth of a Cultural Tradition*. Routledge and Kegan Paul, London.

Waardenburg, J. (1980) Faith and reason in the argumentation of the Qurʾān. *Perennitas: Studi in Onore di Angelo Brelich*. Edizioni dell'Ateneo, Rome, pp. 619–33.

Waardenburg, J. (1981) Towards a periodization of earliest Islām according to its relations with other religions. In: Peters, R. (ed.) *Proceedings of the 9th Congress of the Union Européenne des Arabisants et Islamisants (Leiden 1971)*. E. J. Brill, Leiden, pp. 304–26 (reprinted in Rippin 2001a: 93–115).

Wadud, Amina (1999) *The Qurʾān and Woman*. Oxford University Press, New York.

Al-Wāḥidī Abū ʾl-Ḥasan ʿAlī al-Nīsābūrī (1968) *Asbāb al-nuzūl*. Muṣṭafā ʾl-Bābī ʾl-Ḥalabī, Cairo.

Al-Wāḥidī, Abū ʾl-Ḥasan ʿAlī al-Nīsābūrī (n.d.) *Asbāb al-nuzūl*. Maktabat al-Mutanabbī, Cairo.

Al-Wasaṭ (2004) http://www.alwasatnews.com/topic.asp?tID=5176&mydate=6-30-2004 January 23, 2005 (issue dated June 30, 2004).

Walker, Paul E. (1993) *Early Philosophical Shiism: The Ismaili Neoplatonism of Abū Yaʿqūb al-Sijistānī*. Cambridge University Press, New York.

Walker, Paul E. (1994) *The Wellsprings of Wisdom: A study of Abū Yaʿqūb al-Sijistānī's Kitāb al-Yanābī*. University of Utah Press, Salt Lake City.

Walker, Paul E. (2003) Knowledge and learning. In: McAulffe, Jane Dammen, *Encyclopedia of the Qurʾān*. Brill, Leiden, vol. III, pp. 100–4.

Wansbrough, J. (1977) *Quranic Studies: Sources and Methods of Scriptural Interpretation*. Oxford University Press, Oxford.

Wansbrough, J. (1978) *The Sectarian Milieu: Content and Composition of Islamic Salvation History*. Oxford University Press, Oxford.

Wansbrough, John (1987) *Res Ipsa Loquitur: History and Mimesis*. The Israel Academy of Sciences and Humanities, Jerusalem.

Watt, William Montgomery (1948) *Free Will and Predestination in Early Islam*. Luzac, London.

Watt, William Montgomery (1953) *Muhammad at Mecca*. Clarendon Press, Oxford.

Watt, William Montgomery (1956) *Muhammad at Medina*. Clarendon Press, Oxford.

Watt, W. Montgomery, and Bell, Richard (1970) *Bell's Introduction to the Qurʾān*. Edinburgh University Press, Edinburgh.

Weiss, Bernard G. (1992) *The Search for God's Law: Islamic Jurisprudence in the Writings of Sayf al-Din al-Amidi*. University of Utah Press, Salt Lake City.

Weiss, Bernard (1996) Ibn Taymiyya on Leadership in the Ritual Prayer. In: Masud, Muhammad Khalid, Messick, Brinkley Morris, and Powers, David Stephan (eds.) *Islamic Legal Interpretation: Muftis and Their Fatwas*. Harvard studies in Islamic law. Harvard University Press, Cambridge, pp. 63–71.

Welch, Alfred T. (1980a) Qurʾānic studies – problems and prospects. *Journal of the American Academy of Religion* 47, 620–34.

Welch, A. (1980b) Allah and other supernatural beings: The emergence of the Qurʾānic doctrine of *tawḥīd*. *Journal of the American Academy of Religion* 47, 733–58.

Welch, A. (1983) Muḥammad's understanding of himself: The Koranic data. In: Hovannisian, R., and Vryonis, S. (eds.) *Islam's Understanding of Itself*. Undena Publications, Malibu, pp. 15–52.
Wensinck, A. J. (1971) *A Handbook of Early Muhammadan Tradition*. E. J. Brill, Leiden.
Wheeler, Brannon (2002) *Moses in the Quran and Islamic Exegesis*. Curzon, Richmond.
Widengren, Geo (1955) *Muhammad, Apostle of God and his Ascension*. A.-B. Lundequistska Bokhandeln, Uppsala.
Wiesmüller, Beate (2002) *Die vom Koran getötteen. At-Taʿlabīs Qatlā l-Qurʾān nach der Istanbuler und den Leidener Handschriften. Edition und Kommentar*. Ergon Verlag, Würzburg.
Wild, Stefan (1996) "We have sent down to thee the book with the truth . . .": Spatial and temporal implications of the Qurʾanic concepts of *nuzūl, tanzīl*, and *ʾinzāl*. In: Wild, Stefan (ed.) *The Qurʾān as Text*. E. J. Brill, Leiden, pp. 137–53.
Willis, John R. (1967) *Jihād fī sabīl Allah* – its doctrinal basis in Islam and some aspects of its evolution in nineteenth-century West Africa. *Journal of African History* 8, 395–415.
Witkam, J. J. (2002) Twenty-nine rules for *Qurʾān* copying: A set of rules for the lay-out of a nineteenth-century Ottoman *Qurʾān* manuscript. *Journal of Turkish Studies* 26:1, 339–48.
Wright, W. (1967 [1896]) *A Grammar of the Arabic Language*. 3rd edn. 2 vols. Cambridge University Press, Cambridge.
Al-Yaʿqūbī, Aḥmad b. Abī Yaʿqūb (1960) *Taʾrīkh al-Yaʿqūbī*. Dār Ṣādir, Beirut.
Yāqūt (1907–27) *Irshād al-arīb ilā maʿrifat al-adīb*, ed. D. S. Margoliouth. E. J. Brill, Leiden.
Yılmaz, H. (1980) *Aziz Mahmūd Hüdâyi ve Celvetiyye Tarikati*. Marmara Üniversitesi İlahiyat Fakültesi Vakfı Yayınları, Istanbul.
Zahniser, Mathias (2000) Major transitions and thematic borders in two long *Sūras*: al-Baqara and al-Nisāʾ. In: Boullata, Issa J. (ed.) *Literary Structures of Religious Meaning in the Qurʾān*. Curzon, Richmond, pp. 22–55.
Zammit, M. R. (2002) *A Comparative Lexical Study of Qurʾānic Arabic*. E. J. Brill, Leiden.
Al-Zarqānī, M. (1943) *Manāhil al-ʿirfān fī ʿulūm al-Qurʾān*, 2 vols. Dār Iḥyāʾ al-Kutub al-ʿArabiyya, Cairo.
Al-Zarkashī, Badr al-Dīn (1413/1992) *Al-Baḥr al-muḥīṭ fī uṣūl al-fiqh*, ed. ʿAbd al-Qādir ʿAbd Allāh al-ʿĀnī, 6 vols. Dār al-Ṣafwa [li-] Wizārat al-Awqāf waʾl-shuʾūn al-Islāmiyya biʾl-Kuwait, Ghardaqa, Kuwait.
Al-Zarkashī, Badr al-Dīn (1959) *Al-Burhān fī ʿulūm al-Qurʾān*, ed. M. A. al-Faḍl Ibrāhīm, 4 vols. Maktabat Dār al-Turāth, Cairo.
Al-Zarkashī, Badr al-Dīn (1988) *Al-Burhān fī ʿulūm al-Qurʾān*, ed. Y. al-Marʿshalī, J. al-Dhahabī, and I. al-Kurdī. Dār al-Maʿrifa, Beirut.
Zebiri, Kate (1997) *Muslims and Christians Face to Face*. Oneworld Publications, Oxford.
Zebiri, Kate (2004) Polemic and polemical language. In: McAuliffe, Jane Dammen (ed.) *Encyclopaedia of the Qurʾān*. Brill, Leiden, vol. IV, pp. 114–25.
Zimmern, H. (1917) *Akkadische Fremdwörter als Beweis für babylonischen Kultureinfluß*. A. Edelmann, Leipzig.
Zubaidi, A. M. (1983) The impact of the Qur'ān and *ḥadīth* on medieval Arabic literature. In: Beeston, A. F. L., Johnstone, T. M., Serjeant, R. B., and Smith, G. R. (eds.) *Arabic Literature to the End of the Umayyad Period*. Cambridge University Press, Cambridge, pp. 322–43.
Zwettler, M. (1978) *The Oral Tradition of the Classical Arabic Poetry: Its Characters and Implications*, Ohio State University Press, Columbus.
Zwettler, M. (1991) A mantic manifesto. In: Kugel, J. (ed.) *Poetry and Prophecy: The Beginning of a Literary Tradition*, Cornell University Press, Cornell, pp. 75–120.
Zysow, Aron (1984) The economy of certainty: An introduction to the typology of Islamic legal theory. PhD thesis, Harvard University.

Index of People, Places and Topics

Note: "n" after a page reference indicates a note on that page.

Index of Qur'ān Verses

Note: "n" after a page reference indicates a note on that page.